Fodor's

Pacific North Coast

Portions of this book appear in Fodor's Canada and Fodor's Alaska

Fodor's Travel Publications, Inc.
New York • Toronto • London • Sydney • Auckland

Fodor's Pacific North Coast

Editor: Chelsea S. Mauldin

Contributors: Robert Andrews, Robert Blake, Tom Barr, Susan Brown, Janet Foley, Tom Gaunt, Jeff Kuechle, Melissa Rivers, Mary Ellen Schultz, M. T. Schwartzman (Gold Guide editor), Glenn W. Sheehan, Dinah Spritzer, Loralee Wenger, Adam Woog

Creative Director: Fabrizio La Rocca

Cartographer: David Lindroth

Cover Photograph: D. Carriere/H. Armstrong Roberts

Text Design: Between the Covers

Copyright

Special Sales

CONTENTS

On the Road with Fodor's   v

About Our Writers *v*
What's New *v*
How to Use This Book *vi*
Please Write to Us *vi*

The Gold Guide   xiv

Important Contacts A to Z *xiv*
Smart Travel Tips A to Z *xxviii*

1   Destination: The Pacific North Coast   1

"The Lay Of the Land," by Tom Gaunt *2*
What's Where *4*
Pleasures & Pastimes *5*
Fodor's Choice *8*
Great Itineraries *13*
Festivals and Seasonal Events *18*

2   Portland   20

3   Oregon   52

The Oregon Coast *56*
The Willamette Valley and the Wine Country *74*
The Columbia River Gorge and the Oregon Cascades *93*
Oregon Essentials *103*

4   Seattle   108

5   Washington   152

Whidbey Island *153*
The San Juan Islands *160*
Bellingham and Whatcom & Skagit Counties *167*
Tacoma *175*
Mt. Rainier National Park *182*
The Olympic Peninsula *188*
Long Beach Peninsula *197*
Crossing the Cascades *204*
Yakima Valley Wine Country *210*
Washington Essentials *213*

6   Vancouver   219

7   British Columbia   265

8   Southeast Alaska   312

9 Portraits of the Pacific North Coast   360

"Pacific Northwest Microbrews: Good for What Ales You,"
by Jeff Kuechle 361
"In the Footsteps of the First Settlers," by Glenn W. Sheehan 365
More Portraits 369

Index   370

Maps

Pacific North Coast *viii–ix*
The United States *x–xi*
World Time Zones *xii–xiii*
Downtown Portland 23
Portland Dining 36–37
Portland Lodging 42–43
Oregon 54–55
Oregon Coast and Willamette
Valley/Wine Country 57
Salem 77
Crater Lake National Park 80
Eastern Oregon 94
Downtown Seattle 112–113
Northern Seattle 116
Downtown Seattle Dining
126–127
Metropolitan Seattle Dining 128
Seattle Lodging 136–137
Washington 154–155
Puget Sound 157
Whatcom and Skagit Counties
169
Tacoma 177
Mt. Rainier Natonal Park
184–185

Olympic Peninsula 190
Long Beach Peninsula 199
Yakima Valley 212
Vancouver Exploring 222–223
Tour 1: Downtown Vancouver
224
Tour 2: Stanley Park 229
Tour 3: Granville Island 231
Downtown Vancouver Dining
241
Greater Vancouver Dining
242
Vancouver Lodging 250
British Columbia 268–269
Downtown Victoria 270
Vancouver Island 274
Southeast Alaska 314
Ketchikan 317
Wrangell 320
Petersburg 323
Sitka 325
Juneau 328
Haines 331
Skagway 334

ON THE ROAD WITH FODOR'S

A GOOD TRAVEL GUIDE is like a wonderful traveling companion. It's charming, it's brimming with sound recommendations and solid ideas, it pulls no punches in describing lodging and dining establishments, and it's consistently full of fascinating facts that make you view what you've traveled to see in a rich new light. In the creation of this 11th edition of *Fodor's Pacific North Coast*, we at Fodor's have gone to great lengths to provide you with the very best of all possible traveling companions—and to make your trip the best of all possible vacations.

About Our Writers

The information in these pages is a collaboration of a number of extraordinary writers.

Tom Gaunt works as editor of the magazine section of the *Business Journal of Portland*. A native of the state, Tom has covered Northwest politics and culture for the past 12 years. His writing has appeared in *Pacific Northwest, OMNI,* and the *Oregon Magazine of Nature, Exploration and Science*.

Portland-based writer **Jeff Kuechle** does his best to support the Northwest's burgeoning microbrewery industry. His contributions have appeared in *Pacific Northwest, Ford Times, Emmy,* and *L.A. Times*.

Travel junkie **Melissa Rivers,** updater of the British Columbia and Vancouver chapters, lives in Oregon and travels throughout the Pacific Northwest and eastern Mexico on assignments for Fodor's.

A principal investigator at SJS Archaeological Services, Inc., in Bridgeport, Pennsylvania, **Glenn W. Sheehan** has worked extensively in the Pacific Northwest and Arctic regions.

Loralee Wenger is the former travel editor for *Pacific Northwest* magazine and a freelance writer whose articles have appeared in the *San Francisco Examiner, Washington Post, Parade* magazine, and *Glamour* magazine.

Adam Woog is a Seattle-based freelance writer whose works have appeared in the *Village Voice, Seattle Times,* and *Japan Times*.

What's New

A New Design

If this is not the first Fodor's guide you've purchased, you'll immediately notice our new look. More readable and easier to use than ever? We think so—and we hope you do, too.

Let Us Do Your Booking

Our writers have scoured the Pacific North Coast to come up with an extensive and well-balanced list of the best B&Bs, inns, and hotels, both small and large, new and old. But you don't have to beat the bushes to come up with a reservation. Now we've teamed up with an established hotel-booking service to make it easy for you to secure a room at the property of your choice. It's fast, it's free, and confirmation is guaranteed. If your first choice is booked, the operators can line up your second right away. Just call ☎ 800/FODORS-1 or 800/363-6771 (0800-89-1030 in Great Britain; 0014-800-12-8271 in Australia; 1-800/55-9101 in Ireland).

Travel Updates

In addition, just before your trip, you may want to order a Fodor's Worldview Travel Update. From local publications all over the Pacific North Coast, the lively, cosmopolitan editors at Worldview gather information on concerts, plays, opera, dance performances, gallery and museum shows, sports competitions, and other special events that coincide with your visit. See the order blank at the back of this book, call 800/799-9609, or fax 800/799-9619.

How to Use This Book

Organization

Up front is the **Gold Guide,** comprising two sections on gold paper that are full of practical information listed in alphabetical order by topic. **Important Contacts A to Z** gives addresses and telephone numbers of organizations and companies that offer destination-related services, detailed information, or useful publications. This is also where you'll find information about how to get to the Pacific North Coast from wherever you are. **Smart Travel Tips A to Z,** the Gold Guide's second section, gives specific tips on how to get the most out of traveling, as well as hints for having a (relatively) hassle-free trip to the Pacific North Coast.

Chapter 1, **Destination: Pacific North Coast,** contains an introduction to the area by Oregon native Tom Gaunt, plus several sections to help you enjoy the best of the Pacific North Coast: **What's Where** offers short descriptions of the cities and regions covered in this guide. **Pleasures & Pastimes** covers all the sights and activities that make the Northwest such a rich and exciting vacation destination. **Fodor's Choice** has our picks for the very best there is to do and see—from remarkable inns and delicious dining to natural wonders and fascinating attractions. **Great Itineraries** suggests routes for themed driving tours, and **Festivals and Seasonal Events** covers the top fairs, crafts' shows, sporting events, and exhibitions.

Area chapters in *Fodor's Pacific North Coast* are arranged from south to north, with cities preceding the state or province to which they belong. Each chapter ends with a section called Essentials, which tells you how to get there and get around and lists important local addresses and telephone numbers.

At the back of the book you'll find **Portraits,** wonderful essays about facets of Pacific North Coast culture, followed by suggestions for pretrip reading and viewing.

Stars

Stars in the margin are used to denote highly recommended sights, attractions, hotels, and restaurants.

Restaurant and Hotel Criteria and Price Categories

Restaurants and accommodations are chosen with a view to giving you the cream of the crop in each location and in each price range. In all restaurant price charts, costs are per person, excluding drinks, tip, and tax. We note a dress code only when men are required to wear a jacket or a jacket and tie.

In hotel price charts, rates are for standard double rooms, excluding city and state sales taxes. Note that in general you incur charges when you use many hotel facilities. We wanted to let you know what facilities a hotel has to offer, but we don't always specify whether or not there's a charge, so when planning a vacation that entails a stay of several days, it's wise to ask what's included in the rate.

Credit Cards

The following abbreviations are used: **AE,** American Express; **D,** Discover; **DC,** Diners Club; **MC,** MasterCard; and **V,** Visa. Discover is not accepted outside the United States.

Please Write to Us

Everyone who has contributed to *Fodor's Pacific North Coast* has worked hard to make the text accurate. All prices and opening times are based on information supplied to us at press time, and Fodor's cannot accept responsibility for any errors that may have occurred. The passage of time will bring changes, so it's always a good idea to call ahead and confirm information when it matters—particularly if you're making a detour to visit specific sights or attractions. When making reservations at a hotel or inn, be sure to mention if you have a disability or are traveling with children, if you prefer a private bath or a certain type of bed, or if you have specific dietary needs or any other concerns.

Were the restaurants we recommended as described? Did our hotel picks exceed your expectations? Did you find a museum we recommended a waste of time? We would love your feedback, positive and negative. If you have complaints, we'll look into them and revise our entries when the facts warrant it. If you've happened upon a special place that we haven't included, we'll pass the information along to the writers so they can check it out. So please send us a letter or postcard—you can address it to Pacific North Coast Editor, 201 East 50th Street, New York, NY 10022. We'll look forward to hearing from you. And in the meantime, have a wonderful trip!

Karen Cure

Karen Cure
Editorial Director

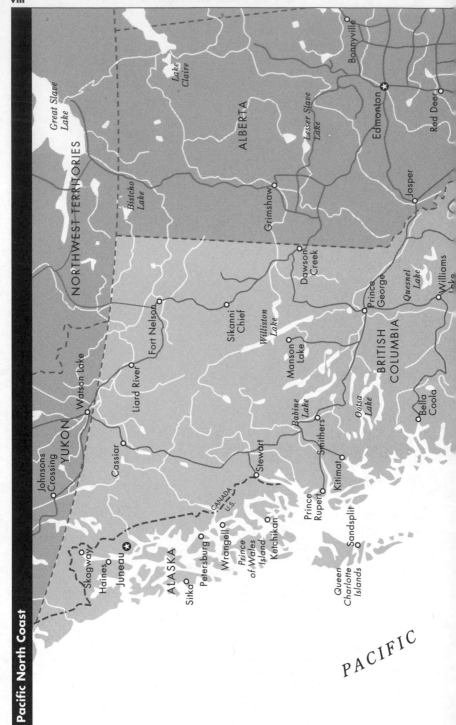

PACIFIC

OCEAN

Port Hardy

Williams Lake

Vancouver Island

Nanaimo

Victoria

Port Angeles

Bremerton

Tacoma

Olympia

Seattle

Vancouver

New Westminster

Kamloops

Kelowna

Golden

Calgary

Lethbridge

Shelby

CANADA
U.S.

MONTANA

Missoula

Helena

Butte

Idaho Falls

Pocatello

Rupert

NEVADA

Salmon

IDAHO

Boise

Ontario

Lewiston

Spokane

Franklin D. Roosevelt Lake

WASHINGTON

Yakima

Walla Walla

Columbia River

Portland

Vancouver

Salem

Corvallis

Eugene

Maupin

Bend

Redmond

Burns

Malheur Lake

OREGON

Upper Klamath Lake

Klamath Falls

Medford

CALIFORNIA

N

0   100 miles
0   150 km

The United States

CANADA

ONTARIO

QUÉBEC

NEW BRUNSWICK

Québec

Fredericton ★

MAINE

Lake Superior

MINNESOTA

Duluth

MICHIGAN

Lake Huron

Ottawa

Montpelier

VT.

Montréal

95

Augusta

Concord

N.H.

MASS.

Boston

R.I.

WISCONSIN

St. Paul

Green Bay

Lake Michigan

Lake Ontario

Toronto ★

Lake Erie

Buffalo

NEW YORK

Albany

Hartford

Providence

CONN.

Minneapolis

Milwaukee

Lansing

Madison ★

Cleveland

Detroit

Pittsburgh

PENNSYLVANIA

Harrisburg

New York

N.J.

Trenton

Philadelphia

IOWA

Chicago

ILLINOIS

INDIANA

OHIO

Columbus

Charleston

WEST VIRGINIA

MD.

Dover

DEL.

Baltimore

Annapolis

Washington, D.C.

Des Moines

Omaha

Indianapolis

Springfield

Cincinnati

Louisville

Frankfort

Richmond

VIRGINIA

Norfolk

Topeka

Kansas City

Jefferson City

MISSOURI

St. Louis

KENTUCKY

Raleigh

NORTH CAROLINA

Tulsa

ARKANSAS

Nashville

TENNESSEE

Memphis

Columbia

SOUTH CAROLINA

Little Rock

Birmingham

Atlanta

GEORGIA

ATLANTIC OCEAN

Jackson

MISSISSIPPI

ALABAMA

Montgomery

Savannah

Baton Rouge

Mobile

Tallahassee

FLORIDA

Jacksonville

Orlando

Houston

New Orleans

LOUISIANA

Gulf of Mexico

Bahama Islands

Miami

Nassau ★

N

0   200 miles

0   300 km

World Time Zones

Numbers below vertical bands relate each zone to Greenwich Mean Time (0 hrs.).
Local times frequently differ from these general indications,
as indicated by light-face numbers on map.

Algiers, **29**	Berlin, **34**	Delhi, **48**	Istanbul, **40**
Anchorage, **3**	Bogotá, **19**	Denver, **8**	Jerusalem, **42**
Athens, **41**	Budapest, **37**	Djakarta, **53**	Johannesburg, **44**
Auckland, **1**	Buenos Aires, **24**	Dublin, **26**	Lima, **20**
Baghdad, **46**	Caracas, **22**	Edmonton, **7**	Lisbon, **28**
Bangkok, **50**	Chicago, **9**	Hong Kong, **56**	London
Beijing, **54**	Copenhagen, **33**	Honolulu, **2**	(Greenwich), **27**
	Dallas, **10**		Los Angeles, **6**
			Madrid, **38**
			Manila, **57**

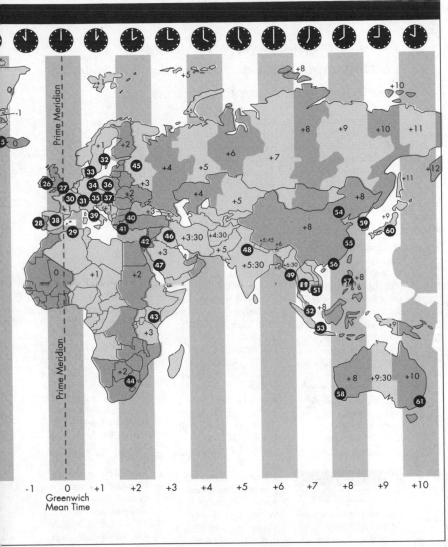

-1 0 +1 +2 +3 +4 +5 +6 +7 +8 +9 +10
Greenwich Mean Time

Mecca, **47**
Mexico City, **12**
Miami, **18**
Montréal, **15**
Moscow, **45**
Nairobi, **43**
New Orleans, **11**
New York City, **16**

Ottawa, **14**
Paris, **30**
Perth, **58**
Reykjavík, **25**
Rio de Janeiro, **23**
Rome, **39**
Saigon (Ho Chi Minh City), **51**

San Francisco, **5**
Santiago, **21**
Seoul, **59**
Shanghai, **55**
Singapore, **52**
Stockholm, **32**
Sydney, **61**
Tokyo, **60**

Toronto, **13**
Vancouver, **4**
Vienna, **35**
Warsaw, **36**
Washington, D.C., **17**
Yangon, **49**
Zürich, **31**

THE GOLD GUIDE / IMPORTANT CONTACTS

IMPORTANT CONTACTS A TO Z

An Alphabetical Listing of Publications, Organizations, and Companies That Will Help You Before, During, and After Your Trip

No single travel resource can give you every detail about every topic that might interest or concern you at the various stages of your journey—when you're planning your trip, while you're on the road, and after you get back home. The following organizations, books, and brochures will supplement the information in *Fodor's Pacific North Coast.* For related information, including both basic tips on visiting the Pacific North Coast and background information on many of the topics below, study Smart Travel Tips A to Z, the section that follows Important Contacts A to Z.

A

AIR TRAVEL

The major gateways to the Pacific North Coast are Seattle, Portland, and Vancouver. Nonstop flying time from New York to Seattle or Portland is approximately five hours; flights from Chicago are about 4–4½ hours; flights between Los Angeles and Seattle take 2½ hours. Flights from New York to Vancouver take about eight hours with connections; from Chicago, about 4½ hours nonstop; and from Los Angeles, about three hours nonstop.

British travelers reach the Pacific North Coast via the main international gateways of Seattle and Vancouver. Southeast Alaska is served by regular, connecting flights to Anchorage from the United Kingdom.

CARRIERS

MAJOR AIRLINES➤ Flying into Seattle and Portland from points throughout the United States are **Alaska** (☎ 800/426–0333), **American** (☎ 800/433–7300), **Continental** (☎ 800/525–0280), **Delta** (☎ 800/221–1212), **Northwest** (☎ 800/225–2525), **TWA** (☎ 800/221–2000), **United** (☎ 800/241–6522), and **USAir** (☎ 800/428–4322). Flying into Vancouver from U.S. points are **American Airlines, Delta,** and **United.** Flying into Vancouver from Canadian cities are **Air Canada** (☎ 800/663–8868) and **Canadian Airlines International** (☎ 800/426–7000).

Most Alaska-bound flights touch down in Anchorage. Nonstop service is also available to Fairbanks, Juneau, and Ketchikan. Southeastern Alaska cities are connected through Seattle. The major U.S. carriers serving Alaska are **Alaska, Continental, Delta, Northwest,** and **United.**

For inexpensive, no-frills flights, contact **MarkAir** (☎ 800/627–5247), based in Anchorage, Alaska, or **Southwest Airlines** (☎ 800/444–5660), based in Salt Lake City and serving Oregon and Washington.

From the United Kingdom, **British Airways** (☎ 0181/897–4000 in London or 0345/222111 in all other areas) services Seattle and Vancouver from Heathrow. **KLM** (☎ 081/751–9000; in U.S. ☎ 800/777–5553) travels to Vancouver from 25 U.K. and Irish airports via Amsterdam. **Air Canada** (☎ 0181/759–2636 in London or 0345/181313 elsewhere) flies from Heathrow and Glasgow to Vancouver; **Canadian Airlines International** (☎ 0181/577–7722 or 0345/616767 outside London) services Vancouver from Heathrow.

For budget-priced flights into Vancouver, contact **Globespan Ltd.** (☎ 0141/332–6600) and **Bluebird Express** (☎ 01444/235–678). At press time, prices began at £400 round-trip. You can also find good deals through specialized ticket agencies (*see* Tour Operators, *below*).

REGIONAL AIRLINES➤ Leading regional carriers in the Pacific North Coast are **Horizon Air** (☎ 800/547–9308) and **United Express** (☎ 800/241–6522). The two airlines provide frequent service between cities in Washington and Oregon. Horizon Air also flies internationally from Seattle to Vancouver and Victoria and Calgary, Alberta.

The two major regional carriers in Canada are **Air BC** (☎ 800/663–8868 or 800/776–3000) and **Canadian Partner** (☎ 800/426–7000). They serve communities throughout western Canada and have daily flights from Vancouver and Victoria into Seattle. **Air BC** also has several daily flights between Vancouver and Portland. **Helijet Airways** (☎ 604/273–1414) provides jet helicopter service from Vancouver to Victoria.

In addition to its regular airport service, Air BC has float-plane service between Vancouver and Victoria harbors. **Kenmore Air** (☎ 206/486–8400 or 800/543–9595) has scheduled flights from Seattle's Lake Union to Victoria and points in the San Juan Islands. Along with several other floatplane companies, Kenmore provides fly-in service to remote fishing resorts along the coast of British Columbia.

COMPLAINTS

To register complaints about charter and scheduled airlines, contact the U.S. Department of Transportation's **Office of Consumer Affairs** (400

7th St. NW, Washington, DC 20590, ☎ 202/366–2220 or 800/322–7873).

CONSOLIDATORS

An established consolidator selling to the public is **TFI Tours International** (34 W. 32nd St., New York, NY 10001, ☎ 212/736–1140 or 800/745–8000). **FLY-ASAP** (3824 E. Indian School Rd., Phoenix, AZ 85018, ☎ 800/359–2727) isn't a discounter, but gets good deals from among published fares, and gets discount tickets from consolidators.

PUBLICATIONS

For general information about charter carriers, ask for the Office of Consumer Affairs' brochure **"Plane Talk: Public Charter Flights."** The Department of Transportation also publishes a 58-page booklet, **"Fly Rights"** ($1.75; Consumer Information Center, Dept. 133B, Pueblo, CO 81009).

For other tips and hints, consult the Consumers Union's monthly **"Consumer Reports Travel Letter"** ($39 a year; Box 53629, Boulder, CO 80322, ☎ 800/234–1970) and the newsletter **"Travel Smart"** ($37 a year; 40 Beechdale Rd., Dobbs Ferry, NY 10522, ☎ 800/327–3633); *The Official Frequent Flyer Guidebook,* by Randy Petersen ($14.99 plus $3 shipping; 4715-C Town Center Dr., Colorado Springs, CO 80916, ☎ 719/597–8899 or 800/487–8893); *Airfare Secrets Exposed,* by

Sharon Tyler and Matthew Wonder (Universal Information Publishing; $16.95 plus $3.75 shipping from Sandcastle Publishing, Box 3070-A, South Pasadena, CA 91031, ☎ 213/255–3616 or 800/655–0053); and *202 Tips Even the Best Business Travelers May Not Know,* by Christopher McGinnis ($10 plus $3 shipping; Irwin Professional Publishing, 1333 Burr Ridge Parkway, Burr Ridge, IL 60521, ☎ 800/634–3966).

B
BETTER BUSINESS BUREAU

Contact the **Alaska Better Business Bureau** (2805 Bering St., Suite 2, Anchorage 99503-3819, ☎ 907/562–0704) or the **Washington Better Business Bureau** (Box 68926, Sea-Tac 98168-0926, ☎ 206/431–2222). For other local contacts, consult the **Council of Better Business Bureaus** (4200 Wilson Blvd., Arlington, VA 22203, ☎ 703/276–0100).

BUS TRAVEL

Contact **Greyhound Lines** (☎ 800/231–2222) for bus service to Washington, Oregon, and British Columbia from various points in the United States and Canada.

WITHIN THE PACIFIC NORTH COAST

SCHEDULED SERVICE➤ **Greyhound Lines** (☎ 800/231–2222) operates regular intercity bus routes to points throughout the region.

Gray Line of Seattle (☎ 206/624–5077) has daily bus service between Seattle and Victoria via the Washington State ferry at Anacortes. Smaller bus companies provide service within local areas. One such service, **Pacific Coach Lines** (☎ 800/661–1725), runs from downtown Vancouver to Victoria (via the British Columbia ferry system). Bus service to Alaska from the lower 48 states is possible via Greyhound, with connections to other bus companies via Whitehorse in the Yukon Territory. **Quick Coach Lines** (☎ 604/244–3744; 800/665–2122 in the U.S.) provides bus service between Seattle's Sea-Tac Airport and Vancouver's major hotels and cruise terminal.

CHARTERS➤ Several companies operate charter bus service and scheduled sightseeing tours that last from a few hours to several days. Most tours can be booked locally and provide a good way for visitors to see the sights comfortably within a short period of time. **Gray Line** companies in Portland (☎ 503/226–6755), Seattle (☎ 206/624–5077), Vancouver (☎ 604/681–8687), and Victoria (☎ 604/388–5248) run such sightseeing trips.

DISCOUNTS➤ The AlaskaPass (*see* Discount Passes, *below*) offers one-price travel on bus and other modes of transportation in Alaska, British Columbia, and the Yukon.

C

CAR RENTAL

Major car-rental companies represented in the Pacific North Coast include **Avis** (☎ 800/331–1212, 800/879–2847 in Canada), **Budget** (☎ 800/527–0700, 0800/181–181 in the U.K.), **Dollar** (known as Eurodollar outside North America, ☎ 800/800–4000, 0181/952–6565 in the U.K.), **Hertz** (☎ 800/654–3131, 800/263–0600 in Canada, 0181/679–1799 in the U.K.), and **National** (☎ 800/227–7368, 0181/950–5050 in the U.K., where it is known as Europcar). Rates in Anchorage begin at $37 a day and $269 a week for an economy car with unlimited mileage. Rates in Seattle begin at $22 a day and $139 a week. Rates in Portland begin at $22 a day and $121 a week. Rates in Vancouver begin at $23 a day and $130 a week.

CHILDREN AND TRAVEL

FLYING

Look into **"Flying With Baby"** ($5.95 plus $1 shipping; Third Street Press, Box 261250, Littleton, CO 80126, ☎ 303/595–5959), cowritten by a flight attendant. **"Kids and Teens in Flight,"** free from the U.S. Department of Transportation's Office of Consumer Affairs, offers tips for children flying alone. Every two years the February issue of *Family Travel Times* (*see* Know-How, *below*) details children's services on three dozen airlines.

GAMES

The gamemeister, Milton Bradley, has games to help keep little (and not so little) children from getting fidgety while riding in planes, trains, and automobiles. Try packing the Travel Battleship sea battle game ($7), Travel Connect Four, a vertical strategy game ($8), the Travel Yahtzee dice game ($6), the Travel Trouble dice and board game ($7), and the Travel Guess Who mystery game ($8).

KNOW-HOW

Family Travel Times, published four times a year by Travel With Your Children (TWYCH, 45 W. 18th St., New York, NY 10011, ☎ 212/206–0688; annual subscription $40), covers destinations, types of vacations, and modes of travel.

The *Family Travel Guides* catalogue ($1 postage; Box 6061, Albany, CA 94706, ☎ 510/527–5849) lists about 200 books and articles on family travel. Also check *Take Your Baby and Go! A Guide for Traveling with Babies, Toddlers and Young Children,* by Sheri Andrews, Judy Bordeaux, and Vivian Vasquez ($5.95 plus $1.50 shipping; Bear Creek Publications, 2507 Minor Ave., Seattle, WA 98102, ☎ 206/322–7604 or 800/326–6566). Also from Globe Pequot are *The 100 Best Family Resorts in North America,* by Jane Wilford with Janet Tice

($12.95), and the two-volume (eastern section and western editions) set of *50 Great Family Vacations in North America* ($18.95 each plus $3 shipping).

TOUR OPERATORS

Contact **Grandtravel** (6900 Wisconsin Ave., Suite 706, Chevy Chase, MD 20815, ☎ 301/986–0790 or 800/247–7651), which has tours for people traveling with grandchildren ages seven to 17; or **Rascals in Paradise** (650 5th St., Suite 505, San Francisco, CA 94107, ☎ 415/978–9800 or 800/872–7225).

If you're outdoorsy, look into the Conservation Summits, nature camps sponsored by the **National Wildlife Federation** (8925 Leesburg Pike, Vienna, VA 22184-0001, ☎ 703/790–4000 or 800/245–5484); **Ecology Tours** (c/o the Audubon Center of the North Woods, Box 530, Sandstone, MN 55072, ☎ 612/245–2648), which mix travel and nature study; as well as programs from **American Wilderness Experience** (Box 1486, Boulder, CO 80306, ☎ 303/444–2622 or 800/444–0099), the **American Museum of Natural History** (79th St. and Central Park W, New York, NY 10024, ☎ 212/769–5700 or 800/462–8687).

CRUISING

More than 30 ships, of all sizes, offer cruises to Alaska. You can sail the Inside Passage on a small ship carrying a handful of passengers

or cross the Gulf of Alaska in the company of more than 1,000 other people. For the latest information on which cruise lines and ships are sailing to Alaska, see *Fodor's Cruises and Ports of Call* or *Fodor's Alaska*. For general information on cruising, contact **Cruise Lines International Association** (Suite 631, New York, NY 10004, ☎ 212/921–0066).

CUSTOMS

U.S. CITIZENS

The **U.S. Customs Service** (Box 7407, Washington, DC 20044, ☎ 202/927–6724) can answer questions on duty-free limits and publishes a helpful brochure, "Know Before You Go." For information on registering foreign-made articles, call 202/927–0540.

CANADIAN CITIZENS

Contact **Revenue Canada** (2265 St. Laurent Blvd. S, Ottawa, Ontario K1G 4K3, ☎ 613/993–0534) for a copy of the free brochure **"I Declare/Je Déclare"** and for details on duties that exceed the standard duty-free limit.

U.K. CITIZENS

HM Customs and Excise (Dorset House, Stamford St., London SE1 9NG, ☎ 0171/202–4227) can answer questions about U.K. customs regulations and publishes **"A Guide for Travellers,"** detailing standard procedures and import rules.

D
FOR TRAVELERS
WITH DISABILITIES

COMPLAINTS

To register complaints under the provisions of the Americans with Disabilities Act, contact the U.S. Department of Justice's **Public Access Section** (Box 66738, Washington, DC 20035, ☎ 202/514–0301, FAX 202/307–1198, TTY 202/514–0383).

ORGANIZATIONS

Barrier Free Alaska (7233 Madelynne Dr., Anchorage, AK 99504-4656, ☎ 907/337–6315) gives travelers with disabilities information about accessible facilities throughout the state.

Shared Outdoor Adventure Recreation (SOAR; ☎ 503/238–1613), a Portland organization, provides local listings of recreational activities for individuals with disabilities.

The **Canadian Paraplegic Association** (780 S.W. Marine Dr., Vancouver, BC V6P 5Y7, ☎ 604/324–3611) provides information on touring British Columbia. Information for people with hearing impairments is available from the **Western Institute for the Deaf** (2125 W. 7th Ave., Vancouver, BC V6K 1X9, ☎ 604/736–7391, TTY 604/736–2527). The annual *British Columbia Accommodation Guide* (☎ 800/663–6000) includes a list of hotel facilities for individuals with disabilities.

Access Alaska (3710 Woodland Dr., Suite 900, Anchorage, AK 99517, ☎ 907/248–4777) provides information and referral to visitors with disabilities. **Challenge Alaska** (Box 110065, Anchorage, AK 99511-0065, ☎ 907/563–2658) provides recreational opportunities for people with disabilities. Activities include downhill and cross-country skiing, sea kayaking, canoeing, camping, fishing, swimming, dogsledding, and backpacking.

FOR TRAVELERS WITH HEARING IMPAIRMENTS> Contact the **American Academy of Otolaryngology** (1 Prince St., Alexandria, VA 22314, ☎ 703/836–4444, FAX 703/683–5100, TTY 703/519–1585).

FOR TRAVELERS WITH MOBILITY PROBLEMS> Contact the **Information Center for Individuals with Disabilities** (Fort Point Pl., 27–43 Wormwood St., Boston, MA 02210, ☎ 617/727–5540, 800/462–5015 in MA, TTY 617/345–9743); **Mobility International USA** (Box 10767, Eugene, OR 97440, ☎ and TTY 503/343–1284, FAX 503/343–6812), the U.S. branch of an international organization based in Belgium (*see below*) that has affiliates in 30 countries; **MossRehab Hospital Travel Information Service** (1200 W. Tabor Rd., Philadelphia, PA 19141, ☎ 215/456–9603, TTY 215/456–9602); the **Society for the Advancement of Travel for the Handi-capped** (347 5th Ave., Suite 610, New York, NY 10016, ☎ 212/447–7284, FAX 212/725–8253); the **Travel Industry and Disabled Exchange** (TIDE, 5435 Donna Ave., Tarzana, CA 91356, ☎ 818/344–3640, FAX 818/344–0078); and **Travelin' Talk** (Box 3534, Clarksville, TN 37043, ☎ 615/552–6670, FAX 615/552–1182).

FOR TRAVELERS WITH VISION IMPAIRMENTS> Contact the **American Council of the Blind** (1155 15th St. NW, Suite 720, Washington, DC 20005, ☎ 202/467–5081, FAX 202/467–5085) or the **American Foundation for the Blind** (15 W. 16th St., New York, NY 10011, ☎ 212/620–2000, TTY 212/620–2158).

IN THE U.K.

Contact the **Royal Association for Disability and Rehabilitation** (RADAR, 12 City Forum, 250 City Rd., London EC1V 8AF, ☎ 0171/250–3222) or **Mobility International** (Rue de Manchester 25, B1070 Brussels, Belgium, ☎ 00–322–410–6297), an international clearinghouse of travel information for people with disabilities.

PUBLICATIONS

The Easter Seal Society (521 2nd Ave. W, Seattle, WA 98119, ☎ 206/281–5700) publishes *Access Seattle,* a free guide to the city's services for people with disabilities.

Circling the City—A Guide to the Accessibility of Public Places in and Near Portland, Oregon, a 144-page book, is available from the Junior League (4838 S.W. Scholls Ferry Rd., Portland, OR 97225, ☎ 503/297–6364).

Several publications for travelers with disabilities are available from the **Consumer Information Center** (Box 100, Pueblo, CO 81009, ☎ 719/948–3334). Call or write for a free catalogue of current titles.

Fodor's *Great American Vacations for Travelers with Disabilities* ($18; available in bookstores, or call 800/533–6478) details accessible attractions, restaurants, and hotels in U.S. destinations. The 500-page *Travelin' Talk Directory* ($35; Box 3534, Clarksville, TN 37043, ☎ 615/552–6670) lists people and organizations who help travelers with disabilities. For specialist travel agents worldwide, consult the *Directory of Travel Agencies for the Disabled,* by Helen Hecker ($19.95 plus $3.50 handling; Disability Bookshop, Box 129, Vancouver, WA, 98666, ☎ 206/694–2462). The Sierra Club publishes *Easy Access to National Parks* ($16 plus $3 shipping; 730 Polk St., San Francisco, CA 94109, ☎ 415/776–2211 or 800/935–1056).

TRAVEL AGENCIES AND TOUR OPERATORS

The Americans with Disabilities Act requires that travel firms serve the needs of all travelers. However, some agencies and operators specialize in making group and individual arrangements for travelers with disabilities, among them **Access Adventures** (206 Chestnut Ridge Rd., Rochester, NY 14624, ☎ 716/889–9096), run by a former physical-rehab counselor; and **Travel Trends** (2 Allan Plaza, 4922 51st Ave., Box 3581, Leduc, Alberta T9E 6X2, ☎ 403/986–9000 or 800/661–2109 in Canada), which has group tours and is especially good for cruises. In addition, many operators and agencies (*see* Tour Operators, *below*) can also arrange vacations for travelers with disabilities.

FOR TRAVELERS WITH MOBILITY IMPAIRMENTS➤ A number of operators specialize in working with travelers with mobility impairments: **Accessible Journeys** (35 W. Sellers Ave., Ridley Park, PA 19078, ☎ 610/521–0339 or 800/846–4537, FAX 610/521–6959), a registered nursing service that arranges vacations; **Hinsdale Travel Service** (201 E. Ogden Ave., Suite 100, Hinsdale, IL 60521, ☎ 708/325–1335 or 800/303–5521), a travel agency that will give you access to the services of wheelchair traveler Janice Perkins; and **Wheelchair Journeys** (16979 Redmond Way, Redmond, WA 98052, ☎ 206/885–2210), which can handle arrangements worldwide.

FOR TRAVELERS WITH DEVELOPMENTAL DISABILITIES➤ Contact the nonprofit **New Directions** (5276 Hollister Ave., Suite 207, Santa Barbara, CA 93111, ☎ 805/967–2841) as well as the general-interest operations above.

DISCOUNT CLUBS

Options include **Entertainment Travel Editions** (fee $28–$53, depending on destination; Box 1068, Trumbull, CT 06611, ☎ 800/445–4137), **Great American Traveler** ($49.95 annually; Box 27965, Salt Lake City, UT 84127, ☎ 800/548–2812), **Moment's Notice Discount Travel Club** ($25 annually, single or family; 163 Amsterdam Ave., Suite 137, New York, NY 10023, ☎ 212/486–0500), **Privilege Card** ($74.95 annually; 3391 Peachtree Rd. NE, Suite 110, Atlanta, GA 30326, ☎ 404/262–0222 or 800/236-9732), **Travelers Advantage** ($49 annually, single or family; CUC Travel Service, 49 Music Sq. W, Nashville, TN 37203, ☎ 800/548–1116 or 800/648–4037), and **Worldwide Discount Travel Club** ($50 annually for family, $40 single; 1674 Meridian Ave., Miami Beach, FL 33139, ☎ 305/534–2082).

DISCOUNT PASSES

The **AlaskaPass Travelpass** (Box 351 Vashon Island, WA 98070, ☎ 800/248–7598) provides transportation aboard any Alaska or British Columbia ferry as well as many connecting bus and train services. Passes of varying lengths enable the independent traveler to exercise a high degree of flexibility in choosing an itinerary.

VIA Rail Canada (☎ 800/665–0200) offers a **Canrailpass** that is good for 30 days. System-wide passes cost $282 (Jan. 6–June 6 and Oct. 1–Dec. 14) and $420 (June 7–Sept. 30). Youth passes (age 24 and under) are $377 in peak season and $257 during the off-season. Prices are quoted in U.S. dollars. Tickets can be purchased in the United States or the United Kingdom from a travel agent, from **Long Haul Leisurail** (Box 113, Peterborough PE1 1LE, ☎ 0733/51780), or upon arrival in Canada. This offer does not apply to Canadian citizens.

F

FERRIES

ALASKA

The transportation lifeblood of southeastern Alaska is the **Alaska Marine Highway System** (Box 25535, Juneau, AK 99802-5535, ☎ 907/465–3941, 907/465–3942, or 800/642–0066 from the lower 48 states). From their southern terminus in Bellingham, Washington, the Alaska ferries carry passengers and vehicles through the Inside Passage year-round, with stops at Skagway, Haines, Ketchikan, Sitka, Wrangell, Petersburg, Stewart, and Juneau. Smaller car ferries serve several other towns and villages in southeast

THE GOLD GUIDE / IMPORTANT CONTACTS

Alaska and Prince Rupert, British Columbia.

BRITISH COLUMBIA

The **British Columbia Ferry Corporation** (1112 Fort St., Victoria, BC V8V 4V2, ☎ 604/386–3431 in Victoria or 604/669–1211 in Vancouver; for recorded schedule information, ☎ 604/656–0757 in Victoria or 604/277–0277 in Vancouver) operates one of the largest and most modern ferry fleets in the world, with 38 ships serving 42 ports of call along the coast of British Columbia. More than 15 million passengers ride this fleet each year.

Clipper Navigation (2701 Alaskan Way, Pier 69, Seattle, WA 98121, ☎ 800/888–2535) operates three passenger-only jet catamarans between Seattle and Victoria; the largest holds 300 people, the smallest 250. Each boat makes the scenic crossing in just under three hours.

Black Ball Transport's (430 Belleville St., Victoria, BC V8V 1W9, ☎ 604/386–2202 in Victoria or 360/457–4491 in Port Angeles) MV *Coho* makes daily crossings year-round, from Port Angeles to Victoria. The *Coho* can carry 800 passengers and 100 cars across the Strait of Juan de Fuca in 1½ hours. Advance reservations are not accepted.

Victoria Line (185 Dallas Rd., Victoria, BC V8V 1A1, ☎ 604/480–5555) operates a

car/passenger ferry, the *Royal Victorian,* from mid-May to late September between Seattle and Victoria with one round-trip daily. Sailing time is 4½ hours.

Gray Line Cruises (☎ 206/738–8099 or 800/443–4552) operates the passenger-only *Victoria Star,* which provides boat service between Bellingham and Victoria from mid-May to mid-October.

Victoria Rapid Transit operates the passenger-only *Victoria Express* (Box 1928, Port Angeles, WA 98362, ☎ 206/452–8088 or 800/633–1589 for reservations in WA) and offers a one-hour crossing of the Strait of Juan de Fuca between Port Angeles and Victoria from the end of May through the end of October.

WASHINGTON

The **Washington State Ferry System** (Colman Dock, Seattle, WA 98104, ☎ 206/464–6400 or 800/843–3779 in WA) has 25 ferries in its fleet, which carries more than 23 million passengers a year between points on Puget Sound and the San Juan Islands. Reservations are not available on any domestic routes.

G
GAY AND
LESBIAN TRAVEL

ORGANIZATIONS

The **International Gay Travel Association** (Box 4974, Key West, FL 33041, ☎ 800/448–8550), a consortium

of 800 businesses, can supply names of travel agents and tour operators.

PUBLICATIONS

The premier international travel magazine for gays and lesbians is *Our World* ($35 for 10 issues; 1104 N. Nova Rd., Suite 251, Daytona Beach, FL 32117, ☎ 904/441–5367). The 16-page monthly *"Out & About"* ($49 for 10 issues; ☎ 212/645–6922 or 800/929–2268) covers gay-friendly resorts, hotels, cruise lines, and airlines.

TOUR OPERATORS

Cruises and resort vacations are handled by **R.S.V.P. Travel Productions** (2800 University Ave. SE, Minneapolis, MN 55414, ☎ 800/328–7787) for gays, **Olivia** (4400 Market St., Oakland, CA 94608, ☎ 800/631–6277) for lesbian travelers. For mixed gay and lesbian travel, contact **Toto Tours** (1326 W. Albion, Suite 3W, Chicago, IL 60626, ☎ 312/274–8686 or 800/565–1241).

TRAVEL AGENCIES

The largest agencies serving gay travelers are **Advance Travel** (10700 Northwest Freeway, Suite 160, Houston, TX 77092, ☎ 713/682–2002 or 800/695–0880), **Islanders/ Kennedy Travel** (183 W. 10th St., New York, NY 10014, ☎ 212/242–3222 or 800/988–1181), **Now Voyager** (4406 18th St., San Francisco, CA 94114, ☎ 415/626–1169 or 800/255–6951), and

Yellowbrick Road (1500 W. Balmoral Ave., Chicago, IL 60640, ☎ 312/561–1800 or 800/642–2488). **Skylink Women's Travel** (746 Ashland Ave., Santa Monica, CA 90405, ☎ 310/452–0506 or 800/225-5759) works with lesbians.

I

INSURANCE

Travel insurance covering baggage, health, and trip cancellation or interruptions is available from **Access America** (Box 90315, Richmond, VA 23286, ☎ 804/285–3300 or 800/284–8300), **Carefree Travel Insurance** (Box 9366, 100 Garden City Plaza, Garden City, NY 11530, ☎ 516/294–0220 or 800/323–3149), **Near Travel Services** (Box 1339, Calumet City, IL 60409, ☎ 708/868–6700 or 800/654–6700), **Tele-Trip** (Mutual of Omaha Plaza, Box 31716, Omaha, NE 68131, ☎ 800/228–9792), **Travel Insured International** (Box 280568, East Hartford, CT 06128-0568, ☎ 203/528–7663 or 800/243–3174), **Travel Guard International** (1145 Clark St., Stevens Point, WI 54481, ☎ 715/345–0505 or 800/826–1300), and **Wallach & Company** (107 W. Federal St., Box 480, Middleburg, VA 22117, ☎ 703/687–3166 or 800/237–6615).

IN THE U.K.

The **Association of British Insurers** (51 Gresham St., London EC2V 7HQ, ☎ 0171/600–3333; 30 Gordon St., Glasgow G1 3PU, ☎ 0141/226–3905; Scottish Provident Bldg., Donegall Sq. W, Belfast BT1 6JE, ☎ 01232/249176; and other locations) gives advice by phone and publishes the free **"Holiday Insurance,"** which sets out typical policy provisions and costs.

L

LODGING

APARTMENT AND VILLA RENTAL

Among the companies to contact are **Property Rentals International** (1008 Mansfield Crossing Rd., Richmond, VA 23236, ☎ 804/378–6054 or 800/220–3332), **Rent-a-Home International** (7200 34th Ave. NW, Seattle, WA 98117, ☎ 206/789–9377 or 800/488–7368), and **Vacation Home Rentals Worldwide** (235 Kensington Ave., Norwood, NJ 07648, ☎ 201/767–9393 or 800/633–3284). Members of the travel club **Hideaways International** ($99 annually; 767 Islington St., Portsmouth, NH 03801, ☎ 603/430–4433 or 800/843–4433) receive two annual guides plus quarterly newsletters, and arrange rentals among themselves.

BED-AND-BREAKFASTS

Reservation services in the Pacific North Coast include **Best Canadian Bed & Breakfast Network** (1090 W. King Edward Ave., Vancouver, BC V6H 1Z4, ☎ 604/738–7207), **Hometours International, Inc.** (1170 Broadway, Suite 614, New York, NY 10001, ☎ 212/689–0851 or 800/367–4668), **Northwest Bed & Breakfast Travel Unlimited** (610 S.W. Broadway, Portland, OR 97205, ☎ 503/243–7616), and **Traveller's Bed & Breakfast** (Box 492, Mercer Island, WA 98040, ☎ 206/232–2345). The **Oregon Bed and Breakfast Guild** (Box 3187, Ashland, OR 97520) publishes a directory of establishments within the state. Before leaving the United Kingdom, you can book a B&B through **American Bed & Breakfast, Inter-Bed Network** (31 Ernest Rd., Colchester, Essex CO7 9LQ, ☎ 0206/223162).

HOME EXCHANGE

Principal clearinghouses include **HomeLink International/Vacation Exchange Club** ($60 annually; Box 650, Key West, FL 33041, ☎ 305/294–1448 or 800/638–3841), which gives members four annual directories, with a listing in one, plus updates; **Intervac International** ($65 annually; Box 590504, San Francisco, CA 94159, ☎ 415/435–3497), which has three annual directories; and **Loan-a-Home** ($35–$45 annually; 2 Park La., Apt. 6E, Mount Vernon, NY 10552-3443, ☎ 914/664–7640), which specializes in long-term exchanges.

HOTELS

Vancouver, Seattle, and Portland have all experienced major hotel building booms during

THE GOLD GUIDE / IMPORTANT CONTACTS

the past 10 years. Most of the major chains have properties in one or all of these cities. For more information, contact **Canadian Pacific** (☎ 800/828–7447), **Delta** (☎ 800/877–1133), **Doubletree** (☎ 800/528–0444), **Four Seasons** (☎ 800/332–3442), **Hilton** (☎ 800/445–8667), **Holiday Inn** (☎ 800/465–4329), **Hyatt** (☎ 800/233–1234), **Marriott** (☎ 800/228–9290), **Ramada** (☎ 800/228–2828), **Red Lion Hotels and Inns** (☎ 800/547–8010), **Sheraton** (☎ 800/325–3535), **Stouffer** (☎ 800/468–3571), **West Coast Hotels/Coast Hotels** (☎ 800/426–0670), and **Westin** (☎ 800/228–3000).

Examples of all-suite hotels are **Courtyard By Marriott** (☎ 800/321–2211) and **Embassy Suites Hotels** (☎ 800/362–2779).

MOTELS/ MOTOR INNS

Nationally recognized chains include **Best Western** (☎ 800/528–1234), **Days Inn** (☎ 800/325–2525), **La Quinta Inns** (☎ 800/531–5900), **Motel 6** (☎ 800/440–6000), **Quality Inns** (☎ 800/228–5151), **Super 8 Motels** (☎ 800/848–8888). **Travelodge** (☎ 800/255–3050), **Nendel's** (☎ 800/547–0106), **Sandman Inns** (☎ 800/726-3626), and **Shilo Inns** (☎ 800/222–2244) are regional chains.

M
MONEY MATTERS

ATMS

For specific **Cirrus** locations in the United States and Canada, call 800/424–7787. For U.S. **Plus** locations, call 800/843–7587 and enter the area code and first three digits of the number you're calling from (or of the calling area where you want an ATM).

WIRING FUNDS

Funds can be wired via **American Express MoneyGram**^{SM} (☎ 800/926–9400 from the U.S. and Canada for locations and information) or **Western Union** (☎ 800/325–6000 for agent locations or to send using MasterCard or Visa, 800/321–2923 in Canada).

P
PASSPORTS
AND VISAS

Canadian and U.S. citizens do not need a passport to travel between the United States and Canada.

U.K. CITIZENS

For fees, documentation requirements, and to get an emergency passport, call the **London Passport Office** (☎ 0171/271–3000). For visa information, call the **U.S. Embassy Visa Information Line** (☎ 0891/200–290; calls cost 48p per minute or 36p per minute cheap rate) or write the **U.S. Embassy Visa Branch** (5 Upper Grosvenor St., London W1A 2JB). If you live in Northern Ireland, write the **U.S. Consulate General** (Queen's House, Queen St., Belfast BTI 6EO).

PHOTO HELP

The **Kodak Information Center** (☎ 800/242–2424) answers consumer questions about film and photography. Fodor's also publishes the *Kodak Guide to Shooting Great Travel Pictures* ($16.50; available at bookstores or from Fodor's Travel Publications, ☎ 800/533–6478), which has hundreds of tips and photos on everything from how to shoot common travel subjects—markets, beaches, architectural details, and so on—to how to compensate for various light and weather conditions.

R
RAIL TRAVEL

Amtrak (☎ 800/872–7245), the U.S. passenger rail system, has daily service to the Pacific North Coast from the Midwest and California. The *Empire Builder* takes a northern route from Chicago to Seattle. The *Pioneer* travels from Chicago to Portland via Denver and Salt Lake City. The *Coast Starlight* begins in Los Angeles, makes stops throughout western Oregon and Washington, and terminates its route in Seattle. At present, there are no trains that cross the border from Seattle into Canada.

Canada's passenger service, **VIA Rail Canada** (☎ 800/665–0200), operates transcontinental routes on the *Canadian* three times weekly between eastern Canada and Vancouver. A second train, the *Skeena,* runs three times weekly between Jasper, Alberta, to the British

Columbia port city of Prince Rupert.

WITHIN THE PACIFIC NORTH COAST

The Pacific North Coast has a number of scenic train routes in addition to those operated by Amtrak and VIA Rail Canada. The **Rocky Mountaineer** (Great Canadian Railtour Co., Ltd., 340 Brooksbank Ave., Suite 104, North Vancouver, BC V7J 2C1, ☎ 800/665–7245) is a two-day rail cruise between Vancouver and the Canadian Rockies, May–October. There are two routes one to Banff/Calgary and the other to Jasper—through landscapes considered to be the most spectacular in the world. An overnight hotel stop is made in Kamloops.

On Vancouver Island, VIA Rail (☎ 604/383–4324) runs the *E&N Railway* daily from Victoria north to Nanaimo. **BC Rail** (Box 8770, Vancouver, BC V6B 4X6, ☎ 604/631–3500) operates daily service from its North Vancouver terminal to the town of Prince George. At Prince George, it is possible to connect with VIA Rail's *Skeena* service east to Jasper and Alberta or west to Prince Rupert. BC Rail also operates a summertime excursion steam train, the *Royal Hudson,* between North Vancouver and Squamish, at the head of Howe Sound.

A dramatic and scenic excursion in southeastern Alaska is the **White Pass and Yukon Route** (Box 435, Skagway, AK 99840, ☎ 800/343–7373). The narrow-gauge railroad carried passengers and ore from the Klondike gold mines of the Yukon to Skagway until it was closed down in the early 1980s. In 1988 the line was reopened as far as Fraser, British Columbia. Bus service is available from Fraser to Whitehorse in the Yukon Territory.

Tours that include travel aboard the Alaska Railroad and often the White Pass and Yukon are available from Princess Tours and Holland America Westours (*see* Tour Operators, *below*).

DISCOUNTS➤ The AlaskaPass (*see* Discount Passes, *above*) offers one-price travel on bus and other modes of transportation in Alaska, British Columbia, and the Yukon.

S
SENIOR CITIZENS

EDUCATIONAL TRAVEL

The nonprofit **Elderhostel** (75 Federal St., 3rd Floor, Boston, MA 02110, ☎ 617/426–7788), for people 60 and older, has offered inexpensive study programs since 1975. The nearly 2,000 courses cover everything from marine science to Greek myths and cowboy poetry. Fees for programs in the United States and Canada, which usually last one week, run about $300, not including transportation.

ORGANIZATIONS

Contact the **American Association of Retired Persons** (membership $8 per person or couple annually; 601 E St. NW, Washington, DC 20049, ☎ 202/434–2277). Its Purchase Privilege Program gets members discounts on lodging, car rentals, and sightseeing, and the AARP Motoring Plan furnishes domestic trip-routing information and emergency road-service aid for an annual fee of $39.95 per person or couple ($59.95 for a premium version).

For other discounts on lodgings, car rentals, and other travel products, along with magazines and newsletters, contact the **National Council of Senior Citizens** (membership $12 annually; 1331 F St. NW, Washington, DC 20004, ☎ 202/347–8800) and **Mature Outlook** (subscription $9.95 annually; 6001 N. Clark St., Chicago, IL 60660, ☎ 312/465–6466 or 800/336–6330).

PUBLICATIONS

The 50+ Traveler's Guidebook: Where to Go, Where to Stay, What to Do, by Anita Williams and Merrimac Dillon ($12.95; St. Martin's Press, 175 5th Ave., New York, NY 10010, ☎ 212/674–5151 or 800/288–2131), offers many useful tips. **"The Mature Traveler"** ($29.95; Box 50400, Reno, NV 89513, ☎ 702/786–7419), a monthly newsletter, covers travel deals.

THE GOLD GUIDE / IMPORTANT CONTACTS

SPORTS

BICYCLING

Bicycling is a popular sport in the Pacific North Coast, appealing to both families out for a leisurely ride and avid cyclists seeking a challenge on rugged mountain trails.

Several cycling organizations sponsor trips of various lengths and degrees of difficulty, both on- and off-road. For further information, contact **Portland Wheelmen Touring Club** (Box 40753, Portland, OR 97240, ☎ 503/257–7982), **Cascade Bicycle Club** (☎ 206/522–2453), and **Bicycling Association of British Columbia** (332–1367 W. Broadway, Vancouver, BC V6H 4A9, tel 604/737–3034.

Rentals are available from bicycle shops in most cities.

BOATING

The **Trade Association of Sea Kayaking (TASK)** (Box 84144, Seattle, WA 98124, ☎ 206/621–1018) provides information on outfitters, rentals, seminars, and safety.

CLIMBING/MOUNTAINEERING

For information, contact **Mazama Club** (909 N.W. 19th Ave., Portland, OR 97209, ☎ 503/227–2345), **The Mountaineers** (300 3rd Ave. W, Seattle, WA 98119, ☎ 206/284–6310), and **Rainier Mountaineering Inc.** (Paradise, WA 98397, ☎ 206/569–2227).

FISHING

For information on fishing regulations, contact **Washington Department of Fisheries** (Administration Bldg., Room 115, Olympia, WA 98504, ☎ 206/586–1425 for Washington salmon fishing or marine licenses), **Washington State Department of Wildlife** (600 Capitol Way N, Olympia, WA 98501, ☎ 206/753–5700 for freshwater fishing), **Oregon Department of Fish and Wildlife** (506 S.W. Mill St., Portland, OR 97208, ☎ 503/229–5403), or **Alaska Department of Fish and Game** (Box 25535, Juneau, AK 99802, ☎ 907/465–4112). In British Columbia, separate licenses are required for saltwater and freshwater fishing. Information and licenses for saltwater fishing can be obtained from the **Department of Fisheries and Oceans** (555 W. Hastings St., Suite 400, Vancouver, BC V6B 5G3, ☎ 604/666–0384). For freshwater fishing, contact the **Ministry of Environment, Fish and Wildlife Information** (Parliament Bldgs., Victoria, BC V8V 1X5, ☎ 604/387–9740).

HIKING

There are many trails in the Pacific North Coast that are geared to both beginning and experienced hikers. The **National Parks and Forests Outdoor Recreation Information Center** (915 2nd Ave., Room 442, Seattle, WA 98174, ☎ 206/220–7450) can provide maps of trails that are well marked and well maintained. Guidebooks that describe the best trails in the area are readily available in local bookstores. The *Footsore* series of books, published by the Mountaineers (306 2nd Ave. W, Seattle, WA 98119, ☎ 206/285–2665), are among the best.

HUNTING

For information on hunting facilities and licenses, contact **Washington State Department of Wildlife** (600 Capitol Way N, Olympia, WA 98501, ☎ 206/753–5700), **Oregon Department of Fish and Wildlife** (506 S.W. Mill St., Portland, OR 97208, ☎ 503/229–5403), **British Columbia Ministry of Environment, Wildlife Branch** (810 Blanshard St., Victoria, BC V8W 2H1, ☎ 604/387–9740), or **Alaska Department of Fish and Game** (Box 3-200, Juneau, AK 99802, ☎ 907/465–4112).

SCUBA DIVING

The crystal-clear waters of Puget Sound and the Inside Passage—with their diversity of marine life—present excellent opportunities for scuba diving and underwater photography. For information on dive shops, equipment rentals, and charter boats in British Columbia, contact **Dive B.C.** (707 Westminster Ave., Powell River, BC V8A 1C5, ☎ 604/485–6267).

SKIING

CROSS-COUNTRY➣ Cross-country skiing is a popular and relatively inexpensive way to enjoy the winter wilderness. Many downhill ski resorts also have well-marked and well-groomed cross-country trails. Washington operates a system of more than 40 **SnoParks** (Office of Winter Recreation, Parks and Recreation Commission, 7150 Cleanwater La., KY-11, Olympia, WA 98504, ☎ 206/586–0185) that are a series of groomed cross-country trails within state parks in which, for the price of a one-day ($7), three-day ($10), or seasonal ($20) pass, skiers have access to trails in 70 locations statewide.

STUDENTS

GROUPS

A major tour operator is **Contiki Holidays** (300 Plaza Alicante, Suite 900, Garden Grove, CA 92640, ☎ 714/740–0808 or 800/466–0610).

HOSTELING

Contact **Hostelling International–American Youth Hostels** (733 15th St. NW, Suite 840, Washington, DC 20005, ☎ 202/783–6161) in the United States, **Hostelling International–Canada** (205 Catherine St., Suite 400, Ottawa, Ontario K2P 1C3, ☎ 613/237–7884) in Canada, and the **Youth Hostel Association of England and Wales** (Trevelyan House, 8 St. Stephen's Hill, St. Albans, Hertfordshire AL1 2DY, ☎ 01727/855215 and 01727/845047) in the United Kingdom. Membership ($25 in the U.S., C$26.75 in Canada, and £9 in the U.K.) gets you access to 5,000 hostels worldwide that charge $7–$20 nightly per person.

I.D. CARDS

To get discounts on transportation and admissions, get the **International Student Identity Card** (ISIC) if you're a bona fide student or the **Go 25 Card** if you're under 26. In the United States, the ISIC and Go 25 cards cost $18 each and include basic travel accident and illness coverage, plus a toll-free travel hot line. Apply through the Council on International Educational Exchange (*see* Organizations, *below*). Cards are available for $15 each in Canada from **Travel Cuts** (187 College St., Toronto, Ontario M5T 1P7, ☎ 416/979–2406 or 800/667–2887) and in the United Kingdom for £5 each at student unions and student travel companies.

ORGANIZATIONS

A major contact is the **Council on International Educational Exchange** (CIEE, 205 E. 42nd St., 16th Floor, New York, NY 10017, ☎ 212/661–1450) with locations in Boston (729 Boylston St., 02116, ☎ 617/266–1926), Miami (9100 S. Dadeland Blvd., 33156, ☎ 305/670–9261), Los Angeles (10904 Lindbrook Dr., 90024, ☎ 310/208–3551), 43 college towns nationwide, and the United Kingdom (28A Poland St., London W1V 3DB, ☎ 0171/437–7767). Twice a year, it publishes *Student Travels* magazine. The CIEE's Council Travel Service offers domestic air passes for bargain travel

within the United States and is the exclusive U.S. agent for several student-discount cards.

Campus Connections (325 Chestnut St., Suite 1101, Philadelphia, PA 19106, ☎ 215/625–8585 or 800/428–3235) specializes in discounted accommodations and airfares for students. The **Educational Travel Centre** (438 N. Frances St., Madison, WI 53703, ☎ 608/256–5551) offers rail passes and low-cost airline tickets, mostly for flights departing from Chicago.

In Canada, also contact **Travel Cuts** (*see above*).

PUBLICATIONS

See the *Berkeley Guide to the Pacific North Coast & Alaska* ($16.95; available in bookstores or through Fodor's Travel Publications, ☎ 800/533–6478).

T
TOUR OPERATORS

Among the companies selling tours and packages to the Pacific North Coast, the following have a proven reputation, are nationally known, and offer plenty of options.

GROUP TOURS

For a deluxe escorted tour to the Pacific North Coast, contact **Maupintour** (Box 807, Lawrence, KS 66044, ☎ 913/843–1211 or 800/255–4266) and **Tauck Tours** (11 Wilton Rd., Westport, CT 06880, ☎ 203/226–6911 or 800/468–2825). Another operator falling between deluxe and first class is **Globus** (5301 S. Federal Circle, Littleton, CO 80123, ☎ 303/797–2800 or 800/221–0090). In the first-class and tourist range, try **Collette Tours** (162 Middle St., Pawtucket, RI 02860, ☎ 401/728–3805 or 800/832–4656), **Gadabout Tours** (700 E. Tahquitz Canyon Way, Palm Springs, CA 92262, ☎ 619/325–5556 or 800/952–5068), and **Mayflower Tours** (1225 Warren Ave., Downers Grove, IL 60515, ☎ 708/960–3430 or 800/323–7604), **Trieloff Tours** (24301 El Toro Rd., Suite 140, Laguna Hills, CA 92653, ☎ 800/248–6877 or 800/432–7125 in CA). For budget and tourist class programs, contact **Cosmos** (*see* Globus, *above*).

AIR TOURS➤ **Alaska Airlines Vacations** (Box 68900, SEARV, Seattle, WA 98168, ☎ 800/468–2248) teams up with local operators in Alaska to offer air and land packages.

CRUISE TOURS➤ The major cruise/tour operators in Alaska for big ships are **Princess Cruises** (2815 2nd Ave., Suite 400, Seattle, WA 98121, ☎ 206/728–4202 or 800/426–0442), **Holland America Westours** (300 Elliott Ave. W, Seattle, WA 98119, ☎ 206/281–3535 or 800/426–0327). For a small-ship cruise-tour, contact **Alaska Sightseeing/Cruise West** (Suite 700, 4th St. and Battery Bldg., Seattle, WA

98121, ☎ 206/441–8687 or 800/426–7702).

PACKAGES

Independent vacation packages to the Pacific North Coast are available from major tour operators and airlines. Contact **American Airlines Fly AAway Vacations** (☎ 800/321–2121), **SuperCities** (139 Main St., Cambridge, MA 02142, ☎ 617/621–0099 or 800/333–1234), **Continental Airlines' Grand Destinations** (☎ 800/634–5555), **Delta Dream Vacations** (☎ 800/872–7786), **Certified Vacations** (Box 1525, Ft. Lauderdale, FL 33302, ☎ 305/522–1414 or 800/233–7260), **United Vacations** (☎ 800/328–6877), **Kingdom Tours** (300 Market St., Kingston, PA 18704, ☎ 717/283–4241 or 800/872–8857), and **USAir Vacations** (☎ 800/455–0123). For rail packages, try **Amtrak** (☎ 800/872–7245).

Basic hotel and air packages to Alaska are rare because most travelers want—and need—the guidance and planning an escorted tour provides. Nevertheless, a few operators and travel agencies specialize in putting together independent packages. One of the oldest is **Knightly Tours** (Box 16366, Seattle, WA 98116, ☎ 206/938–8567 or 800/426–2123), which has specialized in arranging independent travel to Alaska for 25 years.

Packages include fly/drive itineraries with bed-and-breakfast accommodations or ferry-liner tours.

If you plan to travel without any prepackaged itinerary, you may wish to invest in an AlaskaPass (*see* Discount Passes, *above*).

FROM THE U.K.

Travel agencies that offer cheap fares to the Pacific North Coast include **Trailfinders** (42–50 Earl's Court Rd., London W8 6FT, ☎ 0171/937–5400), **Travel Cuts** (295a Regent St., London W1R 7YA, ☎ 0171/637–3161; *see* Students, *above*), and **Flightfile** (49 Tottenham Court Rd., London W1P 9RE, ☎ 0171/700–2722).

THEME TRIPS

For information on themed tours of the Pacific North Coast, *see* Guided Tours *in* the Essentials section at the end of each chapter.

ORGANIZATIONS

The **National Tour Association** (546 E. Main St., Lexington, KY 40508, ☎ 606/226–4444 or 800/755–8687) and **United States Tour Operators Association** (USTOA, 211 E. 51st St., Suite 12B, New York, NY 10022, ☎ 212/750–7371) can provide lists of member operators and information on booking tours.

PUBLICATIONS

Consult the brochure **"On Tour"** and ask for a

current list of member operators from the National Tour Association (*see* Organizations, *above*). Also get a copy of the **"Worldwide Tour & Vacation Package Finder"** from the USTOA (*see* Organizations, *above*) and the Better Business Bureau's **"Tips on Travel Packages"** (publication No. 24-195, $2; 4200 Wilson Blvd., Arlington, VA 22203).

TRAVEL AGENCIES

For names of reputable agencies in your area, contact the **American Society of Travel Agents** (1101 King St., Suite 200, Alexandria, VA 22314, ☎ 703/739–2782).

 U

U.S.
GOVERNMENT
TRAVEL BRIEFINGS

The U.S. Department of State's Overseas Citizens Emergency Center (Room 4811, Washington, DC 20520; enclose SASE) issues **Consular Information Sheets,** which cover crime, security, political climate, and health risks as well as embassy locations, entry requirements, currency regulations, and other routine matters. For the latest information, stop in at any U.S. passport office, consulate, or embassy; call the interactive hot line (☎ 202/647–5225 or fax 202/647-3000); or, with your PC's modem, tap into the Bureau of Consular Affairs' computer bulletin board (☎ 202/647–9225).

V
VISITOR
INFORMATION

IN THE U.S.
Alaska Division of Tourism (Dept. 909, Box 110801, Juneau, AK 99811-0801, ☎ 907/465–2010).

Oregon Tourism Division (775 Summer St. NE, Salem, OR 97310, ☎ 800/543–8838 in OR or 800/547–7842 out of state).

Washington Tourism Development Division (Box 45213, Olympia, WA 98504, ☎ 206/586–2088, 206/586– 2102, or 800/544–1800).

IN CANADA
Tourism British Columbia (1117 Wharf St., Victoria, BC V8W 2Z2, ☎ 800/663–6000).

IN THE U.K.
For touring tips and brochures, contact the **United States Travel and Tourism Administration** (Box 1EN, London WIA 1EN, ☎ 071/495–4466), **Canadian High Commission, Tourism Division** (Canada House, Trafalgar Sq., London SW1Y 5DJ, ☎ 071/930–6857), or **Tourism British Columbia** (1 Regent St., London SW1Y 4NS, ☎ 071/930–6857).

W
WEATHER

For current conditions and forecasts, plus the local time and helpful travel tips, call the **Weather Channel Connection** (☎ 900/932–8437; 95¢ per minute) from a touch-tone phone.

SMART TRAVEL TIPS A TO Z

Basic Information on Traveling in the Pacific North Coast and Savvy Tips to Make Your Trip a Breeze

The more you travel, the more you know about how to make trips run like clockwork. To help make your travels hassle-free, Fodor's editors have rounded up dozens of tips from our contributors and travel experts all over the world, as well as basic information on visiting the Pacific North Coast. For names of organizations to contact and publications that can give you more information, *see* Important Contacts A to Z, *above.*

A
AIR TRAVEL

If time is an issue, **always look for nonstop flights,** which require no change of plane and make no stops. If possible, **avoid connecting flights,** which stop at least once and can involve a change of plane, although the flight number remains the same; if the first leg is late, the second waits.

CUTTING COSTS

The Sunday travel section of most newspapers is a good source of deals.

MAJOR AIRLINES➤ The least-expensive airfares from the major airlines are priced for round-trip travel and are subject to restrictions. You must usually **book in advance and buy the ticket within 24 hours** to get cheaper fares, and

you may have to **stay over a Saturday night.** The lowest fare is subject to availability, and only a small percentage of the plane's total seats are sold at that price. It's good to **call a number of airlines, and when you are quoted a good price, book it on the spot**—the same fare on the same flight may not be available the next day. Airlines generally allow you to change your return date for a $25 to $50 fee, but most low-fare tickets are nonrefundable. However, if you don't use it, you can apply the cost toward the purchase price of a new ticket, again for a small charge.

Fares on scheduled flights from the United Kingdom vary considerably. January to March are the cheapest months to fly, and midweek flights nearly always offer some reductions.

CONSOLIDATORS➤ Consolidators, who buy tickets at reduced rates from scheduled airlines, sell them at prices below the lowest available from the airlines directly—usually without advance restrictions. Sometimes you can even get your money back if you need to return the ticket. Carefully read the fine print detailing penalties for changes and cancellations. If you doubt the

reliability of a consolidator, **confirm your reservation with the airline.**

ALOFT

AIRLINE FOOD➤ If you hate airline food, **ask for special meals when booking.** These can be vegetarian, low cholesterol, or kosher, for example; commonly prepared to order in smaller quantities than standard catered fare, they can be tastier.

JET LAG

To avoid this syndrome, which occurs when travel disrupts your body's natural cycles, try to maintain a normal routine. At night, **get some sleep.** By day, move about the cabin to **stretch your legs, eat light meals, and drink water—not alcohol.**

SMOKING➤ Smoking is banned on all flights within the United States of less than six hours' duration and on all Canadian flights; the ban also applies to domestic segments of international flights aboard U.S. and foreign carriers. Delta has banned smoking system-wide. On U.S. carriers flying to Canada and other destinations abroad, a seat in a no-smoking section must be provided for every passenger who requests one, and the section must be enlarged to accommodate such passengers if necessary as long as they have complied with the airline's deadline for check-in and seat assignment. If smoking bothers you, request a seat far from the smoking section.

Foreign airlines are exempt from these rules but do provide no-smoking sections (British Airways has banned smoking; some nations have banned smoking on all domestic flights, and others may ban smoking on some flights). Talks continue on the feasibility of broadening no-smoking policies.

B
BUS TRAVEL

Bus service in North America—though fairly economical—has not been a first-class means of travel in recent years. But Greyhound and other bus companies are taking great pains to improve service. New amenities may include an onboard host/hostess, meals, and VCRs.

BUSINESS HOURS

WASHINGTON AND OREGON

Most retail stores in Washington and Oregon are open 9:30–6 seven days a week in downtown locations and later at suburban shopping malls. Downtown stores sometimes stay open late Thursday and Friday nights. Normal banking hours are weekdays 9–6; some branches are also open on Saturday morning.

BRITISH COLUMBIA

In British Columbia, many stores close on Sunday. Outlets that cater to tourists are the notable exception. Normal banking hours in Canada are 10–3 on weekdays, with extended hours in many locations. Some banks in major cities are now open on Saturday morning.

ALASKA

In Alaska, most city retail outlets open Monday–Saturday 10–6 or 10–7. Shopping malls stay open until 8 or 9. Most banks operate 10–3.

C
CAMERAS, CAMCORDERS, AND COMPUTERS

LAPTOPS

Before you depart, **check your portable computer's battery,** because you may be asked at security to turn on the computer to prove that it is what it appears to be. At the airport, you may prefer to **request a manual inspection,** although security X-rays do not harm hard-disk or floppy-disk storage. Also, **register your foreign-made laptop with U.S. Customs.** If your laptop is U.S.-made, call the consulate of the country you'll be visiting to find out whether or not it should be registered with local customs upon arrival. You may want to **find out about repair facilities at your destination** in case you need them.

PHOTOGRAPHY

If your camera is new or if you haven't used it for a while, **shoot and develop a few rolls of film** before you leave. Always **store film in a cool, dry place**—never in the car's glove compartment or on the shelf under the rear window.

Every pass through an X-ray machine increases film's chance of clouding. To protect it, carry it in a clear plastic bag and **ask for hand inspection at security.** Such requests are virtually always honored at U.S. airports, and are usually accommodated abroad. Don't depend on a lead-lined bag to protect film in checked luggage—the airline may increase the radiation to see what's inside.

VIDEO

Before your trip, **test your camcorder, invest in a skylight filter to protect the lens, and charge the batteries.** (Airport security personnel may ask you to turn on the camcorder to prove that it's what it appears to be.)

Videotape is not damaged by X-rays, but it may be harmed by the magnetic field of a walk-through metal detector, so **ask that videotapes be hand-checked.**

CHILDREN AND TRAVEL

Many local organizations, such as public libraries, museums, parks and recreation departments, and YMCA/YWCAs, have special events throughout the year for children of all ages. Check local newspaper listings for such activities as plays, storytelling, sporting events, and so forth.

BABY-SITTING

For recommended local sitters, **check with your hotel desk.**

DRIVING

If you are renting a car, **arrange for a car seat when you reserve.** Sometimes they're free.

FLYING

Always **ask about discounted children's fares.** On international flights, the fare for infants under age two not occupying a seat is generally either free or 10% of the accompanying adult's fare; children ages 2–11 usually pay half to two-thirds of the adult fare. On domestic flights, children under two not occupying a seat travel free, and older children currently travel on the lowest applicable adult fare. Some routes are considered neither international nor domestic and have still other rules.

BAGGAGE➤ In general, the adult baggage allowance applies for children paying half or more of the adult fare. Before departure, **ask about carry-on allowances,** if you are traveling with an infant. In general, those paying 10% of the adult fare are allowed one carry-on bag, not to exceed 70 pounds or 45 inches (length + width + height) and a collapsible stroller; you may be allowed less if the flight is full.

SAFETY SEATS➤ According to the Federal Aviation Administra-

tion, it's a good idea to **use safety seats aloft.** Airline policy varies. U.S. carriers allow FAA-approved models, but airlines usually require that you buy a ticket, even if your child would otherwise ride free, because the seats must be strapped into regular passenger seats. Foreign carriers may not allow infant seats, may charge the child's rather than the infant's fare for their use, or may require you to hold your baby during takeoff and landing, thus defeating the seat's purpose.

FACILITIES➤ When making your reservation, **ask for children's meals or freestanding bassinets** if you need them; the latter are available only to those with seats at the bulkhead, where there's enough legroom. If you don't need a bassinet, **think twice before requesting bulkhead seats**—the only storage for in-flight necessities is in the inconveniently distant overhead bins.

LODGING

Most hotels allow children under a certain age to stay in their parents' room at no extra charge, while others charge them as extra adults; be sure to **ask about the cut-off age.**

CRUISES

Cruise ships travel the Inside Passage and Gulf of Alaska from mid-May through late September. The most popular ports of embarkation are Vancouver and Seward (port

city for Anchorage), but cruises also leave from San Francisco and Seattle. One of the best ways to see the state is to **combine your cruise with a land tour.**

To get the best deal on a cruise, **consult a cruise-only travel agency.** For a low-priced cruise alternative, **consider traveling by ferry.**

CUSTOMS
AND DUTIES

IN THE U.S.

RESIDENTS➤ You may bring home $400 worth of foreign goods duty-free if you've been out of the country for at least 48 hours and haven't already used the $400 exemption, or any part of it, in the past 30 days.

Travelers 21 or older may bring back 1 liter of alcohol duty-free, provided the beverage laws of the state through which they reenter the United States allow it. In addition, 100 non-Cuban cigars and 200 cigarettes are allowed, regardless of your age. Antiques and works of art more than 100 years old are duty-free.

Duty-free, travelers may mail packages valued at up to $200 to themselves and up to $100 to others, with a limit of one parcel per addressee per day (and no alcohol or tobacco products or perfume valued at more than $5); outside, identify the package as being for personal use or an unsolicited gift, specifying the contents and their retail value. Mailed items do not count as part of your exemption.

VISITORS➤ Visitors aged 21 or over may import the following into the United States: 200 cigarettes or 50 cigars or 2 kilograms of tobacco; 1 U.S. liter of alcohol; gifts to the value of $100. Restricted items include meat products, seeds, plants, and fruits. Never carry illegal drugs.

IN CANADA

RESIDENTS➤ Once per calendar year, when you've been out of Canada for at least seven days, you may bring in C$300 worth of goods duty-free. If you've been away less than seven days but more than 48 hours, the duty-free exemption drops to C$100 but can be claimed any number of times (as can a C$20 duty-free exemption for absences of 24 hours or more). You cannot combine the yearly and 48-hour exemptions, use the C$300 exemption only partially (to save the balance for a later trip), or pool exemptions with family members. Goods claimed under the C$300 exemption may follow you by mail; those claimed under the lesser exemptions must accompany you.

Alcohol and tobacco products may be included in the yearly and 48-hour exemptions but not in the 24-hour exemption. If you meet the age requirements of the province through which you reenter Canada, you may bring

in, duty-free, 1.14 liters (40 imperial ounces) of wine or liquor *or* 24 12-ounce cans or bottles of beer or ale. If you are 16 or older, you may bring in, duty-free, 200 cigarettes, 50 cigars or cigarillos, and 400 tobacco sticks or 400 grams of manufactured tobacco. Alcohol and tobacco must accompany you on your return.

An unlimited number of gifts valued up to C$60 each may be mailed to Canada duty-free. These do not count as part of your exemption. Label the package "Unsolicited Gift— Value under $60." Alcohol and tobacco are excluded.

VISITORS➤ American and British visitors may bring in the following items duty-free: 200 cigarettes, 50 cigars, and 2 pounds of tobacco; one bottle (1.1 liters or 40 imperial ounces) of liquor or wine, or 24 355-milliliter (12-ounce) bottles or cans of beer for personal consumption; gifts up to the value of C$60 per gift. A deposit is sometimes required for trailers (refunded upon return). Cats and dogs must have a certificate issued by a licensed veterinarian that clearly identifies the animal and certifies that it has been vaccinated against rabies during the preceding 36 months. Plant material must be declared and inspected. With certain restrictions (some fruits and vegetables), visitors may bring food with them for their own use, providing the

quantity is consistent with the duration of the visit.

Canada's firearms laws are significantly stricter than those of the United States. All handguns, semi-automatic, and fully automatic weapons are prohibited and cannot be brought into the country. Sporting rifles and shotguns may be imported provided they are to be used for sporting, hunting, or competition while in Canada. All firearms must be declared to Canada Customs at the first point of entry. Failure to declare firearms will result in their seizure and criminal charges may be made. (New legislation has just been introduced in Parliament to further tighten Canada's gun laws.)

IN THE U.K.

From countries outside the European Union, including the United States and Canada, you may import duty-free 200 cigarettes, 100 cigarillos, 50 cigars or 250 grams of tobacco; 1 liter of spirits or 2 liters of fortified or sparkling wine; 2 liters of still table wine; 60 milliliters of perfume; 250 milliliters of toilet water; plus £136 worth of other goods, including gifts and souvenirs.

D

FOR TRAVELERS
WITH DISABILITIES

When discussing accessibility with an operator or reservationist, **ask hard questions.** Are there any stairs, inside *or* out? Are there grab bars next to the toilet *and* in the shower/tub? How wide is the doorway to the room? To the bathroom? For the most extensive facilities, meeting the latest legal specifications, **opt for newer facilities,** which more often have been designed with access in mind. Older properties or ships must usually be retrofitted and may offer more limited facilities as a result. Be sure to **discuss your needs before booking.**

DISCOUNT CLUBS

Travel clubs offer members unsold space on airplanes, cruise ships, and package tours at as much as 50% below regular prices. Membership may include a regular bulletin or access to a toll-free hot line giving details of available trips departing from three or four days to several months in the future. Most also offer 50% discounts off hotel rack rates. Before booking with a club, **make sure the hotel or other supplier isn't offering a better deal.**

DRIVING

FROM THE U.S.

The U.S. interstate highway network provides quick and easy access to the Pacific North Coast in spite of imposing mountain barriers. From the south, I–5 runs from the U.S.–Mexican border through California, into Oregon and Washington, and ends at the U.S.–Canadian border. Most of the population is clustered along this corridor. From the east,

I–90 stretches from Boston to Seattle. I–84 runs from the midwestern states to Portland.

The main entry point into Canada by car is on I–5 at Blaine, Washington, 30 miles south of Vancouver. Two major highways enter British Columbia from the east: the Trans-Canada Highway (the longest highway in the world, running more than 5,000 miles from St. John's, Newfoundland, to Victoria, British Columbia) and the Yellowhead Highway, which runs through northern British Columbia from the Rocky Mountains to Prince Rupert.

Border-crossing procedures are usually quick and simple (*see* Passports and Visas *and* Customs, *above*). The I–5 border crossing at Blaine, Washington, is open 24 hours a day and is one of the busiest border crossings anywhere between the United States and Canada. Peak traffic times at the border northbound into Canada are daily at 4 PM. Southbound, delays can be expected evenings and weekend mornings. Try to plan on reaching the border at off-peak times. There are smaller highway border stations at various other points between Washington and British Columbia but they may be closed at night.

WITHIN THE PACIFIC NORTHWEST

Except for a short distance north of Van-

couver, there are no roads along the rugged mainland coast of British Columbia and southeast Alaska.

Alaskan cities such as Juneau have no direct access by road; cars must be brought in by ferry. Skagway and Haines are the only towns in southeast Alaska accessible directly by road. The trip—a grueling 1,650 miles from Seattle—passes through British Columbia and the Yukon Territory.

AUTO CLUBS

The American Automobile Association (AAA) and the Canadian Automobile Association (CAA) provide full services to members of any of the Commonwealth Motoring Conference (CMC) clubs, including the Automobile Association, the Royal Automobile Club, and the Royal Scottish Automobile Club. Services are also available to members of the Alliance Internationale de l'Automobile (AIT), the Federation Internationale de l'Automobile (FIA), and the Federation of Interamerican Touring and Automobile Clubs (FITAC). Members receive travel information, itineraries, maps, tour books, information about road and weather conditions, emergency road services, and travel-agency services.

INSURANCE

Vehicle insurance is compulsory in the United States and Canada. Motorists are required to produce evidence of insurance if they become involved in an accident. Upon arrival, visitors from foreign countries should contact an insurance agent or broker to obtain the necessary insurance for North America.

SPEED LIMITS

The speed limit on U.S. interstate highways is 65 miles per hour in rural areas and 55 miles per hour in urban zones and on secondary highways. In Canada (where the metric system is used), the speed limit is usually 100 kilometers (62 miles) per hour on expressways and 80 kilometers (50 miles) per hour on secondary roads.

WINTER DRIVING

Winter driving in the Pacific North Coast can sometimes present some real challenges. In coastal areas, the mild, damp climate contributes to roadways that are frequently wet. Winter snowfalls are not common (generally only once or twice a year), but when snow does fall, traffic grinds to a halt and the roadways become treacherous and stay that way until the snow melts.

Tire chains, studs, or snow tires are essential equipment for winter travel in mountain areas. If you're planning to drive into high elevations, be sure to check the weather forecast beforehand. Even the main-highway mountain passes can be forced to close because of snow conditions.

During the winter months, state and provincial highway departments operate snow advisory telephone lines that give pass conditions.

F
FERRIES

Ferries play an important part in the transportation network of the Pacific North Coast. In some areas, ferries provide the only form of access into and out of communities. In other places, ferries transport thousands of commuters a day to and from work in the cities. For visitors, ferries are one of the best ways to get a feel for the region and its ties to the sea.

ALASKA

Staterooms are available in the ferries on the Alaska Marine Highway System, but cabin space is always booked months in advance. Reservations for staterooms usually become available in early December for the following year. If all the staterooms are booked when you call, then **contact a tour operator** (*see* Tour Operators *in* Important Contacts A to Z, *above*.) If you still can't secure a cabin, **sleep in public lounges or on deck.**

During the summer, U.S. forest rangers ride the larger ferries, offering interpretive programs along the route. Short local land tours, coinciding with ferry stopovers, are available in many communities. During the fall, winter, and spring, ferry rates

are lower and senior citizens are entitled to free passage between ports in Alaska.

BRITISH COLUMBIA

The British Columbia Ferry Corporation's busiest ferries operate between the mainland and Vancouver Island, carrying passengers, cars, campers, RVs, trucks, and buses. Peak traffic times are Friday afternoon, Saturday morning, and Sunday afternoon, especially during summer months and holiday weekends. The company also provides scheduled service on the *Queen of the North* between Port Hardy at the northern end of Vancouver Island and the port city of Prince Rupert. From there, connections can be made to Alaskan ferries that travel still farther north, or to a VIA Rail train heading east through the Canadian Rockies. Connections to the Queen Charlotte Islands (reservations strongly recommended) can also be made via another British Columbia ferry.

The *Queen of the North* sails every two days during the summer and once a week during the winter. Summer cruises (June–September) take 15 hours (all in daylight, so passengers can enjoy every bit of the spectacular coastal scenery). Reservations are strongly recommended. For reservations, contact British Columbia Ferry Corporation (*see* Ferries *in* Important Contacts A to Z, *above*).

WASHINGTON

If you are planning to use the Washington State Ferry System, try to **avoid peak commuter hours.** The heaviest traffic flows are eastbound in the mornings and on Sunday evening, and westbound on Saturday morning and weekday afternoons. The best times for travel are 9–3 and after 7 PM on weekdays. In July and August, you may have to wait up to two hours to take a car aboard one of the popular San Juan Islands ferries. Walk-on space is always available; if possible, **leave your car behind.**

I
INSURANCE

Travel insurance can protect your investment, replace your luggage and its contents, or provide for medical coverage should you fall ill during your trip. Most tour operators, travel agents, and insurance agents sell specialized health-and-accident, flight, trip-cancellation, and luggage insurance as well as comprehensive policies with some or all of these features. Before you make any purchase, **review your existing health and homeowner policies** to find out whether they cover expenses incurred while traveling.

BAGGAGE

Airline liability for your baggage is limited to $1,250 per person on domestic flights. On international flights, the airlines' liability is $9.07 per pound or $20 per kilogram for checked baggage (roughly $640 per 70-pound bag) and $400 per passenger for unchecked baggage. Insurance for losses exceeding the terms of your airline ticket can be bought directly from the airline at check-in for about $10 per $1,000 of coverage; note that it excludes a rather extensive list of items, shown on your airline ticket.

FLIGHT

You should **think twice before buying flight insurance.** Often purchased as a last-minute impulse at the airport, it pays a lump sum when a plane crashes, either to a beneficiary if the insured dies or sometimes to a surviving passenger who loses eyesight or a limb. Supplementing the airlines' coverage described in the limits-of-liability paragraphs on your ticket, it's expensive and basically unnecessary. Charging an airline ticket to a major credit card often automatically entitles you to coverage and may also embrace travel by bus, train, and ship.

HEALTH

If your own health insurance policy does not cover you outside the United States, **consider buying supplemental medical coverage.** It can provide $1,000 to $150,000 worth of medical and/or dental expenses incurred as a result of an accident or illness during a trip. These policies also may include a personal-accident, or death-and-dismemberment, provision, which pays a lump sum ranging from $15,000 to $500,000 to your beneficiaries if you die or to you if you lose one or more limbs or your eyesight, and a medical-assistance provision, which may either reimburse you for the cost of referrals, evacuation, or repatriation and other services, or may automatically enroll you as a member of a particular medical-assistance company.

FOR U.K. TRAVELERS

According to the Association of British Insurers, a trade association representing 450 insurance companies, it's wise to **buy extra medical coverage when you visit the United States.** You can buy an annual travel-insurance policy valid for most vacations during the year in which it's purchased. If you go this route, make sure it covers you if you have a preexisting medical condition or are pregnant.

TRIP

Without insurance, you will lose all or most of your money if you must cancel your trip due to illness or any other reason. Especially if your airline ticket, cruise, or package tour is nonrefundable and cannot be changed, it's essential that you **buy trip-cancellation-and-interruption insurance.** When considering how much coverage you need, look for a policy that will cover the cost of your trip plus the nondiscounted price of a one-way airline ticket should you need to return home early. Read the fine print carefully, especially sections defining "family member" and "preexisting medical condition." Also **consider default or bankruptcy insurance,** which protects you against a supplier's failure to deliver. However, such policies often do not cover default by a travel agency, tour operator, airline, or cruise line if you bought your tour and the coverage directly from the firm in question.

L

LANGUAGE

Canada is officially a bilingual country (English and French). You will see many signs and services offered in both languages; however, little French is spoken on Canada's west coast.

LODGING

Although the hotel and motel price categories are standard, the prices listed under each may vary from one area to another. This variation reflects local price standards. In all cases, price ranges for each category are clearly stated before each listing.

APARTMENT AND VILLA RENTALS

If you want a home base that's roomy enough for a family and comes with cooking facilities, **consider a furnished rental.** It's generally cost-wise, too, although not always— some rentals are luxury properties (economical

only when your party is large). Home-exchange directories do list rentals—often second homes owned by prospective house swappers—and some services search for a house or apartment for you (even a castle if that's your fancy) and handle the paperwork. Some send an illustrated catalogue and others send photographs of specific properties, sometimes at a charge; up-front registration fees may apply.

BED-AND-BREAKFASTS

Bed-and-breakfasts are private homes that reflect the personalities and tastes of their owners. Generally, B&Bs have 2–10 rooms, some with private baths and others with shared facilities. Breakfast is always included in the price of the room.

B&Bs have flourished in recent years. Some homes advertise to the public, while others maintain a low profile. Most belong to a reservation system through which you can book a room.

CAMPING

Camping is a popular and inexpensive way to tour the Pacific Northwest. Oregon, Washington, Alaska, and British Columbia all have networks of excellent government-run parks that offer camping and organized activities. A few state and provincial parks will accept advance camping reservations, but most do not. Privately operated

campgrounds sometimes have extra amenities such as laundry rooms and swimming pools. For more information, contact the local state or provincial tourism department.

HOME EXCHANGE

If you would like to find a house, an apartment, or other vacation property to exchange for your own while on vacation, **become a member of a home-exchange organization,** which will send you its annual directories listing available exchanges and will include your own listing in at least one of them. Arrangements for the actual exchange are made by the two parties to it, not by the organization.

HOTELS

Most big-city hotels cater primarily to business travelers, with such facilities as restaurants, cocktail lounges, swimming pools, exercise equipment, and meeting rooms. Room rates often reflect the range of amenities offered. Most cities also have less-expensive hotels, which are clean and comfortable but have fewer upscale facilities. A new accommodations trend is all-suite hotels, which offer more intimate facilities and are gaining popularity with business travelers.

Many properties offer special weekend rates, sometimes up to 50% off regular prices. However, these deals are usually not extended during peak

THE GOLD GUIDE / SMART TRAVEL TIPS

summer months, when hotels are normally full.

INNS

These establishments generally are located outside cities and have anywhere from eight to 20 rooms. Lodging is often in an old restored building with some historical or architectural significance. Inns are sometimes confused with bed-and-breakfasts because they may include breakfast in their basic rate.

MOTELS/MOTOR INNS

The familiar roadside motel of the past is fast disappearing from the landscape. In its place are economical chain-run motor inns that are strategically located at highway intersections. Some of these establishments offer very basic facilities; others provide restaurants, swimming pools, and other amenities.

RESORTS

The Pacific North Coast has quite a variety of resorts—from rural fishing lodges to luxury destination showpieces. Dozens of small fishing resorts nestle along the coast and within the interior of British Columbia and southeast Alaska. Most are rustic lodges, providing basic accommodations for sports enthusiasts, but others offer such deluxe comforts as gourmet meals and hot tubs in a wilderness setting.

The Whistler Village resort in British Columbia is best known for its world-class skiing. But Whistler is equally impressive as a year-round destination with golf, tennis, swimming, mountain biking, and horseback riding.

Locals and visitors alike favor the grand settings at the Inn at Semi-Ah-Moo in Blaine, Washington, and the Rosario Resort in the San Juan Islands for getaway trips. A new resort on the Washington side of the Columbia River is Skamania Lodge. Most of the Oregon coast is resort country; one of the state's most famous resorts, Salishan Lodge at Gleneden Beach, is located there.

YMCAS/YWCAS

YMCAs or YWCAs are usually a good bet for clean, no-frills, reliable lodging in large towns and cities. These buildings are often centrally located, and their rates are significantly lower than those at city hotels. Nonmembers are welcome, but they may pay slightly more than members. A few very large Ys have accommodations for couples, but sleeping arrangements are usually segregated.

M
MAIL

Postage rates vary for different classes of mail and destinations. Check with the local post office for rates before mailing a letter or parcel. At press time, it cost 32¢ to mail a standard letter anywhere within the United States. Mail to Canada costs 40¢ per first ounce, and 23¢ for each additional ounce; mail to Great Britain and other foreign countries costs 50¢ per half ounce.

First-class rates in Canada are 46¢ for up to 30 grams of mail delivered within Canada, 52¢ for up to 30 grams delivered to the United States, 70¢ for up to 50 grams. International mail and postcards run 92¢ for up to 20 grams, $1.26 for 20–50 grams.

RECEIVING MAIL

Visitors can have letters or parcels sent to them while they are traveling by using the following address: Name of addressee, c/o General Delivery, Main Post Office, City and State/Province, U.S./Canada, Zip Code (U.S.) or Postal Code (Canada). Contact the nearest post office for further details. Any item mailed to "General Delivery" must be picked up by the addressee in person within 15 days or it will be returned to the sender.

MONEY MATTERS

The United States and Canada both use the same currency denominations—dollars and cents—although each currency has a different value on the world market. In the United States, the most common paper currency comes in $1, $5, $10, and $20 bills. Common notes in Canada include the $2, $5, $10, and $20 bills. (Canada recently phased out its $1 bill, replacing it with a $1 gold-colored coin nicknamed the "loonie" by Canadians because it contains a picture of a loon on one side.) Coins in both countries come in denominations of 1¢ (penny), 5¢ (nickel), 10¢ (dime), 25¢ (quarter), and 50¢.

ATMS

Cirrus, Plus and many other networks connecting automated-teller machines operate internationally. Chances are that you can **use your bank card at ATMs** to withdraw money from an account and get cash advances on a credit-card account if your card has been programmed with a personal identification number, or PIN. Before leaving home, **check on frequency limits** for withdrawals and cash advances. Also **ask whether your card's PIN must be reprogrammed** for use in Canada. Four digits are commonly used overseas. Note that Discover is accepted only in the United States.

On cash advances you are charged interest from the day you receive the money from ATMs as well as from tellers. Transaction fees for ATM withdrawals outside your home turf may be higher than for withdrawals at home. Although transaction fees for ATM withdrawals abroad may be higher than fees for withdrawals at home, Cirrus and Plus exchange rates are excellent because they are based on wholesale rates only offered by major banks.

COSTS

Prices for meals and accommodations in the Pacific North Coast are generally lower than in other major North American regions. Prices for first-class hotel rooms in major cities (Seattle, Portland, Vancouver, and Victoria) range from $100 to $200 a night, although you can still find some "value" hotel rooms for $65 to $90 a night. Most hotels offer weekend packages that offer discounts of up to 50%. Don't look for these special deals during the peak summer season, however, when hotels are nearly filled to capacity.

As a rule, costs outside the major cities are lower, but prices for rooms and meals at some of the major deluxe resorts can rival those at the best big-city hotels. In Alaska, food costs are higher because the state has to import virtually all of its produce, as well as its manufactured goods, from the "lower" 48 states.

Prices in Canada are always quoted in Canadian dollars. When comparing prices with those in the United States, costs should be calculated via the current rate of exchange. At press time (fall 1995), the Canadian dollar was worth US$.75, but this exchange rate can vary considerably. Check with a bank or other financial institution for the current rate. A good way to be sure you're getting the best exchange rate is by using your credit card. The issuing bank will convert your bill at the current rate.

Sales tax varies among areas. Oregon and Alaska have no sales tax, although some cities levy a tax on hotel rooms. Portland, for example, has a 9% room tax. The sales tax in Washington is 7.9%. Seattle adds 5% to the rate for hotel rooms. Canada's 7% Goods & Services Tax (GST) is added to hotel bills but will be rebated to foreign visitors. In British Columbia, consumers pay an 8%–10% provincial and municipal tax. The percentage varies from one municipality to another.

EXCHANGING CURRENCY

American money is readily accepted in much of Canada (especially in communities near the border). For the most favorable rates, **change money at banks.** You won't do as well at exchange booths in airports, rail, and bus stations, or in hotels, restaurants, and stores, although you may find their hours more convenient. To avoid lines at airport exchange booths, **get a small amount of currency before you leave home.**

TAXES

GST➤ Canada's Goods and Services Tax (GST) is 7%, applicable on virtually every purchase except basic groceries and a small number of other items. Visitors to Canada may claim a full rebate of the GST on any goods taken out of the country as well as on short-term accommodations. Rebates can be claimed either immediately on departure from Canada at participating duty-free shops or by mail. Rebate forms can be obtained at most stores and hotels in Canada or by writing to Revenue Canada (Visitor's Rebate Program, Ottawa, Ontario K1A 1J5, ☎ 613/991–3346 or 800/668–4748 in Canada). Claims must be for a minimum of $7 worth of tax and can be submitted up to a year from the date of purchase. Purchases made during multiple visits to Canada can be grouped together for rebate purposes.

SALES➤ Oregon and Alaska charge no sales tax; Washington's tax is 7%–8.2%, depending on municipality; provincial sales tax in British Columbia is 7%.

TRAVELER'S CHECKS

Whether or not to buy traveler's checks depends on where you are headed; **take cash to rural areas and small towns, traveler's checks to cities.** The most widely recognized are American Express, Citicorp, Thomas Cook, and Visa, which are sold by major commercial banks for 1% to 3% of the checks' face value—it pays to **shop around.** Both American Express and Thomas Cook issue checks that can be countersigned and used by you or your travel-

ing companion, and they both provide checks, at no extra charge, denominated in Canadian dollars. You can cash them in banks without paying a fee (which can be as much as 20%) and use them as readily as cash in many hotels, restaurants, and shops. So you won't be left with excess foreign currency, **buy a few checks in small denominations** to cash toward the end of your trip. Record the numbers of the checks, cross them off as you spend them, and keep this information separate from your checks.

WIRING MONEY

You don't have to be a cardholder to send or receive funds through MoneyGram^{SM} from American Express. Just go to a MoneyGram agent, located in retail and convenience stores and in American Express Travel Offices. Pay up to $1,000 with cash or a credit card, anything over that in cash. The money can be picked up within 10 minutes in the form of U.S. dollar traveler's checks or local currency at the nearest Money-Gram agent or, abroad, the nearest American Express Travel Office (in Vancouver, ☎ 604/687–7686). There's no limit, and the recipient need only present photo identification. The cost, which includes a free long-distance phone call within the United States, runs from 3% to 10%, depending on the amount sent, the destination, and how you pay.

You can also send money using Western Union. Money sent from the United States or Canada will be available for pickup at agent locations in 100 countries within 15 minutes. Once the money is in the system, it can be picked up at any one of 25,000 locations. Fees range from 4% to 10%, depending on the amount you send.

P
PACKAGES AND TOURS

A package or tour to the Pacific North Coast can make your vacation less expensive and more convenient. Firms that sell tours and packages purchase airline seats, hotel rooms, and rental cars in bulk and pass some of the savings on to you. In addition, the best operators have local representatives to help you out at your destination. Arctic tours are particularly good for travelers who would otherwise move about independently.

A GOOD DEAL?

The more your package or tour includes, the better you can predict the ultimate cost of your vacation. Make sure you know exactly what is included, and **beware of hidden costs.** Are taxes, tips, and service charges included? Transfers and baggage handling? Entertainment and excursions? These can add up.

Most packages and tours are rated deluxe, first-class superior, first class, tourist, and budget. The key difference is usually accommodations. If the package or tour you are considering is priced lower than in your wildest dreams, **be skeptical.** Also, **make sure your travel agent knows the hotels** and other services. Ask about location, room size, beds, and whether it has a pool, room service, or programs for children, if you care about these. Has your agent been there or sent others you can contact?

BUYER BEWARE

Each year consumers are stranded or lose their money when operators go out of business—even very large ones with excellent reputations. If you can't afford a loss, take the time to **check out the operator**—find out how long the company has been in business, and ask several agents about its reputation. Next, **don't book unless the firm has a consumer-protection program.** Members of the United States Tour Operators Association and the National Tour Association are required to set aside funds exclusively to cover your payments and travel arrangements in case of default. Nonmember operators may instead carry insurance; look for the details in the operator's brochure— and the name of an underwriter with a solid reputation. Note: When it comes to tour operators, **don't trust escrow accounts.** Although there are laws governing those of charter-

flight operators, no governmental body prevents tour operators from raiding the till.

Next, **contact your local Better Business Bureau and the attorney general's office** in both your own state and the operator's; have any complaints been filed? Last, **pay with a major credit card.** Then you can cancel payment, provided that you can document your complaint. Always **consider trip-cancellation insurance** (*see* Insurance, *above*).

BIG VS. SMALL➤ An operator that handles several hundred thousand travelers annually can use its purchasing power to give you a good price. Its high volume may also indicate financial stability. But some small companies provide more personalized service; because they tend to specialize, they may also be experts on an area.

USING AN AGENT

Travel agents are an excellent resource. In fact, large operators accept bookings only through travel agents. But it's good to **collect brochures from several agencies,** because some agents' suggestions may be skewed by promotional relationships with tour and package firms that reward them for volume sales. If you have a special interest, **find an agent with expertise in that area;** the American Society of Travel Agents can give you leads in the United States. (Don't rely solely on your agent,

though; agents may be unaware of small niche operators, and some special-interest travel companies only sell direct.)

SINGLE TRAVELERS

Prices are usually quoted per person, based on two sharing a room. If traveling solo, you may be required to pay the full double-occupancy rate. Some operators eliminate this surcharge if you agree to be matched up with a roommate of the same sex, even if one is not found by departure time.

PACKING FOR THE PACIFIC NORTH COAST

Residents of the Pacific North Coast are generally informal by nature and wear clothing that reflects their disposition. Summer days are warm but evenings can cool off substantially. Your best bet is to **dress in layers**—sweatshirts, sweaters, and jackets are removed or put on as the day progresses. If you plan to explore the region's cities on foot, or if you choose to hike along mountain trails or beaches, bring comfortable walking shoes.

Dining out is usually an informal affair, although some restaurants require a jacket and tie for men and dresses for women. Residents tend to dress conservatively when going to the theater or symphony, but it's not uncommon to see some patrons wearing jeans. In other words, almost

THE GOLD GUIDE / SMART TRAVEL TIPS

anything is acceptable for most occasions.

If you're heading for Alaska, **bring a collapsible umbrella or a rain slicker.** Passengers aboard Alaska-bound cruise ships should check with their travel agents about the dress code on board. Some vessels expect formal attire for dinner, while others do not. In all cases, you will need a waterproof coat and warm clothes if you plan to spend time on deck.

If you plan on hiking or camping during the summer, insect repellent is a must. Bring an extra pair of eyeglasses or contact lenses in your carry-on luggage, and if you have a health problem, **pack enough medication** to last the trip or have your doctor write a prescription using the drug's generic name, because brand names vary from country to country (you'll then need a prescription from a doctor in the country you're visiting). In case your bags go astray, **don't put prescription drugs or valuables in luggage to be checked.** To avoid problems with customs officials, carry medications in original packaging. Also don't forget the addresses of offices that handle refunds of lost traveler's checks.

LUGGAGE

Free airline baggage allowances depend on the airline, the route, and the class of your ticket; ask in advance. In general, on domestic flights and on international flights between the United States and foreign destinations, you are entitled to check two bags—neither exceeding 62 inches, or 158 centimeters (length + width + height), or weighing more than 70 pounds (32 kilograms). A third piece may be brought aboard; its total dimensions are generally limited to less than 45 inches (114 centimeters), so it will fit easily under the seat in front of you or in the overhead compartment. In the United States, the FAA gives airlines broad latitude to limit carry-on allowances and tailor them to different aircraft and operational conditions. Charges for excess, oversize, or overweight pieces vary.

If you are flying between two foreign destinations, note that baggage allowances may be determined not by piece but by weight—generally 88 pounds (40 kilograms) in first class, 66 pounds (30 kilograms) in business class, and 44 pounds (20 kilograms) in economy. If your flight between two cities abroad *connects* with your transatlantic or transpacific flight, the piece method still applies.

SAFEGUARDING YOUR LUGGAGE➤ Before leaving home, **itemize your bags' contents** and their worth, and label them with your name, address, and phone number. (If you use your home address, cover it so that potential thieves can't see it.) Inside your bag, **pack a copy of your itinerary.** At check-in, **make sure that your bag is correctly tagged** with the airport's three-letter destination code. If your bags arrive damaged or not at all, file a written report with the airline before leaving the airport.

PASSPORTS AND VISAS

U.S. AND CANADIAN CITIZENS

Citizens and permanent residents of the United States and Canada are not required to have passports or visas to visit each other's country. However, native-born citizens should carry identification showing proof of citizenship, such as a birth certificate, a voter-registration card, or a valid passport. Naturalized citizens should carry a naturalization certificate or some other proof of citizenship. Individuals under the age of 18 who are not accompanied by their parents should bring a letter from a parent or guardian giving them permission to travel in another country. Permanent residents of the United States who are not U.S. citizens should carry their Alien Registration Receipt Cards. U.S. citizens interested in visiting Canada for more than 90 days may apply for a visa that allows them to stay for six months.

U.K. CITIZENS

British citizens need a valid passport. If you are staying fewer than 90 days and traveling on a vacation, with a return or onward ticket, you will probably not need a visa. However, you will need to fill out the Visa Waiver Form, 1-94W, supplied by the airline. British visitors are not required to have a visa to enter Canada. Their stay in Canada, however, cannot exceed six months without authorization from Canadian immigration.

While traveling, **keep one photocopy of your passport's data page** separate from your wallet and leave another copy with someone at home. If you lose your passport, promptly call the nearest embassy or consulate, and the local police; having the data page can speed replacement.

R
RENTING A CAR
CUTTING COSTS

To get the best deal, **book through a travel agent and shop around.** When pricing cars, **ask where the rental lot is located.** Some off-airport locations offer lower rates—even though their lots are only minutes away from the terminal via complimentary shuttle. You may also want to **price local car-rental companies,** whose rates may be lower still, although service and maintenance standards may not be up to those of a national firm. Also **ask your travel agent about a company's customer-service record.** How has it responded to late plane arrivals and vehicle mishaps? Are there often lines at the rental counter, and, if you're traveling during

a holiday period, does a confirmed reservation guarantee you a car?

Always **find out what equipment is standard** at your destination before specifying what you want; **do without automatic transmission or air-conditioning** if they're optional.

INSURANCE

When you drive a rented car, you are generally responsible for any damage or personal injury that you cause as well as damage to the vehicle. Before you rent, **see what coverage you already have** by means of your personal auto-insurance policy and credit cards. For about $14 a day, rental companies sell insurance, known as a collision damage waiver (CDW), that eliminates your liability for damage to the car; it's always optional and should never be automatically added to your bill.

REQUIREMENTS

In Canada your own driver's license is acceptable. An International Driver's Permit, available from the American or Canadian Automobile Association, is a good idea.

FOR U.K. CITIZENS

In the United States you must be 21 to rent a car; rates may be higher for those under 25. Extra costs cover child seats, compulsory for children under five (about $3 per day), and additional drivers (about $1.50 per day). To pick up your reserved car you will need the reservation voucher,

a passport, a U.K. driver's license, and a travel policy covering each driver.

SURCHARGES

Before picking up the car in one city and leaving it in another, **ask about drop-off charges or one-way service fees,** which can be substantial. Note, too, that some rental agencies charge extra if you return the car before the time specified on your contract. To avoid a hefty refueling fee, **fill the tank just before you turn in the car.**

S
SENIOR-CITIZEN DISCOUNTS

To qualify for age-related discounts, **mention your senior-citizen status up front** when booking hotel reservations, not when checking out, and before you're seated in restaurants, not when paying your bill. Note that discounts may be limited to certain menus, days, or hours. When renting a car, **ask about promotional car-rental discounts**—they can net lower costs than your senior-citizen discount.

STUDENTS ON THE ROAD

To save money, **look into deals available through student-oriented travel agencies.** To qualify, you'll need to have a bona fide student I.D. card. Members of international student groups also are eligible. *See* Students *in* Important Contacts A to Z, *above.*

SHOPPING

When souvenir shopping, **make sure that local crafts are genuine.** The state of Alaska has adopted two symbols that guarantee the authenticity of crafts made by Alaskans. A hand symbol indicates the item was made by one of Alaska's native peoples. A polar bear symbolizes that the item was made in Alaska.

T
TELEPHONES

The telephone area codes in the Pacific North Coast are 503 for Oregon; 206 for the metropolitan Seattle area; 360 for the rest of western Washington; 509 for eastern Washington; 604 for British Columbia; and 907 for Alaska, except for the town of Hyder in southeast Alaska, which uses the 604 area code.

Pay telephones cost 25¢ for local calls. Charge phones are also found in many locations. These phones can be used to charge a call to a telephone-company credit card, your home phone, or the party you are calling: You do not need to deposit 25¢. For directory assistance, dial 1, the area code, and 555–1212. For local directory assistance, dial 1 followed by 555–1212. You can dial most international calls direct. Dial 0 to reach an operator.

Many hotels place a surcharge on local calls made from your room and include a service charge on long-distance calls. It may be cheaper for you to make your calls from a pay phone in the hotel lobby rather than from your room.

LONG-DISTANCE

The long-distance services of AT&T, MCI, and Sprint make calling home relatively convenient and let you avoid hotel surcharges; typically, you dial an 800 number in the United States. The long-distance services of AT&T, MCI, and Sprint make calling home relatively convenient and let you avoid hotel surcharges; typically, you dial a local number. Before you go, **find out the local access codes** for your destinations.

TIPPING

Tips and service charges are usually not automatically added to a bill in the United States or Canada. If service is satisfactory, customers generally give waiters, waitresses, taxi drivers, barbers, hairdressers, and so forth, a tip of 15%–20% of the total bill. Bellhops, doormen, and porters at airports and railway stations are generally tipped $1 for each item of luggage.

W
WHEN TO GO

The Pacific North Coast's mild, pleasant climate is best from June through September. Hotels in the major tourist destinations are often filled in July and August, so it's important to book reservations in advance. Summer temperatures generally range in the 70s, and rainfall is usually minimal. Nights, however, can be cool, so if you're going to enjoy the nightlife, take along a sweater or jacket.

Spring and fall are also excellent times to visit. The weather usually remains quite good, and the prices for accommodations, transportation, and tours can be lower (and the crowds much smaller!) in the most popular destinations.

In winter, the coastal rain turns to snow in the nearby mountains, making the region a skier's dream. World-class ski resorts such as British Columbia's Whistler Village are luring a growing number of winter visitors from around the world.

CLIMATE

Tempered by a warm Japan current and protected by the mountains from the extreme weather conditions found inland, the coastal regions of Oregon, Washington, British Columbia, and Southeast Alaska experience a uniformly mild climate.

Average daytime summer highs are in the 70s; winter temperatures are generally in the 40s. Snow is uncommon in the lowland areas. If it does snow (usually in December or January), everything grinds to a halt—but children love it!

The area's reputation for rain is somewhat misleading, as the amount of rainfall in the Pacific North Coast varies greatly from one locale to another. In the coastal mountains, for example, 160 inches of rain falls annually, creating temperate rain forests. In eastern Oregon, Washington, and British Columbia, near-desert conditions prevail, with rainfall as low as 6 inches per year.

Seattle has an average of only 36 inches of rainfall a year—less than New York, Chicago, or Miami. The wetness, however, is concentrated during the winter months, when cloudy skies and drizzly weather persist. More than 75% of Seattle's annual precipi-tation occurs from October through March.

The following are average daily maximum and minimum temperatures for major cities in the Pacific North Coast region.

Climate in the Pacific North Coast

PORTLAND

Jan.	44F	7C	May	67F	19C	Sept.	74F	23C
	33	1		46	8		51	10
Feb.	50F	10C	June	72F	22C	Oct.	63F	17C
	36	2		52	11		45	7
Mar.	54F	12C	July	79F	26C	Nov.	52F	11C
	37	3		55	13		39	4
Apr.	60F	15C	Aug.	78F	25C	Dec.	46F	8C
	41	5		55	13		35	2

SEATTLE

Jan.	45F	7C	May	66F	19C	Sept.	69F	20C
	35	2		47	8		52	11
Feb.	50F	10C	June	70F	21C	Oct.	62F	16C
	37	3		52	11		47	8
Mar.	53F	12C	July	76F	24C	Nov.	51F	10C
	38	3		56	13		40	4
Apr.	59F	13C	Aug.	75F	24C	Dec.	47F	8C
	42	5		55	13		37	3

VANCOUVER

Jan.	41F	5C	May	63F	17C	Sept.	64F	18C
	32	0		46	8		50	10
Feb.	46F	8C	June	66F	19C	Oct.	57F	14C
	34	1		52	11		43	6
Mar.	48F	9C	July	72F	22C	Nov.	48F	9C
	36	2		55	13		37	3
Apr.	55F	13C	Aug.	72F	22C	Dec.	45F	7C
	41	5		55	13		34	1

JUNEAU

Jan.	29F	−2C	May	55F	13C	Sept.	56F	13C
	18	−8		38	3		42	6
Feb.	34F	1C	June	62F	16C	Oct.	47F	8C
	22	−6		44	7		36	2
Mar.	38F	3C	July	64F	18C	Nov.	37F	3C
	26	−4		48	9		28	−2
Apr.	47F	8C	Aug.	62F	17C	Dec.	32F	0C
	31	−1		46	8		23	−5

THE GOLD GUIDE / SMART TRAVEL TIPS

1 Destination: Pacific North Coast

THE LAY OF THE LAND

IT WAS GETTING DARK high in the Oregon Cascades as we rowed ashore at the small, isolated lake. The peaks, just wrapped in an autumn snow, were blurred by the dusk. With less than an hour of light left, we decided one of us should get back to camp quickly, unencumbered, while the other deflated the raft and carried it back the 4 miles to camp, with little chance of making it out before pitch blackness fell over the dense forest.

Maybe it was because my brother is older and has bad knees, or perhaps it was just because I was soaking wet and needed to change anyway. But I elected to be the one who walked in the dark.

Soon I was alone with the lake as a wispy fog slipped in from the upper basin; the tall firs creaked in the wind and to the east, barely visible now, three rugged peaks shrugged in the distance. I knew that my brother, rapidly moving away, was the only other human near me. Behind me were hundreds of tiny lakes like this one, all empty and quiet in their own seldom-explored basins.

I was very alone, feeling at once joyous and frightened, exalted and exhausted, both overwhelmed and completely free. I had not just *connected* with nature in some fleeting, superficial way; I had melded with it. Things of the world below the meadows, canyons, and forests simply did not exist. There were only those moments of scary wonder as I got into some dry clothes and prepared to walk through the woods in the dark.

The sensation of being alone with nature, of being in the very cup of her hands, is something that is familiar to those who live in the Pacific Northwest. There are certainly more remote areas, but here nature can be enjoyed for what it is. Here man seems to have found his niche in the ecosystem and, more or less, stays there as pleased with his failures to conquer nature as with his occasional, temporary successes.

To understand the people of the Pacific Northwest—and there are roughly 10 million of us in an area about the size of Western Europe—one has to understand the land and the climate and how the two combine to cast their spell. For even in the cities of the Pacific Northwest, nature is never far away. In Seattle, Mt. Rainier and the Olympics entrance commuters stuck in traffic; in Vancouver, British Columbia, the Coast Range juts out over downtown, keeping the metropolis in line; and in Portland, city fathers have kept 4,700 acres of primitive forestlands that harbor deer, elk, and the odd bear and cougar in the hills just north of the city center. It's not a zoo, it's just there, a piece of primeval forest that serves as a constant reminder of nature's enduring presence here. No matter how many planes Seattle's Boeing Corporation churns out, or how many chips come out of Oregon's high-tech Silicon Forest, or how many shares of stock change hands in the volatile Vancouver Stock Exchange, the relationship with nature and the wilds is not altered. There is always this mixture of respect and love, fear and admiration, topped off with simple awe.

These feelings come naturally when you survey the landscape—an array of shapes, colors, textures—but still there are the simultaneous sensations of solitude and inclusion. To understand, look at the far corners of this land: southern Alaska and southeastern Oregon.

SWATHED IN SITKA SPRUCE, the islands scattered below the Alaskan mountains are like small individual worlds. Roads and people are few. The intrepid can kayak through the inlets and fjords for days on end, catching salmon or watching the glaciers peel majestically off into the sea, sheet by sheet. Roughly in the middle of this region is Juneau, the only state capital that is inaccessible by road. Here it is common for legislative aides to live in makeshift camps in the hills above town and ski to the state's modest capitol building. Behind the coast ranges are deep, remote river canyons and lakes that stretch all the way east to where the mighty Rockies dribble off into a few bumps on the tundra. Moving south along Coastal British Columbia, the terrain is no less steep, but the glaciers shrink back into the hanging valleys, leaving only a few waterfalls. Other than fishing vessels and the occasional cruise ship, this is lonely country, beautiful, but often pelted with wild rain storms and blizzards that blast straight across the north Pacific.

Likewise, southeast Oregon is solitary country. It is a land of extremes, a high desert where it is not at all uncommon, especially in the spring or fall, to find the highest and lowest temperature reading in the lower 48 states in the same county. A 100-mile drive across the desert and scrub land is not likely to turn up another soul. What people there are—many of them descendants of Basque settlers a century ago—tend to their stock on the arid plains. The land is dominated by Steens' Mountain, a 60-mile-long slab of desert floor that over the millennia gradually tilted upward. From the west, the gain in elevation is barely noticeable at first, just a steppe rolling into the distance. But after 30 miles of bad road, the mountain simply breaks off into space, the Alvord Desert a gasping 5,000 feet below. And beyond, the gray horizon fades into Nevada and Idaho.

WHETHER IT IS the cathedral-like island forests of southern Alaska or the sagebrush-covered frontier of southeastern Oregon, the awe is there—subtle yet omnipresent. In many ways, the land here shapes us, mellowing and hypnotizing us until other ways of life seem improbably complicated. I don't know how many people I've known who come back from visiting New York or San Francisco or some other famously bustling place and say something along the lines of, "It was very exciting, but I don't know why anyone would go to the trouble of living there."

Go to the trouble . . . A key phrase. In the Pacific Northwest, going to the trouble is more likely to be the consequence of some recreational choice. You go to the trouble of rafting a river just for the hell of it; you go to the trouble of hiking to the top of a butte you've never climbed before; or you go to the trouble of taking a road in the baking deserts of eastern Oregon and Washington just to see the mirages disappear as you approach them.

Okay, so Pacific Northwesterners may seem a bit flaky—carefree, perhaps—but some say this contagious attitude simply comes with the land. The Native Americans of the Pacific Northwest had it pretty easy compared with their brethren on the Great Plains. Whereas a family of Sioux might need to scour 100 square miles of land to get enough food to live on, West Coast Indians only needed to dip into the river for fish or take a few steps out of the village for game. Sure, the weather was damp, but wood for shelter and warmth was plentiful and the time saved gathering food went toward monumental projects of art such as the totems of Coastal British Columbia.

Even today this plenty is obvious. While Pacific Northwest cuisine has become popular on some menus, picking a single cuisine here is a difficult task. Most distinctive cuisines of the world have developed because of shortages, not bounty; folks had only a few basic items, and they had to be creative in cooking them up in different ways. But in the Pacific Northwest, food is seldom a problem. The ocean and rivers teem with scallops, crab, salmon, crayfish, sturgeon, and everything in between. The region abounds with fresh water. Wineries and breweries are liberally scattered throughout the area. The Hood River and Yakima, Okanagan, and Rogue valleys are famous for their orchards. Dairies dot the western areas and cattle graze the eastern expanses on ranches the size of Delaware.

In the Pacific Northwest, rich is defined as living a clean life; nature deals the bonuses. What people here compromise in salaries, they are compensated for by having the opportunity to hike, fish, hunt, or just wake up every morning with a view of a forest. Some might call this simple living, others just call it wacky. Some examples: Portland has twice elected as mayor a local tavern owner who bikes around the city in lederhosen and calls out "Whoop, whoop" at the drop of a photo opportunity. And a few years ago, there was a strong effort (serious does not seem to be the right word) to make the rock-and-roll classic "Louie, Louie" the state song of Washington.

Is there some sort of pattern here? Perhaps all the rain twists great and creative minds? When Lewis and Clark arrived almost 200 years ago, the rain almost drove them crazy, and that was after only one winter! Imagine a lifetime of gray winters; you look out of your window in October at a line of dark clouds rolling in from the west and know there will be only a handful of clear days (probably below freezing) until mid-March. Northwest author Ken Kesey has blamed everything from impotence to union problems on this drizzly season. True, residents of the Pacific Northwest drink more and are more likely to commit suicide than others in the country, but it may be that the weather helps us keep a sense of the absurd and the macabre; for example, in Portland's new Oregon Convention Center the men's rooms have etchings of Oregon waterfalls perched above the urinals.

So we're a little eccentric. But remember, when an impulse sends you ripping down an untracked ski run or landing a thrashing steelhead in a river at flood stage, the humdrum details of daily life become pretty ridiculous, like some sort of cosmic joke, and you fade back to a private place, to *your* lake beneath the peaks. Just before dark.

By Tom Gaunt

WHAT'S WHERE

The sections below correspond to regional chapters in this book; major cities that have their own chapters are indicated below in boldface type.

Oregon
Although the climate and landscape of Oregon varies dramatically from place to place, much of the state enjoys a constant level of natural splendor. The Pacific coast is a wild and rocky 300-mile stretch dotted with quaint small towns. In the northeast are the Columbia River Gorge and Mt. Hood, dramatic examples of the

power of earth and water. On the gentler side, the Willamette valley is a lush wine-producing region and home to the state's most important cities. Oregon's largest city, **Portland,** is considered by many to be the nation's most livable—a not unreasonable boast, given its unspoiled setting and host of urban amenities.

Washington
From the islands that dot Puget Sound to the peak of Mt. Rainier to the Yakima Valley's vineyards, Washington presents hundreds of opportunities to appreciate the great outdoors. Watch whales from coastal lighthouses, dine on fresh seafood in waterside towns, tramp through dripping rain forests, hike high mountains—or head straight to **Seattle,** the Pacific North Coast's hippest city, where the green hills and bay views are best appreciated from a coffee bar and the music and art scene changes as frequently as the tides.

British Columbia
Canada's westernmost province harbors Pacific beaches, forested islands, year-round skiing, world-class fishing—a wealth of outdoor action and beauty. Its towns and cities, from Anglophile Victoria to the re-created Native American village of 'Ksan, reflect the diversity of its inhabitants. Cosmopolitan **Vancouver,** Canada's answer to San Francisco, enjoys a spectacular setting. Tall fir trees stand practically downtown, rock spires tower close by, the ocean is at your doorstep, and residents who have come from every corner of the earth create a young and vibrant atmosphere.

Southeast Alaska
The glacier-filled fjords of the Inside Passage are Southeast Alaska's most famous attraction; what a century ago was the route to the Klondike goldfields is today the centerpiece of many Alaskan cruises. Juneau, the state's capital, is also in the Southeast, as are a number of interesting small towns. Petersburg and Ketchikan (which is also known for its totem-pole carving) are traditional fishing villages; an onion-dome cathedral accents Sitka, the one-time capital of Russian America; and each fall up to 4,000 eagles gather just outside of Haines.

PLEASURES & PASTIMES

Beaches

The Pacific coasts of Oregon, Washington, and British Columbia have long, sandy beaches that run for miles at a stretch. But the waters are often too cold or treacherous for swimming. Even in summertime, beachgoers must be prepared to dress warmly.

The most accessible—and warmest—ocean beaches in the region are in Oregon, where a number of resort communities are established. Most of the Oregon coastline has been protected as public land, so it can be enjoyed by everyone.

The beaches of Washington are more remote from the major centers of population. Seattle is a two- to three-hour drive from the nearest ocean beaches. Even in summer, the beaches are never crowded.

Most of the west coast of Vancouver Island is totally isolated. Pacific Rim National Park is one of the few places where ocean beaches are accessible. On the eastern coast of Vancouver Island, there are a number of good swimming beaches around the town of Parksville.

The gravel beaches of Washington's Puget Sound and British Columbia's Inside Passage attract few swimmers or sunbathers, but the beaches are popular for beachcombing and viewing abundant marine life.

Boating

The sheltered waters of Puget Sound and the Inside Passage, plus the area's many freshwater lakes, make boating one of the most popular outdoor activities in the Pacific North Coast. On sunny days, a virtual fleet of boats dots the waterways; in fact, some experts say that there are more boats per capita in the Puget Sound area than anywhere else in the world. For charters, outfitters, and information, see the boating section in each chapter.

Because of the region's mild climate, it is possible to enjoy boating throughout the year. Charters, which are available with or without a skipper and crew, can be rented for a period of a few hours to several days. The calm waterways are also rated among the best in the world for sea kayaking, an appealing way to explore the intertidal regions.

Cruising and particularly deep-sea-fishing charters are available from many ports throughout the Pacific North Coast. Campbell River on British Columbia's Vancouver Island, Neah Bay and Port Angeles on Washington's Olympic Peninsula, Westport on the Long Beach Peninsula in southern Washington, and Depoe Bay in Oregon are leading fishing and charter ports.

The area's swift rivers also provide challenges to avid canoers and kayakers. A word of warning, however: Many of these rivers should be attempted only by experienced boaters. Check with local residents or outfitters to find out what dangers may lie downstream before taking to the waterways.

Climbing and Mountaineering

The mountains of the Pacific North Coast have given many an adventurer quite a challenge. It is no coincidence that many members of the U.S. expedition teams to Mt. Everest have come from this region.

With expert training and advanced equipment, mountaineering can be a safe sport, but you should never go climbing without an experienced guide. Classes are available from qualified instructors.

Dining

Many restaurants in the Pacific North Coast serve local specialties such as salmon, crab, oysters, and other seafood delicacies. Seattle's Pike Place Market and Vancouver's Granville Island Market display bountiful supplies of local seafood and produce, and these are good places to scan what you might find on restaurant menus. Ethnic foods are also becoming increasingly popular, especially Asian cuisines such as Japanese, Korean, and Thai.

There is tremendous emphasis on and enjoyment of the hearty and savory fare available in this area. Chefs of all stripes key their menus to the seasonal availability of local produce. In June strawberries are in season, July brings in Walla Walla Sweets (a softball-size mild onion and a local delicacy), blackberries (which grow wild, and can be picked from the roadside) take the forefront in August, and the Washington apple crop comes in in the fall.

Portions of Washington, Oregon, and British Columbia are major wine-producing regions. Local wines are often featured in the best restaurants. Beer, too, is a popular local product, and microbreweries have enjoyed increasing popularity throughout the Northwest. Often located in or connected with a local pub, some of these breweries produce only enough specialty beers (called microbrews) for their own establishments. Some, however, such as Red Hook Ale, Ballard Bitter, and Anchor Ale, are also available from regular beer outlets. Some wineries and microbreweries offer tours and tastings.

Coffee has become a passion in Seattle. Lattés (the local version of café au lait), cappuccinos, and espressos are the beverages of choice in the finer—and even not so fine—restaurants around town (you can get a latté at the downtown McDonald's). Espresso stands do a brisk business on almost every other downtown corner. The latest phenomenon are drive-through espresso stands that are popping up in suburban areas. The coffee craze is also spreading to Portland and Vancouver. Enjoy!

As a general rule, restaurants in metropolitan areas are more expensive than those outside the city. But many city establishments, especially those that feature foreign cuisines, are surprisingly inexpensive. Because of space limitations, we have listed only restaurants recommended as the best within each price range.

Fishing

The coastal regions and inland lakes and rivers of the Pacific Northwest are known for their excellent fishing opportunities. Fishing lodges, many of which are accessible only by floatplane, cater to anglers in search of the ultimate fishing experience.

Visiting sportsmen must possess a nonresident license for the state or province in which they plan to fish. Licenses are easily obtainable at sporting-goods stores, bait shops, and other outlets in popular fishing areas.

Most coastal towns have charter boats and crews that are available for deep-sea fishing. State and provincial tourism departments can provide further information on charters.

Golf

The Pacific North Coast has many excellent golf courses, but not all of them are open to the public. Consequently, visitors may find it difficult to arrange a tee time at a popular course. If you are a member of a golf club at home, check to see if your club has a reciprocal playing arrangement with any of the private clubs in the areas that you will be visiting.

Sailboarding

The Columbia River, particularly at Hood River, Oregon, is known as the best spot in the world for windsurfing. Puget Sound and some of the inland lakes are also popular venues for the sport. Sailboard rentals and lessons are available from local specialty shops. In British Columbia, the town of Squamish is quickly becoming another major windsurfing destination.

Shopping

The Pacific North Coast offers shoppers quite a selection of locally made crafts and souvenirs. Some of the most distinctive items are produced by Native American artists, who manufacture prints, wood carvings, boxes, masks, and other items. Shops in Seattle, Portland, and Vancouver carry a wide variety of these objects, but collectors can find the best selection and prices in the small communities located on Vancouver Island.

Another popular "souvenir" for visitors is freshly caught salmon. Fish vendors can pack a recent catch in a special airlines-approved box that will keep the fish fresh for a couple of days. A package of smoked salmon—which will keep even longer—is another alternative.

Public markets are among the best places to purchase salmon and other gifts. Seattle's historic Pike Place Market and Vancouver's Granville Island Market offer a wonderful array of fish stalls, fresh fruit and vegetable stands, arts and crafts vendors, and small shops that sell practically everything.

Shoppers in Alaska will find good buys on gold-nugget jewelry, woven baskets, items made from jade, and specialty foods, including salmon and wild-berry products. Also available and unique to Alaska are carvings made from fossilized walrus ivory that are produced only by indigenous native carvers. Look for the "Made in Alaska" logo, which indicates an item that was genuinely manufactured in Alaska.

Because residents of the Pacific North Coast have such an active lifestyle, many leading manufacturers and retailers of outdoor equipment and apparel have their headquarters there. Recreation Equipment Inc. (REI) has several stores in the Seattle area that sell everything from high-quality sleeping bags and backpacks to freeze-dried food and mountain-climbing equipment. Eddie Bauer, the famous recreational clothing and equipment catalogue distributor and retailer, was founded in Seattle and still has outlets there. One of the world's leading athletic shoe manufacturers, Nike, is based in Oregon and has retail shops in Portland. Its space-age store in downtown Portland is worth a visit. A similar Nike shoe store is being built in downtown Seattle.

Skiing

Skiing is by far the most popular winter activity in the area. Moist air off the Pacific Ocean dumps snow on the coastal mountains, providing excellent skiing from November through the end of March and sometimes into April. Local newspapers regularly list snow conditions for ski areas throughout the region during the winter season. Resort and lift-ticket prices tend to be less expensive here than at the internationally known ski destinations. Most Washington ski resorts cater to those who've come for a day of skiing rather than a longer stay.

The Whistler and Blackcomb mountains, north of Vancouver, comprise the biggest ski area in the region. Whistler Village resort boasts the longest and second-longest vertical drops (more than a mile each) of any ski area in North America. Aside from Whistler/Blackcomb, British Columbia has many other excellent ski resorts scattered throughout the province, including several that are only minutes from downtown Vancouver.

Washington has 20 ski areas, several of which are located just east of Seattle in the Cascade Mountains. Snoqualmie Pass, the ski area closest to Seattle—about 45 minutes east—contains three ski areas: Snoqualmie, Ski Acres, and Alpental. Other major ski resorts nearby include Mt. Baker, Crystal Mountain, Stevens Pass, and Mission Ridge.

Oregon's primary ski facility, Mt. Bachelor, in central Oregon, is rated one of the best ski areas in North America. Located 50 miles east of Portland, Mt. Hood's five ski areas offer skiing (on glaciers!) well into the summer months.

Swimming

Despite all the water surrounding the region, there is not as much swimming as one might expect along the Pacific North Coast. While the sandy ocean beaches attract throngs of people during the summer, most sun worshipers spend little time in the water—it's just too cold!

Similarly, the waters of Puget Sound are generally too cold for swimming, and the beaches are mostly rocky. The best swimming beaches can be found around the Parksville area of Vancouver Island, where the combination of low tide, sandy beaches, and shallow water creates fairly warm swimming conditions.

Wildlife Viewing

The Pacific North Coast offers ample opportunities for viewing wildlife, both on land and on water. Bald eagles, sea lions, dolphins, and whales are just a few of the animals that can be observed in the region. The best way to identify native creatures is with a pair of binoculars and a good nature guide at hand. Books on regional wildlife can be found in local bookstores.

FODOR'S CHOICE

Portland

Sights & Attractions

★ **International Rose Test Garden.** Three breathtaking terraced gardens, set on 4 acres, are planted with some 10,000 rose bushes in more than 400 varieties.

★ **Oregon Museum of Science and Industry** (OMSI). A great place for children, the OMSI houses the Northwest's largest astronomy center (with an OMNIMAX theater and a 200-seat planetarium), a hands-on computer facility, a space wing with a mission-control center, and even its own 240-foot submarine, the USS *Blueback*.

★ **Pioneer Courthouse Square.** This broad, art-filled brick piazza is downtown Portland's heart and soul, as well as its premier people-watching venue.

★ **Portland Saturday Market.** At North America's largest open-air handicraft market, merchants sell crystals, beaded hats, stained glass, jewelry, flags, rubber stamps, decorative boots, and other handmade items. An assortment of street entertainers and food booths adds to the festive atmosphere.

Restaurants

★ **Atwater's.** Come for the outstanding view of the Willamette River, the Cascade Mountains, and the city's skyline, and stay for the delicious Northwest cuisine. *$$$$*

★ **L'Etoile.** Intimate and romantic, filled with fresh flowers and flickering candlelight, this tiny restaurant specializes in the delicately sauced pillars of classical French cuisine. *$$$*

★ **Zefiro.** Scandinavian-blonde hardwood floors and gracefully curved walls of honey-color stucco set the mood at Zefiro, where clarity and attractive detail are the thematic touchstones of both the dining room and kitchen. *$$$*

★ **Bangkok Kitchen.** Chef-owner Srichan Miller juggles the lime, cilantro, coconut milk, lemongrass, curry, and (above all) hot peppers of classic Thai cuisine with great virtuosity. *$*

Hotels & Inns

★ **Governor Hotel.** Although tucked amid the modern high-rises, the Governor is small, quiet, and the most atmospherically "Northwestern" of Portland's many renovated luxury accommodations, more like a rustic hunting lodge than a bustling downtown hotel. *$$$$*

★ **Red Lion/Lloyd Center.** This property, a busy and well-appointed business-oriented hotel, is the flagship of the popular Northwest-based Red Lion chain. *$$$–$$$$*

★ **Portland Guest House.** This "working-class Victorian" house, with its coffee-and-cream paint job and scarred oak floors, has been transformed into a cozy B&B. *$$*

★ **Best Western/Fortniter Motel.** Rooms here have a lived-in, put-your-feet-up feel, and each includes a living area with queen-size bed, a kitchenette with full-size refrigerator, and a separate bedroom. *$*

Oregon

Sights & Attractions

★ **Columbia River Gorge.** From Crown Point, a 730-foot-high bluff, there's an unparalleled 30-mile view down the gorge created by America's second-largest river slashing through the Cascade Range.

★ **Columbia River Maritime Museum, Astoria.** Exhibits range from the observation tower of the World War II submarine USS *Rasher* (complete with working periscopes) to personal belongings of ill-fated passengers from ships wrecked in the area since 1811.

★ **Crater Lake National Park.** Rain and snowmelt have filled the caldera left by the eruption of Mt. Mazama, creating a sapphire-blue lake (at a depth of 1,900 feet, the nation's deepest) that is so clear that sunlight penetrates to a depth of 400 feet.

★ **Oregon Coast Aquarium, Newport.** This 2½-acre complex contains painstaking re-creations of offshore and near-shore Pacific marine habitats, all teeming with life: playful sea otters, comical puffins, fragile jellyfish, even a 60-pound octopus, among other creatures.

★ **Oregon Shakespeare Festival, Ashland.** More than 100,000 theater lovers come to the Rogue Valley every year to see some of the finest Shakespearean productions this side of Stratford—plus works by Ibsen, Williams, and other writers. There are backstage tours, noon lectures, and Renaissance music and dancing before each outdoor performance.

Restaurants

★ **The Bistro, Cannon Beach.** A profusion of flowers and candlelight make this 12-table restaurant Cannon Beach's most romantic dining establishment. *$$$*

★ **Chateaulin, Ashland.** One of Oregon's most romantic restaurants occupies a little ivy-covered storefront a block from the Shakespeare Festival center, where it dispenses elegant French food, local wine, and impeccable service with equal facility. *$$$*

★ **Nick's Italian Café, McMinnville.** Ask any wine maker in the valley to name his favorite wine-country restaurant, and chances are that Nick's would head the list. *$$$*

★ **Inn at Orchard Heights, Salem.** This handsome hilltop restaurant, filled with the sound of trickling water and soft classical music, has panoramic views of the capital city. *$$–$$$*

★ **Blue Heron Bistro, Coos Bay.** There are no flat spots on the far-ranging menu at this busy bistro, where you'll get subtle preparations of local seafood and homemade pasta with an international flair. *$$*

Hotels & Inns

★ **Timberline Lodge, Mt. Hood.** This National Historic Landmark, which has withstood howling winter storms for more than 50 years, still manages to warm guests with its hospitality, hearty food, and rustic guest rooms. *$$$*

★ **Mt. Ashland Inn, Ashland.** The giant lodge, which has views of Mt. Shasta as magnificent as its forested setting, is built from cedar logged on the property, located just miles from the ski area on Mt. Ashland. *$$–$$$*

★ **The Steamboat Inn, Steamboat.** A veritable Who's Who of the world's top fly fishermen have visited Oregon's most famous fishing lodge; others come simply to relax in the reading nooks or on the broad decks of the riverside cabins. *$$–$$$*

★ **Chetco River Inn, Brookings.** Acres of forest surround this splendidly remote inn, 17 miles up the Chetco River from Brookings, where guests hike, hunt wild mushrooms, or relax in front of the fireplace. *$$*

★ **This Olde House B&B, Coos Bay.** You'll never sleep better—or eat better once you awake—than at this sprawling Victorian. *$$*

★ **The Sylvia Beach Hotel, Newport.** This 1912 beachfront hotel has a literary theme—each of the antiques-filled rooms is named for a famous writer, and no two are decorated alike. *$$*

Seattle

Sights & Attractions

★ **Ballard Locks.** Follow the fascinating progress of fishing boats and pleasure craft through the locks, part of the Lake Washington Ship Canal, then watch as salmon and trout make the same journey from salt water to fresh: Several seaquarium-like viewing rooms run alongside a fish ladder that allows migrating fish to swim upstream on a gradual incline.

★ **Museum of Flight.** Boeing Field is home to the city's top museum. Exhibits on the history of human flight fill the Red Barn, Boeing's original airplane factory, and the Great Gallery contains more than 20 classic airplanes, dating from the Wright brothers to the jet era.

★ **Pike Place Market.** Read the hundreds of names etched into the floor tiles as you wander among the stalls selling fresh seafood, produce, cheese, Northwest wines, bulk spices, tea, coffee, and arts and crafts.

★ **Space Needle.** There's nothing like the view of the city at night from the observation deck of this Seattle landmark.

Restaurants

★ **Campagne.** The snowy linens, fresh flowers, white walls, and picture windows at this intimate French restaurant evoke Provence, as does the menu: French cuisine here means the robust flavors of the Midi, not the more polished tastes of Paris. *$$–$$$*

★ **Painted Table.** Sand-colored walls and warm mahogany paneling provide an elegant backdrop for the Northwest cuisine of chef Tim Kelly, who selects from the freshest produce available from nearby small vendors, farms, and the Pike Place Market. *$$–$$$*

⋆ **Wild Ginger.** This restaurant near the Pike Place Market specializes in seafood and Southeast Asian fare, ranging from mild Cantonese to spicier Vietnamese, Thai, and Korean dishes. The satay bar, where you can sip local brews and eat tangy, elegantly seasoned skewered tidbits until 2 AM, has quickly become a favorite local hangout. *$$*

⋆ **Saigon Gourmet.** This small café in the International District is about as plain as it gets, but the Vietnamese food is superb and the prices are incredibly low. *$*

Hotels & Inns

⋆ **Four Seasons Olympic Hotel.** Seattle's most elegant hotel has a 1920s Renaissance Revival–style grandeur; public rooms are appointed with marble, wood paneling, potted plants, and thick rugs, and furnished with plush armchairs. *$$$$*

⋆ **Sorrento.** Sitting high on First Hill, this deluxe European-style hotel, designed to look like an Italian villa, has wonderful views overlooking downtown and the waterfront. *$$$*

⋆ **Inn at the Market.** This sophisticated but unpretentious hotel, located right up the street from the Pike Place Market, combines the best aspects of a small French country inn with the informality of the Pacific Northwest. *$$–$$$*

⋆ **Meany Tower Hotel.** Built in 1931 and remodeled many times since, this pleasant hotel just a few blocks from the University of Washington has managed to retain much of its old-fashioned charm. *$$*

Washington

Sights & Attractions

⋆ **A ferry ride through the San Juan Islands.** Nothing beats the view of the islands from the waters of Puget Sound.

⋆ **Mt. Rainier National Park.** Besides magnificent 14,411-foot Mt. Rainier, the park encompasses 400 square miles of surrounding wilderness, within which are hundreds of miles of hiking and cross-country ski trails, lakes and rivers for fishing, glaciers, and ample camping facilities.

⋆ **Point Defiance Zoo and Aquarium, Tacoma.** For an impressive example of humane and innovative trends in zoo administration, take advantage of the superclose vantage points that allow you to observe whales, walruses, sharks, polar bears, octopuses, apes, reptiles, and birds in re-creations of their natural habitats.

⋆ **Snoqualmie Falls.** Spring and summer snowmelt turns the Snoqualmie River into a thundering torrent as it cascades through a 268-foot rock gorge (100 feet higher than Niagara Falls) to a 65-foot-deep pool below.

⋆ **Whale watching on Long Beach Peninsula.** Climb the North Head Lighthouse and watch for a whale blow—the vapor that spouts into the air when a whale exhales—as gray whales pass by on their way back and forth from breeding grounds in warmer waters.

Restaurants

⋆ **Il Fiasco, Bellingham.** An ambitious northern Italian menu, sophisticated decor, knowledgeable staff, and a good wine list that mixes Italian and local vintages makes this one of the best restaurant in Bellingham. *$$$–$$$$*

⋆ **The Herbfarm, Snoqualmie.** To devotees of Northwest cuisine, the Herbfarm ranks as a temple. But the attraction here is more than the fine, fresh food—try intimate, elegant dining among wildflower bouquets, Victorian-style prints, and a friendly staff. *$$$*

⋆ **Alice's Restaurant, Tenino.** This homey restaurant, set in a rural farmhouse next to a winery in the Olympic Peninsula's lovely Skookumchuck Valley, serves elegant, six-course, fixed-price dinners of innovative yet classic American cuisine. *$$*

⋆ **Fountain Café, Port Townsend.** Fine linens and fresh flowers dress up the unpretentious dining room of this small café, where you can count on seafood and pasta specialties with imaginative and always-changing twists. *$$*

Hotels & Inns

⋆ **Majestic Hotel, Anacortes.** An old mercantile in the San Juan Islands has been turned into one of the finest small hotels in the Northwest. $$$–$$$$

★ **Inn at Langley, Langley.** This concrete-and-wood Frank Lloyd Wright–inspired structure on Whidbey Island perches on the side of a bluff that descends to the beach. $$$

★ **Alexander's Country Inn, Ashford.** Built in 1912 as a luxury hotel, this bed-and-breakfast near the southwest entrance of Mt. Rainier National Park has built a fiercely loyal clientele. $$–$$$

★ **James House, Port Townsend.** Overlooking downtown and the waterfront, this splendid antiques-filled Victorian-era B&B presents an elegant atmosphere in a terrific location. $$–$$$

Vancouver

Sights & Attractions

★ **Granville Island.** This small sandbar, once a derelict factory district, was redeveloped—now the refurbished industrial buildings and tin sheds, painted in upbeat primary colors, house restaurants, a public market, marine activities, and artisans' studios.

★ **Museum of Anthropology.** Vancouver's most spectacular museum displays aboriginal art from the Pacific Northwest and around the world. See dramatic totem poles, ceremonial archways, and dugout canoes; exquisite carvings of gold, silver, and argillite; and masks, tools, and costumes from many cultures.

★ **Stanley Park.** An afternoon in this 1,000-acre wilderness park, just blocks from downtown, can include beaches, the ocean, the harbor, Douglas fir and cedar forests, and a good look at the North Shore mountains.

Restaurants

★ **Chartwell.** Named after Sir Winston Churchill's country home, the flagship dining room at the Four Seasons Hotel offers robust, inventive Continental food in a British-club atmosphere. $$$–$$$$

★ **Star Anise.** Pacific Rim cuisine with French flair shines in this intimate restaurant on the west side of town. $$$

★ **Chez Thierry.** This cozy, unpretentious bistro knows how to add pizzazz to a celebration: Charming owner Thierry Damilano stylishly slashes open champagne bottles with a cavalry sabre on request. For the past 18 years, he has also worked with chef Francois Launay to create delicious country-style French fare. $$

★ **Phnom Penh Restaurant.** Part of a small cluster of Southeast Asian shops on the fringes of Chinatown, Phnom Pehn serves unusually robust Vietnamese and Cambodian fare. $

Hotels & Inns

★ **Sutton Place.** This property feels more like an exclusive guest house than a large hotel: Its lobby has sumptuously thick carpets, enormous displays of flowers, and elegant European furniture; rooms are even better. $$$$

★ **Hotel Vancouver.** The copper roof of this grand château-style hotel dominates Vancouver's skyline. The hotel itself, opened in 1939 by the Canadian National Railway, commands a regal position in the center of town across from the art gallery and Cathedral Place. $$$

★ **English Bay Inn.** In this renovated 1930s Tudor house a block from the ocean, the guest rooms have wonderful sleigh beds with matching armoires. A small, sunny English country garden brightens the back of the inn. $$

British Columbia

Sights & Attractions

★ **Butchart Gardens, Victoria.** This world-class horticultural collection grows more than 700 varieties of flowers and has Italian, Japanese, and English rose gardens.

★ **Minter Gardens, Rosedale.** This compound contains beautifully presented theme gardens—Chinese, rose, English, fern, fragrance, and more—along with aviaries and ponds. There are playgrounds and a giant evergreen maze.

★ **O'Keefe Historic Ranch, Vernon.** For a window on cattle-ranch life at the turn of the century, visit the O'Keefe house, a late-19th-century Victorian mansion opulently furnished with original antiques. Also on the 50 acres are a cooks' house, St. Ann's Church, a blacksmith shop, a reconstructed general store, a display of the old Shuswap and Okanagan Railroad, and a contemporary restaurant and gift shop. There's a ranching gallery in the museum, and a reproduction stagecoach offers rides around the grounds.

⋆ **Pacific Rim National Park, Vancouver Island.** The first national marine park in Canada comprises hard-packed whitesand beach, a group of islands, and a demanding coastal hiking trail where you'll find panoramic views of the sea, the rain forest, sandstone cliffs, and wildlife.

Restaurants

⋆ **The Marina Restaurant, Victoria.** This lovely, round restaurant overlooking the Oak Bay Marina is so popular with the locals that it's always crowded and a bit noisy. *$$–$$$*

⋆ **Mahle House, Nanaimo.** Care for detail, an intimate setting, and innovative Northwest cuisine make this casually elegant place one of the finest dining experiences in the region. *$$*

⋆ **The Old House Restaurant, Courtenay.** This bilevel restaurant offers casual dining in a restored 1938 house with large cedar beams and a stone fireplace. *$$*

⋆ **Royal Coachman Inn, Campbell River, Vancouver Island.** Informal, blackboard-menu restaurants like this one dot the landscape of the island, but here the menu, which changes daily, is surprisingly daring. *$–$$*

Hotels & Inns

⋆ **Hastings House, Salt Spring, Gulf Islands.** One of the finest country inns in North America and a member of the prestigious Relais et Châteaux group, this luxurious 30-acre seaside resort knows how to pamper its guests. *$$$$*

⋆ **April Point Lodge and Fishing Resort, Campbell River, Vancouver Island.** Spread across a point of Quadra Island and stretching into Discovery Passage across from Campbell River, the 1944 cedar lodge is surrounded by refurbished fishermen's cabins and guest houses. *$$$–$$$$*

⋆ **Harrison Hot Springs Hotel, B.C. interior.** Ever since fur traders and gold miners discovered the soothing hot springs in the late 1800s, Harrison has been a favored stopover spot. Amenities include a PGA-rated nine-hole golf course and, of course, hot spring–fed pools. *$$$–$$$$*

⋆ **Mulberry Manor, Victoria.** This Tudor mansion is special for a number of reasons: The grounds were designed and, until recently, maintained by a gardener at the world-famous Butchart Gardens, and the manor has been restored and decorated to magazine-cover perfection with antiques, sumptuous linens, and tile baths. *$$$*

⋆ **Ocean Pointe Resort, Victoria.** Public rooms and half of the guest rooms offer romantic evening views of downtown Victoria and the parliament buildings, bedecked with some 3,000 twinkling lights. Guest rooms are spacious; some come with floor-to-ceiling windows and small balconies. *$$$*

Southeast Alaska

Sights & Attractions

⋆ **Abraham Lincoln Totem Pole.** At Saxman Village in Ketchikan, the top-hatted image of Abe Lincoln crowns one of Alaska's most curious totem poles.

⋆ **Alaska State Museum, Juneau.** On view at one of Alaska's top museums are stuffed brown bears, a replica of a two-story-high eagle nesting tree, a 40-foot walrus-skin *umiak* (whaling boat), a re-created interior of a Tlingit tribal house, mining exhibits, and contemporary art.

⋆ **Glacier Bay National Park and Preserve.** One of few places where you get within inches of a glacier, the park comprises 16, which line narrow fjords at the northern end of the Inside Passage and rise up to 7,000 feet above the bay. Seeing the glaciers from the water (from a cruise ships or, particularly, a small craft like a kayak) is a great thrill.

⋆ **Trail of '98.** The actual path of gold prospectors, worn into the coastal mountains a century ago, is visible from period railcars that take excursions to the White Pass Trail outside Skagway.

Hotels & Inns

⋆ **Salmon Falls Resort, Ketchikan.** Perched above scenic Behm Canal, Salmon Falls maintains its own fleet of fishing boats. *$$$$*

⋆ **Glacier Bay Country Inn, Gustavus.** Local, hand-logged timbers were used to build this picturesque but fully modern rambling structure, which has a profusion of marvelous cupolas, dormers, gables, and porches. $$–$$$$

★ **Westmark Shee Atika, Sitka.** Artwork throughout the hotel illustrates the history, legends, and exploits of the Tlingit people. Many rooms overlook Crescent Harbor and the islands in the waters beyond; others have mountain and forest views. $$–$$$$

★ **June's B&B, Skagway.** At this B&B, a genuine gold miner's daughter regales guests with tall tales from Nome's storied past. $$

Restaurants

★ **Channel Club, Sitka.** If you've never dined on halibut cheeks, you don't know what you're missing. The decor is nautical, with fishnet floats, whale baleen, and whalebone carvings hanging on the walls. $$–$$$

★ **Salmon Falls Resort, Ketchikan.** Seafood is caught fresh from adjacent waters of Clover Passage and served up in this huge, octagonal restaurant built of pine logs; at the center of the dining room, supporting the roof, rises a 40-foot section of 48-inch pipe manufactured to be part of the Alaska pipeline. $$

★ **The Fiddlehead, Juneau.** This is probably Juneau's favorite restaurant, a delightful place of light woods, gently patterned wallpaper, stained glass, historic photos, and hanging plants. The food is healthy, generously served, and eclectic. $–$$

★ **Beachcomber Inn, Petersburg.** Seafood with a distinctly Norwegian flair is the specialty in this restored cannery building on the shores of Wrangell Narrows. $

GREAT ITINERARIES

Native Culture of the Pacific North Coast

Hundreds of years before the first white explorers reached the region, scores of Native American nations were comfortably settled in the Pacific North Coast. These "First People" profoundly influenced the development of the region, and many art forms and artifacts are displayed in museums up and down the coast.

It should be noted that this is an ambitious agenda, requiring extensive use of both the British Columbia and the Alaska Marine Highway ferry systems. Distances between points of interest in this part of North America can be great, and it is necessary to spend considerable time in transit. Because of the time involved, you may want to travel only as far as the B.C. ferries go, instead of continuing your journey into Alaska. If you do continue on, and for any of the longer legs, it is advisable to book a stateroom when reserving passage. Nevertheless, seeing this heritage in combination with breathtaking displays of nature more than offsets any inconveniences that may be encountered.

LENGTH OF TRIP➣ 17–19 days

GETTING AROUND➣ From Vancouver, take the B.C. Ferry from Tsawwassen to Victoria, on Vancouver Island; Route 14 West from Victoria will take you to Sooke. All stops between Victoria and Port Hardy can be reached from Route 19, traveling northwest. The B.C. Ferry takes you from Port Hardy to Prince Rupert, on the mainland, where you can pick up Route 16 east to Hazelton. The Alaska Ferry System supplies transportation to all destinations north of Prince Rupert.

THE MAIN ROUTE➣ **2 Nights: Vancouver.** A great starting point, Vancouver offers much background on what you will see and experience in the tour to follow. Visit the Vancouver Museum and the Museum of Anthropology to acquaint yourself with the various tribes that have inhabited the regions you'll be exploring. You can see the first of many totem poles in Stanley Park, and stop by the Wickaninnish Gallery on Granville Island, where temporary exhibits of Native American crafts can be seen. A meal at Quilicum and a shopping stop at Images for a Canadian Heritage should be part of your downtown Vancouver agenda.

1 Night: Victoria. Take the ferry from Tsawwassen to Victoria, capital of British Columbia, and spend some time at the Royal British Columbia Museum, where you'll find—among many other fascinating exhibits—the Kwakiutl Indian Bighouse. In nearby Sooke, visit the Sooke Regional Museum, which offers extensive historical background on the Salish tribe that once flourished in this region. Call ahead for the schedule of weaving demonstrations held at the museum periodically.

1 Night: Duncan. The main draw here is the Native Heritage Centre, a complex devoted entirely to the culture of the tribes that have populated Vancouver Island. You can study the many facets of Indian life addressed here, from interpretive dance and storytelling, to carving, weaving, and native cuisine. Authentic Native American items may be purchased at Big Foot, Modeste Mill, and Hills Indian Crafts. Visit the nearby town of Chemainus. In 1983, the town was dying after the closure of the local sawmill. The town turned to tourism for survival by inviting artists to paint murals on buildings. Today, 32 murals depict the early settlement and industry of the area. Shops and galleries feature local crafts and art.

1 Night: Nanaimo. Petroglyph Provincial Park is named for the many distinctive rock carvings found in this area. A visit to the Nanaimo Centennial Museum will explain the significance of these curiosities. While you're there, you can take a look at the dioramas representing various aspects of Native American life.

1 Night: Campbell River. A 15-minute ferry ride from Campbell River takes you to the Kwagiulth Museum and Cultural Centre in the Cape Mudge Reserve on Quadra Island. The Kwagiulth tribe operates Tsa-Kwa-Luten Lodge where you can dine on authentic native food and experience tribal ceremonies in the resort's Big House. Here you will find masks and costumes used in the Potlatch ceremonies (an event in which gifts are exchanged), spiritual gatherings convened to honor rites of passage such as birth, marriage, and death. In addition to the Potlatch regalia, the center offers tours (phone ahead), videos, dancing, and crafts demonstrations.

1 Night: Port McNeill. The B.C. Ferry takes you from Port McNeill to Alert Bay in about 40 minutes. There you'll find the U'mista Cultural Center (☎ 604/974–5403), which features its own collection of Potlatch masks and tribal dress, as well as jewelry, artifacts, a burial box, and

videos on the prohibition of the Potlatch (which documents what happened to the native peoples) and on Spirit Lodge (a tape combining video presentations and live performers), which was previously seen at Expo '86 in Vancouver. The center focuses on the Kwakwaka'wakw, a group of 16 tribes in the area who shared the same language, Kwak'wala.

1 Night: Port Hardy–Prince Rupert (15-hour ferry)

1 Night: Prince Rupert. While in Prince Rupert, plan to visit the Museum of Northern British Columbia, which has an excellent collection of coastal Indian art as well as demonstrations of wood carving and other crafts. A boat tour of the Metlakatla Indian Village is also available through the museum.

1 Night: Hazelton. 'Ksan Village, about 120 miles east of Prince Rupert on Route 16, is a side trip well worth taking. The village offers just about everything you could ask for in one location: Guided tours, native dancing, pre-European artifacts, and Potlatch entertainment can be experienced in a truly authentic setting framed by the majestic Skeena Mountains.

1–2 Nights: Prince Rupert–Ketchikan (6-hour ferry). Your first port in Alaska, Ketchikan, is the fourth-largest city in the state, with the added distinction of having more totem poles than any other city in the world. Recommended stops here include the Tongass Historical Museum, Totem Bight State Historical Park, and Saxman Indian Village. Also try to get a look at the mural on the campus of the University of Alaska, Southeast, titled *Return of the Eagle.*

1 Night: Ketchikan–Wrangell (6-hour ferry). Some of the most interesting totem poles in Alaska can be found in this timber and fishing community. Visit Kik-Sadi Indian Park, Shakes Island, and Chief Shakes gravesite for some prime examples. Wrangell City Museum houses an eclectic collection that includes Indian artifacts and petroglyphs. For more of the latter, walk along Petroglyph Beach at low tide.

1 Night: Wrangell–Sitka (21-hour ferry). Evidence of native cultures abound in Sitka, and two attractions in particular should not be missed: the Sheldon Jackson Museum, which has a variety of pieces representing the full spectrum of Alaska's Native American life, and Sitka National Historical Park, which offers audiovisual presentations that provide interesting and informative background on native cultures.

1–2 Nights: Sitka–Juneau (8½-hour ferry). The Alaska State Museum, located in Juneau—the state's capital and its third-largest city—has one of the finest Native American exhibits in the Pacific North Coast, and you should plan to spend as much time here as your schedule will allow. Wickersham House offers a more personal collection of photographs, carvings, basketry, and other artifacts.

For those whose appetites are *still* not sated, the Alaska ferry continues from Juneau to Haines, taking 4½ hours, where the Sheldon Museum and Cultural Center and the Chilkat Center for the Arts offer extensive exhibits as well as native dancing and demonstrations of various crafts, such as carving and weaving. For more information, *see* Off the Beaten Track *in* Chapter 8, Southeast Alaska, for excursions to Kake, Angoon, and/or Hoonah.

FURTHER INFORMATION➣ Although schedules, fares, and hours of operation are listed in appropriate chapters, it is always advisable to confirm these by calling ahead; they often change seasonally, sometimes for reasons that seem almost arbitrary. For ferry information, *see* Important Contacts A to Z *in* the Gold Guide. If you wish to book staterooms, and it is advised for some of the longer legs, do so well in advance because they go quickly, especially during peak season. For details on specific attractions, consult Chapter 6, Vancouver; Chapter 7, British Columbia; and Chapter 8, Southeast Alaska.

Sampling the Wines of the Northwest

Whether you're an experienced oenophile or just making the leap from simply ordering a glass of house red, you will find much to delight and instruct you among the vineyards and wineries of the Pacific North Coast. Only California produces more domestic wine than does Washington State, and Oregon boasts many gold-

medal winners among its varietals. This itinerary takes you through the Yakima and Willamette valleys, two major wine-producing regions of the United States. In addition to enhancing your appreciation of the grape, your route will take you through some of the most magnificent countryside in an area that is known for its scenery.

LENGTH OF TRIP➣ 12 days

GETTING AROUND➣ By car from Seattle, take I–90 east to Ellensburg and I–82 south to Yakima; 97 south takes you into Oregon. Go west on I–84 toward Hood River and pick up 35 south to 26 west; from there head west on 212 to I–205 south and 213 south into Salem. From Salem, take 22 west to 99 west, where you can go south to Corvallis or north into Portland. From Portland, take 8 west to Forest Grove.

THE MAIN ROUTE➣ **2 Nights: Seattle.** Take the Winslow ferry from the Seattle terminal to the Bainbridge Island Vineyard and Winery, or visit the Ste. Michelle Winery in Woodinville, 15 miles northeast of Seattle. Be sure to stop by some of the city's wine merchants who carry a wide selection of local products.

1 Night: Ellensburg. On the way to this former trading post, make a stop at the Snoqualmie Winery, about 30 minutes from downtown Seattle. While in Ellensburg, spend an hour or two exploring the town's historical district, or visit Olmstead Park, before heading on to Yakima.

2 Nights: Yakima. You're in the heart of Washington's wine country now, with literally dozens of operations to visit. Pick up the brochure offered by the Yakima Valley Wine Growers Association; it will help you choose three or four good stops.

1 Night: Hood River. Route 97 south takes you through the Yakima Indian Reservation to this lovely town at the junction of the Hood and Columbia rivers. If your interests include sailboarding, you'll want to spend more time here, because Hood River is rapidly becoming this sport's most popular destination. The surrounding area is covered with orchards, and several wineries await your inspection.

2 Nights: Salem. Route 35 south from Hood River loops through some magnificent orchard country and around Mt. Hood before becoming Route 26 west. Pick up Route 212 west to Route 205 south; a few miles farther takes you to Route 213 south, which you'll follow right into Salem. Along this stretch you might want to stop at the Mt. Angel Abbey, a century-old Benedectine seminary whose architecture alone warrants attention.

You could spend weeks exploring the Willamette Valley Wineries that border Route 99W (driving south) from Salem, but the concentration of establishments is so great that you'll be able to get a representative survey within a couple of days. Before leaving Salem, climb to the top of the capitol dome for a panoramic view of the city, valley, and mountains.

1 Night: McMinnville. Take Route 99W north to the home of Oregon's International Pinot Noir Celebration, which is held in August. What was true of the southern leg of this highway is even more so as you head north; use the brochure published by the Oregon Wine Center to distinguish among wineries.

2 Nights: Portland. Continuing north on 99W will take you through the wine towns of Lafayette, Dundee, Newberg, and Tualatin, each of which has at least one site you'll want to explore. Beaverton, Hillsboro, and Forest Grove—west of Portland on Route 8—have several noteworthy establishments.

FURTHER INFORMATION➤ Phone ahead to the places you plan to visit; changes in season, weather, or management that might affect your itinerary can occur at any time. *See* Exploring sections *in* Chapter 2, Portland; Chapter 3, Oregon; Chapter 4, Seattle; and Chapter 5, Washington, for phone numbers and addresses.

Formal and Informal Florals:

The Gardens of British Columbia and Washington

British Columbia and Washington State share many things; among these are a moist climate, relatively moderate temperatures, and fertile soil. As a result, the Pacific North Coast is an area rich in varied vegetation, and residents have capitalized on this desirable condition by fashioning numerous formal gardens, shrubbery mazes, parks, and commercial flower farms throughout the area.

This excursion through Vancouver, Victoria, and Seattle and its vicinity offers you an opportunity to experience the pastoral charms of many diverse arrangements and species of vegetation, as well as a close look at many types of birds and animals, both native and exotic.

LENGTH OF TRIP➤ 7 days

GETTING AROUND➤ From Vancouver, take the B.C. Ferry from Tsawwassen to Victoria. From Victoria, take one of the Victoria Clippers or the *Royal Victorian* car ferry (May to September only) to Seattle. From Seattle, take Route 90 east to Route 405 north to Route 522 east to Route 202 into Woodinville. From Seattle, take Route 5 north to Mount Vernon, or south to Tacoma.

THE MAIN ROUTE➤ **2 Nights: Vancouver.** The Dr. Sun Yat-Sen Gardens, which re-create design elements found in several authentic Chinese arrangements, were constructed by native Chinese artisans using traditional methods and tools. You can appreciate the difference between the Chinese and the Japanese styles with a visit to the Nitobe Garden, considered to be the most authentic of its kind outside of Japan. Queen Elizabeth Park is the site of the Bloedel Conservatory, in which you can see free-flying tropical birds among the botanical displays. Plan to spend some time at the Van Dusen Botanical Garden, which contains one of the largest collections of ornamental plants in the country. Two hours east of Vancouver, just off the Trans-Canada Highway near the resort town of Harrison Hot Springs, is Minter Gardens, a beautifully designed oasis of color.

1 Night: Victoria. Crystal Gardens offers a dazzling array of flowers, tropical birds, and monkeys in a glass-roofed structure that was once a swimming pool. The world-renowned Butchart Gardens boasts Italian, Japanese, and English rose gardens on its 25-acre site. Also worth a look is the Fable Cottage Estate, 3½ acres of brightly colored blooms.

3 Nights: Seattle. Stop by the visitor center at the north end of Washington Park for information on the Washington Park Arboretum, where the walkways are named after flowers. In nearby Woodinville is the Chateau Ste. Michelle Winery, where you can stroll through formal gardens, picnic on the grounds (designed by the Olmsted family, architects of New York City's Central Park), and enjoy complimentary tastings at the winery.

About one hour north of Seattle on Route 5 is the town of Mount Vernon, home to the commercial farms of La Conner Flats and Roozengaarde, which are open to the public. The heady fragrance, dazzling flowers, and sheer expanse of color are well worth the trip. In April, the Skagit Valley is carpeted with thousands of tulips and daffodils in an extraordinary display of color.

Tacoma, less than an hour south of Seattle on Route 5, has two noteworthy attractions. The Seymour Botanical Conservatory, located in Wright Park, features an extensive selection of exotic plant life inside an imposing Victorian-style greenhouse. After admiring the flower gardens and waterfront views in 700-acre Point Defiance Park, check out the world-class zoo and aquarium exhibits.

FURTHER INFORMATION> Obviously, the time of year you choose to visit the gardens will have much to do with the kinds of flowers you'll see; hours of operation and admission charges may change throughout the year as well. Telephone ahead for information for the season. Address and telephone listings can be found in Chapter 4, Seattle; Chapter 5, Washington; Chapter 6, Vancouver; and Chapter 7, British Columbia.

FESTIVALS AND SEASONAL EVENTS

OREGON

MID-FEB.–LATE OCT.➤ **Oregon Shakespearean Festival,** held in Ashland annually since 1935, presents a repertoire of classic and contemporary plays (☎ 800/533–1311 in OR or 800/547–8052 outside OR).

MID-MAY➤ **Sandcastle Day** transforms Cannon Beach into a sculpted fantasyland of fanciful castles and creatures (☎ 503/436–2623).

LATE MAY➤ **Fleet of Flowers Memorial Service,** which begins at Depoe Bay, scatters a mass of flowers into the ocean to commemorate those lost at sea (☎ 503/765–2889).

LATE MAY–MID-JUNE➤ **Portland Rose Festival** features 24 days of diverse events, such as ski racing on nearby Mt. Hood, an air show, a hot-air-balloon classic, the Grand Floral parade, and auto racing (☎ 503/227–2681).

MID-JUNE–EARLY SEPT.➤ **Peter Britt Gardens Music and Arts Festival** features folk, country, bluegrass, and jazz music, as well as musical theater and dance, on the stages of Jacksonville (☎ 800/332–7488 in OR or 800/882–7488 outside OR).

LATE JUNE–EARLY JULY➤ **Oregon Bach Festival,** sponsored by the University of Oregon School of Music, brings the works of the great composer to Eugene (☎ 503/346–5666).

EARLY AUG.➤ **Mt. Hood Festival of Jazz** brings nationally acclaimed jazz musicians to Gresham for performances in an outdoor setting (☎ 503/666–3810).

LATE AUG.–EARLY SEPT.➤ **Oregon State Fair,** which is held in Salem for 11 days prior to Labor Day, hosts concerts, flea markets, horse and livestock shows, and sporting events (☎ 503/378–3247).

WASHINGTON

EARLY–MID-APR.➤ **Skagit Valley Tulip Festival** showcases millions of colorful tulips and daffodils in bloom (☎ 206/428–8547).

MID-MAY➤ **Viking Fest** celebrates the Norwegian community of Poulsbo's proud heritage (☎ 206/779–4848).

LATE MAY➤ **Northwest Folklife Festival** lures musicians and artists to Seattle for one of the largest folkfests in the United States (☎ 206/684–7300).

LATE JUNE–EARLY JULY➤ **Fort Vancouver Days** in Vancouver is a citywide celebration with rodeo, a bluegrass festival, a chili cook-off, and the largest fireworks display west of the Mississippi (☎ 206/693–1313).

MID-JULY➤ **Bite of Seattle** serves up sumptuous specialties from the city's finest restaurants (☎ 206/232–2982).

MID-JULY–EARLY AUG.➤ **Seafair,** Seattle's biggest event of the year, kicks off with a torchlight parade through downtown and culminates in the Blue Angels air show and hydroplane races on Lake Washington (☎ 206/728–0123).

LATE JULY➤ **Pacific Northwest Arts and Crafts Fair** in Bellevue highlights some of the best work of Northwest artists and craftspeople (☎ 206/454–4900).

LATE AUG.➤ **Washington State International Kite Festival** sends kites of all shapes and sizes flying above Long Beach (☎ 206/451–2542).

LATE AUG.–EARLY SEPT.➤ **Bumbershoot,** a Seattle festival of the arts, presents more than 400 performers in music, dance, theater, comedy, and the visual and literary arts (☎ 206/684–7200).

EARLY–MID-SEPT.➤ **Western Washington Fair** brings top entertainment, animals, food, exhibits, and rides to the town of Puyallup (☎ 206/841–5045).

MID-SEPT.➤ **Wooden Boat Festival** has historic boat displays, demonstrations, and a street fair in Port Townsend (☎ 206/385–3628).

BRITISH COLUMBIA

JAN.➤ The **Polar Bear Swim** on New Year's Day in Vancouver is said to bring good luck all year; **skiing competitions** take place at most alpine ski resorts throughout the province (through Feb.).

MAR.➤ **Pacific Rim Whale Festival** on Vancouver Island's west coast celebrates the spring migration of gray whales with guided tours by whale experts and accompanying music and dancing; the **Vancouver International Wine Festival** is held.

APR.➤ **TerrifVic Jazz Party,** in Victoria, has top international Dixieland bands.

MID-MAY➤ **Cloverdale Rodeo** in Surrey is rated sixth in the world by the Pro Rodeo Association; **Vancouver Children's Festival,** the largest event of its kind in the world, presents dozens of performances in mime, puppetry, music, and theater (☎ 604/687–7697).

LATE MAY➤ **Swiftsure Race Weekend** draws more than 300 competitors to Victoria's harbor for an international yachting event (☎ 604/592–2441). **Victoria Day,** a national holiday, is usually celebrated throughout Canada on the penultimate weekend in May.

LATE JUNE➤ **Canadian International Dragon Boat Festival,** in Vancouver, features races between long, slender boats decorated with huge dragon heads, an event based on a Chinese "awakening the dragons" ritual; the festival also includes community and children's activities, dance performances, and arts exhibits (☎ 604/684–5151). **Du Maurier International Jazz Festival** celebrates a broad spectrum of jazz, blues, and related improvised music, with more than 200 performances in 20 locations in Vancouver (☎ 604/682–0706).

LATE JUNE–SEPT.➤ **Whistler Summer Festivals** present daily street entertainment and a variety of music festivals at the

international ski and summer resort.

JULY 1➤ **Canada Day** inspires celebrations around the country in honor of Canada's birthday.

MID-JULY➤ **Harrison Festival of the Arts,** in Harrison Hot Springs, offers a spectrum of artistic expression with a unique blend of international, national, and regional artists and performers (☎ 604/796–3664). **Vancouver Sea Festival** celebrates the city's nautical heritage with the World Championship Bathtub Race, sailing regattas, and windsurfing races, plus a parade, fireworks, entertainment, and a carnival (☎ 604/684–3378).

LATE JULY–EARLY AUG.➤ **Squamish Days** is the largest logging sport show in the world, featuring sports events, a chair-carving contest, and a parade (☎ 604/892–9244).

EARLY AUG.➤ **Abbotsford International Air Show** takes off with a three-day extravaganza of military and civilian flight performances and presents a large aircraft display (☎ 604/852–8511).

MID-AUG.–EARLY SEPT.➤ **Pacific National Exhibition,** western Canada's biggest annual fair, brings top-name entertainment and a variety of displays to Vancouver (☎ 604/253–2311).

SEPT.➤ Cars speed through downtown Vancouver in the **Molson Indy Formula 1 race.**

OCT.➤ The **Vancouver International Film Festival** is held. **Okanagan Wine**

Festivals take place in the Okanagan-Similkameen area.

ALASKA

EARLY FEB.➤ **Tent City Winter Festival,** in Wrangell, captures the flavor of Alaska's early days (☎ 907/874–3901).

LATE MAR.➤ **Seward's Day** is celebrated around the state on the last Monday in March and commemorates the signing of the 1867 treaty purchasing Alaska from Russia.

EARLY APR.➤ **Alaska Folk Festival,** in Juneau, is a mix of music, handmade crafts, and foods (☎ 907/789–0292).

MID-MAY➤ **Little Norway Festival,** in picturesque Petersburg, salutes the town's Scandinavian heritage (☎ 907/772–3646 or 907/772–4636). **Southeast Alaska State Fair,** which takes place in Haines, features entertainment; a timber show; workshops; contests; and agriculture, home-arts, fine-arts, and crafts exhibits (☎ 907/766–2478).

LATE MAY➤ **Juneau Jazz and Classics Festival** features performances by nationally known musicians (☎ 907/364–2801).

JUNE➤ **Sitka Summer Music Festival** is a month-long series of chamber-music performances (☎ 907/747–6774).

MID-OCT.➤ **Alaska Day Celebration** brings out the whole town of Sitka to celebrate the day (Oct. 18) the United States acquired Alaska from Russia. The weeklong festival includes a period costume ball and a parade (☎ 907/747–8086).

2 Portland

Oregon's largest city is considered by many to be the nation's most livable—a not unreasonable boast, given its unspoiled setting and host of urban amenities. Stroll through the city's astonishing gardens, take a gander at one of the unusual museums in East Portland, or just kick back with a foamy pint of ale and a movie at one of the town's best inventions, the "brew theater."

PORTLAND IS A BIG CITY with small-town charm. Beyond its unparalleled natural setting, the city boasts striking examples of up-to-the-minute postmodern architecture, an effective and intelligent transit system, clean air and water, an extensive system of colorful parks and gardens, and a lively arts scene. If this is the city of the future (and many think so), it is one that retains a human scale, and one in which the quality of life of its citizens is a high and constant priority.

By Tom Barr

Updated by
Jeff Kuechle

Since the 1970s, the arts, environmental issues, and history have been as important to Portlanders as economic development. This focus has brought about successful neighborhood revitalization and preservation projects as well as ambitious cultural programs, such as the establishment of a resident professional Shakespeare company and innovative neighborhood theaters. The result, for residents and visitors alike, is an attractive city in which there's much to do day or night, rain or shine.

As far back as 1852, with the establishment of the Boulevard, Portland began setting aside city land as parks, leaving a legacy of an urban setting in which one can enjoy nature, as in 4,700-acre Forest Park, which contains the last ancient forest left in any U.S. city. The recreational system has grown to 250 parks, public gardens, and greenways, and within Portland's city limits are the world's smallest park (officially recognized in *The Guinness Book of World Records*), the nation's largest urban wilderness, and the only extinct volcano within city limits in the continental United States.

The arts in Portland flourish in unexpected places: You'll find creations in police stations, office towers, banks, playgrounds, and on the sides of buildings. Downtown, the brick-paved transit mall is a veritable outdoor gallery of elaborate fountains and sculptures, although, like most artistic endeavors, it elicits some ambivalence; since the mall is restricted to bus and pedestrian traffic, many motorists would gladly trade a statue and fountain or two for a few extra parking spaces.

Known as the City of Roses, Portland takes full advantage of its temperate climate. Since 1907 it has celebrated its award-winning flowers, and today the Portland Rose Festival is a multiweek extravaganza with auto and boat races, visiting navy ships, and a grand floral parade second in size only to Pasadena's. Other annual events are a citywide Neighborhood Fair and an Art Quake featuring everything from painting and sculpture to mime, rock and blues, symphony orchestras, and dance.

The city, which began as a 1-square-mile Indian clearing, has become a metropolis of 485,000 people; the 132 square miles now include 90 diverse and distinct neighborhoods. A center for sports and sportswear, as well, Portland and its surroundings are home to headquarters and factories for Jantzen, Nike, and Pendleton. A variety of high-tech, shipbuilding, furniture, fabricated-metals, and other manufacturers has helped to give it a broad economic base. The city's prime geographic location, at the confluence of the Columbia and Willamette rivers, has helped it achieve its rank as the third-largest port on the West Coast. Five main terminals export automobiles, steel, livestock, grain, and timber. Shipyards repair tankers and tugboats, cruise ships, and navy vessels.

For all its emphasis on looking forward, Portland has not forgotten its past. Preserving the city's architecture is of major importance; in such areas as the Skidmore–Old Town, Yamhill, and Glazed Terra-Cotta National Historic Districts, 1860s brick buildings with cast-iron columns and 1890s ornate terra-cotta designs uphold the legacy of Portland's origins. This city has created an enviably livable present without neglecting its past or mortgaging its future.

EXPLORING

Tour 1: Downtown Portland

Numbers in the margin correspond to points of interest on the Downtown Portland map.

The Willamette River is Portland's east–west dividing line, and Burnside Street separates north from south. While the city's 200-foot-long blocks make them easy walking for most visitors, others may wish to explore the core by either MAX light rail or Tri-Met bus (*see* Getting Around *in* Portland Essentials, *below*).

★ ❶ Start at **Pioneer Courthouse Square** (S.W. Broadway and S.W. Morrison St., ☎ 503/223–1613), a broad, art-filled brick piazza that is downtown Portland's heart and soul. The square's design echoes the classic central plazas of European cities, and it is frequently the scene of special events. It's also Portland's premier people-watching venue, where the neatly dressed office crowd mingles harmoniously with some of the city's stranger elements. Each of the 64,000 bricks that covers the piazza is engraved with the name of someone who made a contribution to help pay for the square. The best time to be here is noon, when a goofy weather machine blasts a fanfare, and a shining sun, stormy dragon, or blue heron rises out of a misty cloud to confirm the day's weather.

❷ From the square, walk south on 6th Avenue for two blocks. Here, at the corner of 6th Avenue and Salmon Street, is **Nike Town,** a sort of F.A.O. Schwarz for the athletically inclined. The international sportswear giant is headquartered in Beaverton, just outside Portland. This futuristic, almost surreal-looking factory outlet is a showplace for the mind-bogglingly broad Nike line. A life-size plaster cast of Michael Jordan captured in mid-jump dangles from the ceiling near the basketball shoes. A display of waterproof sandals—for joggers who fancy mountain streambeds—have a tank of live rainbow trout for a backdrop. Autographed sports memorabilia, video monitors, and statuary compete for your attention with the many products for sale. The children's department upstairs offers kid-size versions of almost everything in the store. Don't expect any bargains, however: Prices are full retail ($60 for a golf shirt?) and the word "sale" is almost as taboo around here as the word "Reebok." *930 S.W. 6th Ave., ☎ 503/221–6453. ⊙ Mon.–Thurs. 10–7, Fri. 10–8, Sat. 10–7, Sun. 11:30–6:30.*

❸ The **Portland Center for the Performing Arts** (corner of S.W. Broadway and S.W. Main St., ☎ 503/248–4496) is nearby. The "old building" and the hub of activity is the **Arlene Schnitzer Concert Hall,** host to the Oregon Symphony and musical events from classical recitals to rock concerts. Across Main Street, but still part of the center, is the 292-seat **Delores Winningstad Theater,** used for plays and lectures. Its stage design and dimensions are based on those of an Elizabethan-era stage. The 916-seat **Intermediate Theater,** which houses Portland Center Stage, a highly regarded resident theater company, is also part of the complex. The section of the street connecting the old and new buildings is often blocked off for food fairs, art shows, and other events.

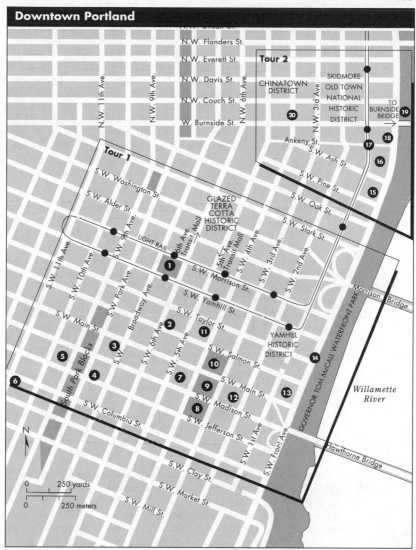

Downtown Portland

Central Fire
Station, **16**
Chapman Square, **9**
Chinatown Gate, **20**
Japanese-American
Historical Plaza, **19**
Justice Center, **12**
Lownsdale Square, **10**
Mill Ends Park, **14**
Nike Town, **2**
Old Church, **6**

Oregon History
Center, **4**
Oregon Maritime
Center and
Museum, **15**
Pioneer Courthouse
Square, **1**
Portland Art
Museum, **5**
Portland Building, **7**

Portland Center for
the Performing Arts, **3**
Portland/Oregon
Visitors
Association, **13**
Portland Saturday
Market, **18**
Skidmore Fountain, **17**
State of Oregon
Sports Hall of Fame, **11**
Terry Shrunk Park, **8**

One block west are the tree-lined **South Park Blocks,** where you'll find a pleasant green-canopied place for a fine-weather stroll. On Park Avenue, on the east side of the South Park Blocks, is an impressive six-story-high mural of Lewis and Clark and the Oregon Trail (the route the pioneers took from St. Joseph and Independence, Missouri, to the Oregon Territory). The paintings signal the entrance to the **Oregon History Center,** which documents the state's history from prehistoric times to the present. Permanent and special exhibits include archaeological and anthropological artifacts, ship models, and memorabilia from the Oregon Trail. A research library is open to the public. A bookstore (corner of Broadway and Madison St.) is the best source for maps and publications on Northwest history. *1200 S.W. Park Ave.,* ☎ *503/306–5200.* ☛ *$4.50 adults and senior citizens (senior citizens free on Thurs.), $1.50 students.* ☉ *Tues.–Sat. 10–5, Sun. noon–5.*

Between Madison and Jefferson streets, across the park, is the **Portland Art Museum.** The museum, which includes a film center, is the region's oldest visual- and media-arts facility. Its treasures span 35 centuries of Asian, European, and American art, with collections of Native American, regional, and contemporary art. The film center features the annual Portland International Film Festival in February and March, and the Northwest Film Festival in early November. *1219 S.W. Park Ave.,* ☎ *503/226–2811; 503/221–1156 for film schedule.* ☛ *$5 nonmembers, $3.50 senior citizens, $2.50 children 6–12 and students; free 1st Thurs. of month 4–9 PM, senior citizens free Thurs.* ☉ *Tues.–Sat. 11–5, Sun. 1–5.*

On the corner of Columbia Street and 11th Avenue, three blocks from the museum, is the **Old Church.** Built in 1882, it's a prime example of Carpenter Gothic architecture, as demonstrated by the exterior's rough-cut lumber, tall spires, and original stained-glass windows. The acoustically resonant church hosts free classical concerts at noon each Wednesday. If you're lucky, you'll get to hear one of the few operating Hook and Hastings tracker pipe organs. *1422 S.W. 11th Ave.,* ☎ *503/222–2031.* ☛ *Free.* ☉ *Weekdays 11–3, Sat. by appointment.*

Return north to Madison Avenue and follow it several blocks east to 5th Avenue. There you'll find the **Portland Building,** where *Portlandia,* the world's second-largest hammered-copper statue (after the Statue of Liberty) kneels on the second-story balcony. She stands 36 feet high and was installed in 1985. The building itself, one of the United States' first postmodern designs, generates strong feelings; chances are you'll either love it or hate it. The controversial structure, designed by architect Michael Graves, is buff colored with brown trim and has what seems to be a wrinkled blue ribbon wrapped around its top. The **Metropolitan Center for Public Art,** on the second floor, is well worth a visit. From a huge fiberglass mold of *Portlandia's* face to original works by local artists, the gallery specializes in images of Portland in sculpture, painting, and photography. *1120 S.W. 5th Ave.,* ☎ *503/823–5111.* ☛ *Art center free.* ☉ *Weekdays 8–6.*

A block farther east, between 4th and 3rd avenues, are three small parks. **Terry Shrunk Park** is a terraced amphitheater of green lawn and brick, shaded by flowering cherry trees, and a popular lunch spot for the office crowd. During the 1920s, **Chapman and Lownsdale squares** were segregated by sex: Chapman (between Madison and Main streets) was reserved for women, and Lownsdale (between Main and Salmon streets) was for men. Beware the public rest rooms, which are grungy and considered unsafe by the locals. The elk statue on Main Street, which separates the parks, was given to the city by former mayor David Thompson; supposedly, it honors an elk that grazed here in the 1850s.

⑪ The **State of Oregon Sports Hall of Fame** is just north of the parks on 4th Avenue, between Salmon and Taylor streets. It houses 3,300 square feet of sports memorabilia associated with such prominent Oregonian athletes and teams as Heisman Trophy winner Terry Baker, the 1977 NBA champion Portland Trailblazers basketball team, and Mickey Lolich, who played for Detroit in three World Series. *900 S.W. 4th Ave. (concourse level of the Standard Insurance Ct.),* ☎ *503/227–7466.* ☛ *Free.* ۞ *Mon.–Sat. 10–3.*

⑫ On Main Street, between 3rd and 2nd avenues, is the **Justice Center,** a beautiful building with glass bricks built into portions of the east and west sides. Because of a city ordinance requiring that 1% of the development costs of new buildings be allotted to the arts, the center's hallways are lined with travertine sculptures, ceiling mosaics, stained-glass windows, and photographic murals. Visitors are welcome to peruse the artwork. The center houses the county court and support offices and, on the 16th floor, the **Police Museum,** which has uniforms, guns, and badges worn by the Portland Police Department. *1111 S.W. 2nd Ave.,* ☎ *503/823–0019.* ☛ *Free.* ۞ *Mon.–Thurs. 10–3.*

The World Trade Center, northeast of the Justice Center, is a trio of buildings connected by sky bridges and designed by prominent Portland architect Robert Frasca. On the ground floors of the buildings are retail stores, a restaurant, coffee shops, banks, and travel agencies. In ⑬ World Trade Center Three is the **Portland/Oregon Visitors Association,** where you can pick up maps and literature about the state. *25 S.W. Salmon St.,* ☎ *503/222–2223.* ۞ *Weekdays 8:30–6:30, Sat. 9–5.*

Cross Front Avenue and enter **Governor Tom McCall Waterfront Park** and **Salmon Street Plaza.** The park stretches north for approximately a mile to Burnside Street and offers what may be the finest ground-level view of downtown Portland's river, bridges, and skyline. The broad, grassy park, which occupies the site of a former expressway, is the site of some of Portland's top special events—the Rose Festival, a series of classical and blues concerts, and the Oregon Brewers' Festival in July. At other times of the year, Waterfront Park is a favorite venue for bikers, joggers, and roller skaters. The arching jets of water at the **Salmon Street Fountain** change configuration every few hours, and are a favorite cooling-off spot during the dog days of summer.

⑭ Follow the park one block north to where **Mill Ends Park** sits in the middle of a traffic island on Front Avenue. At 24 inches in diameter, it has been recognized by the *Guinness Book of World Records* as the world's smallest official city park.

★ You are now in the heart of the **Yamhill National Historic District,** a six-square-block district in which many examples of 19th-century cast-iron architecture have been preserved. Since the cast-iron facade helped support the main structure, these buildings traditionally did not need big, heavy walls to bear the weight; the interior spaces could therefore be larger and more open.

North and west of this district, along 2nd Avenue, you'll find several galleries featuring fine art, ceramics, photography, and posters. On the first Thursday of each month, new shows and exhibits are unveiled and most galleries stay open until 9 PM. For details call the Portland Art Museum (☎ 503/226–2811).

TIME OUT The **Rock Bottom Brewing Co.** (210 S.W. Morrison, at S.W. 2nd Ave., ☎ 503/796–2739) is one of the newest and ritziest examples of that authentically Portland experience, the brew-pub. Have a pint of ale—brewed on the premises, of course—and sample the fine array of pub foods and snacks.

If you are interested in art and architecture, you may wish to zigzag back and forth between Southwest 5th and Southwest 6th avenues and the intersecting streets of Oak and Yamhill. This is the heart of the **Glazed-Terra Cotta National Historic District.** Buildings from the late 1890s to the mid-1910s still stand here and are used as commercial and public properties. At the turn of the century, terra-cotta was an often-used material because of its availability and inexpensive cost; it could also be easily molded into the decorative details that were popular at the time. Elaborate lions' heads, griffins, floral displays, and other classical motifs adorn the rooflines of many of these buildings.

Public art also lines 5th and 6th avenues. On 5th Avenue you'll find a sculpture that reflects light and changing colors, a nude woman made of bronze, a copper and redwood sculpture inspired by the Norse god Thor, and a large limestone cat in repose. Sixth Avenue has a steel-and-concrete matrix, a granite-and-brick fountain, and an abstract modern depiction of an ancient Greek defending Crete.

Tour 2: The Skidmore District and Chinatown

Numbers in the margin correspond to points of interest on the Downtown Portland map.

Bounded by Oak Street to the south and Everett Street to the north, the **Skidmore Old Town National Historic District,** commonly called the Skidmore District or Old Town, is where Portland was born. The 20-square-block district includes a variety of buildings of varying ages and architectural designs. Before it was renovated, this was the city's skid row, and vestiges of that condition remain. Even in daylight, you may feel more comfortable sightseeing with a companion; don't walk here at night. The area is easily accessible from downtown via the MAX light-rail system.

⑮ The exterior of the **Oregon Maritime Center and Museum** features prime street-level examples of cast-iron architecture. Inside, you'll find models of ships that plied the Columbia River, most of which were made from scratch by local model makers, some of whom work at the museum. Photographic displays cover World War II, when Portland was a major military shipbuilding center. *113 S.W. Front Ave., ☎ 503/224–7724. ☛ $4 adults, $3 senior citizens, $2 students, $4.50 families. ☉ Memorial Day–Labor Day, Fri.–Sun. 11–4; Labor Day–Memorial Day, Thurs.–Sun. 11–4.*

⑯ Next door, at the **Central Fire Station** (111 S.W. Front Ave.) is the Jeff Morris Memorial Fire Museum, where you can see antique pumps and other equipment through large plate-glass windows on the north side of the building. Cast-iron medallions, capitals, and grillwork taken from other buildings are also displayed on the north wall.

⑰ Facing the station is **Skidmore Fountain,** the centerpiece of Ankeny Square, a plaza around which many community activities take place. The fountain, built in 1888, is renowned for its granite troughs and spouting lions' heads from which water was collected for quenching the thirsts of both men and horses.

★ ⑱ From March through Christmas, the fountain's environs are home to the **Portland Saturday Market** (also open on Sunday), North America's largest open-air handicraft market. Some 300 merchants sell an assortment of arts and crafts, all one-of-a-kind creations by the artisans. Whatever you're looking for—crystals, yard goods, beaded hats, stained glass, birdhouses, jewelry, flags, wood and rubber stamps, or custom footwear and decorative boots—you stand a good chance of finding it here. Street entertainers and food and produce booths add to the festive atmosphere. *1 S.W. Front Ave.,* ☎ *503/222–6072.* ☉ *Sat. 10–5, Sun. 11–4:30; closed Jan.–Feb.*

Other shopping options are just around the corner: The **Skidmore Fountain Building** (28 S.W. 1st Ave.) has three floors of baskets, jewelry, pottery, women's wear, leather crafts, imports, and other specialty shops. The **New Market Theater Building** (50 S.W. 2nd Ave.) was considered the grandest theater in the West when it opened in 1875. During its heyday it staged everything from Shakespeare to a prize fight with John L. Sullivan. Today its splendidly restored interior houses fast-food restaurants, shops, and offices.

TIME OUT If you need a break from sightseeing and shopping, the cool, dark oasis of **Kell's Irish Restaurant & Pub** (112 S.W. 2nd Ave., between Ash and Pine, ☎ 503/227–4057) is close at hand. Settle into this quiet pub for a pint of Guinness and authentic Irish pub fare, and be sure to ask the bartender how all those folded-up dollar bills got stuck to the ceiling.

⑲ Just north of the Burnside Bridge is the block-square **Japanese-American Historical Plaza.** Take a moment to study the evocative figures cast into the bronze columns at the plaza's entrance; they show Japanese-Americans before, during, and after World War II—living daily life, fighting in battle for the United States, marching off to internment camps. More than 110,000 Japanese-Americans were interned by the American government during the war, and this park was created to commemorate their experience and contributions. The park is an oasis of meticulous landscaping and flowering cherry trees; simple blocks of granite, carved with haiku poems describing the war experience offer powerful testimony to this dark episode in American history.

Walk west from the Skidmore/Old Town neighborhood on Burnside Street to reach Portland's **Chinatown District.** During the 1890s, Portland had the second-largest Chinese community in the United States. Today the neighborhood is compressed into several blocks of northwest Portland and is known for its restaurants, shops, and grocery stores. ⑳ **Chinatown Gate** (N.W. 4th Ave. and Burnside St.)—recognizable by its five roofs, 64 dragons, and two huge lions—is the official entrance to Chinatown.

Around Greater Portland

Washington Park and Forest Park

Some 322 acres of Portland's western hills are covered by **Washington Park,** which is home to a number of the city's best loved attractions.

★ Despite its name, the **International Rose Test Garden** isn't an experimental greenhouse laboratory but three breathtaking terraced gardens, set on 4 acres, where 10,000 bushes and 400 varieties of roses are grown. The flowers, many of them new varieties, are at their peak in June and July, and September and October. This is one of the nation's oldest continually operating sites of its kind. From the gardens, there are highly photogenic views of the downtown skyline and, on fine days, the Fuji-shaped slopes of Mount Hood, 50 miles to the east. *400 S.W. Kingston Ave.,* ☎ *503/823–3636.* ☛ *Free.* ⊙ *Dawn–dusk.*

★ The **Japanese Gardens,** situated above the test garden, meander through 5½ acres of Washington Park. A ceremonial teahouse, an Oriental pavilion, a strolling pond, a sand-and-stone garden, and three other gardens are among the highlights. *611 S.W. Kingston Ave.,* ☎ *503/223– 4070.* ☛ *$5 adults, $2.50 senior citizens and students.* ⊙ *Apr.–May and Sept., daily 10–6; June–Aug, daily 9–8; Oct.–Mar., daily 10–4.*

During summer a 4-mile round-trip narrow-gauge **train ride** operates from the International Rose Test Garden and the Japanese Gardens to the Washington Park Zoo. ☛ *$2.50 adults, $1.75 senior citizens and children 3–11.*

The **Washington Park Zoo,** established in 1887, has been a prolific breeding ground for Asian elephants. Major exhibits include an African section with rhinos, hippos, zebras, and pythons, plus an aviary with 15 species of birds. Other popular attractions include an Alaska Tundra exhibit, a penguinarium, bears, and animals such as beavers, otters, and reptiles that are native to the west side of the Cascade Mountains. *4001 S.W. Canyon Rd.,* ☎ *503/226–7627.* ☛ *$5.50 adults, $4 senior citizens, $3.50 children 3–11; free 2nd Tues. of month after 3* PM. ⊙ *Daily 9:30 to 4–6* PM, *depending on season.*

The **World Forestry Center,** across from the Washington Park Zoo, takes its arboreal interests seriously—its spokesperson is a 70-foot-tall talking tree! Outside, a 1909 locomotive and antique logging equipment are displayed, and inside are two floors of exhibits, a multi-image "Forests of the World," a collection of 100-year-old wood, and a gift shop. *4033 S.W. Canyon Rd.,* ☎ *503/228–1367.* ☛ *$3 adults, $2 senior citizens and children 2–18.* ⊙ *Summer, daily 9–5; Labor Day–Memorial Day, daily 10–5.*

Hoyt Arboretum, adjacent to Washington Park, has more than 700 species of plants, plus one of the nation's largest collection of coniferous trees. Ten miles of trails wind through the park to the Winter Garden and a Vietnam memorial. The Visitor's Center is open most days 9–4 for information and trail maps. *4000 S.W. Fairview Blvd.,* ☎ *503/228–8733.* ☛ *Free.* ⊙ *Daily 6* AM–10 PM.

Pittock Mansion, north of Washington Park and 1,000 feet above the city, offers superb views of the skyline, rivers, and Cascade Mountains. The 1909 mansion, which combines French Renaissance–and Victorian-style decor, was built by Henry Pittock, former editor of the *Oregonian.* Set in its own park, the opulent manor has been restored and is filled with art and antiques of the 1880s. *3229 N.W. Pittock Dr.,* ☎ *503/823–3624.* ☛ *$4 adults, $3.50 senior citizens, $1.50 children 6– 18.* ⊙ *Daily noon–4.*

Forest Park is one of the nation's largest (4,700 acres) urban wildernesses. It is home to more than 100 species of birds and 50 species of mammals, and it includes more than 50 miles of trails. The **Portland Audubon Society** (5151 N.W. Cornell Rd., ☎ 503/292–6855), within the park, offers a bevy of bird activities in the heart of the only old-growth forest left in any major U.S. city. Nature trails, guided bird-watching events, a hospital for injured and orphaned birds, and a gift shop stocked with books, feeders, and other bird lover's paraphernalia fill out the bill. *Take N.W. Lovejoy St. west to where it becomes*

Cornell Rd. and follow to the park, ☎ *503/823–4492.* ☛ *Free.* ☉
Dawn–dusk.

Eastern Portland

★ The new home of the **Oregon Museum of Science and Industry** (OMSI)
is on the east side of the Willamette River, across the Morrison Bridge.
A great place for children, it houses the Northwest's largest astronomy
educational facility, including an Omnimax theater and a 200-seat planetarium, a hands-on computer center, a space wing with a mission-control center, and a variety of other permanent and touring exhibits, which
explain things scientific to 1 million visitors a year. The museum even
has its own 240-foot submarine, the USS *Blueback,* moored in the
Willamette as part of the museum. There's also a fine technology-ori-
ented gift shop. *1945 S.E. Water Ave.,* ☎ *503/797–4000.* ☛ *Museum:*
$7 adults, $6 senior citizens, $4.50 children 3–17; museum and Om-
nimax: $9.75 adults, $8.25 senior citizens, $6 children; planetarium:
$4.50 adults, $4 senior citizens, $3.50 children. Call for show times.
☉ *Summer, daily 9:30–7 (Thurs. and Fri. until 9:30); rest of year,*
Tues.–Sun. 9:30–5:30 (Thurs. until 8).

The **American Advertising Museum** bills itself as the only museum devoted exclusively to advertising. Exhibits include examples of memorable campaigns, print advertisements, radio and TV commercials,
and a variety of novelty and specialty promotion products, along with
changing exhibits. A gift counter stocks books and reproductions of
such specialty items as pens, cups, and pins. *524 N.E. Grand Ave., be-*
tween Lloyd Blvd. and Irving St., ☎ *503/226–0000.* ☛ *$3 adults, $1.50*
senior citizens and children 6–12. ☉ *Wed.–Fri. 11–5, weekends*
noon–5.

At the **Cowboys Then & Now Museum,** on the northeast corner of Oregon Street and Seventh Avenue, visitors can get an intimate glimpse of
what life was *really* like for cowboys in the Old West (as well as
today). A chronologically organized collection of authentic tack and
other personal possessions, a 100-year-old chuck wagon (complete with
cow pies) and exhibits on the 20 most popular cattle breeds enliven
this small museum, which traces the evolution of the cowboy and the
cattle industry from its Spanish roots. *729 N.E. Oregon, Suite 190,* ☎
503/731–3333. ☛ *$2 adults, $1 children 12–17; senior citizens free*
1st Thurs. of month. ☉ *Wed.–Fri. 11–5, weekends noon–5.*

The Grotto (officially known as the Sanctuary of Our Sorrowful Mother)
is a 64-acre tract staffed by the Order of the Servants of Mary. More
than 100,000 visitors per year come here to walk the Stations of the
Cross trail, which leads through a thick forest, and to visit a cave set
in a 110-foot cliff that enshrines a marble replica of Michelangelo's
Pietà. Corner of N.E. 85th Ave. and Sandy Blvd., ☎ *503/254–7371.*
☛ *Free; elevator: $1.* ☉ *May–Sept., daily 9–8; Sept. 16–Apr., daily*
9–5:30.

Fort Vancouver

The **Ft. Vancouver National Historic Site** is a reconstruction of the
1825 fur-trading headquarters of the Hudson Bay Company. Tours,
conducted by National Park Service staff and volunteers, take you into
the smithy, the bakery, and other shops. Some furnishings are from the
original fort. A visitor center has a museum, an audiovisual program,
and a gift shop. *612 E. Reserve St., Vancouver,* ☎ *206/696–7655.* ☛
$2 adults, $4 families Memorial Day–Labor Day; free rest of year. ☉
Memorial Day–Labor Day, daily 9–5; rest of year, daily 9–4.

Outside the front entrance of Ft. Vancouver is the **Officers' Row Historic District,** a string of 21 Victorian-style homes built between 1850 and 1906. Although they are not part of the fort, the houses were often occupied by officers stationed there. Some of the more notable residents include Ulysses S. Grant and George Marshall. Some of the houses are still private residences; others have been converted into restaurants and commercial businesses.

To reach the fort and Officers' Row, leave Portland northbound on I–5 (across the Columbia River toward Vancouver, WA); take Exit 1-C and follow the signs to Officers' Row.

Oregon City

Oregon City (population 19,000) was the western terminus of the Oregon Trail. The city was founded in 1829, when Dr. John McLoughlin claimed the land for his employer, the Hudson Bay Company. In 1843, Oregon country's first provisional legislature was held here, and the town served as territorial capital from 1849 to 1852. McLoughlin's 1846 home, now the **John McLoughlin House National Historic Site,** contains many of his possessions and artifacts from the era. *713 Center St., Oregon City,* ☎ *503/656–5146.* ☛ *$3 adults, $2.50 senior citizens 62 and older, $1 students 6–17.* ☉ *Tues.–Sat. 10–4, Sun. 1–4.*

The **McLoughlin Historic District** that surrounds the home, originally part of McLoughlin's property, is now a neighborhood of picturesque houses and churches in architectural styles dating from the 1840s to the 1930s.

The **End of the Trail Interpretive Center** highlights Oregon Trail travel with displays that include covered wagons, river rafts, firearms, and other artifacts. *1726 Washington St., Oregon City,* ☎ *503/657–9336.* ☛ *$4.50 adults, 2.50 senior citizens and students 6–17.* ☉ *Mon.–Sat. 10–4, Sun. noon–4.*

From Portland, you can reach Oregon City by taking McLoughlin Boulevard (U.S. 99E) south 13 miles.

What to See and Do with Children

The **Children's Museum** offers hands-on play for children (infant–10) through changing arts-and-crafts exhibits, a clay shop, and a child-size grocery store. *3037 S.W. 2nd Ave.,* ☎ *503/823–2227.* ☛ *$3.50.* ☉ *Daily 9–5.*

Japanese Gardens (*see* Around Greater Portland, *above*).

Oaks Amusement Park may not be Disneyland, but it has a small-town charm that delights children and adults alike. There are thrill rides and miniature golf in summer, and roller-skating year-round. Also in the park is the **Ladybug Theater** (☎ 503/232–2346 for show times), which presents shows for children. *At the foot of S.E. Spokane St.,* ☎ *503/233–5777.* ☛ *$7.50.* ☉ *Memorial Day–Labor Day, daily noon–5; rest of year, weekends noon–9.*

Oregon Maritime Center and Museum (*see* Tour 2, *above*).

Oregon Museum of Science and Industry (*see* Around Greater Portland, *above*).

Washington Park Zoo (*see* Around Greater Portland, *above*).

World Forestry Center (*see* Around Greater Portland, *above*).

SHOPPING

Shopping Districts, Malls, and Department Stores

Downtown/City Center

The main shopping area in the city center is concentrated between S.W. 3rd and 10th avenues and between S.W. Stark and Morrison streets. **Second Avenue,** north and west of Yamhill Marketplace, has many fine art galleries. Northwest Portland's funky and fashionable **Pearl District,** north of downtown along Northwest 21st and Northwest 23rd streets, is home to an eclectic array of clothing, gift, and food shops, as well as art galleries, ethnic restaurants, and bookstores. The quiet tree-shaded residential neighborhoods to the east and west make for pleasant walking tours.

The Galleria (921 S.W. Morrison St., in Fareless Sq., ☎ 503/228–2748) covers a full block, with three floors of specialty stores, gift shops, and restaurants.

Meier and Frank (621 S.W. 5th Ave., in Fareless Sq., ☎ 503/223–0512) dates from 1857 and offers 10 floors of general merchandise at the main store downtown.

Nordstrom (701 S.W. Broadway, ☎ 503/224–6666) features fine-quality apparel, accessories, and a large footwear department.

Pioneer Place (700 S.W. 5th Ave., in Fareless Sq., ☎ 503/228–5800) has 70 specialty shops anchored by Saks Fifth Avenue, which offers two floors of high-quality men's and women's clothing and jewelry, among other merchandise. The Cascades Food Court, in the basement, offers good, inexpensive ethnic food from 18 different vendors.

Portland Saturday Market (100 S.W. Ankeny St., ☎ 503/222–6072) is a good place to find unique handcrafted items (*see also* Tour 2, *above*).

Northeast Portland

In 1960, when it opened, **Lloyd Center** (adjacent to MAX light rail; bounded by E. Multnomah, Broadway, and 16th and 19th Aves., ☎ 503/282–2511) was the largest shopping mall in the United States. Extensively remodeled in 1990, the center contains more than 170 shops, including four department stores, a large food court, a multiscreen cinema, and an ice-skating pavilion.

Southwest Portland

Washington Square (S.W. Hall Blvd. and Hwy. 217, ☎ 503/639–8860) has five major department stores, 120 specialty shops, parking accommodations for more than 6,000 cars, vaulted skylights, and indoor landscaping. Washington Square Too has 15 additional stores.

John's Landing (5331 S.W. Macadam, ☎ 503/228–9431) is a pleasant smaller mall with 35 specialty shops and six restaurants.

Southeast Portland

Sellwood, 5 miles from the city center, offers a combination historical walking tour and venture into unusual antiques and collectibles. More than 50 antiques shops line Southeast 13th Street, along with shops specializing in specific products as well as outlet stores for sporting goods. Building dates and original occupants are identified by plaques at each store.

Clackamas Town Center (Exit 14 off I–205 at Sunnyside Rd., ☎ 503/653–6913), with more than 180 shops and five major department stores, has one of the largest selections of merchandise in the Northwest.

Specialty Stores

Antiques

Portland Antique Company (1211 N.W. Glisan St., ☎ 503/223–0999) spreads over 35,000 square feet and houses the Northwest's largest selection of European and English antiques.

Sellwood Antique Row (*see* Shopping Districts, Malls, and Department Stores, *above*).

Art Dealers and Galleries

Jamison/Thomas Gallery (1313 N.W. Glisan St., ☎ 503/222–0063), located downtown, represents contemporary West Coast artists and specializes in art for the knowledgeable collector.

The **Photographic Image Gallery** (208 S.W. 1st Ave., ☎ 503/224–3543) features prints by nationally known nature photographers Ansel Adams and Ray Atkinson, among others.

Quintana Galleries of Native American Art (139 N.W. 2nd Ave., ☎ 503/223–1729) focuses on Navajo, Hopi, and other Native American jewelry.

Books

Powell's City of Books (1005 W. Burnside St., ☎ 503/228–4651), the largest bookstore in the United States, carries new and used books, as well as rare and hard-to-find editions; it's open 365 days a year.

Clothing

Norm Thompson Outfitters (420 S.W. Morrison, ☎ 503/243–2680; 1805 N.W. Thurman St., ☎ 503/221–0764) has two locations offering classic fashions for men and women, innovative footwear, and one-of-a-kind gifts.

Gifts

Shoppers who wish to take home local products will want to seek out the several **Made in Oregon** shops, at Portland International Airport, Lloyd Center, The Galleria, Old Town, Washington Square, or Clackamas Town Center. Merchandise ranges from books and local wines to woolen goods and distinctive carvings made of myrtle wood.

Jewelry

Zell Brothers Jewelers (800 S.W. Morrison, ☎ 503/227–8471) has sold fine jewelry and other precious trinkets to Portlanders since 1912.

Perfume

Perfume House (3328 S.E. Hawthorne Blvd., ☎ 503/234–5375) has more than 600 brand-name fragrances for women and 200 for men.

Records

Django Records (1111 S.W. Stark St., ☎ 503/227–4381) is a must for collectors of tapes, compact discs, 45s, and albums.

Toys

Finnegan's Toys and Gifts (922 S.W. Yamhill St., ☎ 503/221–0306), downtown Portland's largest toy store, stocks artistic, creative, educational, and other types of toys.

SPORTS AND THE OUTDOORS

Participant Sports

Bicycling

Cyclists are common on Portland's streets, and numerous bike paths meander through parks and along the shoreline of the Willamette

River. Designated routes include a 30-mile path along U.S. 30, through Forest Park into northwest and southwest Portland and on to the suburb of Lake Oswego. Other options are the 2 miles of promenade along the Willamette River between the Broadway and Marquam bridges and an east-side route between the Hawthorne and Burnside bridges. Bikes can be rented at **Cascadden's Outdoor Shop** (1533 N.W. 24th Ave., ☎ 503/224–4746) and at **Bike Central** downtown (835 S.W. 2nd Ave., ☎ 503/227–4439).

Fishing

The Columbia and Willamette rivers are both major sportfishing streams with opportunities for angling virtually year-round. The Willamette River offers prime fishing for rainbow and cutthroat trout, as well as bass, channel catfish, and sturgeon. It is also a good winter steelhead stream, and salmon action lasts into June. June is also the top shad month, with some of the best fishing occurring below Willamette Falls at Oregon City. The Columbia River is known for its abundance of trout, salmon, and sturgeon.

REGULATIONS

Local sport shops are the best source of information on current fishing hot spots, which change from year to year. Detailed fishing regulations are available at local tackle shops or from the **Oregon Department of Fish and Wildlife** (2501 S.W. 1st Ave., Portland 97201, ☎ 503/229–5403).

OUTFITTERS

There are numerous outfitters throughout Portland who offer guide services, including **G.I. Joe's** (1140 N. Hayden Meadows Dr., ☎ 503/283–0312) and **Stewart Fly Shop** (23830 N.E. Halsey St., ☎ 503/666–2471). Few outfitters rent equipment anymore, so either bring your own or be prepared to buy.

Golf

Golfers have a choice of 18 public courses in the greater Portland area. Among the best are **Broadmoor** (3509 N.E. Columbia Blvd., ☎ 503/281–1337), 18 holes; **Colwood National** (7313 N.E. Columbia Blvd., ☎ 503/254–5515), 18 holes; **Glendoveer** (14015 N.E. Glisan St., ☎ 503/253–7507), two 18-hole courses; and **Heron Lakes** (3500 N. Victory Blvd., ☎ 503/289–1818), 36 holes.

Skiing

For detailed information on cross-country and downhill ski trails, *see* Chapter 3, Oregon. Two places for ski rentals are **Cascadden's Outdoor Shop** (1533 N.W. 24th Ave., ☎ 503/224–4746) and the **Mountain Shop** (628 N.E. Broadway, ☎ 503/288–6768).

Tennis

Public indoor tennis is available at **Glendoveer Golf Course** (14015 N.E. Glisan St., ☎ 503/253–7507) and at the **Lake Oswego Indoor Tennis Center** (2900 S.W. Diane Dr., ☎ 503/635–5550). The **Portland Tennis Center** (324 N.E. 12th Ave., ☎ 503/823–3189) operates four indoor courts. The **St. John's Racquet Center** (7519 N. Burlington Ave., ☎ 503/823–3629) has three indoor courts.

Portland Parks and Recreation (☎ 503/823–2223) operates 117 outdoor tennis courts (many with night lighting) at Washington Park, Grant Park, and many other locations. The courts are open on a first-come, first-served basis year-round, but you can reserve courts, starting March 1, for play from May 1 to September 30.

Spectator Sports

Auto Racing

Portland International Raceway (N. Victory Blvd. at West Delta Park, ☎ 503/285–6635) features bicycles, drag racing, and motocross on weeknights, and sports cars, motorcycles, and go-carts on weekends from April through September.

Portland Speedway (9727 N. Martin Luther King Blvd., ☎ 503/285–2883) hosts demolition derbies, NASCAR, and stock-car races from April through September. In June, it hosts the Budweiser Indy Car World Series, a 200-mile race featuring the top names on the Indy Car circuit.

Basketball

The **Rose Garden** (1 Center Court, ☎ 503/234–9291) is the brand-new, 21,700-seat home court for the NBA's Portland Trail Blazers.

Greyhound Racing

The season at **Multnomah Greyhound Park** (223rd and N.E. Glisan Sts., ☎ 503/667–7700) starts in May and continues through September.

Hockey

The **Portland Winter Hawks** of the Western Hockey League play home games at Memorial Coliseum (1401 N. Wheeler Ave., ☎ 503/238–6366) and at the Rose Garden (1 Center Court).

Horse Racing

Thoroughbred and quarter horses race, rain or shine, at **Portland Meadows** (1001 N. Schmeer Rd., ☎ 503/285–9144) from October through April.

DINING

First-time visitors to Portland are likely to be surprised by both the diversity of restaurants and the low prices. Although this city has never been known as a melting pot, lovers of ethnic foods can choose from restaurants serving Chinese, French, Indian, Mexican, Middle Eastern, Japanese, Thai, and Vietnamese specialties. Of course, there's also Northwest cuisine, an emerging style that features local fish and domestic game, such as venison, duck, and pheasant, plus locally grown wild mushrooms and other produce. Northwest chefs try to avoid fats by searing and broiling meats.

CATEGORY	COST*
$$$$	over $25
$$$	$18–$25
$$	$10–$18
$	under $10

per person for a three-course meal, excluding drinks and service charge

Cafés, Delis, and Pizza Joints

$$ **Papa Haydn.** While many patrons come here just for the luscious, fresh-baked desserts, temptingly displayed in glass cases, this corner restaurant, situated near the center of Northwest 23rd Avenue's boutiques, also makes a convenient lunch or dinner stop. Top sandwiches include Gruyère cheese and Black Forest ham grilled on French bread, and the mesquite-grilled chicken breast on a roll with bacon, avocado, basil, and tomato. Favorite dinner entrées are the sautéed veal chop in thyme and raspberry vinegar, and the combination plate with mesquite-grilled top sirloin, Italian sausage, and breast of chicken. More versions of grilled and rotisseried meat, fish, and poultry are available next door at the trendy Jo Bar. ✕ *701 N.W. 23rd Ave., ☎ 503/228–7317. Reservations advised for Sun. brunch. AE, MC, V.*

$ Bridgeport Brew Pub. The only food on the menu here is thick, hand-thrown pizza on sourdough beer-wort crust, served up inside a cool, ivy-covered, century-old industrial building near the Willamette River. The boisterous crowds wash down the pizza with frothing pints of Bridgeport's English-style ale, brewed on the premises (there's also wine and nonalcoholic seltzers). During the summer, the flower-festooned loading dock is transformed into an outdoor beer garden. ✕ *1313 N.W. Marshall, ☎ 503/241–7179. MC, V.*

$ Kornblatt's. You won't find a better bagel anywhere in Portland than the ones they serve at Kornblatt's—moist, chewy, and still warm from the oven. This authentic kosher deli has been transplanted from New York to Northwest Portland's trendy 23rd Avenue. The decor is clean and modern; the fresh-cooked pastrami, corned beef, and tongue are lean and tender; and the home-smoked salmon and sablefish are simply the best. For breakfast, try the poached eggs with spicy homemade corned-beef hash. ✕ *628 N.W. 23rd Ave., ☎ 503/242–0055. No reservations. MC, V.*

Eclectic

$$ Indigene. Chef-owner Millie Howe wows regulars with her unique cuisine, which draws on the flavors of India, Latin America, Indonesia, and Europe. Depending on the season, diners may encounter rabbit with mustard, fresh rosemary, cream, and green peppercorns; fresh razor clams seared for 20 seconds a side in butter and garlic; or a four-course Indian feast with Howe's own fresh homemade chutneys. This intimate (11-table) restaurant has a pleasingly spare look, accented with fresh flowers and lots of natural wood. The small garden deck out back is one of the best places in town for a romantic dinner on a summer evening. ✕ *3723 S.E. Division, ☎ 503/238–1470. Reservations advised. MC, V. Closed Sun.–Mon. No lunch Tues.–Sat.*

French

$$$$ L'Auberge. In this French restaurant, you can dine à la carte beside the lounge fireplace or order a six-course meal in the formal dining room. The menu changes weekly and emphasizes seasonal specialties, but you can always count on entrées of steak, rack of lamb or veal, and a poultry or fish offering that might include duckling, pheasant, squab, quail, sturgeon, or swordfish. ✕ *2601 N.W. Vaughn St., ☎ 503/223–3302. Reservations advised. AE, D, DC, MC, V. No lunch.*

$$$ **L'Etoile.** Intimate and romantic, filled with fresh flowers and flicker-★ ing candlelight, this tiny (12-table) restaurant in Northeast Portland specializes in the delicately sauced pillars of classical French cuisine: escargot, rack of lamb, duck with cassis. Chef and owner John Zweben has a deft and artful touch with fresh local ingredients. Try the house specialty, veal sweetbreads in a truffle-infused *sauce Financier.* From Memorial Day to Labor Day (if the weather's good), be sure to get a table outside in the brick-terraced herb garden. The cozy, intimate L'Etoile bar serves delicious light meals at reasonable prices. ✕ *4627 N.E. Fremont St., ☎ 503/281–4869. Reservations advised. AE, MC, V. Closed Sun.–Mon. No lunch.*

36

Abou Karim, **12**

Alexis, **10**

Atwater's, **9**

Bangkok Kitchen, **20**

Bridgeport
Brew Pub, **2**

Dan & Louis's
Oyster Bar, **11**

Esparza's Tex-Mex
Cafe, **18**

Esplanade at
Riverplace, **13**

Genoa Restaurant, **19**

The Heathman, **8**

Hokkaido Japanese
Restaurant, **17**

Indigene, **21**

Jake's Famous
Crawfish, **6**

Kornblatt's, **4**

L'Auberge, **1**

L'Etoile, **15**

Newport Bay at
Riverplace, **14**

Papa Haydn, **3**

Pazzo, **7**

Yen Ha, **16**

Zefiro, **5**

Portland Dining

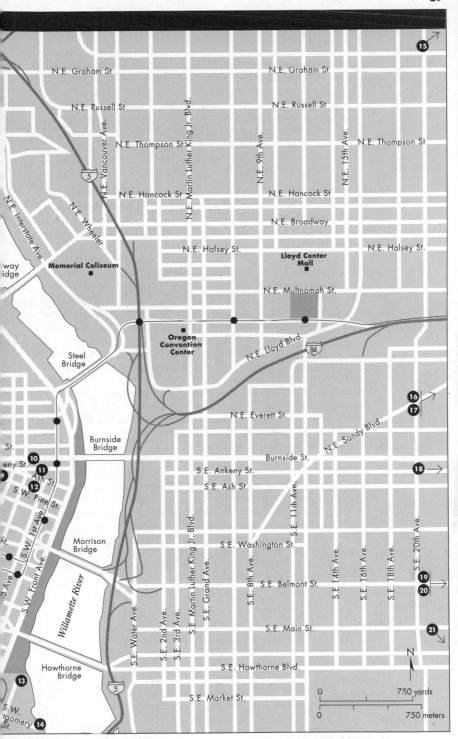

Greek

$ **Alexis.** The Mediterranean decor here consists only of white walls and basic furnishings, but the authentic Greek flavor keeps the crowds coming. You'll find such traditional dishes as *kalamarakia* (deep-fried squid served with *tzatziki*, a yogurt dip) and *horiatiki* (a green salad combination with feta cheese and Kalamata olives, tossed in olive oil, vinegar, and oregano). Greek beers and wines are served at the bar. If you have trouble making up your mind, the gigantic Alexis platter includes a little of everything. ✕ *215 W. Burnside St.,* ☎ *503/224–8577. AE, D, DC, MC, V. No lunch weekends.*

Italian

$$$$ **Genoa Restaurant.** This crowded, intimate restaurant seats only about 35 people and serves a four-course meal at 5:30, 6, and 10:30, and a seven-course dinner every half hour from 5:30 to 9:30. Since there are no windows in the somewhat dark dining room, the consistently delicious meals have become the attraction. Emphasizing fresh meat and seafood, the menu changes frequently but promises creative picks. Fillet of swordfish and veal loin chops are featured, along with fish soups and seafood ravioli. ✕ *2832 S.E. Belmont St.,* ☎ *503/238–1464. Reservations required. AE, D, DC, MC, V. Closed Sun. No lunch.*

$$$ **Zefiro.** Scandinavian-blonde hardwood floors and gracefully curved walls
★ of honey-color stucco set the mood at Zefiro, where clarity and attractive detail are the thematic touchstones of both the dining room and kitchen. The ever-changing menu, based primarily on the specialties of Northern Italy, is unified by an emphasis on simple but impeccable preparations—grilled prawns skewered on a leafy, arrowlike sprig of rosemary, or a T-bone of veal, grilled with sage and lemon butter and accompanied by a creamy potato-and-artichoke gratin. ✕ *500 N.W. 21st Ave.,* ☎ *503/226–3394. Reservations required. AE, DC, MC, V. Closed Sun. No lunch Sat.*

$$ **Pazzo.** By relying on deceptively simple new-Italian cuisine—pastas, risottos, and perfectly grilled meats, fish, and poultry—Pazzo has quickly elbowed its way to the forefront of Portland's fine-dining scene. The menu is small and changes frequently, but get the grilled lamb chops with fennel and the artichoke risotto when they're offered. The aromas of roasted garlic and wood smoke greet guests at the door to the bustling dining room, at street level of the swanky Hotel Vintage Plaza downtown. The decor is a soothing mix of dark wood, terracotta, red-checkered tablecloths, and dangling Parma hams. Booths and glass partitions keep the restaurant surprisingly quiet. ✕ *422 S.W. Broadway,* ☎ *503/228–1515. Reservations advised. AE, D, DC, MC, V.*

Japanese

$$ **Hokkaido Japanese Restaurant.** The soothing sound of water flowing through a rock fountain greets diners at this newly remodeled, reasonably priced restaurant. The sushi and sashimi are impeccably fresh and show occasional flashes of inspiration. Try the spider roll, a whole soft-shell crab surrounded by seaweed, rice, and wasabi. ✕ *6744 N.E. Sandy Blvd.,* ☎ *503/288–3731. MC, V. Closed Mon. No lunch.*

Lebanese

$ **Abou Karim.** Although more than half of the menu is vegetarian, the leg of lamb served on a bed of rice with lentil soup, including a full salad and pita bread, is a favorite. A special menu of meals low in saturated fats is also featured, and there is an outside area for dining in summer. The only nod to atmosphere consists of a few plants and a Lebanese sword or two hanging on a wall. ✗ *221 S.W. Pine St.,* ☏ *503/223–5058. Weekend reservations advised. AE, D, MC, V.*

Northwestern

$$$$ **Atwater's.** Perched on the 30th floor of the U.S. Bancorp Tower, At-
★ water's has an outstanding view of the Willamette River, the Cascade Mountains, and the city's skyline. The decor is a mix of classical pillars, Oriental art, and tile. Northwest cuisine features a variety of mushrooms, huckleberries, venison, Pacific salmon, lamb, and pheasant. A 300-label wine list of Northwest, California, and Italian vintages ranges in price from $15 to $800 per bottle. Sunday brunch is served. ✗ *111 S.W. 5th Ave.,* ☏ *503/275–3600. Reservations advised. AE, D, DC, MC, V. No lunch.*

$$$ **Esplanade at Riverplace.** Tall windows frame a view of the sailboat-filled marina and the Willamette River, providing a dramatic backdrop to this elegant restaurant in the Riverplace Alexis Hotel. The cuisine is gourmet Northwest—Dungeness crab cakes; plump scallops seared with fennel, red onion, and oyster mushrooms; duck with blackberry sauce—and the award-winning wine list features many hard-to-find Northwest vintages in a gratifyingly wide range of prices. ✗ *Riverplace Alexis Hotel, 1510 S.W. Harbor Way,* ☏ *503/228–3233. Reservations advised. AE, D, DC, MC, V. No lunch Sat.*

$$$ **The Heathman.** Chef Philippe Boulot, the French-trained former head chef at New York's Mark Hotel, revels in the cornucopia of fresh fish, game, wild mushrooms, and other produce for which the Northwest is renowned. The menu changes daily depending on what's in season, but some recent offerings include seared ahi tuna wrapped in locally cured prosciutto, served with Oregon-truffle risotto, and pheasant with foie gras on portobello mushroom chips. The elegant dining room, scented with wood smoke and hung with Andy Warhol prints, is a special-occasion favorite. ✗ *Heathman Hotel, 1001 S.W. Broadway,* ☏ *503/241–4100. Reservations advised. AE, D, DC, MC, V.*

Seafood

$$ **Jake's Famous Crawfish.** Diners have been enjoying fresh Northwest seafood in Jake's warren of individual, wood-paneled dining rooms for more than a century—the back bar came around Cape Horn during the 1880s, and the chandeliers hanging from the high ceilings date from 1881—but it wasn't until 1920, when crayfish was added to the menu, that the restaurant began to get a national reputation. White-coated waiters can take your order from a lengthy sheet of daily seafood specials year-round, but try to come during crawfish season, from May to September, when you can sample the tasty crustacean in pie, cooked Creole style, or in étouffé. ✗ *401 S.W. 12th Ave.,* ☏ *503/226–1419. Reservations advised. AE, D, DC, MC, V. No lunch weekends.*

$$ **Newport Bay at Riverplace.** When it comes to views, there's not a bad seat in this house—the restaurant literally floats on the water of the Willamette River. The circular glass dining room affords a 360° view of the marina, bridges, river, and city skyline. Newport Bay seeks out whatever is in season worldwide, which might include Oregon spring salmon, sturgeon, Maine lobster, Australian lobster tail, Alaskan halibut, or New Zealand roughy, as well as swordfish, marlin, and shark. ✗ *0425 S.W. Montgomery St., at Riverplace,* ☏ *503/227–3474. Reservations advised. AE, D, DC, MC, V.*

$ **Dan & Louis's Oyster Bar.** You can have your oysters fried, stewed, or
★ on the half shell. Crab stew—virtually impossible to find elsewhere—
is also a specialty. You'll also find local wines and microbrews. Founder
Louis Wachsmuth, who started his restaurant in 1907, was an avid collector of steins, plates, and marine art. The collection has grown over
the years to fill beams, nooks, crannies, and nearly every inch of wall.
Allow time to examine the ship models, paintings on glass, and the many
photographs. ✕ *208 S.W. Ankeny St.,* ☎ *503/227–5906. Reservations
required for 5 or more. AE, D, DC, MC, V.*

Southwestern

$$ **Esparza's Tex-Mex Cafe.** Be prepared for some south-of-the-border crazi-
ness at this much-beloved local eatery. Wild-west kitsch festoons the
walls, but it isn't any wilder than some of the entrées that emerge from
chef/owner Joe Esparza's kitchen. Look for offerings like lean smoked-
buffalo enchiladas—Esparza's is renowned for its home-smoked meats—
and, for the truly adventurous diner, calf-brain tacos. ✕ *2725 S.E.
Ankeny St., at S.E. 28th Ave.,* ☎ *503/234–7909. Reservations for 6
or more only. AE, MC, V. Closed Sun.–Mon.*

Thai

$ **Bangkok Kitchen.** Chef-owner Srichan Miller juggles the lime, cilantro,
★ coconut milk, lemongrass, curry, and (above all) hot peppers of clas-
sic Thai cuisine with great virtuosity. Pay no attention to the '60s
diner decor, and be sure to try one of the noodle dishes—the tender
rice-stick noodles with shrimp, egg, fresh mint, chilies, and coconut
are memorable. Order your dishes mild or medium-hot unless you have
an asbestos tongue, and don't forget the cold Singh Ha beer. ✕ *2534
S.E. Belmont St.,* ☎ *503/236–7349. Reservations advised. No credit
cards. Closed Sun.–Mon. No lunch Sat.*

Vietnamese

$ **Yen Ha.** The vibrant flavors of Vietnam find full expression at Yen Ha,
which is thronged nightly with Asians and Americans alike. Superb rice-
paper rolls—translucent cylinders filled with pungent bean threads, fresh
mint, and shrimp, then dipped in peanut sauce—and wonderful noo-
dle dishes are among the star attractions. ✕ *8640 S.W. Canyon Rd.,*
☎ *503/292–0616; 6820 N.E. Sandy Blvd.,* ☎ *503/287–3698. Reser-
vations advised. MC, V.*

LODGING

Travelers to Portland will find a variety of accommodations. Lodgings
range from high-rise all-suite complexes near the airport, especially con-
venient for business travelers, to elegant hotels near the city center and
waterfront, appealing because of their proximity to the city's attrac-
tions. For families, all-suite hotels in the southwest suburbs provide a
lot of space without requiring you to give up the extras. Budget trav-
elers will need to sacrifice convenience to the airport and downtown.
Many establishments allow small pets, and some offer senior-citizen
discounts and family plans; unless noted, all places include room ser-
vice and color TVs.

CATEGORY	COST*
$$$$	over $110
$$$	$80–$110
$$	$50–$80
$	under $50

All prices are for a standard double room, excluding 6%–9% tax.

Airport Area

$$$–$$$$ Shilo Inn Suites Hotel. This all-suite hotel provides amenities that border on the excessive. Each room has three TV sets, a VCR, a microwave, four telephones, refrigerator and wet bar, and two oversize beds; complimentary Continental breakfast is also included. The contemporary decor runs to soothing pale blues, light pinks, and light grays in both public and private areas. ☎ *11707 N.E. Airport Way, 97220,* ☎ *503/252–7500 or 800/222–2244. 200 rooms. Restaurant, bar, no-smoking rooms, indoor pool, hot tub, steam room, exercise room, business services, airport shuttle. AE, D, DC, MC, V.*

$$$ ★ Ramada Inn Airport. This facility caters to business travelers; it has conference rooms and a business center with computers, fax machines, and individual workstations. The 108 execu-suites have microwaves, wet bars, refrigerators, and sitting areas. Spacious one- and two-bedroom suites come equipped with a hot tub; standard rooms, with king-size beds, are tastefully decorated in quiet grays, browns, and pinks. ☎ *6221 N.E. 82nd Ave., 97220,* ☎ *503/255–6511 or 800/228–2828,* FAX *503/255–8417. 202 rooms. Restaurant, bar, pool, hot tub, sauna, exercise room, business services, airport shuttle, car rental. AE, D, DC, MC, V.*

$$ Courtyard by Marriott. This modern hotel is conveniently located ¾ mile from I–205. Rooms are of average size and are brightly decorated in teals, maroons, and yellows. The lounge features a large TV screen and grill. ☎ *11550 N.E. Airport Way, 97220,* ☎ *503/252–3200 or 800/325–2525. 150 rooms. Restaurant, bar, no-smoking rooms, pool, hot tub, airport shuttle. AE, D, DC, MC, V.*

$ ★ Best Western/Fortniter Motel. Each room has a living area with queen-size bed or queen-size hide-a-bed, coffee table, full kitchenette, full-size refrigerator, and a separate bedroom. Rooms have a lived-in, put-your-feet-up feel. Although there is no room service, a complimentary Continental breakfast is offered, and there is a nearby restaurant that can be reached by free shuttle provided by the motel. ☎ *4911 N.E. 82nd Ave., 97220,* ☎ *503/255–9771 or 800/528–1234,* FAX *503/255–9774. 52 rooms. Pool, laundry facilities, airport shuttle. AE, D, DC, MC, V.*

Downtown

$$$$ Benson Hotel. Portland's premier hotel, built in 1912, has maintained its elegance. Downstairs, note the hand-carved Russian Circassian walnut paneling and Italian white-marble staircase; in the guest rooms expect to find small crystal chandeliers, inlaid mahogany doors, and original ceilings. All rooms have state-of-the-art movie systems. The London Grill and Trader Vic's are among the city's finest restaurants. ☎ *309 S.W. Broadway, 97205,* ☎ *503/228–2000 or 800/426–0670. 290 rooms. 2 restaurants, bar, coffee shop, exercise room, laundry service, concierge, airport shuttle. AE, D, DC, MC, V.*

$$$$ ★ Governor Hotel. Although tucked amid the modern high-rises, the Governor is small, quiet, and the most atmospherically "Northwestern" of Portland's many renovated luxury accommodations, more like a rus-

42

Benson Hotel, **7**

Best Western/ Fortniter Motel, **24**

Best Western Inn at the Convention Center, **18**

Courtyard by Marriott, **22**

Embassy Suites, **4**

Governor Hotel, **6**

Greenwood Inn, **3**

Heathman Hotel, **10**

Heron Haus, **1**

Hotel Vintage Plaza, **8**

Lamplighter Inn, **2**

Mallory Hotel, **5**

Marriott Hotel, **11**

Portland Guest House, **19**

Ramada Inn Airport, **23**

Red Lion/Coliseum, **15**

Red Lion/Columbia River, **14**

Red Lion/Jantzen Beach, **13**

Red Lion/Lloyd Center, **20**

Riverplace Hotel, **12**

Riverside Inn, **9**

Shilo Inn/Lloyd Center, **17**

Shilo Inn Suites Hotel, **21**

Travelodge Hotel, **16**

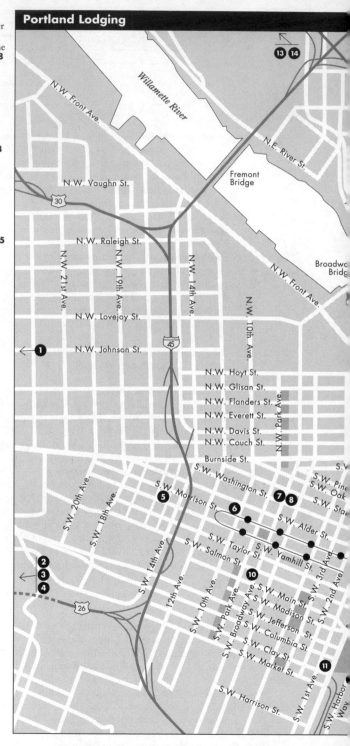

Portland Lodging

tic hunting lodge than a bustling downtown hotel. The public rooms are an oasis of soft amber light, dark wood, crackling fireplaces, well-stocked bookshelves, and comfortable, old-fashioned furniture. The 100 guest rooms and suites, in contrast, are furnished in '30s-flavored Wodehousian opulence, designed to soothe weary business travelers and vacationers alike; some even have working fireplaces. ☎ *S.W. 10th and Alder, 97205,* ☎ *503/224–3400 or 800/554–3456,* FAX *503/224–9426. 100 rooms. Restaurant, bar, health club, business services. AE, D, DC, MC, V.*

$$$$ **Heathman Hotel.** Superior service, a renowned restaurant, a central
★ downtown location (adjoining the Performing Arts Center), and elegantly beautiful public areas have earned the Heathman its reputation for quality. From the teak-paneled lobby hung with Warhol prints to the rosewood elevators and marble fireplaces, this hotel exudes elegance. The earth-tone guest rooms are luxuriously comfortable, if not overly spacious, and the bathrooms have lots of marble and mirrors. The Heathman's clientele, from wealthy Far Eastern businessmen to famous Italian tenors, is as select as its prices. ☎ *1009 S.W. Broadway,* ☎ *503/241–4100 or 800/551–0011. 152 rooms. Restaurant, bar, no-smoking rooms, health club. AE, D, DC, MC, V.*

$$$$ **Heron Haus.** This lovely B&B occupies a stately 90-year-old Tudor mansion, near Forest Park in Portland's West Hills. Each of the five large guest rooms has its own private bath, phone, and work desk, as well as such graceful touches as a tulip-shape bath tub, a tiled, seven-headed antique shower, and a graceful eyebrow window overlooking the downtown skyline and distant mountains. Breakfast (included in the price), is a gourmet Continental affair. ☎ *2545 N.W. Westover, 97210,* ☎ *503/274–1846,* FAX *503/274–1846. 5 rooms. Pool. No smoking. AE, MC, V.*

$$$$ **Hotel Vintage Plaza.** This historic landmark takes its theme from the area's vineyards and features rooms with four distinct styles. Two-story town-house suites are named after local wineries. Guests can fall asleep counting stars in top-floor rooms, where skylights and wall-to-wall conservatory-style windows rate highly among the special details. Hospitality suites feature extra-large rooms with a full living area, and the deluxe rooms have a bar. All rooms are appointed in hunter green, deep plum, cerise, taupe, and gold; more than 20 rooms have hot tubs. Complimentary coffee and newspapers are available in the morning; wine is offered in the evening, and an extensive collection of Oregon vintages is displayed in the tasting room. ☎ *422 S.W. Broadway, 97205,* ☎ *503/228–1212 or 800/243–0555. 91 rooms, 16 suites. Restaurant, piano bar, minibars, exercise room, business services. AE, D, DC, MC, V.*

$$$$ **Marriott Hotel.** The emphasis on service starts with uniformed doormen and continues to the 12th floor, the concierge level. The large rooms are decorated in off-whites; the best rooms look east to the Willamette and the Cascades. Champions Lounge, filled with sports memorabilia, is a singles' hot spot on weekends. ☎ *1401 S.W. Front Ave., 97201,* ☎ *503/226–7600 or 800/228–9290. 500 rooms. 2 restaurants, bar, coffee shop, no-smoking rooms, indoor pool, beauty salon, health club. AE, D, DC, MC, V.*

$$$$ **Riverplace Hotel.** This hotel has the feeling of a private home, with its large, airy rooms, wing-back chairs, teak tables, and feather pillows. It has one of the best views in Portland, overlooking the river and the marina, the city skyline, and a courtyard. Amenities include a complimentary Continental breakfast and parking in a locked garage. ☎ *1510 S.W. Harbor Way, 97201,* ☎ *503/228–3233 or 800/227–1333. 84 rooms. 2 restaurants, bar, no-smoking rooms. AE, D, DC, MC, V.*

$$$ **Riverside Inn.** This five-story hotel overlooking Waterfront Park and the Willamette is the top choice for visitors who want both location and value. The downtown core and the MAX light-rail line are right outside the back door; the hotel itself is scrupulously maintained and has fresh paint, carpeting, and furnishings. East-facing rooms offer a good view of the river and park across busy Front Avenue; rooms on the west side are a trifle quieter and have views of the downtown skyline. The rooms themselves are clean and furnished in white, green, and rattan with comfortable beds and prints of modern artwork. The airy café and bar features a seafood-and-steak menu. ☎ *50 S.W. Morrison St., 97204, ☎ 503/221–0711 or 800/899–0247. 138 rooms. Restaurant, bar, no-smoking rooms. AE, D, DC, MC, V.*

$ **Mallory Hotel.** This 1920s-vintage hotel, eight blocks from the downtown core, has aged gracefully. Its gilt-ceilinged lobby has fresh white paint and floral carpeting, and crystal chandeliers and a leaded-glass skylight hark back to a more elegant era. The rooms are old-fashioned but clean and cheerful; corner suites and rooms on the east side of the building have impressive skyline views. The hotel is a favorite with visiting singers, writers, and artists of every stripe. The staff is friendly and knowledgeable, and most of them have been here for years. ☎ *729 S.W. 15th Ave., 97205, ☎ 503/223–6311 or 800/228–8657. 144 rooms. Restaurant, bar. AE, DC, MC, V.*

West Side

$$$$ **Embassy Suites.** This nine-story structure, within a block of Washington Square shopping center, surrounds an atrium filled with tropical plants and waterfalls. Every room here is a suite, and each has a separate sitting room, bedroom, wet bar with refrigerator, two color TVs, and two telephones. A cooked-to-order breakfast and a two-hour manager's reception with live entertainment are included. ☎ *9000 S.W. Washington Sq. Rd., Tigard 97223, ☎ 503/644–4000 or 800/362–2779, ☒ 503/641–4654. 353 rooms. Restaurant, bar, no-smoking rooms, indoor pool, hot tub, sauna. AE, D, DC, MC, V.*

$$$ **Greenwood Inn.** The guest rooms at this large suburban Portland hotel (a 10-minute drive west of downtown) are comfortably furnished in southwestern shades of sand, ocher, pale green, and red; ask for one with a courtyard view and avoid the noisier rooms on the hotel's west side. The location is popular with both business and pleasure travelers. There is dancing to live bands six nights a week. ☎ *10700 S.W. Allen Blvd., Beaverton 97005, ☎ 503/643–7444 or 800/289–1300. 250 rooms. Dining room, bar, kitchenettes, no-smoking rooms, 2 pools, hot tub, exercise room. AE, D, DC, MC, V.*

$ **Lamplighter Inn.** Although it's close to the freeway, noise coming into the hotel is muffled by highway embankments. The inn's color scheme runs through blues and mauves. The small shopping mall across the street has a supermarket, lounge, and sporting-goods and equipment stores; a Mongolian restaurant is nearby. ☎ *10207 S.W. Pkwy., Beaverton 97225, ☎ 503/297–2211. 56 rooms. Kitchenettes. AE, D, DC, MC, V.*

East Side

$$$–$$$$ **Red Lion/Lloyd Center.** One of the largest hotels in the state, this prop-
★   erty is the flagship of the popular Northwest-based Red Lion chain. It's a busy and well-appointed business-oriented hotel, with a huge traffic in meetings and special events. The public areas are a tasteful mix of marble, rose-and-green carpet, and antique-style furnishings. The chain prides itself on its attentive service and its food. The MAX light-

rail line runs just south of the hotel, Lloyd Center is next door, and the Oregon Convention Center is a five-minute walk away. ☎ *1000 N.E. Multnomah St., 97232, ☎ 503/281–6111 or 800/547–8010. 476 rooms. 3 restaurants, 3 bars, no-smoking rooms, pool, exercise room, airport shuttle. AE, D, DC, MC, V.*

$$–$$$ **Best Western Inn at the Convention Center.** Rooms here are done in pleasing creams and rusts; those with king-size beds come with wet bars. Conveniently located, the inn is four blocks west of Lloyd Center, directly across the street from the Portland Convention Center, and on the MAX line. ☎ *420 N.E. Holladay St., 97232, ☎ 503/233–6331 or 800/528–1234. 97 rooms. Restaurant. AE, D, DC, MC, V.*

$$–$$$ **Travelodge Hotel.** The light and airy rooms here come with king-or queen-size beds and sofas, plus full-length mirrors and cable TVs. The Rose Garden arena, Memorial Coliseum, and Oregon Convention Center are within walking distance. ☎ *1441 N.E. 2nd Ave., 97232, ☎ 503/233–2401 or 800/578–7878. 237 rooms. Restaurant, bar, no-smoking rooms, airport shuttle. AE, D, DC, MC, V.*

$$ **Portland Guest House.** This Northeast Portland "working-class Victorian" house, with its coffee-and-cream-color paint job and scarred oak floors, was transformed into a cozy B&B in 1987. There are no TVs, but each room has its own phone—a rarity among Portland's B&Bs and a concession to business travelers. A gourmet breakfast is included in the rate. ☎ *1720 N.E. 15th St. (near Lloyd Center), 97212, ☎ 503/282–1402. 7 rooms, 5 with bath. AE, DC, MC, V.*

$$ **Red Lion/Coliseum.** The restaurant and many of the rooms here overlook the Willamette River. Unfortunately, a railroad line is between the river and the hotel, making courtside rooms the better choice if you want peace and quiet. The rooms are standard but pleasing enough; they're decorated in pinks, whites, mauve, and sea-foam green, and modern oak furnishings. ☎ *1225 N. Thunderbird Way, 97227, ☎ 503/235–8311 or 800/547–8010. 212 rooms. 2 restaurants, bar, pool, airport shuttle. AE, D, DC, MC, V.*

$$ **Shilo Inn/Lloyd Center.** Location is what this hotel is all about. The Rose Garden arena, Memorial Coliseum, and Oregon Convention Center are only three blocks away. A complimentary Continental breakfast is served, and several dining establishments, including a Chinese restaurant/lounge, are within easy walking distance. Rooms and public areas were freshly renovated in 1994. ☎ *1506 N.E. 2nd Ave., 97232, ☎ 503/231–7665 or 800/421–7665. 44 rooms. No-smoking rooms, airport shuttle. AE, D, DC, MC, V.*

North

$$$$ **Red Lion/Columbia River.** Rooms here, which were completely refurbished in 1995, are quite large and overlook the mighty Columbia River. The public areas—with lots of brass, dark wood, green, and mauve colors—were redecorated in 1991. The hotel is on Hayden Island, a 100-yard stroll away from Jantzen Beach Shopping Center and the tennis courts at neighboring Red Lion/Jantzen Beach (*see below*). ☎ *1401 N. Hayden Island Dr., 97217, ☎ 503/283–2111 or 800/547–8010. 351 rooms. 2 restaurants, bar, no-smoking rooms, pool, putting green, airport shuttle. AE, D, DC, MC, V.*

$$$$ **Red Lion/Jantzen Beach.** Because it was designed and built for this West Coast chain, rather than purchased and refurbished, this property has been given special attention. The results are larger-than-average guest rooms with good views (particularly those facing the Columbia River and Vancouver, Washington), public areas that glitter with brass and with bright lights that accentuate the greenery and burgundy, green, and rose color scheme. The dining room features a seasonal menu based on ingredients fresh from Northwest fields, farms, and waters. ⛅ *909 N. Hayden Island Dr., 97217,* ☎ *503/283–4466 or 800/547–8010. 320 rooms. 2 restaurants, bar, no-smoking rooms, pool, tennis courts, exercise room, airport shuttle. AE, D, DC, MC, V.*

THE ARTS AND NIGHTLIFE

"A&E, The Arts and Entertainment Guide," published each Friday in the *Oregonian,* contains current listings of performers, productions, events, and club entertainment. *Willamette Week,* published free each Wednesday and widely available throughout the metro area, contains similar, but hipper, listings.

Clubs

Blues

Candlelight Cafe and Bar (2032 S.W. 5th Ave., ☎ 503/222–3378) features blues seven nights a week.

Dandelion Pub (1033 N.W. 16th Ave., ☎ 503/223–0099) offers blues nightly in a dark, *L*-shape room with dance floor.

Rock and Folk

Dublin Pub (6821 S.W. Beaverton/Hillsdale Hwy., ☎ 503/297–2889) has more than 100 beers on tap, plus wine, Irish bands, and rock groups.

East Avenue Tavern (727 E. Burnside St., ☎ 503/236–6900) features a potpourri of styles, from Cajun and Irish to bluegrass and French acoustic-guitar music.

Kell's (112 S.W. 2nd Ave., ☎ 503/227–4057) serves up terrific Irish food and Celtic music every night except Sunday and Tuesday.

Key Largo Restaurant and Night Club (31 N.W. 1st Ave., ☎ 503/223–9919) is in a historic building with brick walls, an outdoor courtyard, and a dance floor. The club features Cajun food and top-name local and national rock, blues, and folk acts.

La Luna (215 S.E. 9th Ave., ☎ 503/241–5862) hosts hot rock acts—with occasional world beat, blues, and ethnic concerts—in a nightclub setting.

Moody's (424 S.W. 4th Ave., ☎ 503/223–4241) is where to go for hard rock.

Satyricon (125 N.W. 6th Ave., ☎ 503/243–2380) is the most venerable Portland club for grunge, punk, and other alternative rock music.

Country and Western

Jubitz Truck Stop (33 N.E. Middlefield Rd., ☎ 503/283–1111) presents live country music nightly.

The Drum (14601 S.E. Division St., ☎ 503/760–1400) is Portland's top country club, with traditional country and contemporary country-rock played nightly.

Jazz

Brasserie Montmarte (626 S.W. Park Ave., ☎ 503/224–5552) presents duos on weeknights and quartets and larger groups on weekends.

Jazz de Opus (33 N.W. 2nd Ave., ☎ 503/222–6077) features local musicians with national reputations Tuesday–Saturday.

Parchman Farm (1204 S.E. Clay St., ☎ 503/235–7831) offers prominent local jazz performers nightly.

Comedy

Harvey's Comedy Club (436 N.W. 6th Ave., ☎ 503/241–0338) presents stand-up comics Tuesday through Sunday nights.

Concert and Performance Venues

Arlene Schnitzer Concert Hall (in Portland Center for the Performing Arts, S.W. Broadway and Main St., ☎ 503/248–4496) hosts rock stars, Broadway shows, symphonies, and classical concerts.
Memorial Coliseum (1401 N. Wheeler Ave., ☎ 503/248–4496) has 12,000 seats and books popular rock groups and touring shows.
Portland Center for the Performing Arts (1111 S.W. Broadway, ☎ 503/248–4496) includes four theaters and schedules rock stars, symphonies, lectures, and Broadway musicals.
Portland Civic Auditorium (222 S.W. Clay St., ☎ 503/248–4496), with 3,000 seats and outstanding acoustics, attracts name country and rock performers and touring shows.
Roseland Theater (8 N.W. 6th St., ☎ 503/224–2038) specializes in rock and blues in a club that accommodates up to 1,400 people.

Microbreweries and Brew Theaters

Portland may be known as the City of Roses, but beer lovers have come to regard it as the City of Microbreweries. At last count, there were more than a dozen small breweries operating in the metropolitan area, producing an astonishing variety of pale ales, bitters, bocks, barley wines, and stouts. Some have attached pub operations, where you can sample a foaming pint of house ale. **Bridgeport Brewing** (1313 N.W. Marshall, ☎ 503/241–7179), **Portland Brewing** (1339 N.W. Flanders, ☎ 503/222–7150) or **McMenamins on Broadway** (1504 N.E. Broadway, ☎ 503/288–9498) are just a few among the many.

One especially interesting facet of the microbrewery phenomenon is the "brew theater," former neighborhood movie houses, lovingly restored, where you can enjoy food, suds, and recent theatrical releases. The **Bagdad Theater** (3702 S.E. Hawthorne, ☎ 503/230–0895) and the **Mission Theater** (1624 N.W. Glisan, ☎ 503/223–4031) are the top venues for this uniquely Portland form of entertainment.

Opera and Orchestral Music

Oregon Symphony (711 S.W. Alder St., ☎ 503/228–1353) presents more than 40 classical, pop, children's, and family concerts per season at the Arlene Schnitzer Concert Hall.
Portland Opera (1516 S.W. Alder St., ☎ 503/241–1401) and its orchestra and chorus stage five productions annually at the Portland Civic Auditorium.

Theater and Dance

For current information on theater productions, call **Portland Area Theatre Alliance Hot Line** (☎ 503/241–4902).

Artists Repertory Theatre (1111 S.W. 10th Ave. in the YWCA's Wilson Center, ☎ 503/294–7373) stages five productions a year, featuring regional premiers, occasional commissioned works, and selected classics appropriate to contemporary issues.
Oregon Ballet Theatre (1120 S.W. 10th Ave., ☎ 503/227–6867) produces four classical and contemporary works a year, including a much-

beloved holiday *Nutcracker.* The affiliated ballet school offers drop-in classes for adults.

Oregon Puppet Theater (☎ 503/236–4034) stages five children's productions per year at different locations in town.

Portland Center Stage (1111 S.W. Broadway, ☎ 503/248–6309) produces five contemporary and classical productions between November and April in the 916-seat Intermediate Theater.

Portland Repertory Theater (World Trade Ctr., 25 S.W. Salmon St., ☎ 503/224–4491) presents a varied season with six productions a year by the region's oldest professional theatrical company.

Tygres Heart Shakespeare Co. (1111 S.W. Broadway, ☎ 503/222–9220) mounts a Shakespearean production each in fall, winter, and spring.

PORTLAND ESSENTIALS

Arriving and Departing

By Bus
Greyhound (550 N.W. 6th Ave., ☎ 503/243–2316 or 800/231–2222) travels to points across the country.

By Car
I–5 enters from north and south; I–84 is the major east-side corridor, while U.S. 26 and U.S. 30 are primary east–west thoroughfares. Bypass routes are I–205, which loops through east Portland, and I–405, which arcs around western downtown.

By Plane
Portland International Airport (☎ 503/335–1234) is located in northeast Portland, approximately 12 miles from the city center. It is served by Alaska (☎ 503/224–2547 or 800/426–0333), Air Canada (☎ 800/776–3000), American (☎ 800/433–7300), America West (☎ 800/235–9292), Delta (☎ 800/221–1212), Hawaiian Air (☎ 503/282–3790), Horizon (☎ 800/547–9308), Northwest (☎ 800/225–2525), Reno Air (☎ 800/736–6247), Southwest Airlines (☎ 800/435–9792), TWA (☎ 800/892–2746), and United (☎ 800/241–6522).

BETWEEN THE AIRPORT AND CITY CENTER

By Bus: Raz Tranz (☎ 503/246–3301) operates buses to specified downtown Portland hotels, to the Best Western Inn at the Convention Center, and to Amtrak and Greyhound depots. Departures are approximately every 30 minutes between 5:05 AM and 12:05 AM. The one-way fare is $8.50 for adults, $2 for children 6–12; children under six are free. **Tri-Met** (☎ 503/238–7433) runs about every 15 minutes to and from the airport, making regular stops every two blocks. Service begins daily at 6 AM and ends at about 11:50 PM. Exact times vary depending on the direction in which you're headed; call for specific schedules. The fare is $1 for one- and two-zone trips, $1.30 for three zones.

By Car: From the airport, take I–84 (Banfield Freeway) west to the City Center exit. Going to the airport, take I–84 east to I–205N; follow I–205N to the airport exit.

By Taxi: The trip between downtown Portland and the airport takes about 30 minutes by taxi. The fare is approximately $25.

By Train
Amtrak service departs from Union Station (800 N.W. 6th Ave., ☎ 800/872–7245), with destinations throughout the country.

Getting Around

By Bus
Tri-Met (☎ 503/238–7433) operates bus service throughout the greater Portland area. Fares are the same for both Tri-Met and the light-rail system (*see below*), and tickets can be used on either system. There is a Tri-Met information office at Pioneer Square (6th and Morrison Sts. downtown; open weekdays 9–5).

By Car
Most city-center streets are one-way only, and Southwest 5th and 6th avenues, between Burnside Street and Southwest Madison, are limited to bus traffic. Unless posted, it is legal to turn right on a red light. Left turns from a one-way street onto another one-way street on a red light are also legal. While most parking meters run 8 AM–6 PM, many streets have special posted rush-hour regulations. Sunday parking is free.

By Light Rail
Metropolitan Area Express (☎ 503/228–7246), or MAX, transports passengers from Southwest 11th Avenue and Morrison Street in the city center to Lloyd Center and to the eastern suburban community of Gresham. There are 27 stations along the 15-mile route. Transportation operates daily, 5:30 AM–1 AM, with a fare of $1 for one- and two-zone trips, $1.30 for three zones, and $3.25 day tickets and monthly passes. Senior citizens and persons with disabilities pay 45¢.

By Taxi
Taxi fare is $2 at flag drop plus $1.50 per mile. The first person pays by the meter, and each additional passenger pays 50¢. Cabs cruise the city streets, but it's a better bet to phone for one. Major companies are **Broadway Deluxe Cab** (☎ 503/227–1234), **New Rose City Cab** (☎ 503/282–7707), **Portland Taxi Company** (☎ 503/256–5400), and **Radio Cab** (☎ 503/227–1212).

Guided Tours

Orientation
Gray Line Sightseeing (☎ 503/285–9845) operates city tours year round; call for departure times. **Yachts-O-Fun Riverboat Cruises** (☎ 503/234–6665) has scheduled dinner cruises, Sunday brunches, Portland harbor excursions, historical tours, and charter cruises; schedules are seasonal, so call for times.

Walking
The **Portland/Oregon Visitors Association** (☎ 503/222–2223) has brochures detailing self-guided tours, plus maps and guides to art galleries and select neighborhoods. Walking tours range from a six-block jaunt in the Yamhill Historic District to a 7-mile marathon through several historic areas.

Important Addresses and Numbers

Radio Stations
KEX-AM (1190), news and features; **KINK-FM (101.9)**, contemporary rock; **KKGR-AM (1230)**, contemporary country music and news; **KOPB-FM (91.5)**, National Public Radio—classical, music, news, and features; **KXYQ-FM (105.1)**, contemporary hard rock; **KXL-AM (750)**, news and talk; and **KYL-FM (95.5)**, easy listening.

Emergencies
Dial 911 for fire, police, or medical assistance.

HOSPITALS
Eastmoreland Hospital (2900 S.E. Steele St., ☎ 503/234–0411),
Emanuel Hospital and Health Center (2801 N. Gantenbein Ave., ☎ 503/
280–3200), **Good Samaritan Hospital & Medical Center** (1015 N.W.
22nd, ☎ 503/229–7711), **Providence Medical Center** (4805 N.E.
Glisan St., ☎ 503/230–6000), **St. Vincent Hospital** (9205 S.W. Barnes
Rd., ☎ 503/297–4411).

DENTISTS
Willamette Dental Group PC (1933 S.W. Jefferson St., ☎ 503/644–3200)
has nine offices throughout the metro area and is open Saturdays.

LATE-NIGHT PHARMACIES
Fred Meyer has branches downtown (100 N.W. 20th, ☎ 503/226–7179)
and near Lloyd Center (3030 N.E. Weidler, ☎ 503/280–1333); both
stores are open until 10 PM.

Visitor Information
Portland/Oregon Visitors Association (25 S.W. Salmon St., at World
Trade Ct. 3, ☎ 503/222–2223; ⊘ Weekdays 8:30–6:30, Sat. 9–5).

3 Oregon

Welcome to Oregon, *where natural splendor is the rule, not the exception. The bounty includes some 300 miles of wild and rocky Pacific coast, dotted with quaint small towns, as well as knockouts like the Columbia River Gorge and Mt. Hood, dramatic examples of the power of earth and water. On the gentler side, the Willamette valley is a lush wine-producing region that's also home to such attractions as Crater Lake and Ashland's famous Shakespeare fest.*

By Jeff Kuechle

AT ITS EASTERN END, Oregon begins in a high, sage-scented desert plateau that covers nearly two-thirds of the state's 96,000 square miles (roughly the same size as the United Kingdom). Moving west, the landscape rises to 10,000-foot-high alpine peaks, meadows, and lakes; plunges to fertile farmland and forest; and ends, at last, at the cold, green Pacific.

Thus, within 90 minutes' drive from Portland or Eugene you can lose yourself in the recreational landscape of your choice: a thriving wine country; scenic and uncrowded ocean beaches; lofty, snow-silvered mountain wilderness; or a monolith-studded desert used as a backdrop for many a Hollywood western. Oregonians, who have been called both the hardest-working and the hardest-playing Americans, take full advantage of this bounty. They are uncomplicated people, with down-to-earth ideals. There is a story, never confirmed, that early pioneers arriving at a crossroads of the Oregon Trail found a pile of gold quartz or pyrite pointing the way south to California. The way north, on the other hand, was marked by a hand-lettered sign: TO OREGON. Thus, Oregonians like to think that the more literate of the pioneers found their way here, while the fortune hunters continued south.

It was, however, the promise—and achievement—of wealth that quite naturally fueled Oregon's early exploration. In 1792, Robert Gray, an American trading captain, followed a trail of debris and muddy water inland and discovered the Columbia River. Shortly thereafter, British Army Lieutenant William Broughton was dispatched to investigate Gray's find, and he sailed as far upriver as the rapids-choked mouth of the Columbia River Gorge.

Within a few years, a thriving seaborne fur trade sprang up, with both American and British entrepreneurs exchanging baubles, cloth, tools, weapons, and liquor with the natives for high-quality beaver and sea-otter pelts. By 1804, American explorers Meriwether Lewis and William Clark had arrived at the site of present-day Astoria after their epic overland journey, spurring an influx of white pioneers—clerks, trappers, and traders—sent by John Jacob Astor's Pacific Fur Company in 1810. They came to claim the land from the unfortunate natives for the United States and to trade for furs. The trading part was accomplished readily enough, but the massive fir trees—some so huge that the clasped arms of 10 men couldn't encircle their bases—proved formidable, and after two months Astor's men had managed to clear just an acre.

But the "soft gold" of the fur trade proved an irresistible attraction. The English disputed American claims to the territory, on the basis of Broughton's exploration, and soon after the War of 1812 began, they negotiated the purchase of Astoria from Astor's company. It wasn't until 1846 that they formally renounced their claims in the region with the signing of the Oregon Treaty.

"Oregon Country" grew tremendously between 1841 and 1860, as more than 50,000 settlers from the eastern United States made the journey over the plains in their 10-by 4-foot covered wagons. Most settled in the Willamette Valley, where the vast majority of Oregon's 2.7 million residents still live. As settlers capitalized on gold-rush San Francisco's need for provisions and other supplies, Oregon reaped its own riches and the lawless frontier gradually acquired a semblance of civilization. The territory's residents voted down the idea of statehood three separate times, but in 1859, Oregon became the 33rd U.S. state.

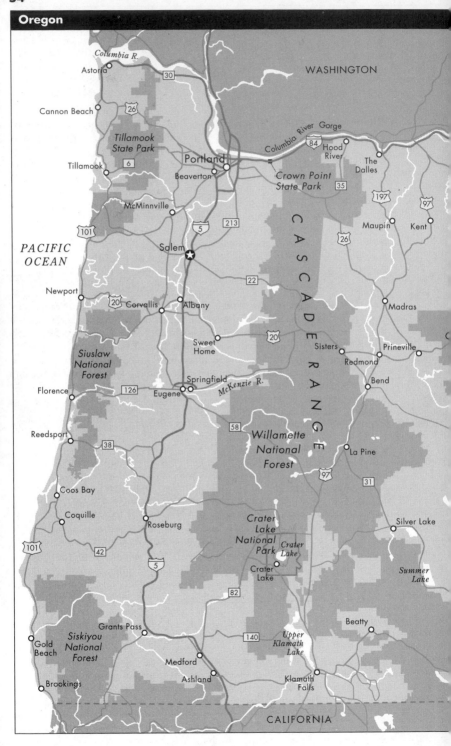

Columbia R.

Astoria

Cannon Beach

WASHINGTON

30

26

Tillamook
State Park

Columbia River Gorge

84 Hood
River

The
Dalles

Tillamook

6

Portland

Beaverton

Crown Point
State Park

35

197

97

McMinnville

213

Maupin

Kent

5

PACIFIC
OCEAN

101

Salem

C
A
S
C
A
D
E

26

22

Newport

20

Corvallis

Albany

Madras

Siuslaw
National
Forest

Sweet
Home

20

Sisters

Redmond

Prineville

R
A
N
G
E

Springfield

McKenzie R.

Bend

Florence

126

Eugene

58

Reedsport

38

Willamette
National
Forest

La Pine

97

31

Coos Bay

Coquille

Roseburg

Crater
Lake
National
Park

Crater
Lake

Silver Lake

101

42

5

Crater
Lake

Summer
Lake

82

Grants Pass

140

Beatty

Gold
Beach

Siskiyou
National
Forest

Upper
Klamath
Lake

Brookings

Medford

Ashland

Klamath
Falls

CALIFORNIA

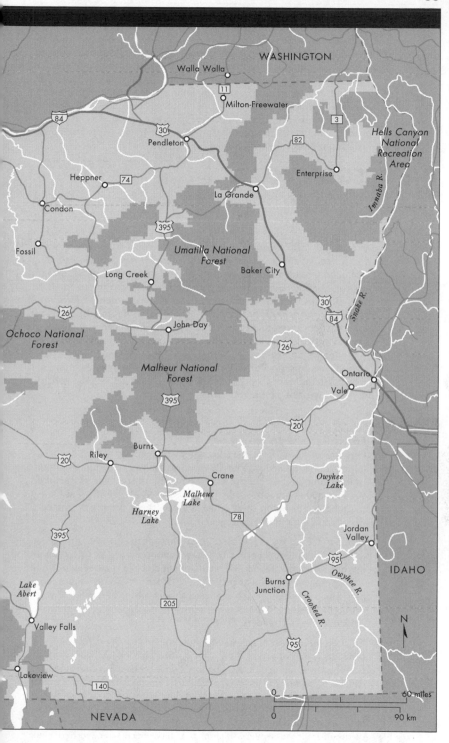

Today the state's economy is still heavily dominated by timber (Oregon is America's largest producer of softwood), agriculture (hazelnuts, fruit, berries, wine, seed crops, livestock, and dairy products), and fishing. A major high-tech center known as the Silicon Forest, producing high-speed computer hardware and sophisticated instruments, has taken root west of Portland in the Tualatin Valley, side by side with the wine industry. Tourism grows in importance here every year—Oregonians have discovered that the scenic and recreational treasures that thrill them also thrill visitors from all over the world. To cater to visitors' needs, a sophisticated hospitality network has appeared, making Oregon more accessible than ever before.

THE OREGON COAST

Numbers in the margin correspond to points of interest on the Oregon Coast and Willamette Valley/Wine Country map.

Oregon has 300 miles of white-sand beaches, not a grain of which is privately owned. Highway 101 parallels the coast from Astoria south to California, past stunning monoliths of sea-tortured rock, brooding headlands, hidden beaches, haunted lighthouses, tiny ports, and, of course, the Pacific, a gleaming gunmetal gray stretching to the horizon. With its charming hamlets (Coos Bay–North Bend–Charleston, the largest metropolis on the coast, has only 25,000 inhabitants) and endless small hotels and resorts, the Oregon Coast seems to have been created with pleasure in mind. That's even more true today, as the awesome forests and salmon runs that once produced immense fortunes dwindle and disappear. Now the locals pursue tourists who come for the endless miles of empty beaches, deep-sea charter fishing, golf, cycling, hiking, shopping, and eating.

Exploring

From Astoria to Newport

① Our journey begins in **Astoria,** where the mighty Columbia River meets the Pacific. (More than 2,000 ships have been lost at the mouth of the Columbia, where the river's powerful current meets the ocean surge over shallow sandbanks.) Founded in 1811, the city was named for John Jacob Astor, then America's wealthiest man, who financed the original fur-trading colony here.

Modern Astoria is a placid amalgamation of turn-of-the-century small town and hardworking port city. Settlers built sprawling Victorian houses on the flanks of **Coxcomb Hill,** many of which have since been restored and are no less splendid as bed-and-breakfast inns. With its museums, inns, and fine recreational offerings, it should be one of the Northwest's prime tourist destinations, yet Astoria remains relatively undiscovered, even by Portlanders.

★ The **Columbia River Maritime Museum,** located on the downtown waterfront, is one of the two most interesting man-made tourist attractions on the Oregon Coast (Newport's Oregon Coast Aquarium is the other). It beguiles visitors—particularly young ones—with exhibits ranging from the observation tower of the World War II submarine USS *Rasher* (complete with working periscopes) and the fully operational U.S. Coast Guard lightship *Columbia* to the personal belongings of some of the ill-fated passengers of ships that have been wrecked here since 1811. *1792 Marine Dr. at 17th St.,* ☎ *503/325–2323.* ☛ *$5 adults, $4 senior citizens, $2 children 6–18.* ☉ *Daily 9:30–5.*

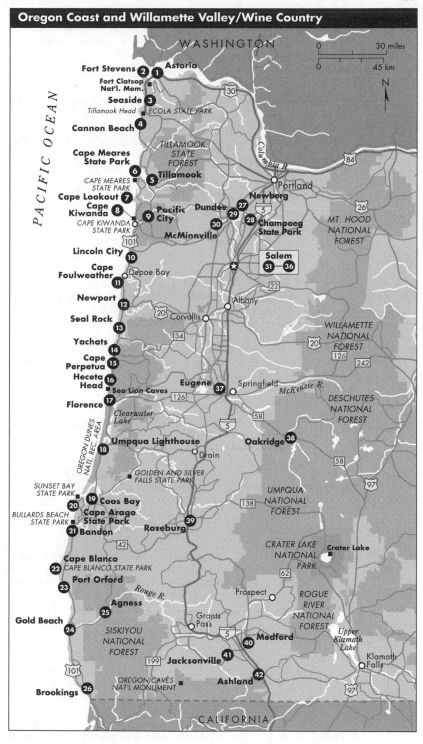

Oregon Coast and Willamette Valley/Wine Country

WASHINGTON

0   30 miles
0   45 km

N

PACIFIC OCEAN

Fort Stevens ② ① Astoria
Fort Clatsop
Nat'l. Mem.
Seaside ③
Tillamook Head ④ ECOLA STATE PARK
Cannon Beach ④

TILLAMOOK
STATE
FOREST

Columbia R.

84

Cape Meares
State Park ⑥
CAPE MEARES ⑤ Tillamook
STATE PARK
Cape Lookout ⑦
Cape
Kiwanda ⑧ ⑨ Pacific
CAPE KIWANDA City
STATE PARK
101

Newberg
Dundee ㉗
㉙ ㉘ Champoeg
State Park
Portland

26

MT. HOOD
NATIONAL
FOREST

McMinnville ㉚

Lincoln City ⑩

Salem
㉛ ㊱

Cape
Foulweather ⑪ Depoe Bay

22

Newport ⑫

Albany

20 Corvallis

WILLAMETTE
NATIONAL
FOREST

Seal Rock ⑬

34

Yachats ⑭
Cape ⑮
Perpetua
Heceta ⑯
Head Sea Lion Caves
Florence ⑰

20
126
242

Eugene ㊲ Springfield
McKenzie R.
126

DESCHUTES
NATIONAL
FOREST

58

Clearwater
Lake

OREGON DUNES NATL. REC. AREA

Umpqua Lighthouse ⑱ Oakridge ㊳

58

Drain

97

GOLDEN AND SILVER
FALLS STATE PARK

UMPQUA
NATIONAL
FOREST

SUNSET BAY
STATE PARK
⑲ Coos Bay
⑳ Cape Arago
BULLARDS BEACH State Park
STATE PARK
㉑ Bandon Roseburg ㊳

138

42

CRATER LAKE
NATIONAL
PARK Crater Lake

Cape Blanco ㉒
CAPE BLANCO STATE PARK
Port Orford
㉓

62

Rouge R.

Prospect

ROGUE
RIVER
NATIONAL
FOREST

Upper
Klamath
Lake

Agness ㉕

Grants
Pass

Gold Beach
㉔

SISKIYOU
NATIONAL
FOREST

5

Medford
㊵

Klamath
Falls

199 Jacksonville ㊶
㊷ Ashland

101

OREGON CAVES
NAT'L MONUMENT

Brookings ㉖

97

CALIFORNIA

A mile up 16th Street from downtown, the **Astoria Column**—a 125-foot-high monolith atop Coxcomb Hill that was patterned after Trajan's Column in Rome—rewards the 164-step spiral stair climb with breathtaking views over Astoria, the Columbia River, the Coast Range, and the Pacific. *Follow signs from downtown.* ☛ *Free.* ⊙ *Daily 9–dusk.*

Follow 16th Street downhill to Duane Street, then walk west about seven blocks to the **Flavel House,** a prim and proper Victorian built between 1883 and 1885. The house's period furnishings, many selected by Captain George Flavel, give insight into the lifestyle of a wealthy 19th-century shipping tycoon. The admission price also includes a visit to the Heritage Museum, housed in the former City Hall. It's an interesting look at the history of Clatsop County, the oldest American settlement west of the Mississippi. *441 8th St.,* ☎ *503/325–2203.* ☛ *$4 adults and senior citizens, $2 children 6–12.* ⊙ *May–Sept., daily 10–5; Oct.–Apr., daily 11–4.*

"Ocean in view! O! The joy!" recorded William Clark, standing near this spot in the fall of 1805. After building a fort and wintering over here, however, the explorers wrote "O! How horriable is the day waves brakeing with great violence against the shore . . . all wet and confined to our shelters." **Ft. Clatsop National Memorial** is a faithful replica of the log stockade depicted in Clark's journal. Park rangers, who dress in period garb during the summer and perform such early 19th-century tasks as making fire with flint and steel, lend an air of authenticity, as does the damp and lonely ambience of the fort itself; a well-appointed visitors center tells the story of the great adventure. *Follow signs 6 mi south of Astoria on Hwy. 101,* ☎ *503/861–2471.* ☛ *Apr.–Sept., $2 adults, $4 families; free rest of year.* ⊙ *Mid-June–Labor Day, daily 8–6; rest of year, daily 8–5.*

To round out your historical view of the West Coast's largest river, journey west on Highway 101, then follow signs to Warrenton Drive toward Oregon's northwestern tip and **Ft. Stevens,** in **Hammond.** The earthworks of this 37-acre fortress were mounded up during the Civil War, to guard the Columbia against a rather improbable Confederate attack. During World War II, Ft. Stevens became the only mainland U.S. military installation to come under enemy (Japanese submarine) fire since the War of 1812. Today the fort's abandoned gun mounts and eerie subterranean bunkers are a memorable destination, especially for children. The corroded skeleton of the *Peter Iredale,* a turn-of-the-century English four-master ship, protrudes from the sand just west of the campground, offering stark evidence of the malevolence of the Pacific. The nearby state park has 605 campsites. *Ft. Stevens State Park, Hwy. 101 (follow signs toward Hammond),* ☎ *503/861–2000.* ☛ *$3 per vehicle for historic area; summer guided truck tours of fort, $2, and underground Battery Mishler, $2.50.* ⊙ *Mid-May–Sept., daily 10–6; Oct.–mid-May, Wed.–Sun. 10–4.*

❸ For years, **Seaside,** 10 miles farther south on Highway 101, had a reputation as the sort of garish, arcade-filled town you would expect to find near Atlantic City, New Jersey. In the past decade it has cleaned up its act, and it now supports a bustling tourist trade with a cluster of hotels, condominiums, and restaurants surrounding the long beach. A 2-mile boardwalk parallels the shore and the stately old beachfront homes. Because it's only 90 miles from Portland, Seaside is often crowded, so it may not be the place for you if you crave solitude. Peak times include February, during the Trail's End Marathon; mid-March, when hordes of teenagers descend on the town during spring break; and July, when the annual Miss Oregon Pageant is in full swing.

❹ For more contemplative surroundings, go 10 miles south to Seaside's refined, artistic alter ego—**Cannon Beach**—a more mellow but trendier place for Portlanders to take the sea air. With its beautiful beachfront homes and tasteful, weathered-cedar shopping district downtown, this tiny hamlet (population 1,200) is undoubtedly one of the most charming on the coast. However, the Carmel of the Oregon Coast is expensive, crowded, and afflicted with a subtle, moneyed hauteur (such as the town's recently enacted ban on vacation-home rentals) that may grate on less-aristocratic nerves.

The town got its name when a cannon from the wrecked schooner USS *Shark* washed ashore in 1846 (the piece is now on display a mile east of town on Highway 101). Towering over the broad sandy beach is **Haystack Rock,** a vast 235-foot-high monolith that is supposedly the most-photographed feature of the Oregon Coast. The rock is temptingly accessible during some low tides, but don't be beguiled: The Coast Guard regularly airlifts stranded climbers from its precipitous sides, and falls have claimed numerous lives over the years. Every May the town hosts the **Cannon Beach Sandcastle Contest,** when thousands throng the beach to view imaginative and often startling works in this most transient of art forms. While in the town, take a walk down the main thoroughfare, **Hemlock Street** (*see* Shopping, *below*), a fine shopping district of art galleries, clothiers, and gift shops.

About a mile north of Cannon Beach is **Tillamook Head** and **Ecola State Park,** a popular playground of sea-sculpted rocks, sandy beaches, tide pools, green headlands, and panoramic views. Less crowded **Indian Beach,** in the same park complex, is one of Oregon's rare rocky beaches. With its small, often deserted cove, mussel-encrusted rocks, and tide pools, this beach is a welcome departure from crowded Ecola.

A brisk 2-mile hike leads to the 1,100-foot-high viewpoint atop Tillamook Head. From there you'll see the old **Tillamook Rock Light Station,** which stands a mile or so out to sea. The lonely beacon, built in 1881 on a straight-sided rock, towers 41 feet above the surrounding ocean. In 1957, the lighthouse was abandoned; it is now a columbarium, or repository for the cremated remains of those who yearn for the sea.

Heading south again on Highway 101, follow signs for 10 miles to the trail head at **Neahkahnie Mountain.** Cryptic carvings on beach rocks near here, and centuries-old Native American legends of shipwrecked Europeans, gave rise to a tale that the survivors of a wrecked Spanish mystery galleon buried a fortune in doubloons somewhere on the side of this 1,661-foot-high mountain. The treasure has never been found, but the trail to the summit provides the intrepid with a different kind of reward: unobstructed views over surf, sand, forest, and mountain. Those who visit in December and April often see pods of gray whales on their annual 14,000-mile migration.

Adventurous travelers will enjoy a sojourn at **Oswald West State Park** at the mountain's base, one of the best-kept secrets on the Pacific Coast. Park your car in the lot on Highway 101 and use a park-provided wheelbarrow to trundle your camping gear down a half-mile trail. There you'll find 36 campsites, surrounded by Cape Falcon's lush old-growth forest. The beach, with its caves and little-visited tide pools, is spectacular. There are no reservations for the campsites, but a call to the park office (☎ 503/731–3411) will yield information on vacancies.

More than 600,000 visitors annually press their noses against the spotlessly clean windows at the **Tillamook County Creamery,** the largest cheese-making plant on the West Coast. Here the rich milk from the area's thousands of Holstein and brown Swiss cows becomes ice cream, butter, and fine Cheddar and Monterey Jack cheeses. There are wide display windows and exhibits on the cheese-making process at the visitor center, free samples, and, of course, a gift shop. *Hwy. 101, about 2 mi north of Tillamook,* ☎ *503/842–4481.* ☛ *Free.* ☉ *Mid-Sept.–May, daily 8–6; June–early Sept., daily 8–8.*

Not to be outdone, **Blue Heron French Cheese Company,** a mile closer to Tillamook, specializes in such French-style cheeses as Camembert and Brie. There's a new petting zoo for kids, as well as a sit-down deli. The factory gift shop also sells a selection of Oregon wines and such other Oregon products as jams and mustards. *2001 Blue Heron Dr., watch for signs from Hwy. 101,* ☎ *503/842–8281.* ☛ *Free.* ☉ *Memorial Day–Labor Day, daily 8–8; rest of year, daily 9–5.*

❺ **Tillamook,** south of Cannon Beach, is a kind of wet Wisconsin-on-the-Pacific. The town, situated about 2 miles inland, lacks the aristocratic charm of Cannon Beach but has much to offer the traveler in search of a quiet, natural retreat. Surrounded by rich dairy land and blessed with abundant fresh and saltwater fishing, it has some of the finest scenery on the Oregon Coast, which contributes to the placid atmosphere.

In Tillamook's 1905 county courthouse, the **Pioneer Museum** has marvelous exhibits on local natural history, Native Americans, pioneers, and logging, as well as a collection of military artifacts dating back two centuries. *2106 2nd St.,* ☎ *503/842–4553.* ☛ *$1 adults, 50¢ children 12–17, $5 family.* ☉ *Mar. 16–Sept., Mon.–Sat. 8–5, Sun. noon–5; Oct.–Mar. 15, Tues.–Sat. 8–5, Sun. noon–5.*

Tillamook Bay, where the Miami, Kilchis, Wilson, Trask, and Tillamook rivers enter the Pacific, is a sportfishing mecca. The quarry includes silver and chinook salmon, steelhead, sea-run cutthroat trout, bottom fish, mussels, oysters, a variety of clams, and the delectable Dungeness crab. There are abundant charter-fishing services available at **Garibaldi,** a mast-filled fishing harbor just north of Tillamook. For some of the best rock fishing in the state, try Tillamook Bay's North Jetty.

Leaving downtown Tillamook, going west via 3rd Street, you'll find the start of scenic **Three Capes Loop,** one of the coast's most rewarding driving experiences. Turning west on Bay Ocean Drive will take you past what was once the thriving resort town of **Bay Ocean.** More than 30 years ago, Bay Ocean washed into the sea, taking with it lots,

❻ houses, a bowling alley—almost everything. Still on the loop, at **Cape Meares State Park,** you'll have a chance to climb 100-year-old **Cape Meares Lighthouse,** open to the public from May through September. From the tower, there's a spectacular view over the cliff of the caves and the sea-lion rookery on the rocks below. A titanic, many-trunked Sitka spruce known as the Octopus Tree grows near the lighthouse parking lot.

❼❽ **Cape Lookout,** next on the loop, has equally fine views, as well as a year-round campground. **Cape Kiwanda,** 15 miles farther south, is a favorite spot for hang gliders and surf watchers. Some of the world's best nature photographers have fallen in love with **Cape Kiwanda State Park,** where huge waves pound jagged sandstone cliffs and caves.

❾ The beach at **Pacific City,** a mile or two farther south, is one of the only places in the state where fishing dories (flat-bottom boats with high flaring sides) are launched directly into the surf instead of from harbors or docks. During the commercial salmon season in late summer, it's possible to buy salmon directly from fishermen.

⑩ If you continue south on Highway 101, you'll encounter **Lincoln City,** the most popular destination city on the Oregon Coast. Here, clustered like barnacles on the offshore reefs, you'll find fast-food restaurants, gift shops, supermarkets, and hotels. Lincoln City even has its own brew pub, the westernmost outlet of Portland's McMenamin chain, as well as a bustling factory-outlet mall. Lincoln City's only other real claim to fame is the 445-foot-long D River, stretching from its source in Devil's Lake to its mouth in the Pacific; the *Guinness Book of World Records* lists this as the world's shortest river.

High above placid Siletz Bay, just south of Lincoln City, is **Salishan** (*see* Dining and Lodging, *below*), the most famous resort on the Oregon Coast. This elegant and expensive collection of guest rooms, vacation homes, condominiums, restaurants, golf fairways, tennis courts, and covered walkways blends into a 750-acre forest preserve; if it weren't for the signs, you would hardly be able to find it.

The tiny (6-acre) harbor at **Depoe Bay** may look vaguely familiar; it was used as a setting for the Academy Award–winning film *One Flew Over the Cuckoo's Nest.* With its narrow channel and deep water, the bay is one of the most protected on the coast, and it supports a thriving fleet of commercial- and charter-fishing boats. The **Spouting Horn,** a natural cleft in the basalt cliffs on the waterfront, blasts seawater skyward during heavy weather.

If you take the **Otter Crest Loop** a mile or two south of Depoe Bay, you'll
⑪ shortly arrive at **Cape Foulweather,** with its lighthouse gift shop. British explorer Captain James Cook named this 500-foot-high headland on a blustery March day in 1778, and the backward-leaning shore pines lend mute witness to the 100-mile-an-hour winds that still strafe this exposed spot in winter.

Rejoining the highway near **Yaquina Head,** you'll find the northern city
⑫ limits of **Newport,** a busy harbor and fishing town with about 8,000 residents. Newport exists on two levels: the highway above, threading its way through the community's main business district; and the charming old bayfront below, which you'll find by heading east on Herbert Street. With its high-masted fishing fleet, well-worn buildings, art galleries and shops, fragrantly steaming crab kettles, and the finest collection of fresh seafood markets on the coast, Newport's bayfront is an ideal place for an afternoon stroll.

Just across the Yaquina Bay is the most recent jewel in the trove of Ore-
★ gon Coast tourist attractions: the **Oregon Coast Aquarium.** This 2½-acre complex contains painstaking re-creations of a variety of offshore and near-shore Pacific marine habitats, all teeming with life: playful sea otters, comical puffins, fragile jellyfish, even a 60-pound octopus, among other creatures. Visitors follow a drop of rain from the forested uplands of the Coast Range, through the tidal estuary, and out to sea. There's a salty hands-on interactive area for children, as well as North America's largest seabird aviary. *2820 S.E. Ferry Slip Rd., Newport,* ☎ *503/867–3474.* ☛ *$7.35 adults, $5.25 senior citizens and children 13–18, $3.15 children 4–12.* ☉ *Mid-May–mid-Oct., daily 9–6; mid-Oct.–mid-May, daily 10–4:30.*

Right next door to the Oregon Coast Aquarium, Oregon State University's **Hatfield Marine Science Center** offers a different kind of underwater experience. Interpretive exhibits in the center's public aquarium explain the cycle of life in the North Pacific, as well as the natural history of the Yaquina estuary. The star of the show is the large octopus in a low, round tank near the entrance—he seems as interested in human visitors as they are in him, and he has been known to reach up and gently stroke children's hands with his suction-tipped tentacles. *2030 Marine Science Dr. (head south across Yaquina Bay Bridge—Hwy. 101—and follow signs),* ☎ *503/867–0100.* ☛ *Free.* ☉ *Memorial Day–Labor Day, daily 10–6; rest of year, daily 10–4.*

From Seal Rock to Umpqua River Lighthouse

South of Newport, following the highway, you'll enter a slower-paced, less-crowded section of the Oregon Coast. The scenery, fishing, and other outdoor activities are just as rich as those in the other towns along the way, but the commercialism and the crowds seem curiously absent.

⑬ At **Seal Rock,** chain-saw sculpture—a peculiar Oregon art form—reaches its pinnacle in one of the state's most unusual tourist attractions: **Sea Gulch,** a full-size ghost town inhabited by more than 300 fancifully carved wood figures. Carver Ray Kowalski wields his Stihl chain saw with virtuosity to create unique cowboys, Indians, hillbillies, trolls, gnomes, and other humorous figures. Visitors can watch him work in his adjoining studio. *East side of Hwy. 101 in Seal Rock,* ☎ *503/563–2727.* ☛ *$4.50 adults, $3.50 senior citizens, $3 children.* ☉ *Daily 8–5.*

⑭ A few miles south of Seal Rock is **Yachats** (pronounced "Ya-hots"), a Native American word meaning "foot of the mountain." Among Oregon beach lovers, this tiny burg of 600 inhabitants has acquired a reputation that is disproportionate to its size. Yachats offers a microcosm of all the coastal pleasures: bed-and-breakfasts, excellent restaurants, deserted beaches, surf-pounded crags, fishing, and crabbing. It is also one of the few places in the world where silver smelt come inland. Every year, from May to September, hundreds of thousands of these delectable sardinelike fish swarm up the Yachats River, where dip-net fishermen eagerly await them. A community smelt-fry celebrates this bounty each July.

⑮ Three miles south of Yachats is **Cape Perpetua,** another lovely headland that towers hundreds of feet over the waves. Watch for the **U.S. Forest Service Visitors Center** on the east side of the highway, where you can obtain handy free maps of Cape Perpetua's miles of hiking trails, as well as of such geological features as the Devil's Churn, where the furious sea rushes into a volcanic fissure in the cliff.

⑯ Ten miles farther south, in **Heceta Head,** the lighthouse—visible for more than 21 miles—is the most powerful beacon on the Oregon Coast. The structure is said to be haunted by the wife of a lighthouse keeper, who fell to her death from the cliffs shortly after the beacon was built in 1874. Excellent views and photographic perspectives can be found at **Devil's Elbow State Park,** a few hundred yards to the south.

In 1880, a sea captain named Cox rowed a small skiff into a fissure in a 300-foot-high sea cliff. Inside, he was startled to discover a vaulted chamber in the rock, 125 feet high and 2 acres in area. Hundreds of massive sea lions—the largest bulls weighing 2,000 pounds or more—covered every available horizontal surface. Cox had no way of knowing it, but his discovery would eventually become one of the Oregon Coast's most venerable and popular tourist attractions, known today as **Sea Lion Caves,** located about a mile south of Heceta Head. Visitors ride an elevator from the cliff-top ticket office down to the floor of the cavern, near sea level, to watch the antics of the fuzzy pups and their parents from above. An ancient sea-lion skeleton is on display, proof that these animals have lived here for many centuries. *91560 Hwy. 101N,* ☎ *503/547–3111.* ☛ *$5.50 adults, $3.50 children 6–15.* ☺ *Oct.–June, daily 9–dusk; July–Sept., daily 8–dusk.*

Six miles south of the caves is **Darlingtona Botanical Wayside,** another surefire child pleaser. Here, a half-mile nature walk leads through clumps of carnivorous, insect-catching cobra lilies, so named because they look like spotted cobras ready to strike. This park is most interesting in May, when the lilies are in bloom. *Mercer Lake Rd., on the east side of Hwy. 101, no* ☎. ☛ *Free.*

Just past Heceta Head, Highway 101 jogs inland, and the frowning headlands and cliffs of the north coast give way to the endless beaches and rolling dunes of the south. Here you'll enter **Florence,** a popular destination for both tourists and retirees. The picturesque waterfront Old Town has restaurants, antiques stores, fish markets, and other wet-weather diversions.

TIME OUT While in Old Town, stop off at **Mo's** (1436 Bay St., ☎ 503/997–2185) for clear bayfront views and a rich, creamy bowl of clam chowder. This coastal institution has been around for more than 40 years, consistently providing the freshest seafood and friendly, down-home service.

Florence is the gateway to the **Oregon Dunes National Recreation Area,** a 41-mile swath of undulating camel-color sand. **Honeyman State Park,** 522 acres within the recreation area, is a popular base camp for the thousands of dune-buggy enthusiasts, mountain bikers, boaters, horseback riders, and dogsledders (the dunes are an excellent training ground) who converge here; there are also numerous hiking trails. The dunes, some more than 500 feet high, are a vast and exuberant playground for children, particularly the sandy slopes surrounding cool **Cleawox Lake.** Facilities in the park include 381 campsites, 66 with full hookups, showers, and a boat ramp; reservations are a must for weekends and holidays. *Oregon Dunes National Recreation Area office, 84505, Hwy. 101, Florence 97439,* ☎ *503/997–3641.* ☛ *$3 per vehicle for day use, $14–$16 overnight stays; to reserve, send $20 deposit (check or money order) to address above.* ☺ *Apr.–Sept., Wed.–Sat. 10–5.*

For coastal sportsmen, **Winchester Bay's Salmon Harbor** is always spoken of with reverence. A public pier, built especially for crabbers and fishermen, juts out over the bay and yields excellent results. The rock-fishing from the **Winchester Bay** jetty is also popular. Salmon Harbor's excellent full-service marina was designed to provide everything an avid fisherman could possibly need, including a fish market in case the day's quest was unsuccessful. For further information, the **Lower Umpqua Chamber of Commerce** (☎ 503/271–3495) can assist you.

The first **Umpqua River Lighthouse,** built on the dunes at the mouth of the Umpqua River in 1857, lasted only four years before it toppled over in a storm. It took chagrined local residents 33 years to build another one. The "new" lighthouse, built on a bluff overlooking the south side of Winchester Bay, is still going strong, flashing a warning beacon out to sea every five seconds. The adjacent **Douglas County Coastal Visitors Center** has a museum featuring local history exhibits.

The 50-acre **Umpqua Lighthouse Park** contains 500-foot sand dunes, among the very highest in the United States. *On Umpqua Hwy., west side of Hwy. 101,* ☎ *503/271–4631.* ☛ *Free.* ☺ *Apr. 1–Oct 1., Wed.–Sat. 10–5, Sun. 1–5.*

From Coos Bay to Brookings

⑲ **Coos Bay** is synonymous with the tall timbers that thrive here. The largest metropolitan area on the Oregon Coast, it lies next to the largest natural harbor between San Francisco Bay and Seattle's Puget Sound. Log trucks freighted with some of the biggest old-growth logs being cut anywhere in the world support Coos Bay's claim that it's still the world's largest lumber-shipping port. But the glory days of the timber industry are over, and Coos Bay has begun to look in other directions, such as tourism, for economic prosperity. Fortunately, the Coos Bay and **North Bend** metro area is also the gateway to some of the coast's most rewarding recreational experiences.

The **Golden and Silver Falls State Park,** where Glenn Creek pours over a high rock ledge deep in the old-growth forest, is home to two of the region's natural wonders. The 210-foot-high **Golden Falls** is the more forceful, but 200-foot-high **Silver Falls,** plunging over the same abyss a quarter-mile to the northwest, is perhaps more beautiful. *Take the Eastside-Allegany exit from Hwy. 101 at the south end of Coos Bay; follow signs to Golden and Silver Falls State Park, about 24 mi northeast; no* ☎. ☛ *Free.* ☉ *Daily dawn–dusk.*

Backtrack to Coos Bay and head west, following signs from Highway 101 to **Charleston,** a fishing village at the mouth of Coos Bay that has an almost Mediterranean quaintness about it. Four miles farther south, on Seven Devils Road, is the **South Slough National Estuarine Reserve,** where the rich, productive mudflats and tidal estuaries of Coos Bay support a wide range of life—everything from algae to bald eagles and black bears. More than 300 species of birds have been sighted here; an interpretive center, guided walks (summer only), and nature trails give visitors a chance to see things up close. *Seven Devils Rd.,* ☎ *503/ 888–5558.* ☛ *Free.* ☉ *Trails: daily dawn–dusk; interpretive center: Memorial Day–Labor Day, daily 8:30–4:30; rest of year, weekdays 8:30–4:30.*

Returning to Charleston, follow the Cape Arago Highway south toward **Sunset Bay State Park.** This placid semicircular lagoon, protected from the sea by overlapping fingers of rock, is the safest swimming beach on the Oregon Coast. Leaving the park, you'll continue southbound to **Shore Acres State Park,** situated on the estate of lumber baron Louis J. Simpson. Today all that remains are the gardens, a beautifully landscaped swath of formal English and Japanese horticulture. *10965 Cape Arago Hwy.,* ☎ *503/888–4902.* ☛ *$3 per vehicle May–Sept., otherwise free.* ☉ *Daily 8–dusk.*

⑳ Just down the road from Shore Acres is **Cape Arago State Park** (end of Cape Arago Hwy., ☎ 503/888–4902), surrounded by a trio of tide pool–pocked coves connected by short but steep trails. Here you'll find some of the richest and least-visited tidal rockery in the state.

㉑ Still traveling south on Highway 101, you'll reach **Bandon,** a small coastal village that bills itself as the Cranberry Capital of Oregon. Bandon, built above a walking beach with weathered monoliths, might be the most beautiful section along the coast. Follow the signs from Bandon south along Beach Loop Road to **Face Rock Wayside** and descend a stairway to the sand, where you can watch the sunset through a veritable gallery of natural sculptures, including Elephant Rock, Table Rock, and Face Rock.

If the weather turns inclement, you might consider a stop at **Bullards Beach State Park,** which houses the photogenic **Bandon Lighthouse** as well as the **Bandon Historical Museum.** At the latter, a historic white-clapboard Coast Guard station, you'll see exhibits on the three fires that have leveled Bandon. *1st St.,* ☎ *503/347–2164.* ☛ *$1, children under 12 free.* ☉ *Tues.–Sat. noon–4.*

㉒ About 20 miles south of Bandon you'll come to **Cape Blanco,** the westernmost point in the continental United States. **Cape Blanco Lighthouse,** accessible after a pleasant 6-mile drive from Highway 101 (follow signs), has been in continual use since 1870. The 1,880-acre **Cape Blanco State Park** (☎ 503/332–6774) has campsites, hiking, and spectacular views of offshore rocks and reefs.

㉓ Many knowledgeable coastal travelers consider the stretch of Highway 101 between **Port Orford** and Brookings (*see below*) to be the most beautiful in all of Oregon, perhaps on the entire Pacific Coast. The ocean here is bluer and clearer—though not appreciably warmer—than it is farther north. The highway soars up green headlands, some hundreds of feet high, and past awesome sea-sculpted scenery: caves, towering arches, and bridges, including the man-made **Thomas Creek Bridge,** the highest span in Oregon. Ten-mile-long **Boardman State Park** offers particularly outstanding hiking trails and cliff-top views. A word of caution: Take plenty of time to admire the scenery, but make use of the many turnouts and viewpoints along the way. Some stretches of Highway 101 are heavily trafficked, and rubbernecking can be dangerous.

㉔ **Gold Beach,** about 20 miles north of the California border, is famous mainly as the place where the much-renowned Rogue River meets the ocean. Daily jet-boat excursions roar upstream from **Wedderburn,** Gold Beach's sister city across the bay, from late spring to late fall. Some
㉕ go to **Agness,** 32 miles upstream, where the riverside road ends and the wild and scenic portion of the Rogue begins. Other boats penetrate farther, to the wet-knuckle rapids at **Blossom Bar,** 52 miles upstream.

Gold Beach also marks the entrance to Oregon's banana belt, where mild, California-like temperatures take the sting out of winter and encourage a blossoming trade in lilies and daffodils. It's said that 90% of the pot lilies grown in the United States come from a 500-acre area
㉖ just inland from **Brookings.** You'll even see a few palm trees here, a rare sight in Oregon.

Brookings is equally famous as a commercial and sportfishing port at the mouth of the incredibly clear, startlingly turquoise-blue Chetco River. If anything, the Chetco is more highly esteemed among fishermen and wilderness lovers alike than is the Rogue. A short jetty, popular with local crabbers and fishermen, offers easy and productive access to the river's mouth; salmon and steelhead running 20 pounds or larger are caught here. At **Loeb State Park** (on the north bank of the Chetco, 10 miles east of Brookings; follow signs from Highway 101), you'll find 53 riverside campsites and some fine hiking trails, including one that leads to a hidden, little-known redwood grove. Tree-lovers should also seek out the grove of myrtlewood trees—impressive because the species grows nowhere else in the world.

Shopping

From Astoria to Newport
Josephson's (106 Marine Dr., Astoria, ☎ 503/325–2190 or 800/772–3474 outside OR) is one of the Oregon Coast's oldest commercial smokehouses (tours offered), preparing Columbia River chinook salmon in the traditional alder-smoked and lox styles. Smoked shark, tuna, oys-

ters, mussels, sturgeon, scallops, and prawns are also available by the pound or in sealed gift packs.

Hemlock Street, the main thoroughfare in **Cannon Beach,** is lined with shops and galleries selling everything from kites to upscale clothing, local artwork, gourmet food, wine, and coffee.

On **Newport's** Bay Boulevard, you'll find the finest group of fresh seafood markets on the coast, as well as wood crafts from the **Wood Gallery** (818 S.W. Bay Blvd., ☎ 503/265–6843) and nautical supplies, including fishing equipment, hardware, and gear from **Englund Marine Supply** (424 S.W. Bay Blvd., ☎ 503/265–9275).

Sports and the Outdoors

Beaches
Virtually the entire 300-mile coastline of Oregon is a clean, quiet white-sand beach, publicly owned and accessible to all. A word of caution: The Pacific off the Oregon Coast is not the mild-mannered playmate it becomes in southern California. It is 45°–55°F year-round, a temperature that can be described as brisk at best and numbing at worst. Tides and undertows are strong, and swimming is not advised. When fishing from the rocks, always watch for sneaker or rogue waves, and never play on logs near the water—they roll in the surf without warning and have cost numerous lives over the years. Above all, watch children closely while they play in or near the ocean.

Everyone has a favorite beach, but Bandon's **Face Rock Beach** is justly renowned as perhaps the state's loveliest for walking, while the beach at **Sunset Bay State Park** on Cape Arago, with its protective reefs and encircling cliffs, is one of the few places along the Oregon Coast where you can swim without worrying about the currents and undertows, although the water temperature is still on the chilly side. Nearby, **Oregon Dunes National Recreation Area** adds extra cachet to Florence's beaches. Fossils, clams, mussels, and other aeons-old marine creatures, easily dug from soft sandstone cliffs, make **Beverly Beach State Park** (5 miles north of Newport) a favorite with young beachcombers.

Bicycling
The **Oregon Coast Bike Route** parallels Highway 101 and the coastline from Astoria to Brookings. There are numerous detours for scenic loops, hikes, and waysides; though the terrain is far from mountainous, it does have its share of hills and headlands. For mountain bikers, the **Oregon Dunes National Recreation Area** near Florence offers a unique challenge.

Fishing
Silver and chinook salmon and the delectable Dungeness crab are the prime quarry the entire length of Oregon's shoreline. Steelhead, flounder, sea-run cutthroat trout, red snapper, lingcod, perch, greenling (whose flesh is a startling electric blue), and dozens of other species are accessible from jetties, docks, and riverbanks from Astoria to Brookings.

There are a bewildering number of options available to visiting fishermen, from self-guided boat and shore trips to guided adventures and seagoing charters. Major charter fleets are available from most towns along the coast; the amenities and fruitful waters of Astoria, Reedsport, and Brookings are particularly esteemed. Ocean salmon season begins in earnest in late June and usually runs through mid-September. For information about fishing options in the specific area you'll be visiting, it's best to contact the local chamber of commerce or visitor center (*see* Important Addresses and Numbers *in* Oregon Essentials, *below*).

Golf

FROM ASTORIA TO NEWPORT

Agate Beach Golf Club (4100 N. Coast Hwy., Newport, ☎ 503/265–7331), nine holes.

Alderbrook Golf Club (7300 Alderbrook Rd., Tillamook, ☎ 503/842–6413), 18 holes.

Lakeside Golf & Racquet Club (3245 Clubhouse Dr., Lincoln City, ☎ 503/994–8442), 18 holes.

FROM SEAL POINT TO UMPQUA RIVER LIGHTHOUSE

Ocean Dunes Golf Links (3345 Munsel Lake Rd., Florence, ☎ 503/997–3232), 18 holes.

FROM COOS BAY TO BROOKINGS

Cedar Bend Golf Course (34391 Squaw Valley Rd., Gold Beach, ☎ 503/247–6911), nine holes.

Kentuck Golf Course (675 Golf Course La., North Bend, ☎ 503/756–4464), 18 holes.

Sunset Bay Golf Course (11001 Cape Arago Hwy., Coos Bay, ☎ 503/888–9301), nine holes.

Dining and Lodging

Unless otherwise noted, casual but neat dress is appropriate at all of the restaurants reviewed below. For price-category definitions, *see* Dining *and* Lodging *in* Oregon Essentials, *below.*

Astoria

DINING

$$ Pier 11 Feed Store Restaurant & Lounge. Housed in a renovated warehouse located on a pier, the windows of this spacious restaurant overlook the Columbia River. The tables are set with fine linen and crystal, and the friendly staff serves hearty and abundant fish, steaks, and prime rib. The cioppino is a massive helping packed with clams, crab, oysters, shrimp, and fish, and it is large enough to feed three people. ✕ *Foot of 11th St.,* ☎ *503/325–0279. D, MC, V.*

$ Columbian Café. The locals love this small, unpretentious diner with its tongue-in-cheek south-of-the-border decor that's heavy on chili pepper–shaped Christmas lights and religious icons. Fresh, simple food—crepes with broccoli, cheese, and homemade salsa for lunch; grilled salmon and pasta with lemon-cream sauce for dinner—is served by a modest staff that usually includes the owner. Come early, though, since this place always draws a crowd. ✕ *1114 Marine Dr.,* ☎ *503/325–2233. No reservations. No credit cards. Closed Sun. No dinner Mon.–Tues.*

LODGING

$$ Franklin Street Station Bed & Breakfast. The ticking of grandfather clocks
★ and the mellow marine light filtering through leaded-glass windows set the tone at this quiet, velvet-upholstered Victorian, built in 1900 on the slopes above downtown Astoria. Each of the six immaculate guest rooms has a private bath. Breakfasts are huge, hot, and satisfying; there's always a plate of goodies and a pot of coffee in the kitchen. ⌂ *1140 Franklin St., 97103,* ☎ *503/325–4314 or 800/448-1098. 6 rooms. MC, V.*

$$ Grandview Bed & Breakfast. This huge, turreted mansion lives up to its name, and then some—decks and telescopes look out over Astoria, with the Columbia River and Washington beyond. The interior is bright and airy, with scrubbed hardwood floors and comfortable, lace-filled rooms. The breakfast specialty is bagels with cream cheese and smoked salmon from Josephson's (*see* Shopping, *above*). 🏠 *1574 Grand Ave., 97103, ☎ 503/325–5555 or 800/488–3250. 9 units, 7 with private bath. D, MC, V.*

$$ **Red Lion Inn.** The only north-coast outlet of this reliable regional chain sits right on the Columbia River, beneath the Astoria Bridge; there's a view of the river and the bridge from the guest-room balconies. The small rooms and public areas are decorated in soothing earth tones. 🏠 *400 Industry St., 97103, ☎ 503/325–7373 or 800/547–8010. 124 rooms. Restaurant, bar. AE, D, DC, MC, V.*

Bandon

DINING

$$ **Bandon Boatworks.** A local favorite, this romantic jetty-side eatery serves up its seafood, steaks, prime rib, and rack of lamb with a view of the Coquille River harbor and the historic Bandon Lighthouse. Try the pan-fried oysters flamed with brandy and anisette, or the quick-sautéed seafood combination that's heavy on scampi and scallops. ✗ *275 Lincoln SW, ☎ 503/347–2111. Reservations advised. AE, D, MC, V. Closed Mon. in Jan.*

$$ **Lord Bennett's.** Some come to this modern cliff-top restaurant for the rich food; the prawns sautéed with butter, brandy, cream, and mustard are especially fine. Even better is the house lobster, sautéed with shallots, mushrooms, brandy, and cream, then broiled in hollandaise sauce. On weekends the lounge features live music, and Sunday breakfasts are particularly good. Most guests, however, are drawn here by the sunsets visible through picture windows that overlook Face Rock Beach. ✗ *1695 Beach Loop Rd., ☎ 503/347–3663. Reservations advised. AE, D, MC, V.*

LODGING

$$–$$$ **Inn at Face Rock.** This modern, cheerful resort sits just across Beach Loop Drive from Bandon's fabulous walking beach. The rooms are spacious, soothing, and well furnished; nearly half have ocean views. The interior is clean and contemporary, decorated in a cream-and-sand color scheme, and some rooms have kitchenettes and fireplaces. 🏠 *3225 Beach Loop Rd., 97411, ☎ 503/347–9441. 55 rooms. Restaurant, bar, hot tub, 9-hole golf course, horseback riding. AE, D, DC, MC, V.*

Brookings

DINING

$ **Mama's Authentic Italian Food.** The decor is down-home trattoria, styled to accompany the home-style Italian food served here. The tender pasta, crusty pizza, and slow-simmered sauces keep this small and simply furnished restaurant always busy. ✗ *703 Chetco Ave., ☎ 503/469–7611. AE, MC, V.*

LODGING

$$ **Best Western Beachfront Inn.** This comfortable, businesslike inn opened in 1990. It offers fine ocean views and beachfront access, as well as some units with a kitchen—perfect for those who can't wait to cook what they catch. 🏠 *Lower Harbor Rd. south of Port of Brookings, 97415, ☎ 503/469–7779 or 800/468–4081. 78 rooms. Pool. AE, D, DC, MC, V.*

DINING AND LODGING

$$ **Chetco River Inn.** Thirty-five acres of private forest surround this splen-
★ didly remote inn, located 17 miles up the pale blue Chetco River from Brookings. Guests come here to hike, hunt wild mushrooms, or relax in

the library or in front of the fireplace in the common room. The host cooks delicious dinners that sometimes star a nickel-bright salmon fresh from the stream. Rooms feature thick comforters and panoramic views of river and forest. ⌂ *21202 High Prairie Rd. (follow North Bank Rd., which follows the Chetco River's north bank), 97415,* ☎ *503/469–8128 (radio phone) or 800/327–2688. 3 rooms. Restaurant. MC, V.*

Cannon Beach

DINING

$$$ **The Bistro.** This 12-table restaurant is not inexpensive, but it does
★   serve arguably the best meal in town. Additionally, a profusion of flowers, candlelight, and classical music make it Cannon Beach's most romantic dining establishment. The four-course, fixed-price menu features imaginative, Continental-influenced renditions of fresh local seafood dishes; expect monstrous scampi and Pacific seafood stew to appear as specials. ✕ *263 N. Hemlock St.,* ☎ *503/436–2661. Reservations advised. MC, V. No smoking.*

$–$$ **Dooger's.** The original Dooger's in Seaside, as well as the newer branch a few miles south in Cannon Beach, are both much beloved by local families. The seafood is fresh and expertly prepared, and the contemporary decor—warm floral tones and wood paneling—makes this a comfortable place in which to enjoy a meal. The creamy clam chowder may also be the best on the coast. ✕ *505 Broadway,* ☎ *503/738–3773; 1371 S. Hemlock St.,* ☎ *503/436–2225. No reservations. MC, V. No smoking.*

$–$$ **Lazy Susan Café.** This cheerful spot is the place to come for breakfast in Cannon Beach. Excellent entrées include quiche, omelets, oatmeal, and a substantial order of waffles topped with fruit and orange syrup. Whatever your choice, don't leave without tasting the fresh-baked muffins and home fries. ✕ *126 N. Hemlock St., in Coaster Sq.,* ☎ *503/436–2816. No reservations. No credit cards. No smoking. Closed Tues. No dinner.*

LODGING

$$$–$$$$ **Hallmark Resort at Cannon Beach.** Cozy rooms with fireplaces, whirlpool tubs, and the best views in Cannon Beach make this triple-decker oceanfront resort the destination of choice for the north coast. Rooms, adorned with oak-tiled baths and spacious balconies, favor a soothing color scheme. Their large size makes them ideal for families or couples looking for a romantic splurge. ⌂ *1400 S. Hemlock St., 97110,* ☎ *503/436–1566 or 800/345–5676. 131 rooms, 5 oceanfront rental homes. Restaurant, bar, refrigerators, indoor pool, wading pool, sauna, exercise room, laundry services. AE, D, DC, MC, V.*

$$ **Webb's Scenic Surf.** This quiet, small, family-operated hotel is a throwback to simpler times in Cannon Beach, before trendiness translated into big resorts and $500 weekends. Located on the beach, Webb's provides panoramic views of the ocean. The austerely furnished rooms, many with kitchens and fireplaces, are functional, clean, and have comfortable beds. For the budget traveler, this is the best deal in town, but call ahead—reservations are a must. ⌂ *255 N. Larch St., 97110,* ☎ *503/436–2706. 14 rooms. MC, V.*

Charleston

DINING

$$ **Portside Restaurant.** This unpretentious place overlooking the busy Charleston boat basin is a gem, with fresh fish brought to the kitchen straight from the dock outside. Preparation is simple, usually with a touch of garlic butter, tomato, white wine, or cream. Try the steamed Dungeness crab with drawn butter or, better, come Friday night for the scrump-

tious all-you-can-eat seafood buffet. The nautical decor reinforces the view of the harbor through the restaurant's picture windows. ✗ *8001 Kingfisher Rd. (follow Cape Arago Hwy. from Coos Bay),* ☎ *503/888–5544. AE, DC, MC, V.*

Coos Bay

DINING

$$ **Blue Heron Bistro.** You'll get subtle preparations of local seafood,
★ chicken, and homemade pasta with an international flair at this busy bistro. There are no flat spots on the far-ranging menu; even the innovative soups and desserts are excellent. The skylit, tile-floor dining room seats about 70 amid natural wood and blue linen. The seating area outside has blue awnings and colorful Bavarian window boxes that add a festive touch. For breakfast, the omelets are as filling as they are innovative. ✗ *100 W. Commercial St.,* ☎ *503/267–3933. Reservations advised for large groups. MC, V.*

$ **Kum-Yon's.** If you have a hankering for something Asian but can't decide on a cuisine, this small multiethnic restaurant on Coos Bay's main drag will fit the bill. You'll find everything from sushi to *kung pao* shrimp to Korean short ribs on the voluminous menu. The preparations are average, and the ambience resembles nothing so much as a Seoul Burger King, but the portions are satisfying and the prices are ridiculously low. ✗ *835 S. Broadway,* ☎ *503/269–2662. MC, V.*

LODGING

$$ **This Olde House B&B.** The charm and care that have gone into the cre-
★ ation of this sprawling Victorian, four blocks up the hill from downtown Coos Bay, are matched only by the warmth of its owners. Each room is a treasure trove of antiques and oddities collected over the past 40 years. You'll never sleep better, or eat better once you awake—breakfast, including heavenly French toast with fresh berries, homemade caramel syrup, and great coffee, is included in the room rate. ▦ *202 Alder Ave., 97420,* ☎ *503/267–5224. 4 rooms, 1 with private bath. No credit cards; personal checks accepted.*

Florence

DINING

$$–$$$ **Windward Inn.** One of the south coast's most elegant eateries, this tightly run ship prides itself on its vast menu, master wine list, home-baked breads and desserts, and array of fresh seafood. The rich, grand-piano atmosphere is perhaps a bit florid, but the prices are quite reasonable. During the summer months, there's live jazz and classical music in the courtyard lounge on Friday and Saturday nights. ✗ *3757 Hwy. 101 N,* ☎ *503/997–8243. Reservations advised. AE, D, MC, V.*

$$ **Bridgewater Seafood Restaurant.** The venerably salty ambience of Florence's photogenic bayfront Old Town permeates this spacious fish house. Fresh-caught seafood is the mainstay at this creaky-floored Victorian-era restaurant. On any given night, there are 25 to 30 fish dishes from which to choose. Try the shrimp and crab enchiladas, a house specialty. ✗ *1297 Bay St.,* ☎ *503/997–9405. MC, V.*

LODGING

$$ **Driftwood Shores Surfside Resort Inn.** The chief amenity at this resort is the location, just north of Florence and directly above one of the longest, emptiest walking beaches on the coast. The rooms and public areas fall a bit short of elegance but they're comfortable, and equipped with kitchens. Some rooms have fireplaces and balconies. ▦ *88416 1st Ave. (take Heceta Beach Rd. from Hwy. 101, about 3 mi north of Florence), 97439,* ☎ *503/997–8263 or 800/824–8774 out-*

side OR. 136 rooms. Restaurant, bar, indoor pool, hot tub, sauna. AE, D, DC, MC, V.

Gleneden Beach

DINING

$$$ Chez Jeanette. This whitewashed, French-country cottage nestles in the shore pine between Highway 101 and the ocean and seems a continent or so away from the frenetic tourism of downtown Lincoln City. The atmosphere is quiet, with a fireplace, antiques, and tables set with linen and crystal. The food is wonderful: Try the carpetbagger steak, a thick fillet stuffed with tiny local oysters, wrapped in bacon and sauced with crème fraîche, scallions, spinach, and bacon. The rest of the menu puts a Parisian spin on the local bounty from the sea, sky, and pasture. ✗ *7150 Old Hwy. 101 (turn west from Hwy. 101 at the Salishan entrance; take 1st left and go ¼ mi south),* ☎ *503/764–3434. Reservations required. AE, MC, V. Closed Sun.–Mon. Labor Day–June. No lunch.*

$$$ Gourmet Dining Room at Salishan. The Salishan resort's main dining
★ room, a multilevel expanse of hushed waiters, hillside ocean views, and snow-white linen, has built an enviable reputation for showy Continental cuisine. House specialties include fresh local fish, game, beef, and lamb; the fettuccine with fat scallops and salmon caviar is heavenly. By all means make a selection from the wine cellar, which at 20,000 bottles holds the largest collection in the state. ✗ *Hwy. 101 at Gleneden Beach,* ☎ *503/764–2371. Reservations advised. Jacket and tie. AE, D, DC, MC, V. No lunch.*

LODGING

$$$$ Salishan Lodge. For most visitors, this is *the* resort on the Oregon Coast. From the soothing, silvered-cedar ambience of its guest rooms, divided into eight units nestled into a 750-acre hillside forest preserve, Salishan embodies a uniquely Oregonian elegance. Each of the quiet, spacious rooms has a wood-burning fireplace, a balcony , and original artwork by Northwest artists. Given all this, plus fine dining (*see above*), you'll understand why the timeless atmosphere also carries what may well be the steepest price tag on the coast. 🏠 *Hwy. 101 at Gleneden Beach, 97388,* ☎ *503/764–2371 or 800/547–6500 outside OR. 205 rooms. 3 restaurants, bar, indoor pool, hot tubs, saunas, 18-hole golf course, 4 tennis courts, exercise rooms, beach, playground, meeting rooms. AE, D, DC, MC, V.*

Gold Beach

DINING

$$ Captain's Table. You can trust this popular local eatery for ultratender Midwest corn-fed beef, a solid touch with fresh seafood, and a nice view out over the ocean. The antiques-filled dining room is on the smallish side, providing a cozy atmosphere; the service is excellent. ✗ *1295 S. Ellensburg Ave.,* ☎ *503/247–6308. No reservations. D, MC, V. No lunch.*

LODGING

$–$$ Ireland's Rustic Lodges. Seven original one- and two-bedroom cabins filled with rough-hewn charm, plus 28 newer motel rooms and two new cabins, are available in this spectacularly landscaped setting. Some units have fireplaces and a deck overlooking the sea, with venerable furnishings in a black, brown, rust, and beige color scheme. For the price, you can't beat this accommodation. 🏠 *1120 S. Ellensburg Ave., 97444,* ☎ *503/247–7718. 40 units. No-smoking rooms. No credit cards; personal checks accepted.*

DINING AND LODGING

$$$$ **Tu Tu Tun Lodge.** This well-known and richly appointed fishing resort
★   (pronounced "Too Tootin"') sits right on the clear blue Rogue River,
7 miles upriver from Gold Beach. Excellent salmon and steelhead fishing made the Tu Tu Tun's name, but jet-boat excursions, golf, and other
activities are also available. All the units in this small establishment
are rustically elegant. Some have hot tubs, others have fireplaces, and
a few have both; private decks overlook the river and the surrounding old-growth forest. Two deluxe rooms have tall picture windows,
a tiled bath, and an outdoor soaking tub with a river view. The dining room serves breakfast, lunch, and dinner; the latter is open to
nonguests with reservations and consists of a five-course fixed-price
meal that changes nightly. Portions are dauntingly huge. ⌨ *96550 N.
Bank Rogue, 97444,* ☎ *503/247–6664. 16 rooms, 2 suites, 3-bedroom
house. Restaurant, bar, pool, 4-hole golf course, hiking, horseshoes,
dock, boating, fishing. MC, V.*

Lincoln City

DINING

$ **Lighthouse Brew Pub.** This westernmost outpost of the Portland-based
★   McMenamin brothers' microbrewery empire has the same virtues as their
other establishments: fresh local ales, including several brewed on the
premises; good unpretentious sandwiches, burgers, and salads; and
cheerfully eccentric decor—of particular note is the psychedelic artwork
by Northwest painters. Be sure to try a house specialty, the stout-ale
milk shake. Families are welcome. ✗ *4157 N. Hwy. 101,* ☎ *503/994–
7238. No reservations. Restaurant. MC, V.*

LODGING

$$ **Ester Lee Motel.** Perched on a bluff overlooking the cold green Pacific
through panoramic windows, this small whitewashed motel has attracted
a devoted repeat business through a simple, elegant approach to the
innkeeping business. For the price, there are some nice amenities, in-
cluding wood-burning fireplaces, cable TV, and full kitchens. Be sure
to request a unit in the older section of the hotel; the rooms are larger,
furnished in rustic knotty pine, with brick fireplaces and picture win-
dows. ⌨ *3803 S.W. Hwy. 101, 97367,* ☎ *503/996–3606. 54 units.
D, MC, V.*

Manzanita

DINING

$$ **Blue Sky Café.** There is a quirky, cheerful atmosphere here, conveyed
through the eclectic table furnishings, the jungle of plants, stained
glass, and butcher paper–covered tables. Menu specialties such as
pesto prawns; creamy homemade soups like ham, apple, and blue-cheese
bisque; and memorably rich desserts make this tiny hole-in-the-wall
restaurant worth a trip from Cannon Beach or Tillamook. ✗ *154
Laneda St.,* ☎ *503/368–5712. MC, V. No lunch.*

Newport

DINING

$$–$$$ **Tables of Content.** This restaurant at the outstanding Sylvia Beach
Hotel offers a well-plotted eight-course, fixed-price ($16.50 per per-
son) menu that changes nightly. Chances are the main character will
be fresh local seafood, perhaps a moist grilled salmon fillet in sauce
Dijonnaise, with a supporting cast of sautéed vegetables, fresh-baked
breads, rice pilaf, and a decadent dessert. The interior is functional and
unadorned, with family-size tables, but then decor isn't the reason to
come here. ✗ *267 N.W. Cliff St. (from Hwy. 101, turn west on 3rd*

St., to Cliff St.), ☎ *503/265–5428. Reservations required. AE, MC, V. No lunch.*

Don Petrie's Italian Food Co. A little hole-in-the-sand place near the beach, this tidy, spartan restaurant has a strong local following and serves some of the best seafood lasagna you'll ever eat. Get here early, especially on weekends, as the place fills up fast. ✕ *613 N.W. 3rd St.,* ☎ *503/265–3663. No reservations. MC, V.*

$ **Mo's.** There are several Mo's restaurants scattered from Lincoln City to Coos Bay. All are always busy, attesting to the quality of the food and the friendly, hardworking staff. Mo's chowder—a creamy, velvet-textured potion flavored with bacon and onion and studded with tender potatoes and clams—is famous; the grilled oysters and cioppino are merely delicious. The decor is hoary and nautical, but just consider yourself lucky to get a table. ✕ *622 S.W. Bay Blvd.,* ☎ *503/265–2979; 860 S.W. 51st St., Lincoln City,* ☎ *503/996–2535; 1436 Bay St., Florence,* ☎ *503/997–2185; 700 S. Broadway, Coos Bay,* ☎ *503/269–1323. No reservations. D, MC, V.*

LODGING

$$–$$$ **The Embarcadero.** This luxurious bayfront resort has everything you're looking for in coastal accommodations. The location—at the east end of Bay Boulevard—is outstanding, offering great views over Yaquina Bay and its graceful bridge; a private dock and equipment rentals please fishing enthusiasts. The rooms (all of which have bay views) and public areas are modern and posh, heavily decorated with rough-hewn native woods and ceramic tiles. Spacious suites have one or two bedrooms, with a bayside deck, fireplace, and kitchen. ⌂ *1000 S.E. Bay Blvd., 97365,* ☎ *503/265–8521 or 800/547–4779. 136 rooms and suites. Restaurant, bar, indoor pool, hot tub, sauna, dock, boating, fishing. AE, D, DC, MC, V.*

$$ **Sylvia Beach Hotel.** Reserve far in advance for this unique, 1912-vintage
★ beachfront hotel (some weekends are fully booked as much as a year ahead), which the owners have restored along a literary theme. Each of the 20 antiques-filled guest rooms is named for a famous writer, and no two are decorated alike. The Poe Room, for instance, sports a pendulum swinging over the bed. The Christie, Twain, and Colette rooms are the most luxurious; all have fireplaces, decks, and great ocean views. As suits the contemplative, literary theme, there are no phones or TVs in the rooms, but upstairs is a well-stocked, split-level library with decks, a fireplace, slumbering cats, and too-comfortable chairs. Complimentary mulled wine is served there nightly at 10. In the morning, a hearty breakfast buffet (included in the room rate) with homemade pastries, cereals, and hot entrée is offered. ⌂ *267 N.W. Cliff St., 97365,* ☎ *503/265–5428. Restaurant, library. AE, MC, V.*

Waldport
LODGING

$$ **Cliff House Bed-and-Breakfast.** The view from Yaquina John Point, on
★ which this extraordinary B&B sits, is exquisite. The huge romantic old house, once a bordello, is filled with an Aladdin's trove of antiques, a mishmash of Asian and European items, including a 500-year-old sleigh bed that once adorned a French manor house. Lacquered screens, Chinese porcelains, plush furnishings, and a garden filled with fairy lights complete the ambience. The breakfasts are as sumptuous as the surroundings. ⌂ *1 block west on Adahi Rd. off Hwy. 101, 97394,* ☎ *503/563–2506. 4 rooms. Hot tub. MC, V.*

Yachats

DINING

$$ **La Serre.** Don't be dismayed by the vaguely steak-and-salad-bar am-
★ bience at this skylit, plant-filled restaurant—the chef's deft touch with
impeccably fresh seafood attracts knowledgeable diners from as far away
as Florence and Newport. Try the tender geoduck clam, breaded with
Parmesan cheese and flash-fried in lemon-garlic butter. A reasonably
priced wine list and mouth-watering desserts complete the package.
La Serre also serves Sunday brunch. ✗ *2nd and Beach Sts.,* ☎ *503/547–*
3420. Reservations advised. AE, MC, V. Closed Tues. No lunch.

$ **New Morning Coffeehouse.** Exquisite fresh-baked breads and desserts,
salads, sandwiches, and fine coffee make this airy sunlit café worth a
stop. The spacious deck makes for pleasant outdoor seating on fine
days. ✗ *4th St. and Hwy. 101,* ☎ *503/547–3848. No reservations.*
No credit cards. No dinner. Closed Mon.–Tues. Oct.–June.

LODGING

$$–$$$ **Ziggurat.** You have to see this four-story cedar-and-glass pyramid,
surrounded by tidal grasslands, to believe it, and you need to spend a
night or two here, serenaded by the wind and the sea, to fully appre-
ciate it. Odd angles, Scandinavian furnishings, and artwork gathered
on the owner's world travels lend an eccentric but welcoming air. Ask
for the fourth-floor master bedroom—the best views in the house
make it the most romantic. One of the ground-floor rooms has its own
sauna. ⊞ *95330 Hwy. 101, 97498,* ☎ *503/547–3925. 3 rooms. No*
credit cards. No smoking.

DINING AND LODGING

$$ **The Adobe.** Yachats is a beautiful and relaxed alternative to some of
the more intensely touristy communities to the north, and this quiet,
unassuming resort motel is right at home here. Rooms are on the
smallish side but warm and inviting, with the low-key, knotty-pine ambience you look for in a coastal getaway. High-beamed ceilings and
picture windows framing noble views mix nicely with such creature
comforts as fridges, cable TV, and coffeemakers; many rooms also have
wood-burning fireplaces. The Adobe Restaurant offers sweeping views
and quality Continental cuisine. The loft above the bar offers a
panoramic vantage for storm- and whale-watching. ⊞ *1555 Hwy. 101,*
97498, ☎ *503/547–3141 or 800/522–3623. 90 units. Restaurant, bar,*
hot tub, sauna. AE, D, DC, MC, V.

THE WILLAMETTE VALLEY AND THE WINE COUNTRY

During the 1940s and 1950s, researchers at Oregon State University
concluded that the Willamette Valley had the wrong climate for the prop-
agation of fine varietal wine grapes. Fortunately for wine lovers everywhere, the researchers' techniques were faulty, as has been proven by
the success of Oregon's burgeoning wine industry. More than 60 wineries dot the hills between Portland and Salem, and two dozen more are
scattered from Roseburg along the I–5 corridor as far south as Ashland,
on the California border. Their products—mainly such cool-climate varietals as Pinot Noir, chardonnay, and Riesling—have won numerous
gold medals in blind tastings against the best wines that California or
Europe have to offer. Oregon's wine country occupies the wet, temperate
trough between the Coast Range to the west and the Cascades to the
east. The main concentration lies in the north, among the Willamette
(locals say "Wil-*lam*-it") and Yamhill Valleys, near Portland. The

warmer, drier Umpqua and Rogue valleys (near Roseburg and Ashland respectively) also produce their share of fine bottlings.

Exploring

The following driving tour suggests sightseeing stops at various sites of historic and natural interest, but does not incorporate winery tours. Those who are interested can easily incorporate a few visits into this itinerary; consult the list of area wineries for suggested establishments (*see* Guided Tours *in* Oregon Essentials, *below*).

From Newberg to McMinnville
Numbers in the margin correspond to points of interest on the Oregon Coast and Willamette Valley/Wine Country map.

㉗ **Newberg** is a graceful old pioneer town located at a broad bend in the Willamette River about a half hour southwest of Portland. The oldest and most significant of its original structures is the **Hoover-Minthorne House,** boyhood home of President Herbert Hoover. Built in 1881, the beautifully preserved and well-landscaped frame house includes many of the original furnishings, as well as the woodshed that no doubt played an important role in shaping young "Bertie" Hoover's character. *115 S. River St., ☎ 503/538–6629. ☛ $1.50 adults, $1 senior citizens and students over 12. ☉ Mar.–Nov., Wed.–Sun. 1–4; Dec. and Feb., weekends 1–4.*

㉘ From Newberg, Highway 219S (toward Donald) will take you to lovely **Champoeg** (pronounced "shampooey") **State Park,** former seat of the first provisional government in the Northwest. The site of a Hudson's Bay Company trading post, granary, and warehouse built in 1813, the settlement was abandoned after a catastrophic flood in 1861, then rebuilt and abandoned again after the flood of 1890. Now the park's wide-open spaces, groves of oak and fir, modern visitor's center, museum, and historic buildings (such as the Pioneer Mother's Memorial Cabin) give visitors a vivid glimpse of pioneer life. *8239 Champoeg Rd. NE, St. Paul 97137, ☎ 503/678–1251. ☛ $3 per vehicle May–Sept., free Oct.–Apr. ☉ Labor Day–Memorial Day, weekdays 8–4, weekends noon–4; rest of year, daily 10–6.*

㉙ If you retrace your route to Highway 99W and continue south, you'll pass through the idyllic orchard land around **Dundee.** This haven of produce stands and tasting rooms is home to 90% of America's hazelnut crop.

㉚ Twelve miles farther southwest is **McMinnville**—the largest (population 20,000) and most sophisticated of the wine-country towns—which hosts a fine collection of bed-and-breakfasts, small hotels, and restaurants. **Linfield College,** a perennial football powerhouse, is an oasis of brick and ivy in the midst of McMinnville's farmers-market bustle and annually hosts Oregon's **International Pinot Noir Celebration.** The college, founded in 1849, is the second oldest in Oregon, next to Willamette University. *Admissions office: 900 S. Baker St., Melrose Hall, ☎ 503/472–4121, ext. 213. Free guided walking tours of campus arranged by appointment. ☉ Weekdays 8–5.*

Salem and Environs
Continuing south on Highway 99W, take Highway 22 west toward
㉛ **Salem,** the state capital, which is precisely halfway between the North Pole and the equator on the 45th parallel, about 45 miles south of Portland along I–5. The brightly gilded 23-foot-high bronze statue of the

Oregon Pioneer atop the 140-foot capitol dome is the centerpiece of Salem's **Capitol Mall,** where Oregon's legislators convene every two years.

Numbers in the margin correspond to points of interest on the Salem map.

③ **Oregon's State Capitol complex**—graceless blocks of gray Vermont marble—looks as if it was designed by a committee of career bureaucrats to frighten away the commoners. But don't be deterred—the interior is softened by some fine relief sculptures and the surprisingly deft historical murals. Tours of the rotunda, the house and senate chambers, and the governor's office leave from the information counter under the dome. *900 Court St.,* ☎ *503/378–4423.* ☛ *Free.* ⊙ *Weekdays 8–5, Sat. 9–4, Sun. noon–4. Guided tours available Memorial Day–Labor Day, daily on the hr; rest of year by appointment.*

③ Just across State Street but half a world away are the tradition-steeped brick buildings and immaculate greens of **Willamette University,** the oldest college in the West. Founded in 1842, Willamette has long been a mecca for aspiring politicians (Oregon senator Mark Hatfield and retired senator Bob Packwood are alumni). Stunning **Hatfield Library,** built in 1986 of gracefully curved brick and glass, is an oasis of silent scholarship on the banks of the merry Mill Stream; tall, prim **Waller Hall,** built in 1841, is one of the five oldest buildings in the Pacific Northwest. The university hosts theatrical and musical performances, athletic events, guest lecturers, and art exhibits year-round. For information and tours, contact the university's public relations office (☎ 503/370–6340).

③ From 12th Street cross over to the **Mission Mill Village** and **Thomas Kay Woolen Mill Museum,** where teasel gigging, napper flock bins, and the patented Furber double-acting napper are but a few of the venerable machines and processes on display. The museum complex (circa 1889), complete with working waterwheels and millstream, looks as if the workers have just stepped away for a lunch break, giving visitors a vivid glimpse of 19th-century manufacturing. In the same complex, the **Marion County Museum of History** (☎ 503/364–2128) displays a fine collection of pioneer and Calipooya Indian artifacts. The spare simplicity of the Jason Lee House, John D. Boon Home, and Methodist Parsonage, also part of the village, invites the visitor to steal a glimpse of domestic life in the wilds of Oregon in the 1840s. In the warehouse a few steps away, specialty shops offer antiques, clothing, quilts, toys, and other handmade goods from local craftspeople. *Museum complex, 1313 Mill St. SE,* ☎ *503/585–7012.* ☛ *$5 adults, $4.50 senior citizens 65 and older, $4 children 6–18 (includes tour).* ⊙ *Daily 10–4:30. Guided tours of historic houses and woolen mill museum leave from mill's admission tent every hr on the hr.*

③ **Bush's Pasture Park,** situated just south of Salem's downtown district, has 105 acres of rolling lawn and formal English gardens. On the grounds is the 1878 **Bush House,** a creaky, gaslit Italianate oddity with 10 marble fireplaces. The house and gardens are on the National Historic Register. *600 Mission St. SE,* ☎ *503/363–4714.* ☛ *$1.50 adults, $1 senior citizens, 75¢ students, 50¢ children.* ⊙ *Oct.–May, Tues.–Sun. 2–5; June–Sept., Tues.–Sun. noon–5.*

③ Across from the park the fanciful 1894 **Deepwood Estate,** built in the Queen Anne style, is worth a visit just for its splendid interior woodwork and original stained glass. The estate is also on the National Historic Register. *1116 Mission St. SE,* ☎ *503/363–1825.* ☛ *$2 adults,*

Bush's Pasture Park, **35**

Deepwood Estate, **36**

Mission Mill Village, **34**

State Capitol, **32**

Willamette University, **33**

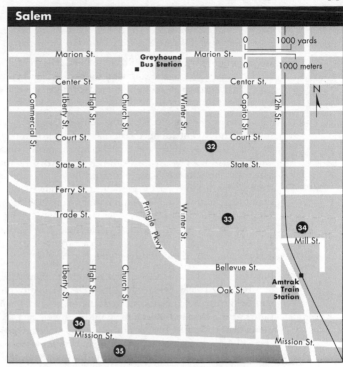

Salem

$1.50 senior citizens and students. ⊘ *Oct.–Apr., Sun., Mon., Wed., Fri. 1–4; May–Sept., Sun.–Fri. noon–4:30.*

The Willamette Valley near Salem is known as the **"Bulb Basket of the Nation"** to local farmers. Irises and tulips create fields of brilliant color in near-perfect growing conditions. Two-hundred-acre **Schreiner's Iris Gardens** is especially esteemed. Established in 1925, this rhizome grower now ships bulbs all over the world; during the short spring growing season (mid-May to early June), the 10-acre display gardens are ablaze with such fancifully named varieties as Hello Darkness, Well Endowed, and Ringo. *3625 Quinaby Rd. NE (Brooks exit off I–5, then west on Brooklake Rd., left on River Rd., then left on Quinaby), Salem 97303,* ☎ *503/393–3232.* ☛ *Free. Display gardens open 8– dusk during blooming season.*

In the lush Cascades, 26 miles east of Salem, shallow Silver Creek roars over the lip of a mossy basalt bowl and into a deep pool far below. The 177-foot South Silver Falls is the main attraction in the 8,700-acre **Silver Falls State Park,** the largest state park in Oregon. Thirteen other waterfalls—half of which are more than 100 feet high—are accessible to hikers within the park. There are picnic facilities and a WPA-era day lodge; during the winter, the cross-country skiing is excellent. Follow Highway 22 east to its junction with Highway 214 and follow the signs to Silver Falls. *Headquarters, 20024 Silver Falls Hwy. SE, Sublimity,* ☎ *503/873–8681.* ☛ *$3 per vehicle May–Sept.*

About halfway between Salem and Eugene is **Corvallis,** which lies off I–5 on Highway 34. It's a good spot to stop for a meal or spend the night.

Eugene and South

Numbers in the margin correspond to points of interest on the Oregon Coast and Willamette Valley/Wine Country map.

㊲ Continuing south on I–5, you'll come to **Eugene,** 63 miles farther. The second-largest city in the state and the mid-valley's cultural hub, Eugene has more than 300 restaurants, a world-class performing-arts center, and outdoor recreation "from sea level to ski level."

The centerpiece of the city is the **University of Oregon,** where Nike shoes founder Phil Knight attended school. The self-proclaimed sobriquet for Eugene—Tracktown USA—and the many joggers thronging the streets and parks of the city are part of his legacy. Also, visitors may recognize the campus as the location for the filming of National Lampoon's *Animal House.* However, Oregon's liberal arts university thrives on more than the reputation of one alumnus and recognition from Hollywood. The grounds are lush and green, with more than 400 varieties of trees shading the 250-acre brick-and-ivy campus. *Admissions office: 1585 E. 13th Ave.,* ☎ *503/346–3201.* ☉ *Weekdays 8–noon and 1–5. Maps and guided tours of campus available.*

In addition to the athletic events at **Autzen Stadium, MacArthur Court,** and **Hayward Field,** where the U of O's perennially powerful track-and-field team holds its meets, there are visiting arts exhibits and lecturers at the **Maude I. Kerns Art Center,** as well as a highly regarded permanent collection of Oriental art at the **University of Oregon Museum of Art.** The university's **Museum of Natural History** is a small museum of Pacific Northwest anthropology and natural sciences. Its ever-changing exhibits are drawn from the university's own vast collections. *Art Museum: 1430 Johnson La.,* ☎ *503/346–3027.* ☛ *Free.* ☉ *Wed.–Sun. noon–5. Natural History Museum: 1680 E. 15th Ave.,* ☎ *503/346–3024.* ☛ *$1.* ☉ *Wed.–Sun. noon–5.*

If you're in the mood for a stroll along the river, the **Willamette Science and Technology Center,** next to Autzen Stadium, is a good place to end your journey. The city's well-equipped and imaginative hands-on scientific museum and planetarium (known to the locals as "Wiz-Tek") features rotating exhibits designed with children in mind; one recent offering, "Pets and People," featured lectures, demonstrations, and a petting zoo equipped with everything from puppies and kittens to pythons and cockroaches. The adjacent planetarium offers a rotating slate of stars and shows. *2300 Leo Harris Pkwy. Museum:* ☎ *503/687–3619;* ☛ *$8 families, $3 adults, $2 children 4–16;* ☉ *Wed.–Sun. noon–6. Planetarium:* ☎ *503/689–6500; admission and hrs vary.*

TIME OUT If you have hungry children, or have a tough time deciding what sounds good for lunch, the food options at the **5th Street Public Market Food Pavilion** (5th and High Sts., ☎ 503/484–0383), a downtown landmark, will give you plenty of options. They range from sit-down restaurants (Mekala's Thai Cuisine, Casablanca Mediterranean Cuisine) to decadent bakeries (the Metropol Bakery on the building's lower level is especially fine) to the bewildering international diversity of the clean, airy second-floor food esplanade, offering Greek, Mexican, English, Chinese, Italian, and nouvelle American foods.

The wineries and memorable scenic drives continue both east and west of Eugene. Highway 58 climbs into the Cascades and the Deschutes Forest toward Willamette Pass east of the city. There, in addition to a popular ski area, you'll find the 286-foot-high Salt Creek Falls, not far **㊳** from the town of **Oakridge.**

Also near Oakridge is **Waldo Lake.** Situated deep in the old-growth forest, this incredibly pure, shield-shape lake is thought by some to be the cleanest landlocked body of water in the world. The lake is accessible after a short hike, so bring comfortable walking attire. *Take Hwy. 58 to Oakridge, then follow signs northwest to Waldo Lake; no ☎.*

Westward, toward the coast, Highway 126 gives access to several wineries and trout-filled rivers before coming to Florence (*see* The Oregon Coast, *above*), on the central Oregon shore.

㊴ Continuing south on I–5, take note of **Roseburg,** where the highway crosses the Umpqua River, a name sacred to steelhead fishermen the world over. Six wineries (Callahan Ridge, Girardet, Henry Estate, Hillcrest, LaGarza, and Davidson) are within an easy drive west of this sleepy farming community.

In town, the **Douglas County Museum,** one of the best county museums in the state, gives visitors a window on 8,000 years of human activity in the region. Its fossil collection, which includes a million-year-old sabertoothed tiger, is worth a stop. *At Douglas County Fairgrounds (take Exit 123 from I–5 and follow the signs), ☎ 503/440–4507. ☛ Free (donations accepted). ⊘ Tues.–Sat. 10–4, Sun. noon–4.*

Crater Lake to Jacksonville

Oregon's only national park got its start 6,800 years ago, when a cascade peak called Mt. Mazama erupted in a volcanic explosion that spewed hot ash and pumice for hundreds of miles. Rain and snowmelt eventually filled the resulting caldera—as the crater in the center of the decapitated mountain peak is called—creating a sapphire-blue lake so clear that sunlight penetrates to a depth of 400 feet. This geological curiosity, the crown jewel of the Cascades and Oregon's most famous ★ tourist attraction, is now **Crater Lake National Park.** Visitors can drive, bicycle, or hike Crater Lake's 25-mile rim; feed the chipmunks along either Godfrey Glen Nature Trail or the 4-mile Castle Crest Wildflower Trail; or take a boat ride out to famous Wizard Island, a perfect miniature cinder cone protruding 760 feet above the surface of the lake. Private boats are not allowed on Crater Lake, so these tours ($10 adults, $5.50 children) offer a unique surface-level view of the caldera. Tours leave every two hours from late June to early September from Cleetwood Cove on the lake's north side.

Historic **Crater Lake Lodge** (Box 128, Crater Lake 97604, ☎ 503/594–2511), perched on the rim of the caldera, finally reopened in the summer of 1995 after a foundation-to-roof renovation. Overnight accommodations are also available at the 40-room Forest Service rental-cabin complex at **Annie Creek Canyon,** south of the lake. These accommodations are far from luxurious, however; you might prefer one of the 198 campsites at nearby **Mazama Campground.** The surrounding National Forest campgrounds offer 900 additional sites. Campsites are not reserved; first-come, first-served camping information available through the lodge. Due to conditions caused by the 6,000-foot elevation, access to the park in winter is restricted to the south and west entry roads.

㊵ Crater Lake is accessible from Roseburg via Highway 138 (about 85 miles) and via Highway 62 from **Medford,** which lies about 70 miles south of Roseburg on I–5. About halfway along this second, 71-mile route, nature lovers who want a glimpse of the Rogue River's loveliest angle can take a side trip to the **Avenue of the Boulders, Mill Creek Falls,** and **Barr Creek Falls,** just off Highway 62, near **Prospect.** Here

Crater Lake National Park

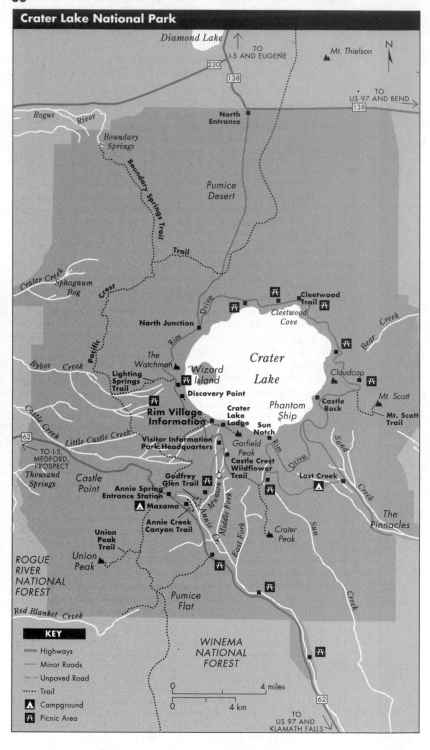

Diamond Lake

↑ TO I-5 AND EUGENE

▲ Mt. Thielson

N

[230]
[138]

TO US 97 AND BEND → [138]

North Entrance

Rogue River

Boundary Springs

Pumice Desert

Boundary Springs Trail

Trail

Crater Creek

Sphagnum Bog

Crest

Pacific

▲ Mt. Scott

Rim Drive

North Junction

The Watchman ▲

Lighting Springs Trail

Bybee Creek

Cleetwood Cove

Cleetwood Trail

Bear Creek

Claudcap ▲

Crater Lake

Wizard Island

Discovery Point

Rim Village Information

Mt. Scott

Castle Rock

Mt. Scott Trail

Crater Lake Lodge

Phantom Ship

Sun Notch

Castle Creek

[62]

Little Castle Creek

Visitor Information Park Headquarters

TO I-5: MEDFORD PROSPECT

Thousand Springs

Garfield Peak

Castle Crest Wildflower Trail

Lost Creek

Sand Creek

The Pinnacles

Godfrey Glen Trail

Castle Point

Annie Spring Entrance Station

▲ **Mazama**

Annie Creek Canyon Trail

Union Peak Trail

Union Peak

Annie

Munson Cr

Middle Fork

East Fork

▲ *Crater Peak*

Sun Creek

ROGUE RIVER NATIONAL FOREST

Red Blanket Creek

Pumice Flat

Rim Drive

KEY

— Highways
— Minor Roads
-- Unpaved Road
···· Trail
▲ Campground
🅰 Picnic Area

WINEMA NATIONAL FOREST

0   4 miles
0   4 km

[62]

TO US 97 AND KLAMATH FALLS ↓

the wild waters of the upper Rogue foam through volcanic boulders and the dense greenery of the Rogue River National Forest.

🔳 In many ways **Jacksonville,** 5 miles west of Medford and I–5 on Route 238, has become more important to the cultural life of Oregon than has Portland or Eugene; its town hosts the **Peter Britt Festival** (*see* the Arts, *below*), which attracts some of the world's best-known classical, jazz, and popular musicians each summer. Even if you won't be in town for the festival, however, downtown Jacksonville deserves a visit for the simple reason that the entire hamlet is on the National Register of Historic Places. Clumping along the boardwalks, it's easy to imagine the gold-rush heyday of 1853, as several of the 80 privately owned landmark buildings date from this era. For free maps and guides to Jacksonville's many historic structures, stop by the **Jacksonville Chamber of Commerce** (185 N. Oregon St., ☎ 503/899–8118).

The **Jacksonville Museum,** located in the old Jackson County Courthouse, houses an intriguing collection of gold rush–era artifacts and a permanent exhibit called "Jacksonville! Boomtown to Home Town," outlining the rich local history. An exhibit installed in 1993 features the images of Peter Britt, the pioneer photographer who homesteaded here. The adjoining **Children's Museum,** occupying the 80-year-old Jackson County Jail, contains hands-on exhibits on pioneer life, as well as a splendid collection of antique toys. *206 N. 5th St., ☎ 503/773–6536. ☛ $2 for both museums. ☉ Memorial Day–Labor Day, daily 10–5; rest of year, Tues.–Sun. 10–5.*

If you follow Route 238 west to Highway 199, then continue south, you'll reach Cave Junction, the turn-off point for the **Oregon Caves National Monument.** The "Marble Halls of Oregon," high in the verdant Siskiyou Mountains, have been entrancing visitors since local hunter Elijah Davidson chased a bear into them in 1874. Huge stalagmites and stalactites, the Ghost Room, Paradise Lost, and the River Styx are all part of a half-mile subterranean tour that lasts about 75 minutes. The tour includes more than 200 stairs and is not recommended for anyone who experiences difficulty in walking or has respiratory or coronary problems. The historic **Oregon Caves Chateau** offers food and lodging at the monument May 28–September 30. *20 mi southeast of Cave Jct. on Hwy. 46, ☎ 503/592–3400. ☛ $5.75 adults, $3.50 children 6–11. Children under 7 not allowed in cave; child care available. ☉ June 13–Sept. 30, daily 8–7; Oct.–Apr., daily 8:30–4; May–June 12, daily 9–5.*

Ashland

In spite of its small size and relative isolation from other towns in the state, **Ashland** is also a major cultural center for Oregon. Home to the 🔳 ★ Tony Award–winning **Oregon Shakespeare Festival** (*see* the Arts, *below*), Ashland draws more than 100,000 theater lovers to the Rogue Valley every year. The influx is especially dramatic during the peak festival months of June–September, when reservations get very tight. A critical mass of excellent restaurants, bed-and-breakfasts (more than 50 at last count), shops, and galleries combines with a salubrious climate to make Ashland one of Oregon's most popular tourist destinations.

At Ashland's **Shakespeare Festival Exhibit Center** in the festival complex, theater fans can try on costumes and view exhibits about the history of the festival. A visit to the center is included with a guided backstage tour, which takes you on a fascinating trip from the indoor Angus Bowmer Theatre, through backstage production shops, and all the way to the very heavens above the Elizabethan stage. *Festival box* *office, 15 S. Pioneer St., ☎ 503/482–4331. ☛ $7.50 adults, $5 children 5–17 (under 5 not admitted). ☛ Exhibit center: $2 adults, $1.50 children 5–17. ⊘ Oct. 5–June 6, Tues.–Sun. 10:30–1:30; June 7–Oct. 4, Tues.–Sun. 10–4. Tours run Feb.–Oct., Tues.–Sun. at 10 AM. Reservations required in summer.*

The Elizabethan Theatre overlooks lovely **Lithia Park,** a 99-acre swath of green in the center of the town. An old-fashioned band shell, a duck pond, a children's playground, nature trails, and **Ashland Creek** make this a perfect spot for a pretheater picnic. Each June, to mark the opening of the outdoor season, the festival hosts a Renaissance dinner (the Feast of Will) in the park, complete with period music, dancing, and food. Tickets (around $13 each) are available through the festival box office (*see* the Arts, *below*).

Ashland's brand-new **Pacific Northwest Museum of Natural History** emphasizes hands-on exploration of the natural world through "multisensory" exhibits that visitors can touch and manipulate as well as see. A series of interactive video adventures allow you to explore various natural processes; there's also a hall with such rotating displays as an exhibition on Africa and its vanishing wildlife. *1500 E. Main St. (1 mi east of downtown), ☎ 503/488–1084. ☛ $6 adults, $5 senior citizens 62 and over, $4.50 children 5–15. ⊘ Apr.–Oct., daily 9–5; Nov.–Mar., daily 10–4.*

Shopping

From Newberg to McMinnville
Oregon's largest permanent antiques show is housed in a lovingly restored 1910 schoolhouse at the **Lafayette Schoolhouse Antique Mall** (Hwy. 99W, 5 mi north of McMinnville, ☎ 503/864–2720). A vast assortment of antiquities, from china and toys to Native American artifacts, are on sale in a three-story showroom.

Salem and Environs
You'll find a cornucopia of handmade local toys, books, dollhouses, quilts, sweaters, and other items at Salem's **Mission Mill Village Warehouse** (1313 Mill St. SE, ☎ 503/585–7012).

Eugene and South
When you need to replenish your supply of mottled turkey-wing quills, primed popper bodies, or bleached beaver, the place to go to is the **Caddis Fly Angling Shop** (168 W. 6th Ave., Eugene, ☎ 503/342–7005 or 800/825–7005). Eugene's **5th Street Public Market** (5th and High Sts., ☎ 503/484–0383) crams nearly 100 shops—specializing in everything from clothing to local art—into a 60-year-old warehouse surrounding a brick-paved courtyard. Every Saturday between April and Christmas (10–5), local craftsmen, farmers, and chefs come together to create the weekly **Eugene Saturday Market** (8th and Oak Sts., ☎ 503/686–8885), where you can buy local artwork, dine cheaply and well, or simply watch the people go by.

Crater Lake to Jacksonville
Harry and David's and **Jackson & Perkins** (2518 S. Pacific Hwy., Medford, ☎ 503/776–2121 or 800/345–5655) are two of the largest mail-order companies in the world: Harry and David for fruit and gift packs; Jackson & Perkins for roses. **Harry and David's Country Store,** located in the same complex, is a retail outlet for their products, most of which are grown in the famous Bear Creek Orchards. Free tours leave the store hourly on the half hour on weekdays.

Sports and the Outdoors

Bicycling

The 25 miles of **Highway 18** between Dundee and Grand Ronde, in the Coast Range, roll through the heart of the Yamhill Valley wine country; wide shoulders and relatively light traffic earned the route a "most suitable" rating from the "Oregon Bicycling Guide."

Eugene is particularly esteemed as a cyclists' town. **Pedal Power** (535 High St., downtown Eugene, ☎ 503/687–1775) rents bikes by the hour, day, or week. The **River Bank Bike Path,** originating in Alton Baker Park on the Willamette's north bank, is a level and leisurely introduction to this exercise-oriented city's two-wheel topography. Also in the park, try the **Prefontaine Trail,** which travels through level fields and forests for 1½ miles.

Canoeing and Rafting

Virtually all rivers flowing from the Willamette Valley and the I–5 corridor offer memorable rafting and canoeing experiences ranging from a placid float through lush forests to an adrenaline-pumping plunge through roaring maelstroms of rock and frigid water. For wet-knuckle enthusiasts (rafters), two rivers stand out: the exuberant **McKenzie,** west of Eugene, and the especially challenging **Rogue,** near the California border. Many parts of the Rogue are still true wilderness, with no road access. Deer, bears, eagles, and other wild creatures are abundant here.

Oregon Guides and Packers (Box 10841, Eugene 97440, ☎ 503/683–9552) publishes a free 80-page directory of Oregon guides and will help you find a professional guide service—an absolute necessity on both the McKenzie and the Rogue rivers. Many guide services offer overnighters and longer trips, aboard either rafts or powerful jet boats, which roar upstream from Gold Beach on the coast.

Fishing

The mountains and bountiful rainfall in western Oregon have given birth to some of the finest fishing lakes and rivers in North America. Though overfishing and logging-caused siltation have vastly depleted the runs, many types of fish can still be caught: Native rainbow and sea-run cutthroat trout; wily steelhead reaching 20 pounds and larger; sturgeon; and, greatest prize of all, the fat chinook salmon (weighing up to 50 pounds) that return every spring. Although it's hard to go wrong on any of the Coast Range streams or high-mountain lakes, fly-and-bait fishing is internationally famous on the **McKenzie, Umpqua, Rogue,** and **Chetco** rivers. In **Crater Lake,** massive rainbow trout, some 3 feet in length, cruise the depths in profusion. The fish thrive because there is no boat fishing allowed. You'll need to bring your own tackle, and no license is necessary, but you're not allowed to use organic baits that might cloud the lake—it's lure fishing only.

Golf

Bayou Golf & Country Club (9301 S.W. Bayou Dr., McMinnville, ☎ 503/472–4651), nine holes; **Riverwood Golf Club** (21050 S.E. Riverwood Rd., Dundee, ☎ 503/864–2667), nine holes.

Battle Creek Golf Club (6161 Commercial St. SE, Salem, ☎ 503/585–1402), 18 holes. **Golf Club of Oregon** (905 Spring Hill Dr. N, Albany, ☎ 503/928–8338), 18 holes; **McNary Golf Club** (6255 River Rd. N,

Keizer, ☎ 503/393–4653), 18 holes; **Pineway Golf Club** (30949 Pineway Rd., Lebanon, ☎ 503/258–8919), nine holes; **Salem Golf Club** (2025 Golf Course Rd., Salem, ☎ 503/363–6652), 18 holes; **Trysting Trees Golf Club** (34028 Electric Rd., Corvallis, ☎ 503/752–3332), 18 holes.

EUGENE AND SOUTH

Emerald Valley Golf Course (83293 Dale Kuni Rd., Creswell, ☎ 503/895–2174), 18 holes; **Fiddler's Green Golf Course** (91292 Hwy. 99 N, Eugene, ☎ 503/689–8464), 18 holes; **Laurelwood Golf Course** (2700 Columbia St., Eugene, ☎ 503/687–5321), nine holes; **McKenzie River Golf Course** (41723 Madrone St., Springfield, ☎ 503/896–3454), nine holes; **Oakway Golf Course** (2000 Cal Young Rd., Eugene, ☎ 503/484–1927), 18 holes; **Riveridge Golf Course** (3800 N. Delta Hwy., Eugene, ☎ 503/345–9160), 18 holes.

ASHLAND

Cedar Links Golf Course (3155 Cedar Links Dr., Ashland, ☎ 503/773–4373), 18 holes; **Oak Knoll Golf Course** (3070 Hwy. 66, Ashland, ☎ 503/482–4311), nine holes.

Skiing

CROSS-COUNTRY

The Willamette Valley itself is temperate and generally receives only a few inches of snow a year, but the **Coast Range,** the **Cascades,** and, farther south, the **Siskiyous** are all Nordic skiers' paradises, crisscrossed by hundreds of miles of trails. Every major ski resort in the state offers Nordic skiing; you can also set off down your choice of Forest Service trails and logging roads. If you're unsure where to begin, the **City of Eugene Parks and Recreation Department** (☎ 503/687–5329) takes cross-country snow campers on overnight loops around both **Crater Lake** and Waldo Lake.

See also Willamette Pass and Mt. Bailey, *below.*

DOWNHILL

Willamette Pass. Though most Oregon downhillers congregate around Mt. Hood and Mt. Bachelor (*see* the Columbia River Gorge and the Oreon Cascades, *below*), there is excellent skiing to the south as well. Willamette Pass, 6,666 feet high in the Cascades Mountains, packs an annual average snowfall of 300 inches atop 18 runs. With a vertical drop of 1,563 feet, there are four triple chairs and one double chair; lift lines are refreshingly short. Other facilities include 13 miles of Nordic trails, Nordic and downhill rentals, repairs, instruction, ski shop, day care, bar, and restaurant. *Hwy. 58, 69 mi southeast of Eugene,* ☎ *503/484–5030.* ☉ *Nov.–Dec., Wed.–Sun. 9–4; Jan.–Mar., Wed.–Sat. 9–9, Sun. 9–4; Apr.–June (depending on snow conditions), weekends, 9–4.*

Mt. Ashland. This cone-shape Siskiyou peak has some of the steepest runs in the state. There are two triple and two double chairlifts, accommodating a vertical drop of 1,150 feet; the longest of the 22 runs is 1 mile. Facilities include rentals, repair, instruction, ski shop, restaurant, and bar. *18 mi southwest of downtown Ashland; follow the signs from I-5,* ☎ *503/482–2897 or 800/547–8052.* ☉ *Winter, daily 9–4; night skiing Thurs.–Sat. 4–10.*

SNOWCAT SKIING

Mt. Bailey. If you *really* crave solitude (and detest lift lines), this is the guide service for you. First you ride in heated Snow-Cats to the summit of Mt. Bailey, an 8,300-foot peak not far from Crater Lake. Then you attack the virgin powder on 4 miles of runs, with a vertical drop of 3,000 feet. The excursions are limited to 12 skiers a day, but be warned—this is downhill for advanced intermediates and experts only. Tours leave Diamond Lake Resort daily at 7 AM. Facilities at the resort include three restaurants, a bar, lodging, downhill and Nordic ski rentals, and Nordic trails. *Diamond Lake Resort, 76 mi east of Roseburg on Hwy. 138, ☎ 503/793–3333. Reservations required. Season runs Nov.–May.*

Spectator Sports

BASEBALL
The **Eugene Emeralds,** the Kansas City Royals' Northwest League (Class A) affiliate, play 38 home games at **Civic Stadium** (2077 Willamette St., Eugene, ☎ 503/342–5367) from June to September.

BASKETBALL
The **Oregon State Beavers** play their home games at **Gill Coliseum** (26th and Washington Sts., on the OSU campus, Corvallis, ☎ 503/737–4455). The **University of Oregon's Ducks** seldom fare as well as the Beavers, but seeing a home game at the eccentrically designed, and somewhat claustrophobic, **MacArthur Court** (1601 University St., on the U of O's campus, Eugene, ☎ 800/932–3668) is a real experience.

FOOTBALL
The **University of Oregon Ducks** play their home games at **Autzen Stadium** (2700 Centennial Blvd., ☎ 800/932–3668). The **Oregon State Beavers** play theirs at **Parker Stadium** (26th and Western Sts., on the OSU campus, ☎ 503/737–4455).

Dining and Lodging

In wine districts everywhere, eating and living well is high on the list of priorities. The Oregon wine country, which includes the Willamette and Rogue valleys from Newberg to Ashland, is no exception. The regional gastronomy is enlivened by an extensive collection of excellent ethnic restaurants, from Italian to Vietnamese to Eastern European, as well as by some expert practitioners of nouvelle cuisine. Eugene, with its longtime emphasis on good living, and Ashland, with its world-famous Oregon Shakespeare Festival, are particularly noted for the excellence and diversity of their restaurants.

Lodging choices are equally varied. In addition to the ever-popular and flourishing number of bed-and-breakfasts, Wild West resorts (complete with buffalo and stagecoach), rustic fisherman's lodges, and plenty of chain facilities are available in all price ranges. The Oregon Shakespeare Festival has stimulated one of the most extensive networks of B&Bs in the country—more than 50 in all. High season for Ashland-area B&Bs is June–October. Expect to pay $90–$150 per night, which includes breakfast for two; during the off-season, $60–$100. Deciding which one to patronize can be a bewildering task. The **Ashland B&B Clearinghouse** (☎ 503/488–0338) and **Ashland B&B Reservation Network** (☎ 503/482–2337) offer free, unbiased advice to connect travelers with more than 450 options available in the area.

Unless otherwise noted, casual but neat dress is appropriate at all of the restaurants reviewed below. For price-category definitions, *see* Dining *and* Lodging *in* Oregon Essentials, *below.*

Ashland

DINING
$$$ **Chateaulin.** One of southern Oregon's most romantic restaurants oc-
★ cupies a little ivy-covered storefront a block from the Shakespeare Festival center, where it dispenses elegant French food, local wine, and

impeccable service with equal facility. Try the fresh loin of lamb with a sauce of balsamic vinegar, shallots, veal stock, and cream, accompanied by a bottle of Ponzi Pinot Noir. ✗ *50 E. Main St.,* ☎ *503/482–2264. Reservations required June–Oct., advised year-round. AE, DC, MC, V. No lunch.*

$$ Chata. There are plenty of great restaurants in and around Ashland, but the locals rave about the food, the service, and the warm atmosphere at this Eastern European restaurant, run by a Polish immigrant couple and their children. Try the *piroshki* (meat or vegetable-filled dumplings in a delicate sour-cream sauce). ✗ *1212 S. Pacific Hwy. (Hwy. 99), Talent, about 2 mi north of Ashland,* ☎ *503/535–2575. Reservations advised. MC, V. No lunch.*

$$ Thai Pepper. Spicy Thai-style curries and stir-fries are the specialties at this elegantly appointed restaurant perched above musical Ashland Creek. With an interior filled with local art, rattan, linen, and crystal, the restaurant feels like a French café in downtown Bangkok. The house special is spicy curry, but try the coconut prawns as well as the Thai beef-salad appetizer for starters. ✗ *84 N. Main St.,* ☎ *503/482–8058. Reservations advised. MC, V. Lunch on Fri. only.*

$–$$ Gepetto's. Kids love this unpretentious local favorite, open daily for breakfast, lunch, and dinner. The vaguely Italian menu features hearty renditions of standard pasta dishes, as well as delicious and unusual sandwiches, salads, and soups. The staff is friendly and fast-moving. Try the fresh-grilled marinated turkey sandwich, served on the crispy house cheese bread. ✗ *345 E. Main,* ☎ *503/482–1138. Reservations advised. MC, V.*

$ Rogue Brewery & Public House. Ashland's first brew-pub (a no-smoking establishment indoors) serves pizza and other hearty pub food. Also available is a rotating selection of four to six ales brewed on the premises, including Rogue Golden, Ashland Amber, and Shakespeare Stout. Two decks overhang the creek, a pleasant venue for ale and conversation during Ashland's warm summer evenings. ✗ *31 B Water St.,* ☎ *503/488–5061. No reservations. MC, V.*

DINING AND LODGING

$$$ Winchester Country Inn. A favorite with locals and knowledgeable visitors, this 1886-vintage restaurant-inn has guest rooms upstairs and two separate cottages with suites. Superb food is served from a small but imaginative menu in the airy, high-windowed dining rooms, which are set among manicured gardens and have a feeling of casual elegance. The duck à la bigarade (roast duck in a sauce of duck stock, caramel, brandy, and fresh fruit) is ambrosial; the homemade scones, crab Benedict, and duck hash with orange hollandaise, served for Sunday brunch, are equally memorable. ▣ *35 S. 2nd St., 97520,* ☎ *503/488–1113 or 800/972–4991. Restaurant (reservations advised; no lunch). 7 rooms, 2 suites. MC, V. Closed Mon. Nov.–May.*

LODGING

$$–$$$ Best Western Bard's Inn. If you're looking for a nicely appointed commercial hotel, close to the theaters but not too expensive, this property fits the bill. The pool's a little small if you've got kids along, but there are Rogue Valley views from every window. Inside, original artwork created by contemporary local artists hangs on the walls. The rooms, though on the small side, are freshly furnished in oak and knotty pine and neutral tones. ▣ *132 N. Main St., 97520,* ☎ *503/482–0049 or 800/528–1234. 79 units. Restaurant, bar, refrigerators, pool, hot tub. AE, D, DC, MC, V.*

$$–$$$ **Mt. Ashland Inn.** Deserving special mention, this is one of the most un-
★   usual B&Bs in the area. The 5,000-square-foot lodge was hand built
from cedar logs cut from the owners' 160-acre property, located just
a mile or two from the summit ski area on Mt. Ashland. The views of
Mt. Shasta and the rest of the Siskiyou Mountains are as magnificent
as the forested setting; the Pacific Crest Trail runs through the parking lot. On the inside, a huge stone fireplace, hand-stitched quilts, and
natural wood provide welcoming warmth. A separate guest house has
a tub for soaking. ⌨ *550 Mt. Ashland Rd. (take Exit 6 from I–5 and
follow the signs toward ski area), 97520,* ☎ *503/482–8707. 5 rooms,
1 cottage. AE, D, MC, V.*

Bellevue

DINING

$$ **Augustine's.** First explore the Lawrence Gallery, with its fine collec-
tion of local art. Then enter the adjoining Oregon Wine Tasting Room
to sample the wares of more than 20 Yamhill Valley wineries. Finally,
go upstairs to the tastefully decorated dining room, with its modern
furnishings and rustic views, where you'll enjoy fresh local seafood,
lamb, and beef, all simply prepared and lightly sauced. The wine list
is as extensive as it is reasonably priced; many local vintages are avail-
able by the glass, a nice concession to those with moderation in mind.
Give the Sunday brunch a try, too. ✗ *19706 Hwy. 18 (7 mi west of
McMinnville),* ☎ *503/843–3225. Reservations advised. D, MC, V.
Closed Tues. year-round, Mon.–Tues. Labor Day–Memorial Day.*

Corvallis

DINING

$$–$$$ **The Gables.** This quiet, elegant eatery, with all dark wood, has earned
a reputation over the years as Corvallis's most romantic restaurant.
The menu is about what you would expect: steaks, straightforward
seafood, local lamb, and prime rib. The portions are huge and satis-
fying. The well-stocked wine cellar can be reserved as a dining room
for small groups and special occasions. ✗ *1121 N.W. 9th St.,* ☎ *503/
752–3364. Reservations advised. AE, D, DC, MC, V. No lunch.*

$–$$ **Novak's Hungarian Paprikas.** Locals can't say enough about this unpretentious family-run restaurant, located a few miles east of Corval-
lis in Albany. Its Hungarian owners turn out such native specialties as
kolbasz (homemade sausages with sweet-and-sour cabbage) and *beef
szelet* (crispy batter-fried cutlets) with virtuosity. The restaurant's only
drawback is its lack of a liquor license, so no alcohol is permitted. ✗
2835 Santiam Hwy. SE, Albany, ☎ *503/967–9488. Reservations advised. MC, V. No lunch Sat.*

LODGING

$$ **Madison Inn.** One of the Willamette Valley's most venerable B&Bs—
opened more than a decade ago by the current owner's mother—is this
sprawling five-story Tudor that overlooks Central Park in downtown
Corvallis. There's also a guest cottage. ⌨ *660 S.W. Madison Ave., 97333,*
☎ *503/757–1274. 2 rooms with bath, 6 rooms share 3 baths. AE, D,
DC, MC, V.*

Eugene

DINING

$$$ **Chanterelle.** In a city quietly renowned for its restaurants, this is where
the smart money comes when it wants a superb meal in a memorably
romantic setting. Seasonal, regional European-inspired cuisine is on the
menu here; the chef's touch is equally deft with game and local beef
or lamb as it is with seafood. The 14-table restaurant, in an old warehouse across from the 5th Street Public Market, is warm and intimate,

and is filled with crystal and fresh flowers. ✗ *207 E. 5th Ave.,* ☎ *503/ 484–4065. Reservations advised. AE, DC, MC, V. Closed Sun.–Mon., last 2 wks of Mar., last wk of Aug., 1st wk of Sept. No lunch.*

$$ **Excelsior Café.** This elegant Victorian restaurant, with its hardwood floors, closet-size bar, and accomplished chefs, is a university tradition. The sparely decorated dining room, shaded by blossoming cherry trees in the spring, has a quiet, scholarly ambience. Despite the simple setting, there is nothing spare about the food: Glorious fresh-baked breads and desserts and imaginative, well-executed sandwiches, pastas, sautées, and grills form the backbone of the menu. Also try the excellent Sunday brunch. ✗ *754 E. 13th Ave.,* ☎ *503/342–6963. AE, MC, V.*

$$ **Zenon Café.** You never know what you'll find on the menu here—Thai, Indian, Italian, South American, down-home barbecue—but it's sure to be both memorable and expertly prepared. The patio-slate floors, picture windows, Parisian street lamps, marble-top tables, and café chairs give this much-beloved local eatery a romantic, open-air bistro feel. There's an admirably stocked wine cellar, and the desserts are formidable—two full-time bakers produce an eye-popping array of some 20 to 30 desserts daily. Look for the *zuccotto Fiorentino,* a dove-shape Italian wedding cake with rum, orange, and flavored whipped cream. ✗ *898 Pearl St.,* ☎ *503/343–3005. No reservations. MC, V.*

$ **Poppi's Anatolia.** For years a joyful, slightly seedy taverna called Poppi's near the University of Oregon's campus distributed home-style Greek food, retsina (white wine strongly flavored with pine resin), Aegean beer, and music with equal liberality. Now Poppi's has moved downtown, altered its name slightly, and generally spruced up. The food—particularly a lovely moussaka and *kalamarakia* (fried squid)— is still great, even if the menu has something of a split personality— Poppi's also serves East Indian specialties from Monday to Saturday. ✗ *992 Willamette St.,* ☎ *503/343–9661. MC, V. No lunch Sun.*

LODGING

$$$–$$$$ **Eugene Hilton.** Location, amenities, and a complete, room-by-room face-lift completed in 1993 make this property Eugene's finest hotel. All 270 rooms are furnished and decorated in shades of rose and forest green, and all have views. The hotel and its extensive convention facilities adjoin Eugene's Hult Center for the Performing Arts. ▥ *66 E. 6th Ave., Eugene 97401,* ☎ *503/342–2000 or 800/445–8667,* ℻ *503/342–6661. 270 rooms. 2 restaurants, 2 bars, indoor pool, beauty salon, hot tub, exercise room, airport shuttle. AE, D, DC, MC, V.*

$$ **Campus Cottage B & B.** Eugene's first bed-and-breakfast, this 1922 French ★ country–style cottage is within lecturing distance of the U of O campus and enjoys an enduring popularity with visiting academics and parents. The rustic European ambience extends to the cozy guest rooms, each of which is furnished with antiques and fresh flowers and has a private bath. A full breakfast is included. ▥ *1136 E. 19th Ave., Eugene 97403,* ☎ *503/342–5346. 4 rooms. Refrigerators. No credit cards.*

$$ **New Oregon Best Western.** This handsomely appointed midsize motel is directly across Franklin Boulevard from the university. Furnishings—such as the leather couches in the lobby—are unexpectedly plush. Completely refurbished in 1992 with upgrades planned at two-year intervals, the property is clean, fresh, and modern. There are some surprising amenities for this price range. ▥ *1655 Franklin Blvd., Eugene 97401,* ☎ *503/683–3669 or 800/528–1234,* ℻ *503/484–5556. 129 rooms. 2 restaurants, bar, indoor pool, saunas, racquetball. AE, D, DC, MC, V.*

Jacksonville

DINING AND LODGING

$$$–$$$$ **Jacksonville Inn.** The guest rooms and basement dining room of this
★   1863-vintage inn evoke what the Wild West might have been, had Leona
Helmsley been in charge. Four-poster beds, scrubbed floors, and spot-
less old antiques are maintained with scrupulous attention to detail.
Those in a romantic frame of mind should try the honeymoon cottage.
The Continental fare and 600-label wine cellar in the dining room are
among the best in southern Oregon. Fresh razor clams and veal dishes
are house specialties here. You'll need to book well in advance, par-
ticularly from late June to August, when the Peter Britt Festival draws
thousands of visitors here. ☒ *175 E. California St., 97530, ☏ 503/899–
1900 or 800/321–9344. Restaurant (reservations advised; no lunch
Mon.). 8 rooms, 1 cottage. AE, D, DC, MC, V.*

McKenzie Bridge

DINING AND LODGING

$$ **Log Cabin Inn.** This inn, on the banks of the wild, fish-filled McKenzie River, is equally appropriate for a fishing vacation or a romantic
weekend getaway. Inside the log cabin–style buildings, you'll find antique furniture and new beds and baths; each room has a river view.
The delightful restaurant features a decadent homemade beer-cheese
soup, buffalo, wild boar, quail, salmon, and a famous marionberry cob-
bler. ☒ *McKenzie Hwy., 97413, ☏ 503/822–3432. 8 cabins. Restaurant, bar, fishing. MC, V.*

McMinnville

DINING

$$$ **Nick's Italian Café.** Ask any wine maker in the valley to name his fa-
★   vorite wine-country restaurant, and chances are that Nick's would head
the list. It's not the decor—Nick's occupies a modestly furnished for-
mer dinette—but it might be Nick's voluminous wine cellar, a verita-
ble New York Public Library of local vintages. The food is spirited and
simple, reflecting the owner's northern Italian heritage. The five-course
fixed-price menu changes nightly. Diners have their choice of three en-
trées; there's always at least one fish choice. ✕ *521 E. 3rd St., ☏ 503/
434–4471. Reservations advised. No credit cards; personal checks ac-
cepted. Closed Mon. No lunch.*

$$–$$$ **Cafe Azul.** This McMinnville favorite benefits from the fortuitous pair-
ing of a Chez Panisse–trained chef and terrific local produce. The
menu features regional Mexican cuisine that's a startling departure from
the traditional beans and enchiladas. The emphasis is on fresh vegetables,
handmade corn tortillas, wild herbs, salted fish, and salads. Unusual
specialties include both yellow and black moles (the latter with fiery
charred peppers) and a spicy marinated pork that's wrapped in banana
leaves and braised in the juice of Seville oranges. The decor is sunny
and warm; walls are festooned with folk art from Oaxaca and other
regions. ✕ *313 3rd St., ☏ 503/435–1234. MC, V. Closed Sun. No break-
fast Sat.; no dinner Mon.–Wed.*

LODGING

$$ **Mattey House Bed & Breakfast.** This 100-year-old Victorian-style home
★   was built by English immigrant Joseph Mattey, a prosperous local
butcher. Its current owners, the Seeds, took over in 1993. The inn had
been fully renovated in 1986, and the owners decorated the property
with family antiques and hand-screened wallpapers. Now, with its
cheerful faux-marble fireplace and gourmet breakfasts (poached pears
with raspberry sauce and scrambled eggs with smoked salmon are typical fare), this B&B is an area favorite. ☒ *10221 N.E. Mattey La., off*

Hwy. 99 W, ¼ mi south of Lafayette, 97128, ☎ 503/434–5058. 4 rooms, 1 with private bath. MC, V. No smoking.

$ **Safari Motor Inn.** This motel on McMinnville's main drag is more functional than fancy. However, it has modest rates, a wonderfully central wine-country location, and clean, comfortable accommodations with up-to-date furnishings. 🖼 *345 N. Hwy. 99 W (corner of 19th St.), 97128, ☎ 503/472–5187 or 800/472–5187. 90 rooms. Restaurant, bar, hot tub, exercise room. AE, D, DC, MC, V.*

Medford

LODGING

$$$ **Under the Greenwood Tree.** Regular guests at this B&B are hard-
★ pressed to decide which they like most: the luxurious and romantic rooms, the stunning 10-acre gardens, or the breakfasts cooked by the owner, a Cordon Bleu–trained chef. The interior is decorated with Renaissance splendor. Gigantic old oaks hung with hammocks shade the inn itself, a 130-year-old farmhouse exuding genteel charm. There's a manicured 2-acre lawn and a creaky three-story barn for exploring; an outbuilding holds the buckboard wagon that brought the property's original homesteaders westward on the Oregon Trail. 🖼 *3045 Bellinger La. (midway between Medford and Ashland; take Exit 27 from I–5 and follow Stewart to Bellinger, about 3 mi), 97501, ☎ 503/776–0000. 5 rooms. MC, V.*

$ **Motel 6.** It's not the Savoy, but it's clean and cheap. Color schemes are primary; a typical room might contain a durable bed with a green bedspread and quarter-operated "magic fingers," a color TV, table and chairs, and a spartan bath. Perhaps one of the best attributes of this chain hotel is its close proximity to not only the Shakespeare Festival but also the Mt. Ashland ski area and Crater Lake. 🖼 *950 Alba Dr. (Exit 27 off I–5), 97504, ☎ 503/773–4290. 167 units. Pool. AE, D, DC, MC, V.*

Oakland

DINING

$$ **Tolly's.** Stroll past the Victorian ice-cream parlor downstairs to the opulent oak- and antique-filled dining room upstairs, where steaks, chicken, veal, shellfish, and salmon receive tender and expert treatment. The menu features such favorites as lamb loin in a pan-juice demiglaze and fillet royale, topped with scampi, artichoke hearts, and lobster sauce. ✗ *115 Locust St. (take Exit 138 from I–5 to Oakland), ☎ 503/459–3796. Reservations advised. MC, V.*

Salem

DINING

$$–$$$ **Inn at Orchard Heights.** This handsome hilltop restaurant is filled with
★ the sound of trickling water and soft classical music, and panoramic views overlook the lights of the capital city. The deftly handled Continental menu, enlivened by the European chef/owner's rich sauces, relies heavily on fresh local seafood, beef, and pasta. Standbys include fresh prawns stuffed with crabmeat and a pan-fried New York steak with pepper-cream sauce. ✗ *695 Orchard Heights Rd. NW (across the Willamette River from downtown Salem off Hwy. 221), ☎ 503/378–1780. Reservations advised. AE, DC, MC, V. No lunch Sun.*

$ **Gerry Frank's Konditorei.** Furnished in the style of a European sidewalk café, with cheerful flower boxes out front, this is *the* place to go in Salem for rich desserts. Sandwiches, salads, soup, and other simple entrées are served, but most people head straight for the tall glass display cases, where homemade cakes, tortes, and cheesecakes with such tempting names as "Orange Cloud" or "Blackout" are piled high. ✗ *310 Kearney St. SE,* ☎ *503/585–7070. D, MC, V.*

$ Thompson Brewery & Public House. The small, intimate rooms at this atmospheric pub, the southern outpost of a Portland-based brew-pub empire, are decked out in a funky mix of '60s rock-and-roll memorabilia and hand-painted woodwork. There are 21 beer taps behind the bar, most pouring fresh local microbrews. Several, including Java Ale and Terminator Stout, are made on the premises in a tiny brewery enlivened by colorful original artwork. (The surrealistic rendering of the state capitol as a spaceship, with Uncle Sam waving his hat astride the dome, is especially noteworthy.) The food—mostly hearty sandwiches, salads, and pasta dishes—is remarkably cheap. ✗ *3575 Liberty Rd. S (a 10-min drive south of the Capitol Mall),* ☎ *503/363–7286. No reservations. MC, V.*

LODGING

$$ Quality Inn. The chief virtue of this clean, functional hotel is its location, about five minutes from the capitol; in addition, there are a few unexpected luxuries, such as the spacious hot tubs in the presidential suites. Views of the freeway are not particularly desirable, but a million-dollar remodeling of the rooms and public areas, completed in late 1991, left them fresh and modernized. ⊞ *3301 Market St. NE, 97301,* ☎ *503/370–7888 or 800/248–6273. 146 rooms. Restaurant, bar, no-smoking rooms, indoor pool, sauna, laundry facilities, airport shuttle. AE, D, DC, MC, V.*

$$ State House Bed & Breakfast. Though the capital's first B&B tends to get a bit of noise from State Street, its location and luxury make up for that inconvenience. Only a five-minute walk from the Capitol Mall and Willamette University, it has a large hot tub overlooking Mill Creek. The decor, in lacy, floral fabrics of sky blue and salmon, is a little fussy but warm. Ask for the Grand Suite—Hank Aaron once slept there, and besides, it's the nicest room in Salem. Cabins, perfect for families, are available in addition to rooms in the main building. ⊞ *2146 State St., 97301,* ☎ *503/588–1340. 4 rooms (2 with private bath), 2 cottages. D, MC, V.*

Steamboat

DINING AND LODGING

$$–$$$ **Steamboat Inn.** Oregon's most famous fishing lodge was first brought
★ to the world's attention in travel articles by western writer Zane Grey in the 1930s. Every fall a veritable Who's Who of the world's top fly fishermen still converge here, high in the Cascades above the emerald North Umpqua River, to try their luck against the 20-pound steelhead that haunt these waters. (Guide services are available, as are fishing equipment rentals and sales.) Others come simply to relax in the reading nooks or on the broad decks of the riverside guest cabins. Another renowned attraction is the nightly Fisherman's Dinner, a multicourse feast served around a massive 50-year-old sugar-pine dinner table. In all, there are eight riverside cabins, five forest bungalows, and two riverside suites; the bungalows and suites have their own kitchens. You'll need to make reservations well in advance, especially for a stay during July–October, the prime fishing months. ⊞ *Steamboat, 97447 (38 mi east of Roseburg on Hwy. 138),* ☎ *503/498–2411. Restaurant, library, meeting room. MC, V.*

Yamhill

LODGING

$$–$$$ **Flying M Ranch.** The mysterious red *M* signs begin in downtown
★ Yamhill and continue west for 10 miles into the Chehalem Valley, in

the foothills of the Coast Range. Following them will bring you to the 625-acre Flying M Ranch, perched above the steelhead-filled Yamhill River. The centerpiece of this rustic complex is the great log lodge, decorated in a style best described as Daniel Boone eclectic and featuring a bar carved from a single 6-ton tree trunk. Guests have their choice of the somewhat austere cabins (the cozy, hot tub–equipped Honeymoon Cabin is the nicest) or the 28 riverside hotel units. In keeping with the rustic tone, there are no TVs or telephones. Be sure to book ahead for a Flying M specialty: the Steak Fry Ride, where guests, aboard their choice of horse or a tractor-drawn wagon, ride into the mountains to the ranch's elk camp for a feast of barbecued steak with all the trimmings. ☎ *From Newberg, take Hwy. 240 west to Yamhill, then follow small red Flying M signs west to 23029 N.W. Flying M Rd., 97148, ☎ 503/662–3222. 28 units, 7 cabins, more than 100 campsites. Restaurant, bar, swimming hole, tennis court, basketball, hiking, horseback riding, horseshoes, fishing. AE, D, DC, MC, V.*

The Arts

Ashland

Every year, from February through October, more than 100,000 bard-quoting fanatics descend on Ashland for the **Oregon Shakespeare Festival** (Box 158, Ashland 97520, ☎ 503/482–4331), presented in three different theaters. The accomplished repertory company stages some of the finest Shakespearean productions you're likely to see on this side of Stratford—plus works by Ibsen, Williams, and other more modern writers. There are backstage tours, noon lectures, and Renaissance music and dancing before each outdoor performance. The best time to go is from June through October, when the 1,200-seat Elizabethan Theatre, an atmospheric re-creation of Shakespeare's Globe, is operating. Be forewarned that tickets are difficult to come by—the festival generally operates at 98% of capacity, and you'll need to book ahead.

Eugene

The **Hult Center For the Performing Arts** (1 Eugene Center, Eugene 97401, ☎ 503/342–5746) is an airy, spacious confection of glass and native wood, containing two of the most acoustically perfect theaters on the West Coast. In the course of a typical year, the complex hosts everything from Broadway shows to ballet, from heavy-metal music to Haydn.

Jacksonville

Every summer some of the finest musicians in the world gather in this historic Wild West town for the **Peter Britt Festival** (Box 1124, Medford 97501, ☎ 503/773–6077 or 800/882–7488), a weekly series of outdoor concerts and theater presentations lasting from mid-June to early September. Contemporary and classical performances are held in a natural amphitheater on the estate of early photographer Peter Britt.

Nightlife

Lounges, restaurants, and bars throughout western Oregon provide the outlet for the region's nightly entertainment. In Salem, visit the **Union Street Oyster Bar** (445 State St., ☎ 503/362–7219). In Ashland, the after-theater crowd (including many of the actors) congregates in the bar at **Chateaulin** (50 E. Main St., ☎ 503/482–2264) for a nightcap. The **Rogue Brewery and Public House** (31 B. Water St., ☎ 503/488–5061) caters to a younger crowd.

THE COLUMBIA RIVER GORGE AND THE OREGON CASCADES

There's only one reason to drive to the Columbia River Gorge and Oregon Cascades: pleasure. Sightseers, sailboarders, hikers, skiers, waterfall lovers, and fans of the Old West will all find contentment in this rugged region. The following tour will take you through the highlights of the Columbia River Gorge, where America's second-largest river (after the Mississippi) slashes through the Cascade Range. Along the way you'll pass Multnomah Falls and Bonneville Dam, the world-class windsurfing hub and rich orchardland of Hood River, and skiing and other alpine attractions of the 11,245-foot-high Mt. Hood. Finally, you'll arrive in Bend, a stronghold of outdoor pleasures steeped in the traditions of the Old West.

An important note: The Columbia Gorge, the Mt. Hood area, and Bend all receive much heavier winter weather than does Portland and western Oregon. At times, even I–84, Oregon's main east–west highway, is closed because of snow and ice. If you're planning a winter visit, be sure your car has traction devices, and carry plenty of warm clothes with you. One further note: If you stop to explore, take your valuables with you—in spite of the idyllic surroundings, car prowlers are not unknown in the Gorge.

Exploring

Numbers in the margin correspond to points of interest on the Eastern Oregon map.

The Columbia River Gorge

❶ The tour begins at **Troutdale,** the gateway to the gorge, where the 22-mile-long Columbia River Scenic Highway leaves the interstate. Traveling on the well-signed route for a few miles will take you to Crown Point, a 730-foot-high bluff with an unparalleled 30-mile view down the gorge. Then the highway heads downhill, over graceful stone bridges built by Italian immigrant masons, past quiet forest glades and lichen-covered cliffs, over which a dozen waterfalls pour in a single 10-mile stretch. Among the most spectacular are **Latourell, Bridal Veil, Wah-**
❷ **keena, Horsetail,** and—finest of all—**Multnomah Falls,** at 620 feet. All the falls have parking areas and hiking trails, so visitors can take a close look. Multnomah Falls is by far the most popular and accessible; there's a paved (but steep) hiking path to the bridge over the lower falls, and an even steeper trail to a viewpoint overlooking the upper falls.

❸ A few miles farther along the old highway from Crown Point is **Oneonta Gorge.** During the hot summer months, you can walk up the bed of a shallow stream and through a cool green canyon that's hundreds of feet high (at other times of year, take the trail that follows along the west side of the canyon). The clearly marked trail head is 100 yards west of the gorge, on the south side of the road. The walls of the narrow rift drip moisture year-round; hundreds of plant species—some found nowhere else—flourish under these conditions. About a half mile up the stream, the trail ends at lovely Oneonta Falls. You'll need boots or submersible sneakers—plus a strong pair of ankles—because the rocks are slippery.

Just past Oneonta Gorge, the old Scenic Highway rejoins I–84. Head
❹ east to **Bonneville Dam,** Oregon's most impressive man-made attraction. The first dam ever to span the Columbia, Bonneville was dedicated by President Franklin D. Roosevelt in 1937. Its great turbines (visible from

94

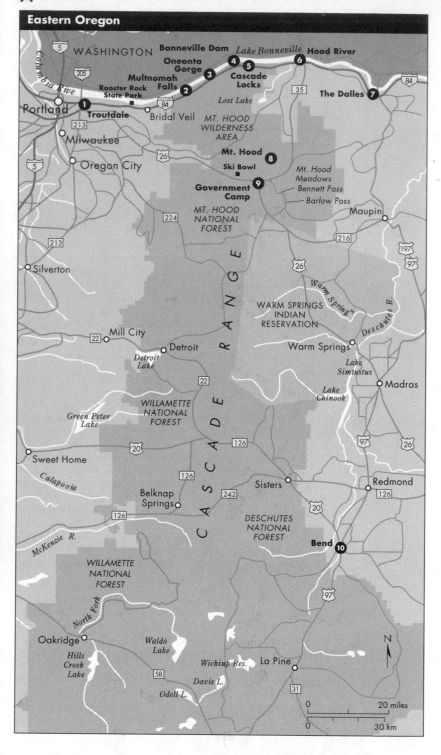

special walkways during self-guided powerhouse tours) can produce nearly a million kilowatts, which is enough to supply 40,000 single-family homes. There is a modern visitor center on Bradford Island, complete with underwater windows for viewing migrating salmon and steelhead as they struggle up the fish ladders (April–October are the best viewing times). *Visitor center on Bradford Island, Bonneville Lock and Dam, Cascade Locks 97014 (drive over powerhouse), ☎ 503/374–8820. ☛ Free. ☉ Summer, daily 9–8; rest of year, daily 9–5.*

Nearby, the **Bonneville Fish Hatchery** has ponds teeming with fingerling salmon, as well as fat rainbow trout and 6-foot-long sturgeon. A gift shop is on the premises. *Star Rte. B, Box 12, Cascade Locks (on Oregon shore), 97014, ☎ 503/374–8393. ☛ Free. ☉ Daily dawn–dusk.*

⑤ The rapids that once bedeviled river travelers near the town of **Cascade Locks** have been inundated by the 48-mile-long **Lake Bonneville.** In pioneer days, boats needing to pass the rapids had to portage around them. In 1896, the locks that gave the town its name were completed, allowing waterborne passage for the first time. Today the locks are used by Native Americans for their traditional dip-net fishing, and Cascade Locks is notable mainly as the home port of the 600-passenger sternwheeler *Columbia Gorge,* which you might recognize from the Mel Gibson–Jodie Foster movie, *Maverick.* From June through September, the comfortable, pleasantly appointed ship churns its way upriver, then back again, on daily two-hour excursions through some of the gorge's most awesome scenery. The company also offers lunches and brunches, and dinner-and-dancing cruises in the evenings. *Cruises leave from Marine Park in Cascade Locks, ☎ 503/223–3928 or 503/374–8427. Departures June–Sept., daily at 10, 12:30, and 3. ☛ $10.95 adults, $5.45 children 4–12. Dinner cruises embark Wed.–Sat. 7 PM; weekends 6 PM. Cruises vary in length from 2 to 4 hrs. Meal and cruise prices range from $17.95 to $32.95 for adults. Reservations required for any cruise with meal. AE, MC, V.*

⑥ For years the incessant easterly winds at **Hood River,** where the gorge widens and the scenery changes to tawny, wheat-covered hills, were nothing but a nuisance. Then somebody bolted a sail to a surfboard, and a new recreational craze was born. A fortuitous combination of factors—mainly the reliable gale-force winds blowing against the current—have made Hood River the self-proclaimed boardsailing capital of the world. Now, especially in the summer, this once-somnolent fruit-growing town swarms with colorful "boardheads," many of whom have journeyed from as far away as Europe and Australia. A collection of restaurants, equipment shops, and inns have sprung up to service this trade, and Hood River is rapidly becoming one of the state's busiest tourist destinations.

Columbia Gorge Sailpark (Port Marina, ☎ 503/386–2000), located on the river downtown, was one of the amenities added to encourage the boardsailing craze. It offers a boat basin, swimming beach, jogging trails, picnic tables, and rest rooms.

Situated 28 miles southwest of Hood River, via signed Forest Service roads, is **Lost Lake** (☎ 503/386–6366 for cabin reservations), one of the most photographed sites in the Pacific Northwest. Lake waters reflect the mountain and thick forests that line the shore.

⑦ **The Dalles,** 20 miles east, presents a placid alternative to frenetic Hood River. With its plethora of 19th-century brick storefronts and historic homes, The Dalles has a small-town, Old West feel to it, possibly because it's the traditional end of the Oregon Trail, where the wagons were loaded onto barges for the final leg of their 2,000-mile journey. The 130-year-old **Wasco County Courthouse** and the 1857-vintage **Ft. Dalles Surgeon's Quarters** have been converted into museums; both contain outstanding displays and collections illustrating the incredible pioneer ordeal. *The Courthouse Museum, 406 W. 2nd St.,* ☎ *503/296–4798.* ☛ *Free (donations accepted).* ⊙ *Apr.–May, Tues.–Sat. 11–3; June–Sept., Tues.–Sat. 10–4. Ft. Dalles Museum, 15th and Garrison Sts.,* ☎ *503/296–4547.* ☛ *$2 adults, children free.* ⊙ *Nov.–Feb., Wed.–Fri. noon–4, weekends 10–4; Mar.–Oct., weekdays 10:30–5, weekends 10–5.*

Mt. Hood

From Hood River, Highway 35 climbs south toward the regal snow-covered bulk of **Mt. Hood,** believed to be an active volcano that is quiet now but capable of the same violence that decapitated nearby Mt. St. Helens in 1980. The mountain is just one feature of the 1,079,169-acre **Mt. Hood National Forest,** an all-season playground that attracts more than 4 million visitors annually. You'll find 95 campgrounds and 150 lakes stocked with brown, rainbow, cutthroat, brook, and steelhead trout. The Sandy, Salmon, and other rivers are known for their fishing, rafting, canoeing, and swimming. Both forest and mountain are crossed by an extensive trail system for hikers, cyclists, and horseback riders. Some are half-milers, while others are day-or-longer treks. The **Pacific Crest Trail,** which begins in British Columbia and ends in Mexico, crosses here at the 4,157-foot-high Barlow Pass, the highest point on the highway.

Two miles off Highway 26, near the pass, sits **Trillium Lake** (☎ 503/666–0771), a beautiful spot for picnicking, overnight camping, and fishing for brown and rainbow trout.

Farther on, Highway 35 joins Highway 26 at 4,670-foot-high **Bennett Pass.** Turning west, you'll encounter signs to historic **Timberline Lodge** (*see* Dining and Lodging, *below*), an exquisite 1930s stone and timber structure, graced with hand-forged wrought iron, intricately carved woodwork, and great stone fireplaces. The lodge has been used as a setting in many films, including *The Shining* with Jack Nicholson. At the front desk of the lodge you can pick up maps that will direct you along the network of trails, leading through alpine meadow and old-growth forest. Today Timberline offers comfortable lodging and gourmet dining high (6,000 feet) on the mountain's flank and is a favorite destination of skiers, romantics, and sightseers alike.

Government Camp, just off Highway 26 west of the Timberline exit, is an alpine-flavored resort village with an abundance of lodging, restaurants, and nightlife. It's a convenient drive to each of Mt. Hood's five ski resorts: **Timberline, Mt. Hood Meadows, Summit Ski Area, Ski Bowl** and **Cooper Spur Ski Area** (*see* Sports and the Outdoors, *below*).

During the summer months, the **Alpine Slide** at Ski Bowl, just across Highway 26 from Government Camp, gives the intrepid a chance to whiz down the slopes on a European-style toboggan run. This is heady stuff, with a marvelous view. The nearby Eastside Action Park features more than 20 kid-oriented attractions, including something called the Rapid Riser, a sort of reverse bungee-jumping device that catapults riders 80 feet in the air. *Hwy. 26 at milepost 53,* ☎ *503/272–3206.* ☛ *$18.* ⊙ *June–Sept., weekdays 11–6, weekends 10–7.*

Bend

Bend, a city of 20,000, very nearly sits in the center of Oregon, about two hours southeast of Mt. Hood. It occupies a landscape that many visitors wouldn't even recognize as Oregon: a tawny high desert plateau, perfumed with juniper and surrounded by 10,000-foot Cascade peaks. Called Bend because it was built on Farewell Bend in the Deschutes River—here an easy-flowing river that becomes a roaring cataract a few miles downstream—the city is a good fueling-up spot. It's filled with decent restaurants, dance bars, pro shops and equipment-rental places, and a surprising number of good, reasonably priced hostelries.

While in Bend, visit the **High Desert Museum,** where you can walk through a stone-age Indian campsite; a pioneer wagon camp; a groaning, echoing old mine; an Old West boardwalk; and other lovingly detailed dioramas. Many are complete with authentic relics, sounds, and even odors. There are outstanding exhibits on local Native American cultures as well. The high point of the complex is the 150-acre outdoor section, which features fat porcupines, baleful birds of prey, and crowd-pleasing river otters at play aboveground and underwater. *59800 S. Hwy. 97, 6 mi south of Bend,* ☎ *503/382–4754.* ☛ *$5.50 adults, $5 senior citizens, $2.75 children 5–12.* ⊙ *Daily 9–5.*

Sports and the Outdoors

Beaches
The Columbia River is lined with sandy beaches, the most famous of which is at **Rooster Rock State Park** (☎ 503/695–2261), where both nudists and conventional bathers soak up the sun. There is a $3 daily-per-vehicle fee.

Bicycling
With a wide bicycle path paralleling I–84, the entire length of the gorge is suitable for bicycling. The terrain is generally flat, but there are stiff and constant winds from the east. The Bend area offers many memorable venues for cyclists, including the entire **Sunriver complex** (☎ 503/593–1221 or 800/547–3922), with 26 miles of paved bike paths and rentals available. Also, Highway 97 north to the **Crooked River Gorge** and the spectacular **Smith Rocks** promise breathtaking scenery and a good workout.

Canoeing and Rafting
The **Deschutes River** flows north from the Cascades west of Bend, gaining volume and momentum as it nears its rendezvous with the Columbia River at The Dalles. Its upper stretches, particularly those near Sunriver and Bend, are placid and suitable for leisurely canoeing. The stretch between Madras and Maupin offers some of Oregon's most famous white-water rafting. Due to heavy use, this portion of the Deschutes is accessible by permit only; for details, call the **Central Oregon Recreation Association** (☎ 503/389–8799 or 800/800–8334).

Skiing
CROSS-COUNTRY
There are nearly 120 miles of cross-country ski trails in the **Mt. Hood National Forest;** try the trail heads at Government Camp, Trillium Lake, or the Cooper Spur Ski Area, on the mountain's northeast flank. The **Deschutes National Forest,** surrounding Bend, is even richer in Nordic trails, with more than 165 miles of them at last count. The **Mt. Bachelor Nordic Center** (☎ 503/382–2442), a lodge surrounded by 36 miles of trails, is an excellent place to begin. **Summit Ski Area** (☎ 503/272–0256) and Ski Bowl/Multipor (☎ 503/272–3206), among other resorts, can supply cross-country rentals, accessories, maps, and guidebooks. For ski conditions, call ☎ 503/222–2211, 503/222–2695, or 503/227–7669.

DOWNHILL

Cooper Spur Ski Area, on the eastern slope of Mt. Hood, caters to families and has two rope tows and a T-bar. The longest run is ⅔ mile, with a 500-foot vertical drop. Facilities and services include rentals, instruction, repairs, a ski shop, day lodge, snack bar, and restaurant. *Follow signs from Hwy. 35 for 3½ mi to ski area,* ☎ *503/352–7803.*

Mt. Bachelor, which is generally regarded as one of the 10 best ski areas in the United States, is the Northwest's largest and most complete facility. The U.S. ski team trains here in the spring. There are 11 lifts, including one that takes skiers all the way to the mountain's 9,065-foot summit. The vertical drop is 3,100 feet; the longest of the 54 runs is 2½ miles. Facilities and services include equipment rental and repair, a ski school, ski shop, Nordic skiing, weekly races, and day care; visitors can enjoy restaurants, bars, and six lodges (including the new mid-mountain Pine Marten Lodge at 7,700 feet). *22 mi southwest of Bend off Hwy. 97 (follow signs),* ☎ *503/382–7888 or 800/829–2442.* ⊘ *Weekdays 9–4, weekends 8–4.*

Mt. Hood Meadows is Mt. Hood's largest ski resort, with more than 2,000 skiable acres, dozens of runs, seven double chairs, one triple chair, one quad chair, a top elevation of 7,300 feet, a vertical drop of 2,777 feet, and a longest run of 3 miles. Facilities include a day lodge, three restaurants, two lounges, a ski school, and a ski shop; equipment rental and repair are also available. *10 mi east of Government Camp on Hwy. 35,* ☎ *503/337–2222.* ⊘ *Mon.–Tues. 9–4, Wed.–Sat. 9 AM– 10 PM, Sun. 9–7.*

Ski Bowl, the ski area closest to Portland (only 50 miles away), boasts "the most extensive night skiing in America." The complex has 63 trails serviced by four double chairs and five rope tows, a top elevation of 5,050 feet, a vertical drop of 1,500 feet, and a longest run of 3 miles. Visitors can take advantage of two day lodges, a mid-mountain warming hut, two restaurants, and two lounges. Sleigh rides are also available; in the summer, there are go-carts, mountain- and alpine-bike rentals, horseback rides, and the Alpine slide (*see* Exploring, *above*). *53 mi east of Portland, across Hwy. 26 from Government Camp,* ☎ *503/272– 3206.* ⊘ *Mon.–Thurs. 9 AM–10 PM, Fri. 9 AM–11 PM, Sat. 8:30 AM– 11 PM, Sun. 8:30 AM–10 PM.*

Summit Ski Area has one chairlift and one rope-tow. Its longest run is a half mile, with a 400-foot vertical drop. Services include instruction and downhill and Nordic rentals; a ski shop, day lodge, and cafeteria are on-site. Bike rentals are available in summer. *Box 250, Government Camp,* ☎ *503/272–0256.*

Timberline, a full-service family-oriented ski area, is also a favorite of snowboard skiers. The U.S. ski team conducts summer training at Timberline (*also see* Dining and Lodging, *below*), a resort famous for its Palmer Chairlift, which takes skiers to a high glacier for summer skiing. There are five double chairs, including one quad chair; the top elevation is 8,500 feet, with 3,600 feet of vertical drop. Facilities include a day lodge with fast food and a ski shop; lessons and equipment rental and repair are available. *60 mi east of Portland on Hwy. 26,* ☎ *503/231–5400.* ⊘ *Sun.–Tues. 9–5, Wed.–Sat. 9 AM–10 PM. Summer lift hrs: 7 AM–1:30 PM.*

Dining and Lodging

Unless otherwise noted, casual but neat dress is appropriate at all of the restaurants reviewed below. For price-category definitions, *see* Dining *and Lodging in* Oregon Essentials, *below.*

Bend

DINING

$$$ Le Bistro. The best restaurant in Bend has prices to match the quality. The menu features traditional French cuisine with an emphasis on fresh Oregon meat and seafood. Try the critics' choices, the highly regarded seafood Wellington and roast rack of lamb. ✗ *1203 N.E. 3rd St. (Hwy. 97),* ☎ *503/389–7274. Reservations advised. AE, DC, MC, V. No lunch.*

$$ Pescatore. This unpretentious new restaurant favors simple Italian preparations of fresh Pacific seafood. Try the penne Pescatore, which tosses mussels, clams, shrimp, calamari, and other *frutti di mare* with a hearty marinara sauce. ✗ *119 N.W. Minnesota,* ☎ *503/389–6276. AE, MC, V.*

$ Deschutes Brewery & Public House. This cheery, popular brew pub features upscale Northwest cuisine and local ales and wines. Give close attention to the extensive list of lunch and dinner specials on the blackboard above the open kitchen, and try the admirable Black Butte Porter. Portions are large. ✗ *1044 N.W. Bond St.,* ☎ *503/382–9242. No reservations. MC, V.*

LODGING

$$$ Sunriver. Many residents consider this to be Oregon's premier outdoor resort destination, and with good reason. There's golf (two 18-hole championship courses designed by Robert Trent Jones); skiing at 9,000-foot Mt. Bachelor 20 minutes to the west; Class-4 white-water rafting on the Deschutes River, which flows right through the complex; high-desert hiking and mountain-biking; fishing; riding; tennis; and swimming. The Sunriver complex itself, once the site of an Army base, is now a self-contained community, with stores, restaurants, contemporary homes, condominiums, lodge and recreational facilities, and even a private airstrip—all set in a warm, pine-scented desert landscape. Visitors can rent condos, hotel rooms, or houses; a host of outdoorsy paraphernalia is also for rent. ☒ *Sunriver (just west of Hwy. 97, 15 mi south of Bend), 07707,* ☎ *503/593–1221 or 800/547–3922. 710 condos, 211 hotel rooms. 8 restaurants, 2 pools, hot tubs, saunas, 2 18-hole golf courses, 28 tennis courts, horseback riding, racquetball, boating, fishing, bicycles, convention center. AE, D, DC, MC, V.*

$$ Lara House Bed & Breakfast Inn. This nicely restored former boardinghouse is in a residential district overlooking Drake Park and Mirror Pond, a five-minute walk from downtown. One of the six spacious rooms has a water bed. Public areas are sunny and inviting. ☒ *640 N.W. Congress St. (west on Franklin from Hwy. 97), 97701,* ☎ *503/ 388–4064. 6 rooms. Hot tub. AE, D, MC, V.*

$$ The Riverhouse. This 1970s hotel is a cut or two above what you'd expect for the very reasonable price. The surprisingly large, well-appointed guest rooms are furnished in contemporary oak pieces, and many have river views (well worth the extra $5 charge). Perhaps the best feature is the sound of the rushing Deschutes River, which you can hear from your room. ☒ *3075 N. Hwy. 97, 97701,* ☎ *503/389– 3111 or 800/547–3928. 3 restaurants, bar, indoor and outdoor pools, hot tub, sauna, 18-hole golf course, 2 tennis courts, exercise room, jogging. AE, D, DC, MC, V.*

Cascade Locks

DINING

$ Cascade Inn. At this family-style restaurant, you can eat breakfast, lunch, and dinner at the counter or in booths. A number of the home-cooked specials are showcased on the Captain's Platter, which includes prawns, fresh fish, oysters, and clams. ✕ *Columbia Gorge Ct., ☎ 503/374–8340. No reservations. AE, D, MC, V.*

$ Char Burger Restaurant. In the 225-seat dining room overlooking the Columbia River you can enjoy a variety of hamburgers, plus salmon, seafood, steak dinners, and a full breakfast menu. Arrowhead collections, rifles, and wagon-wheel chandeliers carry out the western motif. ✕ *745 S.W. Wanapa St., ☎ 503/374–8477. Reservations required for Sun. brunch. MC, V.*

LODGING

$ Scandian Motor Lodge. Oregon pine furniture and wood paneling, colorful bedspreads, and Scandinavian wall hangings brighten otherwise standard but inexpensive rooms. A restaurant, bar, and general store are adjacent. ☒ *Box 217, Columbia Gorge Ct. 97014, ☎ 503/374–8417. 30 rooms. AE, D, DC, MC, V.*

The Dalles

DINING

$$ Ole's Supper Club. Local folk like this establishment for its excellent food, friendly and competent service, and its straightforward, no-nonsense approach. The menu of Western-style food with a Continental twist lists everything from thick slabs of prime rib to veal Oscar. It's hard to go wrong when choosing an entrée, especially when it's accompanied by a selection from the excellent wine list. ✕ *2620 W. 2nd St., ☎ 503/296–6708. Reservations advised. AE, MC, V. Closed Sun.–Mon. No lunch.*

LODGING

$$ Williams House Inn. This Victorian home furnished with antiques is on the Register of National Historic Places. Sitting on 3 acres of landscaped grounds, it has a three-room suite with private bath and two rooms, each with a private balcony and shared bath. ☒ *608 W. 6th St., 97058, ☎ 503/296–2889. 3 rooms. AE, D, MC, V.*

Hood River

DINING

$$ 6th Street Bistro and Loft. The menu at this friendly local favorite changes weekly but concentrates on Pacific Northwest flavors, right down to the coffee and salads. Depending on the season, choices may include local fresh steamer clams and wild coral mushrooms, along with grilled swordfish and chicken. ✕ *Corner of 6th and Cascade Sts., ☎ 503/386–5737. Weekend reservations advised. AE, MC, V.*

$–$$ The Mesquitery. You'll get fish of the season plus lean beef, chicken, and pork grilled over aromatic mesquite—without the usual rich, cloying sauces. Instead, the owners use fresh herbs and tangy marinades with satisfying results. There's also a modest wine and beer list at this sunny, western-flavored restaurant. ✕ *1219 12th St. (atop the hill south of the downtown core), ☎ 503/386–2002. No reservations. MC, V.*

White Cap Brew Pub. The largest microbrewery in Oregon, this glass-walled brew pub with a windswept deck overlooking the Columbia has won major awards at the Great American Beer Festival. The pub offers a variety of savory snack foods to complement the brewery-fresh ales. ✕ *506 Columbia St. (in the old Diamond cannery overlooking* *downtown Hood River),* ☎ *503/386–2247. No reservations. No credit cards.*

DINING AND LODGING

$$$$ Columbia Gorge Hotel. The grande dame of gorge hotels, built by lumber baron Simon Benson as the final destination of his Scenic Highway, was restored to its original magnificence in 1979. The ambience is a bit florid, but the major attraction—the 208-foot-high waterfall—is magnificent. Public areas are decorated in coral, green, and rose, and guest rooms reveal lots of brass, wood, and antiques. Rooms with two beds overlook the formal gardens. A huge seven-course breakfast—the World Famous Farm Breakfast—is included in the price of a room (nonguests pay $22.95 for the meal). While watching the sun set on the Columbia River, you can dine on breast of pheasant with pear wine, hazelnuts, and cream; grilled venison; breast of duck; Columbia River salmon; and sturgeon. ☎ *4000 Westcliff Dr. (take Exit 62), 97031,* ☎ *503/386–5566 or 800/345–1921. 46 rooms. Restaurant, bar. AE, D, DC, MC, V.*

LODGING

$$ Best Western-Hood River Inn. This modern hotel, built on the river within paddling distance of Hood River's Columbia Gorge Sailpark, is the address of choice for visiting windsurfers. Be sure to ask for a room with a river view. ☎ *1108 E. Marina Way, 97031,* ☎ *503/386–2200 or 800/828–7873. 150 rooms. Restaurant, bar, pool. AE, D, DC, MC, V.*

$$ Hood River Hotel. This local landmark, built in 1913 and abandoned for more than 20 years, reopened in 1989 after undergoing a floor-to-ceiling restoration. The results are spectacular. Public areas are rich in beveled glass, warm wood, and tasteful jade-and-cream-color fabrics. Each room is unique, but all have bare fir floors softened by Oriental carpets, four-poster beds, and skylights. Suites have a kitchen and can house five. There's a lively lobby bar and a Mediterranean-inspired kitchen, plus—a thoughtful touch—plenty of locked storage for boardsailors. ☎ *102 Oak St., 97031,* ☎ *503/386–1900. 33 rooms, 9 suites. Restaurant, bar, café. AE, D, DC, MC, V.*

$$ Lakecliff Estate. This small bed-and-breakfast inn, just up the road from
★ the Columbia Gorge Hotel, was a summer home designed by architect A. E. Doyle, who designed Portland's Classic Revival public library, U.S. Bank Building, and the Multnomah Falls Lodge. The 1908 house, built on a cliff overlooking the river, is beautifully maintained and exceptionally comfortable. A pleasant deck at the back of the house and wood-burning fireplaces in three of the rooms ensure a relaxing stay. ☎ *3820 Westcliff Dr. (Exit 62), 97031,* ☎ *503/386–7000. 4 rooms. No smoking. No credit cards.*

Mt. Hood
DINING AND LODGING

$$$ Timberline Lodge. This National Historic Landmark, which has with-
★ stood howling winter storms on an exposed flank of the mountain for more than 50 years, still manages to warm guests with its hospitality, hearty food, and guest rooms with fireplaces. Built as a WPA project during the Depression, everything about the lodge has a handcrafted, rustic feel, from the wrought-iron chairs with rawhide seats to the massive hand-hewn beams. The elegant Cascade Dining Room features expertly prepared cuisine made from the freshest Oregon products. ☎ *Follow the signs from Hwy. 26 a few mi east of Zig Zag; Timberline 97028,* ☎ *503/272–3311 or 800/547–1406. 71 rooms, some with fire-*

places. Restaurant, bar, pool, hot tub, sauna, downhill and cross-country skiing. AE, D, MC, V.

LODGING

$$$ **Valu-Inn/Mt. Hood.** The inn opened in 1990, and although everything looks and smells new, it also has a comfortable, relaxed feel. The Mt. Hood National Forest is outside the east windows; rooms facing the southwest are great for watching the spectacle of night skiing at Ski Bowl, which is literally across the street. Accommodations come in a variety of sizes, from roomy standards to king-size suites with refrigerators and hot tubs to double queens with kitchenettes. There are free ski lockers and a ski tuning room, and a Continental breakfast is provided. ▦ *87450 Government Camp Loop, 97028,* ☎ *503/272–3205. 56 rooms. No-smoking rooms, hot tub, laundry facilities. AE, D, DC, MC, V.*

Troutdale

DINING

$–$$ **Multnomah Falls Lodge.** The lodge, with high, vaulted ceilings and classic stone fireplaces, was built in 1925. Freshwater trout, salmon, and a platter of prawns, halibut, and scallops are specialties. The lodge is justly famous for its wild-huckleberry daiquiris and desserts. A gift shop and nature center are part of the complex. ✕ *Hwy. I–84 and Columbia River Scenic Hwy.,* ☎ *503/695–2376. AE, MC, V.*

Warm Springs

DINING AND LODGING

$$–$$$ **Kah-Nee-Tah Resort.** The culture of the native Wasco, Warm Springs, and Paiute tribes permeates this luxurious resort 11 miles north of Warm Springs off Highway 26. Traditional Indian salmon bakes, festivals, arts, and dances enliven an austerely beautiful setting in the middle of the 640,000-acre high-desert Warm Springs Reservation. Mineral hot springs bubbling up from the desert floor fill baths and pools. If you don't mind spending a little extra, reserve the splendid Warm Springs, Wasco, or Paiute suites, with their tiled fireplaces and hot tubs, big-screen TVs, king-size beds and spectacular desert views. If you'd rather rough it (sort of), and don't mind bringing your own bedroll, check into one of the tepees here. Replicas of traditional Native American dwellings, these wood-frame, canvas-covered conical structures are set on a concrete slab with a fire pit in the center. Rest rooms and shower facilities are campground-style. The resort's new casino opened in 1995. ▦ *Warm Springs 97761,* ☎ *503/553–1112 or 800/831–0100. 139 rooms, 21 tepees. 2 restaurants, bar, 2 pools, hot tubs, saunas, 18-hole golf course, tennis court, exercise room, hiking, horseback riding, water slide, kayaking, fishing, mountain bikes, casino, convention center. AE, DC, MC, V.*

Welches

DINING

$$$ **Chalet Swiss.** The atmosphere is authentically alpine in this country-Swiss restaurant, but it's the food that will make you want to yodel. From the creamy fondue and the nutty *buendnerfleisch*—tissue-thin slices of dry-cured beef—to the rich sautées and fresh seafood, the kitchen displays a sure and artful hand. ✕ *Hwy. 26 at Welches Rd.,* ☎ *503/622–3600. Reservations advised. AE, MC, V. Closed Mon.–Tues. No lunch.*

DINING AND LODGING

$$$$ **Resort at the Mountain.** This sprawling resort complex, nestled among the burly Cascade foothills, has changed hands more often than a track baton. Still, it offers the mountain's most complete resort facil-

ities, with attractive modern public areas and reasonably well-appointed rooms. With the last renovation—in 1990—came the Scottish motif, including tartans on lounge tables and light pink-and-teal floral patterns in guest rooms. Accommodations include standard rooms, huge deluxe rooms, and limited numbers of two-bedroom condos. The Highland Dining Room features Northwest cuisine, including fillet of salmon with fresh herbs and Pinot Noir wine, venison with black-currant sauce, and quail sautéed with mustard. ☎ *68010 E. Fairway Ave. (follow signs from Hwy. 26), 97067, ☎ 503/622–3101 or 800/669–7666. 158 rooms. 2 restaurants, 2 bars, pool, hot tubs, 27 holes of golf, 6 tennis courts (2 lighted), health club, bicycles, meeting rooms. AE, D, DC, MC, V.*

OREGON ESSENTIALS

Arriving and Departing

By Car

If you are entering Oregon from the north or south, take I–5, which runs 300 miles through the Willamette Valley and the heart of Oregon. Entering from the east, take I–84, which runs from the Idaho border to Portland.

By Plane

Most communities along the Oregon coast have municipal airports, but there is no major commercial service anywhere on the coast.

Eugene Airport (☎ 503/687–5430), the best mid-valley air destination, is serviced by Horizon (☎ 800/547–9308), United (☎ 800/241–6522), and United Express (☎ 800/241–6522). Farther south, **Jackson County Airport** (☎ 503/772–8068), in Medford, is served by Horizon (☎ 800/547–9308), United (☎ 800/241–6522) and United Express (☎ 800/241–6522).

Bend-Redmond Municipal Airport (☎ 503/548–6059) is serviced by Horizon (☎ 800/547–9308) and United Express (☎ 800/241–6522).

Getting Around

Greyhound (☎ 800/231–2222) bus routes crisscross the state from the I–5 and I–84 corridors to the Highway 101 coastal route and Highways 20 and 97 in central and eastern Oregon. Be warned, however, that buses—particularly those running on the less-populated routes—leave sporadically and at inconvenient hours.

Amtrak's (☎ 800/872–7245) *Coast Starlight* follows I–5 south to Eugene, then enters the rugged Cascades at Oakridge; from there it follows Highways 58 and 97 south past Diamond Peak and Crater Lake, on its way to California. The *Pioneer* runs daily from Portland to the Columbia Gorge, and parallels I–84 to the Idaho border and beyond.

The Oregon Coast

BY CAR

Highway 101 runs the length of the coast, through vistas of shore pine and churning waves, sometimes turning inland for a few miles, then rewarding you with an awesome coastal vista. **Three Capes Loop** leaves Highway 101 at Tillamook and winds past the dense forests and windswept cliffs of three protruding peninsulas: Capes Meares, Lookout, and Kiwanda.

The Willamette Valley and Wine Country

BY CAR

I–5, the main north-south route, runs the length of the Willamette Valley. **Highway 34** leaves I–5 just south of Albany and heads west, past Corvallis and into the Coast Range, where it follows the fish-filled Alsea River. Watch for a sign marked Alsea Falls/South Fork Road/Monroe a mile south of Alsea. It will take you to the lovely Alsea Falls, where salmon in the spring and steelhead in the fall make prodigious leaps to clear the falls. **Highway 138** leads you through the spectacular waterfall country of the Umpqua River, east of Roseburg (watch for signs along the road), to the back door of Crater Lake National Park; in the winter, however, the road to Crater Lake is closed.

The Columbia River Gorge and the Oregon Cascades

BY CAR

Mt. Hood is about 50 miles from Portland; Bend is 160 miles away. Virtually all travel in eastern and central Oregon is by car. I–84 follows the Columbia River all the way to Idaho, terminating at Salt Lake City. U.S. 197 (later U.S. 97) leaves I–84 at The Dalles and heads south to California, passing Bend along the way.

The **Scenic Gorge Highway** (Route 30) leaves I–84 at Troutdale and climbs past the lush, fern-covered greenery, awesome cliff-top vistas, and thundering waterfalls. The old highway, built in the 1910s by lumber magnate Simon Benson, is a narrow and serpentine 22-mile road made expressly for sightseeing. The route is especially lovely in the fall but often impassable in winter.

The **Highway 97–Highway 218 Loop** is a 25-mile tour through some of the state's most forbiddingly beautiful high desert country. From Shaniko, take Highway 218 south to Antelope, near the now-abandoned commune of Rajneeshpuram. Follow the signs back to Highway 97 and Bend.

BY TRAIN

Once you've reached Hood River, consider taking the **Mt. Hood Railroad** (☎ 503/386–3556 or 800/872–4661), built in 1906, on a 44-mile round-trip scenic tour to Parkdale. Call for schedule information.

Guided Tours

Orientation

Gray Line Sightseeing Tours (Box 17306, Portland 97217, ☎ 503/285–9845) offers guided tours of scenic Oregon for both individuals and groups. Regular destinations include the Mt. Hood Loop and Oregon Coast.

Winery

The best way to see the wine country here is to rent a car and map out your own itinerary. A copy of "Discover Oregon Wineries," the free map and guide published by the **Oregon Wine Center** (1200 N.W. Front Ave., Suite 400, Portland 97209, ☎ 503/228–8336), is an indispensable tool for touring the state's wineries. It provides profiles and service information about each winery and is available at no charge where Oregon wine is sold. Strangely enough, there are no regularly scheduled bus tours at this time, though the Oregon Wine Center may be able to arrange one for larger groups.

For hours and tour schedules at individual wineries, it's best to call in advance. Some of the state's most accomplished and hospitable wineries include (from the northern valley to the south) **Tualatin Vineyards**

(Forest Grove, ☎ 503/357–5005), **Shafer Vineyard Cellars** (Forest Grove, ☎ 503/357–6604), **Ponzi Vineyards** (Beaverton, ☎ 503/628–1227), **Laurel Ridge Winery** (Forest Grove, ☎ 503/359–5436), **Rex Hill Vineyards** (Newberg, ☎ 503/538–0666), **Veritas Vineyard** (Newberg, ☎ 503/538–1470), **Autumn Wind Vineyard** (Gaston, ☎ 503/538–6931), **Knudsen Erath** (Dundee, ☎ 503/538–3318), **Yamhill Valley Vineyards** (McMinnville, ☎ 503/843–3100), **Amity Vineyards** (Amity, ☎ 503/835–2362), **Bethel Heights Vineyard** (Salem, ☎ 503/581–2262), **Eola Hills Wine Cellars** (Rickreall, ☎ 503/623–2405), **Tyee Wine Cellars** (Corvalis, ☎ 503/753–8754), **Alpine Vineyards** (Alpine, ☎ 503/424–5851), **Henry Estate Winery** (Umpqua, ☎ 503/459–5120), **Girardet Wine Cellars** (Roseburg, ☎ 503/679–7252), and **Callahan Ridge Winery** (Roseburg, ☎ 503/673–7901).

Dining

Dollar-sign ratings for restaurants are based on the following price categories for a three-course meal (not including tip or beverages):

CATEGORY	COST
$$$$	over $25
$$$	$18–$25
$$	$10–$18
$	under $10

Lodging

Dollar-sign ratings for accommodations are based on the following price categories for a standard double room (not including tip 6%–9% tax):

CATEGORY	COST
$$$$	over $110
$$$	$80–$110
$$	$50–$80
$	under $50

Sports and the Outdoors

Bicycling

For the past 20 years, Oregon has set aside 1% of its highway funds for the development and maintenance of bikeways throughout the state, resulting in one of the most extensive networks of bicycle trails in the country. Write or call the **Oregon Bicycling Program** (Bicycle Program Manager, Oregon Dept. of Transportation, Room 200, Transportation Bldg., Salem 97310, ☎ 503/986–3200 or 503/986–3555) for the free "Oregon Bicycling Guide." A second excellent publication, "Mountain Bike Guide to Oregon" is available from the **Oregon Parks and Recreation Dept.** (525 Trade St. SE, Salem 97310, ☎ 503/378–6305) for $5.50, plus postage.

Fishing

To fish in most areas of Oregon, out-of-state visitors need a yearly ($40.50), seven-day ($30.50), or daily ($6.75) nonresident angler's license. Additional tags are required for those fishing for salmon or steelhead ($10.50), sturgeon ($6), or halibut ($6); these tags are available from any local sporting-goods store. For more information, contact the **Sport Fishing Information Line** (☎ 800/275–3474).

Important Addresses and Numbers

Emergencies

In most parts of the state, calling 911 will summon **police, fire,** or **ambulance** services; dialing "0" will give you the operator. In some rural areas, it may be necessary to dial the **Oregon State Police** (☎ 800/452–7888).

Visitor Information

All Oregon tourist-information centers are marked with blue I signs from main roads. Opening and closing times vary, depending on season and individual office; call ahead for hours.

For general information on the state, contact the **Oregon State Welcome Center** (12348 N. Center Ave., Portland 97217, ☎ 503/285–1631) or the **Oregon Economic Development Tourism Division** (595 Cottage St. NE, Salem 97310, ☎ 800/547–7842). There is also a **road conditions' hot line** (☎ 503/889–3999).

THE OREGON COAST

Astoria Area Chamber of Commerce (111 W. Marine Dr., 97103, ☎ 503/325–6311).

Brookings Harbor Chamber of Commerce (16330 Lower Harbor Rd., 97415, ☎ 503/469–3181 or 800/535–9469).

Cannon Beach Chamber of Commerce (2nd and Spruce Sts., 97110, ☎ 503/436–2623).

Florence Area Chamber of Commerce (270 Hwy. 101, 97439, ☎ 503/997–3128).

Greater Newport Chamber of Commerce (555 S.W. Coast Hwy., 97365, ☎ 503/265–8801 or 800/262–7844).

Lincoln City Visitors Center (801 S.W. Hwy. 101, 97367, ☎ 503/994–8378 or 800/452–2151).

North Bend Tourist Information Center (1380 Sherman St., 97459, ☎ 503/756–4613).

Seaside Visitors Bureau (7 N. Roosevelt Ave., 97138, ☎ 503/738–6391 or 800/1444–6740).

Tillamook Chamber of Commerce (3705 Hwy. 101 N, 97141, ☎ 503/842–7525).

Yachats Chamber of Commerce (Hwy. 101, near 2nd St., 97498, ☎ 503/547–3530).

THE WILLAMETTE VALLEY AND WINE COUNTRY

Ashland Chamber of Commerce and Visitors Information Center (110 E. Main St., 97520, ☎ 503/482–3486).

Corvallis Convention and Visitors Bureau (420 N.W. 2nd St., 97330, ☎ 503/757–1544 or 800/334–8118).

Eugene-Springfield Convention & Visitors Bureau (305 W. 7th Ave., Eugene 97401, ☎ 800/452–3670 or 503/484–5307).

Grant's Pass Visitor & Convention Bureau (1501 N.E. 6th St., 97526, ☎ 503/476–7717 or 800/547–5927).

McMinnville Chamber of Commerce (417 N. Adams St., 97128, ☎ 503/472–6196).

Roseburg Area Chamber of Commerce (410 S.E. Spruce St., 97470, ☎ 503/672–2648).

Salem Convention & Visitors Center (Mission Mill Village, 1313 Mill St. SE, 97301, ☎ 503/581–4325 or 800/874–7012).

THE COLUMBIA RIVER GORGE AND THE OREGON CASCADES

Bend Chamber of Commerce (63085 N. Hwy. 97, Bend 97701, ☎ 503/382–3221).

Hood River County Chamber of Commerce (Port Marina Park, Hood River 97031, ☎ 503/386–2000 or 800/366–3530).

Mt. Hood National Forest Ranger Stations are located in Gresham (☎ 503/666–0771), Troutdale (☎ 503/695–2276), Zigzag (☎ 503/666–0704), Mt. Hood Information Center (☎ 503/622–3191), and Hood River (☎ 503/352–6002).

Mt. Hood Recreation Association (65000 E. Hwy. 26, Welches 97067, ☎ 503/622–3162 or 503/622–4822 for recreation information on recreational facilities).

4   Seattle

In the Pacific North Coast's hippest city, the green hills and bay views are best appreciated from a coffee bar, and the music and art scenes seem to change with the tides. But Seattle has more to offer than steaming lattes and hot bands—you can wander historic neighborhoods, browse amidst the sights and smells of the Pike Place Market, explore the lakes and islands of this port city, or just eat, eat, eat— Seattle enjoys a spectrum of restaurants that is one of the nation's most innovative and diverse.

SEATTLE IS DEFINED BY WATER. There's no use denying the city's damp weather, or the fact that its skies are cloudy for much of the year. Residents of Seattle don't tan—goes the joke—they rust. But Seattle is also defined by a different kind of water. A variety of rivers, lakes, and canals bisect steep hills, creating a series of distinctive areas along the water's edge that provide for a wide range of activities. Funky fishing boats, floating homes, swank yacht clubs, and waterfront restaurants exist side by side.

By Adam Woog and Loralee Wenger

But a city is defined by its people as well as by its geography, and the people of Seattle—some half million within the city proper, another 2 million in the surrounding Puget Sound region—are a diversified bunch. Seattle has long had an active Asian and Asian-American population, as well as well-established communities of Scandinavians, African Americans, Jews, Native Americans, Latinos, and other ethnic groups.

Although it's impossible to accurately generalize about such a varied group, the prototypical Seattleite was once pithily summed up by a *New Yorker* cartoon in which one arch-eyebrowed East Coast matron says to another, "They're backpacky, but nice." Aided by the proximity of high mountains—the Cascades to the east, the Olympics to the west—and all that water, Seattle's vigorous outdoor sports are indeed perennial favorites. And the city's extensive park system (designed by Frederick Law Olmsted, creator of New York City's Central Park) and miles of secluded walking and bicycling paths add to one's appreciation of the city's surroundings.

At the same time, the climate fosters an easygoing, indoor lifestyle as well. Overcast days and long winter nights help make Seattle a haven for moviegoers and book readers. The city is often used by Hollywood as a testing ground for new films, and according to independent bookstore sales and per-capita book purchases, the city ranks in the highest category. The town that Sir Thomas Beacham once described as a "cultural wasteland" now has all the artistic trappings of a full-blown big city, with ad agencies and artists' co-ops, symphonies and ballet companies. Several magazines compete with the two daily newspapers. There's an innovative new convention center, a covered dome for professional sports, a world-renowned theater scene, an excellent opera company, and a strong music community.

Other signs that Seattle is shedding its sleepy-town image abound. For years, giant aerospace manufacturer Boeing was the only major factor in the area's economy besides lumber and fishing—the staples of the Northwest. But just as the 1962 World's Fair (and its enduring symbol, the Space Needle) signaled a change from small town to medium-size city, so the 1990 Goodwill Games announced the city's new role as a respected international hub. Seattle, one of the fastest-growing communities in the United States, is now a major seaport and a vital link in Pacific Rim trade. Evidence of this internationalism is everywhere, from the discreet Japanese script identifying downtown department stores (i.e., "Nordstrom" written as "Katakana") to the multilingual recorded messages at Seattle-Tacoma International Airport.

As the city grows, though, it is also beginning to display full-blown big-city problems. Increases in crime, drug abuse, homelessness, and poverty are coupled with a decline in the quality of the public schools.

Suburban growth is also rampant; nearby Bellevue, the largest suburb, has swollen in just a few years from a quiet farming community to the second-largest city in the state. Furthermore, the area is plagued with one of the worst traffic problems in the country. But Seattleites are an active political bunch with a great love for their city and a firm commitment to maintaining its reputation as one of the most livable in the country.

EXPLORING

Tour 1: Downtown

Downtown Seattle is bounded by the Kingdome to the south, the Seattle Center to the north, I–5 to the east, and the waterfront to the west. You can reach most points of interest by foot, bus, or the monorail. Bear in mind that Seattle is a city of hills, so comfortable walking shoes are a must.

Numbers in the margin correspond to points of interest on the Downtown Seattle map.

1 Start at the **Visitor Information Center** on the street level of the Washington State Convention and Trade Center to pick up maps, brochures, and listings of events. *800 Convention Pl. (at 8th Ave. and Pike St.), ☎ 206/461–5840. ☉ Labor Day–Memorial Day, weekdays 8:30–5; summer, daily 8:30–5.*

2 From the Information Center, proceed west three blocks on Pike Street to 5th Avenue, turn right, and head one block north to **Westlake Center** (*see* Shopping, *below*), a complex completed in 1989 in spite of the controversy surrounding its construction. Some city residents objected to plans for the structure—a 27-story office tower and three-story shopping structure with enclosed walkways—and favored, instead, a large grassy park without commercial buildings. While the center was built, the block of Pine Street between 4th and 5th avenues is now a pedestrian mall and outdoor plaza. *1601 5th Ave., ☎ 206/467–1600. ☉ Weekdays 9:30–9.*

Beyond its commercial purpose, the center is also a major terminus for buses and for the monorail. If you head up to the monorail terminal (on the Pine Street and 5th Avenue corner), you can take a short jaunt over to **Seattle Center.** Like the monorail itself, this 74-acre complex was built for the 1962 Seattle World's Fair. It includes an amusement park, theaters, the Coliseum, exhibition halls, museums, shops, and the popular Space Needle with its restaurants and observation deck.

★ 3 The distinctive silhouette of the **Space Needle** (rather like something from the old "Jetsons" cartoon show) can be seen from almost any spot in the downtown area. The view from the inside out, however, is even better—at over 500 feet high, the observation deck offers panoramic vistas of the entire region. Have a drink at the Space Needle Lounge or a latte at the adjacent coffee bar and take in Elliott Bay, Queen Anne Hill, and on a clear day, the peaks of the Cascades. The needle also houses two revolving restaurants. ☛ *Observation deck: $7 adults, $6.50 senior citizens, $3.50 children 5–12. ☉ Daily 8 AM–midnight.*

Take the monorail back downtown and head west on Pine Street. From the corner of Pine and 2nd Avenue, you can head three blocks **4** south on 2nd to the **Seattle Art Museum.** The five-story building, completed in 1991, was designed by postmodern theorist Robert Venturi and is a work of art in itself. The building features a limestone exterior with large-scale vertical fluting, accented by terra-cotta, cut granite, and marble. The museum displays an extensive collection of Asian, Native American, African, Oceanic, and pre-Columbian art and has a café and gift shop. *1320 2nd Ave., ☎ 206/625–8900. ☛ $6 adults, $4 senior citizens and students, free for children under 12 and 1st Tues. of month. ⊙ Tues.–Sun. 10–5 (Thurs. until 9); call for tour schedule.*

★ ❺ From 2nd Avenue, you can go west on Pine or Pike streets to the **Pike Place Historical District,** home of the **Pike Place Market,** a Seattle institution. It began in 1907 when the city issued permits to farmers allowing them to sell produce from their wagons parked at Pike Place. Later the city built stalls that were allotted to the farmers on a daily basis. At one time the market was a madhouse of vendors hawking their produce, haggling over prices; some of the fishmongers still carry on this kind of frenzied banter, but chances are you won't get them to waver on their prices. Urban renewal almost killed the market, but city voters, led by the late architect Victor Steinbreuck, rallied and voted it a historical asset. Many of the buildings have been restored, and the project is now connected to the waterfront by stairs and elevators. Besides a number of restaurants, you'll find booths selling fresh seafood—which can be packed in dry ice for your flight home—produce, cheese, Northwest wines, bulk spices, tea, coffee, and arts and crafts. *Pike Place, between Pike and Pine Sts., ☎ 206/682–7453. ⊙ Mon.–Sat. 9–6, Sun. 11–5.*

TIME OUT If the weather is nice, gather a picnic of market foods—fresh fruit and smoked salmon, of course, but soups, sandwiches, pastries, and various ethnic snacks are also available in the market or from the small shops facing it along Pike Place. Carry your bounty north to just past the market buildings, where you'll find **Victor Steinbreuk Park,** a small green gem named for Pike Place's savior.

From the market, take a set of stairs or an elevator down to the waterfront. In the early days, the waterfront was the center of activity in Seattle. Today it stretches some 19 blocks, from Pier 70 (a converted warehouse with shops and restaurants) and Myrtle Edwards Park in the north, down to Pier 51 in Pioneer Square. A vintage trolley runs the length of the waterfront before turning inland and continuing on to Pioneer Square and the International District (*see below*).

❻ At the base of the Pike Street Hillclimb at Pier 59 is the **Seattle Aquarium,** showcasing Northwest marine life. The Discovery Lab offers visitors a chance to see baby barnacles, minute jellyfish, and other "invisible" creatures through high-resolution video microscopes. The Tide Pool exhibit re-creates Washington's rocky coast and sandy beaches at low tide; there's even a 6,000-gallon wave that sweeps in over the underwater life—spectators standing close by may get damp from the simulated sea spray. Sea otters and seals swim and dive in their pools, and the "State of the Sound" exhibit shows the aquatic life and ecology of Puget Sound. *Pier 59, ☎ 206/386–4320. ☛ $6.95 adults, $5.50 senior citizens, $4.50 children 6–18, $2.25 children 3–5; call for group rates. ⊙ Daily 10–5, 10–8 in summer.*

❼ Next to the aquarium is the **Omnidome Film Experience,** where short films on such subjects as the eruption of Mt. St. Helens, mountain gorillas, and the Great Barrier Reef play on a large curved screen. *Pier 59, ☎ 206/622–1868. ☛ $6 adults, $5 senior citizens and youths 13–18, $4 children 3–12; call for prices of combination tickets to the Omnidome and aquarium. ⊙ Daily 10–5.*

112

Kingdome, **10**

Klondike Gold Rush National Historical Park, **9**

Omnidome Film Experience, **7**

Pike Place Market, **5**

Pioneer Park, **8**

Seattle Aquarium, **6**

Seattle Art Museum, **4**

Seattle Visitor Information Center, **1**

Space Needle, **3**

Uwajimaya, **11**

Westlake Center, **2**

Wing Luke Museum, **12**

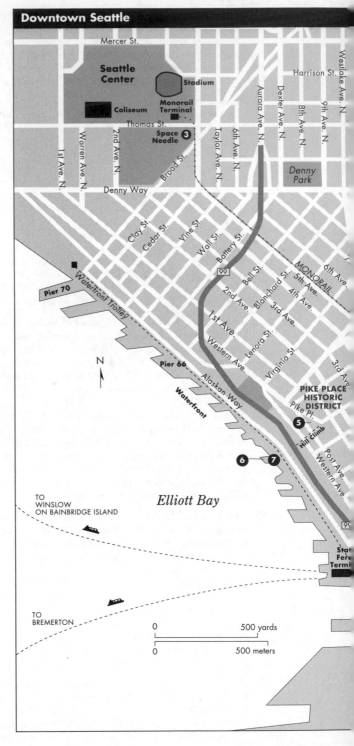

Downtown Seattle

Mercer St.

Seattle Center

Stadium

Coliseum

Monorail Terminal

Thomas St.

Space Needle ❸

Denny Way

Harrison St.

Aurora Ave. N.

Dexter Ave. N.

8th Ave. N.

9th Ave. N.

Westlake Ave. N.

Taylor Ave. N.

6th Ave. N.

Denny Park

1st Ave. N.

Warren Ave. N.

2nd Ave. N.

Broad St.

Clay St.

Cedar St.

Vine St.

Wall St.

Battery St.

99

MONORAIL

6th Ave.

5th Ave.

4th Ave.

3rd Ave.

Bell St.

Blanchard St.

2nd Ave.

1st Ave.

Western Ave.

Lenora St.

Virginia St.

3rd Ave

PIKE PLACE HISTORIC DISTRICT

Pike Pl. ❺

Post Ave.

Western Ave.

Hill Climb

Pier 70

Waterfront Trolley

Pier 66

Waterfront

Alaskan Way

❻ ❼

Elliott Bay

TO WINSLOW ON BAINBRIDGE ISLAND

TO BREMERTON

N

99

Sta Fer Termi

| 0 | | 500 yards |
| 0 | | 500 meters |

North of the aquarium, at Pier 66 along Alaskan Way, is the site of the **Odyssey Contemporary Maritime Museum,** scheduled to open in 1996–97. This new center will feature cultural and educational maritime exhibits on Puget Sound and ocean trade, and offer visitors tours of ships and boats docked nearby. The development will also include a conference center, short-stay boat basin, fish-processing and fisheries-support terminals, and a restaurant.

Catch the waterfront trolley in front of the aquarium and ride it three stops to the area now known as **Pioneer Square.** Two blocks north of the trolley line, at the corner of 1st Avenue and Yesler Way, an ornate iron-and-glass pergola stands in **Pioneer Park.** This was the site of the pier and sawmill owned by Henry Yesler, one of Seattle's first businessmen. Timber logged off the hills was sent to the sawmill on a "skid road"—now Yesler Way—made of small logs laid crossways and greased so that the freshly cut trees would slide down to the mill. The area grew into Seattle's first business center; in 1889, a fire destroyed many of the district's wood-frame buildings, but the industrious residents and businesspeople rebuilt them with brick and mortar.

With the 1897 Klondike gold rush, however, this area became populated with saloons and brothels; businesses gradually moved north, and the old pioneering area deteriorated. Eventually, only drunks and bums hung out in the neighborhood that had become known as Skid Row, and the name became synonymous with "down and out." Today's Pioneer Square encompasses about 18 blocks and includes restaurants, bars, shops, and the city's largest concentration of art galleries, but it is once again known as a hangout for those down on their luck. Incidents of crime in the neighborhood have increased lately, especially after dark.

If you'd like to know more about the city's pioneer days, visit the interpretive center of the **Klondike Gold Rush National Historical Park,** near the trolley stop on Main Street. The center provides insight into the story of Seattle's role in the 1897–98 gold rush through film presentations, permanent exhibits, and gold-panning demonstrations. *117 S. Main St., ☎ 206/553–7220. ☛ Free. ✆ Daily 9–5; closed major holidays.*

Half block east on Main Street, and two blocks south on Occidental Avenue, is the **Kingdome,** where the Seattle Seahawks NFL team and the Seattle Mariners baseball team play. The 650-foot-diameter covered stadium was built in 1976 and has the world's largest self-supporting roof, which sits 250 feet high. If you're interested in the inner workings, take the one-hour guided tour offered in summer. *201 S. King St., ☎ 206/296–3663 for information. ☛ Tour: $4 adults, $2 senior citizens and children.*

To the east is a 40-square-block area known as the **International District** (the ID), as about ⅓ of the area's residents are Chinese, one third are Filipino, and another third come from elsewhere in Asia. The ID began as a haven for Chinese workers who had immigrated to the United States to work on the Transcontinental Railroad. The community has remained largely intact despite anti-Chinese riots in Seattle during the 1880s and the internment of Japanese-Americans during World War II.

The district, which includes many Chinese, Japanese, and Korean restaurants, also houses herbalists, massage parlors, acupuncturists, and about 30 private clubs for gambling and socializing. The most notorious club is the **Wah Mee Club,** on Canton Avenue, where a multiple murder linked to gangs and gambling occurred in 1983. You'll find **Uwajimaya** (519 6th Ave. S, ☎ 206/624–6248), one of the—if not *the*—largest Japanese stores on the West Coast, on the corner of 6th Avenue South and King Street; besides housing a complete supermarket with an array of Asian foods, the store carries a wide selection of affordable china, gifts, fabrics, and housewares.

TIME OUT If you need to rest your feet a bit by now, stop in at **Okazuya** (519 6th Ave. S, ☏ 206/624–6248), the Asian snack bar in Uwajimaya. You can get noodle dishes, sushi, tempura, *humbow,* and other Asian dishes for carry-out or to eat in.

⑫ From Uwajimaya, continue east on King Street to 7th Avenue and turn left. The final stop on your downtown Seattle tour will be at the **Wing Luke Museum,** named for the first Asian person to be elected to a Seattle city office, where you'll find displays on various aspects of Asian history and culture. An acupuncture exhibit demonstrates how needles are inserted into parts of the body to release blocked energy and promote healing. Other elements of the permanent collection include costumes, fabrics, crafts, basketry, and Chinese traditional medicines. *407 7th Ave. S,* ☏ *206/623–5124.* ☛ *$2.50 adults, $1.50 senior citizens and students, 75¢ children.* ☉ *Tues.–Fri. 11–4:30, weekends noon–4.*

Tour 2: North of Downtown

Numbers in the margin correspond to points of interest on the Northern Seattle map.

North of downtown Seattle are a number of attractions that juxtapose the natural world with the urban—from landscaped gardens and a working fish ladder to a habitat zoo and a natural-history museum. From downtown follow Elliott Avenue (which runs along the waterfront from just north of Pike Place Market) north until it turns into 15th Avenue West; continue on 15th over the Ballard Bridge to Northwest Market Street. Turn left on Market and continue until it jogs to the left and turns into Northwest 54th Street.

★ ❶ Here you'll find the Hiram M. Chittenden Locks, more commonly called the **Ballard Locks,** part of the 8-mile Lake Washington Ship Canal linking lakes Washington and Union with the salt water of Shilshole Bay and Puget Sound. Completed in 1917, the locks currently service some 100,000 boats yearly by raising and lowering water levels anywhere from 6 to 26 feet. On the north side of the locks is a fine 7-acre **ornamental garden** of native and exotic plants, shrubs, and trees. Also on the north side are a staffed visitor center with displays on the history and operation of the locks and several fanciful sculptures by local artists. Along the south side is a lovely 1,200-foot promenade with a footbridge, fishing pier, and an observation deck.

Take some time to watch the fascinating progress of fishing boats and pleasure craft through the locks, then check out how the marine population makes the same journey from saltwater to fresh: The **fish ladder** has 21 levels that allow fish to swim upstream on a gradual incline. Several seaquarium-like viewing rooms run alongside the ladder below the waterline and allow visitors to watch various types of salmon and trout—an estimated half million fish yearly—struggle against the current as they migrate upstream to their spawning grounds. Most of the migration takes place from late June through October. (The fish ladder, by the way, is where various attempts are being carried out to prevent sea lions, including the locally notorious Herschel, from depleting the salmon population.) *North entrance, 3015 N.W. 54th St., Locks*

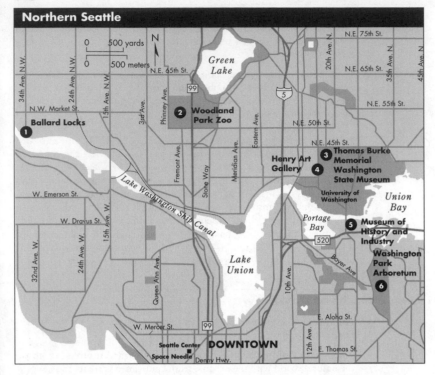

Northern Seattle

☎ 206/783–7001, visitor center ☎ 206/783–7059. ⊙ Locks: year-round, dawn–dusk; visitor center: summer, daily 10–7; winter, Thurs.–Mon. 11–5; call for info on tours.

Head back east on N.W. Market Street, past 15th Avenue Northwest, to Phinney Avenue North, and turn left. At North 55th Street, you'll find the west gate of the 92-acre **Woodland Park Zoo,** where many of the animals roam free in climate-specific habitat areas. The African savanna, the elephant house, and the tropical rain forest are particularly interesting. Wheelchairs and strollers can be rented. 5500 Phinney Ave. N, ☎ 206/684–4800. ☛ $7 adults, $5.25 senior citizens and students, $4.50 children 6–17, $2.25 children 3–5. ⊙ Summer, daily 9:30–6; winter, daily 10–4.

From the Woodland Park Zoo, follow Phinney south to North Market Street and turn left. Take Market east for 2 miles as it crosses Highway 99 (Aurora Ave. N), becomes N. 45th Street, and crosses I–5. A few blocks east of 15th Avenue Northeast is the entrance to the 33,500-student **University of Washington.** Founded in 1861, the university is familiarly known as U-Dub.

On the northwestern corner of the beautifully landscaped campus is the **Thomas Burke Memorial Washington State Museum,** Washington's natural-history and anthropological museum. The museum features exhibits on cultures of the Pacific region and the state's 35 Native American tribes. 17th Ave. NE and N.E. 45th St., ☎ 206/543–5590. ☛ Free (donation requested). ⊙ Daily 10–5 (Thurs. until 8).

Going south, on the west side of the campus is the **Henry Art Gallery,** which displays paintings from the 19th and 20th centuries, textiles, and traveling exhibits. The museum was closed at press time for remodeling and expansion, but is scheduled to reopen in early 1997. *15th Ave. NE and N.E. 41st St.,* ☎ *206/543–2280.*

⑤ South of the channel linking Portage and Union bays, off Montlake and Lake Washington boulevards, is the **Museum of History and Industry.** An 1880s-era room and a Seattle time line depict the city's earlier days. Other displays from the permanent collection are shown on a rotating basis, along with traveling exhibits. *2700 24th Ave. E,* ☎ *206/324–1125.* ☛ *$5.50 adults, $3.50 senior citizens and children 6–12.* ☉ *Daily 10–5.*

⑥ At the museum pick up a brochure of self-guided walking tours of the nearby **Washington Park Arboretum.** The arboretum's Rhododendron Glen and Azalea Way are in full bloom from March through June. During the rest of the year, other plants and wildlife flourish. A visitor center at the north end of the park is open to instruct you on the species of flora and fauna you'll see here. *2300 Arboretum Dr. E,* ☎ *206/325– 4510.* ☛ *Free.* ☉ *Park: daily 7 AM–sunset; visitor center: weekdays 10– 4, weekends noon–4.*

Bainbridge Island

The best short excursion from Seattle may be a ride on the Bainbridge Island ferry to take in great views of the city skyline and the surrounding hills. The ferry leaves from Seattle's busy downtown terminal at Colman Dock on Pier 52, south of the Pike Place Market and just north of Pioneer Square; the trip takes about a half hour each way (*see* Getting Around *in* Seattle Essentials, *below*).

While the ferry trip draws most of the island's visitors, Bainbridge itself has a pleasant small-town atmosphere and plenty of scenic countryside. Once you reach the Bainbridge Island terminal, continue north up a short hill on Olympic Drive to Winslow Way. If you turn west, you'll find yourself in **Winslow,** where there are several square blocks of interesting antiques shops, clothing boutiques, gift stores, galleries, bookstores, restaurants, and other services.

If you pass the Winslow Way turn off and go about a ¼-mile farther north on Olympic you'll find the **Bainbridge Island Vineyard and Winery** (682 S.R. 305, ☎ 206/842–9463), which is open for tastings and tours Wednesday–Sunday noon–5.

Bloedel Reserve, the 150-acre estate of Vancouver, B.C. lumber baron Prentice Bloedel, was opened to the public in 1988. The grounds were designed to recapture the natural, untamed look of the island. Within the park are ponds with ducks and trumpeter swans, Bloedel's grand mansion, and 2 miles of trails. In spring the displays of blooming rhododendrons and azaleas are dazzling, and in fall the leaves of the Japanese maples and other trees colorfully signal the change of seasons. *7571 N.E. Dolphin Dr., Bainbridge Island 98110,* ☎ *206/842– 7631.* ☛ *$6, $4 senior citizens, children under 5 free. Reservations necessary.* ☉ *Wed.–Sun. 10–4.*

On the Trail of Ale

A visit to a brew pub—as drinking establishments attached to actual breweries are called—is a congenial and educational alternative to usual city attractions. Seattle, as well as a good portion of the Pacific Northwest, has become a hotbed for microbrews, high-quality beers made for local distribution. All the pubs listed below also serve food and nonalcoholic beverages. If live music is performed, a cover charge may be required; otherwise admission is free.

The **Pacific Northwest Brewing Co.**, located in the heart of Pioneer Square, offers six mild beers that reflect the taste of its British owner. The elegantly decorated interior—a smooth high-tech design, with antiques and brewing equipment in full view—fits not only the personality of proprietor Richard Wrigley, but the upscale downtown location as well. *322 Occidental Ave. S, ☎ 206/621–7002. ⊘ Tues.–Fri. 11:30 AM–midnight, Sat. 10:30–2 AM, Sun. 11 AM–9 PM.*

The **Trolleyman,** found near the north end of the Fremont Bridge, 8 miles from downtown, is the birthplace of local favorites Ballard Bitter and Red Hook Ale. The pub mixes Northwest style—whitewashed walls and a no-smoking policy—with a cozy atmosphere that includes a fireplace and ample armchairs. Redhook Brewery is right next door—take a 45-minute tour for $1 before you pop in for a pint. *3400 Phinney Ave. N, ☎ 206/548–8000. ⊘ Mon.–Thurs. 8:30 AM–11 PM, Fri. 8:30 AM–midnight, Sat. 11 AM–midnight, Sun. noon–7; call for tour times.*

Big Time Brewery caters to the nearby university crowd and resembles an archetypal college-town pub, what with a moose head on the wall and bits of vintage memorabilia scattered about. Pale ale, amber, and porter are always on tap; specialty brews change monthly. *4133 University Way NE, ☎ 206/545–4509. ⊘ Daily 11:30 AM–1 AM.*

While technically not a brew pub, **Cooper's Northwest Alehouse,** located north of the University District, nonetheless deserves mention for featuring the products of so many regional microbreweries. Its stock of more than 20 brews come from all over the West Coast, and the staff is incredibly knowledgeable about the subtle distinctions between each brew. If you don't come for the drink, come for the dart tournaments that are played on a regular basis. *8065 Lake City Way NE, ☎ 206/522–2923. ⊘ Weekdays 3 PM–2 AM, Sat. 1 PM–2 AM, Sun. 1 PM–midnight.*

Around Town: Wine, Wings, and Hallowed Ground

If your preference is for the grape, not the hop, visit **Ste. Michelle Winery,** one of the oldest wineries in the state. It's located 15 miles northeast of Seattle, nestled on 87 wooded acres that were once part of the estate of lumber baron Fred Stimson. Some of the original 1912 buildings are still on the property, including the family home—the manor house—which is on the National Register of Historic Places. Trout ponds, a carriage house, a caretaker's cottage, and formal gardens are part of the original estate. The landscaping, created by New York's Olmsted family (designers of New York City's Central Park), has been restored, and the gardens feature hundreds of trees, shrubs, and plants. Visitors are invited to picnic and explore the grounds. Delicatessen items, wines, and wine-related gifts are available at the winery shop. In the summer, the company hosts a series of nationally known performers and arts events in the amphitheater. *14111 N.E. 145th St., Woodinville, ☎ 206/488–1133. From downtown Seattle take I–90 east, then go north on I–405. Take Exit 23 east (S.R. 522) to the Woodinville exit. Complimentary wine tastings and cellar tours available daily 10–4:30, except holidays.*

Pilot your way to **Boeing Field** for a fascinating look at the world of aviation. As Boeing, the world's largest builder of airplanes, is based in Seattle, it's not surprising that the **Museum of Flight** is one of the city's best museums. The Red Barn, Boeing's original airplane factory, houses an exhibit on the history of human flight. The Great Gallery, a dramatic structure designed by Seattle architect Ibsen Nelson, contains more than 20 vintage airplanes—suspended from the ceiling and on the ground—dating from the Wright brothers to the jet era. *9404 E. Marginal Way S (take I–5 south to exit 158; turn right on Marginal),* ☏ *206/764–5720.* ☛ *Museum: $6 adults and senior citizens, $3 children 6–15.* ⊙ *Daily 10–5 (Thurs. until 9).*

Two legendary performers—rock guitarist Jimi Hendrix and kung-fu movie star Bruce Lee—are buried in the Seattle area. Their graves are popular sites with fans who wish to pay their respects. In addition, there is a memorial to Hendrix, a Seattle native, overlooking the African Savannah exhibit at Woodland Park Zoo; appropriately enough, it's a big rock.

Jimi Hendrix's grave site is at the Greenwood Cemetery, in Renton. *From Seattle, take I–5 south to Renton exit, then I–405 past Southcenter to Exit 4B. Bear right under freeway, take right along Sunset Blvd. 1 block and right again up 3rd St. Continue 1 mi and go right at 3rd light; cemetery is on the corner of 3rd and Monroe Sts.,* ☏ *206/ 255–1511.* ⊙ *Daily until dusk. Inquire at the office; a counselor will direct you to the site.*

Bruce Lee's grave site is at the Lakeview Cemetery on the north slope of Capitol Hill. *1554 15th Ave. E, directly north of Volunteer Park,* ☏ *206/322–1582.* ⊙ *Weekdays 9–4:30. Inquire at the office for a map.*

What to See and Do with Children

Burke-Gilman Trail (*see* Sports and the Outdoors, *below*) offers good bike trails for children.

Elliott Bay Book Company (*see* Books *in* Shopping, *below*) hosts a children's story hour at 11 AM on the first Saturday of the month.

Green Lake (*see* Sports and the Outdoors, *below*).

Museum of Flight (*see* Around Town *in* Exploring, *above*).

Myrtle Edwards Park (*see* Sports and the Outdoors, *below*).

Seattle Aquarium (*see* Tour 1 *in* Exploring, *above*).

Seattle Children's Museum has tripled its colorful, spacious facility at the Seattle Center's Center House. A global village introduces children to everything from housing and shops to cooking pots and clothing from areas of Ghana, Japan, and the Philippines. The mountain wilderness poking up through one level of the museum educates kids about climbing, camping, and the Northwest environment and features a slide and waterfall. Cog City is a giant maze of pipes and pulleys. The pretend neighborhood provides a post office, café, fire station, grocery store, and more for imaginative play. An infant/toddler area is well padded for climbing and sliding. A large arts-and-crafts area, special exhibits, and workshops are also offered. *Fountain level of Seattle Center House, 305 Harrison St.,* ☏ *206/441–1768.* ☛ *$3.50 adults and children.* ⊙ *Tues.–Sun. 10–5.*

Seattle Children's Theatre performs in the $10 million Charlotte Martin Theatre, which opened in the fall of 1993, and the more intimate 280-seat Eve Alvord Theatre, which opened in 1995. SCT, the second-largest resident, professional children's theater company in the United States, has developed a national reputation for its high-quality and innovative productions and has commissioned more than 55 new plays, adaptations, and musicals, many of which have gone on to be produced by theater companies across the nation. Their season runs September–June. *Charlotte Martin Theatre at Seattle Center, Box 9640, 2nd Ave. N and Thomas St.,* ☎ *206/441–3322.*

Thomas Burke Memorial Washington State Museum (*see* Tour 2 *in* Exploring, *above*).

SHOPPING

Shopping Districts

Broadway Avenue (between E. Roy and E. Pine Sts.) in the Capitol Hill neighborhood is lined with clothing stores selling new and vintage threads, high-design housewares shops, espresso bars, and restaurants. Look for the brass dance steps inlaid on the street corners.

Fremont Avenue, around its intersection with North 35th Street, north of the ship canal and the Fremont Bridge, offers products of a used and funky variety. At Armadillo & Co. (3510 Fremont Pl. N, ☎ 206/633–4241), you'll find jewelry, T-shirts, and other armadillo-theme accessories and gifts. The Daily Planet (3416 Fremont Ave. N, ☎ 206/633–0895) carries vintage everything—jewelry, furniture, clothing, rugs, and so on. Dusty Strings (3406 Fremont Ave. N, ☎ 206/634–1656) is a hammered dulcimer shop. The Frank & Dunya Gallery (3418 Fremont Ave. N, ☎ 206/547–6760) features unique art pieces, from furniture to jewelry. Guess Where (615 N. 35th St., ☎ 206/547–3793) stocks vintage men's and women's clothing and antiques.

Pike Place Market (*see* Tour 1 *in* Exploring, *above*).

University Way Northeast, called "the Ave" between Northeast 41st and Northeast 50th streets in the University District, has a few upscale shops, many bookstores, and an eclectic mixture of such student-oriented imports as ethnic jewelry and South American sweaters.

Malls and Shopping Centers

Bellevue Square, an upscale shopping center about 8 miles east of Seattle, houses more than 200 shops and includes a children's play area, the Bellevue Art Museum, and covered parking. *N.E. 8th St. and Bellevue Way,* ☎ *206/454–8096.* ⊘ *Mon.–Sat. 9:30–9:30, Sun. 11–6.*

Northgate Mall, 10 miles north of downtown, encompasses 118 shops, including Nordstrom's, The Bon, Lamonts, and JCPenney. *I–5 and Northgate Way,* ☎ *206/362–4777.* ⊘ *Mon.–Sat. 9:30–9:30, Sun. 11–6.*

Southcenter Mall contains 140 shops and is anchored by major department stores. *I–5 and I–405 in Tukwila,* ☎ *206/246–7400.* ⊘ *Mon.–Sat. 9:30–9:30, Sun. 11–6.*

Westlake Center lies in the middle of downtown Seattle. The three-story steel-and-glass building contains 80 upscale shops, as well as covered walkways to Seattle's two major department stores, Nordstrom's and The Bon. *1601 5th Ave.,* ☎ *206/467–1600.* ⊘ *Weekdays 9:30–9, Sat. 9:30–8, Sun. 11–6.*

Specialty Shops

Antiques
Antique Importers (640 Alaskan Way, ☎ 206/628–8905), a large warehouselike structure, carries mostly English oak and Victorian pine antiques.

Art Dealers
Michael Pierce Gallery (600 Pine St., ☎ 206/447–9166) specializes in limited-edition prints, oil paintings and paintings on paper.

Art Glass
The **Glass House** (311 Occidental Ave. S, ☎ 206/682–9939), Seattle's only working glass studio open for public viewing, features one of the largest displays of glass artwork in the city.

Books and Maps
The **Elliott Bay Book Company** (101 S. Main St., at 1st Ave. in Pioneer Sq., ☎ 206/624–6600), besides boasting a comprehensive selection of titles, hosts lectures and readings by authors of local and international acclaim. Most such events are free, but phone ahead to be sure.
M. Coy Books (117 Pine St., between 1st and 2nd Aves., ☎ 206/623–5354), in the heart of downtown, carries a large selection of contemporary literature and has a small espresso bar to boot.
Metsker Maps (702 1st Ave., ☎ 206/623–8747), on the edge of Pioneer Square, has a range of regional maps.
Wide World Books and Maps (1911 N. 45th St., ☎ 206/634–3453), north of downtown and west of the university in the Wallingford neighborhood, carries travel books and the city's best selection of maps.

Chocolates
Cafe Dilettante (416 Broadway Ave. E, ☎ 206/329–6463) is well-known for its mouthwatering dark chocolates. Recipes come via Julius Rudolf Franzen, who obtained them from the kitchen of the imperial court of Russia when he was commissioned by Czar Nicholas II as master pastry chef. Franzen emigrated to the United States where he passed his recipes on to the grandfather of Cafe Dilettante's owner.

Clothing
Boutique Europa (1015 1st Ave., ☎ 206/624–5582) features sophisticated women's apparel from Europe.
Littler's (Rainier Sq., ☎ 206/223–1331) offers classic fashions for women.
Local Brilliance (1535 1st Ave., ☎ 206/343–5864) showcases fashions from local designers.
Mario's (1513 6th Ave., ☎ 206/223–1461) offers a wide selection of contemporary menswear.

Crafts
Flying Shuttle Ltd. (607 1st Ave., ☎ 206/343–9762) displays handcrafted jewelry, whimsical folk art, hand knits, and handwoven garments.
Pike Place Market (*see* Tour 1 *in* Exploring, *above*).

Jewelry
Fireworks Gallery (210 1st Ave. S, ☎ 206/682–8707; 400 Pine St., ☎ 206/682–6462) features whimsical earrings and pins.

Leather and Luggage
Bergman Luggage Co. (1930 3rd Ave., ☎ 206/448–3000) carries luggage in a variety of prices and materials.

Outdoor Wear and Equipment

Eddie Bauer (5th Ave. and Union St., ☎ 206/622–2766) features sports and outdoor apparel.

Recreational Equipment, Inc. (1525 11th Ave., between E. Pike and E. Pine Sts., ☎ 206/323–8333)—which everybody calls REI—sells clothing and such outdoor equipment as water bottles, tents, bikes, and freeze-dried food in a creaky, funky building on Capitol Hill; they also rent camping and climbing gear.

Toys

Great Windup (Pike Place Market, ☎ 206/621–9370) carries all sorts of windup action toys.

Magic Mouse Toys (603 1st Ave., ☎ 206/682–8097) has two floors of toys, from small windups to giant stuffed animals.

Wine

Delaurenti Wine Shop (1435 1st Ave., ☎ 206/340–1498) has a knowledgeable staff and a large selection of Northwest Italian–style wines.

Pike & Western Wine Merchants (Pike Pl. and Virginia St., ☎ 206/441–1307 or 206/441–1308) carries a wide selection of Northwest wines from small wineries.

SPORTS AND THE OUTDOORS

Participant Sports

"The best things in life are free" is a homily that holds true, at least in part, when it comes to keeping fit in this most health-oriented of cities. Walking, bicycling, hiking, and jogging require little money; pay-as-you-go alternatives such as golf, kayak, sailboat, or sailboard rentals require only marginally more.

REI (1525 11th Ave., ☎ 206/323–8333), the largest consumer co-op in the United States and Seattle's outdoor-equipment store *ne plus ultra,* hosts free programs on travel, adventure, and outdoor activities every Thursday at 7 PM. Various suburban locations have programs on other nights; call the main branch for times and details.

Bicycling

Although much of Seattle is so hilly that recreational bicycling is strenuous, many residents nonetheless commute by bike. The trail circling **Green Lake** and the **Burke-Gilman Trail** are popular among recreational bicyclists, although at Green Lake the crowds of joggers and walkers tend to impede fast travel. The Burke-Gilman Trail is a city-maintained trail extending 12.1 miles along Seattle's waterfront from Lake Washington nearly to Salmon Bay along an abandoned railroad line; it is a much less congested path. **Myrtle Edwards Park,** north of Pier 70, has a two-lane path for jogging and bicycling. For general information about Seattle's parks and trails, call the Seattle Parks Department (☎ 206/684–4075).

A number of shops around Seattle rent mountain bikes as well as standard touring or racing bikes and equipment. Among them are **Greg's Greenlake Cycle** (7007 Woodlawn Ave. NE, ☎ 206/523–1822) and **Mountain Bike Specialists** (5625 University Way NE, ☎ 206/527–4310).

Boating and Sailboarding

With so much water, it stands to reason that sailboating and power-boating are popular in Seattle. **Sailboat Rentals & Yachts** (301 N. Northlake Way, ☎ 206/632–3302), on the north side of Lake Union near the Fremont area, rents sailboats, with or without skippers, 14–

38 feet in length, by the hour or the day. **Seacrest Boat House** (1660 Harbor Ave. SW, ☎ 206/932–1050), in West Seattle, rents 18-foot aluminum fishing boats, with or without motors, by the hour or the day. **Wind Works Rentals** (7001 Seaview Ave. NW, ☎ 206/784–9386), on Shilshole Bay, rents sailboats ranging from 27 to 42 feet on the more challenging waters of Puget Sound, with or without skippers and by the half day, day, or week. Lake Union and Green Lake are Seattle's prime sailboarding spots. Sailboards can be rented year-round at **Urban Surf** (2100 N. Northlake Way, ☎ 206/545–9463) on Lake Union. Lessons are available.

Fishing

There are plenty of good spots for fishing on Lake Washington, Green Lake, and Lake Union, and there are several fishing piers along the Elliott Bay waterfront. A number of companies operating from Shilshole Bay also offer charter trips for catching salmon, rock cod, flounder, and sea bass. A couple of the many Seattle-based charter companies are **Ballard Salmon Charter** (☎ 206/789–6202) and **Argosy** (☎ 206/623–4253). A two-day fishing license costs $3.50, and some charter companies include it in their charges.

Golf

There are almost 50 public golf courses in the Seattle area. Among the most popular municipally run courses are **Jackson Park** (1000 N.E. 135th St., ☎ 206/363–4747) and **Jefferson Park** (4101 Beacon Ave. S, ☎ 206/762–4513). For more information, contact the **Seattle Parks and Recreation Department** (☎ 206/684–4075).

Jogging, Skating, and Walking

Green Lake is far and away Seattle's most popular spot for jogging, and the 3-mile circumference of this picturesque lake is custom-made for it. Walking, bicycling, roller-skating, fishing, and lounging on the grass and feeding the plentiful waterfowl are also popular pastimes here. In summer, a large children's wading pool on the northeast side of the lake is a popular gathering spot. Several outlets clustered along the east side of the lake offer skate and cycle rentals.

Other good jogging locales are along the **Burke-Gilman Trail,** around the reservoir at **Volunteer Park,** and at **Myrtle Edwards Park,** north of the waterfront.

Kayaking

Kayaking—around both the inner waterways (Lake Union, Lake Washington, the Ship Canal) and open water (Elliott Bay)—is a terrific and easy way to get an unusual view of Seattle's busy waterfront. The **Northwest Outdoor Center** (2100 Westlake Ave. N, ☎ 206/281–9694), on the west side of Lake Union, rents one-or two-person kayaks and equipment by the hour or week and provides both basic and advanced instruction. Canoes and rowing shells are also available.

Skiing

Snoqualmie Pass in the Cascade Mountains, about an hour's drive east of Seattle on I–90, has a number of fine resorts offering both day and night downhill skiing. Among them: **Alpental, Ski Acres, Snoqualmie Summit** (for all areas: 3010 77th St. SE, Mercer Island 98040, ☎ 206/232–8182). All these areas rent equipment and have full restaurant and lodge facilities.

For ski reports for these areas and the more distant White Pass, Crystal Mountain, and Stevens Pass, call ☎ 206/634–0200 or ☎ 206/634–

2754. For recorded messages about road conditions in the passes, call ☎ 206/455–7900.

Tennis

There are public tennis courts in many parks around the Seattle area. For information, contact the **King County Parks and Recreation Department** (☎ 206/296–4258).

Spectator Sports

Baseball

The **Seattle Mariners,** an American-league team, play April through early October at the Kingdome (201 S. King St., ☎ 206/628–3555).

Basketball

The NBA's **Seattle SuperSonics** play October through April at the Seattle Center Coliseum (1st Ave. N, ☎ 206/281–5850).

Boat Racing

The **unlimited hydroplane** (☎ 206/628–0888) races cap Seattle's Seafair festivities from mid-July through the first Sunday in August. The races are held on Lake Washington near Seward Park, and tickets cost $10–$20. Weekly **sailing regattas** are held in the summer on Lakes Union and Washington. Call the Seattle Yacht Club (☎ 206/325–1000) for schedules.

Football

Seattle's NFL team, the **Seahawks,** play August through December in the Kingdome (201 S. King St., ☎ 206/827–9777).

DINING

The abundance of fresh seafood and produce available in the Seattle area, as well as the wines and beers produced by local vineyards and microbreweries, has created a city with a deep appreciation of good food and drink. Additionally, Seattle's Pacific Rim location has resulted in a strong Asian influence on the city's cuisine—traditionally in the many Chinese and Japanese restaurants to be found in the International District and, more recently, in the innovative use of Asian ingredients and cooking techniques in kitchens throughout the city.

CATEGORY	COST*
$$$$	over $35
$$$	$25–$35
$$	$15–$25
$	under $15

per person for a three-course meal, excluding drinks, service, and sales tax (about 7.9%, varies slightly by community)

American/Continental

$$$$ **Canlis.** This sumptuous restaurant is a Seattle institution, dating as it
★ does from a time when steak served by kimono-clad waitresses was the pinnacle of high living in the city by the sound. Little has changed here since the '50s. The restaurant is still very expensive, very good at what it does, and very popular. The view across Lake Union is as good as ever (though curtained off by a forest of recently built high-rises on the far shore). Besides the famous steaks, there are equally famous oysters from Quilcene Bay and fresh fish in season, cooked to a turn. ✕ *2576 Aurora Ave. N, ☎ 206/283–3313. Reservations advised. Jacket required. AE, DC, MC, V. Closed Sun. No lunch.*

$$ Metropolitan Grill. This favorite lunch spot of the white-collar crowd serves custom-aged, mesquite-broiled steaks in a classic steak-house atmosphere. Meals here are not for timid eaters: The steaks—the best in Seattle—are huge and come with baked potatoes or pasta, and even the veal chop is extra thick. You will also find lamb, veal, chicken, and seafood entrées. Among the accompaniments, the onion rings and sautéed mushrooms are tops. ✗ *818 2nd Ave., ☎ 206/624–3287. Reservations advised. AE, DC, MC, V. No lunch weekends.*

Asian

$$ Wild Ginger. This restaurant near the Pike Place Market specializes in
★ seafood and Southeast Asian fare, ranging from mild Cantonese to spicier Vietnamese, Thai, and Korean dishes. House specialties include *satay* (chunks of beef, chicken, or vegetables skewered and grilled, and usually served with a spicy peanut sauce), live crab, sweetly flavored duck, and a variety of wonderful soups. A number of vegetarian dishes are also offered. The satay bar, where you can sip local brews and eat tangy, elegantly seasoned skewered tidbits until 2 AM, has quickly become a favorite local hangout. The clubby, old-fashioned dining room has high ceilings and is decorated with lots of mahogany and Asian art. ✗ *1400 Western Ave., ☎ 206/623–4450. Reservations advised. AE, CB, DC, MC, V. No lunch Sun.*

Chinese

$$ Linyen. This comfortable restaurant comes into its own late at night, when Seattle celebrities come to mingle with chefs from Chinatown restaurants. The standard fare is light-style Cantonese, but you're best off sticking with the blackboard specials: clams in black-bean sauce, spicy chicken, geoduck (a large local clam), and fish dishes. The dart games in the bar are a popular—and heated—diversion. ✗ *424 7th Ave. S, ☎ 206/622–8181. Reservations advised. AE, DC, MC, V.*

$ Chau's Chinese Restaurant. This small, very plain place on the outer limits of Seattle's International District serves great seafood, such as steamed oysters in garlic sauce, Dungeness crab with ginger and onion, and geoduck. Avoid the standard Cantonese dishes, and stick to the seafood and specials. ✗ *310 4th Ave. S, ☎ 206/621–0006. Reservations advised. MC, V. No lunch weekends.*

Deli

$ A. Jay's. Breakfast is the big draw here—on weekend mornings, people come in droves for the eggs Benedict, blintzes, whitefish, and bagels piled high with cream cheese and lox. At lunch there are large sandwiches (try the pastrami), pasta, burgers, and soup. Service is friendly, and you can sit and chat without being rushed. ✗ *2619 1st Ave., ☎ 206/441–1511. Reservations advised. AE, MC, V. No dinner.*

$ Three Girls Bakery. This 13-seat glassed-in lunch counter tucked behind a bakery outlet serves sandwiches, soups, and pastries to hungry folks in a hurry. Go for the chili and a hunk of Sicilian sourdough, or buy a loaf at the take-out counter, get smoked salmon at the fish place next door, and head for a picnic table in Waterfront Park. ✗ *Pike Place Market, 1514 Pike Pl., ☎ 206/622–1045. No reservations. No credit cards. Closed Sun. No dinner.*

126

Campagne, **5**
Casa-U-Betcha, **3**
Chau's Chinese Restaurant, **18**
Dahlia Lounge, **10**
Emmet Watson's Oyster Bar, **4**
Fuller's, **12**
Hunt Club, **13**
Il Terazzo Carmine, **17**
Lampreia, **2**
Linyen, **20**
Marco's Supper Club, **1**
Metropolitan Grill, **15**
Nikko, **11**
Painted Table, **14**
Place Pigalle, **8**
Saigon Gourmet, **19**
Takara, **7**
Three Girls Bakery, **6**
Trattoria Mitchelli, **16**
Wild Ginger, **9**

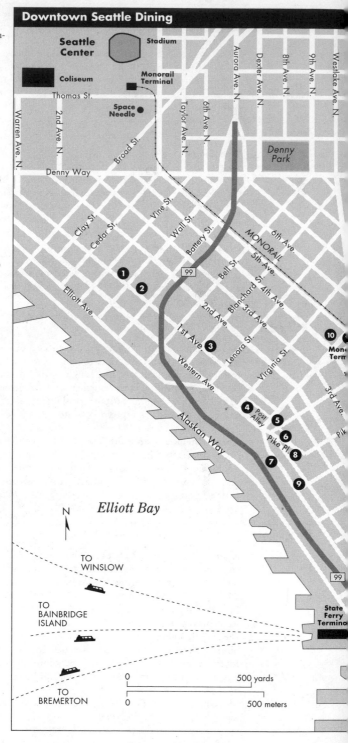

Downtown Seattle Dining

128

A. Jay's, **9**
Adriatica, **7**
Bahn Thai, **8**
Cafe Flora, **13**
Cafe Juanita, **10**
Canlis, **6**
Pirosmani, **5**
Ray's Boathouse, **1**
Raga, **11**
Rover's, **12**
Saleh Al Lago, **3**
Santa Fe Cafe, **2, 4**

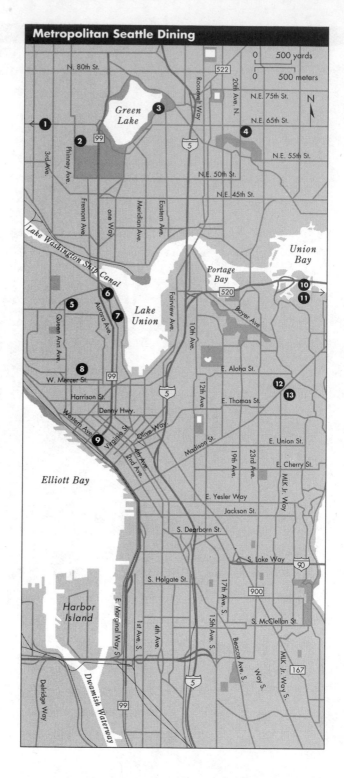

Eclectic

$$ Marco's Supper Club. Multiregional cuisine is the specialty of this one-time tavern, now a casual, fun place with shrimp-color walls and mismatched flatware. Start with the fried sage-leaf appetizer with garlic aioli and salsa, than move on to Moroccan lamb, Jamaican jerk chicken, or a drunken pork loin marinated in juniper berries and served with sautéed greens and mashed potatoes. ✗ *2510 1st Ave.,* ☎ *206/441–7801. Reservations advised. AE, MC, V. No lunch Sat.*

French

$$$ Campagne. Overlooking Pike Place Market and Elliott Bay, Cam-
★ pagne is intimate and urbane. White walls, picture windows, snowy linens, candles, and fresh flowers evoke Provence, as does the menu—French cuisine here means the robust flavors of the Midi, not the more polished tastes of Paris. Dishes traditionally flavored with cream and butter are instead sauced with vegetable essences, oils, or light stocks. To start, try Campagne's own seafood sausage or the calamari fillets with ground almonds. Main plates include such flavorful treats as pan-fried scallops with a green-peppercorn and tarragon sauce, cinnamon-roasted quail served with carrot and orange essence, and Oregon rabbit accompanied by an apricot-cider and green-peppercorn sauce. The wine list includes French country varietals not readily available at other Seattle restaurants. Campagne is open only for dinner, but the nearby Cafe Campagne serves breakfast and lunch daily. ✗ *Inn at the Market, 86 Pine St.,* ☎ *206/728–2800. Reservations advised. Jacket required. AE, MC, V. No lunch.*

$$ Rover's. This is French cooking at its best, with a daily menu based on ingredients that are fresh and locally available. Specialties include salmon, pheasant, quail, venison, and rabbit in elegant yet surprisingly light sauces. The enormous pasta dishes are among Seattle's best. Each of the dishes carries chef-owner Thierry Rautureau's Northwest-French stylings. The setting is highly romantic, in a small house with a garden and herbs and flowers growing in beds just outside the windows. Service is excellent—friendly but unobtrusive. ✗ *2808 E. Madison St.,* ☎ *206/325–7442. Reservations advised. AE, MC, V. Closed Sun.–Mon. No lunch.*

Georgian

$$–$$$ Pirosmani. Named for folk painter Niko Pirosmani, this restaurant resides in a 1906 house on Queen Anne Hill. The Georgian offerings are notable for their innovative use of herbs and lack of heavy sauces: Duck is seared, then braised with coriander and savory. Lamb is skewered; grilled with basil, garlic, and cilantro; and served with a plum sauce. Other entrées have their origins on the shores of the Mediterranean—North Africa, the south of France. The signature dessert is a walnut-date rosewater tart, but you wouldn't go wrong with the baklava-ricotta cheesecake either. ✗ *2220 Queen Anne Ave. N,* ☎ *206/285–3360. Reservations advised. AE, MC, V. Closed Sun.–Mon. No lunch.*

Indian

$$ Raga. The aromas of cardamon, cumin, and jasmine wafting through the air may make you feel like you've been transported to another continent entirely, but along with a sister restaurant, Dawat, in Vancouver, Raga offers some of the best East Indian cuisine in the Northwest. Mouthwatering dishes include *shahee panner* (cheese in a mildly spiced cream sauce) and *matar panner* (green peas with a homemade cottage cheese). Be sure to order a selection of various breads—nan, roti, *paratha, kulcha*—to accompany your meal. ✕ *555 108th Ave. NE, Bellevue,* ☎ *206/450–0336. Reservations advised. MC, V. No lunch Sun.*

Italian

$$$ Il Terrazo Carmine. On the ground floor of a Pioneer Square office building, this restaurant owes its comfortable but refined atmosphere to ceiling-to-floor draperies, genteel service, and quiet music. Chef-owner Carmine Smeraldo prepares flavorful chicken dishes with prosciutto and fontina, and his veal baked with spinach and scallops is simply excellent. The pasta dishes, too, are superb. In the summer, you can choose to eat outdoors on the patio that faces a large fountain. ✕ *411 1st Ave. S,* ☎ *206/467–7797. Reservations advised. AE, D, DC, MC, V. Closed Sun. No lunch Sat.*

$$$ Saleh Al Lago. Some of the best Italian fare in the city can be found north of downtown. The well-lit dining room here is done in soft colors and, with its view of Green Lake and the park, invites simple, slow-paced evening dining. The antipasti, fresh pasta, and veal dishes are always excellent. Be sure to try the ravioli *al mondo mio,* the chef's special ravioli (filling and sauce vary), or the tagliatelle (flat, ribboned egg pasta) with champagne and caviar. Even deceptively plain fare, like grilled breast of chicken with olive oil and fresh herbs, is superb. ✕ *6804 E. Greenlake Way N,* ☎ *206/522–7943. Reservations advised. Jacket required. AE, MC, V. Closed Sun. No lunch Sat.*

$$ Cafe Juanita. This comfortable, casual place with wonderful views is more than just a restaurant: There's a winery in the basement, and the vintages made there—bottled under owner–wine maker Peter Dow's Cavatappi label—are available upstairs. The country Italian menu is best represented by the mustard-marinated rabbit served with wild mushrooms. The veal scaloppine and chicken dishes can be a bit on the rich and buttery side, but there's plenty of inexpensive Italian wine on the lengthy list to dilute the cream. ✕ *9702 N.E. 120th Pl., Kirkland,* ☎ *206/823–1505. Reservations advised. MC, V. No lunch.*

$$ Trattoria Mitchelli. This archetypal Seattle storefront café has a bohemian atmosphere that's fast-paced and friendly, even during the wee hours of the morning—closing time isn't until 4 AM on weekends—when it can get noisy and crowded. The pasta, sandwiches, and antipasti aren't haute cuisine, but they're tasty, moderately priced, and come in generous portions. ✕ *84 Yesler Way,* ☎ *206/623–3885. No reservations. AE, DC, MC, V.*

Japanese

$$–$$$ Nikko. Given that the sushi bar is the architectural centerpiece of this restaurant's sophisticated low-light and black-lacquer decor, it's not surprising that Nikko serves some of the best sushi and sashimi in Seattle. The Kasuzuke cod and teriyaki salmon are also both highly recommended. ✕ *Westin Hotel, 1900 5th Ave.,* ☎ *206/322–4641. Reservations advised. AE, D, DC, MC, V. Closed Sun. No lunch.*

$$ Takara. In full action, the sushi chef here can look like a character from a Japanese wood-block print, perhaps a master swordsman preparing to fight heaven and earth. His real calling, however, seems to be serving up only the freshest seafood for sushi and sashimi. No wonder Japanese businessmen flock to the sushi bar for lunch. The dining room serves classic Japanese dishes using Northwest ingredients. The salmon teriyaki is superb, as is the steamed black cod. ✕ *Pike Place Market Hillclimb, 1501 Western Ave.,* ☎ *206/682–8609. Reservations advised* *for dining room, no reservations for sushi bar. AE, MC, V. Closed Sun. in winter.*

Mediterranean

$$–$$$ Adriatica. This place gathered a loyal local following, became a virtual Seattle institution, and was then discovered by visitors who spread the word. Located in a hillside Craftsman-style house, the dining room and upstairs bar offer views of Lake Union. Over several years, the fare here has evolved into a unique Pacific Northwest–influenced Greek and Italian cuisine. Regular offerings include daily fresh fish, a pasta, a risotto, and seafood souvlaki. Phyllo pastries with honey and nuts are among the tasty and interesting dessert choices. ✕ *1107 Dexter Ave. N, ☎ 206/285–5000. Reservations advised. AE, DC, MC, V.*

Mexican

$$ Casa-U-Betcha. Colorful neon signs and faux granite sculptures standing in for room dividers create a fittingly lively atmosphere for the upscale crowd and cuisine at this trendy spot. Familiar Mexican dishes are served using less grease, less cheese, and black beans rather than refried. The menu isn't too strict, though, so you'll find Caribbean and Latin American influences (south of the border here seems to mean anywhere between Texas and the equator) in such inventive offerings as Coyote Moon Carnitas—lean pork seasoned with herbs and marinated in lime juice, then grilled. ✕ *2212 1st Ave., ☎ 206/441–1989. Reservations advised. AE, DC, MC, V.*

Northwest

$$$ Fuller's. The works of northwest artists hang over the booths in this ★ dining room favored by locals for special occasions. Start with a sesame-crust tuna pizza, vegetable strudel with sun-dried tomatoes and goat cheese, or spinach salad with smoked duck and honey-mustard dressing. Move on to pork loin with an apple-brandy blue-cheese sauce or monk fish with a wild-mushroom and tomato ragout. All the dishes are enhanced by the elegant china and crystal settings atop linen tablecloths. Chef Monique Andree Barbeau specializes in low-fat sauces made from vegetable purees and natural reductions, but you'll forget all about that when you see the wonderfully decadent desserts. ✕ *1400 6th Ave. (in the Seattle Sheraton, at Pike St.), ☎ 206/447–5544 or 800/325–3535. Reservations advised. Jacket required. AE, D, DC, MC, V. Closed Sun. No lunch Sat.*

$$$ Hunt Club. A combination of dark wood and plush seating provides a comfortable if surprisingly traditional setting for Chef Eric Leonard's innovative interpretations of Pacific Northwest meat and seafood. Potato pancakes with caviar or the squash ravioli are excellent starters. Entrées on the seasonal menu include swordfish with an almond-herb crust, pork chops stuffed with artichokes and sun-dried tomatoes, and roast venison sauced with a peppercorn and cranberry game-based demi-glace and served with candied yams. ✕ *Sorrento Hotel, 900 Madison St., ☎ 206/622–6400. Reservations advised. Jacket required. AE, DC, MC, V.*

$$$ Lampreia. The subtle beige-and-gold interior of this Belltown restaurant is the perfect backdrop for owner and chef Scott Carsberg's sophisticated cuisine. After an appetizer of cream of polenta with shiitake mushrooms, try one of the seasonal menu's intermezzo or light main courses (how about squid and cannelloni filled with salmon) or a full entrée such as pheasant with apple-champagne sauerkraut or lamb with pesto and whipped potatoes. The clear flavors of the desserts, such as lemon mousse with strawberry sauce, bring a soothing conclusion to an exciting food experience. ✕ *2400 1st Ave.,* ☎ *206/443–3301. Reservations advised. AE, DC, MC, V. No lunch.*

$$–$$$ **Painted Table.** The sand-color walls and warm mahogany paneling in
★ this sophisticated dining room at the Alexis Hotel provide an elegant backdrop for the room's displays of works by local artists. Meals are equally appealing: Chef Tim Kelly selects from the freshest regional produce available from nearby small vendors, farms, and the Pike Place Market. The resulting vegetable and seafood dishes are attractively presented, framed by hand-painted plates. The seasonal menu features such entrées as herbed prawns with linguine and shiitake mushrooms or herb-crusted lamb with grilled Japanese eggplant, fennel, and polenta. Desserts include a frozen banana soufflé and a jasmine-rice custard made with coconut milk. ✕ *Alexis Hotel, 1007 1st Ave.,* ☎ *206/624–3646. Reservations advised. AE, D, DC, MC, V. No lunch weekends.*

$$ **Dahlia Lounge.** This place feels cozy and romantic at night with low light on the dark red walls. Owner Tom Douglas is credited with introducing Seattle to crab cakes, and his reputation for fine food has only taken off from there. In addition to the famed crab concoctions, served as an entrée or appetizer, the ever-changing menu offers the best of the Northwest's bounty. Vegetarians and other lovers of produce shouldn't miss the apple-onion tart or the corn tamale served with green rice and grilled vegetables. Desserts, such as coconut cream pie and fresh cobblers, are scrumptious. At press time, Douglas had just opened Etta's Seafood Restaurant in the Pike Place Market. ✕ *1404 4th Ave.,* ☎ *206/ 682–4142. Reservations advised. MC, V. No lunch weekends.*

$$ **Place Pigalle.** Large windows look out over Elliott Bay from this intimate restaurant tucked behind a meat market in the Pike Place Market's main arcade; in nice weather, they're left ajar to admit the fresh salt breeze. Bright flower bouquets lighten up the café tables, and the friendly staff makes you feel right at home. Despite its French name, this is a very American restaurant and a popular place with locals. Seasonal meals feature seafood and regional ingredients. Go for the rich oyster stew, the fresh Dungeness crab (available only when it is truly fresh), or the fish of the day baked in hazelnuts. ✕ *Pike Place Market,* ☎ *206/624–1756. Reservations advised. MC, V. Closed Sun.*

Seafood

$$ **Ray's Boathouse.** The view of Puget Sound may be the drawing card
★ here, but the seafood is impeccably fresh and well prepared. Perennial favorites include broiled salmon, kasu sake cod, teriyaki salmon fillets, blackened cod, and oysters prepared almost any way you could want them. Ray's has a split personality: There's a fancy dining room downstairs and a casual café and bar upstairs. Go for the café; the prices are lower and the food is just as good. In warm weather, sit on the deck outside the café and watch a continuous parade of fishing and pilot boats, tugs, and pleasure yachts floating past, almost right below your table. ✕ *6049 Seaview Ave. NE,* ☎ *206/789–3770. Reservations advised for window seats in dining room; no reservations for café. AE, DC, MC, V.*

$ **Emmet Watson's Oyster Bar.** This unpretentious spot can be a bit hard to find—it's in the back of the Pike Place Market's Soames-Dunn Building, facing a small flower-bedecked courtyard—but for Seattleites (and discerning visitors) who know their oysters, it's worth the special effort. Not only are the oysters very fresh and the beer icy cold, but both are inexpensive and available in any number of varieties. If you don't like oysters, try the salmon soup or the fish-and-chips (large flaky pieces of fish with very little grease). ✗ *Pike Place Market, 1916 Pike Pl.,* ☎ *206/448–7721. No reservations. No credit cards. Closed Sun.*

Southwest

$$ **Santa Fe Cafe.** Visitors from New Mexico say that this is about as au-
★ thentic as southwestern fare gets—maybe because that's where the restaurant buys the red and green chilies for its sauces. Interesting brews on tap help mitigate the heat of such delicious dishes as spicy green-chili burritos made with blue-corn tortillas. Other choices are less *picante,* but still flavorful. Try the red or green enchiladas or house specialties like the artichoke ramekin, chili-relleno torte, and roasted-garlic appe-tizer. Of the two locations, the 65th Street restaurant offers a cozier, homey appeal, with its woven rugs and dried flowers, and is popular with grad-uate students and professors. The Phinney Avenue location is slicker and more chic; skylights fill the place with light that brightens the soft pink-and-mauve color scheme. ✗ *2255 N.E. 65th St.,* ☎ *206/524–7736; no lunch Sat.–Mon. 5910 Phinney Ave. N,* ☎ *206/783–9755; lunch Sat. only. Reservations advised at both. MC, V.*

Thai

$ **Bahn Thai.** Thai cooking is ubiquitous in Seattle—it can almost be con-sidered a mainstream cuisine. Because of the variety of dishes and the quality of the preparations, the Bahn Thai, one of the pioneers of local Thai food, is still one of the best and most popular. Start your meal with a skewer of tangy chicken or pork satay, or with the *tod mun goong* (spicy fish cake), and continue with hot-and-sour soup and one of the many prawn or fish dishes. The deep-fried fish with garlic sauce is particularly good—and you can order it very hot. This restaurant promises a relaxed, romantic atmosphere in the evenings. ✗ *409 Roy St.,* ☎ *206/283–0444. Reservations advised. AE, DC, MC, V. No lunch weekends.*

Vegetarian

$–$$ **Cafe Flora.** This lovely place in Madison Valley is attracting vegetari-ans and meat eaters alike for artistically presented, full-flavored meals. The menu includes a portobella mushroom Wellington, a Mediterranean plate, and a four-onion pizza, as well as great salads. ✗ *2901 E. Madi-son St.,* ☎ *206/325–9100. Reservations advised. MC, V. Closed Mon. No dinner Sun.*

Vietnamese

$ **Saigon Gourmet.** This small café in the International District is about
★ as plain as it gets, but the food is superb. Aficionados make special trips for the Cambodian soup and the shrimp rolls. The peanut dip-ping sauce is more flavorful than usual. Do try the papaya with beef jerky—it's unusual but enjoyable. The prices are incredibly low, just one reason why this is one of the best lunch places in town. Parking, however, can be a problem. ✗ *502 S. King St.,* ☎ *206/624–2611. No reservations. MC, V. Closed Mon.*

LODGING

There is no shortage of lodging in Seattle. The variety ranges from the elegant deluxe hotels of downtown to the smaller, less expensive ho-tels in the University District; from a number of budget motels along Aurora Avenue North (Highway 99), many of which are legacies of the 1962 World's Fair, to the large, standard hotels strung along Pacific Highway South (also Highway 99) that accommodate travelers near Seattle-Tacoma International Airport. Always inquire about special rates based on occupancy, weekend stays, or special packages.

A number of bed-and-breakfast accommodations are also available. For more information, contact the **Washington State Bed-and-Breakfast Guild** (2442 N.W. Market St., Seattle 98107, ☎ 800/647–2918) or the **Pacific Bed & Breakfast Agency** (701 N.W. 60th St., Seattle 98107, ☎ 206/784–0539).

CATEGORY	COST*
$$$$	over $170
$$$	$110–$170
$$	$60–$110
$	under $60

All prices are for a standard double room, excluding 14.1% combined hotel and state sales tax

Downtown Seattle

$$$$ ★ **Alexis.** The Alexis is an intimate four-story, European-style hotel in an artfully restored historic 1901 building on 1st Avenue near the waterfront, the Public Market, and the Seattle Art Museum. Guests are greeted with complimentary sherry at this understated and elegant hotel. The rooms are decorated in subdued colors, with at least one piece of antique furniture in each. Some suites feature hot tubs, wood-burning fireplaces, and some have marble fixtures. Unfortunately, none of the rooms have any kind of view, and those facing the avenue can be noisy. Amenities include complimentary Continental breakfast, shoe shines, morning newspaper, and access to workout facilities and private steam room. The Painted Table restaurant is on the hotel's ground floor (*see* Dining, *above*). ▦ 1007 1st Ave., 98104, ☎ 206/624–4844 or 800/426–7033, ℻ 206/621–9009. 54 rooms. Restaurant, bar, café. AE, MC, V.

$$$$ ★ **Four Seasons Olympic Hotel.** The Olympic is Seattle's most elegant hotel. In 1982, Four Seasons restored it to its 1920s Renaissance Revival–style grandeur, with the public rooms appointed with marble, wood paneling, potted plants, and thick rugs, and furnished with plush armchairs. Palms and skylights in the Garden Court provide a relaxing background for lunch, afternoon tea, or dancing to a live swing band on the weekends. The Georgian Room, the hotel's premier dining room, exudes Italian Renaissance elegance, while Shuckers oyster bar is more casual. Guest rooms are less luxurious than the public rooms and have a homey feel. They are furnished with sofas, comfortable reading chairs, and desks and decorated with period reproductions and floral print fabrics. Amenities include valet parking, stocked bar, chocolates on your pillow, complimentary shoe shines, and a bathrobe in the room for each guest. Locals drop in occasionally to pamper themselves with a massage and swim at the health club. ▦ 411 University St., 98101, ☎ 206/621–1700 or 800/223–8772, ℻ 206/682–9633. 450 rooms. 3 restaurants, room service, indoor pool, health club. AE, DC, MC, V.

$$$$ **Hotel Vintage Park.** As a tribute to the state's growing wine industry, each guest room in this small hotel is named for a Washington winery or vineyard. The theme is extended to complimentary servings of local wines each evening in the elegant lobby, where guests can relax on richly upholstered sofas and chairs arranged around the ornate marble fireplace. The rooms, which are decorated in rich color schemes of dark green, plum, deep reds, taupe and gold, are furnished with custom-made

cherry-wood pieces. Each room also contains original works by San Francisco artist Chris Kidd. For literary-minded guests, hotel staff will check out and deliver your choice of books from the nearby Seattle Public Library. ⌧ *1100 5th Ave., 98101,* ☏ *206/624–8000 or 800/624–4433,* ☏ *206/623–0568. 129 rooms. Restaurant, no-smoking floors, room service, health club access, business services. AE, DC, MC, V.*

$$$$ Westin Hotel. This large high-rise hotel in the heart of downtown, the flagship of the Westin chain, is the preferred accommodation of such visiting dignitaries as the President. Located just north and east of the Pike Place Market, it is easily recognizable by its twin cylindrical towers. With this design, all rooms have terrific views over the waterfront and Lake Union. The rooms themselves are airy and bright, and furnished in a plain but high-quality style. A number have been turned into environmentally friendly, "green" accommodations; the children's programs, which include an interactive, kids-only radio network, are equally innovative. The informal Market Cafe, the more formal Palm Court, and Nikko, a stylish Japanese restaurant (*see* Dining, *above*), as well as three lounges, are located in-house. ⌧ *1900 5th Ave., 98101,* ☏ *206/728–1000 or 800/228–3000,* ☏ *206/728–2259. 829 rooms, 48 suites. 3 restaurants, 3 bars, no-smoking floors, room service, indoor pool, hot tub, beauty salon, massage, sauna, exercise room, children's programs, laundry service, concierge, business services, convention center, car rental. AE, D, DC, MC, V.*

$$$ Edgewater. The only hotel on Elliott Bay, the Edgewater is an institution, known for the now-defunct tradition of guests' fishing from their waterside windows. In 1988 the new owners banned hotel fishing but remodeled the 238 rooms, the results of which are magnificent. The lobby features oak furnishings and comfortable chairs and sofas, with a fireplace and a panoramic bay window from which you can sometimes see sea lions frolicking. Spacious rooms on the water provide views of ferries, barges, and the Olympic Mountains, and are decorated in rustic Northwest plaids and unfinished wood furnishings. ⌧ *Pier 67, 2411 Alaskan Way, 98121,* ☏ *206/728–7000 or 800/624–0670,* ☏ *206/441–4119. 238 rooms. Restaurant, bar. AE, DC, MC, V.*

$$$ Seattle Hilton. This Hilton is a favorite for conventions and meetings, especially because of its central location. Rooms are furnished in the same nondescript but tasteful style characteristic of Hiltons worldwide, and have soothing color schemes. One of its two restaurants, the Top of the Hilton, serves well-prepared variations of salmon steak and other local specialties, and has excellent views of the city. An underground passage connects the Hilton with a shopping concourse, Rainier Square, as well as with the 5th Avenue Theater and the Washington State Convention Center. ⌧ *1301 University St., 98101,* ☏ *206/624–0500, 800/542–7700, or 800/426–0535,* ☏ *206/682–9029. 237 rooms, 6 suites. 2 restaurants, piano bar, no-smoking floors. AE, D, DC, MC, V.*

$$$ Seattle Sheraton Hotel and Towers. The Sheraton is a modern, 840-room hotel (renovated in 1991) catering largely to conventioneers, as it is conveniently located near the Washington State Convention & Trade Center. The lobby features an art-glass collection by Dale Chihuly, a Northwest artist of international repute. The Towers (top five floors) feature larger, more elegant rooms with concierge service, and complimentary Continental breakfast. Within the complex is a diverse selection of restaurant and entertainment options, including Banners, which offers an authentic Japanese breakfast, buffet luncheon, and Continental menu; Fullers (*see* Dining, *above*), one of the best restaurants in Seattle, serving nouvelle cuisine using local ingredients; and Gooey's (named after the geoduck, a large, sausagelike northwestern clam that is the subject of many jokes), the bar-disco nighttime hot spot. ⌧ *1400 6th*

136

Alexis, **13**

Camlin Hotel, **7**

Doubletree, **22**

Edgewater, **1**

Four Seasons
Olympic Hotel, **11**

Holiday Inn
Sea-Tac, **20**

Hotel Vintage
Park, **16**

Hyatt Regency
Bellevue, **28**

Inn at the Market, **5**

Mayflower Park
Hotel, **6**

Meany Tower
Hotel, **18**

Pacific Plaza, **14**

Red Lion Bellevue, **26**

Red Lion/Sea-Tac, **21**

Seattle Airport
Hilton, **23**

Seattle Hilton, **12**

Seattle Marriott, **24**

Seattle Sheraton Hotel
and Towers, **9**

Seattle YMCA, **15**

Sixth Avenue Inn, **4**

Sorrento, **8**

Stouffer Madison
Hotel, **17**

University Plaza
Hotel, **19**

Warwick Hotel, **2**

West Coast Bellevue
Hotel, **25**

Westin Hotel, **3**

Woodmark Hotel, **27**

Youth Hostel: Seattle
International, **10**

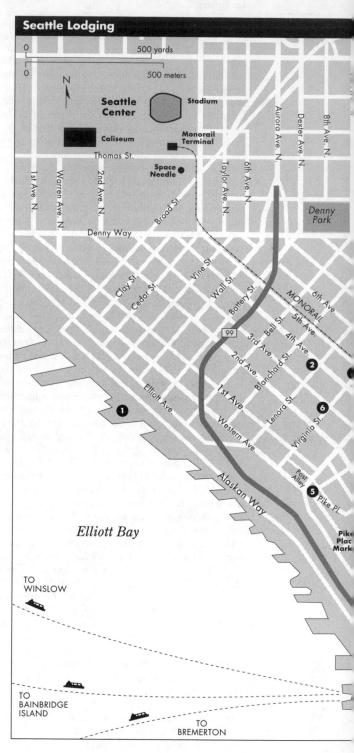

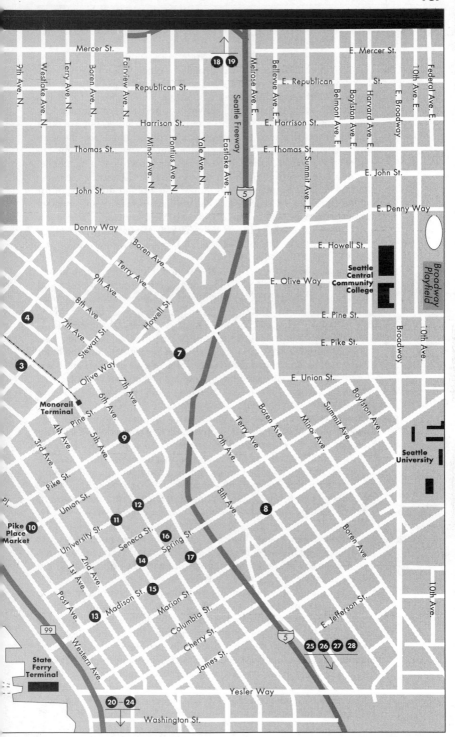

Ave., 98101, ☎ *206/621–9000 or 800/325–3535,* FAX *206/621–8441. 840 rooms. 2 restaurants, 2 bars, indoor pool, health club. AE, D, DC, MC, V.*

$$$ **Sorrento.** This deluxe European-style hotel, built in 1909 for the
★   Alaska-Yukon Exposition, was designed to look like an Italian villa. The dramatic entrance is along a circular driveway around an Italian fountain, and ringed by palm trees. Sitting high on First Hill, it has wonderful views overlooking downtown and the waterfront. The rooms are smaller than those in a more modern hotel, but are quiet and very comfortable; they're decorated in understated, elegant earth tones. The largest rooms are the corner suites, which have some antiques and spacious baths. The stylish Hunt Club (*see* Dining, *above*) restaurant features exquisite Northwest-Asian dishes, while the dark-paneled Fireside Lounge in the lobby is a warm and inviting spot for sipping coffee, tea, or a cocktail. Other amenities include a complimentary limousine service within the downtown area, concierge, and guest privileges at a nearby athletic club. ☎ *900 Madison St., 98104,* ☎ *206/622–6400,* FAX *206/625–1059. 76 rooms, 42 suites. Restaurant, bar. AE, DC, MC.*

$$$ **Stouffer Madison Hotel.** This high-rise hotel, located between downtown and I–5, was built in 1983. Rooms are decorated in peach and green tones, and come equipped with wood cabinets and marble countertops; those on the 10th floor and up have good views of downtown, Elliott Bay, and the Cascade Mountains. Views above the 20th floor are excellent. Club-level floors (25 and 26) feature their own concierge, complimentary Continental breakfast, and a library. Amenities on other floors include complimentary coffee, morning newspaper, and shoe shines. The health club includes a 40-foot rooftop pool and a Jacuzzi. ☎ *515 Madison St., 98104,* ☎ *206/583–0300 or 800/468–3571,* FAX *206/622–8635. 554 rooms. 2 restaurants, bar. AE, D, DC, MC, V.*

$$$ **Warwick Hotel.** The Warwick manages to combine its somewhat large size with intimate European-style charm. Service is friendly and leisurely (but not slow), and the rooms are understated without being bland. All rooms have small balconies and good views of downtown. There is live entertainment in the Liaison restaurant and lounge, and 24-hour courtesy transportation within downtown. ☎ *401 Lenora St., 98121,* ☎ *206/443–4300,* FAX *206/448–1662. 230 units, 4 suites. Restaurant, bar, no-smoking rooms, pool, hot tub, sauna, exercise room. AE, D, DC, MC, V.*

$$–$$$ **Inn at the Market.** This sophisticated but unpretentious hotel has a great
★   location just up the street from the Pike Place Market. It combines the best aspects of a small, French country inn with the informality of the Pacific Northwest, offering a lively setting that's perfect for travelers who prefer originality, personality, and coziness to big-hotel amenities. The rooms are spacious and tastefully decorated with comfortable modern furniture and small touches such as fresh flowers and ceramic sculptures. Ask for a room with views of the Market and Elliott Bay. An added plus is a 2,000-square-foot deck, furnished with Adirondack chairs and overlooking the water and the market. Guests also have access to a health club and spa. Three restaurants share the building: Campagne (*see* Dining, *above*); the Gravity Bar, an ultratrendy hangout with a variety of juices and coffees; and Cafe Dilettante (*see* Dining, *above*) for light meals, fine chocolates, and coffees. ☎ *86 Pine St., 98109,* ☎ *206/443–3600,* FAX *206/448–0631. 65 rooms. 3 restaurants, no-smoking rooms, room service. AE, D, DC, MC, V.*

$$–$$$ **Mayflower Park Hotel.** This pleasant older hotel, built in 1927, is conveniently connected with Westlake Center and the Monorail terminal to Seattle Center. Brass fixtures and antiques give both the public and private spaces a muted Oriental feel, and the service is similarly unobtrusive and smooth. The rooms are somewhat smallish, but the Mayflower Park is so sturdily constructed that it is much quieter than many modern downtown hotels. Guests can use a nearby health club. ☎ *405 Olive Way, 98101,* ☏ *206/623–8700,* FAX *206/382–6997. 168 rooms, 14 suites. Restaurant, bar, no-smoking rooms. AE, DC, MC, V.*

\$\$ Camlin Hotel. This 1926 Seattle apartment-hotel has a gracious lobby featuring Oriental carpets, large mirrors, and lots of marble. Located on the edge of the downtown office area, but close to the convention center, this reasonably priced hotel is popular with business travelers. Rooms ending with 10 are best because they feature windows on three sides, and all have working spaces with a chair and a table, along with cushioned chairs for relaxing. One drawback here, though, is the noisy heating, air-conditioning, and ventilation system. ☎ *1619 9th Ave., 98101,* ☏ *206/682–0100 or 800/426–0670,* FAX *206/682–7415. Restaurant, bar, pool. AE, D, DC, MC, V.*

\$\$ Pacific Plaza. Built in 1929 and refurbished in 1992, this hotel reflects its original character. The rooms and furnishings, reminiscent of the '20s and '30s, are appropriate for singles or couples but are too small to comfortably accommodate a family. Because of its downtown location and modest rates (which include a Continental breakfast), the Plaza is a good choice for anyone who is not seeking contemporary luxury. ☎ *400 Spring St., 98104,* ☏ *206/623–3900 or 800/426–1165,* FAX *206/623–2059. 160 rooms. 2 restaurants. AE, DC, MC, V.*

\$ Seattle YMCA. This accommodation has 198 units and is a member of the American Youth Hostels Association. Rooms are clean and plainly furnished with a bed, phone, desk, and lamp. Rooms cost about \$40; bunk units, designed to accommodate four people each, are about \$20. ☎ *909 4th Ave., 98104,* ☏ *206/382–5000. 198 units. Pool, health club. No credit cards.*

\$ Youth Hostel: Seattle International. Situated near the Pike Place Market is a bright, clean youth hostel with 128 dormitory-style beds for about \$20 a night. Guests can use the kitchen or eat in the dining room. ☎ *84 Union St., 98101,* ☏ *206/622–5443. 128 units. Bar, library. No credit cards.*

Seattle Center

\$\$ Meany Tower Hotel. This pleasant hotel is just a few blocks from the
★ University of Washington's campus. Built in 1931 and remodeled many times since, it has managed to retain much of its old-fashioned charm, with a muted-peach color scheme throughout, brass fixtures, and careful, attentive service. The rooms, especially those on the higher floors, have good views of the college grounds with glimpses of Green Lake and Lake Union. The Meany Grill on the ground floor serves breakfast, lunch, and dinner; there is a large street-level lounge as well. ☎ *4507 Brooklyn Ave. NE, 98105,* ☏ *206/634–2000,* FAX *206/634–2000. 55 rooms. Restaurant, bar, no-smoking rooms, room service. AE, DC, MC, V.*

\$\$ Sixth Avenue Inn. Families and business travelers patronize this small but comfortable motor hotel a few blocks north of downtown; it's also the hotel of choice for musicians playing at Dimitriou's Jazz Alley, the highly regarded club across the street. Rooms are pleasant, with wicker furnishings and standard-issue but well-maintained decor and color schemes; the service is cheerful. ☎ *2000 6th Ave., 98121,* ☏ *206/441–8300,* FAX *206/441–9903. 166 rooms. Restaurant, bar, no-smoking rooms. AE, DC, MC, V.*

$$ **University Plaza Hotel.** This is a full-service motor hotel, just across I-5 from the University of Washington's campus, making it popular with families and others who have business in the area. The mock-Tudor decor gives its lobby and other public areas a slightly outdated feel, but the service is cheerful and the rooms are spacious and pleasantly decorated in teak furniture, with pale pinks and grays being the predominant colors. The rooms on the freeway side, however, can be noisy. ☎ *400 N.E. 45th St., 98105,* ☎ *206/634–0100,* ℻ *206/633–2743. 135 rooms. Restaurant, bar, no-smoking rooms, pool, beauty salon, exercise room. AE, D, DC, MC, V.*

Seattle-Tacoma Airport

$$$ **Red Lion/Sea-Tac.** The Red Lion is a popular, hospitable 850-room, full-service convention hotel. Rooms are spacious and bright, with large panoramic balconies and decor in shades of mauve, teal, and gray. The corner "King Rooms" feature wraparound balconies and have the best views. Furnishings include chests of drawers, comfortable chairs, a dining table, and a desk. ☎ *18740 Pacific Hwy. S, 98168,* ☎ *206/ 246–8600,* ℻ *206/242–9727. 850 rooms. 2 restaurants, 2 bars, coffee shop, pool, health club. AE, D, DC, MC, V.*

$$$ **Seattle Airport Hilton.** This relatively small hotel (for a Hilton) has an intimate, original feel accentuated by the lobby's oak furnishings, cozy fireplace, and paintings of Northwest scenery. The large rooms are bright and decorated in pastel colors. This is also conveniently located only a half-hour drive from downtown and a 10-minute drive from Southcenter shopping mall. ☎ *17620 Pacific Hwy. S, 98188,* ☎ *206/244– 4800,* ℻ *206/439–7439. 173 rooms. Restaurant, bar, pool, health club, airport shuttle. AE, D, DC, MC, V.*

$$–$$$ **Doubletree Inn** and **Doubletree Suites.** These two hotels, situated across the street from each other, are adjacent to Southcenter shopping mall and convenient to the myriad business-park offices there. The inn is a classic Pacific Northwest–style lodge. Rooms are smaller and less lavish than those at the Suites, but otherwise perfectly nice and cost at least $25 less. Suites, decorated in neutrals, mauves, and pinks, feature a sofa, table and chairs, and a wet bar in the living room. The vanity area includes a full-size closet with mirrored doors. ☎ *Doubletree Inn, 205 Strander Blvd., Tukwila 98188,* ☎ *206/246–8220,* ℻ *206/575–4743. 198 rooms. Bar, coffee shop, dining room, pool. Doubletree Suites, 16500 Southcenter Pkwy., Tukwila 98188,* ☎ *206/ 575–8220,* ℻ *206/575–4743. 221 suites. Restaurant, bar, pool, hot tub, sauna, health club, racquetball. AE, D, DC, MC, V (for both).*

$$–$$$ ★ **Seattle Marriott.** A surprisingly luxurious and substantial hotel considering its nondowntown location, this Marriott features a five-story-high, 20,000-square-foot tropical atrium that's complete with waterfall, dining area, indoor pool, and lounge. The rooms are decorated in greens and mauve with dark wood and brass furnishings. Special rates are available to AAA and AARP members. ☎ *3201 S. 176th St., 98188,* ☎ *206/ 241–2000, international reservations* ☎ *800/228–9290,* ℻ *206/248– 0789. 459 rooms. Restaurant, no-smoking rooms, 2 hot tubs, health club, concierge, airport shuttle. AE, D, DC, MC, V.*

$$ **Holiday Inn Sea-Tac.** The atrium lobby of this hotel, built in 1970, has an attractive garden room that's convenient for meeting people. Most of the spacious guest rooms have been redecorated in a color scheme of mauve and peach with maroon and green accents. The Top of the Inn revolving-view restaurant features singing waiters. ☎ *17338 Pacific Hwy. S, 98188,* ☎ *206/248–1000 or 800/465–4329,* ℻ *206/242–*

7089. *260 rooms. Restaurant, bar, coffee shop, indoor pool, hot tub, health club. AE, DC, MC, V.*

Bellevue/Kirkland

$$$ **Hyatt Regency Bellevue.** This deluxe high-rise complex is in the heart of downtown Bellevue, within a few blocks of Bellevue Square and other fine shopping locales. The exterior looks pretty much like any other sleek high-rise, but the interior has such Asian touches as antique Japanese *tansu* (wood chests of drawers) and huge displays of fresh flowers. The rooms are decorated in similarly understated ways, with floor-to-ceiling windows and dark wood and earth tones predominating the color scheme. The service is impeccable. Some rooms have been specially designed for Japanese travelers. Deluxe suites include two bedrooms, bar facilities, and meeting rooms with desks and full-length tables. Guests have access to a health club and pool. The Eques restaurant serves excellent and reasonably priced breakfast, lunch, and dinner; an English-style pub serves a variety of drinks as well as lunch and dinner. 🔲 *900 Bellevue Way NE, 98004, ☎ 206/462–2626, FAX 206/646–7567. 352 rooms, 30 suites. Restaurant, pub, no-smoking rooms, room service. AE, D, DC, MC, V.*

$$$ **Red Lion Bellevue.** This 10-story hotel has a large, airy atrium filled with trees, shrubs, and flowering plants. The property also has a formal dining room, a lounge with two dance floors, and oversize guest rooms decorated in mauve and sea-foam green. Rooms have either king- or queen-size beds, and two-room suites feature wet bars and hot tubs. A new Italian restaurant, Velato's, opened here in 1993. 🔲 *300 112th Ave. SE, Bellevue 98004, ☎ 206/455–1300 or 800/274–1415, FAX 206/454–0466. 353 rooms. 2 restaurants, bar, pool, health club. AE, D, DC, MC, V.*

$$$ **Woodmark Hotel.** Only steps away from downtown Kirkland, this hotel
★ is the only one on the shores of Lake Washington. Its contemporary-style rooms face the water, courtyard, or street and are tastefully decorated in earth tones, with heavy comforters and numerous amenities such as terry-cloth bathrobes and fragrant soaps. Guests can use a nearby health club. Comfortable chairs surround the fireplace in the large, open lobby, and a circular staircase descends to the lounge, passing a huge bay window and vast view of Lake Washington. The Carillon Room restaurant offers pasta and fresh fish dishes and excellent water views. 🔲 *1200 Carillon Point, Kirkland 98033, ☎ 206/822–3700 or 800/822–3700, FAX 206/822–3699. 100 rooms. Restaurant, bar. AE, MC, V.*

$ **West Coast Bellevue Hotel.** This hotel–motor inn features a number of town-house suites, suitable for two to four people, with sleeping lofts and wood-burning fireplaces. Rooms are clean; those in the corporate wing face the courtyard and are larger and quieter than the others. The hotel is about eight blocks or a 20-minute walk from Bellevue Square. A complimentary appetizer buffet, offered in the lounge weekdays between 5 and 7 PM, is substantial and includes seafood and roast beef. 🔲 *625 116th Ave. NE, Bellevue 98004, ☎ 206/455–9444, FAX 206/455–2154. 160 rooms, 16 suites. Restaurant, bar, coffee shop, pool. AE, D, DC, MC, V.*

THE ARTS

Seattle has gained a world-class reputation as a theater town, and it also has a strong music and dance scene for local, national, and international artists. A good handle on what's happening in town can be found in any of several periodicals. Both the *Seattle Times* and *Post-*

Intelligencer have pull-out sections on Friday detailing most of the coming week's events. The *Seattle Weekly,* which hits most newsstands on Wednesday, has even more detailed coverage and arts reviews. *The Rocket,* a lively free monthly, covers music news, reviews, and concert information, with an emphasis on rock and roll.

The Arts for Free

Seattle's summer concerts, the **Out to Lunch Series** (☎ 206/623–0340), runs from mid-June to early September every weekday at noon in various parks, plazas, and atriums in downtown. Concerts feature local and national musicians and dancers. Call ahead for schedules and locations.

Gallery Walk (begin at any gallery in Pioneer Square, ☎ 206/587–0260), an open house hosted by Seattle's art galleries, explores new local exhibits the first Thursday of every month, starting at 5.

Ticket Services

Ticketmaster (☎ 206/628–0888) provides tickets to most productions in the Seattle area; you can charge by phone. The two locations of **Ticket/Ticket** (Broadway Market, 401 Broadway E, 2nd Floor, ☎ 206/324–2744; Pike Place Market Information Booth, 1st Ave. and Pike St., ☎ 206/682–7453, ext. 26) sell half-price tickets for many events on the day of the performance (or the day before for matinees). Sales are cash only and in-person only.

Dance

Allegro Dance Company (Broadway Performance Hall, 1625 Broadway, ☎ 206/323–2623) presents the best in local and regional choreography, with some productions that include other elements of the performing arts. It schedules about 10 concerts a year between September and June.

Meany Hall for the Performing Arts (University of Washington campus, ☎ 206/543–4880) presents important national and international companies, September–May, with an emphasis on modern and jazz dance.

On the Boards (Washington Performance Hall, 153 14th Ave., ☎ 206/325–7901) presents and produces a wide variety of contemporary performances, including not only dance but also theater, music, and multimedia events by local, national, and international artists. Although the main subscription series runs October–May, OTB events happen nearly every weekend year-round.

Pacific Northwest Ballet (Opera House at Seattle Center, ☎ 206/441–2424) is a resident company and school that presents 60–70 performances annually. Its Christmastime production of *The Nutcracker,* with choreography by Kent Stowell and sets by Maurice Sendak, has become a beloved Seattle tradition.

Orchestras and Opera

Civic Light Opera (11051 34th Ave. NE, ☎ 206/363–2809) is a non-Equity, semipro company that offers three or four high-quality productions of large-scale American musical theater per season. The season runs roughly October–May.

Northwest Chamber Orchestra (☎ 206/343–0445) is the Northwest's only professional chamber-music orchestra. At the Moore Theater, the Nippon Kan, and other venues, it presents a full spectrum of music, from Baroque to modern. The season, generally September–May, includes a Bach festival every fall, a spring subscription series, and special holiday performances in December.

Seattle Opera (Opera House at Seattle Center, Mercer St. at 3rd Ave., ☎ 206/389–7600) is a world-class company, generally considered to be one of the top operas in the United States. During the August–May season, it presents six performances of six productions.

Seattle Symphony (Opera House at Seattle Center and other locations, ☎ 206/443–4747) presents some 120 concerts from September to June and—under the musical direction of Gerard Schwartz—continues its long tradition of excellence. A new $99 million Symphony Hall at 2nd Avenue and University Street is set to open in 1997.

Performance Spaces

Part of the legacy left by the 1962 World's Fair is a series of performance halls at **Seattle Center** (305 Harrison St., ☎ 206/684–8582). Seattle also boasts two fine classic early 20th-century music halls—the **Fifth Avenue** (1308 5th Ave., ☎ 206/625–1900) and the 3,000-seat **Paramount** (907 Pine St., ☎ 206/682–1414), which reopened in 1995 after a $37 million renovation.

The **Cornish College of the Arts** (710 E. Roy St., ☎ 206/323–1400) is an internationally recognized school that also serves as home to a number of distinguished professional groups, including jazz and dance, performing September–May.

Other prominent venues are the **Moore Theater** (1932 2nd Ave., ☎ 206/443–1744), the small but acoustically outstanding **Broadway Performance Hall** (1625 Broadway, ☎ 206/323–2623) at Seattle Central Community College, and **Kane** and **Meany halls** on the University of Washington campus (☎ 206/543–4880).

Theater Companies

Annex Theatre (1916 4th Ave., ☎ 206/728–0933) is a cabaret-style, avant-garde theater that performs new works and is run by a collective of artists.

A Contemporary Theater (100 W. Roy St., ☎ 206/285–5110) specializes in developing works by emerging playwrights, including at least one world premiere every year. The season runs May–November, and every December ACT mounts a popular production of Dickens's *A Christmas Carol*. ACT will move to the Eagle's Auditorium (7th Ave. and Union St.), near the Convention Center, in mid-1996.

Bathhouse Theater (7312 W. Greenlake Dr. N, ☎ 206/524–9108) produces six productions on a year-round schedule, specializing in innovative updates on classics. In addition, it mounts numerous free public shows in various Seattle parks.

Crêpe de Paris (1333 5th Ave., ☎ 206/623–4111), a restaurant in the Rainier Tower building downtown, offers some sidesplitting cabaret theater and musical revues, such as The Bouffants, an all-girl group complete with tall beehive hairdos and cat's-eye glasses.

Empty Space Theater (3509 Fremont Ave., ☎ 206/547–7500) has a reputation for introducing Seattle to new playwrights. The season generally runs November–June, with five or six main-stage productions and several smaller shows throughout the season.

Fifth Avenue Musical Theater Company (Fifth Avenue Theater, 1308 5th Ave., ☎ 206/625–1900) is a resident professional troupe that mounts four lavish musicals between October and May each year, with each run lasting about two weeks. (During the rest of the year, this chinoiserie-style historical landmark, carefully restored to its original 1926 condition, hosts a variety of other traveling musical as well as theatrical performances.)

Group Theater (305 Harrison St., on the fountain level of the Center House in Seattle Center, ☎ 206/441–1299) is a multicultural troupe that prides itself on presenting socially provocative works—old and new—by artists of varied cultures and colors. The season runs September–June, and the Group also mounts a special summertime playwrights' festival. Of the regular season's six productions, one is always the popular *Voices of Christmas,* a study of the holidays with consideration to cultural differences and ethnic and emotional barriers.

Intiman Theater (Playhouse at Seattle Center, 2nd and Mercer Sts., ☎ 206/626–0782) presents classics of the world stage in an intimate, high-quality setting. The season generally runs May–November.

New City Theater and Arts Center (1634 11th Ave., ☎ 206/323–6800) is home to a wide range of experimental performances produced by a resident company as well as in conjunction with major national and international artists. Its yearly output includes six plays, a director's festival and a playwright's festival, three dance concerts, a monthly film showing, and a lively, late-night monthly cabaret.

Seattle Repertory Theater (Bagley Wright Theater at Seattle Center, 155 Mercer St., ☎ 206/443–2222) presents a variety of high-quality programming, from classics to new plays. During its October–May season, six main stage productions and three smaller shows (in the adjoining PONCHO Forum) are presented.

Village Theater (303 and 120 Front St. N, Issaquah, ☎ 206/392–2202) produces high-quality family musicals, comedies, and dramas September–May in Issaquah, a town east of Seattle. The main stage is at the 303 Front Street location; the theater's original venue, at 120 Front, is now known as First Stage.

NIGHTLIFE

For a city its size, Seattle has a remarkably strong and diverse nightlife scene. On any given night, you can hear high-quality live sounds—from traditional jazz and ethnic folk music to garage bands—at a variety of venues. Jazz, blues, and R&B have long been Seattle favorites, and each year are showcased on major stages at the Labor Day Bumbershoot Festival at the Seattle Center. Seattle has also gained a certain notoriety as the birthplace of grunge rock; some of the better-known Seattle bands to spring from this scene include Nirvana, Pearl Jam, Screaming Trees, and Alice in Chains. Beyond music, there are plenty of spots to see a comedian, catch a movie, dance, or just have a drink while watching the lights on the water.

Bars and Lounges

Areas with high concentrations of clubs and taverns include Ballard, Pioneer Square, and Capitol Hill, and Belltown, also known as the Denny Regrade, just north of the Pike Place Market. Many of these clubs feature a wide variety of live bands (*see* Music, *below*).

Given Seattle's setting, bars with waterfront views are plentiful—you just have to pick your body of water. **Anthony's Home Port** (6135 Seaview Ave. NW, ☎ 206/783–0780) has great views of Shilshole Bay. **Arnie's Northshore** (1900 N. Northlake Way, ☎ 206/547–3242) overlooks Lake Union. **Ernie's Bar & Grill** (2411 Alaskan Way, Pier 67, ☎ 206/728–7000), in the Edgewater Hotel, has great views of Elliott Bay and the Olympic Mountains. **Kayak Grill** (1200 Westlake Ave. N, ☎ 206/284–

2535) is set on Lake Union. **Pescatore** (5300 34th Ave. NW, ☎ 206/784–1733) has a view of the Ship Canal. **Ray's Boathouse** (6049 Seaview Ave. NW, ☎ 206/789–3770) is on Shilshole Bay.

Other options include **F. X. McRory's** (419 Occidental Ave. S, ☎ 206/623–4800), near the Kingdome, which is famous for its huge selection of single-malt whiskies and fresh oysters. Also downtown, the **Garden Court** (411 University St., ☎ 206/621–1700) at the Four Seasons Olympic is a rather formal and elegant locale. **Salty's** (1396 Harbor Ave. SW, ☎ 206/937–1600), a noisy, sprawling restaurant and lounge in West Seattle, has unparalleled views of downtown.

Comedy

Comedy Underground (222 S. Main St., ☎ 206/628–0303), a Pioneer Square club that's literally underground, beneath Swannie's, presents stand-up comedy nightly, with Monday and Tuesday reserved as open-mike nights.

Giggles (5220 Roosevelt Way NE, ☎ 206/526–5653), in the University District, presents the best local and nationally known comedians five nights a week (Tuesday–Saturday), with late shows on weekend nights.

Dancing

Ballroom Dancing

The local chapter of the **U.S. Amateur Ballroom Dancing Association** (☎ 206/822–6686) holds regular classes and dances throughout the year at the **Avalon Ballroom** (1017 Stewart St.). The **Washington Dance Club** (1017 Stewart St., ☎ 206/628–8939) sponsors nightly workshops and dances on various styles.

Dance Clubs

There are several popular clubs in Pioneer Square that feature recorded dance music; **Fenix** (315 2nd Ave., ☎ 206/467–1111) and **Fenix Underground** (323 2nd Ave. S, ☎ 206/467–1111) are connected by an underground passageway and play very danceable music. In the downtown area, **Fitzgerald's on Fifth** (1900 5th Ave., ☎ 206/728–1000) in the Westin Hotel and **Pier 70 Bay Cafe** (2815 Alaskan Way at Broad St., ☎ 206/728–7071) are dance clubs that feature Top-40 music. A number of Seattle's rock clubs (*see* Music, *below*) also offer dancing.

Movies

Seattle is a movie-loving town, as best exemplified by the popularity of the **Seattle International Film Festival** (☎ 206/324–9996), held each May. For show times and theater locations of current releases, call the **Seattle Times InfoLine** (☎ 206/464–2000, ext. 3456).

Egyptian Theater (801 E. Pine St., at Broadway, ☎ 206/323–4978), an Art Deco movie palace that was formerly a Masonic temple, screens art films and is the prime venue of the film festival.

Gran Illusion Cinema (1403 N.E. 50th St., at University Way, ☎ 206/523–3935), in the U district, seats less than 100 and shows mainly independent and art films.

Neptune Theater (1303 N.E. 45th St., at Brooklyn, ☎ 206/633–5545), located near the university, often shows double features of classic films.

U.A. Seattle Center Theaters (2131 6th Ave., at Blanchard St., ☎ 206/443–9591) shows second-run films for the bargain price of $2.

Music

For $8 you can purchase the Pioneer Square joint cover charge, which will admit you to up to 10 area clubs; contact the Central Saloon (*see* Rock, *below*) for details.

Blues and R&B

Ballard Firehouse (5429 Russell St. NW, ☎ 206/784–3516) is the music mecca in the heart of Ballard, with an emphasis on local and national blues acts.

Chicago's (315 1st Ave. N, ☎ 206/282–7791), a reasonably priced Italian restaurant just west of the Seattle Center, has live blues on the weekend.

Larry's (209 1st Ave. S, ☎ 206/624–7665) features live R&B and blues nightly in an unpretentious, friendly, and usually jam-packed tavern-restaurant in Pioneer Square.

Old Timer's Cafe (620 1st Ave., ☎ 206/623–9800) is a popular Pioneer Square restaurant and bar with live music—mostly R&B—nightly.

Scarlet Tree (6521 Roosevelt Way NE, ☎ 206/523–7153), a neighborhood institution just north of the University District, offers great burgers and live R&B most nights.

Folk

Backstage (2208 N.W. Market St., ☎ 206/781–2805) is an often-packed basement venue in Ballard that hosts a lively mix of national and local acts with the emphasis on world music, offbeat rock, and new folk.

Kells (1916 Post Alley, ☎ 206/728–1916), a snug Irish-style pub, is located near the Pike Place Market and presents live Celtic music Wednesday–Saturday starting at 9 PM.

Murphy's Pub (2110 45th St. NE, ☎ 206/634–2110) is a cozy neighborhood bar that has open-mike Wednesdays, with Irish and other folk music on Friday and Saturday.

Jazz

Dimitriou's Jazz Alley (2037 6th Ave., ☎ 206/441–9729) is a downtown club with nationally known, consistently high-quality performers every night but Sunday. Excellent dinners are served before the first shows.

Latona Tavern (6423 Latona Ave. NE, ☎ 206/525–2238) is a funky, friendly, often jazz-oriented, neighborhood bar at the south end of Green Lake that features a variety of local musicians playing folk, blues, and jazz nightly.

New Orleans Restaurant (114 1st Ave. S, ☎ 206/622–2563) is a popular Pioneer Square restaurant with good food and live jazz nightly—mostly top local performers but occasionally national acts as well.

Rock

The **Moore Theater** (1932 2nd Ave., ☎ 206/443–1744) and the **Paramount** (907 Pine St., ☎ 682–1414, or Ticketmaster, ☎ 206/628–0888) are elegant former movie-music halls that now host visiting big-name acts.

Central Saloon (207 1st Ave. S, ☎ 206/622–0209) is a crowded Pioneer Square tavern with an ever-changing roster of local and national rock acts.

Crocodile Café (2200 2nd Ave., ☎ 206/448–2114) is one of Seattle's most successful rock clubs, featuring a variety of folk-rock, acoustic-rock, hard-rock, and new-wave groups every night but Monday.

Doc Maynard's (610 1st Ave., ☎ 206/682–4649) is a classic rock-and-roll-oriented tavern with a small and always jam-packed dance floor.

Off-Ramp Music Cafe (109 Eastlake E, ☎ 206/628–0232) features a rock band nightly, often the loud and alternative kind.

O.K. Hotel Cafe (212 Alaskan Way S, ☎ 206/621–7903) offers rock, folk, and jazz nightly in a small venue near Pioneer Square.

Re-Bar (1114 Howell St., ☎ 206/233–9873) presents an eclectic mix of music nightly, including acid-jazz, rock, and soul.

Vogue (2018 1st Ave., ☎ 206/443–0673), a club in Belltown, the artists' community just north of the Public Market, hosts au courant local and national rock acts, as well as industrial, reggae, and gothic music.

SEATTLE ESSENTIALS

Arriving and Departing

By Bus

Seattle is served by **Greyhound** (8th Ave. and Stewart St., ☎ 800/231–2222), a nationwide bus line.

By Car

I–5 enters Seattle from the north and south, I–90 from the east. Washington law requires all passengers to be buckled into seat belts. Children under age five should use car seats. Cars are allowed to turn right at a red light after stopping to check for oncoming traffic.

By Plane

Seattle-Tacoma International Airport (Sea-Tac) is 20 miles from downtown Seattle and is served by Air BC (☎ 206/467–7928 or 800/663–8868), Air Canada (☎ 206/467–7928), Alaska (☎ 206/433–3100), American (☎ 800/433–7300), America West (☎ 800/247–5692), British Airways (☎ 206/433–6714), Continental (☎ 206/624–1740 or 800/525–0280), Delta (☎ 206/433–4711), EVA Airways (☎ 206/687–2833 or 800/695–2833), Hawaiian (☎ 800/367–5320), Horizon (☎ 800/547–9308), Japan (☎ 206/624–4737 or 800/225–2525), Northwest (☎ 206/433–3500 or 800/221–2000), Thai Airways (☎ 800/426–5204), TWA (☎ 206/447–9400), United (☎ 206/441–3700 or 800/241–6522), United Express (☎ 206/441–3700), and USAir (☎ 206/587–6229 or 800/428–4322).

BETWEEN THE AIRPORT AND THE CITY

Taxis to the airport take 30–45 minutes; the fare is about $25.

Gray Line Airport Express (☎ 206/626–6088) operates buses from major downtown hotels from 6:10 AM to 11:45, with departures every 20–30 minutes, depending on the hotel. The fare is $7.50 one-way, $13 round-trip.

Shuttle Express (☎ 206/622–1424) offers service to and from the airport. Fares are $18 for singles one-way or $24 for two one-way tickets from downtown.

By Train

Amtrak (303 S. Jackson St., ☎ 800/872–7245) provides rail transportation into Seattle. After a 14-year hiatus, rail service between Seattle and Vancouver was reinstated in 1995; at press time, the trip took about four hours, but Amtrack was hoping to bring that down.

Getting Around

By Bus

Metropolitan Transit (821 2nd Ave., ☎ 206/553–3000) provides a free-ride service in the downtown waterfront area until 7 PM. Fares to other destinations range from 85¢ to $1.60, depending on the zone and time of day.

By Car

Many downtown streets are one-way, so a map with arrows is especially helpful. Main thoroughfares into downtown are Aurora Avenue (the part through downtown is called the Alaskan Way Viaduct) and I–5.

By Ferry

The **Washington State Ferry System** (☎ 206/464–6400; 206/464–2000, ext. 5500; or 800/843–3779) is the largest in the United States. Ferries leave from downtown Seattle for Bainbridge Island and Bremerton (Kitsap Peninsula) several times daily. Ferries for pedestrians travel to Vashon Island and Southworth (Kitsap Peninsula). Car and passenger ferries leave from Fauntleroy, in West Seattle, to Vashon Island and Southworth; from Edmonds, north of Seattle, to Kingston; and from Mukilteo, farther north, to Clinton (Whidbey Island). In Anacortes, about 90 minutes north of Seattle, ferries depart for the San Juan Islands and Vancouver Island, British Columbia. Fares range from as low as $1.15 for senior citizens and children 5–11 traveling the Mukilteo-to-Clinton route, to $33.50 for a car and driver going one-way from Anacortes to Sydney. (*See also* Washington Essentials *in* Chapter 5, Washington.)

Clipper Navigation, Inc.'s (☎ 206/448–5000) passenger catamarans leave from Pier 69. They make the trip to Victoria in under three hours and depart four times daily in the summer, two times daily in the spring and fall, and once daily in winter. The fares are $89 round-trip. The ships offer summer sunset cruises. Clipper Navigation also makes runs to Port Townsend and Friday Harbor on San Juan Island in the summer. Reservations are necessary.

By Monorail

The **Monorail** (☎ 206/684–7200), built for the 1962 World's Fair, shuttles between its terminals in Westlake Center and the Seattle Center every 15 minutes; the trip takes under three minutes. Hours are Sunday to Thursday 9–9 and Friday and Saturday 9 AM–midnight. The fare is 90¢ each way, free for children under 6.

By Taxi

Taxis can be hailed on the street; the fare is $1.80 at the flag drop and $1.80 per mile. Major companies are **Farwest** (☎ 206/622–1717) and **Yellow Cab** (☎ 206/622–6500).

By Trolley

Waterfront trolleys (☎ 206/553–3000) run from Pier 70 into Pioneer Square. The fares (85¢ nonpeak and $1.60 for travel during peak hours) are the same as bus fares.

Guided Tours

Art and Cultural

Seattle's International District is one of the largest Asian-American enclaves in North America. **Chinatown Discovery Tours** offers a program and information on Asian history and cultural traditions, as well as a walk through the area. Tours end with a traditional dim-sum brunch, afternoon tea, or dinner banquet. *Box 3406, 98114,* ☎ *206/236–0657.* ☛ *$29.95 for tour and meal. Tours offered several times during the day and evening.*

You'll find unusual, self-guided tours in **"A Directory of Seattle's Public Art,"** an illustrated brochure published by the Seattle Arts Commission.

It describes walks and drives to see more than 256 innovative works of art in public places. Among these treasures are brass dance-steps inlaid on the sidewalks of Broadway, whirligigs festooning a neighborhood electric power substation, an "ark" of animals at Woodland Park Zoo, murals on downtown high-rises, and a "sound garden" of acoustical sculptures in a lakeside park. To receive the brochure, send a SASE with $1 in postage to the Seattle Arts Commission. *221 1st Ave. W, Suite 100, 98109, ☎ 206/684–7171.*

Tillicum Village Tours sails across Puget Sound to Blake Island, south of Bainbridge Island, for a four-hour examination of traditional Native American life. A dinner including steamed clams and salmon is served, and Native American dancers perform a production, *Dance on the Wind. Pier 56, ☎ 206/443–1244. Tour schedule varies during the year, with up to 3 tours leaving daily during peak months.* ☛ *$46.50 adults, $43 senior citizens, $30 youths 13–18, $18.50 children 6–12, $9.50 children 4–5.*

Ballooning

Balloon Depot (16138 N.E. 87th St., Redmond 98052, ☎ 206/881–9699) offers 60- to 90-minute balloon flights for $99–$145 per person, depending on the length of flight and whether it's a weekday or weekend. **Lighter Than Air Adventures** (21808 N.E. 175th St., Woodinville 98072, ☎ 206/488–4135) has one-hour evening flights for $110 per person, as well as sunset flights for $120 per person.

Boat

Argosy Cruises offers a variety of one-hour tours exploring Elliott Bay and the Port of Seattle. Some seven vessels take visitors on trips through the Hiram Chittenden Locks and Lake Washington. Sailings vary according to season. *Pier 55, Suite 201, 98101, ☎ 206/623–1445.* ☛ *$12.50 adults, $10.50 senior citizens, $5.75 children 5–12.*

Emerald City Charters offers a unique look at Seattle's waterfront from beneath the sails of a refurbished 64-foot 1939 yawl. There are 90-minute harbor sails and a 2½-hour sunset sail. *Pier 56, ☎ 206/624–3931. May–Oct.* ☛ *Harbor sail: $20, sunset sail: $37.*

Gray Line (*see* Orientation, *below*).

The *Spirit of Puget Sound* runs dinner and lunch cruises in Elliott Bay on a sleek, 175-foot yacht. Besides the beef, salmon, and chicken buffet offered on all sailings, the dinner cruise includes a 30-minute Broadway-style revue and one hour of dancing to a five-piece band. Summer moonlight cocktail cruises, which have a nightclub atmosphere, set sail at about 11:30 and return at 2 AM. *2819 Elliot Ave., Suite 204, Seattle 98121, ☎ 206/443–1439.* ☛ *Dinner cruise is about $50, depending on day of wk; call for schedules and details for lunch and moonlight cruises.*

The *Victoria Clipper* offers two-hour sunset cruises in the summer. The itinerary includes Elliott Bay, Agate Passage, and Vashon Island. *Pier 69, ☎ 206/448–5000.* ☛ *$16 adults, $8.50 children.*

Orientation

Gray Line offers some 20 guided bus tours of the city and environs ranging in scope from a daily 2½-hour spin to a six-hour "Grand City Tour." The company also offers specialized tours of, among others, the Boeing 747–767 plants, Mt. Rainier, and Seattle's waterways by boat. From May to October, Gray Line has tours via Seattle Trolleys through downtown. Tours depart from the Seattle/Kings County Convention and Visitors Bureau (800 Convention Pl., ☎ 206/461–5840), at the

I–5 end of Pike Street; the only exceptions are the Seattle Trolley tours and the *Victoria Star* service between Bellingham and Victoria, which operates June 1–Oct. 15. ☎ *206/626–5208. Free transfers from major downtown hotels. Reservations required.*

Train

The ***Spirit of Washington*** is a diesel-powered dinner train that takes passengers along the eastern shore of Lake Washington from the depot in Renton to the Columbia winery in Woodenville. Passengers on this 3½-hour, 45-mile round-trip excursion ride in regular or domed dining cars and are served dinner on the first leg of the trip, then disembark for a tour and wine tasting. Dessert and coffee are served on the return trip. The route offers views of Lake Washington, the Bellevue skyline, and Mt. Rainier. The menu includes entrées such as prime rib, baked cherry-smoked salmon with pineapple chutney, and Dungeness crab cakes. Desserts are flavorful and usually decadent, and bar offerings include Washington wines, beers and ales. There are also Saturday lunch and Sunday brunch trips. *Renton Depot,* ☎ *800/876–7245. Reservations required. No runs Mon. mid-Sept.–mid-May.* ☞ *$57; $69 for dome-car seating.*

Walking

One of the most beloved of Seattle's tours is the **Underground Tour,** begun in 1965 by feisty entrepreneur-historian Bill Speidel as an effort to help preserve the then-derelict Pioneer Square area. This 90-minute walking tour explores (with tongue-in-cheek narration) the rough-and-tumble history of early Seattle; the Great Fire of 1889, which destroyed most of downtown; and the fascinating below-ground sections of Pioneer Square that have been abandoned (and built on top of) since 1907. This tour, however, is not wheelchair- or stroller-accessible, as six flights of stairs are involved. *Departure from Doc Maynard's Public House, 610 1st Ave., reservations* ☎ *206/682–4646, schedules* ☎ *206/682–1511.* ☞ *$5.95 adults, $4.87 senior citizens, $4.33 youths 13–17 or with valid student ID, $2.71 children 6–12. Reservations advised. Tours run daily except major holidays; schedule varies seasonally, with up to 8 tours daily in summer.*

Important Addresses and Numbers

Radio Stations

KBSG-AM (1210)/FM (97.3), '50s, '60s, and '70s music; **KING-FM (98.1),** classical; **KIRO-AM (710),** news, sports, and features; **KMPS-AM (1300)/FM (94.1),** country music; **KUOW-FM (94.9),** National Public Radio—news, classical music, and features; and **KUBE-FM (93.3),** contemporary rock.

Emergencies

For **police, ambulance,** or **other emergencies,** dial 911.

HOSPITALS

Area hospitals with emergency rooms include **Harborview Medical Center** (325 9th Ave., ☎ 206/223–3074) and **Virginia Mason Hospital** (925 Seneca St., ☎ 206/583–6433).

PHARMACIES

Fred Meyer (417 Broadway Ave. E, ☎ 206/323–6586) is open until 10 PM.

Visitor Information

Drop by the **Seattle/King County Convention and Visitors Bureau** (800 Convention Pl., at the I–5 end of Pike St., 98101, ☎ 206/461–5840) or the information booth at Westlake Center (400 Pine St., street level, ☎ 206/467–1600) for maps and information about lodging, restaurants, and attractions throughout the city. You can receive the same through the mail by writing to the **Visitor Information Center** (520 Pike St., Suite 1300, 98101, ☎ 206/461–5840).

The **Bainbridge Island Chamber of Commerce** (590 Winslow Way, Bainbridge Island, ☎ 206/842–3700), two blocks from the ferry dock, has maps and information on restaurants, shops, and sights.

5 Washington

From the islands that dot Puget Sound to the peak of Mt. Rainier to the Yakima Valley's vineyards, Washington presents hundreds of opportunities to appreciate the great outdoors. Whether you watch for whales from coastal lighthouses, dine on fresh seafood in waterside towns, tramp through dripping rain forests, hike high mountains, or sail the cool waters of the Pacific, the state will stun you with its beauty long before you exhaust its possibilities.

By Loralee
Wenger and
Adam Woog

THIRTY YEARS AGO, Washington State was a virtual backwater in the country's landscape. The nation had first awakened to this bit of the world via the press given the 1962 Seattle World's Fair, but even so, the state was still nowheresville, stuck on the corner of the continental map.

For the most part, Washingtonians didn't care what the rest of the country thought of them; they were too busy hiking, backpacking, mountain climbing, and sailing. Before outdoor adventures became popular in the rest of the country, they were commonplace for Washington residents. For northwesterners, adventuring isn't so much the in thing to do as it is the expression of a yearning to join with the mighty and majestic forces of nature. Now the Northwest is one of the country's foremost locations for outdoor activities.

Washington boasts a host of scenic attractions that beckon the sightseer as well as the adventurer. To the west, the Olympic Peninsula's rain forest drips with moss, waterfalls, and sprawling greenery. The 5,200-foot-high Hurricane Ridge offers spectacular views of the Olympic Mountains and the Straits of Juan de Fuca. The state's coastline along the western shores of the Olympic Peninsula and the Long Beach Peninsula is punctured with inlets, coves, and secluded harbors.

Across Puget Sound, Mt. Rainier reigns over the Cascade Mountains. The mild climate and regular rainfall of western Washington make for lush stands of Douglas fir, western red cedar, and the Renoiresque washes of color with the springtime blossoming of rhododendrons and azaleas. Crossing the Cascades into central and eastern Washington, patchwork quilts of irrigated fruit orchards; miles of rolling, treeless prairie; and stands of golden grain prevail—and so does eastern Washington's extreme weather.

The state's contrasts in landscape have spilled over to its residents. Battles have been hard-fought between Native American and non–Native American fishermen, between land developers and environmentalists, and now, between residents and an influx of prospective residents, purportedly Californians hell-bent on Los Angelesizing Puget Sound. These conflicts underscore the vigor with which Washingtonians defend their turf. Visitors can expect to feel welcome here as long as they continue to respect the state's bounty and leave it intact for others to enjoy.

WHIDBEY ISLAND

On a nice day, there's no better excursion from Seattle than a ferry trip across Puget Sound to Whidbey Island. It's a great way to watch seagulls, sailboats, and massive container vessels in the sound—not to mention the surrounding scenery, which takes in the Kitsap Peninsula and Olympic Mountains, Mt. Rainier, the Cascade Mountains, and the Seattle skyline. Even when the weather isn't all that terrific, travelers can stay snug inside the ferry, have a snack, and listen to the folk musicians who entertain the cross-sound commuters.

The island, 30 miles northwest of Seattle, is one of the nearest "escapes" from the city. In fact, some folks escape to it from Seattle every night— they live on Whidbey and commute to work. The island is a blend of bucolic rolling hills, forests, meadows, sandy beaches, and dramatic, high cliffs. It's a great place for country drives, bicycle touring, exploring

Washington

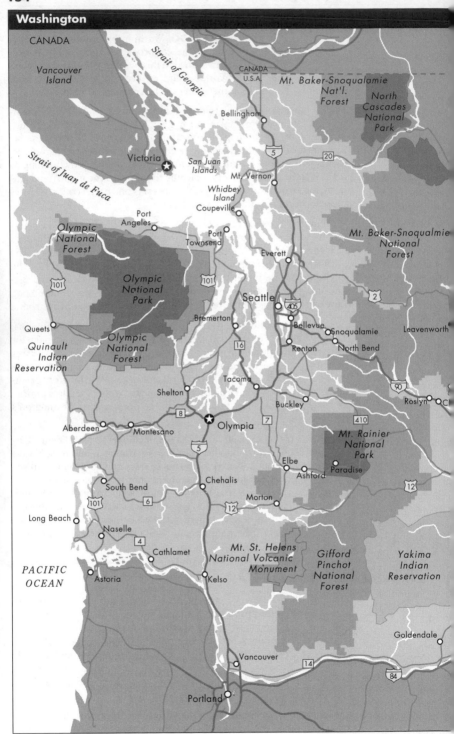

CANADA

Vancouver Island

Strait of Georgia

CANADA
U.S.A

Mt. Baker-Snoqualmie Nat'l. Forest

North Cascades National Park

Bellingham

5

20

Strait of Juan de Fuca

Victoria

San Juan Islands

Mt. Vernon

Whidbey Island

Coupeville

Olympic National Forest

Port Angeles

Port Townsend

Mt. Baker-Snoqualmie National Forest

Everett

101

Olympic National Park

101

Seattle

405

2

Bremerton

Bellevue

Snoqualmie

Leavenworth

Queets

Olympic National Forest

16

Renton

North Bend

Quinault Indian Reservation

495

Tacoma

90

Shelton

Roslyn

C

Buckley

8

Olympia

7

Mt. Rainier National Park

410

Aberdeen

Montesano

5

Elbe

Paradise

South Bend

Chehalis

Ashford

12

6

Morton

Long Beach

101

12

Naselle

4

Mt. St. Helens National Volcanic Monument

Gifford Pinchot National Forest

Yakima Indian Reservation

PACIFIC OCEAN

Cathlamet

Astoria

Kelso

Goldendale

Vancouver

14

84

Portland

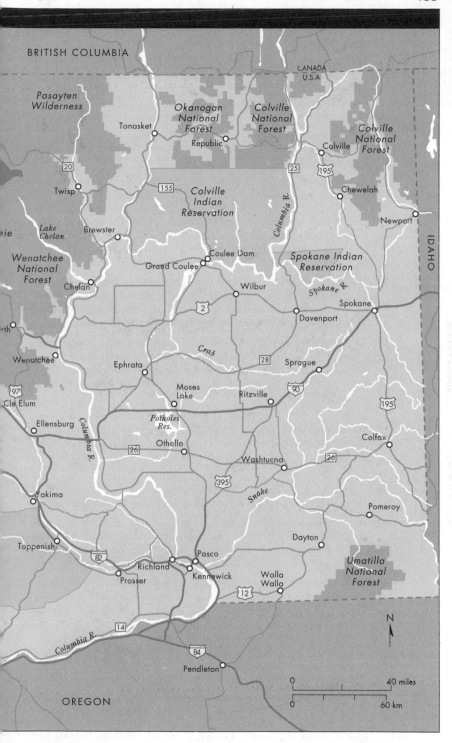

BRITISH COLUMBIA

CANADA
U.S.A.

*Pasayten
Wilderness*

*Okanogan
National
Forest*

*Colville
National
Forest*

*Colville
National
Forest*

Tonasket

Republic

Colville

〔20〕

〔25〕

〔195〕

Twisp

〔155〕

*Colville
Indian
Reservation*

Chewelah

Columbia R.

Newport

IDAHO

*Lake
Chelan*

Brewster

ie

*Wenatchee
National
Forest*

Coulee Dam

Grand Coulee

*Spokane Indian
Reservation*

Chelan

Wilbur

Spokane R.

Spokane

〔2〕

Davenport

th

Wenatchee

Crab

〔28〕

Sprague

Ephrata

〔97〕

Cle Elum

Moses
Lake

Ritzville

〔90〕

〔195〕

Ellensburg

Columbia R.

*Potholes
Res.*

Colfax

〔26〕

Othello

Washtucna

〔26〕

Yakima

〔395〕

Snake

Pomeroy

Toppenish

Dayton

〔82〕

Richland

Pasco

*Umatilla
National
Forest*

Prosser

Kennewick

Walla
Walla

〔12〕

〔14〕

N

Columbia R.

〔84〕

Pendleton

0   40 miles

0   60 km

OREGON

the shoreline by boat or kayak, and viewing sunsets. On the west side of the island, visitors can watch container ships ply the waters of Puget Sound between Asia and ports in Seattle and Tacoma.

Whidbey is easily accessible via the Washington State Ferry system from Mukilteo (pronounced muck-ill-*tee*-oh) to Clinton on the southern part of the island or a drive across Deception Pass on the northern end of the island on Highway 20.

Exploring

Numbers in the margin correspond to points of interest on the Puget Sound map.

At 60 miles long and 8 miles wide, Whidbey Island is the second-longest in the contiguous United States—Long Island in New York takes the honors as the longest. This tour begins at the southern tip of the island, which has a mostly rural landscape of undulating hills, gentle beaches, and little coves. Wildlife is plentiful, and it's not unusual to see eagles, great blue herons, and oystercatchers, as well as orcas, gray whales, dolphins, and otters.

❶ Perhaps the best view of the sea creatures can be had from **Langley,** the quaint town that sits atop a 50-foot-high bluff overlooking the southeastern shore. In the heart of town, along 1st Street and 2nd Street, there are boutiques that sell art, glass, antiques, jewelry, and clothing.

❷ About halfway up this long, skinny island is the town of **Greenbank,** home to the historically recognized **Loganberry Farm.** The 125-acre site is now the place of production for the state's unique spirit, Whidbey's Liqueur. *657 Wonn Rd.,* ☎ *360/678–7700.* ☛ *Free. Self-guided tours offered daily 10–4.*

While in Greenbank, you may want to see the 53-acre **Meerkerk Rhododendron Gardens,** with 1,500 native and hybrid species of rhododendrons, numerous walking trails, and ponds. The flowers are in full bloom in April and May. *Resort Rd., Greenbank,* ☎ *360/678– 1912.* ☛ *$2.* ☾ *Daily 9–4.*

❸ Farther north you'll come to **Keystone,** notable because it is the port of call for the ferry bound for Port Townsend on the Olympic Peninsula.

❹ **Ft. Casey State Park** (☎ 360/678–4519), just north of Keystone, is one of three forts built in 1890 to protect Puget Sound. Today it offers a small interpretive center, camping, picnic sites, fishing, and a boat launch.

❺ About two-thirds the way up the island is **Coupeville,** home of many restored Victorian houses and one of the largest National Historic Districts in the state. The town was founded in 1852 by Captain Thomas Coupe; his house, built in 1853, is one of the state's oldest. The town is also the site of the **Island County Historical Museum** (908 N.W. Alexander St., ☎ 360/678–3310), which has exhibits on the history of the island's fishing, timber, and agriculture industries. The museum also offers historical tours and walks.

❻ **Ebey's Landing National Historic Reserve** (☎ 360/678–4636), a 22-acre area west of Coupeville, was established by Congress in 1980 and is the first and largest reserve of its kind. It is dotted with some 91 nationally registered historical structures, farmland, parks, and trails.

❼ About 11 miles farther north is **Oak Harbor,** which derived its name from the Garry oaks that grow in the area. It was settled by Dutch and

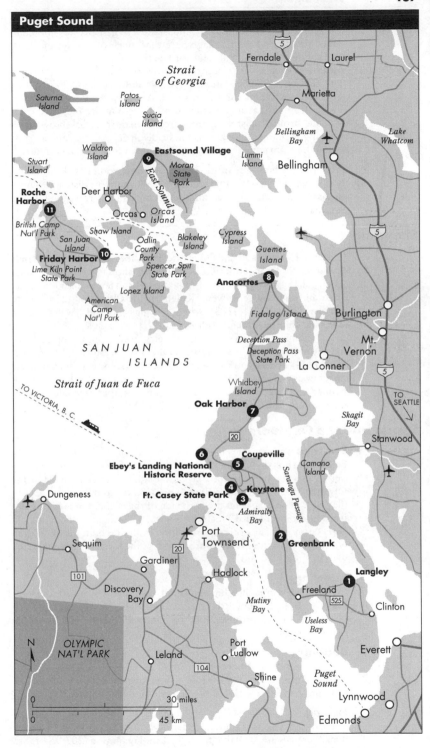

Strait of Georgia

Saturna Island

Patos Island

Sucia Island

Stuart Island

Waldron Island

Eastsound Village

9

Moran State Park

East Sound

Roche Harbor

11

Deer Harbor

British Camp Nat'l Park

Orcas

Orcas Island

Shaw Island

San Juan Island

Odlin County Park

Blakeley Island

Cypress Island

Guemes Island

Friday Harbor **10**

Spencer Spit State Park

Lime Kiln Point State Park

Lopez Island

American Camp Nat'l Park

Anacortes **8**

Fidalgo Island

SAN JUAN

ISLANDS

Deception Pass

Deception Pass State Park

Strait of Juan de Fuca

TO VICTORIA, B.C.

Whidbey Island

Oak Harbor **7**

20

Ebey's Landing National Historic Reserve

6

Coupeville

5

Keystone

Ft. Casey State Park

4

3

Admiralty Bay

Dungeness

Sequim

Gardiner

20

Port Townsend

Hadlock

101

Discovery Bay

Mutiny Bay

2 **Greenbank**

Langley **1**

Freeland

525

Clinton

Useless Bay

OLYMPIC NAT'L PARK

N

Leland

Port Ludlow

104

Shine

Ferndale

5

Laurel

Marietta

Bellingham Bay

Lummi Island

Lake Whatcom

Bellingham

5

Burlington

Mt. Vernon

La Conner

5

TO SEATTLE

Skagit Bay

Stanwood

Camano Island

Saratoga Passage

Everett

Lynnwood

Edmonds

Puget Sound

0   30 miles

0   45 km

Irish immigrants in the mid-1800s, and several Dutch windmills are still in existence. Unfortunately, the island's largest city has not maintained the sleepy fishing-village pace that much of the rest of the island follows. Instead, Oak Harbor has the look of suburban sprawl, with strips of fast-food restaurants and service stations. Just north of Oak Harbor is **Whidbey Island Naval Air Station** (☎ 360/257–2286), at which group tours can be arranged. At **Deception Pass State Park,** 3 miles from the naval base, take some time to notice the spectacular view and stroll among the madrona trees with their reddish-brown peeling bark. While walking across the bridge, you won't be able to miss seeing the dramatic gorge below, well-known for its tidal currents.

From the northern side of the island, the Deception Pass bridge links Whidbey to Fidalgo Island. From here it's just a short distance to **Anacortes,** Fidalgo's main town and the terminus for ferries going to the San Juan Islands.

Shopping

Langley's 1st Street and 2nd Street offer a number of unique items. **Annie Steffen's** (101 1st St., ☎ 360/221–6535) specializes in wearables—handpainted, handwoven, and hand-knit apparel and jewelry. You can meet artist and shop owner Gwenn Knight at the **Glass Knit** (214 1st St., Langley, ☎ 360/221–6283), where her glass art and jewelry are for sale. The **Childers/Proctor Gallery** (302 1st St., Langley, ☎ 360/221–2978) exhibits and sells paintings, jewelry, pottery, and sculpture. Just outside of Langley is the **Blackfish Studio** (5075 S. Langley Rd., ☎ 360/221–1274), where you can see works in progress as well as finished pieces by artist Kathleen Miller, who produces enamel jewelry and hand-painted clothing and accessories, and photographer Donald Miller's depictions of the land and people of the Northwest.

Sports and the Outdoors

Beaches

Beaches are best on Whidbey Island's west side, where the sand stretches out to the sea and you have a view of the shipping lanes and the Olympic Mountains. **Maxwelton Beach** (Maxwelton Beach Rd.), popular with the locals, is on the west side of the island. **Possession Point** (west on Coltas Bay Rd.) includes a park, a beach, and a boat launch. **Forts Casey** and **Ebey** offer more hiking trails and bluff outlooks than wide, sandy beaches. **West Beach,** north of the forts, is a stormy beach with lots of driftwood.

Bicycling

In the Bayview area of Whidbey Island, just off Highway 20, **The Pedaler** (5603½ S. Bayview Rd., ☎ 360/221–5040) bicycle sales and service shop also has around 25 or so mountain bikes and hybrids for rent year-round.

Boating

Langley's **small boat harbor** (☎ 360/221–6765) offers moorage for 35 boats, utilities, and a 160-foot fishing pier, all protected by a 400-foot timber-pile breakwater. No reservations are accepted.

Fishing

You can catch salmon, perch, cod, and bottomfish from the Langley dock. Supplies are available from the **Langley Marina** (202 Wharf St., ☎ 360/221–1771).

Dining

For price-category definitions, *see* Dining *in* Washington Essentials, *below.*

$$$ Country Kitchen. Entering the restaurant at the Inn at Langley (*see* Lodging, *below*), you first see a fireplace and what looks like a living room, until you notice the tables for two unobtrusively lining the walls. On the other side of the fireplace is the "great table," which seats 10. Dinner may include locally gathered mussels in a black-bean sauce, breast of duck in a loganberry sauce, or rich Columbia River salmon. Appetizers, side dishes, salad greens so fresh they've never seen the inside of a refrigerator, and desserts such as a bowl of island-grown strawberries with cream complement the entrées. ✗ *400 1st St., Langley,* ☎ *360/221–3033. Reservations required. Jacket and tie. MC, V.*

$$ Christopher's. Tucked away at the back of Mariner's Court in Coupeville is this small, eclectically furnished restaurant with a warm yet casual ambience. High ceilings bring a light and airy quality to the main dining room, where the tables are laid with linens, fresh flowers, and candles. Chef and owner Christopher Panek favors regional seafood, vegetarian fare, and fresh local produce. Start with local oysters broiled with prosciutto and provolone and served with sun-dried tomatoes and pickled peppers. Try pork medallions dressed in a cream sauce flavored with Whidbey's loganberry liqueur or have one of the vegetarian dishes—lentil *dahl* tossed with roasted vegetables and served on a bed of couscous is recommended. More than 50 French and domestic wines are also availble. ✗ *23 Front St., at Alexander St., Coupeville,* ☎ *360/678–5480. Reservations advised. AE, D, MC, V. Closed Mon., Tues. No lunch Sat.–Thurs.*

$$ Garibyan Brothers Café Langley. Terra-cotta tile floors, antique oak tables, Italian music, and the aromas of garlic, basil, and oregano set the tone for your lunch or dinner. Greek salads, vegetarian eggplant, fresh mussels, lamb loin chops, moussaka, and lamb shish kebabs are just a few of the offerings. ✗ *113 1st St., Langley,* ☎ *360/221–3090. Reservations advised. MC, V.*

$$ Star Bistro. This black, white, and red bistro, atop the Star Store, serves up Caesar salads, shrimp-and-scallop linguine, and gourmet burgers. ✗ *201½ 1st St., Langley,* ☎ *360/221–2627. No reservations. AE, MC, V.*

$ Dog House Backdoor Restaurant. This extremely casual waterfront tavern and restaurant serves large, juicy burgers and has a pool table, as well as a great view of Saratoga Passage. ✗ *230 1st St., Langley,* ☎ *360/ 221–9996. No reservations. No credit cards.*

Lodging

$$$$ Cliff House. This luxury house, situated near Freeland, sleeps one to two couples in a secluded setting overlooking Admiralty inlet. The three-story house, one side nearly all glass, affords romantic views to the guests enjoying the elegant bedroom loft. Rain and occasionally snow whisk through the open-air atrium in the middle of the house. Guests are pampered with fresh flowers, a huge stone fireplace, and miles of driftwood beach. ☒ *5440 Windmill Rd., Freeland 98249,* ☎ *360/221–1566. 1 room. No credit cards.*

$$$ Guest House Cottages. This B&B, just outside Greenbank, includes a luxurious log lodge for one couple, four private cottages, and a three-room suite in a farmhouse located on 25 acres of forest and pastureland. The accommodations are cozy, with fireplaces, stained-glass pieces, and country antique furnishings; some have kitchens and all have microwaves. ⌧ *835 E. Christianson Rd., Greenbank 98253,* ☎ *360/ 678–3115. 6 units. Pool, exercise room. No credit cards.*

$$$ **Inn at Langley.** This concrete-and-wood Frank Lloyd Wright–inspired
★ structure perches on the side of a bluff that descends to the beach. Guest rooms feature Asian-style decor in neutral colors and spectacular views of Saratoga Passage and the Cascade Mountains. Meals are served in the inn's acclaimed restaurant, the Country Kitchen (*see* Dining, *above*). Continental breakfast (for guests) is available Monday–Wednesday, 8– 10. Dinner starts promptly at 7, with a glass of sherry and a tour of the wine cellar. ⌧ *400 1st St., Langley,* ☎ *360/221–3033. 24 rooms. Restaurant. MC, V.*

$$ **Captain Whidbey Inn.** This inn offers a wide variety of accommodations, including the original madrona log inn (listed on the National Register of Historic Places), cottages, a duplex, and houses with views of Penn Cove. Inn rooms are rustic and have shared baths, though they do feature a few antiques and feather beds. Lagoon rooms are large and have private baths. Cottages and the duplex have one or two bedrooms, sitting rooms, and some have kitchens, fireplaces, and private baths. The dining room, serving breakfast, lunch, and dinner, is cozy, with dark paneling, soft lighting, and several tables overlooking Penn Cove. ⌧ *2072 W. Captain Whidbey Inn Rd., Coupeville 98239,* ☎ *360/678– 4097. 33 units. Boating, bicycles. MC, V.*

$$ **Fort Casey Inn.** These restored, two-story, Georgian Revival officers' quarters were built in 1909. Each has a fireplace, two bedrooms, a living room, and a full country kitchen (with breakfast fixings on hand). Owners Gordon and Victoria Hoenig have restored the tin ceilings and decorated the units with rag rugs, old quilts, hand-painted furniture, and sundry Colonial touches. ⌧ *1124 S. Engle Rd., Coupeville 98239,* ☎ *360/678-8792. 9 units. Bicycles. AE, MC, V.*

$$ **Twickenham House.** The weekend-in-the-country ambience of this new cedar-sided inn takes hold as soon as you catch sight of the sheep grazing and ducks wandering in the surrounding pasture. The rooms are decorated simply with trunks, pine armoires, and matching duvets and pillow shams. One of the highlights of a stay here is the gourmet breakfast, made from fresh, local ingredients and reflecting the English and French Canadian heritage of the inn's owners. ⌧ *5023 Langley Rd., Langley 98260,* ☎ *800/874–5009. 4 rooms, 2 suites. MC, V.*

THE SAN JUAN ISLANDS

The San Juan Islands are the jewels of the Northwest. Because the islands are reachable only by ferry or airplane, they beckon to souls longing for a quiet change of pace, whether it be kayaking in a cove, walking a deserted beach, or nestling by the fire in an old farmhouse. Unfortunately, solitude becomes a precious commodity in the summer when the San Juans are overrun by tourists. Island residents enjoy their peace and quiet, and many would just as soon not have their country roads and villages jammed with "summer people." Not surprisingly, tourism and development are hotly contested issues on the islands.

On weekends and even some weekdays, expect to wait at least three hours in line once you arrive at the ferry terminal. You will face the same challenge or worse if you return on Sunday afternoon or evening. One way to avoid crowds and the possibility of a cantankerous island resident is to plan a trip in the spring, fall, or winter. Reservations are a must anytime in the summer and are advised for weekends in the off-season, too.

Exploring

Numbers in the margin correspond to points of interest on the Puget Sound map.

There are 172 named islands in the San Juan archipelago, although at low tide the islands total 743 and at high tide, 428. Sixty are populated and 10 are state marine parks. Ferries stop at Lopez, Shaw, Orcas, and San Juan; other islands, many privately owned, must be reached by private plane or boat. In any case, the San Juan Islands are a gold mine for naturalists, because they are home to more than 94 orcas, a few minke whales, seals, dolphins, otters, and more than 100 active pairs of breeding bald eagles.

Lopez and Shaw Islands

The first ferry stop is Lopez Island, with old orchards, weathered barns, and pastures of sheep and cows. Because of the relatively flat terrain, this island is a favorite for bicyclists. Two popular parks to note are **Odlin County Park** and **Spencer Spit State Park.**

At the next stop, Shaw Island, a local order of nuns wear their traditional habits while running the ferry dock. You may notice that few people get off here; the island is mostly residential, and tourists rarely stop.

Orcas Island

Orcas Island, the next in line, is a large, mountainous, horseshoe-shape island. Roads sweep down through wide valleys and rise to marvelous hilltop views. A number of little shops featuring the island's cottage industries—jewelry, weaving, pottery—are in **Eastsound Village,** the island's business and social center, which is situated in the middle of the horseshoe. Walk along Prune Alley, where you'll find a handful of small shops and restaurants.

On the other side of the horseshoe from the ferry landing, following aptly named Horseshoe Highway, is **Moran State Park** (Star Rte., Box 22, Eastsound 98245, ☎ 360/376–2326). The ranger station will supply information, but applications for camping permits within the park for Memorial Day through Labor Day must be received by mail at least two weeks prior to the requested date. From the summit of the 2,400-foot-tall **Mt. Constitution** are panoramic views of the San Juan Islands, the Cascades, the Olympics, and Vancouver Island.

San Juan Island

The last ferry stop in the San Juan Islands is at **Friday Harbor** on San Juan Island, with a colorful, active waterfront that always conveys a holiday feeling. Friday Harbor—the islands' county seat and the only incorporated town on San Juan Island—is also the most convenient destination in the San Juans for visitors traveling on foot. The shops here cater to tourists, offering clever crafts, gifts, and whimsical toys.

Standing at the ferry dock facing the bluff and downtown, you'll recognize the **Whale Museum** by the mural of the whale painted on the wall. To reach the entrance, walk up Spring Street and turn right on 1st Street. This modest museum doesn't attempt to woo you with expensive exhibits; models of whales, whale skeletons, baleen, recordings of whale sounds, and videos of whales are the attractions. There are also workshops on marine mammals and San Juan ecology. *62 1st St. N,* ☎ *360/378–4710.* ☞ *$3 adults, $2.50 senior citizens, $1.50 children 3–12.* ☼ *June–Sept., daily 10–5; Oct.–May, daily 11–4.*

For an opportunity to see whales cavorting in the Strait of San Juan de Fuca, go to **Lime Kiln Point State Park,** on San Juan's west side, just 6 miles from Friday Harbor. This viewpoint is America's first official whale-watching park. The best seasons to visit are late spring, summer, and fall. *6158 Lighthouse Rd.,* ☎ *360/378–2044.* ☛ *Free.* ☉ *Daily 6:30 AM–10 PM. Day-use only; no camping facilities.*

The **San Juan Island National Historic Park** is a remnant of the "Pig War," a prolonged scuffle between American and British troops who were brought in after a Yank killed a Brit's pig in 1859, setting off tempers on both sides. The mere presence of the soldiers was pretty much the extent of the hostilities (no gunfire was ever exchanged), although troops from both countries remained on the island until 1872. The park encompasses two separate areas: a British camp on the west side of the island, containing a blockhouse, commissary, and barracks; and an American camp with a laundry, fortifications, and a visitor's center. From June through August the park offers hikes and historic reenactments of 1860s-era military life. For information contact the **San Juan Island Visitor Information Service** (☎ 360/468–3663).

⓫ **Roche Harbor,** at the northern end of San Juan, is an elegant little town of well-manicured lawns, rose gardens, cobblestone waterfront, hanging flower baskets on the docks, and the Hotel de Haro, with its restaurant and lounge.

Shopping

Lopez Island

The **Chimera Gallery** (Lopez Village, ☎ 360/468–3265) is a local artists' cooperative exhibiting crafts, jewelry, and fine art. **Grayling Gallery** (3630 Hummel Lake Rd., ☎ 360/468–2779) features the paintings, prints, sculptures, and pottery of about 10 artists from Lopez Island, some of whom live and work on the gallery's premises. The gallery is open Friday–Sunday 10–5.

Orcas Island

Darvill's Rare Print Shop (Eastsound, ☎ 360/376–2351) specializes in antique and contemporary prints.

San Juan Island

Boardwalk Bookstore (5 Spring St., Friday Harbor, ☎ 360/378–2787) is strong in classics and has a collection of good, popular literature selected by a most literate owner, Dorthea Augusztiny. **Cabezon Gallery** (60 1st St. W, ☎ 360/378–3116) features the works of local artists. **Island Wools, Weaving, and Quilting** (30 1st St. S, Friday Harbor, ☎ 360/378–2148) carries wonderful yarns, some hand-spun and hand-dyed; imaginative buttons; quilting supplies; and some hand-knit items. **Waterworks Gallery** (315 Argyle St., Friday Harbor, ☎ 360/378–3060) emphasizes marine art.

Sports and the Outdoors

Beaches

The best beaches on Lopez Island include the low-bank beach at **Odlin County Park** (Rte. 2, Box 3216, ☎ 360/468–2496) and a mile of waterfront at **Spencer Spit State Park** (Rte. 2, Box 3600, ☎ 360/468–2251). On San Juan Island, you'll find 10 acres of beachfront at the **San Juan County Park** (380 Westside Rd. N, Friday Harbor, ☎ 360/378–2992) and 6 miles of public beach at American Camp.

Bicycling

LOPEZ ISLAND

The **Bike Shop** (Rte. 1, Box 1162, Lopez 98261, ☎ 360/468–3497) provides bikes for rent year-round. **Cycle San Juans Tours and Rentals** (Rte. 1, Box 1744, Lopez 98261, ☎ 360/468–3251) provides free bicycle delivery all year.

ORCAS ISLAND

Key Moped Rental (Box 279, Eastsound, ☎ 360/376–2474) rents mopeds during the summer. **Wildlife Cycles** (Box 1048, Eastsound, ☎ 360/376–4708) has bikes for rent in Eastsound.

SAN JUAN ISLAND

San Juan Island Bicycles (380 Argyle St., Friday Harbor, ☎ 360/378–4941) has a reputation for good service as well as equipment. **Susie's Mopeds** (Box 1972, Friday Harbor, ☎ 360/378–5244 or 800/532–0087) rents mopeds.

Boating and Kayaking

Marine State Parks (☎ 360/753–2027) are accessible by private boat only. No moorage or camping reservations are available, and fees are charged at some parks from May through Labor Day. Fresh water, where available, is limited. Island parks are Blind, Clark, Doe, James, Jones, Matia, Patos, Posey, Stuart, Sucia, and Turn. All have a few campsites; there are no docks at Blind, Clark, Patos, Posey, or Turn islands.

Skippered sailing charters are available through **Amante Sail Tours** (☎ 360/376–4231), **Custom Designed Charters** (☎ 360/376–5105), **Harmony Sailing Charters** (☎ 360/468–3310), **Kismet Sailing Charters** (☎ 360/468–2435), **Nor'wester Sailing Charters** (☎ 360/378–5478), and **Wind N' Sails** (☎ 360/378–5343).

If you are kayaking on your own, beware of ever-changing conditions, ferry and shipping landings, and strong tides and currents. Go ashore only on known public property. Day trips and longer expeditions are available from **Shearwater Sea Kayak Tours** (☎ 360/376–4699), **Doe Bay Resort** (☎ 360/376–2291), **San Juan Kayak Expeditions** (☎ 360/378–4436), and **Seaquest** (☎ 360/378–5767).

MARINAS

On Lopez Island, **Islands Marine Center** (☎ 360/468–3377) has most standard marina amenities, repair facilities, and transient moorage. On Orcas Island, **Deer Harbor Resort & Marina** (☎ 360/376–4420), **Lieber Haven Marina Resort** (☎ 360/376–4420), and **West Sound Marina** (☎ 360/376–2314) offer standard marina facilities and more. **Russell's Landing/Orcas Store** (☎ 360/376–4389) has gas, diesel, tackle, and groceries at the ferry landing. On San Juan Island, **Port of Friday Harbor** (☎ 360/378–2688), **San Juan Marina** (☎ 360/378–2841), and **Roche Harbor Resort** (☎ 360/378–2155) have standard marina facilities; Port of Friday and Roche harbors are also U.S. Customs ports of entry.

Fishing

You can fish year-round for bass and trout at Hummel Lake on Lopez Island, and at Egg and Sportsman lakes on San Juan Island. On Orcas, there are three lakes at Moran State Park that are open to fishing from late April through October. You can go saltwater fishing through **Buffalo Works** (☎ 360/378–4612) and **King Salmon Charters** (☎ 360/468–2314).

Dining

For price-category definitions, *see* Dining *in* Washington Essentials, *below.*

Lopez Island

$$ **Bay Café.** Fine entrées served with an international flair, plus an excellent wine list, attract everyone from locals and vacationers to movie stars filming on the island to this modest-looking restaurant near the water in Lopez Village. Highlights of the seasonal menu include grilled pork tenderloin with a honey-mustard glaze, smoked ham aioli, and garlic mashed potatoes. ✗ *Lopez Village,* ☎ *360/468–3700. Reservations advised. MC, V. No lunch.*

Orcas Island

$$–$$$ **Christina's.** The emphasis at this elegant restaurant is on fresh, local seafood. Order the steamed lemongrass and ginger rockfish served with rice noodles, leeks, and carrots, and then relax on the enclosed porch or the rooftop terrace with views of East Sound. Other specialties include a stuffed breast of chicken served with an eggplant relish and grilled vegetables. Desserts include the likes of pumpkin flan with cookies or a Chocolate Blackout Torte. ✗ *N. Beach Rd. and Horseshoe Hwy.,* ☎ *360/376–4904. Reservations advised. AE, DC, MC, V. Closed Tues. Oct.–mid June. No lunch.*

$–$$ **Bilbo's Festivo.** Stucco walls, Mexican tiles, wood benches, and weavings from New Mexico betray the culinary theme of this restaurant with a courtyard. The menu features burritos, enchiladas, and other Mexican favorites like orange-marinated chicken grilled over mesquite and served with fresh asparagus, potatoes, and salad. ✗ *N. Beach Rd. and A St., Eastsound,* ☎ *360/376–4728. No reservations. AE, MC, V. No lunch Oct.–May.*

San Juan Island

$$$ **Duck Soup Inn.** Everything the Duck Soup Inn serves is made from scratch daily, including the fresh bread, Mediterranean-inspired entrées, vegetarian dishes, and delicious ice cream. Start with apple-wood-smoked Westcott Bay oysters, followed with pan-seared sea scallops served in a red-curry coconut sauce on a bed of cashews and greens. There is also a good list of Northwest, California, and European wines. ✗ *3090 Roche Harbor Rd.,* ☎ *360/378–4878. Reservations advised. MC, V. Closed Mon.–Tues. Apr.–Oct.; closed entirely Nov.–Mar. No lunch.*

$$ **Springtree Café.** This bistro-style café in downtown Friday Harbor has an innovative daily menu built around fresh seafood and vegetarian entrées. The kitchen uses fresh, Waldron Island organic produce to create such dishes as ginger shrimp with mango and dark rum or steamed San Juan Island mussels. The restaurant also offers a good wine list. ✗ *Spring St.,* ☎ *360/378–4848. Reservations advised. MC, V. Closed Sun.–Mon. Oct. 11–May 1.*

$ **Front Street Ale House.** This English-style pub serves sandwiches and salads, as well as such traditional pub fare as lamb stew, meat pastries, steak-and-kidney pie, and trifle. For vegetarians, there's a vegetable patty lightly sautéed, then stacked with cheese, mushrooms, lettuce, tomato, and onions. On-tap brews from the San Juan Brewing Company carry such locally inspired names as Pig War Stout. ✗ *1 Front St., Friday Harbor,* ☎ *360/378–2337. No reservations. MC, V.*

Lodging

For price-category definitions, *see* Lodging *in* Washington Essentials, *below.*

Anacortes

$$$-$$$$ **Majestic Hotel.** An old mercantile has been turned into one of the finest small hotels in the Northwest. From the elegant, Victorian-style, two-story lobby, guests can enter the Rose & Crown pub and the banquet rooms or ascend the sweeping stairway to the guest rooms and the dark, English-style library. The top-floor gazebo has views of the marina, Mt. Baker, and the Cascades. Rooms are individually decorated with European antiques and down comforters; several contain whirlpool tubs. A complimentary Continental breakfast is served in the dining room, and the full-service restaurant, the Courtyard Bistro, turns out excellent meals. ☒ *419 Commercial Ave., Anacortes, Fidalgo Island 98221,* ☎ *360/293–3355,* ᶠᴬˣ *360/293–5214. 23 rooms. Restaurant, pub, library. MC, V.*

Lopez Island

$$$ **Edenwild.** The imposing gray Victorian-style farmhouse, surrounded by rose gardens, looks as if it's a restored island building, but dates only from 1990, not 1890. Rooms feature whitewashed oak floors, a muted gray interior, and white painted woodwork, along with botanical prints, lace curtains from Scotland, leaded-glass windows, and some antiques. In summer a three-course breakfast is served in the dining room. ☒ *Box 271, Lopez Island 98261,* ☎ *360/468–3238. 7 rooms. MC, V.*

$$-$$$ **Inn at Swifts Bay.** Robert Herrman and Chris Brandmeir invite guests into their sumptuously comfortable Tudor-style home as if they were welcoming old friends. The English-country ambience is enhanced by eclectic furnishings and well-stocked book and video libraries. Bay windows in the living and dining areas overlook well-kept gardens, and a crackling fire warms the living room on winter evenings. Robes, thongs, and flashlights are available for your walk through the garden to a hot tub under the stars. Guest rooms and suites are all decorated tastefully. In the morning, Chris treats you to a gourmet breakfast, such as eggs Dungeness (poached eggs with hollandaise and fresh crab). ☒ *Rte. 2, Box 3402, Lopez Island 98261,* ☎ *360/468–3636. 2 rooms, 3 suites, waterfront cabin. Hot tub, beach. AE, D, MC, V.*

$$ **Mackaye Harbor Inn.** At the south end of Lopez Island, across the road from MacKaye Harbor, is this two-story inn, a frame 1920s sea captain's house with a half mile of beach. Rooms feature golden oak and brass details and wicker furniture; three have views of the harbor. Owners Robin, who is Swedish, and Mike Bergstrom take turns cooking breakfast, which often includes Scandinavian specialties such as *aebleskiver* (apple pancake) and *panukakku* (Finnish pancake). ☒ *Box 1940, Lopez Island 98261,* ☎ *360/468–2253. 5 rooms. Kayaking, boating, bicycles. MC, V.*

Orcas Island

$$$ **Rosario Spa & Resort.** This 1905 Mediterranean-style mansion, which supports a six-ton copper roof, has finally received its due: The interior of the building, done in teak and mahogany and featuring original Mission-style furniture, has been renovated. Shipbuilding magnate Robert Moran, who commissioned the structure, was told he had six months to live so he went all-out—to the tune of $1.5 million—on this, his last extravagance. As it happened, Moran lived another 30 years, and now the mansion is on the National Register of Historic Places. The villas and hotel units, added after Rosario was converted into a resort in 1960, now have modern bathrooms, soundproofing, and fresh color schemes; many have great views of the water. Avoid long ferry lines in the summer by leaving your car in Anacortes; the resort shuttle meets every ferry and offers transportation into Eastsound. The

resort also is accessible from Seattle by floatplane and Victoria clipper boats. ☎ *Horseshoe Hwy., Eastsound 98245, ☎ 360/376–2222 or 800/562–8820. 179 rooms. Dining room, indoor pool, 2 outdoor pools, hot tub, sauna, spa, 2 tennis courts, hiking, dock, boating, fishing. AE, DC, MC, V.*

$$–$$$ **Orcas Hotel.** On the hill overlooking the Orcas Island ferry landing is this three-story, red-roof Victorian hotel, complete with a wraparound porch and white picket fence. Construction first began in 1900, and the building is on the National Register of Historic Places. Guest rooms feature wicker, brass, antique furnishings, and feather beds, and some units have small sundecks. The dining room (open to nonguests as well) overlooks the ferry landing and gardens; an on-site bakery offers espresso drinks. A complimentary breakfast is served in the dining room, where guests order from the restaurant's regular menu of French toast, omelets, and other egg dishes. ☎ *Box 155, Orcas 98280, ☎ 360/376–4300, FAX 360/376–4399. 12 rooms. Restaurant, bar. AE, DC, MC, V.*

$$–$$$ **Turtleback Farm Inn.** Just 15 minutes from the ferry landing is this forest green inn, trimmed in white, set on 80 acres of meadow, forest, and farmland in the shadow of Turtleback Mountain. The interior is spacious and airy, without frills. Guest rooms have easy chairs, good beds with woolen comforters made from the fleece of resident sheep, some antiques, cream-color muslin curtains, and views of meadows and forest. Breakfast, cooked by Susan Fletcher and served by her husband, Bill, can be taken in the dining room or on the deck overlooking the valley. ☎ *R.R. 1, Box 650, Eastsound 98245, ☎ 360/376–3914. 7 rooms. MC, V.*

$$ **Deer Harbor Inn.** The original 1915 log lodge—situated on a knoll overlooking Deer Harbor—was the first resort built on the island and is now the dining room of the inn. A newer log cabin features eight spacious, airy rooms with peeled-log furniture, lovely views from balconies, and breakfast delivered to the door in a picnic basket. The dining room, which specializes in fresh seafood, is large but cozy, with its natural wood and floral prints, and has an adjoining deck for outdoor dining. ☎ *Box 142, Eastsound 98243, ☎ 360/376–4110. 8 units. Restaurant. AE, MC, V.*

$–$$ **Doe Bay Village Resort.** This is a rustic place that is a personal-growth center and retreat. The resort feels faintly countercultural, a holdover from its earlier days as an artists' colony. Units vary from dormitory rooms to cottages, some with sleeping quarters only and access to shower house and community kitchen; other units feature kitchens and baths. A natural-food café and general store are also on-site. The peaceful, scenic grounds are great for walks or for sitting and reading. ☎ *S.R. 86, Olga 98279, ☎ 360/376–2291. 100 units. Café, hot tub, massage, kayaking. AE, MC, V.*

San Juan Island

$$$ **Friday Harbor House.** On a bluff overlooking the marina, ferry landing, and San Juan Channel, this contemporary villa hotel opened in late 1994. Each of the 20 guest rooms has a fireplace, view, oversized whirlpool tub, and refrigerator; complimentary continental breakfast is included. ☎ *130 West St., Box 1385, Friday Harbor 98250, ☎ 360/ 378–8455. 20 rooms. Restaurant. MC, V.*

$$–$$$ **Roche Harbor Resort.** Here you've got a choice between rather nondescript cottages and condominiums, or rooms in the 1886 restored Hotel de Haro. The old hotel building is better to look at than to stay in; its guest rooms are fairly shabby or, at best, very rustic. On the other hand, the resort has extensive facilities, including boat slips for 200 yachts, full marina facilities, and a 4,000-foot airstrip. ⌨ *Box 1, Friday Harbor 98250, ☎ 360/378–2155. 60 rooms. Restaurant, pool, tennis court. MC, V.*

$$ **Blair House.** This B&B sits on more than an acre of landscaped grounds just four blocks uphill from the ferry landing in Friday Harbor. The two-story gray Victorian house with dormer windows and a wide wraparound porch, now furnished with wicker chairs and table, was built in 1909 and has since been enlarged several times. The rooms are decorated with sophisticated wallpapers, color-coordinated linens, and ivory comforters on the beds. Guests can eat breakfast in the large dining room, on the front porch, or alongside the outdoor pool. ⌨ *345 Blair Ave., Friday Harbor 98250, ☎ 360/378–5907. 7 rooms, 1 cottage. Dining room, pool, hot tub. AE, MC, V.*

$$ **Fridays.** Since it was built in 1891, this house near the ferry terminal has been a hotel, restaurant, private home, and a youth hostel. Debbie and Steve Demarest have converted it into a downtown bed-and-breakfast hideaway with Arts and Crafts–style furniture in the sitting room and several guest rooms that open onto decks flanked by roses, geraniums, and other flowers. All rooms are upstairs and are decorated with antiques, colorful floral-print comforters on the beds, and art on the walls. Continental breakfast features fresh orange juice, scones baked daily, and gourmet coffee. ⌨ *35 1st St., Friday Harbor 98250, ☎ 360/ 378–5848 or 800/352–2632. 4 rooms with bath, 4 rooms share 2 baths, 2 suites. MC, V.*

$$ **Hillside House.** Less than a mile outside of Friday Harbor, this contemporary house sits on a hill, providing stunning views of the harbor and Mt. Baker from a large deck. The Eagle's Nest suite features several windows with expansive views, a king-size bed, sitting area, and spacious bathroom, where guests can luxuriate in the whirlpool tub while gazing up at the moon through large, high windows. Queen-size beds, oak chests, and one- or two-person window seats are in all the rooms. Some feature sophisticated decor while others are more whimsical. Others overlook the 10,000-square-foot full-flight aviary. The Robinsons, who own the inn, encourage guests to use the recycled books in the hallway—take one or leave one. Breakfast includes entrées made with resident hens' eggs, island jams, and fresh berries. ⌨ *365 Carter Ave., Friday Harbor 98250, ☎ 360/378–4730 or 800/232–4730. 6 rooms, 1 suite. AE, MC, V.*

$$ **San Juan Inn.** This restored 1873 inn is comfortably furnished and within walking distance of the ferry terminal. Rooms, which are all on the second floor, are small but have brass, iron, or wicker beds, a few antiques, and decorative wallpaper. Some rooms have views of a lovely courtyard garden. A breakfast of muffins, coffee, and juice is served each morning in a parlor overlooking the harbor. ⌨ *50 Spring St., Box 776, Friday Harbor 98250, ☎ 360/378–2070 or 800/742–8210. 10 rooms. Car rental. MC, V.*

BELLINGHAM AND WHATCOM & SKAGIT COUNTIES

North of Seattle on the way to Vancouver, British Columbia, I–5 passes through the beautiful Skagit River valley and Skagit and Whatcom counties. The gentle farmlands and low foothills along this route are often wrapped in mist, resembling a delicate Japanese pen-and-ink landscape drawing. To the east, however, rising sharply from the foothills, are the anything-but-delicate Cascade Mountains.

Aside from the natural beauty, there are many interesting sights in the area, and a good place to start—and a perfect launching point for exploration—is the town of Bellingham, where you'll witness the best of several worlds, including an intellectual college atmosphere and a bustling fishing and lumber industry in a lush and beautiful setting.

Exploring

Numbers in the margin correspond to points of interest on the Whatcom and Skagit Counties map.

Bellingham and Environs

❶ There are a variety of places to visit in and around **Bellingham,** but a convenient starting point is downtown, at the **Whatcom Museum of History and Art.** The expanded, four-building campus includes a beautiful, huge redbrick Victorian building housing permanent exhibits of the early coal and lumbering industries, Native American artifacts, and local waterfowl; other traveling exhibits, on a variety of subjects, are shown on a regular basis. The complex includes a children's museum, too. *121 Prospect St.,* ☎ *360/676–6981.* ☛ *Free (children's museum $2).* ☉ *Tues.–Sun. noon–5.*

Traveling by car or on foot, go northwest from downtown to Holly Street, across the mouth of Whatcom Creek. Turning right on C Street will bring you to the **Maritime Heritage Center,** an urban park that pays tribute to Bellingham's fishing industry. Self-guided tours allow visitors to learn about hatcheries and salmon life cycles, see salmon-rearing tanks and fish ladders, go angling for salmon and trout, and watch salmon spawning. *1600 C St.,* ☎ *360/676–6806.* ☛ *Free.* ☉ *Weekdays 9–5.*

Go about ¼ mile down Holly Street or Roeder Avenue to F Street and Bellingham's northern waterfront. The harbor here, including the Squalicum Harbor Marina (Roeder Ave. and Coho Way, I–5 Exits 253 and 256), the second-largest marina on Puget Sound and home to more than 1,700 commercial and pleasure boats, makes for good dock walking, fishing, lounging, and picnicking. There are several other points on Bellingham's shoreline from which to engage in any of these activities, including Boulevard Park (S. State St. and Bayview Dr.), an excellent waterfront park with 14 acres and a ½ mile of shoreline located midway between downtown and Old Fairhaven; and Marine Park (foot of Harris St., in Old Fairhaven), a small but popular spot for sunset-watching and crabbing that is close to the Alaska Marine Highway terminal.

On a hill, overlooking downtown and Bellingham Bay, is the picturesque campus of **Western Washington University** (516 High St., ☎ 360/650–3000). To get there, take Garden Street from the north or College Drive from the south. The collection of outdoor sculptures scattered around the campus includes works by Mark DiSuvero, Isamu Noguchi, Richard Serra, and George Rickey.

At the beginning of Chuckanut Drive (Highway 11) is **Fairhaven,** home base for the Bellingham Cruise Terminal, the Alaska Marine Highway System, the 120-foot schooner the *Zodiac,* and seasonal cruise vessels that go to the San Juan Islands. The historic district of Fairhaven includes many Victorian homes and several commercial buildings, including restaurants, shops, galleries, and bookstores.

An option out of the city is to take Highway 11 south for a 23-mile drive into Skagit County, alongside beautiful **Chuckanut Bay.** On one side is the steep and heavily wooded Chuckanut Mountain; on the other

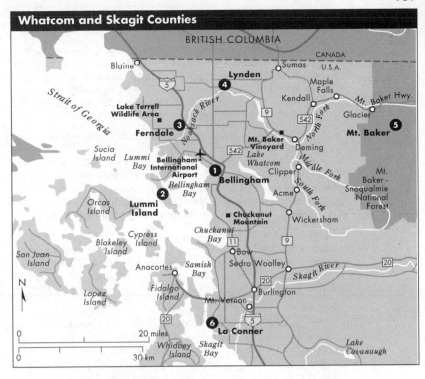

Whatcom and Skagit Counties

are stunning views westward over Puget Sound and the San Juan Islands. Many university professors and others have attractive houses built along this stretch of road. Beginning by **Fairhaven Park** in the Old Fairhaven neighborhood and joining up with I–5 in the flat farmlands near **Bow,** in Skagit County, the full loop can be made in a few hours. Several good restaurants are located toward the southern end of the drive, so planning your excursion to include a lunch stop is a good idea.

While in the area, stop at the **Rose Garden** at Fairhaven Park. It was developed in the early 1900s and is used as a testing site by the American Rose Society; the roses are at their best from June to September. Fairhaven Park also has numerous hiking trails and picnic grounds, a playground, tennis courts, playing fields, a wading pool, and a youth hostel. *107 Chuckanut Dr., ☎ 360/671–1570. ☛ Free. ☼ Daily 9–5.*

Another alternative route from Bellingham is to take Exit 260 west off I–5 to the ferry terminal at Fisherman's Cove dock on the Lummi Indian Reservation. The passenger-car ferry will take you on a 10-minute ❷ ride across to **Lummi Island.** The 10-mile-long mountainous and largely uninhabited spot in Bellingham Bay makes a great day trip, especially if you're going to bike or hike.

Ferndale

❸ Farther north off I–5 is **Ferndale** (Exit 262), a charming town and longtime dairy-farming community in the Nooksack Valley, 18 miles north of Bellingham. Among its chief attractions is **Pioneer Park,** which has a number of 1870s log buildings, including a granary, Whatcom County's first church, a hotel, and several historic houses. The buildings have been restored and converted into period museums through which the public can wander and learn about the town's history. *1st*

and Cherry Sts. (2 blocks south of Main St.), ☎ *360/384–3042.* ☛
Free. ⊙ *May–Oct., Tues.–Sun. noon–5; tours run daily on the hr.*

Also in Ferndale is the **Hovander Homestead Park,** a National Historic
Site with a model farm complete with Victorian-era farmhouse, barnyard animals, water tower, vegetable gardens, and antique farm equipment. Surrounding it are 60 acres of walking trails, picnic grounds, and
access to fishing in the Nooksack. *5299 Nielsen Rd., Ferndale,* ☎ *360/
384–3444.* ☛ *Free. Park open during daylight hrs daily.*

About a mile away is **Tennant Lake Natural History Interpretive Center,** situated in the Nielsen House, an early homestead. There are exhibits and nature walks around the lake within these 200 acres of marshy
habitat, where eagles and other wildlife can be seen. The unusual **Fragrance Garden**—with herbs and flowers—is designed for the sight-im-
paired and can be explored by following Braille signs. *5236 Nielsen
Rd., Ferndale,* ☎ *360/384–3444.* ☛ *Free.* ⊙ *Daily dawn–dusk.*

At **Lake Terrell Wildlife Preserve,** visitors can observe a wide variety
of waterfowl that live throughout this 11,000-acre spread. In the fall
you can hunt pheasants and western Washington waterfowl; catfish,
perch, bass, and cutthroat can be fished year-round. *5975 Lake Terrell Rd., Ferndale,* ☎ *360/384–4723.* ☛ *Free.* ⊙ *Weekdays 8–5.*

Lynden

❹ From Ferndale, take Highway 539 north and east to **Lynden**—a small
dairying town that has preserved its conservative Dutch heritage. Sunday retail-store closure has only recently become voluntary instead of
mandatory, and drinking alcoholic beverages is still prohibited in establishments where dancing occurs. **Lynden Farm Tours** (7026 Noon
Rd., ☎ 360/354–3549) offers tours of working farms in the area. Efforts to keep the Dutch heritage alive have resulted in much kitschy-
cuteness, but several good examples of traditional Dutch architecture
are also evident. **Downtown Lynden** features a four-story windmill
(which doubles as an inn), a minimall called Delft Square, the Dutch
Village Shopping Mall, and a miniature indoor canal. On special occasions, shopkeepers wear traditional Dutch clothing, right down to
the wood clogs.

Mt. Baker and Whatcom County

❺ Probably the single biggest tourist attraction near Bellingham is **Mt. Baker,**
part of the Cascade range. At 10,778 feet high, this sharp peak is visible from virtually everywhere in the area, as is the adjacent and photogenic **Mt. Shuksan,** which stands at an elevation of 9,038 feet. **Mt.
Baker–Snoqualmie National Forest,** as well as the foothills, forests,
streams, and country villages you will pass through on the road from
Bellingham, provides endless opportunity for exploration. Along the
60-mile route east from Bellingham (on the Mt. Baker Highway, also
called Highway 542) are several excellent stopping points. Among the
pleasant mountain towns are Deming, Kendall, Maple Falls, and
Glacier, all of which have a variety of good, old-fashioned cafés and
shops.

Just past the town of Glacier is the turnoff to **Coleman Glacier;** the thundering, 170-foot-high **Nooksack Falls,** only a short walk from the
road; and **Mt. Baker's Heather Meadows ski area** (*see* Sports and the
Outdoors, *below*).

TIME OUT   If you're about ready for a mountain picnic, at Deming go south on
Highway 9 to the town of Van Zandt. **Everybody's Store** (the only public
building in town) is a long-standing local favorite place to stock up on

exotic foods and goodies. Everything from dill pickles to homemade sausage, cheeses, bialys—not to mention toys, imported clothes, and regular foodstuffs—can be found here.

Continue south along the Nooksack River valley, through the small towns of Clipper and Acme, then cut over at Wickersham and back to Bellingham along Lake Whatcom for a splendid afternoon's drive. Special tours by the **Lake Whatcom Steam Train** (Box 91, Acme 98220, ☏ 360/595–2218) offer picturesque rides behind a restored, vintage steam engine through the woods at the south end of Lake Whatcom during the summer and holidays.

La Conner

Driving south for about 30 miles on I–5 and Route 1 from Bellingham will bring you to **La Conner,** a small fishing village and arts community west of Mount Vernon, at the mouth of the Skagit River. Such painters as Morris Graves, Kenneth Callahan, Guy Anderson, and Mark Tobey set up shop here in the '40s, and it has been an artist's haven ever since. A concerted effort has been made in recent years to make La Conner a tourist destination; the number of good shops and restaurants has increased, but so has the traffic, and in summer this usually sleepy town becomes clogged and congested.

Many of the shopkeepers and gallery owners in La Conner carry free copies of a helpful visitor's guide, published by the **Chamber of Commerce** (Lime Dock, 109 N. 1st St., ☏ 360/466–4778). Interesting attractions that you won't want to miss are the **Volunteer Fireman's Museum** (1st St., no ☏), with turn-of-the-century equipment that you can see from the street through large windows in the building; the **Gaches Mansion** (2nd and Calhoun Sts., ☏ 360/466–4288), a Victorian house that is now an exhibition space and museum for area artists, called the Northwest School of La Conner; and the **Skagit County Historical Museum** (501 4th St., ☏ 360/466–3365).

Outside the village of La Conner is the fertile flatland of the Skagit River valley. Many farms grow huge batches of commercial flowers—especially daffodils and tulips—and depending on the season, it is possible to view these huge fields of bright colors as you drive the back roads. One of the commercial gardens open to the public is **La Conner Flats** (1588 Best Rd., ☏ 360/466–3190). At various times throughout the year, tulips (the main crop), rhododendrons, roses, and flowering cherry trees may be seen. Another garden, **Roozengaarde** (1587 Beaver Marsh Rd., ☏ 360/424–8531), one of the largest growers of tulips, daffodils, and irises in the United States, is open to the public.

Shopping

Bellingham

The **Old Fairhaven District** (12th and Harris Sts.) is a number of square blocks of beautifully restored 1890s brick buildings housing a variety of restaurants, taverns, galleries, and specialty boutiques. To get there, take Exit 250 from I–5, then take Old Fairhaven Parkway west.

In **Old Town** (Lower Holly St.), in downtown Bellingham, there are a number of good antiques shops, secondhand stores, fish markets, hobby shops, and outdoor recreation equipment suppliers. The surrounding area also has small shops and a pleasant small-town atmosphere. Public parking is available on the street or at the Parkade (corner of Commercial and Holly Sts.).

Bellis Fair (I–5 Exits 256 and 256B, jct. I–5 and Guide Meridian, ☎ 360/734–5022) is a glossy regional shopping mall a few miles north of downtown. It features major department stores, several restaurants, and more than 120 other shops, including a multiplex movie theater.

Sports and the Outdoors

Bicycling

Chuckanut Drive and **Lummi Island** are favorite bicycling routes. Also good is the flat land around **La Conner,** to the south of Bellingham. To the north, **Lynden** is beautiful country, where tulip farms enliven the scenery in the spring. For rentals, try **Fairhaven Bicycle and Ski** (1103 11th St., ☎ 360/733–4433).

Climbing

The **American Alpine Institute** (1212 24th St., Bellingham 98225, ☎ 360/671–1505) is one of the most prestigious mountain- and rock-climbing schools around.

Golf

A public course designed by Arnold Palmer is at the **Inn at Semiahmoo Golf Club** (☎ 360/371–7005), a luxury resort near Blaine and the Canadian border on Semiahmoo Spit. There are also public 18-hole courses at **Birch Bay** (☎ 360/371–2026), **Sudden Valley** (☎ 360/734–6435), and **Lake Padden Park** (☎ 360/676–6989).

Skiing

Mt. Baker's **Heather Meadows** (1017 Iowa St., ☎ 360/734–6771), with both downhill and cross-country skiing, has the longest season in the state, lasting from roughly November to March. It has new chairlifts, day-lodge facilities, and parking areas.

For equipment rentals, try the **Great Adventure** (201 E. Chestnut, Bellingham, ☎ 360/671–4615).

Spectator Sports

The **Bellingham Giants** baseball team plays June–September (Joe Martin Stadium, 1500 Orleans St., Bellingham, ☎ 360/671–6347). The **Bellingham Ice Hawks** play in the British Columbia Junior Hockey League September–March (Whatcom Sports Arena, 1801 W. Bakerview Rd., Bellingham, ☎ 360/676–8080).

Water Sports

Several lakes near Bellingham offer ample opportunity for water sports, including **Lake Padden Park** (4882 Samish Way, ☎ 360/676–6989) and **Bloedel Donovan Park** (2214 Electric Ave., ☎ 360/676–6888), on the northwest shore of Lake Whatcom. For a list of fishing and sailing charter companies, contact the Bellingham/Whatcom County CVB (☎ 360/671–3990).

Whale Watching

San Juan Islands Shuttle Express (Alaska Ferry Terminal, 355 Harris Ave., No. 105, Bellingham 98225, ☎ 360/671–1137) offers scheduled summer whale-watching trips from Bellingham to the San Juan Islands.

Dining

For price-category definitions, *see* Dining *in* Washington Essentials, *below.*

Bellingham

$$$–$$$$ **Il Fiasco.** Although the food can be pricey, this restaurant (the name means
★   "the flask") is considered one of the best in Bellingham, offering an ambitious northern Italian menu, sophisticated decor, knowledgeable staff, and a good wine list that mixes Italian and local vintages. Many of the entrées, such as the fresh-crab ravioli or a luscious lasagna made with lamb, fontina cheese, spinach, and polenta, can be ordered as appetizers; an entire meal can thus be concocted entirely from the appetizer list, a practice that is not only accepted but encouraged by the friendly waiters and waitresses. ✕ *1309 Commercial St.,* ☎ *360/676–9136. Reservations advised. MC, V. No lunch weekends.*

$$ **Pacific Café.** Seafood and pasta dishes with an Asian twist are the specialty at this restaurant next door to the historic Mt. Baker Theater in downtown Bellingham; typical menu listings include Alaska spot prawns in a garlicky black-bean sauce and rib steak with a plum-oyster sauce. Portions are large, but you'll want to save room for one of the wickedly good desserts, such as the chocolate éclairs. The café's understated decor, like the food, is Asian-influenced: white walls, rice-paper screens, and wood shutters. ✕ *100 N. Commercial St.,* ☎ *360/647–0800. Reservations advised. AE, MC, V. No lunch Sat.; no dinner Sun.*

$–$$ **Orchard Street Microbrewery and Fine Little Restaurant.** This new find occupies a former warehouse in a manufacturing complex. The purple floor, orangish walls, and red tables of the upscale contemporary restaurant complement the industrial ambience. Start with a crab *casidia* and then migrate to the salmon with mushrooms and oysters in a puff pastry. If you want something more casual, select from the list of pizzas baked in the wood oven. ✕ *709 W. Orchard Dr., No. 1, Bellingham,* ☎ *360/647–1614. No reservations 5–9 PM. AE, MC, V.*

$ **Archer Ale House.** "Fresh air, fresh ale" is the slogan of Bellingham's first smoke-free pub, located in the Fairhaven district in the renovated cellar of the historic 1903 Shering Block. A 20-foot oak bar, stained glass windows, an embossed-tin ceiling, and a dartboard create a hearty, English-pub atmosphere that complements the menu—a selection of pasties, hearty soups, deep-dish pizzas, and a few vegetarian dishes. The 10 rotating taps dispense everything from pilsners to stouts. Two beer engines provide cask-conditioned ales, naturally carbonated brews famous for their clear, rich flavor. ✕ *1212 10th St., Bellingham,* ☎ *360/647–7002. No reservations. MC, V.*

$ **Colophon Café.** Incorporated into the Village Bookstore, this restaurant offers such hearty soups as Brazilian peanut butter, as well as good sandwiches and ice cream. ✕ *1208 11th St., Old Fairhaven,* ☎ *360/647–0092. No reservations. MC, V.*

Bow

$$ **Oyster Creek Inn.** This small eatery, best described as Northwest eclectic, is set in a sharp switchback near the southern end of Chuckanut Drive in nearby Skagit County. Window tables overlook the creek and the bay. Oysters, cooked in a variety of imaginative ways, stand out, while an excellent wine list—drawn exclusively from Washington State vineyards—is also featured. Sunday brunch, with classic dishes such as salmon omelets and fries, is offered. ✕ *190 Chuckanut Dr., Bow,* ☎ *360/766–6179. Reservations advised. AE, MC, V.*

$–$$ **Rhododendron Café.** Homemade soups, seafood, and fresh salads comprise the foundation upon which the ever-changing menu is built here. Specials vary according to the market and may include mussel-vegetable soup or marinated snapper with a toasted-nut sauce. The locally famous pies and other luscious desserts should be sampled. The restaurant, located at the very southern (and out-of-the way) end of Chuckanut Drive—near the tiny town of Bow in Skagit County—is pleasant and unpretentious in its decor; the service is usually cheerful and fast, though when things get crowded it can slow up. ✗ *553 Chuckanut Dr., Bow,* ☎ *360/766–6667. MC, V. Closed Mon.–Tues.*

Lodging

For price-category definitions, *see* Lodging *in* Washington Essentials, *below.*

Bellingham

$$$ **Schnauzer Crossing.** A meticulously kept garden surrounds three sides of this elegant B&B, with Lake Whatcom on the fourth. Besides a large and gracious common sitting room, each of its two guest rooms offers something different: The larger has a huge bed, garden views, a fireplace, and a small sitting room, while the smaller has a view of the lake and a choice little library. You'll be greeted with a fruit basket and cookies upon arrival. Friendly owners Donna and Vermont McAllister serve ample gourmet breakfasts. ☎ *1807 Lakeway Dr., 98226,* ☎ *360/733–0055 or 800/562–2808,* ℻ *360/734–2808. 2 rooms. Hot tub, tennis court, boating. MC, V.*

$$ **Best Western Lakeway Inn.** A large, bustling hotel in downtown Bellingham, this accommodation is popular with tourists, especially those from Vancouver. Located near the big Fred Meyers shopping complex, there are plenty of things to keep the whole family occupied. Children under 12 stay for free when sharing a room with their parents. ☎ *714 Lakeway Dr., 98225,* ☎ *360/671–1011,* ℻ *360/676–8519. 132 rooms. Café, piano bar, indoor pool, sauna, exercise room, airport and ferry shuttle. AE, D, DC, MC, V.*

$–$$ **Park Motel.** Because of its "children under 12 free" policy, this is a popular family motel, and since it's close to the university, it's also often occupied by the visiting parents of students. The strictly standard-issue decor and furnishings are functional but comfortable, and some are equipped with kitchens. ☎ *101 N. Samish Way, 98225,* ☎ *360/733–8280,* ℻ *360/738–9186. 56 rooms. No-smoking rooms, hot tub, sauna. AE, DC, MC, V.*

Blaine

$$$ **Inn at Semi-ah-moo.** At the tip of a sandspit on the U.S.–Canadian border, the Inn at Semi-ah-moo (a coastal Native American word for "clam eaters") is housed in the old Semiahmoo Salmon Cannery building. Extensively renovated and refitted to be a hostelry, the inn's guest rooms range from standard motel-like accommodations to rooms and suites with fireplaces, balconies, and expansive views. The draw here, however, is the dramatic waterside location and the plethora of outdoor activities available at this 800-acre resort. Guests can bike, jog, or hike around the nearby nature trails; join a fishing charter or sightseeing cruise; golf a course designed by Arnold Palmer; recreate indoors at the health club or track; and swim in heated pools indoors or out. ☎ *9565 Semiahmoo Pkwy., 98230,* ☎ *360/371–2000 or 800/822–4200,* ℻ *360/371–5490. 188 rooms, 12 suites. 2 restaurants, bar, indoor pool, outdoor pool, golf course, tennis court, health club, jogging, racquetball, squash, dock, boating, bicycles. AE, MC, V.*

La Conner

$$ **Hotel Planter.** This renovated hotel is the oldest in La Conner and is on the National Register of Historic Places. Bright and airy rooms are filled with attractive handmade furniture, and offer fine views of either La Conner's main street or the waterfront. ☎ *715 1st St., 98257,*

☎ *360/466–4710 or 800/488–5409,* FAX *360/466–1320. 12 rooms, some with private bath. Hot tub. AE, MC, V.*

$$ **Rainbow Inn.** Just a half mile east of LaConnor is this stately, three-story, turn-of-the-century country house fringed with a white picket fence. Hosts Sharon Briggs and Ron Johnson left corporate careers in the Bay Area to pursue their love of cooking, gardening, and entertaining. The main floor's parlor has a tile fireplace, antiques, and views out onto open fields. Rooms are large and are furnished with some antiques; one has its own whirlpool tub, but all guests can soak while gazing at Mt. Baker from the hot tub in the gazebo behind the house. From the enclosed porch where breakfast is served, guests can see the gardens and neighboring farms. Breakfast entrées include fresh ginger pancakes with mango topping, mild green-chili frittata with home-made salsa, and zucchini bread with jalapeño jelly. ☎ *1075 Chilberg Rd., 98257,* ☎ *360/466–4578,* FAX *360/466–5700. 5 rooms with bath, 3 rooms share 1 bath. Hot tub. MC, V.*

Mt. Baker

$$ **Mt. Baker Lodging & Travel.** These self-contained cabins are nestled in a lovely wooded setting, 17 miles west of the Mt. Baker National Forest. Each unit—from snug hideaways suitable for couples to larger chalets for families or groups—is clean and charming, if rustic, and has a wood-burning stove or fireplace. All accommodations come stocked with linen, firewood, and towels, and some units are equipped with VCRs; guests with children can be provided with cribs and toys. ☎ *Box 5177, Glacier 98244,* ☎ *360/599–2453 or 800/709–7669. 15 units. Hot tub, sauna. AE, MC, V.*

The Arts and Nightlife

Bellingham

The **Whatcom Museum of History and Art** (121 Prospect St., ☎ 360/676–6981) sponsors regular walks downtown, among the many art galleries. The **Mt. Baker Theater** (104 N. Commercial St., ☎ 360/734–6080) is a restored 62-year-old theater from vaudeville days with a 110-foot Moorish tower and a lobby fashioned after a Spanish galleon. The theater presents movies and national and international touring performances. **Western Washington University** (College of Fine Performing Arts, Western Washington College, 516 High St., ☎ 360/676–3866) has a high-quality performing-arts scene with classical music and theater presentations by local and national performers. In late August and early September, the **Bellinham Festival of Music** (1300 N. State St., Suite 202, ☎ 360/676–5997) offers nearly 20 orchestral, chamber-music, and jazz concerts at Western Washington University and other nearby locations. Informative talks are given an hour prior to chamber and symphony performances. **Speedy O. Tubs Rhythmic Underground** (1305 11th St., Old Fairhaven, ☎ 360/734–1539) features rock and blues, rock and roll, and a drumming circle.

TACOMA

Like many towns in the Northwest, Tacoma's history is tied inextricably with lumber and fishing, and with the two-fisted men and women who did the labor. Today Tacoma is still a hardworking, largely blue-collar town, and it is fighting to upgrade its downtown and its image. Although the city's reputation—based largely on the smell and pollution resulting from the many nearby pulp mills and smelters—is partly deserved, Tacoma is doing much to clean up its act; it appears that the self-proclaimed "City of Destiny" is finally getting a little respect.

Tacoma deserves this respect, too. Looking beyond the surface of this city of 179,000, the visitor will find lovely residential neighborhoods, handsome brick buildings, fine views of Commencement Bay, a world-class zoo, and a tremendously active port (so busy, in fact, that it's stealing the thunder of its larger neighbor to the north). The city is also a convenient jumping-off point for exploring some wonderful locations in south-central Washington: the Cascade Mountains—most notably, the dominating presence of nearby Mt. Rainier (*see* Mt. Rainier National Park, *below*)—and, across the Tacoma Narrows Bridge, the small fishing villages of the Kitsap Peninsula.

Exploring

Numbers in the margin correspond to points of interest on the Tacoma map.

1 **Union Station** (1717 Pacific Ave., at 19th St., ☎ 206/931–7884) is an heirloom from the golden age of railroads, when Tacoma was the western terminus for the transcontinental Northern Pacific Railroad. Built by Reed and Stem, architects of New York City's Grand Central Station, the massive copper-domed, Beaux Arts–style depot was opened in 1911 and shows influences from the Roman Pantheon and the 16th-century Italian Baroque. It now houses federal district courts. The rotunda is open to the public and features a large exhibit of Dale Chihuly art glass.

The renovation of Union Station has prompted more redevelopment **2** in the area. The **Washington State Historical Society** is adjacent to Union Station in a new facility with the same opulent architecture featuring mammoth arches. Its pioneer, Alaskan, and Native American displays are the largest on the Pacific Coast. The permanent exhibit, "Home, Frontier, Crossroads," depicts the many roles the state of Washington has played for its residents. The museum houses exhibits on the Native American, pioneer, maritime, industrial, and natural history of the state. In 1997, the Tacoma branch of the University of Washington will open across from the historical society building. *1911 Pacific Ave.,* ☎ *206/593–2830.* ☛ *$2.50 adults, $2 senior citizens, $1 children.* ☺ *Tues.–Sat. 10–5, Sun. 1–5.*

TIME OUT   Catch a meal at **The Swiss** (1904 S. Jefferson Ave., ☎ 206/572–2821), which is housed in a distinctive 1913 building that was once the Swiss Hall. You'll find good pub fare, a selection of Northwest microbrews, plenty of pool tables, and on certain Sundays, brunch with polka dancing.

3 While downtown visit the **Tacoma Art Museum,** where you'll find a rich collection of American and French paintings, as well as Chinese jades and imperial robes. The museum features a comprehensive collection of work by native Tacoman Dale Chihuly, generally recognized as the greatest living glass sculptor. *12th St. and Pacific Ave.,* ☎ *206/272–4258.* ☛ *$3 adults, $2 senior citizens, students, and children 6–12.* ☺ *Tues.–Sat. 10–5, Sun. noon–5.*

4 The **Pantages Theater,** designed by the famous theater architect B. Marcus Pritica, is a beautifully restored example of early 20th-century Greco-Roman music-hall style, which features classical figures, ornate columns, arches, and reliefs. Once the locale of performances by such varied entertainers as W.C. Fields, Mae West, Charlie Chaplin, Bob Hope, and Stan Laurel, it is now the home of the Tacoma Sym-

Camp Six Logging Museum, **11**

Ft. Nisqually, **10**

Gig Harbor, **12**

Northwest Trek Wildlife Park, **13**

Pantages Theater, **4**

Point Defiance Park, **8**

Point Defiance Zoo and Aquarium, **9**

Port of Tacoma, **7**

Stadium High School, **5**

Tacoma Art Museum, **3**

Union Station, **1**

Washington State Historical Society, **2**

Wright Park, **6**

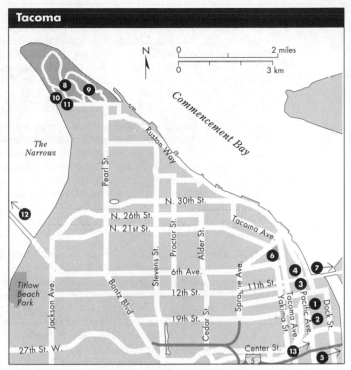

phony and BalleTacoma, as well as visiting musical and theatrical productions. The 1,182-seat Pantages is part of the Broadway Center for the Performing Arts; the center also includes the 748-seat Rialto Theater, just up the street, which once hosted vaudeville performances and showings of silent films and which reopened in 1991 to house the Tacoma Youth Symphony. Adjacent to the Pantages, the very contemporary **Theatre on the Square** opened in 1993 with the Tacoma Actors Guild as its resident company. *901 Broadway,* ☎ *206/591–5890. Tours Thurs. 1–4, free with reservations.*

West of the Pantages building, the **Children's Museum of Tacoma** offers hands-on exhibits in science, the arts, and creative play, especially for children ages 4–12. *925 Court St.,* ☎ *206/627–2436.* ☛ *$3.25, children under 3 free.* ⊙ *Tues.–Sat. 10–4.*

⑤ At the north end of downtown is **Stadium High School,** an elaborate building designed in 1891 as a luxury hotel for the Northern Pacific Railroad (Tacoma was once the railroad's terminus); it was converted into a high school in 1906 after a fire left only the outer shell. The château-style building, with classic European details, is still used as such by the Tacoma School District. *111 N. E St.,* ☎ *206/596–1325.*

⑥ **Wright Park** is a pleasant 28-acre park in the north end of the downtown area. Lawn bowling, a children's playground, and picnicking are big attractions here. The park's chief feature is the **W. W. Seymour Botanical Conservatory,** a lovely Victorian-style greenhouse with an extensive collection of exotic flora. *Park, between 6th and Division Sts., Yakima and Tacoma Aves. Conservatory, nearest corner on 4th and G Sts.,* ☎ *206/591–5331.* ☛ *Free; donations accepted.* ⊙ *Daily 8:30–4:20.*

7 If you take 11th Street or I–5 east from downtown, you find yourself in the **Port of Tacoma.** For a look at a variety of working boats, including container ships, bulk carriers, barges, tugboats, and fireboats, visit the **observation tower,** which has great views of the harbor, one of the five best and naturally deep harbors in the world. Signage and displays explain the workings, activities, and history of the port. *Exit 136 off I–5 to Port of Tacoma Rd., turn left (S.W.) onto E. 11th St. and continue to observation tower,* ☎ *206/383–5841.* ☛ *Free.* ☉ *24 hrs.*

The Port of Tacoma created **Gog-Le-Hi-Te** to replace a small intertidal wetland that had been filled to construct a major container terminal. The name, Gog-Le-Hi-Te, means "where the land and waters meet." The wetland comprises 9 ½ acres of land, marsh, mudflat, fresh water from the Puyallup River, and brackish water from Commencement Bay. There are viewing platforms and interpretive displays. The Tahoma Audubon Society has recorded more than 100 different types of migratory and resident birds, and there are salmon and steelhead there, as well. *Exit 135 off I–5 and follow Portland Ave. to Lincoln Ave.*

8 North of the heart of the city is one of Tacoma's most interesting attractions: 700-acre **Point Defiance Park,** one of the largest urban parks in the country. In addition to its various museums, this huge tract of land that juts out into the western part of Commencement Bay offers extensive footpaths and hiking trails, a variety of flower gardens, the densely wooded Five Mile Drive, and spectacular views of the waterfront. *5400 N. Pearl St.,* ☎ *206/305–1000.* ☛ *Free.* ☉ *June–Aug., daily 10–7; Sept.–May, weekdays 10–4, weekends 10–7.*

★ **9** On the grounds of the park is the **Point Defiance Zoo and Aquarium,** founded in 1888 and generally considered one of the top zoos in the country. Using the Pacific Rim as its theme, it has blossomed (since an extensive renovation in 1986) into an impressive example of humane and innovative trends in zoo administration. Natural habitats and superclose vantage points allow visitors to observe a wide variety of whales, walruses, sharks, polar bears, octopuses, apes, reptiles, and birds. Both the zoo and the aquarium have gained an international reputation for the expert caretakers who treat injured wildlife. ☎ *206/301–1000.* ☛ *$6.25 adults, $5.75 senior citizens and people with disabilities, $4.50 children 5–17, $2.25 children 3–4.* ☉ *Sept.–May, daily 10–4; June–Aug., daily 10–7; closed Thanksgiving and Dec. 25.*

10 Part of Point Defiance is **Ft. Nisqually.** This painstakingly restored Hudson Bay Trading Post was originally built as a British outpost on the Nisqually Delta in the 1830s and relocated as a WPA project to Point Defiance in 1935. Tours of the fort are offered, in which guides point out kitchens, stables, bunkhouses, and other parts of the fur-trading post. *Ft. Nisqually,* ☎ *206/591–5339.* ☛ *$1 adults, 50¢ children.* ☉ *June–Aug., daily noon–4; closed Labor Day–Memorial Day.*

11 Near the fort is the **Camp Six Logging Museum,** a 15-acre museum featuring restored original bunkhouses, hand tools, and historic logging equipment. A 1½-mile-long steam donkey train ride takes you around old bunk cars and a 240-ton skidder. *Logging museum,* ☎ *206/752–0047.* ☛ *Free; train ride $2 adults, $1 senior citizens and children 3–12.* ☉ *May–Sept., Wed.–Fri. 10–6, weekends 10–7; spring and fall, Wed.–Sun. 10–4; closed Nov.–Dec.*

12 From Point Defiance, take Highway 16 8 miles to **Gig Harbor,** once the home and fishing grounds for a small band of Nisqually Indians. Now it is a tiny village retreat inhabited by musicians, artists, sailing enthusiasts, and general layabouts. The beautiful and well-protected harbor is home to a number of unusual bed-and-breakfasts, a string of boutiques and antiques shops, and a lively marina full of both working fishing boats and pleasure crafts. Continuing north along the highway you'll pass many small farms, rolling hills, and fine beaches that are good for beachcombing and clamming.

Although the 35-mile drive southeast along Route 161 will take you away from the city, a trip to the **Northwest Trek Wildlife Park** is time well spent. The land, administered by the Metropolitan Park District of Tacoma, is 600 acres of forest and meadow in which bison, beavers, bobcats, bighorn goats, moose, elk, bald eagles, and more can be observed from a guided tram tour. The **Cheney Discovery Center,** in the park, features a live butterfly atrium and a 150-gallon fish tank with many varieties of native fish, such as salmon and trout. *11610 Trek Dr. E, Eatonville,* ☎ *206/832–6116 or 800/433–8735.* ☛ *$7.50 adults, $6.50 senior citizens, $5 children 5–17, $3 children 3–4.* ☉ *Year-round at 9:30 AM; closing times vary, so call ahead. Tram tours run hourly from 10 AM.*

Shopping

Downtown, **Antique Row** (Broadway and St. Helens St., between 7th and 9th Sts.) is made up of several high-quality antiques stores—perfect for browsing on a rainy afternoon—as well as a few funky boutiques. A surprisingly wide variety of items is available, from high-quality to decidedly odd, from Native American crafts to antique fishing gear, from circus memorabilia to fine furniture. In the unusual category, there's **Good Kitty, Bad Kitty** (765 Broadway, ☎ 206/383–4232) where everything from coffee mugs to fabrics have feline themes; the merchandise is designed by a Tacoma artist. A farmers market is also held here during the summer on Thursdays.

Freighthouse Square Public Market, on the corner of 25th and D streets, is a former railroad warehouse that's been converted into several small, unpretentious shops. The emphasis is on local arts and crafts, and there's also a weekend farmers market, several informal snack bars, and restaurants.

For a small-town ambience within the city, shop the **Proctor District,** with more than 60 businesses, in Tacoma's north end. The **Pacific Northwest Shop** (2702 N. Proctor St., ☎ 206/752–2242) features apparel, books, pottery, food, and wine from more than 800 Northwest artisans and producers. Across the street, neon lights in the shapes of little blue mice herald the movie marquee of the **Blue Mouse Theater** (2611 N. Proctor St., ☎ 206/752–9500).

The biggest shopping mall in the Pacific Northwest is the **Tacoma Mall** (☎ 206/475–4565), 1½ miles south of Tacoma Dome. The mall has more than 150 department stores, specialty shops, services, and restaurants for the devoted shopper.

Sports and the Outdoors

Bicycling

Bicycling is especially popular in the **Puyallup Valley** to the east and the **Kitsap Peninsula.** A number of shops in Tacoma, Puyallup, Gig Harbor, and Port Orchard rent bicycles and equipment.

Golf

Tacoma has several fine golf courses, including **North Shore** (☎ 206/927–1375), with 18 holes and several small unpretentious shops; **Allenmore**

(☎ 206/627–7211), with 18 holes; **Highlands** (☎ 206/759–3622), a nine-hole course; and **Meadowpark** (☎ 206/473–3033), with 18 holes plus a nine-hole course.

Skiing

Sixty-four miles east of Tacoma is **Crystal Mountain** (Rtes. 410 and 123 at Crystal Mountain Rd., ☎ 360/663–2265), a world-class ski resort with activities year-round. The elevation is 7,000 feet, with 34 runs and 2,300 acres of skiable terrain for all levels. Services include full resort amenities and equipment rentals.

Spectator Sports

The Tacoma Dome is home to the **Tacoma Rockets,** an expansion team of the Western Hockey League. The Rockets play about 37 home games, October through March (☎ 360/627–3653). The **Tacoma Rainiers,** an affiliate of the Seattle Mariners baseball team, play at the 10,000-seat Cheney Stadium (Rte. 16, just west of Tyler St., ☎ 206/752–7707). The **Spanaway Speedway** (16413 22nd Ave. E, Spanaway, ☎ 206/537–7551), 7 miles south of Tacoma, has featured the region's most exciting auto racing for more than 30 years. Midweek competition features amateurs racing their "street legal" automobiles. The racetrack offers family packages and a supervised play area for children.

Dining

For price-category definitions, *see* Dining *in* Washington Essentials, *below.*

Gig Harbor

$$ **eville's Shoreline.** This pleasant, accommodating restaurant in the
★ heart of Gig Harbor's marina is rather dark inside, but window tables offer excellent views of the water. Northwest seafood is the specialty here—try especially the simply but well-prepared salmon and clams. There is a fine Sunday brunch. ✕ *8827 N. Harborview Dr.,* ☎ *206/851–9822. Reservations advised. AE, D, MC, V.*

$ **Tides Tavern.** This noisy, cheerful waterfront bar-cum-restaurant has been going strong since 1904. The menu features standard tavern grub—sandwiches, burgers, pizza—but is much better than average; shrimp salad is a house specialty. When the sun's out, the deck is the most popular seating area. If you happen to arrive by boat or seaplane, no problem—you can tie up right at the tavern. ✕ *2925 Harborview Dr.,* ☎ *360/858–3982. No reservations. MC, V.*

Tacoma

$$–$$$ **E.R. Rogers Restaurant.** Housed in an 1891 mansion 10 miles southwest of Tacoma, the restaurant overlooks Puget Sound and historic Steilacoom, with views of the Tacoma Narrows Bridge. The restaurant, one of the best in the Tacoma area, is decorated in a Victorian theme, with lace valances, brass fixtures, some antiques, and the original tongue-in-groove ceiling in the bar. The menu features a wide array of seafood—try the salmon with strawberry butter glaze—as well as steaks, prime rib with Yorkshire pudding, poultry, and an extensive list of wines to accompany them. The restaurant is open seven nights a week and for Sunday buffet brunch. ✕ *1702 Commercial St., Steilacoom,* ☎ *206/582–0280. Reservations advised. MC, V. No lunch.*

$$ **Harbor Lights.** This waterfront institution, appropriately adorned with nautical furnishings, including glass floats, stuffed fish, and life preservers, hasn't changed since the '50s. The specialties are also classics—seafood, steaks, chops, and shellfish—but the steamed clams (in season) and good, ungreasy fish-and-chips are particular favorites. Service is

generally efficient despite the crowds usually found here. There's a good waterfront view of Commencement Bay if you're lucky enough to snag a window seat. ✗ *2761 Ruston Way,* ☎ *206/752–8600. Reservations advised. AE, DC, MC, V.*

$$ **Lobster Shop.** This classic seafood restaurant has two locations; the older, on Dash Point, is cozier than the newer in-town spot, although both have fine views of Commencement Bay. Dash Point's rustic feel makes for an especially good spot to while away a long winter evening. Both restaurants specialize in simply prepared seafood, with salmon the perennial favorite. There's a cocktail lounge in the newer location, and beer and wine are available in the older. ✗ *6912 Soundview Dr. NE (off Dash Point Rd.),* ☎ *206/927–1513; 4013 Ruston Way,* ☎ *206/759–2165. Reservations advised. AE, DC, MC, V.*

$$ **Old House Café.** Among the entrée-sized salads served at this upstairs café, try the warm scallop salad with sweet peppers, veggies, fresh wild greens, and perfectly braised scallops. Also recommended is the king salmon, which is placed on a bed of fresh spinach, smothered in raspberries, wrapped in phyllo, and baked to perfection. Various antique fixtures grace the restaurant, including a large stained-glass window from a Victorian Yakima building, five large light fixtures from a turn-of-the-century Seattle bank, and Victorian fretwork from a mansion in Philadelphia. Frank Pittman, a tea broker and district manager for the Pacific Coast Merchandise Co., often stored goods here, in the home he and his wife Mary purchased in 1907 for $3,000. So it's fitting that today the ground floor is the Mercantile Shop, with gifts, kitchenwares—including Fiestaware like that used upstairs—and, yes, tea. ✗ *2717 N. Proctor St.,* ☎ *206/759–7336. Reservations advised. AE, MC, V. Closed Sun., Mon. night.*

$–$$ **Grazie Ristorante.** In the heart of Old Town in a refurbished 1896 building with a waterfront view, this northern Italian restaurant features homemade pasta, chicken, and seafood dishes, predominantly with white sauces. You will also find a variety of salads and veal entrées. For those sunny, summer days, there is a comfortable deck outside. ✗ *2301 N. 30th St.,* ☎ *206/627–0231. Reservations advised. MC, V.*

$ **Antique Sandwich Company.** Breakfast, lunch, and dinner are served daily at this pleasant deli-style café, which specializes in hearty soups and sandwiches, classic children's food such as waffles and PB&J sandwiches, and well-prepared espresso drinks. Old posters on the walls, plastic bears for serving honey on the tables, and a toy-covered play area for children (which doubles as a music stage) help set the restaurant's cheerful, casual mood. On weekends come hear live folk and classical music; Tuesday evening is open-mike night. ✗ *5102 N. Pearl St., 2 blocks from entrance to Point Defiance Park,* ☎ *206/752–4069. No reservations. AE, MC, V.*

Lodging

For price-category definitions, *see* Lodging *in* Washington Essentials, *below.*

Tacoma

$$$ **Sheraton Tacoma Hotel.** This attractive high-rise is located in the heart of downtown and is a popular site for conventions. The executive suites on the top floors (24th and 25th) have concierge service and Continental breakfasts. Amenities for the other rooms include great views of Commencement Bay and/or Mt. Rainier from almost every angle, and modern decor in elegant muted tones. Also on hand in the hotel are a lively European-style café, the Wintergarden, as well as a less formal restaurant and a lobby-level cocktail lounge. Altezzo, a moderately

priced rustic Italian restaurant at the top of the hotel, features large paintings of Italian city and country scenes and great views of Mt. Rainier and Commencement Bay. ⊠ *1320 Broadway Plaza, 98402, ☎ 206/572–3200. 319 rooms. 2 restaurants, bar, health-club privileges. AE, DC, MC, V.*

$$–$$$ Commencement Bay Bed & Breakfast. This elegant home in north Tacoma proudly displays its AAA rating. There are three guest rooms, each individually decorated. Myrtle's Room features a four-poster queen bed and armoire and is decorated in forest green, rose, and burgundy colors. It features a view of the bay, the Cascade Mountains, and Mt. Rainier. Hosts Sharon, a former nurse, and Bill Kaufmann, who works in advertising and marketing, provide a full breakfast and plenty of helpful information about the area. ⊠ *3312 N. Union Ave., Tacoma 98407, ☎ 206/752–8175, ℻ 206/759–4025. 3 rooms with bath. Hot tub, business services. MC, V.*

$$–$$$ Ramada Hotel–Tacoma Dome. Situated near the Tacoma Dome, this hotel caters to people coming to see the musical, sporting, and other events held there. Basic, standard-issue rooms are offered, with few amenities, but there is free airport service and pets are allowed. ⊠ *2611 E. E St., 98421, ☎ 206/572–7272. 163 rooms. Restaurant, lounge. AE, MC, V.*

$$–$$$ The Villa. This 7,000-square-foot Italian mansion with a large formal entrance and lush gardens brings the Mediterranean to Tacoma. The home was built in 1925 by architect Ambrose Russell. The focal point of the entry is a curved wooden staircase leading to the guest rooms. The Bay View Suite features a sweeping view of Commencement Bay and the Olympic Mountains. You stay isn't complete until you enjoy the gourmet breakfast served by friendly hosts Becky and Greg Anglemyer. ⊠ *705 N. 5th St., Tacoma 98403, ☎ 206/572–1157. 4 rooms with bath. No facilities. MC, V.*

MT. RAINIER NATIONAL PARK

★ The centerpiece of **Mt. Rainier National Park,** located about 60 miles southeast of Tacoma, is the magnificent 14,411-foot Mt. Rainier—the fifth-highest mountain in the lower 48 states. It's so big that it creates its own weather system. The awestruck local Native Americans called it Tahoma, "the mountain that was God," and dared not ascend its eternally ice-bound summit. In 1792 the first European to visit the region, British explorer George Vancouver, gazed in amazement at its majestic dome and named it after his friend Rear Admiral Peter Rainier.

But the park isn't just this incredible volcanic peak; it also encompasses nearly 400 square miles of surrounding wilderness. Within its boundaries are more than 300 miles of hiking trails, from easy to advanced, as well as good lakes and rivers for fishing, glaciers, isolated cross-country skiing spots, and ample camping facilities. Among the wildlife in the park are bears, mountain goats, deer, elk, eagles, beavers, and mountain lions; the abundant flora includes Douglas fir, hemlock, cedar, ferns, and wildflowers. Surrounded by some of the finest old-growth forests left on earth, gnawed at by the most extensive system of glaciers in the contiguous United States, supporting a rich array of plant and animal life, Mt. Rainier rewards day-trippers and experienced mountaineers alike.

Exploring

It is possible to sample Rainier's main attractions—Longmire, Paradise, the Grove of Patriarchs, and Sunrise—in a single day by car, but if at all possible, you should plan on staying a few days to hike the park's multitude of forest, meadow, and high-mountain trails. Be forewarned: A single, narrow, winding paved road links the main attractions at Rainier, and during the peak months of July and August, traffic can be torturously slow and heavy.

The best way to get a complete overview of Mt. Rainier's charms in a day or less is to enter via Nisqually, and begin your tour by browsing in the **Longmire Museum.** The museum's simple glass cases contain hundreds of preserved plants and animals from the park, including a large, friendly-looking stuffed cougar. Other exhibits give an overview of park history. ☉ *Daily 9–4:30.*

The ½-mile **Trail of Shadows** begins just across the road from the National Park Inn at Longmire. It's notable for its insights into meadowland ecology, its colorful soda springs, James Longmire's old homestead cabin, and the foundation of the old Longmire Springs Hotel, which was destroyed around the turn of the century.

From Longmire, the road climbs northeast into the mountains toward Paradise. Take a moment to explore gorgeous Christine Falls, just north of the road 1½ miles past Cougar Rock Campground, and Narada Falls, 3 miles farther on; both are spanned by graceful stone footbridges. Fantastic mountain views, alpine meadows crosshatched with nature trails, a welcoming lodge and restaurant, and an excellent visitor center combine to make **Paradise** the primary goal of most park visitors.

Exhibits at the **Henry M. Jackson Visitor Center** focus on geology, mountaineering, glaciology, winter storms, and alpine ecology. Two worthwhile 20-minute multimedia programs repeat at half-hour intervals. ☎ *360/569–2211.* ☉ *Early May–mid-Oct., daily 9–6; off-season, weekends and holidays only, 10–5.*

A number of hiking trails to various points lead off from here. One outstanding (but grueling) way to explore the high country is to hike the 5-mile Skyline Trail to Panorama Point, which has stunning 360-degree views.

Continue eastward 21 miles and leave your car for an hour to explore the incomparable **Grove of the Patriarchs,** one of the park's most stunning features. A 1⅓-mile loop trail begins just west of the Stevens Canyon entrance and passes through a lush old-growth forest of Douglas fir, cedar, and hemlock. Over a bridge to a small island is a grove of thousand-year-old trees, among the oldest in the Northwest; they have been protected from forest fires and other disasters by the rushing waters.

Afterward, turn your car north toward White River and the **Sunrise Visitor Center** (☉ *July–Labor Day, daily 9–6*), from which you can watch the alpenglow fade from Mt. Rainier's domed summit. The visitor center has exhibits on that region's sparser alpine and subalpine ecology.

Sports and the Outdoors

Mountain Climbing

The highly regarded concessionaire **Rainier Mountaineering** (Paradise, WA 98398, ☎ 360/627–6242 in winter, 360/569–2227 in summer), cofounded by Himalayan adventurer Lou Whittaker, makes climbing the Queen of the Cascades an adventure open to anyone in good physical condition. The company teaches the fundamentals of mountaineering at one-day classes held during the climbing season, late

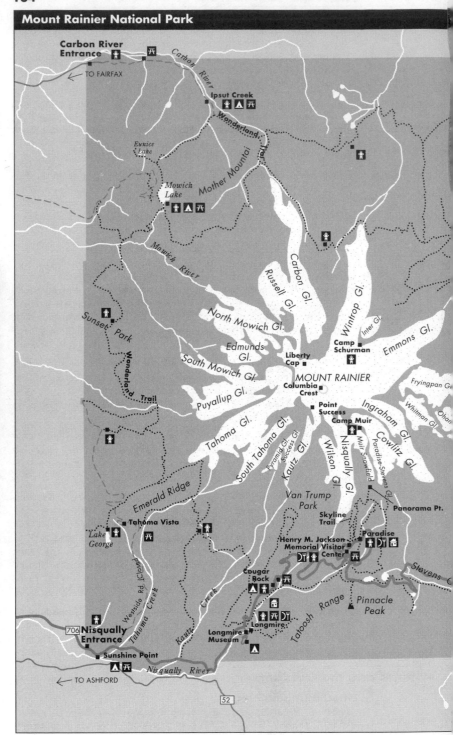

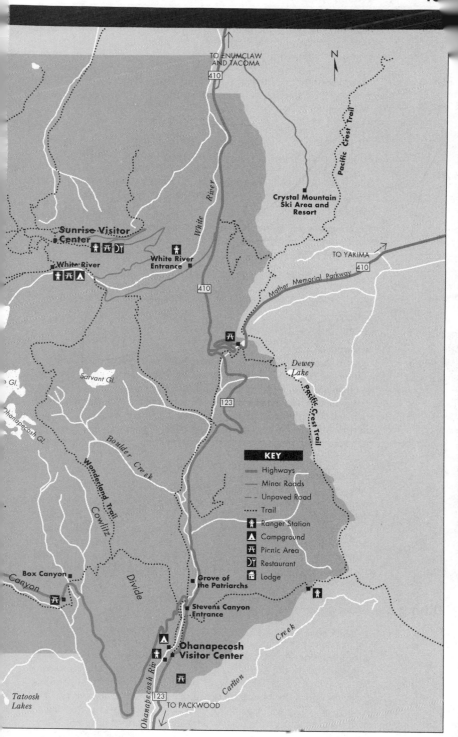

TO ENUMCLAW
AND TACOMA

N

410

Crystal Mountain
Ski Area and
Resort

White River

TO YAKIMA
410

Pacific Crest Trail

Mather Memorial Parkway

Sunrise Visitor
Center

White River
Entrance

White River

Sarvant Gl.

Dewey
Lake

Gl.

Ohanapecosh Gl.

123

Boulder Creek

Wonderland Trail

Pacific Crest Trail

Cowlitz

KEY

Highways
Minor Roads
Unpaved Road
Trail
Ranger Station
Campground
Picnic Area
Restaurant
Lodge

Box Canyon

Grove of
the Patriarchs

Canyon

Divide

Stevens Canyon
Entrance

Creek

Ohanapecosh
Visitor Center

Carlton Creek

Ohanapecosh Riv.

Tatoosh
Lakes

123

TO PACKWOOD

May through early September. Participants in these classes are evaluated for their fitness for the climb; they must be able to withstand a 16-mile round-trip with a 9,000-foot gain in elevation. Those who meet the fitness requirement choose between guided two-and four-day summit climbs, the latter via more-demanding Emmons Glacier. Experienced climbers can fill out a climbing card at the Paradise, White River, or Carbon River ranger stations and lead their own groups of two or more.

Skiing

Mt. Rainier is a major Nordic ski center. Trails, none of which are groomed, can become quite crowded. Those around Paradise are particularly popular; if you want to ski with fewer people, try the trails in and around the Ohanapecosh/Stevens Canyon area, which are just as beautiful. Never ski on the plowed main roads—the snowplow operator can't see you.

The Longmire Ski Touring Center (☎ 360/569–2411), adjacent to the National Park Inn at Longmire, rents cross-country ski equipment and provides lessons from mid-December to early April.

Mt. Tahoma Trails System (Box 942, Eatonville 98328) is a nonprofit group of volunteers that has organized a series of trails near Mt. Rainier for more than 100 miles of cross-country skiing, most of which is beginner to intermediate terrain, and huts for basic overnight accommodations, available by reservation.

Snowmobiling

Snowmobiling is allowed on the east side of the park, on sections of Highway 123 and Stevens Canyon Road—between the ranger station at Ohanapecosh Visitor Center and Box Canyon—and on Highway 410, which is accessible from the north entrance and unplowed after its junction with the road to the Crystal Mountain Ski Area. A State of Washington Sno-Park permit, available at stores and gas stations throughout the area, is required to park in the area near the north park entrance arch.

Snowshoeing

Deep snows make Mt. Rainier a snowshoeing capital. Rentals are available at the **Longmire Ski Touring Center** (*see* Skiing, *above*). From December through April, park rangers lead free, twice-daily snowshoe walks that start at Jackson Memorial Visitor Center at Paradise and cover 1¼ miles in about two hours. The network of trails in the Paradise area makes it most popular for snowshoers, but the park's east side roads, Highways 123 and 410, are unplowed and provide another good snowshoeing venue.

Dining and Lodging

While it's not difficult to find a decent meal around Mt. Rainier, lodging can be a problem; be sure to book in advance for the accommodations below. A good alternative is provided by the five drive-in campgrounds in the park—Cougar Rock, Ipsut Creek, Ohanapecosh, Sunshine Point, and White River—which have almost 700 campsites for tents and RVs. All are first come, first-served, and have parking spaces, drinking water, garbage cans, fire grates, and picnic tables with benches; most have flush or pit toilets, but none have hot water. For price-category definitions, *see* Dining *and* Lodging *in* Washington Essentials, *below.*

Ashford

DINING

$ **Wild Berry Restaurant.** This funky, organic eatery just down the road from Alexander's is where the mountain's laid-back ski-and-hot-tub crowd stokes up for a long day in the woods. Hefty salads, pizzas, crepes, sandwiches, and home-baked desserts are served in relaxed (though far from luxurious) surroundings. ✕ *37720 Hwy. 706 E, 4 mi east of Ashford,* ☎ *360/569–2628. MC, V.*

DINING AND LODGING

$$–$$$ **Alexander's Country Inn.** Since the days when presidents Theodore Roo-
★ sevelt and William Taft stayed here during visits to the mountain, this 1912 inn has towered over its competition like a grand old Douglas fir over seedlings. A large hot tub overlooking the trout pond out back was added since T.R.'s time, but the big second-floor sitting room—with its fireplace, deep couches, stained glass, and complimentary evening wine—has only improved with age. Guest rooms sparkle with fresh paint, carpeting, antiques, and marble-top pine bedside tables; nothing, unfortunately, has been done for the thin walls. A delicious farm breakfast is included in the price of the room. For lunch and dinner, try the excellent restaurant, which is open to guests and nonguests. Bread and desserts are baked on the premises, and a variety of fresh fish and pasta dishes are also specialties. 🖃 *37515 Hwy. 706 E (4 mi east of Ashford), Ashford 98304,* ☎ *360/569–2300 or 800/654–7615,* 🆔 *360/569–2323. 14 rooms, 10 with bath, plus 3-bedroom/2-bath house that sleeps 8. Restaurant (reservations advised; closed weekdays in winter). MC, V.*

LODGING

$$ **Nisqually Lodge.** Built in 1989, this motor lodge has an intimate Swiss-chalet feel, with a big stone fireplace, exposed beams, and lots of knotty pine in the lobby. The earth-tone rooms are spacious; even though the motel is on busy Highway 706, double insulation keeps them quiet. A Continental breakfast is included in the room price. 🖃 *31609 Hwy. 706 E (2 mi east of Ashford), Ashford 98304,* ☎ *360/569–8804. 21 rooms. AE, DC, MC, V.*

Longmire

DINING AND LODGING

$$ **National Park Inn.** This smaller, more modern, and more intimate version of the Paradise Inn (*see below*) lost a little of its old rustic flair but gained a lot of comfort in an extensive 1990 renovation. The old stone fireplaces are still here, but the public areas are freshly painted and carpeted. The small rooms mix budget-motel functionality (though without TVs and telephones) with such wistful backwoods touches as antique bentwood headboards and graceful wrought-iron lamps. A restaurant on the ground serves simple fare—pan-fried snapper with lemon butter and wine, hearty broiled steaks, and spicy pasta with fennel sausage. For breakfast, don't miss the home-baked cinnamon rolls with cream-cheese frosting. Located down the hill at heavily wooded Longmire, the inn is the only year-round lodging in the park, and it makes a great base camp for day explorers. Reservations well in advance are a must. 🖃 *Box 108, Ashford 98304,* ☎ *360/569–2275. 25 rooms, 18 with bath. Restaurant, gift shop, general store. MC, V.*

Paradise

$$–$$$ **Paradise Inn.** With its hand-carved cedar logs, burnished parquet floors, stone fireplaces, Indian rugs, and glorious mountain views, this 75-year-old inn is loaded with high-mountain atmosphere. Its small-ish, sparsely furnished rooms, however, are not equipped with TVs or

telephones and have thin walls and showers that tend to run cold during periods of peak use. The attraction here is the 5,400-foot alpine setting, so lovely you expect Julie Andrews to stroll by singing at any moment. The full-service dining room serves leisurely Sunday brunches in summer; in addition, the lodge has a small snack bar and a snug, crowded lounge. ☎ *Hwy. 706 (c/o Mt. Rainier Guest Services, Box 108, Star Rte., Ashford 98304),* ☎ *360/569–2275,* 🖷 *360/569–2770. 127 rooms, 96 with bath. Reservations advised. MC, V. Closed Nov.–mid-May.*

THE OLYMPIC PENINSULA

The rugged Olympic Peninsula is the most northwestern corner of the continental United States. Much of it is wilderness, with the magnificent Olympic National Park and National Forest at its heart. The peninsula has tremendous variety: the wild Pacific shore, the sheltered waters along the Hood Canal and the Strait of Juan de Fuca, the rivers of the Olympic Rain Forest, and the towering Olympic Mountains.

Although the region's economy—primarily lumber and fishing—assures some ties to the outside world, the peninsula is in many ways isolated and largely self-sufficient. Its inaccessible terrain and the unique climates caused by the Olympic Mountains add to this feeling of separateness: The mountains trap incoming clouds, creating both a rain forest to the west and a dry "rain shadow" area on the east. As a result, the peninsula has both the wettest and the driest climates in the entire coastal Pacific Northwest.

A benefit of this somewhat ambiguous environment is that wildlife takes to it—and flourishes. Visitors in search of the great outdoors, however, should be aware that much of the Olympic Peninsula is stringently protected. Within the National Park, all hunting, firearms, and off-road vehicles are prohibited, as is any disturbance to plants or wildlife. Although hunting and fishing are permitted in portions of the National Forest, many areas are maintained as complete wilderness. Furthermore, Native American tribal regulations restrict access to, and activity within, certain parts of reservations; check with local authorities for details.

Because of the rugged terrain and some difficult roads, much of the peninsula is accessible only to backpackers, but the 300-mile loop made by Highway 101 provides glimpses of some of its most interesting features. The various side roads off 101, meanwhile, offer excellent (if sometimes unpaved) opportunities for further exploration of more remote towns, beaches, and mountains. This section describes a journey clockwise, primarily around Highway 101 (although jaunts from the main drag are suggested), beginning and ending in Olympia.

Exploring

Numbers in the margin correspond to points of interest on the Olympic Peninsula map.

❶ Olympia, Washington State's capital, is often overrun with government activity; the legislative season determines whether this town at the southern end of Puget Sound is bustling or somnolent. But even in full swing, the city still retains a relaxed air. While you are in the capitol area, consider taking a tour of the stately **Legislative Building.** This handsome Romanesque structure boasts a 287-foot dome that closely resembles the Capitol Building in "the other Washington." State Senate and Representative sessions can be viewed from visitors' galleries. The surrounding grounds feature carefully maintained rose gardens (best in summer) and Japanese cherry trees that are in glorious bloom around the end of April. Also worth a look is the modern **State Library,** located directly behind the Legislative Building. It is open to the public during regular business hours and boasts a variety of artwork, including murals by two renowned Washington artists, Mark Tobey and Kenneth Callahan, and exhibits devoted to early state history. *Legislative Bldg., Capitol Way between 10th and 14th Aves., ☎ 360/586–8687. ☛ Free. Tours offered daily, on the hr 10–3.*

Traveling south along Capitol Way to 21st Street—a pleasant walk or a short drive—will bring you to the **State Capitol Museum,** housed in a handsome building that dates from the 1920s and was once the mansion of a local banker. Exhibits of local art, history, and natural history are on display, including a permanent collection of rare local Native American baskets. *211 W. 21st St., ☎ 360/753–2580. ☛ Free; donations accepted. Call for hrs.*

A few blocks east of the Capitol campus on Union Avenue, at its intersection with Plum Street and adjacent to City Hall, the sister cities of Olympia and Yashiro, Japan, have recently collaborated on a beautiful **Japanese garden** complete with a waterfall, bamboo grove, carp pond, and stone lanterns. *Corner of Union and Plum Sts.*

Wolfhaven, just 15 miles south of the city on Old Highway 99, is a unique facility offering walk-through guided tours on the hour of a 60-acre refuge and sanctuary primarily for wolves. On Friday and Saturday evenings in the summer, the facility reopens at 7 PM for the public Howl-in featuring tours, musicians performing around a campfire, and howling with the wolves. *3111 Offut Lake Rd., ☎ 360/264–4695. ☛ Daily tours: $5 adults, $2.50 children 5–12; Howl-in: $6 adults, $3 children 5–12. ☺ Wed.–Mon. 10–4.*

②❸ Leaving Olympia, travel west along Highway 101 and State Routes 8 and 12 to Gray's Harbor and the twin seaports of **Hoquiam** and **Aberdeen.** In spring, thousands of migratory shorebirds and peregrine falcons come to Bowerman Basin, west of Hoquiam on State Route 109.

❹❺ An option from Hoquiam would be to drive north on Route 109, passing through resorts and ample beach areas such as **Copalis Beach, Pa-** **❻** **cific Beach,** and **Moclips** on your way to the Quinault Indian Reservation **❼** and the tribal center of **Taholah.** You should know, however, that access to the coastline at some points here is restricted to tribal members. Taholah is a rustic town, and the main attraction for tourists here, as elsewhere on the peninsula, is the vast amount of pristine scenery, rather than a commercialized town center.

Another route to follow from Hoquiam is Highway 101 north, along the west fork of the Hoquiam River (through the wonderfully named town of Humptulips) to picturesque Quinault Lake and west to the **❽❾** ocean at **Queets** and **Kalaloch.** The stretch of coastal highway north of Kalaloch has many well-marked trails—each ¼ mile or less in length—that lead to spectacular Pacific beaches.

Continue north on 101 for about 20 miles before taking the Hoh Road east to the spectacular Hoh Rain Forest, a complex and rich ecosystem of conifers, hardwoods, grasses, mosses, and other flora that shelter such wildlife as elk, otters, beavers, salmon, and even flying squirrels. The average rainfall here is 145 inches a year. The **Hoh Visitor Center,** located at the campground and ranger center at road's end, has in-

Olympic Peninsula

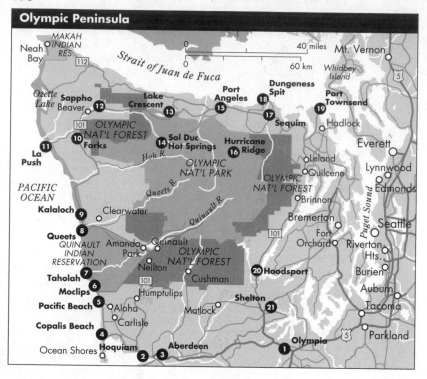

formation, nature trails, and a museum. There are several interpretive facilities to help visitors prepare for the nature trails, and naturalist-led campfire programs and walks are conducted daily in July and August. *Hoh Rd., 1½ mi north of Hoh River Bridge (visitor center is 20 mi farther),* ☎ *360/374–6925.* ☛ *Park: $3.* ☉ *Visitor Center: year-round but often unstaffed Sept.–May.*

⑩ North on Highway 101 is the little town of **Forks,** famous throughout the Northwest for its lavish and enjoyable Fourth of July celebrations (which actually last three days). This is classic Americana with a Northwest twist: parades featuring giant logging trucks along with the Shriners and royalty, demolition derbies, marathon runs and dances, arts and crafts, fireworks, and lots of food. For details, write to Forks Old Fashioned Fourth of July (Box 881, 98331) or Forks Chamber of Commerce (Box 1249, 98331, ☎ 360/374–2531).

⑪ From Forks, take La Push Road west for about 15 miles to the town of the same name. **La Push** is a coastal village and the tribal center of the Quileute Indians. (One theory about the town's name is that it is a variation on the French *la bouche,* "the mouth"; this makes sense, since it's located at the mouth of the Quilayute River.) Several points along this road have short trails with access to the ocean, fabulous views of offshore islands, and stark rock formations. The north branch of the La Push detour is the road to **Rialto Beach,** a picnic area and campsite.

⑫ North and east, Highway 101 enters the **Soleduck River valley,** which has been known for its salmon fishing. At **Sappho,** Burnt Mountain Road branches northward off to Route 112 (paved but slow) and eventually leads to **Neah Bay, Capes Flattery** and **Alava, Shi-Shi Beach,** and **Ozette Lake** (the largest body of freshwater in the state). Eight miles east of Sappho is the **Soleduck Hatchery** (☎ 360/327–3246), operated by the Washington State Department of Fisheries and offering a variety of interpretive displays about the many aspects of fish breeding.

🔞 The deep azure of **Lake Crescent,** about 12 miles farther along, is outstandingly beautiful, and the area has abundant campsites, resorts, trails, canoeing, and fishing. Among Lake Crescent's famous guests was Franklin D. Roosevelt, whose negotiations with U.S. senators and Park Department officials at the Lake Crescent Lodge in 1937 led directly to the creation of the Olympic National Forest. The original lodge buildings of 1915 are still in use, well-worn but comfortable.

Twelve miles south on Soleduck Road (which meets Highway 101 a
🔞 mile west of the western tip of Lake Crescent) is **Sol Duc Hot Springs.** Native Americans have known about the soothing waters of these springs for generations, and since the first resort opened there tourists have learned about it as well. There are three hot sulfur pools, ranging in temperature from 98° to 104°. The Sol Duc Hot Springs Resort, a venerable institution dating from 1910, has a series of cabins, a restaurant, and a hamburger stand. It is not necessary to stay at the resort to use the hot springs. *Soleduck Rd. and Hwy. 101,* ☎ *360/327–3583.* ☛ *$6 per day.* ⊙ *Mid-May–Sept.*

🔞 Back on Highway 101 east, you will soon come to **Port Angeles,** a bustling commercial fishing port and an access route to Canada. Directly across the Strait of Juan de Fuca is Victoria, British Columbia, which can be reached via the private Black Ball Ferry Line (☎ 360/457–4491).

Among the points of interest in P.A., as its residents fondly refer to it, is the **Clallam County Historical Museum.** This handsome Georgian building, constructed in 1914 as a courthouse, has exhibitions of artifacts and photo displays detailing the lifestyles of the people, both Native American and white, who lived in this timber-rich and seagoing community. *4th and Lincoln Sts.,* ☎ *360/452–7831, ext. 364.* ☛ *Free; donations accepted.* ⊙ *June–Aug., Mon.–Sat. 10–4; Sept.–May, weekdays 10–4.*

Also interesting is the casual but well-appointed **aquarium** of the Arthur D. Feiro Marine Laboratory, operated as a joint venture by the City of Port Angeles and Peninsula College. Many kinds of local sea life, including octopuses, scallops, rockfish, and anemones, are on display, with new varieties and specimens arriving often. The tour is self-guided, but friendly volunteers are always on hand to answer questions. *Port Angeles City Pier,* ☎ *360/452–9277.* ☛ *$3.* ⊙ *June–Aug., daily 10–8; Sept.–May, weekends noon–4.*

🔞 **Hurricane Ridge,** 17 miles south of Port Angeles, rises nearly a mile above sea level and offers spectacular views of the Olympics, the Strait of Juan de Fuca, and Vancouver Island. Despite the point's height, the road grade leading to it is easily negotiated by car. In the summer, rangers lead hikes and give interpretive talks on local geology and flora and fauna. The numerous nature trails range from wide, paved paths that are accessible to users of wheelchairs to advanced climbs; they provide an opportunity to see wildflowers such as glacier lilies and lupine, as well as animals such as deer and marmots. In winter, when accessible, the area has miles of cross-country ski routes and a modest downhill ski operation. *National Park Visitor Center, 600 E. Park Ave., Port Angeles 98362,* ☎ *360/452–0330.*

A wide variety of animal life, present and past, can be found in the
🔞 charming town of **Sequim,** 17 miles east of Port Angeles on Highway 101, and in the fertile plain at the mouth of the Dungeness River to
🔞 the north of the town. **Dungeness Spit,** part of the Dungeness National

Wildlife Refuge and one of the longest natural spits in the world, is home to thousands of migratory waterfowl as well as clams, oysters, and seals. This picturesque locale features a lighthouse at the end of the spit in addition to its abundant natural beauty; there is no formal interpretive center, but large displays provide information about what can be seen. A 65-site campground nearby is operated by Clallam County. *About 3 mi north on Kitchen Rd. (4 mi west of Sequim). Campground* ☎ *360/683–5847;* ○ *Feb.–Oct. 1. Wildlife Refuge* ☎ *360/457–8451.*

In 1977, 12,000-year-old mastodon remains were discovered near Sequim and today are displayed at the **Sequim-Dungeness Museum,** where you can look at these Ice Age creatures as well as at exhibits on Captain Vancouver, the early Klallam Indians, and the area's pioneer towns. *175 W. Cedar St.,* ☎ *360/683–8110.* ☞ *Free; donations accepted.* ○ *May–Sept., Wed.–Sun. noon–4; Oct.–Nov. and mid-Feb.–Apr., weekends noon–4; closed Dec.–mid-Feb.*

⑲ About 10 miles east of Sequim, State Route 20 turns northward another 12 miles to **Port Townsend,** a charming town with a fine waterfront along which runs a series of handsome brick buildings that date from the 1870s. These have been carefully restored and now house a variety of attractive shops, restaurants, and services. High up on the bluff are several large gingerbread-trimmed Victorian homes, many of which have been turned into elegant B&Bs. Although Port Townsend is a flourishing arts community, with a high proportion of writers, musicians, and artists in residence, the restored buildings of **Fort Worden,** a former coast artillery army base, are the center for a variety of popular annual arts festivals.

Backtracking from Sequim, Highway 101 travels south along the west side of Hood Canal, past abundant oyster-picking and clam-digging areas. The **Hamma Hamma Oyster Company** is a retail store south of the town of Eldon, where you can buy fresh salmon, mussels, crab, shrimp, and other seafood, as well as a variety of pickled and smoked items. Picnic tables outside provide a fine place in which to have an alfresco meal. Especially worth a look and maybe a sample are the store's live examples of geoducks (pronounced gooey-ducks), giant cousins to the clam. *N. 35959 Hwy. 101,* ☎ *360/877–5811.* ☞ *Free.* ○ *Daily 8:30–5:30.*

⑳ About 10 miles farther, near the southern bend of the canal and the town of **Hoodsport,** is the **Hoodsport Winery,** which produces a number of fine wines—from chardonnays and Rieslings to gooseberry and rhubarb. The winery is open to the public; the friendly staff gives tours and tastings on an informal basis as requested. *N. 23501 Hwy. 101,* ☎ *360/877–9894.* ☞ *Free.* ○ *Daily 10–6.*

Branching off to the west from the middle of town is the Staircase Road, which leads to **Lake Cushman.** This is not only an important source of water for Tacoma's powerhouse on Hood Canal, but it is also the trailhead to numerous hiking trails, including one to the spectacular **Staircase Rapids** on the Skokomish River. Here the steep country gives rise to rushing cataracts and boulder-strewn rapids, broken up by deep pools where Dolly Varden trout rest.

㉑ Driving south on Highway 101 through the sawmill town of **Shelton** will take you back to Olympia.

_ pping

The single best locale for the confirmed shopaholic is the waterfront array of boutiques and stores in **Port Townsend,** all of which feature a good selection of Northwest arts and crafts. Additional shops are uptown on **Lawrence Street,** near the Victorian houses.

Sports and the Outdoors

Fishing

Trout and salmon fishing is particularly abundant in rivers throughout the peninsula. In **Aberdeen** and **Hoquiam,** bottomfish and salmon are the primary catches. For information concerning fishing in the Olympic Peninsula, contact **North Olympic Peninsula Visitors and Convention Bureau** (Box 670, Port Angeles 98362, ☎ 360/452–8552 or 800/942–4042).

Hiking

Both the ocean and mountain areas offer numerous hiking trails for all levels of ability. For details, contact the **National Park Service** (600 E. Park Ave., Port Angeles 98362, ☎ 360/452–0330).

Skiing

Hurricane Ridge (☎ 360/452–4501), south of Port Angeles, has a modest downhill operation, with two rope tows and a poma lift, as well as miles of cross-country ski trails. Contact the **National Park Service** (600 E. Park Ave., Port Angeles 98362, ☎ 360/452–0330) for information.

Dining and Lodging

For price-category definitions, _see_ Dining _and_ Lodging _in_ Washington Essentials, _below._

Copalis Beach

LODGING

$$–$$$ **Iron Springs Resort.** Three miles north of Copalis Beach on Route 109, this string of 25 individual cottages can accommodate anywhere from two to 10 people—perfect for families. Each has its own fireplace and kitchen; older cabins are decorated in a dimly lit but pleasantly funky style, while newer ones (Nos. 22–25) are spiffier; only No. 6 has no view, but others have superb beach, river, and forest views and access. ⌷ _Box 207, Copalis Beach 98535,_ ☎ _360/276–4230,_ ℻ _360/276–4365. 25 units. Pool. AE, MC, V._

Forks

DINING AND LODGING

$$–$$$ **Kalaloch Lodge.** A hodgepodge of old cabins, new log cabins, an old lodge, and a new hotel make up this facility in the lush Olympic National Forest. Lodge rooms are clean, airy, and comfortable, and most have terrific ocean views. Some of the rooms in the modern part—Sea Crest House—have fireplaces and decks. The old cabins can be pretty basic (drafty in winter, with minimal kitchens and other amenities), but they are fine for informal stays and for a sense of what the wild Washington coast was like in "the good old days." The new log cabins convey a similar feeling but are a little spiffier, and the lodge offers few resort-type amenities but abundant opportunities for beachcombing, hiking, and other robust activities. Good, fresh salmon and oysters highlight the menu in the restaurant, though the rest of the fare can be disappointingly ordinary. ⌷ _Hwy. 101 (HC 80, Box 1100), Forks-Kalaloch_

98331, ☎ 360/962–2271, ℻ 360/962–3391. 58 rooms
Restaurant. AE, MC, V.

Moclips

DINING AND LODGING

$$ Ocean Crest Resort. Set high on a bluff above a spectacular s
the Pacific, this resort hotel has one- and two-bedroom units w
decor, fireplaces, cedar paneling, and superb views. Some have ki
and/or fireplaces; access to the beach is down a steep wooded w
way. The Ocean Crest restaurant also features panoramic ocean vie
along with standard but well-prepared food in ample portions: egg
hash browns, good coffee and muffins at breakfast, fresh seafood fo
lunch and dinner. There's also a gift shop and a snug bar decorated
with Native American artifacts. ▣ *Hwy. 109 (18 mi north of Ocean
Shores), 98562, ☎ 360/276–4465 or 800/684–8437, ℻ 360/276–4149.
45 rooms. Restaurant, pool, hot tub, weight room. AE, MC, V.*

Olympia

DINING

$$–$$$ La Petite Maison. Imaginative French food is the specialty in this con-
verted 1890s farmhouse, generally considered to be Olympia's premier
fine-dining establishment. The ambience—one of quiet elegance—is
created by the classical music, unobtrusive service, and crisp linens. En-
trées range from delicately prepared local seafood (look especially for
the Shelton clams) to marinated lamb or duck with blackberry sauce.
A good wine list and excellent desserts, such as a Grand Marnier torte,
round out the menu. ✕ *2005 Ascension Way, ☎ 360/943–8812. Reser-
vations advised. MC, V. Closed Sun. No lunch Sat.; no dinner Mon.*

LODGING

$$ Westwater Inn. This is a large but friendly hotel, close to downtown
Olympia and the capitol grounds, with striking views of Capitol Lake,
the Capitol Dome, and the surrounding hills. The rooms are spacious
and comfortable; those facing the water are especially appealing. There
are two good restaurants on the premises: a modest coffee shop called
Tiffin's, and Ceazan's, a restaurant with a fine view that serves decent
sandwiches and full meals, mostly imaginative American fare, for
modest prices. ▣ *2300 Evergreen Park Dr., 98502, ☎ 360/943–4000
or 800/551–8500, ℻ 360/357–6604. 191 rooms. 2 restaurants, bar,
coffee shop, no-smoking rooms, pool, hot tub. AE, D, MC, V.*

Port Angeles

DINING

$$$ C'est Si Bon. A French expatriate couple, Norbert and Michele Juhasz
run this locally famous French restaurant. Probably the most elegant
eatery on the decidedly informal Olympic Peninsula, C'est Si Bon has
bold art on the walls, fine linen on the tables, and a good view of rose
gardens and the Olympic Mountains. Sophisticated and generally good
service complements the classic menu. Escargots *en Pernod, fruits de
mer au gratin,* or a hearty onion soup are typical appetizers; entrées
include salmon, duck, and prawns with tomato and garlic. There is an
excellent wine list, and desserts are also good, especially the chocolate
mousse. ✕ *2300 Hwy. 101E (4 mi east of Port Angeles), ☎ 360/452–
8888. Reservations advised. AE, DC, MC, V. Closed Mon. No lunch.*

$ First Street Haven. The storefronts of downtown Port Angeles provide
an innocuous setting for this small, informal spot, which nonetheless
serves a high-quality breakfast and lunch. The service is friendly and
fast, and the decor is cheerful but unpretentious. Breakfast (served all
day on Sunday) includes omelets, various renditions of scrambled eggs,

and Belgian waffles with fresh fruit. Fresh salads, thick sandwiches, well-prepared fajitas and chili, and homemade quiche are featured at lunch. All the muffins, coffee cakes, and scones are baked on the premises; good espresso drinks and desserts are offered, too. ✗ *107 E. 1st St. (at Laurel),* ☎ *360/457–0352. No reservations. No credit cards. No alcohol. No dinner.*

DINING AND LODGING

$$ Sol Duc Hot Springs Resort. This comfortable, casual resort dates from the turn of the century and has been spiffed up just enough without becoming slick and soulless. The 32 minimally outfitted cabins have a pleasant and cheery atmosphere; all units have separate bathrooms, and some have kitchens. There is also an outdoor hamburger stand and an attractive inside dining room that serves unpretentious meals (breakfast, lunch, and dinner) drawing on the best of the Northwest: salmon, crab, fresh vegetables, and fruit. ⊡ *12 mi south of Hwy. 101 on Soleduck Rd. (Box 2168), 98362,* ☎ *360/327–3583,* FAX *360/327–3398. 32 units and camping and RV facilities. Restaurant, pool, hot springs. MC, V. Closed mid-Oct.–mid-May.*

$–$$ Lake Crescent Lodge. A big main lodge and small cabins overlook beautiful deep-blue Lake Crescent. Units in the lodge are minimal—bathrooms down the hall, dimly lit rooms—but the setting makes up for sparse amenities. Trout fishing, hiking, evening nature programs, and boating are all on the bill. The food in the restaurant is nothing special, but the service is cheerful and efficient, appealing to young college students enjoying a summer away from the city. ⊡ *6540 E. Beach Rd., 98362,* ☎ *360/928–3211. 52 units. Restaurant, boating, fishing. AE, DC, MC, V. Closed Nov.–Apr.*

LODGING

$$ Tudor Inn. This 1910 Tudor-style house, fully refurbished and turned into a pleasant B&B, is only about 12 blocks from the Victoria-bound ferry dock. Adding to the quiet style of this inn are the antique furnishings and library; from the biggest and most pleasant of the five guest rooms you get spectacular water views (and private bath). The cheerful and efficient owners—the Glasses—serve breakfast in classic English style, which includes eggs, bacon, and muffins, as well as a generous afternoon tea with plenty of fresh scones and other goodies. ⊡ *1108 S. Oak St., 98362,* ☎ *360/452–3138. 5 units. No facilities. No smoking. MC, V.*

Port Townsend

DINING

$$ Fountain Café. This small café, set off the main tourist drag, is one of ★ the best restaurants in Port Townsend. Fine linens and fresh flowers dress up the unpretentious dining room, and a cheerful staff furthers the welcoming tone of this café. You can count on seafood and pasta specialties with imaginative and always-changing twists: smoked salmon in black porter sauce, for instance. This is a local hot spot, as evidenced by the occasional wait for a table. ✗ *920 Washington St.,* ☎ *360/385– 1364. Reservations advised. MC, V.*

$ Salal Café. Featuring home-style cooking and daily specials, this cooperatively run restaurant shines among early-morning breakfast joints. Try one of many variations on the potato-egg scramble. For lunch, seafood and regional American-style meals are good, portions ample, and prices reasonable. Try to get a table in the glassed-in back room, which faces a plant-filled courtyard. ✗ *634 Water St.,* ☎ *360/385– 6532. No reservations. No credit cards. Closed Tues. No dinner.*

$$–$$$ James House. A splendid antiques-filled Victorian-era B&B, located on the bluff overlooking downtown Port Townsend and the waterfront, this inn presents an elegant atmosphere in a terrific location. Each of the two parlors has a fireplace and a library, and several of the guest rooms feature waterfront views. Elegant Continental cuisine breakfasts, inspired by the owners' garden and love for herbs, are served in the formal dining room. In addition to being on the National Register of Historic Places, the James lays claim to being the first B&B in the Northwest. ☎ *1238 Washington St., 98368, ☎ 360/385–1238. 12 rooms. No facilities. Call for restrictions. MC, V.*

$$ Palace Hotel. This friendly, small hotel in the historic downtown section of Port Townsend is tastefully decorated to reflect its 1889 construction date and its former history as a bordello. The narrow, steep brick facade is pleasant to look at, but there is no elevator, a consideration if getting around is difficult for you. On the up side, the Palace is conveniently located close to the town's shopping and sightseeing district. ☎ *1004 Water St., 98368, ☎ 360/385–0773 or 800/962–0741, FAX 360/946–5287. 15 units, 1 with kitchenette. AE, D, MC, V.*

$$ Tides Inn. You might recognize this place from the movie *An Officer and a Gentleman*, which was filmed around Port Townsend and Fort Worden. (The hotel is the setting for those steamy love scenes between Richard Gere and Debra Winger.) There are even *Officer and a Gentleman*-theme rooms available, complete with stills from the movie and a VCR for private viewing of the film. Along the waterfront, about six blocks from downtown, the Tides is a comfortable, unfancy place, with good views of the water. An informal but adequate Continental breakfast is served every morning, and kitchens are available in both single rooms and suites; all the rooms have TVs and phones, and some have private decks and hot tubs. ☎ *1807 Water St., 98368, ☎ 360/385–0595 or 800/822–8696. 21 units. AE, DC, MC, V.*

Quinault

$$$ Lake Quinault Lodge. This lodge is set on a perfect glacial lake in the midst of the Olympic National Forest. Spectacular old-growth forests are an easy hike away, and there is abundant salmon and trout fishing. The medium-size and quite deluxe lodge, built in 1926 of cedar shingles, includes delightful public rooms decorated with antiques and a fireplace. The restaurant food is expensive but generally bland and unadventurous; the old-fashioned bar is lively and pleasant. Hiking and jogging trails are within easy access. Lake Quinault Lodge is especially popular with conventions and other groups. ☎ *S. Shore Rd. (Box 7), 98575, ☎ 360/288–2571, FAX 360/288–2901. 89 rooms. Restaurant, bar, indoor pool, hot tub, sauna, golf course, games room. MC, V.*

Sequim

$$–$$$ Greywolf Inn. Peggy and Bill Melang, from North Carolina and still brimming with southern hospitality, have obviously had fun turning this B&B into a showplace. Each room is (very) individually decorated— one looks imported from China, with a black lacquer four-poster and wardrobe; another room is Bavarian themed, with a feather bed under a pine canopy. One room with a gas fireplace can be combined with the adjacent room to create a two-bedroom suite with its own entrance. A Japanese-style bathhouse outside holds a hot tub. The dining room and decks overlook meadows, and a woodland trail winds through the property's idyllic 5 acres. ☎ *395 Keeler Rd., ☎ 360/683–5889 or 360/683–1487. 6 rooms with bath. Outdoor hot tub. AE, MC, V.*

Tenino
DINING

$$ **Alice's Restaurant.** This homey restaurant, set in a rural farmhouse ad-
★ jacent to the Johnson Creek Winery in the lovely Skookumchuck Val-
ley, offers a cheerful, simple ambience reminiscent of a Norman
Rockwell rendering. The food is surprisingly sophisticated, and fixed-
price dinner costs vary depending on the entrée. These elegant six-course
meals are innovative takes on classic American cuisine and are ac-
companied, naturally, by Johnson Creek wines. Vegetable appetizers,
soup, a fish course, and home-baked bread are among the preludes to
the robust entrées, which might be anything from wild game to oys-
ters or steak. ✗ *19248 Johnson Creek Rd. E, ☎ 360/264–2887.
Reservations required. AE, MC, V. Closed Mon.–Tues. No lunch.*

The Arts and Nightlife

The Arts
In Port Townsend, contact **Centrum** (Box 1158, Port Townsend 98368,
☎ 800/733–3608), the town's well-known and respected performing-
arts organization, which features a variety of performances, workshops,
and conferences each year.

Nightlife
On the Olympic Peninsula, the **Fourth Avenue Tavern** (210 E. 4th Ave.,
Olympia, ☎ 360/786–1444), a cheerful beer-and-wine joint, offers live
rock music on weekends. A favorite with locals, featuring live rock and
roll on weekends, is **Back Alley** (923 Washington St., Port Townsend,
☎ 360/385–2914).

LONG BEACH PENINSULA

If the waters of the Pacific and the mighty Columbia River had met in
a less turbulent manner, a huge seaport might sit at the river's mouth.
Instead, the entrance to the Columbia is only sparsely populated. Dot-
ted with fishing villages and cranberry bogs, it is worlds apart from
Seattle—3½ hours southwest—and Portland—two hours away. Long
Beach Peninsula, just north of the river's mouth, is rich for the natu-
ralist who enjoys bird-watching, hiking, or beachcombing; the history
buff; or the gourmet. It is the perfect place for holing up in front of a
crackling fire and indulging in a good book or venturing out to wit-
ness a winter storm (of which there are plenty). Locals warn that it is
not a place for swimming. Shifting sands underfoot and tremendous
undertows account for several drownings each year.

Long Beach Peninsula's natural bounty comes from its water and
coastline. The peninsula boasts the longest uninterrupted stretch (28
miles) of sandy beach in North America. Unfortunately, the locals act
as if it were private property, greedily claiming their right to drive cars,
trucks, recreational vehicles, and motorcycles up and down this pris-
tine belt of sand. Despite what the practice may do to clamming beds
or the psyche of solitary beachcombers, it continues. At least in 1990
the state legislature decided to close about 40% of the beach to motor
vehicles from April through Labor Day.

In 1990, a ½-mile-long wood boardwalk (stretching from Bolstad
Street south to South 10th Street) was installed in the town of Long
Beach, along with stairs to the beach access, wheelchair-accessible
ramps, plenty of benches, and telescopes. Since no vendors are permitted,
the addition allows for unobstructed views of the beach and bird life.

Inland a mile or two, the peninsula-area marshes are a haven to migrating birds, particularly the graceful, white trumpeter swans. The old-growth red-cedar grove on Long Island is believed to have sprouted some 4,000 years ago and is home to the endangered spotted owl, the marbled murelet, and other birds and small mammals.

Exploring

Numbers in the margin correspond to points of interest on the Long Beach Peninsula map.

① **Fort Columbia State Park and Interpretive Center,** one of 27 coastal defense units of the U.S. Army, was built in 1903 to house as many as 200 men at one time. Many of the fort's 30 structures have been restored to their original state. Illustrating barracks life at the fort is an interpretive center in one of the old accommodations, and a museum in the fort commander's quarters depicts military family life. A hike up Scarborough Hill behind the fort gives a breathtaking view of the peninsula and the Columbia River. *Hwy. 101, 2 mi east of Chinook,* ☎ *360/777–8221.* ☛ *Free. Call the Long Beach Visitors Bureau for hrs.*

② Two miles farther is **Chinook,** named for a Native American tribe that helped William Clark and Meriwether Lewis during their stay on the Pacific Coast. The **Sea Resources Hatchery Complex** offers tours of the hatchery and fish-rearing ponds that are used to teach high-school students the basics of salmon culturing and marine industrial arts. *Houtchen Rd.,* ☎ *360/777–8229.* ☛ *Free. Phone ahead to arrange a tour.*

③ The next town along the coast is **Ilwaco,** a small fishing community of about 600. From 1884 to 1910, gill-net and trap fishermen around here fought one another with knives, rifles, and threats of lynchings over access to and ownership of the fishing grounds. Today, the port is home to salmon, crab, tuna, charter fishing, and other commercial boats. The **Ilwaco Heritage Museum** uses excellent dioramas to present the history of southwestern Washington, beginning with the Native Americans; moving on to the influx of traders, missionaries, and pioneers; and concluding with the contemporary industries of fisheries, agriculture, and forests. The museum also houses a model of the peninsula's "clamshell railroad," a narrow-gauge train that transported passengers and mail along the beach. The rail bed on which the tracks were laid was made of ground-up clam and oyster shells. *115 S.E. Lake St.,* ☎ *360/642–3446.* ☛ *$1.25 adults, $1 senior citizens, 50¢ children under 12.* ☉ *May–Aug., Mon.–Sat. 9–5, Sun. noon–4; Sept.–Apr., Mon.–Sat. 9–5, Sun. noon–5.*

④ **Cape Disappointment Lighthouse,** first used in 1856, is one of the oldest lighthouses on the West Coast. The cape was named by English fur trader Captain John Meares in 1788 because of his unsuccessful attempt to find the Northwest Passage. Construction of the lighthouse suffered when the boat *Oriole,* carrying materials for the project, sank 2 miles offshore.

⑤ **Ft. Canby State Park** was an active military installation until 1957, when it was turned over to the Washington State Parks and Recreation Commission, and many of the bunkers that guarded the mouth of the Columbia remain today. The park attracts beachcombers, ornithologists, and fishermen, and offers viewing spots for watching huge waves crash against the Columbia River bar during winter storms. *Robert Gray Dr. (Box 488), 2½ mi southwest of Ilwaco, off Hwy. 101;* ☎ *360/642–3078 or 800/562–0990.* ☛ *Free. Call the Long Beach Visitors Bureau for hrs.*

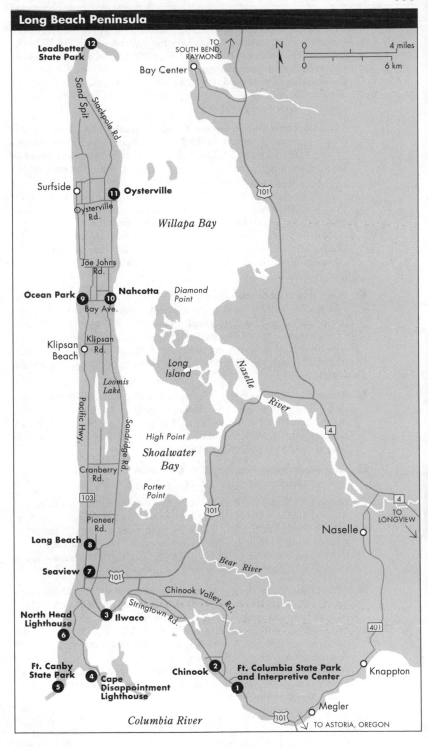

Long Beach Peninsula

TO
SOUTH BEND,
RAYMOND

N

0   4 miles

0   6 km

Bay Center

**Leadbetter
State Park** 12

Sand Spit

Stackpole Rd.

Surfside

11 **Oysterville**

Oysterville
Rd.

Willapa Bay

101

Joe Johns
Rd.

Ocean Park 9 **10** **Nahcotta**

*Diamond
Point*

Bay Ave.

Klipsan
Beach

Klipsan
Rd.

*Long
Island*

Naselle

Pacific Hwy.

*Loomis
Lake*

Sandridge Rd.

High Point

*Shoalwater
Bay*

River

4

Cranberry
Rd.

*Porter
Point*

103

101

4

TO
LONGVIEW

Pioneer
Rd.

Naselle

Long Beach 8

Bear   River

Seaview 7

101

Chinook Valley Rd.

401

**North Head
Lighthouse** 3 **Ilwaco**

Stringtown Rd.

6

**Ft. Canby
State Park** 4 **Cape
Disappointment
Lighthouse**

5

Chinook

2

1 **Ft. Columbia State Park
and Interpretive Center**

Knappton

Columbia River

Megler

TO ASTORIA, OREGON

101

In the park is the **Lewis & Clark Interpretive Center,** which was built in 1976 and covers the 8,000-mile round-trip journey of the Corps of Volunteers for Northwest Discovery from Wood River, Illinois, to the mouth of the Columbia River. Artwork, photographs, and original journal entries are arranged along a series of ramps and take visitors from the planning of the expedition to a view of the Pacific from Cape Disappointment. ☎ *360/642–3029 or 360/642–3078. Check with the Long Beach Visitors Bureau for hrs.*

The **U.S. Coast Guard Station Cape Disappointment** is the largest search-and-rescue station on the Northwest coast, and its operations saved or assisted some 3,000 people in 1989. The **National Motor Life Boat School** is a graduate course in conquering fear. The only school of its kind, it teaches elite rescue crews from around the world advanced skills in navigation, mechanics, fire fighting, lifesaving, the capabilities and limitations of motor lifeboats, and safe rescues. The rough conditions of the Columbia River bar provide a practical training for the regular surf drills. The observation platform on the North Jetty at Ft. Canby State Park is a good viewing spot for watching the motor lifeboats. ☎ *360/642–2384. Informal tours may be available, but phone ahead.*

❻ North Head Lighthouse, also one of the oldest lighthouses in the area, was built in 1899 to help skippers sailing from the north who could not see the Cape Disappointment Lighthouse. Before the lighthouses were built, a variety of less-sophisticated signals, such as notched trees, white rags, or bonfires, were used. Volunteers residing in Astoria had to paddle across the river and hike 12 miles up the cape to place the signals.

❼ Seaview is an unincorporated community that includes several homes dating from the 1800s. The **Shelburne Inn** (*see* Dining and Lodging, *below*), built in 1896, is the last turn-of-the-century hotel that still accommodates visitors. Another historic building is the **Sou'wester Lodge,** built by U.S. Senator Henry Winslow Corbett in 1892.

❽ Long Beach, a community of 1,400, caters to tourists with its go-carts, bumper cars, amusement park, and beach activities.

❾ Ocean Park is the commercial center of the peninsula's north end. It was founded as a camp for the Methodist Episcopal Church of Portland in 1883, but the law that once prohibited the establishment of saloons and gambling houses no longer exists. The **Taylor Hotel,** built in 1892 on Bay Avenue and N Place, houses retail businesses and is the only structure from the early days that is open to the public.

❿ Across the way, on the bay side, is **Nahcotta,** the site of an active oyster industry. Oysters are shucked and canned on the docks on Willapa Bay, and you can sample them at the **Ark** (273 Sandridge Rd., ☎ 360/665–4133), a restaurant on the old Nahcotta Dock. Named for a Native American chief, Nahcotta was once the northernmost point on the peninsula's narrow-gauge railway, and the schedule is still posted in the Nahcotta Post Office. The town's port is a good place from which to view Long Island, home of an old-growth cedar forest that can be reached only by private boat.

⓫ The town of **Oysterville,** established in 1854, did not survive the oyster industry's decline in the late 1800s. The native shellfish were fished to extinction and, although replaced with a Japanese oyster, Oysterville never made a comeback. Tides have washed away homes, businesses, and a Methodist church, but the village still exists, and free maps inside the vestibule of the restored **Oysterville Church** direct you through this town, which is now on the National Register of Historic Places. For more information on the town, write to the **Oysterville Restoration Foundation** (Box 1, Oysterville 98641).

⑫ **Leadbetter State Park,** at the northernmost tip of the peninsula, is a wildlife refuge and good spot for bird-watching, and the dune area at the very tip of the point is closed from April to August to protect the nesting snowy plover. Black brants, sandpipers, turnstones, yellowlegs, sanderlings, knots, and plovers are among the 100 species biologists have recorded at the point. *Off Stackpole Rd. at the northern tip of the peninsula,* ☎ *360/642–3078. Call this number or the Long Beach Visitors Bureau for hrs.*

Shopping

The Bookvendor (101 Pacific Ave., Long Beach, ☎ 360/642–2702) stocks an extensive supply of children's books, classics, and travel books as well as art supplies.

Gray Whale Gallery & Gifts (105 Pacific Ave., Long Beach, ☎ 360/642–2889) features Northwest art, cards, jewelry, and cranberry products from the peninsula.

Long Beach Kites (104 Pacific Ave. N, Long Beach, ☎ 360/642–2202) offers myriad kites, from box kites, dragons, and fighters to 19 varieties of stunt kites, *and* free repairs are made.

North Head Gallery (600 S. Pacific Ave., Long Beach, ☎ 360/642–8884) has the largest selection of Elton Bennett originals, plus Bennett's reproductions and works from other Northwest artists.

Sports and the Outdoors

Bicycling

Good areas for bicycling include Ft. Canby and North Head roads, Sandridge Road to Ocean Park and Oysterville, and Highway 101 from Naselle to Seaview along Willapa Bay.

Fishing

Salmon, rock cod, lingcod, flounder, perch, sea bass, and sturgeon are popular and plentiful for fishing. A free fishing guide is available from the **Port of Ilwaco** (Box 307, 98624, ☎ 360/642–3145).

The clamming season varies depending on the supply but is a popular pastime here. For details, call the **Washington Department of Fisheries** (☎ 360/902–2250) or the **fisheries shellfish lab** (☎ 360/665–4166) in Nahcotta.

Golf

The peninsula has two nine-hole golf courses, the **Peninsula Golf Course** (☎ 360/642–2828), on the northern edge of Long Beach, and the **Surfside Golf and Country Club** (☎ 360/665–4148), located 2 miles north of Ocean Park.

Hiking

Hiking trails are available at **Ft. Canby** (☎ 360/642–3078) and **Leadbetter** (☎ 360/642–3078) state parks.

Horseback Riding

Horseback riding is popular on the beach, and rentals are available at **Skippers** (S. 9th St. and Beach Access Rd., ☎ 360/642–3676). For beach access, riders are asked to use South 10th Street rather than Bolstad Street. Also, **Double "D" Horse Rides** (on 10th St., ☎ 360/642–2576) takes phone reservations.

Whale Watching

★ **Whale watching** is a popular activity on Long Beach Peninsula. Gray whales pass by here twice a year: December through February, on their migration from the Arctic to their winter breeding grounds in Californian and Mexican waters; and March through May, on the return trip north. At press time no charters were being offered in the Long Beach area, but the Northhead Lighthouse offers the best viewpoint. The best conditions exist in the mornings, when seas are calm and overcast conditions reduce the glare. Look on the horizon for a whale blow—the vapor, water, or condensation that spouts into the air when the whale exhales. Once a blow is spotted, there are likely to be others. Whales often make up to six shorter, shallow dives before a longer dive that can last as long as 10 minutes.

Dining

For price-category definitions, *see* Dining *in* Washington Essentials, *below.*

Chinook

$$–$$$ **The Sanctuary.** This restaurant, in a turn-of-the-century church building, offers fine cuisine and a quiet atmosphere with soft lighting and stained-glass windows. Swedish meatballs are a specialty, but the menu also features local seafood, prime rib, veal, an extensive wine list, and delicious homemade desserts. ✗ *Hwy. 101 and Hazel St., Chinook,* ☎ *360/777–8380. Reservations advised. AE, MC, V. No lunch.*

Long Beach

$$–$$$ **Columbia Lightship.** This restaurant, on the beach side of Nendel's Inn, affords some of the best views of the beach and surf in the area. Huge windows and high ceilings lend an open, airy feeling to the place, and the atmosphere is casual and low key. Don't be surprised to see kites or a large wind sock floating in the air as you gaze out at the beach from the open-air bar, which serves an assortment of Washington wines and local microbrews. The lunch menu offers fish-and-chips, fresh salads, quiche, pasta, and sandwiches. Dinner entrées include grilled fresh salmon, fresh Willapa Bay oysters, Cajun chicken, Manilla clams, pasta primavera, and prime rib. Try the Chicken Radiator Pasta, accordion-shape noodles in a white Parmesan cheese sauce, with chicken and artichokes. Breakfast (served in summer only) options include a buffet with meat, eggs, fruit, waffles, pancakes, biscuits, muffins, and porridge. ✗ *409 10th St. SW, Long Beach,* ☎ *360/542–2311. Reservations advised. MC, V.*

$–$$ **Dog Salmon Café & Lounge.** Even if you don't eat here, have a look inside this family restaurant, decorated with replicas of Northwest Coast Native American carvings and paintings of bears, beavers, and salmon on wood-paneled walls. The fare ranges from hamburgers to spicy Cajun shrimp linguine. ✗ *113 Hwy. 103, in downtown Long Beach,* ☎ *360/642–2416. No reservations. MC, V.*

$ **My Mom's Pies.** Although this lunch spot is in a mobile home, and keeps few hours, it's worth dropping by for the specialty pies, such as the banana whipped cream, chocolate almond, pecan, sour-cream raisin, and fresh raspberry. They also serve clam chowder and quiche. ✗ *Hwy. 103 and 12th St. S,* ☎ *360/642–2342. No reservations. MC, V. Closed Sun.–Tues. No dinner.*

Nahcotta

$$$ **The Ark.** The Ark, sitting adjacent to the Nahcotta oyster dock, has excellent cuisine. The house specialty is seafood—especially oysters, but leave room for the splendid desserts—cranberry Grand Marnier mousse and blackberry bread pudding, for example. The bar presents less expensive, lighter fare, including soup and sandwiches. ✗ 273 Sandridge Rd., ☎ 360/665–4133. Reservations advised. AE, MC, V. Closed Jan.–Feb. Call ahead for hrs.

Seaview

$$–$$$ **Shoalwater Restaurant.** The Shoalwater Restaurant at the Shelburne Inn has been acclaimed by Gourmet, Bon Appétit, and Travel & Leisure, so you dine in good company here. Seafood, bought from the fishing boats to the restaurant's back door, is as fresh as it can be; local mushrooms and salad greens are gathered from the peninsula's woods and gardens. Exquisite desserts are the creation of Ann Kischner, a master pastry chef, and an extensive wine list and Northwest microbrews on tap in the Heron & Beaver Pub are featured. Also try the Sunday brunch offered on Easter, Mother's Day, and throughout the summer. ✗ Pacific Hwy. and N. 45th St., Seaview, ☎ 360/642–4142, FAX 360/642–8904. Reservations advised. AE, MC, V. No lunch in restaurant; pub offers lunch.

$–$$ **42nd Street Café.** This much-needed, middle-of-the-road restaurant is nestled comfortably between deep-fried seafood and fries at one end of the peninsula's restaurant spectrum and expensive gourmet fare on the other. The café emphasizes home-cooked food and features a new menu daily. Grilled Willapa Bay oysters are tender and succulent, and halibut and salmon are grilled or poached. The raisin cream pie for dessert is heavenly. Hwy. 103 and 42nd St., Seaview, ☎ 360/642–2323. Reservations accepted for parties of 5 or more. V. Closed Tues. No lunch.

Lodging

For price-category definitions, see Lodging in Washington Essentials, below.

Long Beach

$$–$$$ **Breakers Motel and Condominiums.** These contemporary condominiums have one- and two-bedroom units and are located on the beach. Since they are individually owned, the decor varies, but all are modern, comfortable, and clean. ☎ Box 428, 98631, ☎ 360/642–4414 or 800/288–8890, FAX 360/642–8772. 114 rooms, some with kitchenettes. Indoor pool, spa, playground. MC, V.

$$–$$$ **Nendels Edgewater.** Rooms at this modern motel, set just behind the sand dunes and very close to the beach, have a variety of views, but those in the newer building offer the best scenery. ☎ Box 793, 98631, ☎ 360/642–2311 or 800/561–2456. 84 rooms. Restaurant, bar. AE, D, MC, V.

$$ **Sandpiper Beach Resort.** This resort is a modern, four-story complex of clean, attractive, and fully equipped suites; most have a sitting room, dining area, fireplace, small kitchen, porch, bedroom, and bath. Penthouse suites have an extra bedroom and cathedral ceilings. There are also five cottages and a few one-room studios. Despite a downright ugly playground that mars the beach view, the building is attractive, with the wood exterior blending well with the surrounding woods and water. This is definitely the place for a getaway: no in-room phones, no pool, no TV, no restaurant. ☎ Rte. 109 (1½ mi south of Pacific Beach), Box A, 98571, ☎ 360/276–4580. 30 rooms. 3-night minimum on holidays and summer. MC, V.

Ilwaco

$$$ **Inn at Ilwaco.** This New England–style church, built in 1928, has been renovated as a B&B. All but two of the nine guest rooms are upstairs in the old Sunday-school rooms and all are cozily furnished with some

antiques, armoires, and eyelet or printed chintz curtains and coverlets. The lobby, with upholstered sofas, chairs, and tables with loads of books, and the breakfast area are in the former church parlor. For performances, meetings, classes, and weddings, the inn makes use of its converted sanctuary, which is now a 120-seat theater. Breakfast may include such delicacies as apple-walnut pancakes, homemade muffins, fresh fruit, and cereal. ⌸ *120 Williams St. NE, Ilwaco 98624, ☎ 360/642–8686. 9 rooms, 7 with private bath. MC, V.*

Seaview

$$$ Shelburne Inn. This bright and cheerful antiques-filled inn was built in 1896 by Charles Beaver and is now listed on the National Register of Historic Places. It is also right on the highway, which can make it noisy, so the best picks are rooms on the west side. The indefatigable team of David Campiche and Laurie Anderson have the inn to its current high level of comfort and quality. Most of the rooms have balconies, private baths, queen-size beds with handmade quilts or hand-crocheted bedspreads, and some have lovely stained glass. The gourmet breakfast is unforgettable. ⌸ *Hwy. 103 and N. 45th St., Seaview 98644, ☎ 360/542–2442, ℻ 360/642–8904. 16 rooms. Restaurant, pub. AE, MC, V.*

$–$$ Sou'wester. A stay at the Sou'wester is a rather bohemian experience. Proprietors Len and Miriam Atkins came to Seaview from South Africa, by way of Israel and Chicago, where they worked with the late psychologist Bruno Bettelheim, and they are always up for a stimulating conversation. The historic lodge was built in 1892 as the summer retreat for Henry Winslow Corbett, a Portland banker, timber baron, shipping and railroad magnate, and U.S. senator. Rooms and apartments in the lodge are not "decorated"—instead they are the repository of things carefully collected over the years, including handmade quilts and original paintings and drawings. Soirees and chamber-music concerts sometimes occur in the parlor. Cabins and the classic mobile-home units just behind the beach have cooking facilities, and guests are also welcome to make breakfast in the Atkins' homey kitchen. ⌸ *Beach Access Rd. (Box 102), Seaview 98644, ☎ 360/642–2542. 3 rooms with shared bath and kitchen, 4 cabins, 8 trailers. Beach. D, MC, V.*

CROSSING THE CASCADES

Driving east out of Seattle on I–90, you'll travel through bucolic farmland with snowcapped mountains in the background. Nestled in the foothills is Snoqualmie Falls, one of the area's most popular attractions. Small mining towns dot the mountains, and to the north of the main I–90 route, you'll find Leavenworth, an alpine-style village with excellent sporting opportunities. Crossing over the mountains, you'll emerge in eastern Washington—seemingly a different state, in both attitude and climate. Ellensburg is the gateway to the east, a pleasant college town that makes an excellent jumping-off point for visiting the wineries that lie in the Yakima Valley.

Exploring

Snoqualmie

Spring and summer snowmelt turns the Snoqualmie River into the thundering torrent known as **Snoqualmie Falls** as it cascades through a 268-foot rock gorge (100 feet higher than Niagara Falls) to a 65-foot-deep pool below. These falls are the biggest attraction of Snoqualmie, which is about 30 miles east of Seattle at Exit 27 off I–90, although a sizeable contingent of visitors come to see where David Lynch filmed his short-lived—but deeply loved—TV series *Twin Peaks*.

A 2-acre park, including an observation platform 300 feet above the Snoqualmie River, offers a view of the falls and surrounding area. Hike the **River Trail,** a 3-mile round-trip route through trees and open slopes, ending with a view from the base of the falls. (Note: Be prepared for an uphill workout on the return to the trailhead.)

Steam locomotives power vintage trains on **Puget Sound** and **Snoqualmie Valley Railway.** The 75-minute trip travels through woods and farmland. Railroad artifacts and memorabilia are displayed at both the Snoqualmie Depot (Hwy. 202, in downtown Snoqualmie) and Railroad Park Depot in downtown Northbend. For children, a special Santa train runs the first two weekends in December and a spook train runs the last two weekends in October; tickets for all special trips must be prepurchased. *Box 459, Snoqualmie,* ☎ *206/746–4025 in Seattle or 206/888–0373.* ☛ *$6 adults, $5 senior citizens, $4 children. Trains operate Sept., May, and June, weekends; Oct. and Apr., Sun.; July–Aug., Fri.–Sun. Call for departure times.*

Roslyn and Cle Elum

Across the pass, in the eastern foothills of the Cascades, are two former coal-mining towns. Roslyn, off I–90 on Route 903, has gained a certain notoriety of late as the real-life stand-in for the Alaskan town of Cicely on the TV program *Northern Exposure.* Fans can take a photo under the giant mural seen in the opening credits or have a beer at the **Brick Tavern** (100 Pennsylvania, ☎ 509/649–2643), which has a second claim to fame—it opened in 1889 and is now the oldest operating bar in Washington. Roslyn is also notable for its 23 ethnic cemeteries, established by communities of miners around the turn of the century. Cle Elum (klee *ell*-um) doesn't have much to recommend it sights-wise, but it's right off I–90 and serves as a convenient stop for lunch or to get gas.

Leavenworth

Some of the best skiing, hiking, rock climbing, rafting, canoeing, and snowshoeing in the Northwest (*see* Sports and the Outdoors, *below*) are accessible from Leavenworth, a cute pseudo-Bavarian resort town about 50 miles north of I–90. Take Rte. 970 from Cle Elum to Rte. 97 and continue north 40 miles, or catch Rte. 97 at its junction with I–90 just 4 miles west of Ellensburg. (You can also reach Leavenworth by traveling northeast from Seattle along I–5 and U.S. 2.)

Although it was once a center for mining and railroading, by the early 1960s Leavenworth had become a moribund village. Civic leaders seeking ways to revitalize the area decided to capitalize on the town's spectacular alpine setting; the result is a charming (and only sometimes *too* cute) center for both winter and summer sports. Shopkeepers and hostelers, maintaining the town's buildings in gingerbread Tyrolean style and sponsoring events modeled after those found in a typical Bavarian village, keep a European spirit of simple elegance alive in a setting that is never short of spectacular.

Virtually all the many specialty shops, restaurants, and hotels subscribe to the Bavarian theme. There are restaurants specializing in Bavarian food; candy shops with gourmet Swiss-style chocolate; shops featuring music boxes, nutcrackers, and other Bavarian specialties; and charming European-style pension hotels. (There's even a laundromat called Die Washerie.) Throughout the year the village engages in festivities that reflect the alpine theme.

Ellensburg

The combined attractions of a busy college-town atmosphere and a well-maintained redbrick Victorian district make downtown Ellensburg worth a stop. Cafés and bookstores that serve the 6,000 students at **Central Washington University** (400 E. 8th Ave., ☎ 509/963–1111) are intermixed with the equipment and feed shops that supply the region's largest industry, cattle ranching. In celebration of the cowboy ethic, the town holds the **Ellensburg Rodeo** (☎ 800/637–2444 for tickets and information), acclaimed as one of the best in the country, every Labor Day weekend.

Sports and the Outdoors

Golf

Those hankering for placid, or at least warmer-weather, sports can try the **Leavenworth Golf Club** (Box 247, 98826, ☎ 509/548–7267), an 18-hole, par-71 course with a pro shop and clubhouse.

Hiking and Rock Climbing

Leavenworth also offers hiking trails that take in some of the most breathtaking vistas in the entire Cascades. There are more than 320 miles of scenic trails in the Leavenworth Ranger District alone, including **Hatchery Creek, Icicle Ridge,** the **Enchantments, Tumwater Canyon, Fourth of July Creek, Snow Lake, Stuart Lake,** and **Chatter Creek.** Contact the **Leavenworth Ranger District** (600 Sherburne St., 98826, ☎ 509/782–1413) for more details, or consult one of the many fine books detailing backcountry hikes in the Northwest. Rock climbing is also popular because of the solid granite cliffs in the area.

Horseback Riding

Hourly and daily horseback rides and pack trips are available at **Eagle Creek Ranch** (7951 Eagle Creek Rd., Leavenworth 98826, ☎ 509/548–7798).

Skiing

Snoqualmie Pass is the site of three ski areas—**Alpental, Ski Acres,** and **Snoqualmie Summit** (for all areas: 3010 77th St. SE, Mercer Island 98040, ☎ 206/232–8182). Both downhill and cross-country skiing are available in winter and spring, and there's hiking in the summer. Each area rents equipment and has full restaurant and lodge facilities.

Beginning and advanced skiers will find more than 20 miles of maintained cross-country ski trails in the Leavenworth area. Meanwhile, Stevens Pass has downhill slopes and lifts for skiers of every level. Several shops in Leavenworth rent and sell ski equipment. For more information, contact the **Leavenworth Winter Sports Club** (Box 573, 98826, ☎ 509/548–5115).

White-Water Rafting

Rafting is a popular sport during March–July, with the prime high-country runoff in May and June. The **Wenatchee River,** which runs through Leavenworth, is generally considered the best white-water river in the state—a Class 3 (out of six on a scale of difficulty) on the International Canoeing Association scale. Depending on the season and location, anything from a relatively calm scenic float to an invigorating white-water shoot is possible on the Wenatchee or on one of several other nearby rivers. Some rafting outfitters and guides in the Leavenworth area are **Northern Wilderness River Riders** (10645 Hwy. 209, Leavenworth 98826, ☎ 509/548–4583), **All Rivers Adventures/Wenatchee Whitewater** (Box 12, Cashmere 98815, ☎ 509/782–2254), and **Leavenworth Outfitters** (21588 S.R. 207, Leavenworth 98826, ☎ 509/763–3733).

Dining and Lodging

For price-category definitions, *see* Dining *and* Lodging *in* Washington Essentials, *below.*

Cle Elum

DINING AND LODGING

$$ Mama Vallone's Steakhouse and Inn. The Vallones use traditional recipes from their Italian homeland to design the menu for this cozy and informal restaurant. Although it's renowned for its great pasta, the pasta and *fagioli* soup (a tomato-based soup with vegetables and beans) and the *bagna calda* (a bath of olive oil, garlic, anchovies, and butter for dredging vegetables and meat) are also worthy favorites. Also try the Sunday brunch, which may feature ravioli or tortellini along with a standard eggs-and-ham buffet. The inn upstairs was built in 1906 as a boardinghouse for unmarried miners; today there are three moderately priced rooms with private baths and antique-style furnishings. ⊞ *302 W. 1st St.,* ☎ *509/674–5174. 3 rooms. Restaurant (reservations advised; closed Mon.; no lunch). AE, DC, MC, V.*

Ellensburg

DINING

$ Valley Cafe. This Art Deco eatery, built in the late 1930s, serves light and tasty meals all day. Try the chicken dijon sandwich, the Mediterranean tortellini salad, or the café plate, which combines a cup of soup with an open-faced sandwich. Breakfast is served on the weekend until noon. ✕ *105 W. 3rd St.,* ☎ *509/925–3050. AE, D, DC, MC, V.*

Leavenworth

DINING

$$–$$$ Edelhaus. From its prime spot in downtown Leavenworth, the Edelhaus exudes quiet, European country–style ambience with white stucco walls, old wooden tables, and crisp white linens. The sophisticated menu is closer to that of the Asian-accented Northwest cuisine found in Seattle restaurants than it is to the German-theme restaurants hereabouts. ✕ *320 9th St., Leavenworth,* ☎ *206/548–4412. MC, V.*

$$ Cougar Inn. This stylish family restaurant is on the shores of Lake Wenatchee, about 25 miles outside Leavenworth. Locals often come by boat and tie up at the restaurant's dock for the good country food. The atmosphere is pleasant, with lots of natural wood, airy rooms, great views of the lake and, in summer, a big outdoor deck. Breakfast, lunch, and dinner are served daily, and the hearty American-style Sunday brunch is especially popular. The menu, featuring burgers, steaks, and prime rib, is not particularly adventurous, but the food is well prepared and the service friendly. ✕ *23379 S.R. 207, Lake Wenatchee,* ☎ *509/763–3354. Reservations advised, especially for Sun. brunch. AE, MC, V.*

$$ Pewter Pot. This intimate restaurant with lace curtains and fresh flowers in downtown Cashmere is some 10 miles from Leavenworth, but worth the drive. Owner Kristi Bjornstad focuses on comfort food and very personal service. Start with one of her great soups. Entrées include a stuffed breast of chicken with an apple-cider sauce, turkey and dressing, and sour-cream beef potpie. The deep-dish marionberry pie is memorable. Ms. Bjornstad serves lunch and afternoon tea, but stops serving dinner at 8 PM. ✕ *124 ½ Cottage Ave., Cashmere 98815,* ☎ *509/782–2036. Reservations advised. MC, V.*

$$ Reiner's Gasthaus. Authentic central European cuisine with a Hungarian-Austrian accent is presented in this small, cheerful restaurant. The decor is heavy on the pine furnishings and thick drapes, with lots of vintage photographs and knickknacks on the walls, and the service is bustling and friendly. Music is performed on weekend evenings: Usually a jolly accordion player is featured. Specialties include pork schnitzel and Hungarian goulash; these two dishes, as well as all the reasonably priced and well-prepared dinners, come with hearty soups and salads. ✕ *829 Front St. (upstairs), Leavenworth, ☎ 509/548–5111. No reservations. MC, V.*

$ **Baren Haus.** Hearty, unpretentious food is served in this spacious, noisy, and often crowded high-ceiling beer-hall-style room. The cuisine may not be haute, or even particularly interesting, but the generous servings and low prices will appeal to families and those traveling on a tight budget. Seating is at large booths with blue tablecloths. House specialties include German-style sandwiches (such as bratwurst on grilled whole-wheat bread with sauerkraut and hearty mustards) and pizzas. ✕ *208 9th St., ☎ 509/548–4535. Reservations accepted, except during festival time (Aug. and late Sept.–early Oct.). MC, V.*

$ **Danish Bakery.** Tasty homemade pastries, good strong espresso drinks, and a self-serve coffee bar are the attractions in this small, pleasant shop. The decor is tastefully done with dark woods and mural paintings, and the service is fast and friendly. This is a perfect place to escape the crowds on the sidewalks. ✕ *731 Front St., ☎ 509/548–7514. No reservations. No credit cards.*

$ **Homefires Bakery.** Locals come to this bakery when they want hearty, chewy bread baked in an old brick oven. Try the German sourdough black rye bread—it's great for sandwiches or eaten simply with unsalted butter. The cinnamon rolls and cookies will make a hit with your sweet tooth. ✕ *13013 Bayne Rd., Leavenworth, ☎ 509/548–7362. No reservations. No credit cards.*

LODGING

The number of hotels, motels, B&Bs, and long-term-rental cabins in Leavenworth has increased as the area has become more popular. **Bavarian Bedfinders** (309 8th St., Suite 1, Leavenworth 98826, ☎ 509/548–4410 or 800/323–2920 in WA) matches travelers with more than 100 facilities such as condominiums, private cabins, small lodges, and B&Bs, in Leavenworth and around the state.

$$–$$$ **Pension Anna.** This small, family-run Austrian-style pension in the middle of the village has a farmhouse atmosphere. Rooms and suites are decorated with sturdy, antique pine furniture, with such added touches as fresh flowers and comforters on the beds. Two of the suites have whirlpool baths, and all except the ground-level rooms have small balconies. The two largest suites have fireplaces and handsome four-poster beds. A hearty European-style breakfast (cold cuts, meats, cheeses, soft-boiled eggs), included in the room price, is served in a breakfast room decorated in traditional European style with crisp linens, pine decor, dark green curtains, and (of course) a cuckoo clock. The staircases to the upper floors are quite steep. Two suites are in a 1913 onion dome steepled church building that has been relocated on the property. 🏨 *926 Commercial St., 98826, ☎ 509/548–6273. 14 units. AE, D, MC, V.*

$$ **Evergreen Motel.** Popular with hikers and skiers, the Evergreen was built in the 1930s and still has a lot of the charm of the old-fashioned roadside inn it once was. Some of its two-bedroom suites have fireplaces and/or kitchens (though no utensils), while some have multiple beds and can sleep up to six comfortably. Thus, although there are only 26 units, the motel's capacity is about 80 guests. Complimentary Continental breakfast is offered by a very friendly staff, and the motel is one block from downtown. 🏨 *1117 Front St., 98826, ☎ 509/548–5515 or 800/327–7212. 26 rooms. AE, D, DC, MC, V.*

$$ Haus Rohrbach. This alpine-style B&B sits on the side of a hill overlooking its own pool and hot tub, the village of Leavenworth, and the valley beyond. The center of activity here is a large lodgelike room with a wood stove, a kitchen area, and tables for dining, playing games, socializing, or just taking in the view. Guest rooms have double or queen-size beds (some have a sofa bed or daybed, as well), down comforters, and pine furniture. The suites offer king-size beds, whirlpool tubs, a gas fireplace, easy chairs, and small but fully equipped kitchens. The full breakfast served here typically features Dutch babies or sourdough pancakes and sausage. ☎ *12882 Ranger Rd., 98826, ☎ 509/548–7024. 9 rooms with bath, 4 rooms share 2 baths, 3 suites. Pool, hot tub. AE, D, MC, V.*

$$ Linderhoff Motor Inn. This small place at the west end of Leavenworth is one of the nicest in town for the money. It offers a variety of options: standard rooms, honeymoon suites with whirlpool tubs and fireplaces, and town-house units that sleep up to eight and have fully equipped kitchens and two bathrooms. In contrast to the Bavarian-style exterior, with its overflowing flower boxes, guest rooms are decorated in a contemporary style of soft colors and feature locally crafted pine furnishings. The complimentary Continental breakfast choices of fresh fruit juice and locally baked muffins and Danishes can be taken back to the rooms or eaten outside on the inn's balcony. ☎ *690 Hwy. 2, 98826, ☎ 509/548–5283. 26 units. Pool, hot tub. AE, MC, V.*

$ Edelweiss Hotel. This is an unpretentious hotel above the restaurant of the same name. Small rooms, plainly furnished and with either shared or private baths, are available. This is not the place to go for a romantic weekend, but if you're on a budget and simply need a place to lay your head, the Edelweiss's price ($15 for a single room, no windows or TV) is hard to beat in this hotel-hungry town. The service is genial if sometimes harried, and the staircase is steep. ☎ *843 Front St., 98826, ☎ 509/548–7015. 14 units. MC, V.*

Roslyn

DINING

$–$$ Roslyn Café. This funky café has gained notice from its exterior's appearances on TV's "Northern Exposure," but it's the trappings from its real-life past that, along with its good food, make it popular. High ceilings, a jukebox with the original 78s, and neon in the window bring nostalgia to the place. The hamburgers with spinach and onions are mouthwatering, but entrées also include such offerings as fresh halibut in dill sauce. Desserts are decadent. ✗ *28 Pennsylvania Ave., ☎ 509/649–2763. No reservations. MC, V. No dinner Mon.–Wed.*

Snoqualmie

DINING

$$$ The Herbfarm. If there is such a thing as Northwest cuisine, then The
★ Herbfarm must rank as its temple. But the attraction here is more than the fine, fresh food: This restaurant offers intimate, elegant dining among wildflower bouquets, Victorian-style prints, and a friendly staff. Try such delicacies as goat's milk cheese and parsley biscuits, green pickled walnuts in the husk, fresh salmon with a sauce of fresh garden herbs, and sorbet of rose geranium and lemon verbena. There's only one drawback: The Herbfarm is commonly booked up months ahead of time, which means you should plan a meal long before you're getting to Seattle. Is all that effort worth it? Yes. Wine is the only alcohol served. ✗ *From I–90, Exit 22, go 3 mi. to 32804 Issaquah-Fall City Rd., Fall City, ☎ 206/784–2222. 75% of the 24 seats for each lunch or special dinner are reserved in early Apr. The other 6 seats can be reserved by phoning at 1 PM the Fri. before you wish to go. Allow 2 hrs for lunch*

($60 per person) and the garden tour. Dinners, including 9 courses and 5 fine wines, are scheduled in the summer ($115 per person). MC, V. Closed Mon.–Thurs. No dinner Jan.–early Apr.

$$$ **Salish.** The restaurant at the Salish lodge (see below) serves three meals daily, but gained its widespread reputation for its Saturday and Sunday brunch. Five- or eight-course brunches are available, including such items as eggs, bacon, fish, fresh fruit, pancakes, and the Salish's renowned oatmeal. ✗ 37807 Snoqualmie-Fall City Rd., Fall City 37807, ☎ 206/888–2556. Reservations required. Jacket and tie (for dinner). AE, DC, MC, V.

LODGING

$$$ **Salish.** This lodge at the top of the falls has been rebuilt and is operated by the Oregon-based Salishan Lodge. Eight of the 91 rooms look out over the falls, and others have a view upriver. All the rooms have an airy feeling, wood furniture, and window seats or balconies. You can sit in the whirlpool bath and open a window to view the fire in the flagstone fireplace. ⊡ 37807 Snoqualmie-Fall City Rd., Fall City 37807, ☎ 206/888–2556. 91 rooms. 2 restaurants, bar, health club. AE, DC, MC, V.

Arts and Nightlife

Snoqualmie Falls Forest Theater produces three plays a summer (the Passion Play, a melodrama, and a well-known classic performed by acting students and community theater performers) in the 250-seat outdoor amphitheater near Fall City, usually on Friday and Saturday nights and Sunday afternoons. From I–90 take Exit 22 and go 4 mi; take a right on David Powell Rd., follow signs, continue through gate to parking area. 36800 S.E. David Powell Rd., ☎ 206/222–7044. ☛ $8.50; for another $9 per person, you can enjoy a salmon or steak barbecue after the matinee and before the evening performances. Reservations required for dinner.

YAKIMA VALLEY WINE COUNTRY

Numbers in the margin correspond to points of interest on the Yakima Valley map.

America's second-largest producer of wines, Washington state has been blessed with just the right soil, latitude, growing season, and climate that work together for premium grape and wine production. Its vineyards share the same latitude (46 degrees) and growth cycle of the great French wine-producing regions of Bordeaux and Burgundy. The Columbia and Yakima valleys have a low average rainfall, and irrigation allows for careful moisture control during critical growth phases. Warm, sunny days build heavy sugars and cool nights help to retain high acids in the grapes. The results are balanced wines of superior flavor and quality.

Eastern Washington has some 11,000 acres planted in vineyards of cabernet sauvignon, Johannesburg Riesling, chardonnay, sauvignon blanc, chenin blanc, grenache, merlot, semillon, muscat, and Gewürztraminer grapes. Yakima Valley, the viticultural center of the state, is home to the largest group of wineries. Wine operations vary from small wineries on the back of residential property to large, commercial operations. Barrels are tapped and wine tasting begins about the last week of April. The **Yakima Valley Wine Grower Association** (Box 39, Grandview 98930) publishes a brochure that lists local wineries with tasting-room tours and maps of the region.

❶ The first stop is 10 minutes south of Yakima at **Staton Hills Winery** (71 Gangl Rd., Wapato, ☎ 509/877–2112), just east of I–82. The building, with a huge stone fireplace and commanding view of the valley, is surrounded by three vineyard trellis systems, showing an efficient method of grape growing.

Zillah, a town named after the daughter of a railroad manager, features
❷ six wineries. Small **Bonair Winery** (500 S. Bonair Rd., Zillah, ☎ 509/829–6027), which specializes in chardonnay, is run by the Puryear family who, after years of amateur wine making in California, took up commercial
❸ production in the Yakima Valley. **Hyatt Vineyards Winery** (2020 Gilbert Rd., Zillah, ☎ 509/829–6333) specializes in estate-bottled table wines, and premium dessert wines are produced under the Thurston Wolfe label.
❹ **Zillah Oakes Winery** (Box 1729, Zillah, ☎ 509/829–6990) produces wine from vineyards on the southern slopes of the Rattlesnake Mountains.
❺ **Quail Run Vintners** (1500 Vintage Rd., Zillah, ☎ 509/829–6235), producers of Covey Run wines, is one of the valley's largest wineries, with expansive decks and grounds offering commanding views of the surrounding vineyards and orchards. Inside you can watch the wine making through windows off the tasting room.

❻ **Portteus Vineyards** (5201 Highland Dr., Zillah, ☎ 509/829–6970) limits its production to cabernet sauvignon and chardonnay from grapes
❼ grown at a 1,440-foot elevation in the hills above Zillah. **Horizon's Edge Winery** (4530 E. Zillah Dr., Zillah, ☎ 509/829–6401) takes its name from its tasting-room view of the Yakima Valley, Mt. Adams, and Mt. Rainier. The winery produces champagne, barrel-fermented chardonnays, pinot noir, cabernet sauvignon, and muscat canelli.

❽ Granger's **Eaton Hill Winery** (530 Gurley Rd., Granger, ☎ 509/854–2508), located in the restored Rinehold Cannery building, produces white Riesling and semillon. You may see fruit pickers working out-
❾ side the **Stewart Vineyards** (1711 Cherry Hill Rd., Granger, ☎ 509/854–1882), located atop Cherry Hill. In sunny weather, tastings are held on the large deck overlooking the cherry orchard.

❿ **Washington Hills** (111 E. Lincoln Ave., Sunnyside, ☎ 509/839–9463), in the little town of Sunnyside, produces a variety of white wines, a red,
⓫ and a blush. The **Tucker Cellars** (70 Ray Rd., Sunnyside, ☎ 509/837–8701) family produces some 20,000 gallons of wine annually. Their market, just east of Sunnyside on Highway 12, sells the family's homegrown fruit and vegetables in addition to wine.

⓬ The state's oldest winery is **Chateau Ste. Michelle** (W. 5th and Ave. B, Grandview, ☎ 509/882–3928), in Grandview, where many of the company's red wines are made in a building dating from the '30s. The European-style open-top fermenters and a collection of wood aging tanks are featured.

⓭ Several wineries are found in the Prosser area. The **Yakima River Winery** (Rte. 1, Box 1657, Prosser, ☎ 509/786–2805), specializing in barrel-aged red wines and dessert wines, is southwest of town. The name
⓮ **Pontin del Roza** (Rte. 4, Box 4735, Prosser, ☎ 509/786–2805) comes from the owners, the Pontin family, and the Roza, the irrigated, south-facing slopes of the Yakima Valley where the grapes are grown.

⓯ **Hinzerling Vineyards** (1520 Sheridan Rd., Prosser, ☎ 509/786–2163), operated by the Wallace family, is the valley's oldest family-owned winery, specializing in estate-grown cabernets and late-harvest wines.
⓰ East of Prosser is **Chinook Wines** (Wine Country Rd., Box 387, Prosser,

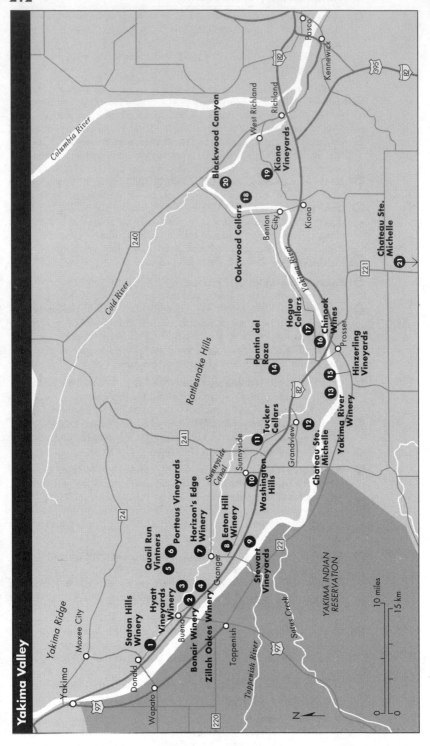

Yakima Valley

No matter where you go, travel is easier when you know the code.^{SM}

dial 1 8 0 0 CALL ATT®

Dial 1 800 CALL ATT and you'll always get through from any phone with any card* and you'll always get AT&T's best deal.** It's the one number to remember when calling away from home.

*Other long distance company calling cards excluded.
**Additional discounts available.

AT&T
Your True Choice

All the best trips start with **Fodor's**.

EXPLORING GUIDES

At last, the color of an art book combined with the usefulness of a complete guide.

"As stylish and attractive as any guide published." —*The New York Times*

"Worth reading before, during, and after a trip." —*The Philadelphia Inquirer*

More than 30 destinations available worldwide. $19.95 each.

BERKELEY GUIDES

The budget traveler's handbook

"Berkeley's scribes put the funk back in travel."
—*Time*

"Fresh, funny, and funky as well as useful."
—*The Boston Globe*

"Well-organized, clear and very easy to read."
—*America Online*

14 destinations worldwide. Priced between $13.00 - $19.50. ($17.95 - $27.00 Canada)

AFFORDABLES

"All the maps and itinerary ideas of Fodor's established gold guides with a bonus—shortcuts to savings." —*USA Today*

"Travelers with champagne tastes and beer budgets will welcome this series from Fodor's." —*Hartfort Courant*

"It's obvious these Fodor's folk have secrets we civilians don't." —*New York Daily News*

Also available: Florida, Europe, France, London, Paris. Priced between $11.00 - $18.00 ($14.50 - $24.00 Canada)

At bookstores, or call **1-800-533-6478**

Fodor's
The name that means smart travel.™

☎ 509/786–2725), operated by Kay Siman and Clay Mackey, vintners known for their dry wines.

⑰ **Hogue Cellars** is housed at the Prosser Industrial Park, east of Chinook Wines. Three generations of the Hogue family have farmed in the Yakima Valley, and in 1982 they produced their first wine in the family's mint shed. Hogue Cellars includes a tasting room, reception room, and gift shop featuring Hogue Farm's foods and wines and other locally made products. *Box 31, Prosser,* ☎ *509/786–4557. Gift shop open daily 10–5.*

⑱ Farther east are three small wineries, including **Oakwood Cellars** (Rte. 2, Box 2321, Benton City, ☎ 509/588–5332), where almost all the work
⑲ is done by hand; **Kiona Vineyards** (Rte. 2, Box 2169E, Benton City, ☎ 509/588–6716), producers of the first commercial Lemberger re-
⑳ leased in this country; and **Blackwood Canyon** (Rte. 2, Box 2169H, Benton City, ☎ 509/588–6249), known for its Old World wine-making techniques.

㉑ The largest winery in the area is **Chateau Ste. Michelle** (Box 231, Hwy. 221, Columbia Crest Dr., ☎ 509/875–2061) at Patterson. The imposing 16-acre estate is situated in the hills above the Columbia River near the Washington–Oregon border, and the winery itself is in a building that covers more than 9 acres.

WASHINGTON ESSENTIALS

Arriving and Departing

By Bus
Greyhound Lines (☎ 800/231–2222) connects Washington with adjoining states and Canada.

By Car
Interstate 5 is the main north–south route through the state. **Interstate 90** enters Washington from the east and runs across the Cascades to Seattle.

By Ferry
A number of ferries run between Washington and Canadian destinations. In Anacortes, about 90 minutes north of Seattle, the **Washington State Ferry System** (☎ 206/464–6400) has departures for Vancouver Island, British Columbia. Bellingham is the current southern terminus for the **Alaska Marine Highway System** (☎ 800/642–0066), providing transportation between Bellingham and Alaska's Inside Passage. The **Lummi Island Ferry** (☎ 360/758–2190) is operated by Whatcom County to provide transportation between Bellingham and the island. **Victoria San Juan Cruises,** operated by Gray Line (☎ 800/443–4552), offers passenger-only service between Bellingham and Victoria, British Columbia, in the summer.

By Plane
Bellingham International Airport offers nonstop flights to Seattle, Calgary, Alberta, and Reno, Nevada, via United Air Express, Horizon Air, and Empire Air/Silver Wings. West Isle Air flies to the San Juan Islands. **Seattle-Tacoma International Airport** (*see* Seattle Essentials *in* Chapter 4, Seattle), about a two-hour drive south from Bellingham, is served by most major airlines. **Vancouver International Airport** (*see* Vancouver Essentials *in* Chapter 6, Vancouver), in British Columbia, is 1½ hours

away by car. Major airlines use this facility, which includes a main terminal building with three levels.

By Train

Amtrak (☎ 800/872–7245) serves major cities and towns throughout the state.

Getting Around

Whidbey Island

BY CAR

Whidbey Island can be reached by going north from Seattle along I–5, then heading west on Highway 20; cross the dramatic Deception Pass via the bridge at the north end of the island.

BY FERRY

For complete information on the **Washington State Ferry System** (☎ 206/464–6400), *see* By Ferry *in* The San Juan Islands, *below.*

BY PLANE

Harbor Airlines (☎ 800/359–3220) flies to Whidbey Island from Friday Harbor and Sea-Tac Airport. **Kenmore Air** (☎ 206/486–1257 or 800/543–9595) can arrange charter float plane flights to Whidbey Island.

The San Juan Islands

BY CAR

To reach the San Juan Islands from Seattle, drive north on I–5 to Mt. Vernon, Exit 230, go west and follow signs to Anacortes; pick up the Washington State Ferry (*see below*). It is convenient to have a car in the San Juan Islands, but taking your car with you may mean waiting in long lines at the ferry terminals. With prior arrangement, most bed-and-breakfast owners can pick up walk-on guests at the ferry terminals.

BY FERRY

The **Washington State Ferry System** (☎ 206/464–6400), the biggest in the United States, includes vessels ranging from the 40-car *Hiyu* to jumbo ferries capable of carrying more than 200 cars and 2,000 passengers each. They connect points all around Puget Sound and the San Juan Islands.

Car and passenger ferries leave from Fauntleroy, in West Seattle, to Vashon Island and Southworth; from Edmonds, north of Seattle, to Kingston; from Port Townsend to Keystone (Whidbey Island); from Mukilteo, farther north, to Clinton on Whidbey Island; and from Anacortes, about 90 miles north of Seattle, to the San Juan Islands.

Sunny weekends are heavy traffic times all around the San Juan Islands, and weekday commuting hours for ferries headed into or out of Seattle are also crowded. Peak times on the Seattle runs are sunny weekends, eastbound in the morning and Sunday nights, as well as westbound Saturday morning and weekday afternoons. Since no reservations are accepted on Washington State Ferries (except for the Sidney–Anacortes run during summer), arriving at least a half hour before a scheduled departure is always advised.

The advantages of walking on board are obvious; it's cheaper than taking your car and hassle-free (no long waits in lines of frustrated drivers during peak commute hours or on weekends). If you do take your car, there are several points to note: Passengers and bicycles always load first unless otherwise instructed. Prior to boarding, lower antennas. Only parking lights should be used at night, and it is considered bad form to start your engine before the ferry docks. Also, no smoking is allowed in public areas.

You don't have to rely solely on the state ferries: **San Juan Islands Shuttle Express** (Alaska Ferry Terminal, 355 Harris Ave., No. 105, Bellingham 98225, ☎ 360/671–1137) takes passengers from Bellingham to Orcas Island and Friday Harbor.

BY PLANE
West Isle Air (☎ 800/874–4434) flies to Friday Harbor on San Juan Island from Sea-Tac and Bellingham airports. **Kenmore Air** (☎ 206/486–8400 or 800/543–9595) flies float planes from Lake Union in Seattle to the San Juan Islands.

Tacoma
BY BUS
Pierce Transit (☎ 206/581–8000) is the public bus system that covers most of the county.

BY CAR
I–5 runs passes through Tacoma, and Highway 16 goes west across the Tacoma Narrows Bridge to Gig Harbor and the Kitsap Peninsula; Highway 410 heads east toward Mt. Rainier.

BY PLANE
Tacoma is about a half-hour's drive south of **Seattle-Tacoma International Airport.** Two smaller fields, the **Tacoma Narrows Airport** (☎ 206/383–4638) and the **Pierce County Airport** (☎ 206/841–3779), offer services to and from smaller destinations in the Northwest.

Mt. Rainier National Park
BY CAR
The vast majority of visitors arrive via Highway 706 and the Nisqually entrance, at the park's southwest corner. Highways 410 and 123 enter the park from the east and southeast, respectively; both routes are usually closed in winter. Highway 165 leads to Ipsut Creek Campground through the Carbon River entrance and to Mowich Lake, in the park's northwest corner. The Nisqually entrance is preferred because of its proximity to I–5, and because the road from it links the popular Paradise area with Ohanapecosh and Sunrise. In winter, this route deadends at Paradise, but the other roads within the park are not plowed at all.

The Olympic Peninsula
BY CAR
Looping around the Olympic Peninsula is Highway 101, branching off via Route 8 from I–5.

BY PLANE
To reach destinations in the Olympic Peninsula, pick up a commuter flight from Seattle-Tacoma airport to fly to the **Jefferson County International Airport** near Port Townsend or **Fairchild International Airport** near Port Angeles.

Long Beach Peninsula
BY CAR
To reach Long Beach Peninsula, take Route 8 (Ocean Beaches exit from I–5) to Highway 107 at Montesano to Highway 101S to Seaview. From Longview, take Highway 4 through Naselle and Highway 101 for a scenic Columbia River view.

Yakima Valley Wine Country
BY CAR

To reach the Yakima Valley, take I–90 east from Seattle across Snoqualmie Pass to Ellensburg and I–82 south to Yakima.

Guided Tours

Cruises and Whale Watching

San Juan Islands Shuttle Express (Alaska Ferry Terminal, 355 Harris
Ave., No. 105, Bellingham 98225, ☎ 360/671–1137) offers whale-
watching trips.

Victoria San Juan Cruises (355 Harris Ave., Bellingham 98225, ☎ 800/
443–4552) operates 3½-hour nature cruises through the San Juan Islands
to Victoria.

Western Prince Cruises (Box 418, Friday Harbor 98250, ☎ 360/378–
5315) in the San Juan Islands charters boats for half-day whale-watching cruises during the summer; in the spring and fall, bird-watching
and scuba-diving tours are offered. Cruises depart from Friday Harbor on San Juan Island.

Orientation

Christy's Escorted Tours (1268 Mt. Baker Hwy., Bellingham 98226, ☎
360/734–3570) offers a variety of trips in the Northwest.

Gray Line (720 S. Forest St., Seattle 98134, ☎ 206/624–5077) offers
some 20 guided bus tours of Seattle's environs, ranging in scope from
a daily 2½-hour spin to trips to Mt. Rainier.

Guided Historical Tours (820 Tyler St., Port Townsend 98368, ☎ 360/
385–1967) offers a number of tours of Port Townsend, the most popular of which is a one-hour walking tour of the waterfront and downtown, focusing on the town's architecture, history, and humor.

Moonlit Rides (3908 River Rd., Yakima 98901, ☎ 509/575–6846) offers tours of the Yakima area.

Sunshine Ventures (6101 100th St. SW, No. 1, Tacoma 98499, ☎ 206/
588–3881) offers walking and general tours of Tacoma.

Special Interest and Sports

Olympic Raft and Guide (239 521 Hwy. 101, West Port Angeles 98362,
☎ 360/452–1443) offers white-water and scenic float trips on the Hoh
and Elwha rivers on the Olympic Peninsula.

Olympic West Arttrek (c/o Forks Chamber of Commerce, Box 1249,
Forks 98331, ☎ 360/374–2531 or 800/443–6757) produces a brochure
for a self-guided auto tour to nearly 30 locations, including artists' studios, galleries, a Native American woodcarving shop, an herb farm,
and gift shops on the western Olympic Peninsula.

Peak Six Tours (HC 80, Box 695, Forks 98331, ☎ 360/374–5254) provides guides for hiking, biking, camping, climbing, and sightseeing on
the Olympic Peninsula.

Winery

Accent! Tours & Charters (3701 River Rd., Suite B, Yakima 98907, ☎
509/452–9402) provides informative tours of Yakima-area wineries.

Blue Mountain Express (1037 Winslow Ave., Richland 99352, ☎ 509/
946–7375) visits wineries throughout eastern Washington.

Olympic Peninsula Winery Loop (North Olympic Peninsula Visitor and
Convention Bureau, Box 670, Port Angeles 98362, ☎ 360/452–8552

or 800/942–4042) provides a brochure for a self-directed auto tour to eight wineries on or near the east side of the Olympic Peninsula.

Transcascade (609 E. Yakima Ave., Yakima 98907, ☎ 509/452–9402) tours Yakima Valley wineries.

Dining

Unless otherwise noted at the bottom of a review, casual and neat apparel is appropriate at all of the establishments listed in this chapter. Dollar-sign ratings for restaurants are based on the following price categories for a three-course meal (excluding drinks, service, and 8.1% sales tax):

CATEGORY	COST
$$$$	over $35
$$$	$25–$35
$$	$15–$25
$	under $15

Lodging

Dollar-sign ratings for hotels and inns are based on the following price categories for a double room (excluding 8.1% sales tax):

CATEGORY	COST
$$$$	over $170
$$$	$110–$170
$$	$60–$110
$	under $60

Important Addresses and Numbers

Emergencies

Throughout Washington State, except on Orcas Island and Long Beach Peninsula, dial 911 for **police, ambulance,** or other emergencies. On Orcas dial "0" or 360/468–3663; on Long Beach dial 360/642–2911 for police and 360/642–4200 for fire.

Visitor Information

Washington State Tourism (101 General Administration Bldg., Olympia 98504, ☎ 800/544–1800).

THE SAN JUAN ISLANDS
San Juan Islands Visitor Information Service (Box 65, Lopez 98261, ☎ 360/468–3663).

BELLINGHAM AND WHATCOM & SKAGIT COUNTIES
Bellingham/Whatcom County Convention and Visitors Bureau (904 Potter St., Bellingham 98227, ☎ 800/487–2032).
North Cascades National Park (2105 Hwy. 20, Sedro Woolley 98264, ☎ 360/856–5700).

TACOMA
Tacoma-Pierce County Visitors and Convention Bureau (906 Broadway, 98402, ☎ 206/627–2836).

MT. RAINIER NATIONAL PARK
Superintendent, Mt. Rainier National Park (Tahoma Woods, Star Route, Ashford, WA 98304, ☎ 360/569–2211).

THE OLYMPIC PENINSULA

North Olympic Peninsula Visitor and Convention Bureau (Box 670, Port Angeles 98362, ☎ 360/452–8552 or 800/942–4042).

Port Townsend Chamber of Commerce (2437 E. Sims Way, Port Townsend 98368, ☎ 360/385–2722).

Superintendent, Olympic National Park (1835 Blacklake Blvd., Olympia 98512-5623, ☎ 360/956–4501).

Supervisor, Olympic National Forest (1835 Blacklake Blvd., Olympia 98512-5623, ☎ 360/956–2400).

LONG BEACH PENINSULA

Long Beach Peninsula Visitors Bureau (Intersection of Hwys. 101 and 103, Box 562, Long Beach 98631, ☎ 360/642–2400 or 800/451–2542).

CROSSING THE CASCADES

Leavenworth Chamber of Commerce (894 Hwy. 2, Box 327, 98826, ☎ 509/548–5807).

Upper Snoqualmie Valley Chamber of Commerce (Box 356, North Bend 98045, ☎ 206/888–4440).

YAKIMA VALLEY WINE COUNTRY

Yakima Valley Visitors & Convention Bureau (10 N. 8th St., Yakima 98901-2515, ☎ 509/575–1300 or 800/221-0751).

6 Vancouver

Cosmopolitan Vancouver, Canada's answer to San Francisco, enjoys a spectacular setting. Tall fir trees stand practically downtown, rock spires tower close by, the ocean is at your doorstep, and people from every corner of the earth create a young and vibrant atmosphere.

Updated by
Melissa Rivers

VANCOUVER IS A YOUNG CITY, even by North American standards. While three to four hundred years of settlement may make cities like Québec and Halifax historically interesting to travelers, Vancouver's youthful vigor attracts visitors to its powerful elements that have not yet been ground down by time. Vancouver is just over a hundred years old; it was not yet a town in 1870, when British Columbia became part of the Canadian confederation. The city's history, such as it is, remains visible to the naked eye: Eras are stacked east to west along the waterfront like some century-old archaeological dig—from cobbled, late-Victorian Gastown to shiny postmodern glass cathedrals of commerce grazing the sunset.

The Chinese were among the first to recognize the possibilities of Vancouver's setting. They came to British Columbia during the 1850s seeking the gold that inspired them to name the province Gum-shan, or Gold Mountain. They built the Canadian Pacific Railway that gave Vancouver's original townsite a purpose—one beyond the natural splendor that Royal Navy captain George Vancouver admired during his lunchtime cruise around its harbor on June 13, 1792. The transcontinental railway, along with the city's Great White Fleet of clipper ships, gave Vancouver a full week's edge over the California ports in shipping tea and silk to New York at the dawn of the 20th century.

Vancouver's natural charms are less scattered than in other cities. On clear days, the mountains appear close enough to touch. Two 1,000-acre wilderness parks lie within the city limits. The salt water of the Pacific and fresh water direct from the Rocky Mountain Trench form the city's northern and southern boundaries.

Bring a healthy sense of reverence when you visit: Vancouver is a spiritual place. For its original inhabitants, the Coast Salish peoples, it was the sacred spot where the mythical Thunderbird and Killer Whale flung wind and rain all about the heavens during their epic battles— how else to explain the coast's occasional fits of climatic temper? Devotees of a later religious tradition might worship in the sepulchre of Stanley Park or in the polished, incense-filled quiet of St. James Anglican Church, designed by English architect Sir Adrian Gilbert Scott and perhaps Vancouver's finest building.

Vancouver has a level of nightlife possible only in a place where the finer things in life have never been driven out to the suburbs and where sidewalks have never rolled up at 5 PM. There is no shortage of excellent hotels and restaurants here either. But you can find good theater, accommodations, and dining almost anywhere these days. Vancouver's real culture consists of its tall fir trees practically downtown and its towering rock spires close by, the ocean at your doorstep, and people from every corner of the earth all around you.

EXPLORING

The heart of Vancouver—which includes the downtown area, Stanley Park, and the West End high-rise residential neighborhood—sits on a peninsula bordered by English Bay and the Pacific Ocean to the west; by False Creek, the inlet home to Granville Island, to the south; and to the north by Burrard Inlet, the working port of the city, past which loom the North Shore mountains. The oldest part of the city—Gastown and Chinatown—lies at the edge of Burrard Inlet, around Main Street, which runs north–south and is roughly the dividing line between the east side and the west side. All the avenues, which are numbered, have east and west designations.

Numbers in the margin correspond to points of interest on the Tour 1: Downtown Vancouver map.

❶ You can logically begin your downtown tour in either of two ways. If you're in for a day of shopping, amble down **Robson Street** (*see* Shopping, *below*), where you'll find any item from souvenirs to high fashions, from espresso to sushi.

❷ If you opt otherwise, start at **Robson Square,** built in 1975 and designed by architect Arthur Erickson to be the gathering place of downtown Vancouver. The complex, which functions from the outside as a park, encompasses the Vancouver Art Gallery and government offices and law courts that have been built under landscaped walkways, a block-long glass canopy, and a waterfall that helps mask traffic noise. An ice-skating rink and restaurants occupy the below-street level.

❸ The **Vancouver Art Gallery,** which heads the square, was a classical-style 1912 courthouse until Erickson converted it in 1980. Notice the detail: lions that guard the majestic front steps and the use of columns and domes—features borrowed from ancient Roman architecture. In back of the old courthouse, a more modest staircase now serves as a speakers' corner. *750 Hornby St., ☎ 604/682–5621. ☛ $5 adults, $2.50 students and senior citizens; free Thurs. eve. ☻ Mon., Wed., Fri., and Sat. 10–5; Thurs. 10–9; Sun. and holidays noon–5.*

❹ Directly across Hornby Street is the **Hotel Vancouver** (1939), one of the last of the railway-built hotels. (The last one built was the Chateau Whistler, in 1989.) Reminiscent of a medieval French castle, this château style has been incorporated into hotels in almost every major Canadian city. With the onset of the Depression, construction was halted here, and the hotel was finished only in time for the visit of King George VI in 1939. It has been renovated twice: During the 1960s it was unfortunately modernized, but the more recent refurbishment is more in keeping with the spirit of what is the most recognizable roof on Vancouver's skyline. The exterior of the building has carvings of malevolent-looking gargoyles at the corners, an ornate chimney, Indian chiefs on the Hornby Street side, and an assortment of grotesque mythological figures.

TIME OUT If you're in the vicinity of the Hotel Vancouver between 2 PM and 4:30 PM, stop in for afternoon tea in the lobby lounge. Tea sandwiches, fruit, scones with Devonshire cream, and a large selection of pastries are served in regal style as classical musicians perform in the background.

❺ The tiny **Christ Church Cathedral** (1895), across the street from the Hotel Vancouver, is the oldest church in Vancouver. Built in Gothic style with buttresses and pointed-arch windows, it looks like the parish church of an English village. By contrast, the cathedral's rough-hewn interior is that of a frontier town, with Douglas-fir beams and ornate woodwork that offers excellent acoustics for the vespers, carol services, and Gregorian chants frequently presented here. *690 Burrard St., ☎ 604/ 682–3848. ☻ Weekdays 10–4.*

❻ **Cathedral Place,** on the corner of Hornby and Georgia streets, is a spectacular office tower adjacent to Christ Church Cathedral. Three large sculptures of nurses at the corners of the building are replicas of the statues that ornamented the art deco Georgia Medical-Dental Building, the site's previous structure.

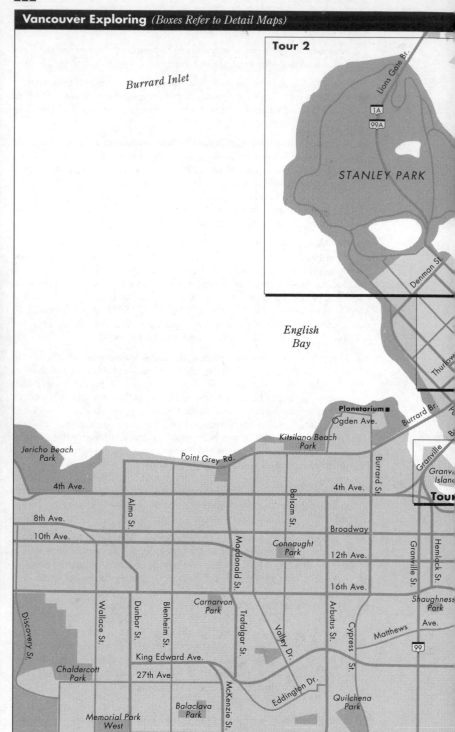

Burrard Inlet

Tour 2

Lions Gate Br.

1A

99A

STANLEY PARK

Denman St.

English Bay

Thurlow

Planetarium ■

Ogden Ave.

Burrard Br.

Kitsilano Beach Park

Burrard St.

Jericho Beach Park

Point Grey Rd.

Granville

Granv
Island

4th Ave.

4th Ave.

Tou

Alma St.

Balsam St.

8th Ave.

Broadway

Granville St.

Hemlock St.

10th Ave.

Connaught Park

12th Ave.

Macdonald St.

16th Ave.

Carnarvon Park

Shaughness
Park

Discovery St.

Wallace St.

Dunbar St.

Blenheim St.

Trafalgar St.

Valley Dr.

Arbutus St.

Cypress St.

Matthews

Ave.

99

King Edward Ave.

Chaldercott Park

27th Ave.

Eddington Dr.

Quilchena Park

McKenzie St.

Balaclava Park

Memorial Park West

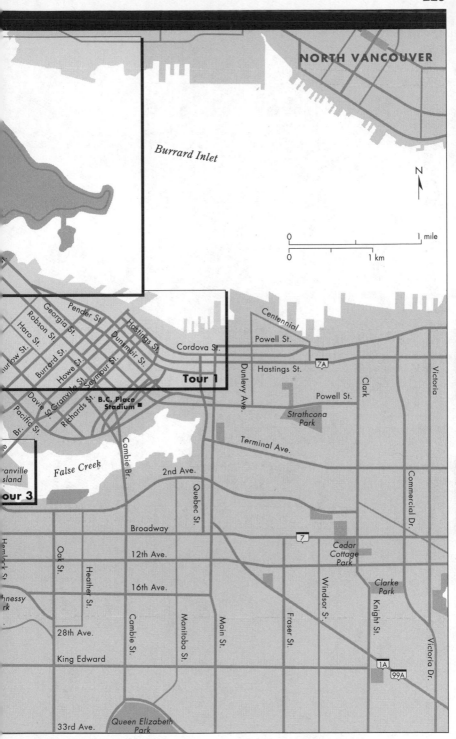

North Vancouver

Burrard Inlet

N

0   1 mile
0   1 km

Centennial
Powell St.
Cordova St.
Hastings St.
Pender St.
Georgia St.
Robson St.
Haro St.
Dunsmuir St.
Hastings St.
Powell St.
Strathcona Park
Burrard St.
Howe St.
Seymour St.
Davie St.
Granville St.
Richards St.
Pacific St.
Br.
Cambie Br.
Dunlevy Ave.
Clark
Victoria
Tour 1
B.C. Place Stadium
Terminal Ave.
2nd Ave.
Quebec St.
Commercial Dr.
False Creek
Granville Island
our 3
Broadway
12th Ave.
16th Ave.
28th Ave.
King Edward
33rd Ave.
Oak St.
Heather St.
Cambie St.
Manitoba St.
Main St.
Fraser St.
Windsor St.
Knight St.
Victoria Dr.
Hemlock St.
hnessy rk
Cedar Cottage Park
Clarke Park
Queen Elizabeth Park
7A
7
1A
99A

Tour 1: Downtown Vancouver

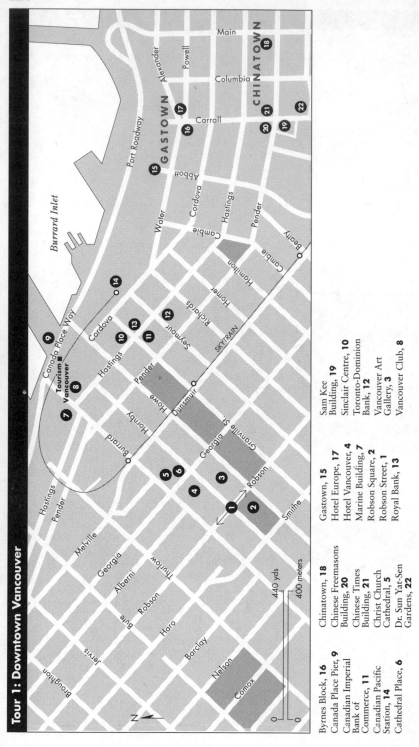

Byrnes Block, **16**
Canada Place Pier, **9**
Canadian Imperial
Bank of
Commerce, **11**
Canadian Pacific
Station, **14**
Cathedral Place, **6**

Chinatown, **18**
Chinese Freemasons
Building, **20**
Chinese Times
Building, **21**
Christ Church
Cathedral, **5**
Dr. Sun Yat-Sen
Gardens, **22**

Gastown, **15**
Hotel Europe, **17**
Hotel Vancouver, **4**
Marine Building, **7**
Robson Square, **2**
Robson Street, **1**
Royal Bank, **13**

Sam Kee
Building, **19**
Sinclair Centre, **10**
Toronto-Dominion
Bank, **12**
Vancouver Art
Gallery, **3**
Vancouver Club, **8**

A restored terra-cotta arch—formerly the front entrance to the medical building—and frieze panels showing scenes of individuals administering care now decorate the **Canadian Craft Museum,** across the courtyard. The Craft Museum, which opened in 1992, is one of the first national cultural facilities dedicated to crafts—historical and contemporary, functional and decorative. Craft embodies the human need for artistic expression in everyday life, and examples here range from elegantly carved utensils with decorative handles to colorful hand-spun and hand-woven garments. The two-level museum offers exhibits, lectures, and the Museum Shop, which specializes, of course, in Canadian crafts. The restful courtyard is a quiet place to take a break. *639 Hornby St.,* ☎ *604/687–8266.* ☞ *$4 adults, $2 senior citizens and students, children under 12 free.* ☉ *Mon. and Wed.–Sat. 10–5, Sun. and holidays noon–5.*

Cathedral Place also is the site of the **Sri Lankan Gem Museum,** which opened in 1993. The museum, with a floor of 9,000 polished Brazilian agates set in pyrite, has some $5 million worth of gemstones, including moonstones, rubies, lapis, garnets, jade, and emeralds. Many of the gems are from Sri Lanka. *925 W. Georgia St.,* ☎ *604/688–8528.* ☞ *$3.50 (proceeds go to the Vancouver Symphony Orchestra).* ☉ *Mon.–Sat. 10:30–5:30.*

⑦ The **Marine Building** (1931), at the foot of Burrard Street, is Canada's best example of Art Deco architecture. Terra-cotta bas-reliefs depict the history of transportation: Airships, biplanes, steamships, locomotives, and submarines are figured. These motifs were once considered radical and modernistic adornments, because most buildings were still using classical or Gothic ornamentation. From the east, the Marine Building is reflected in bronze by 999 West Hastings, and from the southeast in silver by the Canadian Imperial Bank of Commerce. Stand on the corner of Hastings and Hornby streets for the best view of the Marine Building.

You can take a nice walk along Hastings Street—the old financial district. Until the period between 1966 and 1972, when the first of the bank towers and underground malls on West Georgia Street were developed, this was Canada's westernmost business terminus. The temple-style banks, businessmen's clubs, and investment houses survive as evidence of the city's sophisticated architectural advances prior to **⑧** World War I. The **Vancouver Club,** built between 1912 and 1914, was a gathering place for the city's elite. Its architecture evokes that of private clubs in England inspired by Italian Renaissance palaces. The Vancouver Club is still the private haunt of city businessmen. *915 W. Hastings St.,* ☎ *604/685–9321.*

⑨ At the foot of Howe Street, north of Hastings, is **Canada Place Pier.** Originally built on an old cargo pier to be the off-site Canadian pavilion in Expo '86, Canada Place was later converted into Vancouver's Trade and Convention Center. It is dominated at the shore end by the luxurious Pan Pacific Hotel (*see* Lodging, *below*), with its spectacular three-story lobby and waterfall. The convention space is covered by a fabric roof shaped like 10 sails, which has become a landmark of Vancouver's skyline. Below is a cruise-ship facility, and at the north end are an Imax theater, a restaurant, and an outdoor performance space. A promenade runs along the pier's west side with views of the Burrard Inlet harbor and Stanley Park. *999 Canada Pl.,* ☎ *604/775–8687.*

Just across the street (next door to the Waterfront Centre Hotel) is the **Tourism Vancouver Infocentre** (200 Burrard St., ☎ 604/683-2000), with brochures and personnel to answer questions, as well as an attractive Northwest Coast native art collection.

⑩ Walk back up to Hastings and Howe streets to the **Sinclair Centre.** Outstanding Vancouver architect Richard Henriquez has knitted four government office buildings (built 1905–1939) into an office-retail complex. The two Hastings Street buildings—the 1905 post office with the elegant clock tower and the 1913 Winch Building—are linked with the Post Office Extension and Customs Examining Warehouse to the north. Painstaking and very costly restoration involved finding master masons—the original terrazzo suppliers in Europe—and uncovering and refurbishing the pressed-metal ceilings.

⑪ A bit farther up Hastings, at Granville Street, you'll find one of Vancouver's oldest and most impressive charter banks, the former **Canadian Imperial Bank of Commerce (CIBC)** headquarters (1906–1908); the columns, arches, and details are of typically Roman influence. The **⑫** **Toronto–Dominion Bank,** one block east, is of the same style but was built in 1920.

⑬ Backtrack directly across from the CIBC on Hastings Street to the more Gothic **Royal Bank.** It was intended to be half of a symmetrical building that was never completed, due to the Depression. Striking, though, is the magnificent hall, reminiscent of a European cathedral.

⑭ At the foot of Seymour Street is the **Canadian Pacific Station,** the third and most pretentious of three Canadian Pacific Railway passenger terminals. Constructed in 1912–1914, this terminal replaced the other two as the western terminus for Canada's transcontinental railway. After Canada's railways merged, the station became obsolete until a 1978 renovation turned it into an office-retail complex and SeaBus terminal. Murals in the waiting rooms show passengers what kind of scenery to expect on their journeys across Canada.

★ ⑮ From Seymour Street, pick up Water Street, on your way to **Gastown.** Named for the original townsite saloon keeper, "Gassy" Jack Deighton, Gastown is where Vancouver originated. Deighton arrived at Burrard Inlet in 1867 with his Indian wife, a barrel of whiskey, and few amenities. A statue of Gassy Jack stands on the north side of Maple Tree Square, the intersection of five streets, where he built his first saloon.

When the transcontinental train arrived in 1887, Gastown became the transfer point for trade with the Orient and was soon crowded with hotels and warehouses. The Klondike gold rush encouraged further development until 1912, when the "Golden Years" ended. The 1930s–1950s saw hotels being converted into rooming houses and the warehouse district shifting elsewhere. The area gradually became unattended and run-down. However, both Gastown and Chinatown were declared historic areas and have been revitalized.

⑯ The **Byrnes Block** building was constructed on the corner of Water and Carrall streets (the site of Gassy Jack's second saloon) after the 1886 Great Fire. The date is just visible at the top of the building above the door where it says "Herman Block," which was its name for a short time.

Tucked behind 2 Water Street are **Blood Alley** and **Gaoler's Mews.** Once the site of the city's first civic buildings—the constable's cabin and courthouse, and a two-cell log jail—today the cobblestone street with antique street lighting is the home of architectural offices.

⑰ The **Hotel Europe** (1908–1909), a flatiron building at Powell and Alexander streets, once billed as the best hotel in the city, was Vancouver's first reinforced concrete structure. Designed as a functional commercial building, the hotel lacks ornamentation and fine detail, a style unusually utilitarian for the time.

★ ⑱ From Maple Tree Square, walk three blocks up Carrall Street to Pender Street, where **Chinatown** begins. There was already a sizable Chinese community in British Columbia because of the 1858 Cariboo gold rush in central British Columbia, but the greatest influx from China came in the 1880s, during construction of the Canadian Pacific Railway, when 15,000 laborers were imported. The Chinese were among the first inhabitants of Vancouver, and some of the oldest buildings in the city are in Chinatown.

Even while doing the hazardous work of blasting the rail bed through the Rocky Mountains, the Chinese were discriminated against. The Anti-Asiatic Riots of 1907 stopped growth in Chinatown for 50 years, and immigration from China was discouraged by more and more restrictive policies, climaxing in a $500 head tax during the 1920s.

In the 1960s the city council planned bulldozer urban renewal for Strathcona, the residential part of Chinatown, as well as freeway connections through the most historic blocks of Chinatown. Fortunately, the project was halted, and today Chinatown is an expanding, vital district fueled by investment from Vancouver's most notable newcomers—immigrants from Hong Kong. It is best to view the buildings in Chinatown from the south side of Pender Street, where the Chinese Cultural Center stands. From here you'll get a view of important details that adorn the upper stories. The style of architecture in Vancouver's Chinatown is patterned on that of Canton and won't be seen in any other Canadian cities.

The corner of Carrall and East Pender streets, now the western boundary of Chinatown, is one of the neighborhood's most historic spots. Standing at 8 West Pender Street is the **Sam Kee Building,** recognized by *Ripley's Believe It or Not!* as the narrowest building in the world, at just 6 feet wide. The 1913 structure still exists; its bay windows overhang the street and the basement burrows under the sidewalk.

⑳ The **Chinese Freemasons Building** (1901) at 1 West Pender Street has two completely different styles of facade: The side facing Chinatown presents a fine example of Cantonese-imported recessed balconies; on the Carrall Street side, the standard Victorian style common throughout the British Empire is displayed. It was in this building that Dr. Sun Yat-sen hid for months from the agents of the Manchu dynasty while he raised funds for its overthrow, which he accomplished in 1911.

㉑ Directly across Carrall Street is the **Chinese Times Building,** constructed in 1902. Police officers could hear the clicking sounds of clandestine mah-jongg games played after sunset on the building's hidden mezzanine floor. Attempts by vice squads to enforce restrictive policies against the Chinese gamblers proved fruitless, because police were unable to find the players.

㉒ Planning for the **Chinese Cultural Center** and **Dr. Sun Yat-sen Gardens** (1980–1987) began in the late 1960s; the first phase was designed by James Cheng, a former associate of Arthur Erickson. The cultural center has exhibition space, classrooms, and meeting rooms. The Dr. Sun Yat-sen Gardens, located behind the cultural center, were built by 52 artisans from Suzhou, the Garden City of the People's Republic. The gardens incorporate design elements and traditional materials from several of that city's centuries-old private gardens and are the first living classical Chinese gardens built outside China. As you walk through the gardens, remember that no power tools, screws, or nails were used in the construction. Free guided tours are offered throughout the day; telephone for times. *Dr. Sun Yat-sen Gardens. 578 Carrall St.,* ☎ *604/689–7133.* ☛ *$5 adults, $3 senior citizens and students, $10 families.* ☉ *Daily 10–4:30.*

Tour 2: Stanley Park

Numbers in the margin correspond to points of interest on the Tour 2: Stanley Park map.

★ A 1,000-acre wilderness park just blocks from the downtown section of a major city is a rarity. In the 1860s, due to a threat of American invasion, the area that is now **Stanley Park** was designated a military reserve (though it was never needed). When the city of Vancouver was incorporated in 1886, the council's first act was to request that the land be set aside for a park. In 1888 permission was granted and the grounds were named Stanley Park after Lord Stanley, then governor general of Canada.

An afternoon in Stanley Park gives you a capsule tour of Vancouver that includes beaches, the ocean, the harbor, Douglas fir and cedar forests, and a good look at the North Shore mountains. The park sits on a peninsula, and along the shore is a pathway 9 kilometers (5½ miles) long called the seawall. You can walk or bicycle all the way around or follow the shorter route suggested below.

Bicycles are for rent at the foot of Georgia Street near the park entrance. Cyclists must ride in a counterclockwise direction and stay on their side of the path. A good place for pedestrians to start is at the foot of Alberni Street beside **Lost Lagoon.** Go through the underpass and veer right to the seawall past **Malkin Bowl,** an open amphitheater where theater-under-the-stars plays during the summer (call 604/687–0174 for performance information).

㉓ ㉔

㉕ The old wood structure that you pass is the **Vancouver Rowing Club,** ㉖ a private athletic club (established 1903); a bit farther along is the **Royal Vancouver Yacht Club.**

㉗ About ½ kilometer (⅓ mile) away is the causeway to **Deadman's Island,** a former burial ground for the local Salish Indians and the early settlers. It is now a small naval training base called the HMCS Discovery that is not open to the public. Just ahead is the **Nine O'Clock Gun,** ㉘ a cannonlike apparatus that sits by the water's edge. Originally used to alert fishermen to a curfew ending weekend fishing, it now automatically signals every night at 9.

㉙ Farther along is **Brockton Point** and its small but functional lighthouse and foghorn. The **totem poles,** which stand farther inland, make a popular photo stop for tourists. Totem poles were not carved in the Vancouver area; these were brought to the park from the north coast of British Columbia and were carved of cedar by the Kwakiutl and Haida peoples late in the last century. The carved animals, fish, birds, and mythological creatures were like family coats-of-arms or crests.

㉚ At kilometer 3 (mile 2) is **Lumberman's Arch,** a huge log archway dedicated to the workers in Vancouver's first industry. Beside the arch is an asphalt path that leads back to Lost Lagoon. This path also leads ㉛ to the **Vancouver Aquarium.** The humid Amazon rain-forest gallery has piranhas, giant cockroaches, alligators, tropical birds, and jungle veg-

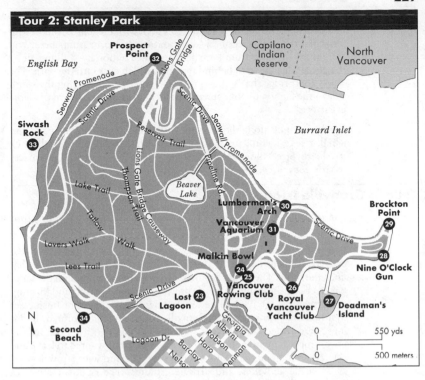

Tour 2: Stanley Park

etation. Other displays show the underwater life of coastal British Columbia, the Canadian arctic, and other areas of the world. *Aquarium,* ☎ 604/682–1118. ☛ *$9.50 adults, $8.25 senior citizens and students, $6.25 children 5–12, $27 families.* ☉ *July–Labor Day, daily 9:30–8; Labor Day–June, daily 10–5:30.*

③② About 1 kilometer (¾ mile) farther is the **Lions Gate Bridge**—the halfway point of the seawall. Just past the bridge is **Prospect Point,** where cormorants build their seaweed nests along the cliff's ledges. The large black diving birds are distinguished by their long necks and beaks; when not nesting, they often perch atop floating logs or boulders. Another remarkable bird found along the park's shore is the beautiful great blue heron, which reaches up to 4 feet tall and has a wing span of 6 feet. The heron preys on passing fish in the waters here; the oldest heron rookery in British Columbia is in the trees near the aquarium.

★
③③ Continuing around the seawall you will come to the **English Bay** side and the beginning of sandy beaches. The imposing rock just offshore is **Siwash Rock.** Legend tells of a young Indian who, about to become a father, bathed persistently to wash his sins away so that his son could be born pure; for his devotion he was blessed by the gods and immortalized in the shape of Siwash Rock. Two small rocks, said to be his wife and child, are up on the cliff just above the site.

TIME OUT Along the seawall is one of Vancouver's best restaurants, the **Teahouse at Ferguson Point** (*see* Dining, *below*). Set on the great lawn among Douglas fir and cedar trees, the restaurant is the perfect stopover for a summer weekend lunch or brunch. For just a snack, try the park concession stand at Ferguson Point.

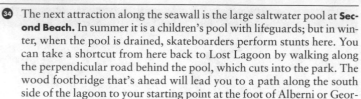

The next attraction along the seawall is the large saltwater pool at **Second Beach.** In summer it is a children's pool with lifeguards; but in winter, when the pool is drained, skateboarders perform stunts here. You can take a shortcut from here back to Lost Lagoon by walking along the perpendicular road behind the pool, which cuts into the park. The wood footbridge that's ahead will lead you to a path along the south side of the lagoon to your starting point at the foot of Alberni or Georgia street.

If you continue along the seawall, you will emerge from the park into a high-rise residential neighborhood, the **West End.** You can walk back to Alberni Street along Denman Street, where there are plenty of places to stop for coffee, ice cream, or a drink.

Tour 3: Granville Island

Numbers in the margin correspond to points of interest on the Tour 3: Granville Island map.

★ **Granville Island** was just a sandbar until World War I, when the federal government dredged False Creek for access to the sawmills that lined the shore. The sludge from the creek was heaped up onto the sandbar to create the island to house much-needed industrial- and logging-equipment plants. By the late 1960s, however, many of the businesses that had once flourished on Granville Island had deteriorated. Buildings were rotted, rat-infested, and dangerous. In 1971, the federal government bought up leases from businesses that wanted to leave and offered an imaginative plan to refurbish the island with a public market, marine activities, and artisans' studios. The opposite shore of False Creek was the site of the 1986 World's Fair and is now part of the largest urban redevelopment plan in North America.

The small island has no residents except for a small houseboat community. Most of the former industrial buildings and tin sheds have been retained but are painted in upbeat reds, yellows, and blues. Through a committee of community representatives, the government regulates the types of businesses that settle on Granville Island; most of the businesses permitted here involve food, crafts, marine activities, and the arts.

To reach Granville Island on foot, make the 15-minute walk from downtown Vancouver to the south end of Thurlow Street. Aquabuses (☎ 604/689–5858) depart from the foot of Hornby Street downtown and deliver passengers across False Creek to Granville Island Public Market. Another option is the Granville Island Ferries (☎ 604/684–7781) which leave every five minutes from a dock behind the Vancouver Aquatic Center. These pudgy boats are a great way to see the sights on False Creek, but for a longer ferry ride, stay on until you reach the Maritime Museum (*see* Other Museums, *below*), where visitors can board a tugboat and chart the coastal waters of British Columbia.

Another way to reach the island is to take a 20-minute ride on a BC Transit (☎ 604/261–5100) bus. Take a University of British Columbia (UBC), Granville, Arbutus, Cambie, or Oak bus from downtown to Granville and Broadway, and transfer to Granville Island Bus 51 or False Creek Bus 50 from Gastown or stops on Granville Street for direct service to Granville Island. Parking is free for one to three hours; paid parking is available in garages on the island.

The ferry to Granville Island will drop you off at the **Granville Island Public Market,** where food stalls are enclosed in the 50,000-square-foot building. As the government allows no chain stores, each outlet is unique,

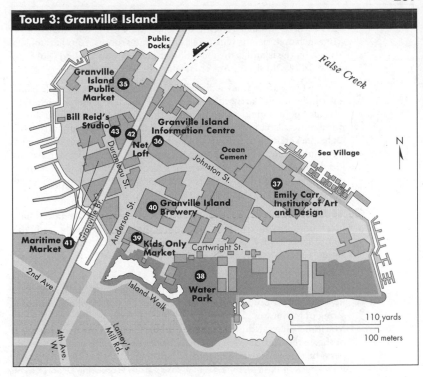

Tour 3: Granville Island

and most are of good quality. You probably won't be able to leave the market without a snack, espresso, or fixings for a lunch out on the wharf. Don't miss the fish chowder or bouillabaisse from the **Stock Market,** fresh fudge at **Olde World Fudge,** or smoked salmon from the **Salmon Shop.** Year-round you'll see mounds of raspberries, strawberries, blueberries, and more exotic fruits like persimmons and litchis. You'll find plenty of outdoor seating on the water side of the market. *Public Market,* ☎ *604/666–6477.* ⊙ *Daily 9–6.*

🟢 The **Granville Island Information Centre,** catercorner to the market, is a good place to get oriented. Maps are available, and a slide show depicts the evolution of Granville Island. Ask here about special-events days; perhaps there's a boat show, an outdoor concert, a dance performance, or some other happening. *1592 Johnston St.,* ☎ *604/666–5784.* ⊙ *Daily 8–6.*

Walk south on Johnston Street to begin a clockwise loop tour of the island. Next is **Ocean Cement,** one of the last of the island's former industries; its lease does not expire until the year 2004.

🟢 Next door is the **Emily Carr Institute of Art and Design.** Just inside the front door, to your right, is the **Charles H. Scott Gallery,** which hosts contemporary multimedia exhibits. *1399 Johnston St.,* ☎ *604/687–2345.* ☛ *Free.* ⊙ *Daily noon–5.*

Past the art school, on the left, is **Sea Village,** one of the only houseboat communities in Vancouver; others have been banned by the city because of problems with sewage and property taxes. The owners of this community appealed the ban and won special status. Take the boardwalk that starts at the houseboats and continues partway around the island.

As you circle around to Cartwright Street, stop in **Kakali** at number 1249, where you can watch the fabrication of fine handmade paper from such materials as blue jeans, herbs, and sequins. Another unusual artisan on the island is the glassblower at the **Small Sterling Glass Studio** at 1404 Old Bridge Street, around the corner.

38 **39** The next two attractions will make any child's visit to Granville Island a thrill. First, on Cartwright Street, is the children's **water park,** with a wading pool, sprinklers, and a fire hydrant made for children to shower one another. A bit farther down, beside Isadora's restaurant, is the **Kids Only Market,** with two floors of small shops selling toys, arts-and-crafts materials, dolls, records and tapes, chemistry sets, and other sorts of kid stuff. *Water park: 1318 Cartwright St., ☎ 604/665–3425; ☛ Free. ☾ June–Aug., daily 10–6. Kids Only Market: 1496 Cartwright St., ☎ 604/689–8447. ☾ Daily 10–6.*

40 At the **Granville Island Brewery,** across the street, you can take a half-hour tour every afternoon; at the end of the tour, sample the Granville Island lager that is produced here and sold locally in most restaurants. *1441 Cartwright St., ☎ 604/687–2739. ☛ Free. Tours daily at 1 and 3.*

41 Cross Anderson Street and walk down Duranleau Street. On your left, **Rowand's Reef Scuba Shop** marks the start of the **Maritime Market,** a string of businesses all geared to the sea. The first walkway to the left, Maritime Mews, leads to marinas and dry docks. There are dozens of outfits in the Maritime Market that charter boats (with or without skippers) or run cruise-and-learn trips. Another way to take to the water is by kayak. Take a lesson or rent a kayak from **Ecomarine Ocean Kayak Centre** (1668 Duranleau St., ☎ 604/689–7575).

TIME OUT **Bridges** (1696 Duranleau St., ☎ 604/687–4400), in the bright yellow building across from the market, is a good spot to have lunch, especially on a warm summer's day. Eat on the spacious deck that looks out on the sailboats, fishing boats, and other water activities.

42 The last place to explore on Granville Island is the blue building next to Ecomarine on Duranleau Street, the **Net Loft.** The loft is a collection of small, high-quality stores, including a bookstore, a crafts store–gallery, a kitchenware shop, a postcard shop, a custom-made hat shop, a handmade paper store, a British Columbian native Indian gallery, a do-it-yourself jewelry store, and more.

43 Behind Blackberry Books, in the Net Loft complex, is **Bill Reid's studio,** belonging to British Columbia's most respected Haida Indian carver. His *The Raven and the First Men*, which took five carvers more than three years to complete, is in the Museum of Anthropology (see *Other Museums,* below); Reid's Pacific Northwest Coast artworks are world renowned. Although you can't visit the studio, there are large windows to peer through. Sadly, Mr. Reid was very ill at press time, and there was talk that the studio might close.

Once you have come full circle, you can either take the ferry back to downtown Vancouver or stay for dinner and catch a play at the **Arts Club** (☎ 604/687–1644) or the **Waterfront Theater** (☎ 604/685–6217).

Other Museums

The **Maritime Museum** traces the history of marine activities on the West Coast. Permanent exhibits depict the port of Vancouver, the fishing industry, and early explorers; the model ships on display are a delight.

Traveling exhibits vary but always have a maritime theme. Guided tours are led through the double-masted schooner *St. Roch,* the first ship to sail in both directions through the treacherous Northwest Passage. A changing variety of restored heritage boats from different cultures is moored behind the museum, and a huge Kwakiutl totem pole stands out front. *1905 Ogden Point at north end of Cypress St.,* ☎ *604/257–8300.* ☞ *$5 adults, $2.50 children, students, and senior citizens, $10 families.* ☺ *Spring–fall, daily 10–5; winter, Tues.–Sun. 10–5. Access via Granville Island Ferries.*

★ The **Museum of Anthropology,** focusing on the arts of the Pacific Northwest natives and aboriginals from around the world, is Vancouver's most spectacular museum. On the campus of the University of British Columbia, it is housed in an award-winning glass-and-concrete structure designed by Arthur Erickson. In the Great Hall are large and dramatic totem poles, ceremonial archways, and dugout canoes—all adorned with carvings of frogs, eagles, ravens, bears, and salmon. Also showcased are exquisite carvings of gold, silver, and argillite (a black stone found in the Queen Charlotte Islands), as well as masks, tools, and costumes from many other cultures. The museum contains a ceramics wing, which houses about 600 pieces from 15th- to 19th-century Europe. *6393 N.W. Marine Dr.,* ☎ *604/822–3825.* ☞ *$5 adults, $2.50 students 6–18 and senior citizens, $12 families; free Tues.* ☺ *Tues. 11–9, Wed.–Sun. 11–5.*

Science World is in a gigantic shiny dome that was built for Expo 86 for an Omnimax Theater. The hands-on museum encourages visitors to touch and participate in the theme exhibits. A special gallery, the Search Gallery, is aimed at younger children, as are the fun-filled demonstrations given in Center Stage. *1455 Quebec St.,* ☎ *604/268–6363.* ☞ *Science World: $8 adults, $5 senior citizens and children.* ☞ *Omnimax: $9; discounted admission to both.* ☺ *Weekdays 10–5, weekends 10–6.*

Vancouver Museum displays permanent exhibits that focus on the city's early history and native art and culture. Life-size replicas of an 1897 Canadian Pacific Railway passenger car, a trading post, and a Victorian parlor, as well as a real dugout canoe are highlights. *1100 Chestnut St.,* ☎ *604/736–4431.* ☞ *$5 adults, $2.50 senior citizens and children; surcharges may apply for special exhibitions.* ☺ *Winter, Tues.–Sun. 10–5; summer, daily 10–9.*

Video documentaries, photographs, costumes, and an array of sporting equipment are displayed at the **B.C. Sports Hall of Fame and Museum.** There's a high-tech, hands-on participation gallery, so bring tennis shoes. *B.C. Place Stadium, 777 Pacific Blvd. S,* ☎ *604/687–5523.* ☞ *$2.* ☺ *Wed.–Sun. 9–5.*

Other Parks and Gardens

The small (2½-acre) **Nitobe Memorial Garden** is considered the most authentic Japanese garden outside Japan. The circular path around the park symbolizes the cycle of life and provides a tranquil view from every direction. In April and May cherry blossoms are the highlight, and in June the irises are magnificent. *1903 West Mall, Univ. of B.C.,* ☎ *604/822–6038.* ☞ *$3 adults, $1.50 senior citizens and students.* ☺ *Summer, daily 10–6; winter, weekdays 10–3.*

Pacific Spirit Park (*4915 W. 16th Ave.,* ☎ *604/224–5739*), more rugged than Stanley Park, has 61 kilometers (30 miles) of trails, a few washrooms, and a couple of signboard maps. Go for a wonderful walk in the West-Coast arbutus and evergreen woods—it's hard to believe you're are only 15 minutes from downtown Vancouver.

Queen Elizabeth Park has lavish gardens and an abundance of grassy picnicking spots. Illuminated fountains; the Bloedel Conservatory, with tropical and desert plants and 35 species of free-flying tropical birds; and other facilities including 20 tennis courts, lawn bowling, pitch and putt, and a restaurant are on the grounds. *Cambie St. and 33rd Ave., ☎ 604/872–5513. ☛ Conservatory: $3 adults, $1.50 senior citizens and children 6–18, $6 families. ☉ Apr.–Sept., weekdays 9–8, weekends 10–9; Oct.–Mar., daily 10–5.*

Van Dusen Botanical Garden was a 55-acre golf course but is now the grounds of one of the largest collections of ornamental plants in Canada. Native and exotic plant displays include a shrubbery maze and rhododendrons in May and June. For a bite to eat, stop in Sprinklers Restaurant (☎ 604/261–0011), on the grounds. *5251 Oak St. at 37th Ave., ☎ 604/266–7194. ☛ $4.50 adults, $2.25 senior citizens and children 6–18, $9 families; half-price off-season. Garden open July–Aug. 10–9; Oct.–Apr. 10–4; May, June, and Sept. 10–6.*

What to See and Do with Children

Take your pint-size chef out to Sunday brunch at **Griffin's** (900 W. Georgia St., ☎ 604/662–1900), the bistro-style restaurant in the Hotel Vancouver, where the little ones don miniature chef's hats and make their own pancakes and churn ice cream.

The **miniature steam train** in Stanley Park, just five minutes northwest of the aquarium, is a big hit with children as it chugs through the forest. The **children's water park** across the road is also popular throughout the summer.

Splashdown Park (Rte. 17, just before the Tsawwassen Ferry causeway, ☎ 604/943–2251), 38 kilometers (24 miles) outside Vancouver, is a giant water slide park with 11 slides (for toddlers to adults), heated water, picnic tables, and miniature golf.

Richmond Nature Park (No. 5 Rd. exit from Rte. 99, ☎ 604/273–7015), with its displays and games in the Nature House, is geared toward children. Guides answer questions and give tours. As the park sits on a natural bog, rubber boots are recommended if it's been wet, but a boardwalk around the duck pond makes some of the park accessible to strollers and wheelchairs.

Maplewood Farms (405 Seymour River Pl., ☎ 604/929–5610), a 20-minute drive from downtown Vancouver, is set up like a small farm, with all the barnyard animals for children to see and pet. Cows are milked every day at 1:15.

Kids Only Market (*see* Tour 3 *in* Exploring Vancouver, *above*).

Science World (*see* Other Museums, *above*).

Vancouver Aquarium (*see* Tour 2, *above*).

Off the Beaten Path

On the North Shore you can get a taste of the mountains and test your mettle at the **Lynn Canyon Suspension Bridge** (off Peters Rd. in Lynn Canyon Park, North Vancouver, ☎ 604/987–5922), which hangs 170 feet above Lynn Creek. Also on the North Shore is the **Capilano Fish**

Hatchery in the Capilano Regional Park (4500 Capilano Park Rd., ☏ 604/666–1790), with exhibits about salmon.

If the sky is clear, the telescope at the **Gordon McMillan Southam Observatory** is focused on whatever stars or planets are worth watching that night. While you're there, visit the planetarium on the site. *1100 Chestnut St., Vanier Park,* ☏ *604/738–7827.* ☉ *Fri.–Sun. and holidays.*

Rock and Roll Heaven, formerly the Beatles Museum, exhibits memorabilia from Jimi Hendrix, Jim Morrison, the Beatles, and other rock icons. *19 Water St.,* ☏ *604/685–8841.* ☛ *$4.* ☉ *Mon.–Sat. 11–7, Sun. noon–7.*

SHOPPING

Unlike many cities where suburban malls have taken over, Vancouver has a downtown that is still lined with individual boutiques and specialty shops. Stores are usually open daily and on Thursday and Friday nights, and Sunday noon to 5.

Shopping Districts

The immense **Pacific Centre Mall** (550–750 W. Georgia St., ☏ 604/688–7236), on two levels and mostly underground, in the heart of downtown, connects Eaton's and the Bay department stores, which stand at opposite corners of Georgia and Granville streets.

A commercial center has developed around **Sinclair Centre** (757 W. Hastings St., ☏ 604/666–4483; *see* Tour 1, *above*), which caters to sophisticated and upscale tastes.

On the opposite side of Pacific Centre is **Robson Street,** stretching from Burrard to Bute streets and chockablock with small boutiques and cafés. Vancouver's liveliest street is not only for the fashion-conscious; it also provides many excellent corners for people-watching and attracts an array of street performers.

Fourth Avenue, from Burrard to Balsam streets, offers an eclectic mix of stores (from sophisticated women's clothing to surfboards).

In addition to the Pacific Centre Mall, **Oakridge Shopping Centre** (650 W. 41st Ave. at Cambie St., ☏ 604/261–2511) has chic, expensive stores that are fun to browse.

Ethnic Districts

Chinatown (*see* Tour 1 *in* Exploring Vancouver, *above*)—centered on Pender and Main streets—is an exciting and animated place for restaurants, exotic foods, and distinctive architecture.

Commercial Drive (around East 1st Avenue) is the heart of the Italian community, here called **Little Italy.** You can sip cappuccino in coffee bars where you may be the only one speaking English, or buy sun-dried tomatoes, real Parmesan, or an espresso machine.

The **East Indian shopping district** is on Main Street around 50th Avenue. Curry houses, sweet shops, grocery stores, and sari shops abound.

A small **Japantown** on Powell Street at Dunlevy Street is made up of grocery stores, fish stores, and a few restaurants.

Department Stores

Among Vancouver's top department stores is **Eaton's** (701 Granville St., ☎ 604/661–4425), which carries everything: clothing, appliances, furniture, jewelry, accessories, and souvenirs. **Holt Refrew** (Pacific Centre, Granville at Georgia, ☎ 604/681–3121) is smaller, focusing more exclusively on high fashion for men and women. Both are Canadian-owned and have stores at most malls as well as downtown.

Flea Markets

A huge flea market (703 Terminal Ave., ☎ 604/685–0666), with more than 360 stalls, is held weekends and holidays from 9 to 5. It is easily accessible from downtown on the SkyTrain, if you exit at the Main Street station.

Auctions

On Wednesday at noon and 7 PM, art and antiques auctions are held at **Love's** (1635 W. Broadway, ☎ 604/733–1157). **Maynard's** (415 W. 2nd Ave., ☎ 604/876–6787) has home furnishings auctions on Wednesday at 7 PM.

Specialty Stores

Antiques

A stretch of antiques stores runs along Main Street from 19th to 35th avenues. **Folkart Interiors** (3715 W. 10th Ave., ☎ 604/228–1011) specializes in whimsical B.C. folk art and Western Canadian antiques. For very refined antiques and decorative arts, see **Artemis** (3050 Granville St.). For Oriental rugs, go to **Granville Street** between 7th and 14th avenues.

Art Galleries

There are many private galleries throughout Vancouver. **Buschlen/Mowatt** (1445 W. Georgia St., ☎ 604/682–1234), among the best of them, is a showcase for Canadian and international artists. **Diane Farris** (1565 W. 7th Ave., ☎ 604/737–2629; call first) also very good, often spotlights hot new artists.

Books

Duthie's (919 Robson St., ☎ 604/684–4496; and 4444 W. 10th Ave., ☎ 604/224–7012), downtown and near the university, is tops of Vancouver's many bookstores when it comes to size and selection. **World Wide Books and Maps** (736A Granville St., downstairs, ☎ 604/687–3320), one of several specialty bookstores in town, offers travel books and maps that cover the world.

Clothing

Fashion is big business in Vancouver, and there are clothing boutiques on almost every corner downtown. If your tastes are traditional, don't miss **George Straith** (900 W. Georgia St., ☎ 604/685–3301) in the Hotel Vancouver, offering tailored designer fashions for both sexes. Handmade Italian suits, cashmere, and leather for men is sold at stylish **E.A. Lee** (466 Howe St., ☎ 604/683–2457); there are also a few women's items to browse through. Buttoned-down businesswomen usually shop at **Wear Else?** (789 W. Pender St., ☎ 604/662–7890), focusing on career women's fashions. For truly unique women's clothing, try **Dorothy Grant** (Sinclair Centre at Hastings and Granville, ☎ 604/681–0201) where traditional Haida native designs meld with modern fashion in a boutique that looks more like an art gallery.

Neto Leather (347 Water St., ☎ 604/682–6424), in Gastown, carries a huge selection of men's and women's leather outfits and accessories. At the architecturally stunning **Versus** (1008 W. Georgia St., ☎ 604/688–8938) boutique, ladies and gents sip espresso as they browse through the fashionable Italian designs of Gianni Versace. **Leone** (757 W. Hastings St., ☎ 604/683–1133) is yet another ultrachic boutique, dividing designer collections in themed areas; there's DKNY, Georgio Armani, and more here. Trendy men's and women's casual wear by Ralph Lauren is available at **The Polo Store** (375 Water St., ☎ 604/682–7656).

Gifts

Want something special to take home from British Columbia? One of the best places in Vancouver for good-quality souvenirs (West Coast native art, books, music, jewelry, and so on) is the **Clamshell Gift Shop** (Public Aquarium, ☎ 604/685–5911) in Stanley Park. The **Salmon Shop** (☎ 604/666–6477) in the Granville Island Public Market will wrap smoked salmon for travel. In Gastown, Haida, Inuit, and Salish native art is available at **Images for a Canadian Heritage** (164 Water St., ☎ 604/685–7046), as is a selection of fine Canadian crafts. Near Granville Island, **Leona Lattimer's** shop (1590 W. 2nd Ave., ☎ 604/732–4556), built like an Indian longhouse, is full of Indian arts and crafts ranging from cheap to priceless.

SPORTS AND THE OUTDOORS

Participant Sports

Biking

Stanley Park (*see* Tour 2 *in* Exploring Vancouver, *above*) is the most popular spot for family cycling. Rentals are available here from **Bayshore Bicycles** (745 Denman St., ☎ 604/688–2453) or **Stanley Park Rentals** (1798 W. Georgia, ☎ 604/681–5581).

Another popular summer biking route is along the north or south shores of **False Creek.** For bikes, try **Granville Island Bike Rentals** (1496 Cartwright, ☎ 604/669–2453) or **Granville Island Water Sports** (Charter Boat Dock, ☎ 604/662–7245).

Boating

Several charter companies offer a cruise-and-learn vacation, usually to the Gulf Islands. **Sea Wing Sailing Group, Ltd.** (Granville Island, ☎ 604/669–0840) offers a five-day trip teaching the ins and outs of sailing. If you'd rather just rent a speedboat to zip around the bay for a day, contact **Granville Island Boat Rentals** (☎ 604/682–6287) or **Granville Island Water Sports** (☎ 604/662–7245); the latter also rents jet skis and offers para-sailing for the more adventurous.

Fishing

You can fish for salmon all year in coastal British Columbia. **Sewell's Marina Horseshoe Bay** (6695 Nelson St., Horseshoe Bay, ☎ 604/921–3474) organizes a daily four-hour trip on Howe Sound or has hourly rates on U-drives. **Bayshore Yacht Charters** (1601 W. Georgia St., ☎ 604/691–6936) has a daily five-hour fishing trip; boats are moored five minutes from downtown Vancouver. **Island Charters** (Duranleau St., Granville Island, ☎ 604/688–6625) arranges charters or boat shares and supplies all gear.

Golf

Lower Mainland golf courses are open all year. Spacious **Fraserview Golf Course** (☎ 604/280–8623), with fairways well defined by hills and mature conifers and deciduous trees, is the busiest in the country. Fraserview is also the most central, about 20 minutes from downtown. **Seymour Golf and Country Club** (☎ 604/929–5491), on the south side of Mt. Seymour, on the North Shore, is a semiprivate club that is open to the public on Monday and Friday. One of the finest public courses in the country is **Peace Portal** (☎ 604/538–4818), near White Rock, a 45-minute drive from downtown.

Health and Fitness Clubs

Both the **YMCA** (955 Burrard St., ☎ 604/681–0221) and the YWCA (580 Burrard St., ☎ 604/662–8188) downtown have drop-in rates that let you participate in all activities for the day. Both have pools, weight rooms, and fitness classes; the YMCA has racquetball, squash, and handball courts. **The Bentall Centre Athletic Club** (1055 Dunsmuir St., lower level, ☎ 604/689–4424), has racquetball and squash courts, weight rooms, and aerobics.

Hiking

Pacific Spirit Park (*see* Other Parks and Gardens *in* Exploring Vancouver, *above*) has 48 kilometers (30 miles) of hiking trails. The **Capilano Regional Park** (*see* Off the Beaten Track *in* Exploring Vancouver, *above*), on the North Shore, provides a scenic hike.

Jogging

The seawall around **Stanley Park** (*see* Tour 2 *in* Exploring Vancouver, *above*) is 9 kilometers (5½ miles) long and gives an excellent minitour of the city. You can take a shorter run of 4 kilometers (2½ miles) in the park around **Lost Lagoon.**

Skiing

CROSS-COUNTRY

The best cross-country skiing is at **Cypress Bowl Ski Area** (☎ 604/926–6007).

DOWNHILL

Vancouver is two hours from **Whistler/Blackcomb,** one of the top-ranked ski destinations in the world (*see* Excursion to Whistler, *below*).

There are three ski areas on the North Shore mountains, close to Vancouver, with night skiing. The snow is not as good as at Whistler, and the runs are generally used by novice, junior, and family skiers or those who want a quick ski after work. **Cypress Bowl** (☎ 604/926–5612; snow report, ☎ 604/926–6007) has the most and the longest runs; **Grouse Mountain** (☎ 604/984–0661; snow report, ☎ 604/986–6262) has extensive night skiing, restaurants, and bars; and **Mt. Seymour** (☎ 604/986–2261; snow report, ☎ 604/879–3999) is the highest in the area, so the snow is a little better.

Tennis

Stanley Park has several well-surfaced outdoor courts near English Bay Beach; many of the other city parks have public courts as well. Contact the **Vancouver Board of Parks and Recreation** (☎ 604/257–8400) for other locations. There are no fees for use of public tennis courts.

Water Sports

KAYAKING

Rent a kayak from **Ecomarine Ocean Kayak Center** (☎ 604/689–7575) on Granville Island (*see* Tour 3 *in* Exploring Vancouver, *above*) to explore the waters of False Creek and the shoreline of English Bay.

WINDSURFING
Boards can be rented at **Windsure Windsurfing School** (Jericho Beach, ☎ 604/224–0615) and **Windmaster** (English Bay Beach, ☎ 604/685–7245).

Spectator Sports

The **Vancouver Canucks** (☎ 604/254–5141) of the National Hockey League play in the Coliseum October–April. The **Canadians** (☎ 604/872–5232) play baseball in an old-time outdoor stadium in the Pacific Coast League; their season runs April–September. The **B.C. Lions** (☎ 604/583–7747) football team scrimmages at the B.C. Place Stadium downtown June–November. The **Vancouver Eighty-Sixers** (☎ 604/299–0086) play soccer in Swangard Stadium from late April through early September. The **Vancouver Grizzlies** (☎ 604/688–5867), members of the National Basketball Association, hoop it up at the new General Motors Place arena near B.C. Place. Tickets are available from Ticketmaster (☎ 604/280–4444).

Beaches

An almost continuous string of beaches runs from Stanley Park to the University of British Columbia. Children and hardy swimmers can take the cool water, but most others prefer to sunbathe; these beaches are sandy, with grassy areas running alongside. Liquor is prohibited in parks and on beaches. For information, call the **Vancouver Board of Parks and Recreation** (☎ 604/257–8400).

Kitsilano Beach. Kits Beach, with a lifeguard, is the busiest of them all—transistor radios, volleyball games, and sleek young people are ever present. The part of the beach nearest the Maritime Museum is the quietest. Facilities include a playground, tennis courts, a heated saltwater pool (good for serious swimmers to toddlers), concession stands, and many nearby restaurants and cafés.

Point Grey Beaches. Jericho, Locarno, and Spanish Banks begin at the end of Point Grey Road. This string of beaches has a huge expanse of sand, especially in summer and at low tide. The shallow water here, warmed slightly by sun and sand, is best for swimming. Farther out, toward Spanish Banks, you'll find the beach becomes less crowded, but the last concession stand and washrooms are at Locarno. If you keep walking along the beach just past Point Grey, you'll hit Wreck Beach, Vancouver's nude beach. It is also accessible from Marine Drive at the university, but there is a fairly steep climb from the beach to the road.

West End Beaches. Second Beach and Third Beach, along Beach Drive in Stanley Park, draw families. Second Beach has a guarded saltwater pool. Both have concession stands and washrooms. The most lively of the West End beaches is English Bay Beach centered at the foot of Denman Street. A water slide, live music, windsurfing outlet, and other concessions located here are jumping all summer long. Farther along Beach Drive, at the foot of Jervis Street, Sunset Beach, surprisingly quiet considering the location, has a lifeguard on duty but no facilities.

DINING

Vancouver offers the visitor a diverse gastronomical experience; restaurants—from the bustling downtown area to trendy beachside neighborhoods—have enticing locales in addition to succulent cuisine. A new wave of Asian immigration and tourism has brought a proliferation of upscale Asian (Chinese, Japanese, Korean, Thai, Vietnamese) restaurants, offering dishes that would be at home in their own leading cities. Restaurants featuring Pacific Northwest fare—including such homegrown regional favorites as salmon and oysters, accompanied by British Columbia and Washington State wines—have become some of the city's leading attractions.

What to Wear

Vancouver dining is usually fairly informal; casual but neat dress is appropriate everywhere except the few expensive restaurants that require jacket and tie (indicated in the text below).

CATEGORY	*COST
$$$$	over $40
$$$	$30—$40
$$	$20—$30
$	under $20

per person for a three-course meal, excluding drinks, service, and sales tax

American

$ **Isadora's.** Not only does Isadora's offer good coffee, a menu that includes lox and bagels and children's specials, but there is also an inside play area packed with toys. Rest rooms with changing-tables accommodate families. In summer, the restaurant opens onto Granville Island's water park, so children can entertain themselves. Service can be slow, but Isadora's staff is friendly. The restaurant is no-smoking. ✕ 1540 Old Bridge St., Granville Island, ☎ 604/681–8816. Reservations required for 6 or more. DC, MC, V. Closed Mon. dinner Sept.–May.

$ **Nazarre BBQ Chicken.** The best barbecued chicken in several hundred miles comes from this funky storefront on Commercial Drive. Owner Gerry Moutal massages his chickens for tenderness before he puts them on the rotisserie and bastes them in a mixture of rum and spices. Chicken comes with roasted potatoes and a choice of mild, hot, extra-hot, or hot garlic sauce. You can eat in, at one of four rickety tables, or take out. ✕ 1859 Commercial Dr., ☎ 604/251–1844. No credit cards.

Cambodian/Vietnamese

$ **Phnom Penh Restaurant.** A block from the bustle of Keefer Street, the
★ Phnom Penh is part of a small cluster of Southeast Asian shops on the fringes of Chinatown. The simple, pleasant decor consists of potted plants and framed views of Angkor Wat on the walls. The hospitable staff serves unusually robust Vietnamese and Cambodian fare, including crisp, peppery garlic prawns fried in the shell and slices of beef crusted with ground salt and pepper mixed in the warm beef salad. The decor in the Broadway location is fancier, but the food is every bit as good as at East Georgia Street. ✕ 244 E. Georgia St., ☎ 604/682–5777; 955 W. Broadway, ☎ 604/734–8898. Dinner reservations advised for 5 or more. AE, MC. Closed Tues.

Chinese

$$–$$$ **Imperial Chinese Seafood.** This elegant Cantonese restaurant in the Art
★ Deco Marine Building offers stupendous views through two-story floor-to-ceiling windows of Stanley Park and the North Shore mountains across Coal Harbour. Any dish featuring lobster, crab, or shrimp from the live tanks is recommended, as is the dim sum served every afternoon from 11 to 2:30. Portions tend to be small and pricey (especially the abalone, shark's fin, and bird's nest delicacies) but never fail to please. 355 Burrard St., ☎ 604/688–8191. Reservations advised. AE, V.

Downtown Vancouver Dining

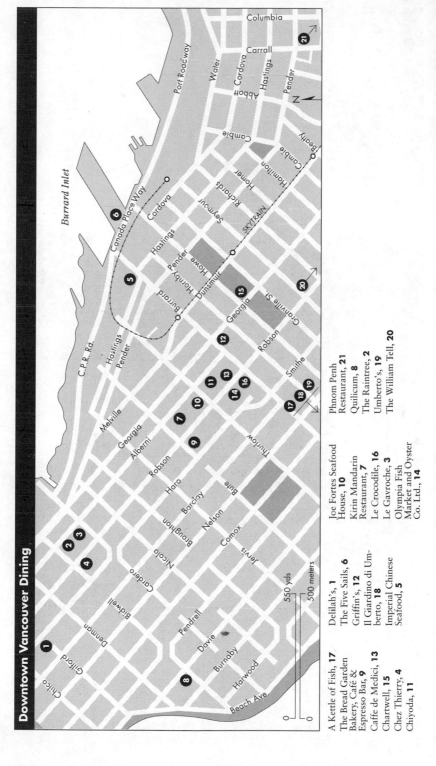

Burrard Inlet

A Kettle of Fish, **17**
The Bread Garden
Bakery, Café &
Espresso Bar, **9**
Caffe de Medici, **13**
Chartwell, **15**
Chez Thierry, **4**
Chiyoda, **11**

Delilah's, **1**
The Five Sails, **6**
Griffin's, **12**
Il Giardino di Um-
berto, **18**
Imperial Chinese
Seafood, **5**

Joe Fortes Seafood
House, **10**
Kirin Mandarin
Restaurant, **7**
Le Crocodile, **16**
Le Gavroche, **3**
Olympia Fish
Market and Oyster
Co. Ltd., **14**

Phnom Penh
Restaurant, **21**
Quilicum, **8**
The Raintree, **2**
Umberto's, **19**
The William Tell, **20**

550 yds

500 meters

242

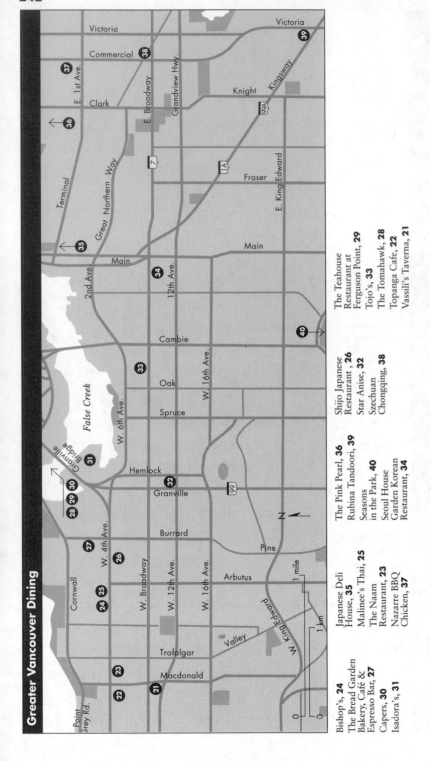

Greater Vancouver Dining

Bishop's, **24**
The Bread Garden
Bakery, Café &
Espresso Bar, **27**
Capers, **30**
Isadora's, **31**

Japanese Deli
House, **35**
Malinee's Thai, **25**
The Naam
Restaurant, **23**
Nazarre BBQ
Chicken, **37**

The Pink Pearl, **36**
Rubina Tandoori, **39**
Seasons
in the Park, **40**
Seoul House
Garden Korean
Restaurant, **34**

Shijo Japanese
Restaurant, **26**
Star Anise, **32**
Szechuan
Chongqing, **38**

The Teahouse
Restaurant at
Ferguson Point, **29**
Tojo's, **33**
The Tomahawk, **28**
Topanga Cafe, **22**
Vassili's Taverna, **21**

$$ **Kirin Mandarin Restaurant.** Fish swim in tanks set into the slate-green walls, part of the lavish decorations of this restaurant serving a smattering of northern Chinese cuisines. Dishes include Shanghai-style smoked eel, Peking duck, and Szechuan hot-and-spicy scallops. Kirin is just two blocks from most of the major downtown hotels. *1166 Alberni St.,* ☏ *604/682–8833. Reservations advised. AE, DC, V.*

$$ **Pink Pearl.** This noisy, 650-seat Cantonese restaurant has tanks of live seafood—crab, shrimp, geoduck, oysters, abalone, rock cod, lobsters, and scallops. Menu highlights include clams in black-bean sauce, crab sautéed with five spices (a spicy dish sometimes translated as crab with peppery salt), and Pink Pearl's version of crisp-skinned chicken. Arrive early for dim sum on the weekend if you don't want to be caught in the lineup. *1132 E. Hastings St.,* ☏ *604/253–4316. Reservations advised. AE, DC, MC, V.*

$ **Szechuan Chongqing.** Although fancier Szechuan restaurants can be found, the continued popularity of this unpretentious, white-tablecloth restaurant in a revamped fried-chicken franchise speaks for itself. Try the Szechuan-style fried green beans, steamed and tossed with spiced ground pork, or the Chongqing chicken—a boneless chicken served on a bed of spinach cooked in dry heat until crisp, giving it the texture of dried seaweed and a salty, rich, and nutty taste. ✗ *2808 Commercial Dr.,* ☏ *604/254–7434. Reservations advised. AE, MC, V.*

Continental

$$$–$$$$ **Chartwell.** Named after Sir Winston Churchill's country home (a painting of which hangs over the green marble fireplace), the flagship dining room at the Four Seasons hotel (*see* Lodging, *below*) looks like an upper-class British club. Floor-to-ceiling dark-wood paneling, deep leather chairs to sink back in while you sip claret, plus a quiet setting make this the city's top spot for a power lunch. The chefs cook robust, inventive Continental food with lighter offerings and a variety of low-calorie, low-fat entrées. Favorites, including tomato basil soup with gin, rack of lamb, and a variety of salmon offerings, are repeated on the seasonal menu. ✗ *791 W. Georgia St.,* ☏ *604/844–6715. Reservations advised. AE, DC, MC, V. Closed Sat. lunch.*

$$$–$$$$ **William Tell.** Silver service plates, embossed linen napkins, and a silver flower vase on each table set the tone of Swiss luxury. The William Tell's well-established reputation for excellent Continental food continues at its quarters on the main floor of the Georgian Court Hotel. Chef Christian Lindner offers sautéed veal sweetbreads with red onion marmalade and marsala sauce and such Swiss specialties as *Zürcher Geschnezeltes* (thinly sliced veal with mushrooms in a light white wine sauce) and *Bündnerfleisch* (paper-thin slices of air-dried beef). Make reservations well in advance for the all-you-can-eat "Swiss Farmer's Buffet" on Sunday night. *765 Beatty St.,* ☏ *604/688–3504. Reservations advised. AE, DC, MC, V.*

$$$ **Seasons in the Park.** Seasons has a commanding view over the park gardens to the city lights and the mountains beyond. A comfortable room with lots of light wood and white tablecloths, this restaurant in Queen Elizabeth Park serves a conservative Continental menu with such standards as grilled salmon with fresh mint and roast duck with sun-dried cranberry sauce. ✗ *Queen Elizabeth Park,* ☏ *604/874–8008. Reservations advised. AE, MC, V. Closed Dec. 25.*

$$$ **Teahouse at Ferguson Point.** The best of the Stanley Park restaurants is perfectly poised for watching sunsets over the water, especially from its glassed-in conservatorylike wing. Although the Teahouse has a less innovative menu than its sister restaurant, Seasons in the Park, certain specialties, such as the cream of carrot soup, lamb with herb crust, and the perfectly grilled fish, don't need any meddling. ✕ *Ferguson Point in Stanley Park,* ☎ *604/669–3281. Reservations required. AE, MC, V. Closed Dec. 25.*

Deli/Bakery

$ **Bread Garden Bakery, Café & Espresso Bar.** What began as a croissant bakery has taken over two neighboring stores and is now the ultimate Kitsilano 24-hour hangout. Salads, quiches, elaborate cakes and pies, giant muffins, and cappuccino draw a steady stream of the young and fashionable. You may be subjected to an irritatingly long wait in line here, or, for that matter, at any of its other locations popping up around the city; quality is suffering with the rapid expansion, but the Garden's following is still strong. *1880 W. 1st Ave.,* ☎ *604/738–6684; 812 Bute St.,* ☎ *604/688–3213. AE, MC, V.*

East Indian

$$ **Rubina Tandoori.** For the best East Indian food in the city, try Rubina
★ Tandoori, 20 minutes from downtown. The large menu spans most of the subcontinent's cuisines, and the especially popular *chevda* (an East Indian salty snack) gets shipped to fans all over North America. Non-smokers get the smaller, funkier back room with the paintings of coupling gods and goddesses; smokers get the slightly more subdued front room. ✕ *1962 Kingsway,* ☎ *604/874–3621. Weekend reservations advised. DC, MC, V. Closed Sun.*

French

$$$ **Le Gavroche.** Time has stood still in this charming, somewhat formal turn-of-the-century house, where a woman dining with a man will be offered a menu without prices. Featuring classic French cooking, lightened—but by no means reduced—to nouvelle cuisine, Le Gavroche's menu also includes such simple listings as smoked salmon with blini and sour cream. Other options may be as complex as smoked pheasant breast on a puree of celeriac, shallots, and wine with a light truffle sauce. The excellent wine list stresses Bordeaux. No reservations are necessary after 9:30, when the late-dessert menu is offered. Tables by the front window promise mountains-and-water views. ✕ *1616 Alberni St.,* ☎ *604/685–3924. Weekend reservations advised. AE, DC, MC, V. Closed weekend lunch and holidays.*

$$ **Chez Thierry.** This cozy, unpretentious bistro on the Stanley Park end
★ of Robson Street adds pizzazz to a celebration: Charming owner Thierry Damilano stylishly slashes open champagne bottles with a cavalry saber on request. For the past 18 years, he has worked together with chef Francois Launay in creating country-style French fare. Try the signature bouillabaisse; fresh tuna grilled with artichokes, garlic, and tomatoes; or filet mignon with a creamy cognac–Dijon black pepper sauce; and apple *tarte Tatin* for dessert. If you have a favorite French dish, call ahead and Thierry will go all-out to accommodate your particular craving. During the week, the intimate dining room is relaxing; on the weekend, however, the restaurant can be crowded and noisy. ✕ *1674 Robson St.,* ☎ *604/688–0919. Reservations advised. AE, DC, MC, V. Closed lunch and Dec. 24–26.*

$$ **Le Crocodile.** In a roomy location off Burrard Street, Chef Michael Jacob serves extremely well-cooked, simple food at reasonable prices. His Alsatian background shines with the caramel-sweet onion tart. Anything that involves innards is superb, and even such old standards as duck à l'orange are worth ordering here. ✕ *100-909 Burrard St.,* ☎ *604/669–4298. Reservations required. AE, DC, MC, V. Closed Sat. lunch, Sun., and holidays.*

Greek

$$ Vassili's Taverna. The menu in this family-run restaurant in the heart of the city's small Greek community is almost as conventional as the decor: checked tablecloths and mandatory paintings of white fishing villages and the blue Aegean Sea. At Vassili's, though, even standards become memorable due to the flawless preparation. The house specialty is a deceptively simple *kotopoulo* (a half-chicken, pounded flat, herbed, and charbroiled). ✕ *2884 W. Broadway,* ☎ *604/733–3231. Weekend reservations advised. AE, DC, MC, V. Closed Mon. and weekend lunch.*

Health Food

$ ★ Capers. Hidden in the back of the most lavish health food store in the Lower Mainland, Capers drips with earth-mother chic: wood tables, potted plants, and heady smells from the store's bakery. Breakfast starts at 8: free-range eggs and bacon with no additives, or feather-light blueberry pancakes crammed with berries. The newer Fourth Avenue location, with its dining room above the store, is by far the nicer of the two; the West Vancouver store is somewhat old and dingy. ✕ *2496 Marine Dr., W. Vancouver,* ☎ *604/925–3316; 2285 W. 4th,* ☎ *604/739–6685. MC, V. Marine Dr. closed Sun. dinner.*

$ Naam Restaurant. Vancouver's oldest alternative restaurant is open 24 hours, so if you need to satisfy a late-night tofu-burger craving, rest easy. The Naam also serves wine, beer, cappuccino, and wicked chocolate desserts, along with the vegetarian stir-fries. Wood tables and kitchen chairs provide a homey atmosphere. On warm summer evenings, try the outdoor courtyard at the back of the restaurant. ✕ *2724 W. 4th Ave.,* ☎ *604/738–7151. Reservations required for 7 or more. MC, V.*

Italian

$$$ ★ Caffe de Medici. You'll need to shift gears as you leave the stark concrete walls of the Robson Galleria behind and step into this elegant, somewhat formal restaurant with its ornate molded ceilings, rich green velvet curtains and chair coverings, and portraits of the Medici family. But after a little wine, an evening's exposure to courtly waiters, and a superb meal, you may begin to wish the outside world conformed more closely to this peaceful environment. Although an enticing antipasto table sits in the center of the room, consider the *bresaola* (air-dried beef marinated in olive oil, lemon, and pepper) as a worthwhile appetizer. Try the rack of lamb in a mint, mustard, and vermouth sauce. Any of the pastas is a safe bet. ✕ *1025 Robson St.,* ☎ *604/669–9322. Reservations advised. AE, D, DC, MC, V. Closed weekend lunch.*

$$$ Il Giardino di Umberto, Umberto's. First came Umberto's, a Florentine restaurant serving classic northern Italian food, installed in a century-old Vancouver home at the foot of Hornby Street. Then, next door, Umberto Menghi built Il Giardino, a sunny, light-splashed restaurant styled after a Tuscan house. A moneyed, see-and-be-seen crowd goes to Il Giardino for braided breast of pheasant with polenta and reindeer fillet with crushed peppercorn sauce. Fish is treated either Italian style—sea bass or salmon grilled and served with sun-dried tomatoes, black olives, and pine nuts—or with a taste of East Asia, as in yellowfin tuna grilled with wasabi butter. ✕ *Il Giardino, 1382 Hornby St.,* ☎ *604/669–2422. Umberto's, 1380 Hornby St.,* ☎ *604/687–6316. Reservations advised. AE, DC, MC, V. Umberto's closed lunch and Mon.; Il Giardino closed Sat. lunch and Sun.*

$$ Griffin's. The Sunday brunch ambience here is cheerful, energetic, and kid-oriented: Kids in aprons (provided by the restaurant) whip up their own pancakes and take turns churning ice cream for dessert. The rest of the week the emphasis is on the adult crowd. This brasserie uniquely blends the charm of old Italy with the flair of sophisticated design and fresh, regional ingredients. Squash-yellow walls, bold black-and-white tiles, and splashy food art by Mary Frances Tuck enhance Griffin's liveliness. The brasserie has an open kitchen that prepares inspired cuisine, including such buffet selections as convict bread, a round loaf stuffed with soft, fresh goat cheese, olives, tomatoes, and peppers in olive oil; smoked salmon; chicken pasta al pesto; and baked Pacific black cod with herbed crumbs. ✗ *900 W. Georgia St.,* ☏ *604/ 662–1900. Reservations advised. AE, D, DC, MC, V.*

Japanese

$$$ **Tojo's.** Hidekazu Tojo is a sushi-making legend here. His handsome
★ blond-wood tatami rooms, on the second floor of a modern green-glass tower in the hospital district on West Broadway, provide proper ambience for intimate dining, but Tojo's 10-seat sushi bar stands as the centerpiece. With Tojo presiding, it is a convivial place for dinner and offers a ringside seat for watching the creation of edible art. Although tempura and teriyaki dinners will satisfy, the seasonal menu is more exciting. In fall, ask for *dobbin mushi,* a soup made from pine mushrooms that's served in a teapot. In spring, try salad made from scallops and pink cherry blossoms. ✗ *777 W. Broadway, No. 202,* ☏ *604/ 872–8050. Weekend reservations advised. AE, DC, MC, V. Closed lunch and Sun.; Dec. 24–26 and Jan. 1 and 2.*

$$ **Chiyoda.** The bar curves through Chiyoda's main room: On one side are the customers and an array of flat baskets full of the day's offerings; on the other side are the chefs and grills. There are 35 choices of things to grill, from squid, snapper, and oysters to eggplant, mushrooms, onions, and potatoes. The finished dishes, dressed with sake, soy, or *ponzu* sauce, are dramatically passed over on the end of a long wooden paddle. If Japanese food means only sushi and tempura to you, check this out. ✗ *1050 Alberni St.,* ☏ *604/688–5050. Reservations accepted. AE, DC, MC, V. Closed lunch Sat., Sun.*

$$ **Shijo Japanese Restaurant.** Shijo has an excellent and very large sushi bar, a smaller robata bar, tatami rooms, and a row of tables overlooking bustling Fourth Avenue. The epitome of modern urban Japanese chic is conveyed through the jazz music, handsome lamps with a patinated bronze finish, and lots of black wood. Count on creatively prepared sushi, eggplant *dengaku* topped with light and dark miso paste and broiled, and shiitake *foil yaki* (fresh shiitake mushrooms cooked in foil with *ponzu* sauce). ✗ *1926 W. 4th Ave.,* ☏ *604/732–4676. Reservations advised. AE, MC, V. Closed weekend lunch.*

$ **Japanese Deli House.** The least expensive sushi in town is served in the high-ceilinged main-floor room of a turn-of-the-century building on Powell Street, once the heart of Vancouver's Japantown. This restaurant is not much to look at, but the food is especially fresh and good if you can make it an early lunch: sushi rectangles and rolls are made at 11 AM for the 11:30 opening, and there are all-you-can-eat sushi and tempura lunch specials on weekdays. ✗ *381 Powell St.,* ☏ *604/681–6484. No credit cards. Closed Sun. and Mon. dinners.*

Korean

$ **Seoul House Garden Korean Restaurant.** The shining star in a desperately ugly section of East Broadway, Seoul House is a bright restaurant, decorated in Japanese style, that serves a full menu of Japanese and Korean food. The best bet is the Korean barbecue, which you cook at your table. A barbecue dinner of marinated beef, pork, chicken, or fish comes complete with a half-dozen side dishes—kimchi, salads, stir-fried rice, and pickled vegetables—as well as soup and rice. Service can be chaotic in this very popular restaurant. ✗ *36 E. Broadway,* ☏ *604/ 874–4131. Reservations advised. MC, V. Closed Sun. lunch.*

Mexican

$ Topanga Cafe. Arrive before 6:30 or after 8 PM to avoid waiting in line for this 40-seat Kitsilano classic. The California-Mexican food hasn't changed much since 1978, when the Topanga started dishing up fresh salsa and homemade tortilla chips. Quantities are still huge and prices low. Kids can color blank menu covers while waiting for food; a hundred or more of the clientele's best efforts are framed on the walls. ✗ *2904 W. 4th Ave.,* ☎ *604/733–3713. No reservations. MC, V. Closed Sun.*

Nouvelle

$$$$ Five Sails. On the fourth floor of the Pan Pacific Hotel, this special-occasion restaurant affords a stunning panoramic view of Canada Place, Lions Gate Bridge, and the lights of the north shore twinkling across the bay. Austrian chef Ernst Dorfler, a past member of the Canadian Culinary Olympic team, has a special flair for presentation, from the swan-shape butter served with breads early in the meal to the chocolate ice-cream bonbon served on a bed of dry ice at the end. Pacific Rim best describes the broad-reaching menu that includes caramelized swordfish, spicy Mongolian-style chicken, and such old favorites as medallions of B.C. salmon or lamb from Salt Spring Island. ✗ *Pan Pacific Hotel, 300–999 Canada Pl.,* ☎ *604/662–8211. Reservations advised. AE, DC, MC, V. Closed lunch and Dec. 24, 26, and Jan. 1.*

$$$ Bishop's. John Bishop established Vancouver's most influential restaurant in 1985 by serving West Coast Continental cuisine with an emphasis on British Columbia seafood. Penne with grilled eggplant, roasted peppers, and basil pasta cohabit on the menu with medallions of venison, rack of lamb, and roasted duck breast. Seasonal specials such as ravioli filled with crab and mascarpone are enticing. The small white rooms—their only ornament some splashy expressionist paintings—are favored by Pierre Trudeau and by Robert De Niro when he's on location in Vancouver. ✗ *2183 W. 4th Ave.,* ☎ *604/738–2025. Reservations required. AE, DC, MC, V. Closed weekend lunch, Dec. 24–26, and first week in Jan.*

$$$ ★ Star Anise. When Sammy Lalji and Adam Busby, top performers from the highly regarded Bishop's (*see above*), left to open their own restaurant, they built a faithful following in record time. Their superior skills in attentive service, imaginative presentation, and excellent preparation of Pacific Rim cuisine with French flair shine in this intimate, no-smoking location just off Granville on the west side of town. Don't miss the cilantro and Dungeness crab cakes with fried ginger threads, rouille, and potatoes that are often on the seasonal menu; spot prawn ravioli, grilled pork chops, and carrot and ginger mousse are also good choices. The wine list offers an array of fine international and West Coast choices. Weekend brunch is a real treat here. ✗ *1485 W. 12th Ave.,* ☎ *604/737–1485. Reservations advised. AE, D, DC, MC, V. Closed Dec. 25, 26, and Jan. 1.*

$$ ★ Delilah's. Cherubs dance on the ceiling, candles flicker on the tables, and martini glasses clink in toasts, but this incredibly popular restaurant is simply too crowded and noisy to be romantic. Under the direction of chef Peg Montgomery, the nouvelle California cuisine is delicious, innovative, and beautifully presented. The fresh daily menu lets you choose two- or five-course prix fixe dinners. Try the salmon in strawberry peppercorn sauce and the pecan-crusted pork loin. Reservations are not accepted, and patrons have been known to line up before the restaurant even opens for dinner. ✗ *Buchan Hotel, 1906 Haro St.,* ☎ *604/687–3424. DC, MC, V. Closed lunch and Dec 24–27.*

Pacific Northwest

\$\$ Quilicum. Only a few blocks from English Bay, this downstairs "longhouse" serves the original Northwest Coast cuisine: bannock bread, baked sweet potato with hazelnuts, alder-grilled salmon, and soapberries for dessert. Try the authentic but odd dish—"oolichan grease"—that's prepared from candlefish. Native music is piped in, and Northwest Coast Indian masks (for sale) peer from the walls. ✗ *1724 Davie St.,* ☎ *604/ 681–7044. Reservations advised. AE, MC, V. Closed lunch.*

\$\$ The Raintree. This cool, spacious restaurant has a local menu and a
★ wine list that offers vintages from British Columbia, Washington, and Oregon. Raintree bakes its own bread, makes luxurious soups, and serves up such old favorites as a slab of apple pie for dessert. The kitchen, focusing on healthy cuisine, teeters between willfully eccentric and exceedingly simple. Seasonal specials may include salmon and crab gnocchi with roasted butternut squash cream; roasted Pacific halibut with oregano pesto; smoked Fraser Valley duck breast with gooseberry compote; and rabbit terrine with basil, mint, and blackberry sauce. Main courses change daily depending on market availability. ✗ *1630 Alberni St.,* ☎ *604/688–5570. Weekend reservations advised. AE, DC, MC, V. Closed weekend lunch and Dec. 24–26.*

\$ The Tomahawk. North Vancouver was mostly trees in 1926, when the Tomahawk first opened. Over the years, the original hamburger stand grew and mutated into part Northwest Coast Indian kitsch museum, part gift shop, and part restaurant. Renowned for its Yukon breakfast—five slices of back bacon, two eggs, hash browns, and toast—the Tomahawk also serves gigantic muffins, excellent French toast, and pancakes. The menu switches to oysters, trout, and burgers named for Indian chiefs at lunch and dinner. ✗ *1550 Philip Ave.,* ☎ *604/988–2612. AE, MC, V.*

Seafood

\$\$ Joe Fortes Seafood House. Reserve a table on the second floor balcony
★ at this Vancouver seafood hot spot to take in the view of the broad wall murals, the mounted blue marlins, and, most especially, the everentertaining scene at the noisy bar downstairs. The signature panfried Cajun oysters, the salmon with smoked apple and cider chutney, and the seared sea scallops in sesame and oyster glaze are tasty and filling, but often overlooked in favor of the reasonably priced daily blue-plate special. ✗ *777 Thurlow St.,* ☎ *604/669–1940. Reservations advised. AE, D, MC, V.*

\$\$ A Kettle of Fish. Since opening in 1979, this family-run restaurant at the foot of Burrard Bridge has developed a strong local following; depend on getting top quality seafood here. The menu varies daily according to market availability, but there are generally 15 kinds of fresh seafood to choose from that are either grilled, sautéed, poached, barbecued, or blackened Cajun-style according to your preference. The B.C. salmon and the seafood combo plate are always good choices. ✗ *900 Pacific St.,* ☎ *604/682–6853. AE, DC, MC, V.*

\$ Olympia Fish Market and Oyster Co. Ltd. Some of the city's best fishand-chips are fried in this tiny shop behind a fish store in the middle of the Robson Street shopping district. The choice is halibut, cod, prawns, calamari, and whatever's on special in the store, served with homemade coleslaw and genuine—never frozen—french fries. It's funky and fun. ✗ *1094 Robson St.,* ☎ *604/685–0716. No reservations. DC, MC, V.*

Thai

\$\$ Malinee's Thai. The city's most consistently interesting Thai food can
★ be found in this typically Southeast Asian–style room, tapestries adorning the walls. The owners, two Canadians who lived for several years

in Thailand, can give you detailed descriptions of every dish. Steamed fish with ginger, pickled plums, and red chili sauce is on the regular menu; steamed whole red snapper marinated in oyster sauce, ginger, cilantro, red pepper, and lime juice is a special worth ordering when it's available. ✗ *2153 W. 4th Ave.,* ☎ *604/737–0097. Reservations advised. AE, DC, MC, V. Closed lunch Sat.–Mon, Dec. 24–26.*

LODGING

The hotel industry has become a major business for Vancouver, a fairly young city that hosts large numbers of Asian businesspeople and others who are used to an above-average level of service. Although by some standards pricey, properties here are highly competitive, and you can expect the service to reflect this.

Note: At press time, the new **Wall Centre Garden Hotel** (1088 Burrard St., ☎ 604/331–1000 or 800/663–9255) had just opened and still had many kinks to work out. However, it does look promising.

CATEGORY	COST*
$$$$	over $200
$$$	$150–$200
$$	$100–$150
$	under $100

*All prices are for a standard double room for two, excluding 10% provincial accommodation tax, 15% service charge, and 7% GST.

$$$$ **Four Seasons**. This bustling 28-story hotel adjacent to the Vancouver Stock Exchange is attached to the Pacific Centre shopping mall. Standard rooms are average in size; roomier corner deluxe or deluxe Four Seasons rooms are recommended. Expect tasteful and stylish decor in the rooms and hallways. Service is outstanding, and the Four Seasons has all the amenities. The formal dining room, Chartwell (*see* Dining, *above*), is one of the best in the city. ☎ *791 W. Georgia St., V6C 2T4,* ☎ *604/689-9333; in Canada, 800/268-6282; in the U.S., 800/332-3442;* ℻ *604/844-6744. 317 rooms, 68 suites. 2 restaurants, bar, indoor-outdoor pool, sauna, aerobics, exercise room. AE, DC, MC, V.*

$$$$ **Pan Pacific Hotel**. Sprawling Canada Place sits on a pier right by the financial district and houses the luxurious Pan Pacific (built in 1986 for the Expo), the Vancouver Trade and Convention Centre, and a cruise-ship terminal; it's very easy to get turned around here. The three-story atrium lobby (once you locate it) has a dramatic totem pole and waterfall, and the lounge, the restaurant, and the café all have huge expanses of glass, so that you are rarely without a harbor view or a mountain backdrop. Earth tones and Japanese detail give the rooms an understated elegance. The hotel's fine dining restaurant, the Five Sails (*see* Dining *above*), offers what is arguably the best panoramic view in town and an imaginative menu to match. The health club has a $15 fee that's well worth the price. The busy hotel seems better suited to conventions than an intimate weekend getaway, but they do have pampering down to a science. ☎ *300–999 Canada Pl., V6C 3B5,* ☎ *604/662-8111; in Canada, 800/663-1515; in the U.S., 800/937-1515;* ℻ *604/685-8690. 467 doubles, 39 suites. 3 restaurants, bar, outdoor pool, massage, sauna, steam room, whirlpool, aerobics, health club, indoor track, paddle tennis, racquetball, squash. AE, DC, MC, V.*

$$$$ **Sutton Place (formerly Le Meridien)**. This property feels more like an
★ exclusive guest house than a large hotel: Its lobby has sumptuously thick carpets, enormous displays of flowers, and elegant European furniture. The rooms are even better, furnished with rich, dark woods reminis-

Vancouver Lodging

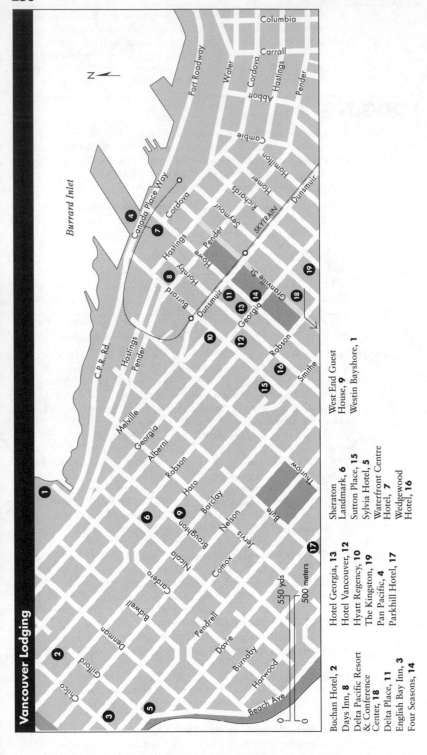

Burrard Inlet

Buchan Hotel, **2**
Days Inn, **8**
Delta Pacific Resort
 & Conference
 Center, **18**
Delta Place, **11**
English Bay Inn, **3**
Four Seasons, **14**

Hotel Georgia, **13**
Hotel Vancouver, **12**
Hyatt Regency, **10**
The Kingston, **19**
Pan Pacific, **4**
Parkhill Hotel, **17**

Sheraton
 Landmark, **6**
Sutton Place, **15**
Sylvia Hotel, **5**
Waterfront Centre
 Hotel, **7**
Wedgewood
 Hotel, **16**

West End Guest
 House, **9**
Westin Bayshore, **1**

cent of 19th-century France. Bathrobes, slippers, and umbrellas in the room attest to the attention to detail here. Despite the size of this hotel, Sutton Place in Vancouver has achieved and maintained a level of intimacy and exclusivity. The Café Fleuri serves one of the best Sunday brunches in town (plus a chocolate buffet on Thursday, Friday, and Saturday evenings), and Le Club, a fine French restaurant, is a special-occasion place. Lots of leather, dark wood, wingback chairs, and a fireplace give the Gérard Lounge the feel of a refined gentlemen's club. The tiny La Boulangerie Bakery, added in 1993, is a hit. An apartment hotel adjoins the Sutton Place. ☎ *845 Burrard St., V6Z 2K6, ☎ 604/ 682–5511, 800/961–7555, FAX 604/682–2926. 350 doubles, 47 suites. Restaurant, bar, café, indoor pool, beauty salon, massage, sauna, steam room, health club, business services. AE, D, DC, MC, V.*

$$$–$$$$ **Westin Bayshore.** The closest thing to a resort that you'll find in the downtown area, the Bayshore is perched right on the best part of the harbor. Because it is only a five-minute walk from Stanley Park, because of the truly fabulous view, and because of its huge outdoor pool, sundeck, and grassy areas, it is the perfect place to stay in summer, especially for a family. The new tower has rooms with the best views of the water; rooms in the main wing were updated in 1993 and are now comparable in contemporary style. The café is okay, and Trader Vic's, the hotel's dining room, is a pleasant, Polynesian-style experience. ☎ *1601 W. Georgia St., V6G 2V4, ☎ 604/682–3377 or 800/228–3000; FAX 604/687–3102. 484 doubles, 33 suites; 2 floors for persons with disabilities. Restaurant, café, 2 bars, indoor and outdoor pools, massage, sauna, health club, boating, fishing, bicycles, billiards, downtown shuttle. AE, D, DC, MC, V.*

$$$ **Delta Pacific Resort & Conference Center.** It's not a view or a shoreline that makes this place (five minutes from the airport) a resort, it's the facilities on the 14-acre site: three swimming pools (one indoor, with a three-story tubular water slide), four all-year tennis courts with a pro (matching list for partners), an outdoor fitness circuit, squash courts, aqua-exercise classes, outdoor volleyball nets, golf practice nets, a play center for children, summer camps for 5- to 12-year-olds, and a playground. In spite of the hotel's size, the atmosphere is casual and friendly. Guest rooms are modern with contemporary decor and a pleasant blue and green color scheme. The Japanese restaurant is expensive and not the best value. ☎ *10251 St. Edwards Dr., Richmond, V6X 2M9, ☎ 604/278–9611; in Canada, 800/268–1133; in the U.S., 800/877–1133; FAX 604/276–1122. 460 doubles, 4 suites. Restaurant, bar, café, saunas, baby-sitting, airport shuttle. AE, DC, MC, V.*

$$$ **Delta Place.** This 18-story hotel built in 1985 by the luxurious Hong Kong Mandarin chain was sold to Delta Hotels in 1987. Although the rates went down, the surroundings did not change: The lobby is still restrained and tasteful—one has to look for the registration desk, which is tucked off to the right. A slight Oriental theme is given to the rich dark-mahogany furnishings. Most rooms have small balconies, and the studio suites—roomier, and only slightly more expensive than a standard room—are recommended. The business and shopping district is a five-minute walk away. ☎ *645 Howe St., V6C 2Y9, ☎ 604/687– 1122; in Canada, 800/268–1133; in the U.S., 800/877–1133; FAX 604/ 643–7267. 181 doubles, 16 suites. Restaurant, bar, lap pool, massage, saunas, exercise room, racquetball, squash. AE, DC, MC, V.*

$$$ **Hotel Vancouver.** The copper roof of this grand château-style hotel dom-
★ inates Vancouver's skyline. Opened in 1939 by the Canadian National Railway, the hotel commands a regal position in the center of town across from the art gallery and Cathedral Place. Even the standard guest rooms have an air of prestige with mahogany furniture, TVs in armoires,

attractive linens, and the original, deep bathtubs. Entrée Gold suites, with French doors, graceful wingback chairs, and fine mahogany furniture take up two floors and come with extra services and amenities, including complimentary breakfast in a private, luxurious lounge. Afternoon tea in the lobby lounge is a real treat. ⊞ *900 W. Georgia St., V6C 2W6,* ☎ *604/684–3131 or 800/441–1414,* ℻ *604/662–1937. 466 doubles, 42 suites. 2 restaurants, bar, lobby lounge, lap pool, health club, exercise room, AE, D, DC, MC, V.*

$$$ Hyatt Regency. The 34-story hotel, which opened in 1973, underwent major renovation in 1992. The Hyatt's standard rooms are spacious and decorated in deep, dramatic colors and dark wood. Ask for a corner room with a balcony on the north or west side. The lobby, with its four-story atrium, can't escape the feel of a large convention hotel. For a small fee, the Regency Club gives you the exclusivity of a floor accessed by keyed elevators, your own concierge, a private lounge with a stereo and large TV, complimentary breakfast, 5 PM hors d'oeuvres, and evening pastries. ⊞ *655 Burrard St., V6C 2R7,* ☎ *604/683–1234 or 800/233–1234,* ℻ *604/689–3707. 612 doubles, 34 suites. Restaurant, 2 bars, café, outdoor heated pool, sauna. AE, D, DC, MC, V.*

$$$ Waterfront Centre Hotel. This dramatically elegant, 23-story glass hotel opened in 1991 across from Canada Place, the Convention Centre, and the cruise-ship terminal—all of which can be reached from the hotel by an enclosed walkway. Views from the caramel-color lobby and 70% of the guest rooms are of Burrard Inlet. The rooms are attractively furnished with contemporary artwork, minibars, and armoires concealing the TV. A live string quartet entertains in the lobby restaurant, Herons, during a lavish Sunday brunch that includes imaginative dishes and decadent desserts. ⊞ *900 Canada Place Way, V6C 3L5,* ☎ *604/691–1991 or 800/441–1414,* ℻ *604/691–1999. 460 doubles, 29 suites. Restaurants, heated outdoor pool, massage, steam room. AE, D, DC, MC, V.*

$$$ Wedgewood Hotel. This hotel upholds its reputation as a small, ele-
★ gant property run by an owner who cares fervently about her guests. The intimate lobby is decorated in fine detail with polished brass, beveled glass, a fireplace, and tasteful artwork. All the extra touches are here, too: nightly turndown service, afternoon ice delivery, darkout drapes, flowers growing on the balcony, terry-cloth robes, and morning newspaper. No tour groups or conventions stop here; the Wedgewood's clients are almost exclusively corporate, except on weekends, when the place turns into a couples' retreat. It's a treasure. ⊞ *845 Hornby St., V6Z 1V1,* ☎ *604/689–7777 or 800/663–0666,* ℻ *604/688–3074. 60 doubles, 33 suites. Restaurant, bar, exercise room. AE, D, DC, MC, V.*

$$–$$$ Parkhill Hotel. Cool pastel shades echo the colors of Impressionist prints decorating the surprisingly spacious rooms in this West End hotel just a block from the seawall and sandy Sunset Beach. Large, comfortable sitting areas, half-moon balconies with city or bay views, in-room safes, minifridges, hair dryers, and complimentary downtown shuttle services are part of the package. ⊞ *1160 Davie St., V6E 1N1,* ☎ *604/685–1311 or 800/663–1525,* ℻ *604/681–0208. 191 rooms. 2 restaurants, lounge, pool, sauna, exercise room, travel services. AE, D, DC, MC, V.*

$$–$$$ Sheraton Landmark. The towering Landmark on Robson Street is still the tallest hotel in downtown Vancouver and, since its renovations in 1994–95, contains some of the prettiest guest rooms in town. The Sheraton has turned to the bold jewel tones (emerald, sapphire, and ruby) of paintings by British Columbia's beloved Emily Carr (whose works hang in every room). All rooms enjoy a fine view, but the Cloud Nine revolving restaurant on the top floor is the place to go for an unobstructed vista of all of Vancouver—it's a great place to watch the sunrise over an early breakfast buffet. ☎ *1400 Robson St., V6G 1B9,* ☎ *604/687–0511 or 800/325–3535,* FAX *604/687–2801. 351 rooms, 7 suites. Restaurant, café, sports bar, no-smoking rooms, saunas, exercise room, travel services. AE, DC, MC, V.*

$$ Days Inn. For the business traveler looking for a bargain, this location is tops. The six-story hotel, which opened as the Abbotsford in 1920, is the only moderately priced hotel in the business core. Recent renovations of the guest rooms and the lobby have made it even more agreeable. Although it's a basic hotel, rooms are bright, clean, and functional; standard units are very large, but there is no room service and few amenities. Suites 310, 410, 510, and 610 have a harbor view. The Bombay Bicycle Club bar is a favorite with businesspeople. ☎ *921 W. Pender St., V6C 1M2,* ☎ *604/681–4335,* FAX *604/681–7808. 74 doubles, 11 suites. Restaurant, 2 bars, no-smoking rooms, free parking. AE, D, DC, MC, V.*

$$ English Bay Inn. This newly renovated 1930s Tudor house is one block
★ from the ocean and Stanley Park in a quiet residential part of the West End. The guest rooms—each with a private bath—have wonderful sleigh beds (in all but one room) with matching armoires, Ralph Lauren linen, and alabaster lighting fixtures. The common areas of this no-smoking inn are generous and elegantly furnished: The sophisticated but cozy parlor has wingback chairs, a fireplace, a gilt Louis XIV clock and candelabras, and French doors opening onto the front garden. A small, sunny English country garden decorates the back of the inn. Breakfast is served in a rather formal room with a Gothic dining room suite, a fireplace, and a 17th-century grandfather clock. ☎ *1968 Comox St., V6G 1R4,* ☎ *604/683–8002. 4 rooms, 1 suite. Free parking. AE, V.*

$$ Hotel Georgia. This handsome 12-story hotel, built in 1927, has such Old World features as a dark-wood-paneled lobby, ornate brass elevators, and a subdued, genteel atmosphere. Rooms are small but well furnished, with nothing worn around the edges. Executive rooms have an almost separate seating area; rooms facing the art gallery have the best views. From this hotel (across from the Four Seasons) it's a five-minute walk to the business district. ☎ *801 W. Georgia St., V6C 1P7,* ☎ *604/682–5566 or 800/663–1111,* FAX *604/682–8192. 310 doubles, 3 suites. Restaurant, 3 bars. AE, D, DC, MC, V.*

$$ West End Guest House. Judge this lovely Victorian house, built in
★ 1906, by its gracious front parlor, cozy fireplace, and early 1900s furniture rather than by its bright pink exterior. Most of the small but extraordinarily handsome rooms have high brass beds, antiques, gorgeous linens, and dozens of old framed pictures of Vancouver. Avoid the basement rooms, however. The inn's genial host, Evan Penner, makes the difference, with small touches such as a pre-dinner glass of sherry, duvets and feather mattress-pads, terry bathrobes, hand-knit slippers, turndown service, and a goodnight tart. The inn is in a residential neighborhood that is a 15-minute walk from Stanley Park and two minutes from Robson Street. Room rates include a full breakfast at this no-smoking establishment. ☎ *1362 Haro St., V6E 1G2,* ☎ *604/681–2889,* FAX *604/688–8812. 7 rooms. Parking. AE, D, MC, V.*

$ Buchan Hotel. This three-story 1930s building is conveniently set in a tree-lined residential street a block from Stanley Park, a block from shops and restaurants on Denman Street, and a 15-minute walk from the liveliest part of Robson Street. For the budget price, guests rent tiny, institutional rooms with very basic furnishings, ceiling fans, and color TV, but no telephone or air-conditioning; sadly, recent reports indicate problems with cleanliness. The pension-style rooms with shared bath down the hall are perhaps the most affordable accommodations in downtown. Since 1993, this has been a no-smoking hotel. ☎ *1906 Haro St., V6G 1H7, ☎ 604/685–5354 or 800/668–6654, FAX 604/685–5367. 60 rooms, 30 with private bath. Lounge, coin laundry, bike storage. AE, DC, MC, V.*

$ **The Kingston.** The Kingston is a small budget hotel convenient for shopping. It is an old-style, four-story building, with no elevator—the type of establishment you'd find in Europe. The spartan rooms are small and immaculate and share a bathroom down the hall. All rooms have phones and a few have TVs. Rooms on the south side are brighter. Continental breakfast is included. ☎ *757 Richards St., V6B 3A6, ☎ 604/684–9024. 60 rooms, 7 with bath. Lounge, sauna, coin laundry, free parking. AE, MC, V.*

$ **Sylvia Hotel.** The Sylvia Hotel is perhaps the best bargain in Vancouver, but don't count on staying here June–August unless you've booked six months ahead. What make this hotel so popular are its low rates and near-perfect location: about 25 feet from the beach, 200 feet from Stanley Park, and a 20-minute walk from downtown. Rooms are unadorned and have worn, plain furnishings that have probably been around for more than 20 years; not much to look at, but the view—particularly from the south and west sides—and price make it worthwhile. Suites are huge, and all have kitchens, making this a perfect family accommodation. There is little difference between the old and new wings. ☎ *1154 Gilford St., V6G 2P6, ☎ 604/681–9321. 97 rooms, 18 suites. Restaurant, lounge, parking. AE, DC, MC, V.*

THE ARTS AND NIGHTLIFE

For information on events, pick up a free copy of the *Georgia Straight* (available at cafés and bookstores around town), or look in the entertainment section of the *Vancouver Sun* (Thursday's paper has listings in the **"What's On"** column). And there's the Arts Hotline (☎ 604/684–2787). For tickets, book through **Ticketmaster** (☎ 604/280–3311).

The Arts

Dance
Watch for **Ballet British Columbia**'s (☎ 604/669–5954) Dance Alive! series, presenting visiting or local ballet companies (from the Kirov to Ballet BC). Most performances by these companies can be seen at the Orpheum or the Queen Elizabeth Theatre (*see below*). Local modern dance companies worth seeing are **Karen Jamison, Judith Marcuse,** and **JumpStart.**

Film
Two theaters have distinguished themselves by avoiding the regular movie fare: **Ridge Theatre** (3131 Arbutus St., ☎ 604/738–6311), which generally plays foreign films and rerun double-bills, and **Pacific Cinématèque Pacifique** (1131 Howe St., ☎ 604/688–3456), which goes for even more esoteric foreign and art films. The **Vancouver International Film Festival** (☎ 604/685–0260) is held during September and October in several theaters around town.

Music
The **Vancouver Symphony Orchestra** (☎ 604/684–9100) and the **CBC Orchestra** (☎ 604/662–6000) play at the restored **Orpheum Theatre** (601 Smithe St.). Choral groups like the **Bach Choir** (☎ 604/921–8012), the **Cantata Singers** (no ☎), and the **Vancouver Chamber Choir** (☎ 604/738–6822) play a major role in Vancouver's classical music

scene. The **Early Music Society** (☎ 604/732–1610) performs medieval, Renaissance, and baroque music throughout the year and hosts the Vancouver Early Music Summer Festival, one of the most important early music festivals in North America. Concerts by the **Friends of Chamber Music** (no ☎) and the **Vancouver Recital Society** (☎ 604/736–6034) are always of excellent quality.

Vancouver Opera (☎ 604/682–2871) stages four high-caliber productions a year, usually in October, January, March, and May, at the **Queen Elizabeth Theatre** (600 Hamilton St.). This theater is also the major venue in Vancouver for traveling Broadway musicals.

Theater

The **Vancouver Playhouse** (Hamilton St. at Dunsmuir, ☎ 604/872–6622) is the most established venue in Vancouver. The **Arts Club Theatre** (1585 Johnston St., ☎ 604/687–1644), with two stages on Granville Island and performances all year, is the most active. Both present mainstream theatrical shows. **Carousel Theatre** (☎ 604/669–3410), which performs off-off Broadway shows at the Waterfront Theatre (1405 Anderson St.) on Granville Island, and **Touchstone** (☎ 604/687–8737), at the Firehall Theatre (280 E. Cordova St.), are smaller but lively companies. The **Back Alley Theatre** (751 Thurlow St., ☎ 604/688–7013) hosts *Theatresports,* a hilarious improv event. The **Vancouver East Cultural Centre** (1895 Venables St., ☎ 604/254–9578) is a multipurpose performance space that always hosts high-caliber shows. The **Starlight Theatre** (West End, ☎ 604/280–3311) is the latest of Vancouver's live performance venues to be refurbished.

Bard on the Beach (☎ 604/875–1533) is a summer series of Shakespeare's plays performed under a huge tent on the beach at Vanier Park. **The Fringe** (☎ 604/873–3646), Vancouver's annual live theatrical arts festival, is staged in September at churches, dance studios, and theater halls around town.

Nightlife

Bars and Lounges

The **Gérard Lounge** (845 Burrard St., ☎ 604/682–5511) at Sutton Place Hotel is probably the nicest in the city because of its fireplaces, wingback chairs, dark wood, and leather. For spectacular views, head up to the **Roof Lounge** (900 W. Georgia St., ☎ 604/684–3131) in the Hotel Vancouver, where a pianist plays nightly. The **Bacchus Lounge** (845 Hornby St., ☎ 604/689–7777) in the Wedgewood Hotel is stylish and sophisticated. The **Gallery Lounge** (655 Burrard St., ☎ 604/687–6543) in the Hyatt is a genteel bar, with lots of windows that let in the sun and provide views of the action on the bustling street. The **Garden Court** (791 W. Georgia St., ☎ 604/689–9333) in the Four Seasons is bright and airy with greenery and a waterfall, plus big soft chairs you won't want to get out of. For a more lively atmosphere, try **Joe Fortes** (777 Thurlow St., 604/669–1940), known in town as the local "meet market." Billiards is now tremendously popular in Vancouver, and the **Soho Café and Billiards** (1144 Homer, ☎ 604/688–1180) is the place to go. Another "hot" pool hall is the **Automotive Billiards Club** (1095 Homer, ☎ 604/682–0040).

On Granville Island, the after-work crowd head to **Bridges** (☎ 604/687–4400) near the Public Market overlooking False Creek. Slightly more upscale is **Pelican Bay** (☎ 604/683–7373), the lounge in the Granville Island Howard Johnson Plaza, at the other end of the island. The **Backstage Lounge** (1585 Johnston St., ☎ 604/687–1354), behind the main stage at the Arts Club Theatre, features one of the largest selections of scotches in town and is the hangout for local and touring musicians and actors.

Casinos

A few casinos have been licensed recently in Vancouver, and proceeds go to local charities and arts groups. No alcohol is served. A good bet is the **Royal Diamond Casino** (535 Davie St., ☎ 604/685–2340) downtown. The **Great Canadian Casino** (2477 Heather St., ☎ 604/872–5543), in the Holiday Inn, is another option for gamblers in downtown Vancouver.

Comedy

Yuk Yuks (750 Pacific Blvd., ☎ 604/687–5233) is good for a few laughs. **Punchlines Comedy Theatre** (15 Water St., ☎ 604/684–3015), another cheerful place, is in Gastown.

Music

DISCOS

Although discos come and go, lines still form every weekend at **Richard's on Richards** (1036 Richards St., ☎ 604/687–6794) for live and taped Top-40 music. **Graceland** (1250 Richards St., ☎ 604/688–2648) attracts a slightly younger dance crowd. The go-go dancers at **Mars** (1320 Richards St., ☎ 604/622–7707) are supposed to be there to get dancers into the swing of things.

JAZZ

A jazz and blues hot line (☎ 604/682–0706) gives you current information on concerts and clubs. The **Alma Street Café** (2505 Alma St., ☎ 604/222–2244), a restaurant, is a traditional venue with good mainstream jazz. The **Glass Slipper** (185 E. 11th Ave., ☎ 604/877–0066) has mainstream to contemporary jazz with a more underground atmosphere.

ROCK

The **Town Pump** (66 Water St., ☎ 604/683–6695) is the main venue for local and touring rock bands. The **Soft Rock Café** (1925 W. 4th Ave., ☎ 604/736–8480) is decidedly more upscale than some other Vancouver rock venues; there's live music with dinner. The **86th Street Music Hall** (750 Pacific Blvd., ☎ 604/683–8687) serves up big-name bands. The **Commodore Ballroom** (870 Granville St., ☎ 604/681–7838), a Vancouver institution, has been restored to its original, Art Deco style and offers live music ranging from B.B. King to zydeco bands.

EXCURSION TO WHISTLER

Exploring

If you think of skiing when you hear mention of Whistler, British Columbia, you're thinking on track. Whistler and Blackcomb mountains, part of Whistler Resort, are the two largest ski mountains in North America and are consistently ranked the first- or second-best ski destinations on the continent. There's winter and summer glacier skiing, the longest vertical drop in North America, and one of the most advanced lift systems in the world. At the base of the mountains is Whistler Village—a small community of lodgings, restaurants, pubs, gift shops, and boutiques. With dozens of hotels and condos within a five-minute walk of the mountains, the site is frenzied with activity. Culinary options in the village range from burgers to French, Japanese to deli cuisine; and nightly entertainment runs the gamut from sophisticated piano bars to casual pubs.

In winter, the village buzzes with skiers taking to the slopes, but as the scenery changes from winter's snow-white to summer's lush-green landscapes, the mood of Whistler changes, too. Things seem to slow down a bit, and the resort sheds some of its competitive edge and relaxes to a slower pace. Even the local golf tournaments and the triathlon are interspersed with Mozart and bluegrass festivals.

Recent developments in this rapidly growing resort include **Whistler North,** with still more boutiques, condo hotels, and dining outlets; **Glacier Creek Lodge,** a visually stunning addition at Blackcomb that expands the dining options on the mountain; and the new **Meadow Park Sports Centre** (☏ 604/938–3133), with a six-lane pool, a hot tub, a sauna, a steam room, and two squash courts.

Adjacent to the area is the 78,000-acre (31,579-hectare) **Garibaldi Provincial Park,** with dense mountainous forests splashed with hospitable lakes and streams. Even if you don't want to roam much farther than the village, there are five lakes for canoeing, fishing, swimming, and windsurfing, and many nearby hiking and mountain-bike trails.

Whistler Village is a pedestrian-only community. Anywhere you want to go within the resort is at most five minutes away, and parking lots are just outside the village. The bases of Whistler and Blackcomb mountains are also just at the edge; in fact, you can ski right into the lower level of the Chateau Whistler Hotel, and all 3,000 of the village's hotel rooms are less than 1,000 feet from the lifts.

If you are interested in a tour of the area, **Alpine Adventure Tours** (☏ 604/932–2705) has a Whistler history tour of the valley and a Squamish day trip.

Scenic Drives
The **Coast Mountain Circle** links Vancouver to Cariboo Country. This 702-kilometer (435-mile) route takes in spectacular Howe Sound, the deep-water port of Squamish, Whistler Resort, and Pemberton Valley before heading back to Vancouver through scenic Fraser Canyon and Harrison Hot Springs. The loop makes a comfortable two- to three-day journey. For more information contact the **Tourism Association of Southwestern B.C.** (204-1755 W. Broadway, Vancouver V6J 4S5, ☏ 604/739–9011 or 800/667–3306, ℻ 604/739–0153).

Sports and the Outdoors
Canoeing and Kayaking
You'll see lots of canoes and kayaks at the many lakes and rivers near Whistler. If you want to get in on the fun, rentals are available at Alta Lake at both **Lakeside Park** and **Waside Park.** Another spot that's perfect for canoeing is the **River of Golden Dreams,** either from Meadow Park to Green Lake or upstream to Twin Bridges. Kayakers looking for a thrill may want to try **Green River** from Green Lake to Pemberton. Call **Whistler Outdoor Experience** (☏ 604/932–3389), **Whistler Sailing and Water Sports** (☏ 604/932–7245) or **Sea to Sea Kayaking** (☏ 604/898-5498) for equipment or guided trips.

Fishing
Whistler Backcountry Adventures (☏ 604/938–1410) or **Whistler Fishing Guides** (☏ 604/932–4267) will take care of anything you need—equipment, guides, and transportation. All five of the lakes around Whistler are stocked with trout, but the area around **Dream River**

Park is one of the most popular fishing spots. Slightly farther afield, try **Cheakamus Lake, Daisy Lake,** and **Callaghan Lake.**

Golf

Arnold Palmer designed the par-72 championship **Whistler Golf Course** (☎ 604/932–4544), a "good four-iron shot from the village." The course is very scenic, fairly flat, and challenging for the experienced but pleasant for beginners. The equally scenic **Chateau Whistler Golf Club** (4612 Blackcomb Way, ☎ 604/938–8000), designed by Robert Trent Jones II and nestled at the foot of the mountain on the opposite side of Whistler Village, was ranked the best new course in Canada by Golf Digest in 1993.

Skiing

DOWNHILL

The vertical drops and elevations at **Blackcomb** (☎ 604/932–3141) and **Whistler** (☎ 604/932–3434) mountains are, perhaps, the most impressive features to skiers here. Blackcomb has a 5,280-foot vertical drop, North America's longest, while Whistler comes in second, with a 5,020-foot drop. The top elevation is 7,494 feet on Blackcomb and 7,160 on Whistler. These mountains also have the most advanced ski-lift technology: Blackcomb has a 27,102-skier-per-hour lift capacity, while Whistler's capacity is 22,815 skiers per hour. Blackcomb and Whistler have more than 100 marked trails each and receive an average of 360 inches of snow per year; Blackcomb is open June–August for summer glacier skiing. **Whistler Ski School** and **Blackcomb Ski School** offer lessons to skiers of all levels.

HELI- AND SNOCAT SKIING

In Whistler, **Mountain Heli-Sports** (☎ 604/932–2070), **Tyax Heli-Skiing** (☎ 604/932–7007), and **Whistler Heli-Skiing** (☎ 604/932–4105) have day trips with up to four glacier runs, or 12,000 vertical feet of skiing for experienced skiers; the cost is about $350.

Dining and Lodging

Dining

Dining at Whistler is informal; casual dress is appropriate everywhere.

For prices *see* Dining *in* Vancouver, *above.*

$$$ **Il Caminetto di Umberto; Trattoria di Umberto; Settebello's.** Umberto Menghi is among Vancouver's best-known restaurateurs because of his fabulously successful Italian restaurants. Now there are three in Whistler. Il Caminetto and the Trattoria are in the village, and Settebello's is in Whistler Creek, about 3 kilometers (2 miles) south. Umberto offers home-style Italian cooking in a relaxed atmosphere; he specializes in such pasta dishes as crab-stuffed cannelloni or a four-cheese lasagna. The Trattoria has a Tuscan-style rotisserie, highlighting a pasta dish served with a tray of chopped tomatoes, hot pepper, basil, olive oil, anchovies, and Parmesan so that you can mix it as spicy and flavorful as you like. Settebello's specialty is lean grilled beef and chicken, and Il Caminetto, perhaps the best restaurant in the Whistler area, is known for its veal, osso buco, and zabaglione. ✕ *Il Caminetto: 4242 Village Stroll,* ☎ *604/932–4442; Trattoria: Mountainside Lodge,* ☎ *604/932–5858; Settebello's: Whistler Creek Lodge,* ☎ *604/932–3000. Dinner reservations advised. AE, DC, MC, V.*

$$$ **Les Deux Gros.** The name means "the two fat guys," which may ex-
★ plain the restaurant's motto, "Never trust a skinny chef." Portions of the country French cuisine are generous indeed. The Alsatian onion pie, steak tartare, juicy rack of lamb, and salmon Wellington are all

superbly crafted and presented, and the service is friendly but unobtrusive. Just southwest of the village, this is the spot for a special romantic dinner; request one of the prime tables by the massive stone fireplace. ✗ *1200 Alta Lake Rd.,* ☎ *604/932–4611. Reservations advised. AE, MC, V. Closed lunch.*

$$$ **The Wildflower Cafe.** Although this is the main dining room of the Chateau Whistler, it's an informal, comfortable restaurant. Huge picture windows overlook the ski slopes. The rustic effect of the Chateau Whistler lobby continues in the Wildflower—more than 100 antique wood birdhouses decorate the room, and chairs and tables have a farmhouse look. An à la carte menu focuses on Northern Italian cuisine and fresh seafood; the restaurant also offers terrific breakfast, lunch, and dinner buffets that may include fresh crepes and omelets, sweet-potato-and-parsnip soup, barbecued salmon, smoked halibut, artichoke-and-mushroom salad, pepper salad, seafood pâté, pasta in a spicy tomato sauce, and cold meats. ✗ *Chateau Whistler Hotel,* ☎ *604/938–2033. Dinner reservations advised. AE, D, DC, MC, V.*

$$ **La Rúa.** One of the brightest lights on the Whistler dining scene is La
★ Rúa, on the ground floor of Le Chamois (*see* Lodging, *below*). Reddish flagstone floors and sponge-painted walls, a wine cellar behind a wrought iron door, modern oil paintings, and sconce lighting give the restaurant an intimate, Mediterranean ambience. Favorites from the Continental menu include Asian prawns, rack of lamb, and baked sea bass with fresh herbs. Start with the filling black-bean soup and end with the pleasing tiramisù. ✗ *4557 Blackcomb Way,* ☎ *604/932–5011. Reservations advised. AE, DC, MC, V. Closed lunch.*

Lodging

All lodgings can be booked through the **Whistler Resort Association** (☎ 604/932–4222 or 800/944–7853); summer rates are greatly discounted.

For price categories, *see* Lodging *in* Vancouver, *above.*

$$$$ **Chateau Whistler.** Whistler's most extravagant hotel is a large and friendly-looking fortress just outside the village. It was built and run by Canadian Pacific and is the same style as the Banff Springs Hotel and the Jasper Park Lodge. The marvelous lobby is filled with rustic Canadiana, handmade Mennonite rugs, enormous fireplaces, and enticing overstuffed sofas. Floor-to-ceiling windows in the lounge, the health club, and the Wildflower Cafe overlook the base of Blackcomb Mountain. The standard rooms, called premier, are average, but the suites are fit for royalty, with specially commissioned quilts and artwork, complemented by antique furnishings. Both the Wildflower Cafe (*see* Dining, *above*) and La Fiesta, a tapas bar, are very good choices for a meal. The resort added an extensive spa facility in late 1993; ask about reasonably priced retreat packages and summer rates that drop by 50%. ⌨ *4599 Chateau Blvd., Box 100, V0N 1B0,* ☎ *604/938–8000 or 800/441–1414 in the U.S. and Canada,* FAX *604/938–2055. 307 doubles, 36 suites. 2 restaurants, bar, indoor-outdoor pool, massage, saunas, steam rooms, golf course, 3 tennis courts, exercise room. AE, D, DC, MC, V.*

$$$$ **Le Chamois.** Sharing the prime ski-in, ski-out location at the base of
★ the Blackcomb runs is this elegant luxury hotel. Of the 62 spacious guest rooms with convenience kitchens, the most popular are the studios with Jacuzzi tubs set in front of the living room's bay windows overlooking the slopes and lifts. Guests can keep an eye on the action also from the glass elevators and the heated outdoor pool. ⌨ *4557 Blackcomb Way,* ☎ *604/932–8700 or 800/777–0185 in the U.S. and*

Canada, FAX 604/938–1888. 62 suites and studios. Restaurant, deli, pool, hot tub, exercise room, ski storage, coin laundry, village shuttle, free parking. AE, DC, MC, V.

$$ Pension Edelweiss. The Edelweiss, one of several charming and very European bed-and-breakfasts around Whistler, is within walking distance of Whistler Village. Rooms have a crisp, spic-and-span feel, in keeping with the Bavarian chalet style of the house; all have private baths and some have balconies and telephones. Each morning a different breakfast (included in the room rate) is served: Scandinavian, American, French, German. A bus stop just outside provides easy access to Whistler Village. 🖾 *7162 Nancy Greene Way, Box 850,* ☎ *604/932–3641 or 800/665–1892 (Whistler B&B Inns),* FAX *604/938–1746. 8 rooms, 1 suite. Hot tub, sauna. AE, MC, V.*

Whistler Essentials

Arriving and Departing

BY BUS

Maverick Coach Lines (☎ 604/255–1171, FAX 604/255–5700) has buses leaving every couple of hours for Whistler Village from the depot in downtown Vancouver. The fare is approximately $26 round-trip. During ski season, the last bus leaves Whistler at 9:45 PM.

Perimiter Bus Transportation (☎ 604/261–2299 or 800/663–4265, FAX 604/266–1628) has daily service, November–April and June–September from Vancouver Airport to Whistler. Reservations are necessary 24 hours in advance; the ticket booth is on the Arrivals level of the airport. The fare is around $26 one way.

BY CAR

Driving time from Seattle to Vancouver is about three hours. Whistler is 2–2½ hours north of Vancouver via Route 99, the Sea-to-Sky Highway.

By Train

BC Rail (☎ 604/984–5246) travels north from Vancouver to Whistler along a beautiful route. The Vancouver Bus Terminal and the North Vancouver Station are connected by bus shuttle. Rates are under $20 one way.

Important Whistler Addresses and Numbers

EMERGENCIES

Dial 0 for **police, ambulance,** or **poison control.**

VISITOR INFORMATION

Contact the **Whistler Resort Association** (4010 Whistler Way, Whistler V0N 1B4; in Whistler, ☎ 604/932–4222 or 800/944–7853 in the U.S. and Canada, FAX 604/932–7231). There is an information booth (☎ 604/932–2394) in Whistler Village at the front door of the Conference Center; hours fluctuate, so call before visiting.

A provincial government **Travel Infocentre** (☎ 604/932–5528) is on the main highway, about 1½ kilometers (1 mile) south of Whistler.

VANCOUVER ESSENTIALS

Arriving and Departing

By Bus

Greyhound Lines (☎ 604/662–3222 or 800/661–8747) is the largest bus line serving Vancouver. The Pacific Central Station (1150 Station

St.) is the depot. **Quick Shuttle** (☎ 604/244–3744 or 800/665–2122 in the U.S.) bus service runs between Vancouver and Seattle five times a day in winter and up to eight times a day in summer.

By Car
From the south, I–5 from Seattle becomes **Route 99** at the U.S.–Canada border. Vancouver is a three-hour drive from Seattle. Avoid border crossings during peak times: holidays and weekends.

Route 1, the **Trans-Canada Highway,** enters Vancouver from the east. To avoid traffic, arrive after rush hour (8:30 AM).

By Ferry
BC Ferries (☎ 604/277–0277, 24-hour recorded schedule information; 604/669–1211, reservations) operates two major ferry terminals outside Vancouver. From Tsawwassen to the south (an hour's drive from downtown), ferries sail to Victoria and Nanaimo on Vancouver Island and to the Gulf Islands (the small islands between the mainland and Vancouver Island). From Horseshoe Bay (30 minutes north of downtown), ferries sail a short distance across the strait and up the coast to Nanaimo on Vancouver Island.

By Plane
Vancouver International Airport is on an island about 14 kilometers (9 miles) south of downtown. Current expansion of the airport facilities is due for completion in 1996; in the meantime, all departing passengers are charged a $15 improvement fee. **American Airlines** (☎ 800/433–7300), Delta (☎ 604/221–1212), **Horizon Air** (☎ 800/547–9308), and **United** (☎ 800/241–6522) fly into the airport. The two major domestic airlines are **Air Canada** (☎ 800/776–3000) and **Canadian Airlines** (☎ 800/426–7000).

Air BC (☎ 604/688–5515) offers 30-minute harbor-to-harbor service (downtown Vancouver to downtown Victoria) several times a day. Planes leave from near the Bayshore Hotel. **Helijet Airways** (☎ 604/273–1414) has helicopter service from downtown Vancouver to downtown Victoria. The heliport is near Vancouver's Pan Pacific Hotel.

BETWEEN THE AIRPORT AND DOWNTOWN
The drive from the airport to downtown is 20–45 minutes, depending on the time of day. Airport hotels offer free shuttle service to and from the airport.

The **Vancouver Airporter Service** (☎ 604/261–2299) bus leaves the international and domestic arrival levels of the terminal building approximately every half hour stopping at major downtown hotels. It operates from 6 AM until midnight. The fare is $9 one-way and $15 round-trip.

Taxi stands are in front of the terminal building on domestic and international arrivals levels. Taxi fare to downtown is about $24. Area cab companies are **Yellow** (☎ 604/681–3311) and **Black Top** (☎ 604/681–2181).

Limousine service from **Airlimo** (☎ 604/273–1331) costs about the same as a taxi to downtown: The current rate is about $28.

By Train
The **Pacific Central Station** (1150 Station St.) is the hub for rail, bus, and SkyTrain service. The **VIA Rail** (☎ 800/561–8630) station is at Main Street and Terminal Avenue. VIA provides trans-continental service through Jasper to Toronto three times a week. Passenger trains leave

the **BC Rail** (☎ 604/631–3500) station in North Vancouver for Whistler and the interior of British Columbia.

Getting Around

By Bus

Exact change is needed to ride **B.C. Transit** (☎ 604/261–5100) buses: $1.50 adults, 75¢ for senior citizens and children 5–13. Books of 25 tickets are sold at convenience stores and newsstands; look for a red, white, and blue "Fare Dealer" sign. Day passes, good for unlimited travel after 9:30 AM, cost $4.50 for adults. They are available from fare dealers and any SeaBus or SkyTrain station. Transfers are valid for 90 minutes and allow travel in both directions.

By Car

Although no freeways cross Vancouver, rush-hour traffic is not yet horrendous. The worst rush-hour bottlenecks are the North Shore bridges, the George Massey Tunnel on Route 99 south of Vancouver, and Route 1 through Coquitlam and Surrey.

By Rapid Transit

Vancouver has a one-line, 25-kilometer (15-mile) rapid transit system called **SkyTrain,** which travels underground downtown and is elevated for the rest of its route to New Westminster and Surrey. Trains leave about every five minutes. Tickets, sold at each station from machines (correct change is not necessary), must be carried with you as proof of payment. You may use transfers from SkyTrain to SeaBus (*see below*) and BC Transit buses and vice versa.

By SeaBus

The **SeaBus** is a 400-passenger commuter ferry that crosses Burrard Inlet from the foot of Lonsdale (North Vancouver) to downtown. The ride takes 13 minutes and costs the same as the transit bus. With a transfer, connection can be made with any B.C. Transit bus or SkyTrain.

By Taxi

It is difficult to hail a cab in Vancouver; unless you're near a hotel, you'd have better luck calling a taxi service. Try **Yellow** (☎ 604/681–3311) or **Black Top** (☎ 604/681–2181).

Guided Tours

North Shore tours usually include any or several of the following: a gondola ride up Grouse Mountain, a walk across the Capilano Suspension Bridge, a stop at a salmon hatchery, the Lonsdale Quay Market, and a ride back to town on the SeaBus. Half-day tours cost anywhere from $30–$45 and are offered by **Landsea Tours** (☎ 604/255–7272), **Harbour Ferries** (☎ 604/687–9558), **Gray Line** (☎ 604/879–3363), and **Pacific Coach Lines** (☎ 604/662–7575).

Air

Tour the mountains and fjords of the North Shore by helicopter for around $200 per person (minimum of three people) for 50 minutes: **Vancouver Helicopters** (☎ 604/270–1484) flies from the Harbour Heliport downtown. Or see Vancouver from the air for $65 for 30 minutes: **Harbour Air**'s (☎ 604/688–1277) seaplanes leave from beside the Bayshore Hotel.

Boat

The Royal Hudson, Canada's only functioning steam train, heads along the mountainous coast up Howe Sound to the logging town of

Squamish. After a break to explore, you sail back to Vancouver via the MV *Britannia*. This excellent excursion costs about $55, takes 8 hours, and is organized by **Harbour Ferries** (☎ 604/687–9558). Reservations are advised.

The SS *Beaver* (☎ 604/682–7284), a replica of a Hudson Bay fur-trading steamship that ran aground here in 1888, offers two trips. One is the Harbour Sunset Dinner Cruise, a three-hour trip with a barbecue dinner; the other is a three-hour daytime trip up Indian Arm with salmon for lunch. Each is under $50 and reservations are necessary for both.

Harbour Ferries (☎ 604/687–9558) takes a 1½-hour tour of Burrard Inlet in a paddle wheeler; the tour operates Wednesday–Sunday and costs under $20.

Fraser River Connection (☎ 604/525–4465) will take you on a six-hour tour of a fascinating working river—past log booms, tugs, and houseboats. Between May and October, ride from New Westminster to Fort Langley aboard a convincing replica of an 1800s-era paddle wheeler for under $50 (half price for children).

Orientation

Gray Line (☎ 604/879–3363), the largest tour operator, offers the 3½-hour Grand City bus tour year-round. Departing from the Sandman Inn in summer and the Plaza of Nations in winter, the tour includes Stanley Park, Chinatown, Gastown, English Bay, and Queen Elizabeth Park and costs about $31. During the spring, summer, and fall, **Westcoast City and Nature Sightseeing** (☎ 604/451–5581) accommodates up to 24 people in vans that run a 3½-hour City Highlights Tour for $27 (pickup available from any downtown location). Using minibuses, **Vance Tours** (☎ 604/941–5660) offers a similar tour (3½ hours, $33) that includes a visit to the University of British Columbia, and a shorter city tour (2½ hours, $30).

The **Vancouver Trolley Company** (☎ 604/451–5581) runs turn-of-the-century–style trolleys through Vancouver from April to October on a 2-hour narrated tour of Stanley Park, Gastown, English Bay, Granville Island, Queen Elizabeth Park, and Chinatown, among other sights. A day pass allows you to complete one full circuit, getting off and on as often as you like. Start the trip at any of the sights and buy a ticket on board. Adult fare is around $20, children half that. During the rest of the year, the trolley runs the same circuit on a 2½-hour trip, but no on-off option is available. Between June and September, **Gray Line** (☎ 604/879–3363) offers a similar narrated tour aboard double-decker buses; passengers get on and off as they choose and are allowed to ride free the following day if they haven't had their fill. Adult fare is $18, children's $9.

Personal Guides

Early Motion Tours (☎ 604/687–5088) covers Vancouver in a Model-A Ford convertible. For about $60, up to four people can take an hour-long trip around downtown, Chinatown, and Stanley Park.

AAA Horse & Carriage (☎ 604/681–5115) has a 50-minute tour of Stanley Park, along the waterfront, and through a cedar forest and a rose garden for about $10.

Individualized V.I.P. tours are available from personal guide **Marcel Jonker** (☎ 604/261–9169).

Opening and Closing Times

Banks traditionally are open Monday–Thursday 10–3 and Friday 10–6, but many banks have extended hours and are open on Saturday, particularly outside of downtown.

Museums are generally open 10–5, including Saturday and Sunday. Most are open one evening a week as well.

Department store hours are Monday–Wednesday and Saturday 9:30–6, Thursday and Friday 9:30–9, and Sunday noon–5. Many smaller stores are also open Sunday.

Important Addresses and Numbers

Radio Stations

CFOX-FM (99.3), contemporary rock; **CFUN-AM (1410)/FM (100.1)**, oldies and hits; **CBU-AM (1370)**, CBS Radio—news and features; and **CJJR-FM (93.7)**, country music.

Consulates

United States (1075 W. Pender St., ☎ 604/685–4311); **United Kingdom** (800–1111 Melville St., ☎ 604/683–4421).

Dentist

The counterpart to Medicentre is **Dentacentre** (1055 Dunsmuir St., lower level, ☎ 604/669–6700), which is next door and is also open weekdays.

Emergencies

Call 911 for **police, fire** department, and **ambulance.**

Hospitals and Clinics

St. Paul's Hospital (1081 Burrard St., ☎ 604/682–2344), a downtown facility, has an emergency ward. **Medicentre** (1055 Dunsmuir St., lower level, ☎ 604/683–8138), a drop-in clinic on the lower level of the Bentall Centre, is open weekdays.

Late-Night Pharmacy

Shopper's Drug Mart (1125 Davie St., ☎ 604/685–6445) offers 24-hour service daily.

Road Emergencies

BCAA (☎ 604/293–2222) has 24-hour emergency road service for members of AAA or CAA.

Travel Agencies

American Express Travel Service (1040 W. Georgia St., ☎ 604/669–2813), **Mirage Holidays** (14–200 Burrard St., tel 604/685–4008), and **P. Lawson Travel** (409 Granville St., Suite 150, ☎ 604/682–4272).

Visitor Information

Vancouver Tourist Info Centre (200 Burrard St., ☎ 604/683–2000) provides maps and information about the city and is open July and August daily 8–6; the remainder of the year, weekdays 8:30–5, Saturday 9–5. A kiosk in Pacific Centre Mall is open daily in summer, Monday–Saturday 9:30–5, Sunday noon–5; in winter, Monday–Saturday 9–5. Eaton's department store downtown also has a tourist information counter that is open all year. **Discover B.C.** (☎ 800/663–6000) is available year round to assist with tourist information and reservations.

7 British Columbia

Canada's westernmost province harbors Pacific beaches, forested islands, year-round skiing, world-class fishing—a wealth of outdoor action and beauty. Its towns and cities, from Anglophile Victoria to the re-created Native American village of 'Ksan reflect the diversity of its inhabitants.

Updated by Melissa Rivers

BRITISH COLUMBIA, CANADA'S WESTERNMOST province, harbors Pacific beaches, forested islands, year-round skiing, world-class fishing—a wealth of outdoor action and beauty. The people of the province are a similarly heterogeneous mix: descendants of the original Native American peoples and 19th-century British and European settlers and more recent immigrants from Asia and Eastern Europe. From Anglophile Victoria to the recreated Native American village of 'Ksan, B.C.'s towns reflect the vigor of its inhabitants.

Canada's third-largest province (only Québec and Ontario are bigger), British Columbia occupies almost 10% of Canada's total surface area, stretching from the Pacific Ocean eastward to the province of Alberta, and from the U.S. border north to the Yukon and Northwest Territories. It spans more than 360,000 square miles, making it larger than every American state except Alaska.

But size alone doesn't account for British Columbia's popularity as a vacation destination. Even easterners, content in the fact that Ontario and Québec form the industrial heartland of Canada, admit that British Columbia is the most spectacular part of the nation, with salmon-rich waters, abundant coastal scenery, and stretches of snow-capped peaks.

The region's natural splendor has ironically become the source of conflict. For more than a century, logging companies have depended on the abundant supply of British Columbia timber, and whole towns are still centered on the industry. But environmentalists and many residents see the logging industry as a threat to the natural surroundings. Compromises have been achieved in recent years, but the issue is far from resolved.

The province used to be very British and predictable, reflecting its colonial heritage; but no longer. Vancouver (*see* Chapter 6), for example, has become an international city whose relaxed lifestyle is spiced by a rich and varied cultural scene embracing large Chinese, Japanese, Italian, and Greek communities. Even Vancouver Island's Victoria, which clings with restrained passion to British traditions and lifestyles, has undergone an international metamorphosis in recent years.

No matter how modern the province may appear, evidence remains of the earliest settlers: Pacific Coast natives (Haida, Kwakiutl, Nootka, Salish, and others) who occupied the land for more than 12,000 years before the first Europeans arrived en masse in the late 19th century. Today's native residents often face social barriers that have kept them from the mainstream of the province's rich economy. Although some have gained university educations and have fashioned careers, many are just now beginning to make demands on the nonnative population. In dispute are thousands of square miles of land claimed as aboriginal territory, some of which is within such major cities as Vancouver, Prince George, and Prince Rupert. Although the issue of ownership remains undecided, British Columbia's roots show throughout the province, from such native arts as wood-carved objects and etched-silver jewelry in small-town boutiques to authentic culinary delights from traditional recipes in big-city dining establishments.

EXPLORING

When you travel by car, keep in mind that more than three-quarters of British Columbia is mountainous terrain. Trips that appear relatively short may take longer, especially in the northern regions and along the coast, where roads are often narrow and winding. In certain areas—most of the uninhabited west coast of Vancouver Island, for example—roads do not exist.

British Columbia encompasses a vast range of climates, largely a result of the province's size, its mountainous topography, and its border on the Pacific. Vancouver Island, surrounded by Pacific waters, has relatively mild winters and summers (usually above 32°F winter, below 80°F summer), although winter brings frequent rains. Likewise, the northern coast around Prince Rupert and the Queen Charlotte Islands has wet winter months and few extremes in temperature. As you move inland, especially toward the Peace River region in the north, the climate becomes much colder. In the southern interior, the Okanagan Valley is arid, with temperatures dropping below freezing in winter and sometimes reaching 90°F in summer.

Tour 1: Victoria

Numbers in the margin correspond to points of interest on the Downtown Victoria map.

Victoria, originally Fort Victoria, was the first European settlement on Vancouver Island and is the oldest city on Canada's west coast. It was chosen in 1842 by James Douglas to be the Hudson's Bay Company's westernmost outpost, and it became the capital of British Columbia in 1868. Today it's a compact seaside town laced with tea shops and gardens. Though it's quite touristy during the high summer season, it's also at its prettiest, with flowers hanging from turn-of-the-century lampposts and strollers feasting on the beauty of Victoria's natural harbor.

1 A logical place to begin this tour is at the **Visitors Information Centre** on the waterfront. The bridge immediately south affords a grand view of the inner harbor and, across the water on Songhees Point, the 182½-foot **Welcome Totem** (now the tallest totem pole in the world) erected in 1994 for the Commonwealth Games. *812 Wharf St.,* ☎ *604/382–2127.* ☯ *July and Aug., daily 9–9; May, June, and Sept., daily 9–7; Oct.–Apr., daily 9–5.*

2 Just across the way is the **Empress Hotel,** which originally opened in 1908 and is a symbol of both the city and the Canadian Pacific Railway. Designed by Francis Rattenbury, whose works dot Victoria, the property is another of the great châteaus built by Canadian Pacific, still the owners, who also built the Château Frontenac in Québec City, Château Laurier in Ottawa, and Château Lake Louise in Alberta. The ingredients that made the 483-room hotel a tourist attraction in the past are still here. Stop in for tea—served at hour-and-a-half intervals during the afternoon. *721 Government St.,* ☎ *604/384–8111. No jeans, shorts, or T-shirts in the tea lobby.*

A short walk around the harbor leads you to the old CPR Steamship Terminal, also designed by Rattenbury, completed in 1924. Today it
3 is the **Royal London Wax Museum,** housing some 300 wax figures, including replicas of Queen Victoria, Elvis, and Marilyn Monroe. *470 Belleville St.,* ☎ *604/388–4461.* ☛ *$7 adults, $6.25 senior citizens, $6 students, $3 children 6–12.* ☯ *May–Aug., daily 9–9; Sept.–Apr., daily 9:30–5.*

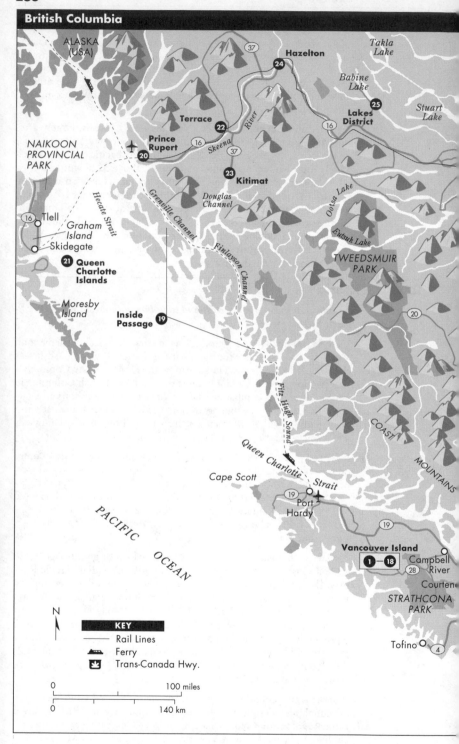

KEY
Rail Lines
Ferry
Trans-Canada Hwy.

0   100 miles

0   140 km

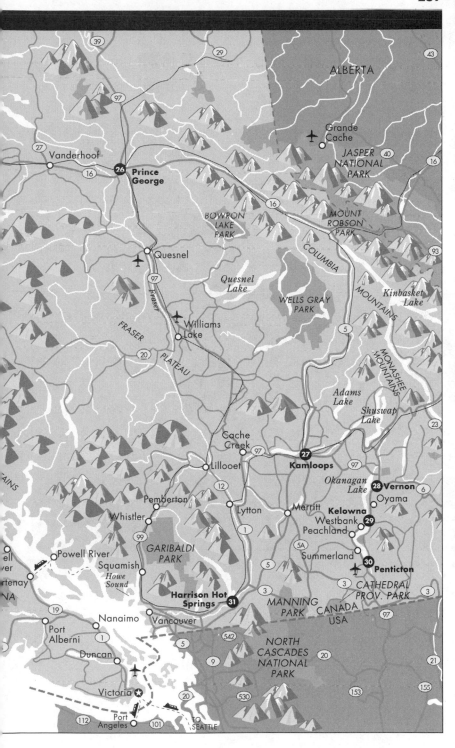

Downtown Victoria

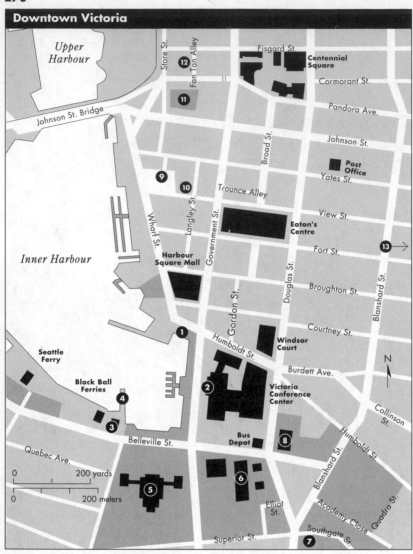

Upper Harbour

Inner Harbour

Johnson St. Bridge

Store St.

Fan Tan Alley

Fisgard St.

Centennial Square

Cormorant St.

Pandora Ave.

Broad St.

Johnson St.

Post Office

Trounce Alley

Yates St.

View St.

Wharf St.

Langley St.

Government St.

Eaton's Centre

Harbour Square Mall

Fort St.

Douglas St.

Broughton St.

Gordon St.

Courtney St.

Humboldt St.

Windsor Court

Blanshard St.

Seattle Ferry

Burdett Ave.

Black Ball Ferries

Victoria Conference Center

Collinson St.

Belleville St.

Bus Depot

Humboldt St.

Quebec Ave.

Elliot St.

Blanshard St.

Academy Close

Quadra St.

Superior St.

Southgate St.

0   200 yards

0   200 meters

N

Bastion Square, 9

Beacon Hill Park, 7

Chinatown, 12

Craigdarroch Castle, 13

Crystal Gardens, 8

Empress Hotel, 2

Maritime Museum of British Columbia, 10

Market Square, 11

Pacific Undersea Garden, 4

Parliament Buildings, 5

Royal British Columbia Museum, 6

Royal London Wax Museum, 3

Visitors Information Centre, 1

4 Next to the wax museum are the **Pacific Undersea Gardens,** where more than 5,000 marine specimens are on display in their natural habitat. You'll also see a short, rather hokey show of performing scuba divers and a giant Pacific octopus. Unfortunately, there are no washrooms, and the site is not wheelchair accessible. This one is usually a disappointment to all but the youngest tourists. *490 Belleville St., ☎ 604/382–5717. ☛ $6.50 adults, $6 senior citizens, $4.75 children 12–17, $3 children 5–11. ⊙ Oct.–May, daily 10–5; summer, daily 9–9. Closed Dec. 25. Shows run about every 45 min.*

5 Across Belleville Street is the **Parliament Buildings** complex. The stone structure, completed in 1897, dominates the inner harbor and is flanked by two statues: Sir James Douglas, who chose the location of Victoria, and Sir Matthew Baille Begbie, the man in charge of law and order during the gold-rush era. Atop the central dome is a gilded statue of Captain George Vancouver, who first sailed around Vancouver Island; a statue of Queen Victoria stands in front of the complex; and outlining the building at night are more than 3,000 lights. Another of Rattenbury's creations, the complex is a good example of the rigid symmetry and European elegance that characterize much of the city's architecture. The public can watch the assembly, when it's in session, from the galleries overlooking the Legislative Chamber. *501 Belleville St., ☎ 604/387–3046. ☛ Free. Tours run several times daily and are conducted in at least 4 languages in summer and 3 in winter. ⊙ Sept.–June, weekdays 8:30–5; summer, daily 8:30–5:30.*

6 Follow Belleville Street one block east to reach the **Royal British Columbia Museum,** easily the best attraction in Victoria. Here you can spend hours wandering through the centuries, back 12,000 years. In the prehistoric exhibit, you can actually smell the pines and hear the calls of mammoths and other ancient wildlife. Other exhibits allow you to explore a turn-of-the-century town, with trains rumbling past. In the Kwakiutl Indian longhouse, the smell of cedar envelops you, while piped-in potlatch songs tell the origins of the genuine ceremonial house before you. *675 Belleville St., ☎ 604/387–3014. ☛ Free Mon., Oct.–Apr.; otherwise $5 adults, $3 students and senior citizens, $2 children 6–18 and people with disabilities. ⊙ Sept.–June, daily 10–5:30; July and Aug., daily 9:30–7. Closed Dec. 25 and Jan. 1.*

Just behind the museum and bordering Douglas Street is **Thunderbird Park,** where totem poles and a ceremonial longhouse constructed by Kwakiutl Chief Mungo Martin stand in one corner of the garden of **Helmcken House,** the oldest house in British Columbia. Built in 1852 by pioneer doctor and statesman John Sebastian Helmcken, it is a treasure trove of history, from the early Victorian furnishings to an intriguing collection of 19th-century medical tools. Audio tours last 20 minutes. For further information on this and other heritage attractions in Victoria (Craigflower Farm and Schoolhouse, Emily Carr House, and Point Ellice House), call 604/387–4697. *Helmcken House, 10 Elliot St., ☎ 604/361–0021. ☛ $4 adults, $3 senior citizens and students, $2 children 6–12, $10 families. ⊙ May–Oct. daily 11–5, early to mid-Nov. noon–4, mid- to late Dec. by reservation.*

7 A walk east on Superior Street to Douglas Street will lead you to **Beacon Hill Park,** a haven for joggers, walkers, and cyclists. The park's southern lawns offer one of the best views of the Olympic Mountains and the Strait of Juan de Fuca. There are also lakes, walking paths, abundant flowers, a wading pool, a petting zoo, and an outdoor amphitheater for Sunday-afternoon concerts.

⑧ From the park, go north on Douglas Street and stop off at the **Crystal Gardens.** Opened in 1925 as the largest saltwater swimming pool in the British Empire, this glass-roof building—now owned by the provincial government—is home to flamingos, macaws, 75 varieties of other birds, hundreds of blooming flowers, and monkeys. At street level there are several boutiques and Rattenbury's Restaurant, one of Victoria's well-frequented establishments. *713 Douglas St.,* ☎ *604/381–1213.* ☛ *$6 adults, $4 senior citizens and children 6–16; discounted admission in winter.* ☉ *Oct.–Apr., daily 10–5:30; May–Sept., daily 9–9.*

From Crystal Gardens continue north on Douglas Street to View Street, then west to **Bastion Square,** with its gas lamps, restaurants, cobblestone streets, and small shops. This is the spot James Douglas chose as the original Fort Victoria in 1843 and the original Hudson's Bay Company trading post. Today fashion boutiques and restaurants occupy the old buildings. While you're here, you may want to stop in at what was Victoria's original courthouse but is now the **Maritime Museum of British Columbia.** Dugout canoes, model ships, Royal Navy charts, photographs, uniforms, and ship's bells chronicle Victoria's seafaring history. A seldom-used 100-year-old cage lift, believed to be the oldest in North America, ascends to the third floor. In 1996, however, a new museum is scheduled to open and replace this facility. *28 Bastion Sq.,* ☎ *604/385–4222.* ☛ *$5 adults, $4 senior citizens, $3 students, $2 children 6–11.* ☉ *Daily 9:30–4:30. Closed Dec. 25 and 26 and Jan. 1.*

⑪ West of Government Street, between Pandora Avenue and Johnson Street, is **Market Square,** which offers a variety of specialty shops and boutiques and is considered one of the most picturesque shopping districts in the city. At the turn of the century this area—once part of Chinatown—provided everything a visitor desired: food, lodging, entertainment. Today the square has been restored to its original, pre-1900s character.

⑫ Just around the corner from Market Square is Fisgard Street, the heart of **Chinatown,** one of the oldest in Canada. It was the Chinese who were responsible for building much of the Canadian Pacific Railway in the 19th century, and their influences still mark the region. If you enter Chinatown from Government Street, you'll walk under the elaborate **Gate of Harmonious Interest,** made from Taiwanese ceramic tiles and decorative panels. Along the street, merchants display fragile paper lanterns, embroidered silks, imported fruits, and vegetables. **Fan Tan Alley,** just off Fisgard Street, holds claim not only to being the narrowest street in Canada but also to having been the gambling and opium center of Chinatown, where mah-jongg, fan-tan, and dominoes games were played.

⑬ A 15-minute walk or a short drive east on Fort Street will take you to Joan Crescent, where **Craigdarroch Castle** stands. This lavish mansion was built as the home of British Columbia's first millionaire, Robert Dunsmuir, who oversaw coal mining for the Hudson's Bay Company. (He died before the castle's completion in about 1890.) Converted into a museum depicting turn-of-the-century lifestyle, the castle is strikingly authentic, with elaborately framed landscape paintings, stained-glass windows, carved woodwork—precut in Chicago for Dunsmuir and sent by rail—and rooms for billiards and smoking. The location offers a wonderful view of downtown Victoria from the fourth-floor tower. *1050 Joan Crescent,* ☎ *604/592–5323.* ☛ *$6 adults, $5 students, $2 children 6–11.* ☉ *Mid-June–early Sept., daily 9–7:30; mid-Sept.–mid-June, daily 10–4:30.*

Tour 2: Vancouver Island

Vancouver Island, the largest island on the west coast, stretches 450 kilometers (280 miles) from Victoria in the south to Cape Scott. Some 97% of the population live between Victoria and Campbell River (halfway up the island); 50% of them live in Victoria itself. The western side is wild, often inhospitable, with just a handful of small settlements. Virtually all of the island's human habitation is on the eastern coast, where the weather is gentler and the topography is low-lying.

The cultural heritage of the island is from the Kwakiutl, Nootka, and Coastal Salish native groups. Native art and cultural centers flourish throughout the region, especially in the lower end of the island, enabling visitors to catch a glimpse of contemporary native culture.

Mining, logging, and tourism are the important island industries. Environmental issues, such as the logging practices of British Columbia's lumber companies, are becoming important to islanders—both native and nonnative. Residents are working to establish a balance between the island's wilderness and its economy.

Numbers in the margin correspond to points of interest on the Vancouver Island map.

① Beginning your driving tour from Victoria (*see* Tour 1, *above*), take Route 14 west to **Sooke** (26 miles, or 42 kilometers, west of Victoria), a logging, fishing, and farming community. **East Sooke Park,** on the east side of the harbor, offers 3,500 acres of beaches, hiking trails, and meadows dotted with wildflowers. You can also visit the **Sooke Region Museum and Travel Infocentre,** where displays of Salish and Nootka crafts and artifacts from 19th-century Sooke occasionally compete with barbecued salmon and strawberry shortcake on the front lawn in summer. *2070 Phillips Rd., Box 774, V0S 1N0, ☎ 604/642-6351. ☛ Free; donations accepted. ☯ Summer, daily 9–6; winter, Tues.–Sun. 9–5.*

TIME OUT **Seventeen Mile House** (5121 Sooke Rd., Sooke, ☎ 604/642-5942) is on the road to Sooke from Victoria. Stop here for British pub fare, a beer, or fresh local seafood. Built as a hotel, the house is an education in turn-of-the-century island architecture.

If you're adventurous, continue on Route 14 west and pick up the logging road from Port Renfrew back to the east coast; conditions on the gravel road may be hazardous, especially on weekdays with truck traffic. The more reliable route backtracks to Victoria, then follows the Trans-Canada Highway up the eastern coast toward Nanaimo, the midisland B.C. Ferries terminal point. On your way you'll pass through **②** **Duncan** (about 60 kilometers, or 37 miles, north of Victoria), nicknamed City of Totems for the many totem poles that dot the small community. The two carvings behind the City Hall are worth a short trip off the main road.

Duncan is also home to the **Native Heritage Centre.** Covering 13 acres on the banks of the Cowichan River, the center features a native longhouse, a theater, occasional interpretive dance presentations, an arts-and-crafts gallery that focuses on carvings and weaving traditions, and native fare served in the Bighouse Restaurant. *200 Cowichan Way, Duncan, ☎ 604/746-8119. ☛ $6.75 adults, $6.25 senior citizens and students, $2 children 6–12, children 5 and under free, $16 families. ☯ Mid-May–mid Oct., daily 9:30–5:30; mid-Oct.–mid-May, daily 10–4:30.*

Vancouver Island

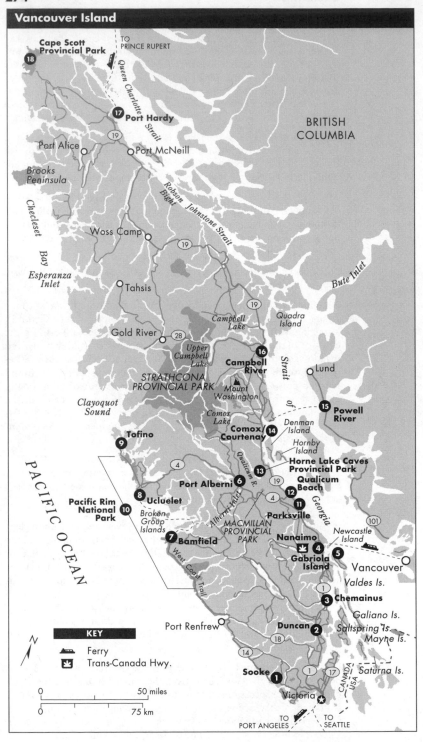

TO PRINCE RUPERT

Cape Scott Provincial Park
18

BRITISH COLUMBIA

17 **Port Hardy**

Port Alice

(19)

Port McNeill

Brooks Peninsula

Robson Johnstone Strait

Queen Charlotte Strait

Checleset Bay

Esperanza Inlet

Woss Camp

(19)

Bute Inlet

Tahsis

(19)

Campbell Lake

Quadra Island

Gold River *(28)*

Upper Campbell Lake

STRATHCONA PROVINCIAL PARK

16 **Campbell River**

Strait

Lund

Clayoquot Sound

Mount Washington ▲

Comox Lake

15 **Powell River**

of

9 **Tofino**

Comox Courtenay **14**

Denman Island

8 **Ucluelet**

(4)

Port Alberni **6**

Qualicum R.

Hornby Island

Horne Lake Caves Provincial Park

13

(19)

Qualicum Beach **12**

Pacific Rim National Park **10**

Broken Group Islands

Alberni Inlet

(4)

11

Parksville

Georgia

(101)

PACIFIC OCEAN

7 **Bamfield**

MACMILLAN PROVINCIAL PARK

Nanaimo

Newcastle Island

West Coast Trail

4
Gabriola Island

5

Vancouver

Valdes Is.

3 **Chemainus**

(1)

Port Renfrew

Duncan **2**

Galiano Is.

Saltspring Is.

Mayne Is.

(18)

(14)

Saturna Is.

Sooke **1**

(1) *(17)*

CANADA / USA

KEY

⛴ Ferry

🍁 Trans-Canada Hwy.

Victoria ✪

0 —————— 50 miles

0 —————— 75 km

TO PORT ANGELES   TO SEATTLE

Also in Duncan is the **B.C. Forest Museum.** More a park than a museum, it spans some 100 acres, combining indoor and outdoor exhibits that focus on the history of forestry in British Columbia. You ride an original steam locomotive around the property and over an old wood trestle bridge. The exhibits feature logging and milling equipment. *R.R. 4, Trans-Canada Hwy.,* ☎ *604/746–1251,* FAX *604/746–1487.* ☛ *$6 adults, $5 senior citizens and children 13–18, $3 children 6–12, children 5 and under free.* ☉ *May–Sept., daily 9:30–6; off-season, by appointment.*

③ Just north of Duncan, **Chemainus** is known for the bold epic murals that decorate its landscape. Once dependent on the lumber industry, the small town began to revitalize itself in the early 1980s when its mill closed down. Since then, more than 30 murals depicting local historical events have been painted around town by international artists. Footprints on the sidewalk lead you on a self-guided tour of the murals. Restaurants, shops, tea rooms, coffee bars, art galleries, antiques dealers, and the new Chemainus Theater (☎ 604/246–9820 or 800/565–7738) have added to the town's growth.

④ **Nanaimo,** across the Strait of Georgia from Vancouver, is about an hour's drive from Victoria. Throughout the region, there are petroglyphs (rock carvings) representing humans, birds, wolves, lizards, sea monsters, and supernatural creatures. The **Nanaimo District Museum** (100 Cameron St., ☎ 604/753–1821) will give you information about local carvings. Eight kilometers (5 miles) south of town at **Petroglyph Provincial Park,** you can see designs carved thousands of years ago along the marked trails that begin at the parking lot.

⑤ From Nanaimo you can take a 20-minute ferry ride to rustic, rural **Gabriola Island,** which has lodging; and a 10-minute ferry ride to **Newcastle Island,** where you can picnic, ride your bicycle, walk on trails leading past old mines and quarries, and catch glimpses of deer, rabbits, and eagles.

⑥ As you continue north on Route 19, you can branch off on Route 4 west to Port Alberni and the lower west-coast towns. **Port Alberni,** about an 80-kilometer (49-mile) drive from Nanaimo, is mainly a pulp- and sawmill town and a stopover on the way to Ucluelet and Tofino. The salmon-rich waters attract fishermen. While you're here, consider a breathtaking trip down the Alberni Inlet to Barkley Sound aboard the *Lady Rose,* a Scottish ship built in 1937. The *Lady Rose* leaves the Argyle Street dock Tuesday, Thursday, and Saturday (and Friday and Sunday **⑦** in July and August) for the four-hour cruise to **Bamfield,** a remote village of about 200. Bamfield's seaside boardwalk affords an uninterrupted view of ships heading up the inlet to Port Alberni. The town is well equipped to handle overnight visitors. The west coast is invaded every summer by fishermen, kayakers, scuba divers, and hikers. Bamfield is also a good base for boating trips to the Broken Group Islands and hikes along the West Coast Trail (*see below*). From early June to mid-September the *Lady Rose* and *Francis Barkley* sail for Ucluelet (*see below*) on Monday, Wednesday, and Friday. It's a unique trip and deserves all the accolades it receives. *Argyle St. dock,* ☎ *604/723–8313 or 800/663–7192 for reservations Apr.-Sept. Bamfield fare: $36; Broken Group Islands fare: $38; Ucluelet fare: $40. Sailings depart daily at 8 AM.*

North of Bamfield are Ucluelet and Tofino—the whale-watching capitals of Canada, if not of the whole west coast of North America. The two towns are quite different in character, though both are relaxed in **⑧** winter and swell to several times their sizes in summer. **Ucluelet,** which in the native language means "people with a safe landing place," is totally focused on the sea. Fishing, water tours, and whale-watching are the primary activities. Whale-watching is big business, with a variety of charter companies that take tourist boats to greet the 20,000 gray whales that pass close to Ucluelet on their migration to the Bering Sea every March–May. Sometimes you can even see the migrating whales from the Ucluelet shore.

⑨ Tofino, on the other hand, is more commercial, with beachfront resorts, motels, and several unique B&Bs. But the surrounding area remains natural. You can walk along the beach discovering caves, cruise around the ancient forests of Meares Island, or take an hour-long water taxi to the hot springs north of town.

★ **⑩** Ucluelet and Tofino bookend the Long Beach section of the **Pacific Rim National Park** (Box 280, Ucluelet, V0R 3A0, ☎ 604/726–7721, FAX 604/726–4720), the first national marine park in Canada. The park itself comprises three separate areas—Long Beach, the Broken Group Islands, and the West Coast Trail. Each accommodates a specific interest.

The **Long Beach** unit gets its name from an 11-kilometer (7-mile) strip of hard-packed white sand strewn with twisted driftwood, shells, and the occasional Japanese glass fishing float. It is a favorite spot in summer, and you often have to fight heavy traffic along the twisting 85 kilometers (53 miles) of Route 4 from Port Alberni.

The 100 **Broken Group Islands** can be reached only by boat. Many commercial charter tours are available from Ucluelet, at the southern end of Long Beach, and from Bamfield and Port Alberni. The islands and their waters are alive with sea lions, seals, and whales. The sheltered lagoons of Gibraltar, Jacques, and Hand islands offer protection and good boating conditions, but go with a guide.

The third element of the park, the **West Coast Trail** (*see* Hiking, *below*), stretches along the coast from Bamfield to Port Renfrew. After the SS *Valencia* ran aground in 1906, killing all but 30 of the crew and passengers, the Canadian government constructed the lifesaving trail to help future victims of shipwrecks reach safe ground. The trail remains, with demanding bogs, steep slopes and gullies, cliffs (with ladders), slippery boardwalks, and insects. Although it presents many obstacles for hikers, the rewards are the panoramic views of the sea, the dense rain forest, sandstone cliffs with waterfalls, and wildlife that includes gray whales and seals.

Heading back to the east coast from Port Alberni, stop off at **Cathedral Grove,** in MacMillan Provincial Park on Route 4. Walking trails lead you past Douglas fir trees and western red cedars, some as much as 800 years old. Their remarkable height creates a spiritual effect, as though you were gazing at a cathedral ceiling. Another stop along the way is **Butterfly World** (Rte. 4, Box 36, Coombs, V0R 1MO, ☎ 604/248–7026), an enclosed tropical garden housing a massive collection of exotic, free-flying tropical butterflies.

⑪ At the junction of Routes 4 and 19 is **Parksville**—one of the east island's primary resort areas, where lodges and waterfront motels cater to families, campers, and boaters. In **Rathtrevor Provincial Park** (☎ 604/248–9449), 1½ kilometers (about 1 mile) south of Parksville, high tide brings ashore the warmest ocean water in British Columbia, so plan to swim then.

⑫ Just 12 kilometers (7 miles) north of Parksville is **Qualicum Beach,** known largely for its salmon fishing and opportunities for beachcombing along the long, sandy beaches. The nonprofit **Old School House Gallery and Art Centre** (122 Fern Rd. W, ☏ 604/752–6133), with nine working studios, shows and sells the work of local artists and artisans.

⑬ Continue north, then head west off the highway and follow signs for about 15 kilometers (9 miles) to Horne Lake and the **Horne Lake Caves Provincial Park.** Three of the six caves are open at all times. If you decide to venture in, bring along a flashlight, warm clothes, and a hard hat, and be prepared to bend and even crawl. Riverbend Cave, 1,259 feet long, requires ladders and ropes in some parts, and can only be explored with a guided tour. Spelunking lessons and tours are offered for all levels, from beginner to advanced. ☏ *604/248–7829. Fees for tours vary depending on ability. Reservations advised for tours.*

Between the Horne Lake turnoff and the twin cities of Comox and Courtenay is tiny Buckley Bay, where ferries leave for **Denman Island,** with connecting service to **Hornby Island.** Denman offers old-growth forests and long sandy beaches, while Hornby's spectacular beaches have earned it the nickname the Undiscovered Hawaii of British Columbia. Many artists have settled on the islands, establishing studios for pottery, jewelry, wood carving, and sculpture.

⑭ **Comox** and **Courtenay** are near **Strathcona Provincial Park** and commonly provide a base for Mt. Washington skiers in winter. Strathcona, the largest provincial park on Vancouver Island, encompasses **Mt. Golden Hinde,** at 7,218 feet the island's highest mountain; and **Della Falls,** Canada's highest waterfall, reaching 1,443 feet. The park's multitude of lakes and 161 campsites attract summer canoers, fishermen, and wilderness campers, and the **Strathcona Park Lodge and Outdoor Education Center,** well known for its wilderness-skills programs, has information on the park's facilities. *Education Center, Rte. 28, on Upper Campbell Lake, about 45 km (28 mi) west of Rte. 19, Box 2160, Campbell River, V9W 5C9,* ☏ *604/286–3122. Hours vary; call ahead.*

⑮ From Comox, you can take a 75-minute ferry ride east across the Strait of Georgia to **Powell River,** a city established around the MacMillan pulp-and-paper mill, which opened in 1912. Renowned as a year-round salmon-fishing destination, the mainland Sunshine Coast town has 30 regional lakes that offer exceptional trout fishing, as well. For information contact **Powell River Travel Info Center** (4690 Marine Dr., ☏ 604/485–4701).

⑯ **Campbell River** is ringed by shopping centers that make it look like a free-zoned mess. But people don't come here for the aesthetics, they come for the fish; some of the biggest salmon ever caught on a line have been landed just off the coast here. At the mouth of the town's namesake, you can try for membership in Campbell River's Tyee Club, which would allow you to fish in a specific area and possibly land a giant chinook. Requirements for membership in the club include registering and landing a tyee (a spring salmon weighing 30 pounds or more). Coho salmon and cutthroat trout are also plentiful in the river. For information contact **Campbell River Tourism** (1235 Shoppers Row, Box 482, Campbell River, V9W 5C1, ☏ 604/286–1616 or 800/463–4386).

Pods of resident Orcas live nearby year-round in Johnstone Strait; and in Robson Bight they like using the beaches to rub against. Because of their presence, Robson Bight has been made into an ecological preserve: Whales there must not be disturbed by human observers. Some of the island's best whale-watching tours, however, are conducted nearby, out of Telegraph Cove, a village built on pilings over water.

⑰ Farther north is **Port Hardy,** the departure and arrival point for B.C. Ferries going through the Inside Passage to and from Prince Rupert, the coastal port serving the Queen Charlotte Islands. In summer the town can be crowded, so book your accommodations well in advance. Ferry reservations for the trip between Port Hardy and Prince Rupert should also be made well in advance.

⑱ To continue to the northernmost point on Vancouver Island, drive about 60 kilometers (about 37 miles) on logging roads to reach **Cape Scott Provincial Park,** a wilderness camping region designed for well-equipped and experienced hikers. At Sand Neck, a strip of land that joins the cape to the mainland of the island, you can see both the eastern and the western shores at once.

Tour 3: The Gulf Islands

Traveling up the northeastern coastline of Vancouver Island in the late 1790s, Captain George Vancouver dubbed the expansive body of water on which he sailed the Gulf of Georgia, thinking that it led to open sea. While the name of the waterway was later changed to the Strait of Georgia when further exploration revealed that the British Columbia mainland lay to the east, the islands dotting the strait continue to be known as the Gulf Islands.

Of the hundreds of islands in this strait, the most popular are Galiano, Mayne, North and South Pender, Saturna, and Salt Spring. A temperate Mediterranean climate (warmer, with half the rainfall of Vancouver), scenic beaches, towering promontories, rolling pasturelands, and virgin forests are common to all, but each also has its unique flavor. Marine birds are numerous, and unusual vegetation such as arbutus trees (also known as madronas, a leafy evergreen with red peeling bark) and Garry oaks differentiate the islands from other areas around Vancouver. Writers, artists, craftspeople, weekend cottagers, and retirees take full advantage of the undeveloped islands.

For a first visit to the Gulf Islands, make a stopover on Salt Spring Island, the most commercialized of the southern islands, or on more subdued, pastoral Mayne Island. Their proximity to Vancouver make each feasible for a one- or two-day trip. Free maps are available on the ferry or in island stores.

Mayne

Middens of clam and oyster shells give evidence that tiny **Mayne Island**—only 21 square kilometers, or 8½ square miles—was inhabited as early as 5,000 years ago. It later became the stopover point for miners headed from Victoria to the gold fields of Fraser River and Barkersville, and by the mid-1800s had developed into the communal center of the inhabited Gulf Islands, with the first school, post office, police lockup, church, and hotel. Farm tracts and orchards established in the 1930s and 1940s and worked by Japanese farmers until their internment during World War II continue to thrive today, and a farmer's market is open each Saturday during harvest season. There are few stores, restaurants, or historic sites here, but Mayne's manageable size (even if you're on a bicycle) and slower pace make it very popular.

Starting at the ferry dock at **Village Bay,** head toward Miners Bay via Village Bay Road. About half a mile from the ferry landing on the left is the unmarked path to **Helen Point** (pull off on the shoulder near the grouping of power lines that cross the road), previously a native reservation, which currently has no inhabitants. You'll pass middens by the bay and log cabin remains in the woods on the hour-long hike out to

Helen Point, where you can look out across Active Pass (named for the turbulent waters).

A quarter mile farther on the right side of Village Bay Road is the carved wooden archway marking the entrance to **Mount Parke,** which was declared a wilderness park in 1989. Drive as far as the gate and the sign that reads NO VEHICLES PAST THIS POINT. From here it's a 15- to 20-minute hike to the highest point on the island and a stunning, almost 360-degree view of Vancouver, Active Pass, and Vancouver Island.

If you continue on Village Bay Road, head toward **Miners Bay,** a little town 1.2 miles away. Here, you'll find **Plumbers Pass Lockup,** built in 1896 as a jail and now a minuscule museum chronicling the island's history (open July–August only).

From Miners Bay head east on Georgia Point Road to **St. Mary Magdalene Church,** a pretty stone chapel built in 1898 that now doubles as an Anglican and United church. The graveyard beyond is also interesting; generations of islanders–the Bennets, Georgesons, Maudes, and Deacons (whose names are all over the Mayne Island map)–are buried here. Across the road, a stairway leads down to the beach.

At the end of Georgia Point Road is the **Active Pass Lighthouse,** built in 1855, which still signals ships into the busy waterway. The grassy grounds, open to the public every day from 1 to 3, are great for picnicking.

Head back down Georgia Point Road and turn left on Waugh Road, which turns into Campbell Bay Road. There's a great pebble beach for beach combing at shallow (and therefore warmer) **Campbell Bay.** Look for a pull-out on the left just past the bottom of the hairpin turn. A fence post marks the entrance to the path leading to the beach. Campbell Bay Road ends at Fernhill Road; turn right there and you'll end up back in Miners Bay.

Salt Spring

Named for the saltwater springs at its north end, Salt Spring is the largest and most developed of the Gulf Islands. Among its first nonnative settlers were black Americans who came here to escape slavery in the 1850s. The agrarian tradition they and other immigrants established remains strong, but tourism and art now support the local economy. A government wharf, two marinas, and a waterfront shopping complex at Ganges serve a community of more than 8,500 residents.

After coming into either Fulford Harbour or Long Harbour by ferry, head to **Ganges,** a pedestrian-oriented seaside village and the island's cultural and commercial center, where dozens of smart boutiques, galleries, and restaurants await exploration. **Mouat's Trading Company** (Fulford–Ganges Rd.), built in 1912 and still functioning as a community store, is worth a peek. Ganges is also the site of **ArtCraft,** a summer-long art, crafts, theater, music, and dance festival. Dozens of working **artists' studios** are open to the public here; pick up a studio tour map at the Chamber of Commerce on Lower Ganges Road.

There are bargains galore to be had at both of the island's **Saturday markets** held each year between April and October. Fresh produce, seafood, crafts, clothing, herbs and aromatherapy mixtures, candles, toys, home-canned items and more are available at the two markets; one is at the top of the hill (next to the Harbour House) overlooking Ganges Harbour, the other in the center of town between Fulford–Ganges Road and Centennial Park.

From Ganges, you can circle the northern tip of the island by bike or car (on Vesuvius Bay Road, Sunset Road, North End and North Beach Roads, Walker Hook Road, and Robson Road) past fields and peek-a-boo views of Stuart Channel, Houston Passage, and Trincomali Channel. You can also cut the trip short by returning to town on North End Road past **St. Mary Lake,** your best bet for warm-water swimming.

The summit of **Mt. Maxwell Provincial Park,** near the center of Salt Spring, affords spectacular views of south Salt Spring, Vancouver Island, and other Gulf Islands. It's also a great picnic spot. Look for the sign on Fulford–Ganges Road; the last portion of the drive on Mt. Maxwell Road is steep, winding, and unpaved. From there, follow Fulford–Ganges Road south, then turn east on Beaver Point Road to reach **Ruckle Provincial Park,** site of an 1872 heritage homestead and extensive fields still being farmed by the Ruckle family. The park also has camping and picnic spots and trails leading to rocky headlands.

Tour 4: North of Vancouver Island

Numbers in the margin correspond to points of interest on the British Columbia map.

⑲ The 274-nautical-mile **Inside Passage,** between Port Hardy on northern Vancouver Island and Prince Rupert, is a sheltered marine highway that follows a series of natural channels behind protective islands along the green-and-blue shaded British Columbia coast. The undisturbed landscape of rising mountains and humpbacked islands has a prehistoric look that leaves an indelible impression.

After a short segment in the open ocean, the 410-foot MV *Queen of the North* ducks in behind Calvert Island into Fitz Hugh Sound. From there, its route is protected from ocean swells all the way through Finlayson and Grenville channels, which are flanked by high, densely wooded mountains that rise steeply, in places, from narrow gorges. The *Queen of the North,* carrying up to 800 passengers and 157 vehicles, takes 15 hours (almost all in daylight during summer sailings) to make the Port Hardy to Prince Rupert trip. The ship has plenty of deck space plus lounge areas, a self-serve cafeteria, and a satisfactory restaurant that offers a plentiful buffet. Day-use cabins are available for an additional fee. Children can play in the Captain Kids Room. *B.C. Ferries, 1112 Fort St., Victoria V8V 4V2, ☎ 604/386–3431. Cost varies according to cabin, vehicle, and season. Reservations required for the cruise and advised for hotel accommodations at ports of call. Oct.–Apr. sailings are once weekly; May sailings twice-weekly; June–Sept. sailings daily, departing on alternate days from Port Hardy and Prince Rupert; departure time 7:30 AM, arrival time 10:30 PM. Schedule and fares subject to change.*

An alternative to the ferry cruise along the Inside Passage is one of the more expensive luxury-liners that sail along the British Columbia coast from Vancouver to Alaska.

⑳ **Prince Rupert,** the final stop on the B.C. Ferries route through the Inside Passage, is about 750 air kilometers (465 miles) northwest of Vancouver, though it takes more than 20 hours to drive the mountainous 1,500 kilometers (936 miles). Prince Rupert has a mild but wet climate, so take rain gear.

The town lives off fishing, fish processing, logging, saw- and pulp-mill operations, and deep-sea shipping. Prince Rupert is also a place where British Columbia's cultural heritage asserts itself. The **Museum of**

Northern British Columbia has one of the province's finest collections of coastal native art, some artifacts dating back 10,000 years. Native artisans carve totem poles in the carving shed and, in summer, the museum runs a 2½-hour boat tour of the harbor and Metlakatla native village. *1st Ave. and McBride St., Prince Rupert,* ☎ *604/624–3207.* ☛ *Free; donations accepted.* ⊙ *Sept.–May, Mon.–Sat. 10–5; June–Aug., Mon.–Sat. 9–9, Sun. 9–5.*

From Prince Rupert you can continue on to explore either the Alaskan Panhandle, the Queen Charlotte Islands, or interior British Columbia. To proceed north through the Alaskan waterways to Skagway, board the **Alaska Marine Highway System ferry** (☎ 604/627–1744 or 800/642–0066), which docks alongside the *Queen of the North* in Prince Rupert. Alaska ferries travel this route about four times a week in the summer, twice a week the rest of the year.

㉑ A popular vacation destination, the **Queen Charlotte Islands,** or Misty Islands, though once the remote preserve of the Haida natives, are now easily accessible by ferry. Today the Haida make up only one sixth of the population, but they continue to infuse the island with a sense of the Haida past and contribute to the logging and fishing industries, as well as to tourism. Haida elders lead tours—an essential service if you want to reach the isolated, abandoned villages. Limited accommodations make it necessary to reserve guest rooms well in advance.

The *Queen of Prince Rupert* (☎ 604/386–3431), a B.C. Ferries ship, sails six times a week between late May and September (three times a week the rest of the year), and can easily accommodate recreational vehicles. Crossing the Hecate Strait from Prince Rupert to Skidegate, near Queen Charlotte on Graham Island, takes about six hours. Schedules vary and reservations are required, so call ahead. The **MV Kwuna,** another B.C. Ferries ship, connects Skidegate Landing to Alliford Bay on Moresby Island, with 12 20-minute sailings daily. Access to smaller islands off Graham Island (the northernmost and largest of the group of 150) and Moresby Island is by boat or air; plans should be made in advance through a travel agent.

In the Queen Charlottes, 150 kilometers (93 miles) of paved road, most of it on Graham Island, connect Queen Charlotte in the south to Masset in the north. Some of the other islands are laced with gravel roads, most of which can be driven with any sturdy car or RV. The rugged, rocky west coast of the archipelago faces the ocean; the east coast has many broad sandy beaches. Throughout, the mountains and shores are often shrouded in fog and rain-laden clouds, adding to the islands' mystery.

★ **Naikoon Provincial Park** (☎ 604/557–4390), in the northeast corner of Graham, preserves a large section of unique wilderness, where low-lying swamps, pine and cedar forests, lakes, beaches, trails, and wildlife combine to create an intriguing environment. Take the 5-kilometer (3-mile) walk from the Tlell Picnic Site to the beach, and on to the bow section of the old wooden shipwreck of the *Pezuta*, a 1928 log-hauling vessel. On the southern end of Graham Island, the **Queen Charlotte Islands Museum** has a small but impressive display of Haida totem poles, masks, and carvings of both silver and argillite (hard black slate). A natural-history exhibit gives interesting background on the wildlife of the islands. *Box 1373, Skidegate V0T 1S1,* ☎ *604/559–4643.* ☛ *$2.50 adults; children 13 and under free.* ⊙ *Apr.–late Oct., weekdays 9–5, weekends 1–5; winter, Wed.–Sun. 1–5.*

If you have time on Graham Island, drive up to Old Masset on the northern coast, site of the **Ed Jones Haida Museum.** Exhibits here include totems and artifacts. Nearby, artists sell their work from their homes. South of Graham, in and around South Moresby National Park Reserve, lie most of the better-known abandoned Haida villages, which are accessible by water. Visiting some of the villages requires at least several days' travel time and lots of planning for the wilderness. You need to contact Parks Canada (☎ 604/559–8818) before you go.

For more information on the Queen Charlotte Islands, contact the **Queen Charlotte Islands Travel Information Center** (Box 337, Queen Charlotte V0T 1S0, ☎ 604/559–4742, FAX 604/559–8188).

㉒ ㉓ ㉔ To see interior British Columbia, take Route 16 east from Prince Rupert. En route you'll pass through or near such communities as **Terrace,** with a hot-springs complex at the Mt. Layton Resort, skiing at Shames Mountain, and excellent fishing in the Skeena River; and **Kitimat** (on Route 37, south of Terrace), at the head of the Douglas Channel, where the fishing is superb. At **Hazelton,** a town rich in the culture of the Gitksan and Wet'suwet'en peoples, you must visit **'Ksan,** just outside town, a re-created Gitksan village. The elaborately painted community of seven longhouses is a replica of the one that stood on the same site when the first explorers arrived in the 19th century. The **National Exhibition Centre and Museum** displays works and artifacts from the Upper Skeena River region. A workshop, often used by 'Ksan artists, is open to the public, and three other longhouses can be visited: One features contemporary masks and robes, another has song-and-dance dramas in the summer. A gift shop and museum are on the grounds. *National Exhibition Centre: Box 333, Hazelton, V0J 1Y0, ☎ 604/842–5723;* ☛ *Free;* ◷ *year-round, Thurs.–Mon. 10:30–4:30. 'Ksan Indian Village: Box 326, Hazelton, V0J 1Y0, ☎ 604/842–5544;* ☛ *$5.50 adults, $3.50 senior citizens, $3 students, $2 children 5–12;* ◷ *May–mid-Oct., daily 9–6; mid-Oct.–Apr., Thurs.–Mon. 9–5. Tours given May–mid-Oct., on the hour.*

㉕ ㉖ North of Route 16 you pass by the serene **Lakes District,** which is popular for camping, fishing, and water sports, before coming to **Prince George** (Tourism Prince George, 1198 Victoria St., V2L 2L2, ☎ 604/ 562–3700), British Columbia's third-largest city. This provincial hub contains the Fraser–Ft. George Regional Museum (☎ 604/562–1612), a railroad museum (☎ 604/563–7351; open late May–Labor Day), and the Prince George Native Art Gallery (☎ 604/562–7385). Not far from town are some exceptional glaciers. From Prince George you can turn south on Route 97 for Kamloops and the Okanagan Valley (*see* Scenic Drives, *below*), or you can continue on Route 16 to Route 5 for a longer (some say even more spectacular) route to the same place.

Tour 5: Okanagan Valley and Environs, Including Rainbow and High Country

The Okanagan Valley is part of a highland plateau between the Cascade range of mountains on the west and the Monashee mountains on the east. Though small in size (only 3% of the province's total land mass), the area contains the interior's largest concentration of people. Dominating the valley is Okanagan Lake, a vacation magnet for tourists from the west coast and Alberta. In summer it can be difficult to find rooms here. The largest towns along the lake are Vernon at the north end, Kelowna in the middle, and Penticton to the south. Between, and along the lake, are the recreational and resort communities of **Summerland, Peachland, Westbank,** and **Oyama,** which are popular tourist destinations and have camping facilities, motels, and cabins.

The valley is the fruit-growing capital of Canada, producing apricots, pears, cherries, plums, apples, grapes, and peaches. A visit to the region from mid-April through early June delights your senses with the brightness and fragrance of the spring blossoms.

㉗ **Kamloops** (which is officially a part of High Country, not Okanagan) is a convenient passageway into the valley from Fraser Canyon and Thompson Valley, and a stop on the Canadian Pacific Railroad. The town is 50 minutes northeast of Vancouver by air and 425 kilometers (260 miles) by road and is surrounded by 500 lakes, which provide an abundance of trout, Dolly Varden, and kokanee. During late September and October, however, attention turns to the sockeye salmon, when thousands of these fish—intent on breeding—return home to their birth waters in Adams River (only 65 kilometers, or 40 miles, east of Kamloops off the Trans-Canada Highway).

Once every four years—the last time was 1994—the sockeye run reaches a massive scale, as more than a million salmon pack the waters and up to 500,000 visitors come to observe. The **Roderick Haig-Brown Conservation Area,** which protects the 11-kilometer (7-mile) stretch of Adams River, is the best vantage point.

The **Kamloops Wildlife Park** (Box 698, Kamloops, V2C 5L7, ☎ 604/573–3242), houses 71 species in fairly natural habitats on 55 acres. Canyon hiking trails, a miniature railway, and adjacent water slides provide something for everyone.

Vernon, Kelowna, and Penticton, running south along Route 97, like to believe each has a distinct personality, but local rivalries aside, the towns are actually one large unit. Okanagan Lake is their glue, offering recreation, lodging, and restaurants.

㉘ Of the three, **Vernon** is the least dependent on tourism, organized instead around forestry and agriculture. The city borders on two other lakes besides Okanagan, the most enticing of which is Kalamalka Lake. The **Kalamalka Lake Provincial Park** has warm waters, and some of the most scenic viewpoints and hiking trails in the region. Twelve
★ kilometers (7.5 miles) north of Vernon, the **O'Keefe Historic Ranch** gives visitors a window on cattle-ranch life at the turn of the century. The O'Keefe house is a late-19th-century Victorian mansion opulently furnished with original antiques. On the 50 acres are a Chinese cooks' house, St. Ann's Church, a blacksmith shop, a reconstructed general store, a display of the old Shuswap and Okanagan Railroad, and a contemporary restaurant and gift shop. There's a ranching gallery in the museum, and a reproduction stagecoach offers rides around the grounds. *9830 Rte. 97, 12 km (7½ mi) north of Vernon,* ☎ *604/542–7868.* ☛ *$5 adults, $4 senior citizens and children 13–18, $3 children 6–12; $15 families.* ☉ *Mid-May–mid-Oct., daily 9–5.*

㉙ **Kelowna,** the largest city in the Okanagan, is home to **Father Pandosy's Mission,** the first nonnative settlement in the region, founded in 1859. *3685 Benvouline Rd.,* ☎ *604/860–8369.* ☛ *Free; donations accepted.* ☉ *Daily 8–dusk.*

Kelowna is the geographic center of the valley's wine industry, with **Calona Wines Ltd.** (1125 Richter St., ☎ 604/762–3332), British Columbia's oldest and largest winemaker. Also around Kelowna are smaller but more intimate wineries, including **Gray Monk Estate Winery** (1051 Camp Rd., 8 km, or 5 mi, west of Winfield, off Rte. 97, ☎ 604/766–3168) and **Cedarcreek Estate Winery** (5445 Lakeshore Rd.,

12 km, or 7½ mi, south of Kelowna, off Rte. 97, Pandosy and Lakeshore Rds., ☎ 604/764–8866).

③ **Penticton** is the most tourist-oriented of the three towns. While its winter population is about 25,000, its population in summer nears 130,000. Sixteen kilometers (10 miles) north of town, you can take a ride on the historic **Kettle Valley Steam Railway** (10112 S. Victoria Rd., Summerland, ☎ 604/494–8422), reopened in 1995, which passes through 10 kilometers of orchards, vineyards and wooded mountain terrain along the 1915 line that opened up the interior of British Columbia by connecting Vancouver with the Kootenays. An 11-kilometer (5-mile) drive south from Penticton on Route 97 takes you to the **Okanagan Game Farm** (☎ 604/497–5405), with more than 650 species of wild animals from around the world. Farther south, off Route 3 and along the U.S. border, **Cathedral Provincial Park** (☎ 604/494–0321) preserves 82,000 acres of lakes and rolling meadows, teeming with mule deer, mountain goats, and California bighorn sheep. To reach the main part of the park, either take the steep, eight-hour hike, or arrange (and pay in advance) for the Cathedral Lakes Lodge (☎ 604/499–5848, ℻ 604/ 499–5266) to transport you by four-wheel drive. There are 16 campsites in the park, which is open mid-June through early October.

Winding farther south, Route 3 connects with the Trans-Canada Highway (Route 1), which parallels the Fraser River through the **Rainbow Country** region. A glimpse through the mists above roiling **Hell's Gate,** off Route 1 in Fraser Canyon, hints at how the region got its name. An air tram (cable car) carries visitors across the foaming canyon above the fishway, where millions of sockeye salmon fight their way upriver to spawning grounds four times a year—April, July, August, and October. In addition to interpretive displays on the life cycle of the salmon, you'll find a fudge factory, a gift shop, and a restaurant at the lower air-tram terminal. *Box 129, Hope,* ☎ *604/867–9277.* ☛ *$8.50 adults, $7.50 senior citizens, $5 children 6–14, $22 families.* ☉ *Mid-Apr.–Oct. at 9* AM; *closing times are seasonal (between 5 and 7* PM).

★ Continue southwest on Route 1 to the well-signed **Minter Gardens** at Exit 135 in Rosedale. This 27-acre compound contains 11 beautifully presented theme gardens—Chinese, rose, English, fern, fragrance, and more—along with aviaries and ponds. There are playgrounds and a giant evergreen maze. *52892 Bunker Rd., Rosedale,* ☎ *604/794–7191 or 800/661–3919 in Canada.* ☛ *$7.50 adults, $6.50 senior citizens, $3.50 children 6–12, children 5 and under free, $20 families.* ☉ *Apr.– Oct., daily 9–dusk.*

It's hard to miss the **Trans-Canada Waterslides,** just across the highway. This tremendously popular water park has slides with such names as Kamikaze, Cannonball, Super Heroes, Black Hole, and Flash Flood, along with wave and soaking pools, snack bars, and sunbathing areas to provide plenty of warm-weather fun. *Bridal Falls Rd., Rosedale,* ☎ *604/794–7455.* ☛ *$12 adults, $8.50 children 4–12, children 3 and under free.* ☉ *Mid-May–mid-June, weekends 10–8, mid-June –early Sept., daily 10–9.*

③ The same exit also leads to **Harrison Hot Springs,** a small resort community at the southern tip of picturesque Harrison Lake. Vacationers flock here to relax in this almost pristine natural setting. Mountains surround the 64-kilometer- (40-mile-) long lake, which, ringed by pretty beaches, provides a broad range of outdoor activities, in addition to the hot springs. Across from the beach is a spring-fed public pool. *100 Esplanade, Harrison Hot Springs,* ☎ *604/796–2244.* ☛ *$7* *adults, $5 senior citizens and children, children under 5 free; unlimited-entry day passes $10 adults, $8 children.* ⊙ *Sun.–Thurs. 8 AM–9 PM, Fri. and Sat. 8 AM–10 PM.*

★ A tour of **Historic Kilby Store and Farm,** a heritage attraction in nearby Harrison Mills, takes you back in time to the British Columbia of the 1920s. Visitors tour the general store and farm buildings of T. Kilby and other pioneers of the area, chat with the shopkeeper, sniff whatever is simmering on the wood-burning stove, and tramp through the orchards, stockroom, fueling station, barn, and dairy house on the grounds. There is also a teahouse. This is a fine slice of living history. *215 Kilby Rd. (1½ km off Rte. 7 on north shore of Frazer River; follow signs), Harrison Mills,* ☎ *604/796–9576.* ☞ *$4 adults, $3.50 senior citizens, $1.50 children 6–14, $9 families.* ⊙ *Mid-May–June and early Sept.–mid-Oct., Thurs.–Mon. 10–5; July–early Sept., daily 10–5.*

Scenic Drives

The **Gold Rush Trail** is a 640-kilometer (400-mile) route along which frontiersmen traveled in search of gold in the 19th and early 20th centuries. The interior British Columbia trail begins just below Prince George in the north and extends to Lillooet in the south, but juts off at points in between. Following the route you can travel through Quesnel, Williams Lake, Wells, and Barkerville and along the Fraser Canyon and Cache Creek. Most towns and communities through which the trail passes have re-created villages, history museums, or historic sites that help to tell the story of the gold-rush era. For more information contact the **Cariboo Chilcotin Coast Tourist Association** (Box 4900, Williams Lake V2G 2V8, ☎ 604/392–2226; in U.S. 800/663–5885, FAX 604/392–2838) and **Heritage Attractions of British Columbia** (Ministry of Small Business, Tourism, and Culture, 800 Johnson St., Victoria, V8V 1X4, ☎ 604/387–5129).

Completion of a new highway opened the **Coast Mountain Circle,** linking Vancouver to Cariboo Country. This 702-kilometer (435-mile) route takes in spectacular Howe Sound, the deep-water port of Squamish, Whistler Resort, and Pemberton Valley before heading back to Vancouver through scenic Fraser Canyon and Harrison Hot Springs. The loop makes a comfortable two- to three-day journey. For more information contact the **Tourism Association of Southwestern B.C.** (204–1755 W. Broadway, Vancouver V6J 4S5, ☎ 604/739–9011 or 800/667–3306).

What to See and Do with Children

Anne Hathaway's Cottage, tucked away in a unique English village complex in Victoria, is a full-size replica of the original thatched home in Stratford-Upon-Avon, England. The building and the 16th-century antiques inside are typical of Shakespeare's era. The Olde England Inn, on the grounds, is a pleasant spot for tea or a traditional English-style meal. You can also stay ($76–$198; AE, DC, MC, V) in one of the 50 antiques-furnished rooms, some complete with four-poster beds. *429 Lampson St., V9A 5Y9,* ☎ *604/388–4353.* ☞ *$6.50 adults, $4.25 senior citizens and children 8–17, children under 8 free.* ⊙ *June–Sept., daily 9–9; Oct.–May, daily 10–4. Guided tours leave from inn in winter and from cottage in summer. From downtown Victoria, take Munro bus to door.*

Pacific Undersea Gardens (*see* Tour 1: Victoria, *above*).

Swan Lake Christmas Hill Nature Sanctuary. This 23-acre lake, in 110 acres of open fields and wetlands, is 10 minutes from downtown Victoria. From the 1½-mile chip trail and floating boardwalk, birders can spot a variety of waterfowl in winter and nesting birds in the tall grass. *3873 Swan Lake Rd. (take Bus 70 or 75),* ☎ *604/479–0211.* ☛ *Free. Nature House open weekdays 8:30–4; weekends and holidays noon–4.*

Royal London Wax Museum (*see* Tour 1: Victoria, *above*).

Off the Beaten Path

★ **Butchart Gardens,** on the 130-acre Ross estate about 21 kilometers (13 miles) north of downtown Victoria, grows more than 700 varieties of flowers and has Italian, Japanese, and English rose gardens. In summer, many of the exhibits are illuminated at night. Also on the premises are a teahouse and restaurants. *800 Benvenuto Ave., Brentwood Bay,* ☎ *604/652–5256.* ☛ *$11 adults, $5.75 children 13–17, $1.50 children under 13, excluding GST; discounted rates in winter. Hours vary seasonally; call ahead.*

SHOPPING

Okanagan Valley
The **Okanagan Pottery Studio** (☎ 604/767–2010), on Route 97 in Peachland, sells handcrafted ceramics. At **Geert Maas Sculpture Gardens, Gallery, and Studio** (R.R. 1250, Reynolds Rd., Kelowna, V1Y 7P9, ☎ 604/860–7012), in the hills above Kelowna, world-class sculptor Geert Maas exhibits his distinctive bronze, stoneware, and mixed media abstract figures in an indoor gallery and a 1-acre garden. He also sells medallions, original paintings, and etchings.

Prince Rupert
Native art and other local crafts are available at **Studio 9** (516 3rd Ave. W, ☎ 604/624–2366).

Queen Charlotte Islands
The Haida carve valuable figurines from the hard, black slate called argillite. The specific variety used by the Haidas is found only on the islands. Their works are sold at the **Adams Family House of Silver** (☎ 604/626–3215), in Old Masset, behind the Ed Jones Haida Museum. **Joy's Island Jewellers** (☎ 604/559–4742) in Queen Charlotte also carries a good selection. Other island specialties are silk-screen prints and silver jewelry.

Vancouver Island
Watercolor artist and author **Sue Coleman** (☎ 604/478–0380) in Metchosin, 35 minutes west of Victoria on road to Sooke, invites visitors to the island to tour her studio. Duncan is the home of Cowichan wool sweaters, hand knitted by the Cowichan people. A large selection is available from **Hills Indian Crafts** (☎ 604/746–6731) on the main highway, about 1½ kilometers (1 mile) south of Duncan. **Modeste Wool Carding** (2615 Modeste Rd., Duncan, ☎ 604/748–8983), about a half mile off the highway, also carries a selection of handmade knitwear.

Victoria
Shopping in Victoria is easy: Virtually everything can be found in the downtown area on or near Government Street stretching north from the Empress. You'll smell the sweets well before you get to **Roger's Chocolates** (913 Government St., ☎ 604/384–7021), purveyor of fine chocolates and an array of other candies. If the British spirit of Victoria has

you searching for fine teas, head to **Murchie's** (1110 Government St., ☎ 604/381–5451), where they have over 40 varieties to choose from (not to mention blended coffees, tarts, and cakes). Next door, **Munro's Books** (1108 Government St., ☎ 604/382–2464) sells a wide selection of books, and the building itself, with its high ceiling, elaborate moldings, and murals, is worth a peek. **The Best of British Columbia** (910 Government St., ☎ 384–7773) focuses on products produced in British Columbia, from maple syrup to original art.

The **Cowichan Trading Co., Ltd.** (1328 Government St., ☎ 604/383–0321) sells native jewelry, moccasins, and Cowichan Indian sweaters. **Hill's Indian Crafts** (665 Fort St. at Government St., ☎ 604/383–8224) has a mixture; you'll have to plow through some schlocky souvenirs to find the good-quality West Coast native art.

The **House of Traditions** (910 Government St., ☎ 604/361–3020) offers frilly lace blouses and skirts, some Victorian in fashion. Men's designer clothes by Ralph Lauren are available at **The Polo Store** (1200 Government St., ☎ 604/381–7656). As the name would suggest, **Irish Linen Stores** (1090 Government St., ☎ 604/383–6812) offers fine linen and lace items—hankies, napkins, tablecloths, and place mats.

For a wide selection, head to the larger shopping centers downtown. **Eaton Centre** (1 Victoria Eaton Centre, at Government and Fort streets, ☎ 604/382–7141) is a department store and mall with around 100 boutiques and restaurants. **Market Square** (560 Johnson St., ☎ 604/386–2441) has three stories of specialty shops and offbeat stores; there's everything from fudge, music, and comic books to jewelry, local arts, and New Age accoutrements.

A 10-minute drive (or the No. 1 or No. 2 bus) from downtown out Fort Street to Oak Bay Avenue will take you to one of the few residential shopping areas that is not a mall. **Oak Bay Village** is great for browsing, buying, or an afternoon cuppa'. Start at the corner of Oak Bay and Foul Bay and work your way east toward the water.

At last count, Victoria had 60-plus antiques shops specializing in coins, stamps, estate jewelry, rare books, crystal, china, furniture, or paintings and other works of art. A short walk on Fort Street going away from the harbor will take you to Antique Row between Blanshard and Cook streets. You will also find antiques on the west side of Government Street near the Old Town.

SPORTS AND THE OUTDOORS

Canoeing and Kayaking

Canoeing and kayaking are favorite ways to explore the miles of extended, interconnected waterways and the breathtaking coastline of British Columbia. The **Inside Passage, Queen Charlotte Strait,** the **Strait of Georgia,** and the other island-dotted straits and sounds that border the mainland provide fairly protected sea-going from Washington state to the Alaskan border, with numerous marine parks to explore along the way. Another particular favorite among paddlers is the **Powell Forest Canoe Route,** a 60-kilometer (45-mile) circuit of 12 lakes connected by streams, rivers, and well-maintained portage trails along the Powell River.

For rentals on Vancouver Island, contact **Tofino Sea-Kayaking Company** (Box 620, Tofino, V0N 3J0, ☎ 604/928–3117 or 604/725–4222) and **Stubbs Island Charters** (Box 7, Telegraph Cove, ☎ 604/928–3185). For multiple-day, guided sea-kayak expeditions, contact **Wild**

Heart Adventures (Site P, C-5, R. R. 4, Nanaimo, V9R 5X9, ☎ 604/ 722–3683, FAX 604/722–2175). On the mainland, try **Okanagan Canoe Holidays** (R.R. 1, 2910 N. Glenmore Rd., Kelowna V1Y 7P9, ☎ and fax 604/762–8156) or **Mount Robson Adventure Holidays** (Box 687, Valemount V0E 2Z0, ☎ 604/566–4386).

Fishing

Miles of coastline and thousands of lakes, rivers, and streams bring more than 750,000 fishermen to British Columbia each year. The waters of the province hold 74 species of fish (25 of them sport fish), including Chinook salmon and rainbow trout. A saltwater-fishing license for one day costs $3.75 for both Canadian residents and non-Canadians and is available at virtually every fishing lodge and sporting-goods outlet along the coast. Annual licenses are about $11 for non–British Columbia Canadians and $38 for non-Canadians.

For updated fishing information and regulations, contact the **B.C. Fish Branch** (Ministry of Environment, 780 Blanshard St., Victoria V8V 1X4, ☎ 604/387–5987). For a guide to saltwater fishing, contact the **Department of Fisheries and Oceans** (Recreational Fisheries Division, 400– 555 W. Hastings St., Vancouver V6B 5G3, ☎ 604/666–3271).

Golf

There are more than 225 golf courses in British Columbia, and the number is growing. The province is now an Official Golf Destination of the PGA Tour in Canada and of the American PGA tour. Greens fees are about $20–$40. The topography in British Columbia tends to be mountainous, and many courses have fine views as well as treacherous approaches to greens.

OKANAGAN VALLEY AND ENVIRONS

The Okanagan has a central tee-time booking service for out-of-town golfers that lists all of the Okanagan/Interior British Columbia courses below. *412–4004 Blue Bird Rd., Kelowna, V1W 1Y6,* ☎ *604/764– 4118 or 800/930–4622.* ☉ *May 15–Oct. 15, weekdays 9–5.*

Gallaghers Canyon Golf and Country Club (4320 McCulloch Rd., Kelowna, ☎ 604/861–4240) is one of the most challenging semi-private courses in British Columbia, with long, rolling, and twisting fairways. **Osoyoos Golf and Country Club** (62 Ave. off Rte. 99, Osoyoos, ☎ 604/495–7003) provides a green setting in the parched hills; only two of the 12 par fours on the course are under 350 yards. Visitors are welcome. The relatively new **Predator Ridge Golf Resort** (360 Commonage Rd., Vernon, ☎ 604/542–3436) is a very challenging public course. **Rivershore Golf Club** (off Old Shuswap Rd., Kamloops, ☎ 604/ 573–4622), a Robert Trent Jones–designed course, is one of British Columbia's longest, at 7,007 yards. Recently overshadowing the Rivershore course in length is the new **Harvest Golf Club** (2725 KLO Rd., East Kelowna, ☎ 604/862–3103), at 7,151 yards.

VICTORIA

Though **Victoria Golf Club** (1110 Beach Dr., ☎ 604/598–4321) is private, it's open to other private-club members; the windy course is the oldest (built in 1893) in British Columbia and offers a spectacular view of the Strait of Juan de Fuca. The **Cordova Bay Golf Course** (5333 Cordova Bay Rd., ☎ 604/658–4444), Victoria's newest public course, is an 18-hole, par-72 course set on the shoreline overlooking Haro Strait and the San Juan Islands. The **Olympic View Golf Club** (643 Latoria Rd., ☎ 604/474–3673), 20 minutes from downtown, offers both challenging and forgiving tees and stunning views of the Strait of Juan de Fuca and the Olympic Mountains.

Golf is also very popular elsewhere on Vancouver Island, where there are many good courses to choose from, including the **Fairwinds Golf and Country Club** (3730 Fairwinds Dr., Nanoose Bay, ☎ 800/667–7060) and the **Morningstar Golf Course** (525 Lowery Rd., Parksville, ☎ 604/248–8161), neither far from Nanaimo; the **Storey Creek Golf Club** (Box 727, Campbell River, ☎ 604/923–3673), a bit farther up the coast; and the **Long Beach Golf Course** (Pacific Rim Hwy., Tofino, ☎ 604/725–3332), on the west side of the island.

Hiking

One of the most challenging hikes in British Columbia is along the **West Coast Trail** (*see* Exploring, Tour 2) in Pacific Rim National Park (☎ 604/726–7721, FAX 604/726–4720), on Vancouver Island. The demanding 77-kilometer (47-mile) trail is for experienced hikers and follows part of the coast known as the "Graveyard of the Pacific" because of the large number of shipwrecks that have occurred there. It can be traveled only on foot, takes an average of six days to complete, and is open from May to late September. A permit is necessary to hike this trail; reservations are available from March through September.

In the Okanagan Valley, you can hike the rail beds of the **Kettle Valley Railway** network, stretching along Lake Okanagan between Penticton and Kelowna. The going is mild, and you're likely to want a camera along to record all the views. The Visitors Bureaus for Kelowna (☎ 604/861–1515) and Penticton (☎ 604/493–4055) can provide maps and information.

Virtually all of British Columbia's provincial parks have fine hiking-trail networks; the **Ministry of Parks** (800 Johnson St., 2nd Floor, Victoria, V8V 1X4, ☎ 604/387–5002) offers detailed information.

Heli-hiking is very popular in this province; helicopters deliver hikers to high alpine meadows and verdant mountain tops that have remained virtually untouched because of their inaccessibility. **Highland Helicopter** (1685 Tranmer, Agassiz V0M 1K0, ☎ 604/796–9610) and **Mount Robson Adventure Holidays** (Box 687, Valemount V0E 2Z0, ☎ 604/566–4386) on the mainland can provide further information. On Vancouver Island, contact **Island Sauvage** (131 Beach St., Campbell River, V9W 5G4, ☎ 604/286–0205 or 800/667–4354 in Canada).

Rafting

With such beautiful rivers as the Adams, Chilcotin, Fraser, Illecillewaet, and Thompson lacing the High Country, Okanagan Valley, and Fraser Canyon, there is a diverse range of rafting trips from which to choose. Operators such as **Mount Robson Adventure Holidays** (Box 687, Valemount V0E 2Z0, ☎ 604/566–4386), **Fraser River Raft Expeditions Ltd.** (Box 10, Yale V0K 2S0, ☎ 604/863–2336 or 800/363–7238 in Canada), **Hyak Wilderness Adventures** (204B–1975, Maple St., Vancouver V6J 3S9, ☎ 604/734–8622 or 800/663–7238 in Canada), **Canadian River Expeditions** (302–3524 W. 16th Ave., Vancouver, V6R 3C1, ☎ 604/738–4449), and **Alpine Rafting Company** (Box 1409, Golden V0A 1H0, ☎ 604/344–5016) provide options ranging from lazy half-day floats to exhilarating white-water journeys of up to a week.

Skiing

British Columbia has hundreds of kilometers of groomed cross-country (Nordic) ski trails in the provincial parks and more than 40 cross-country resorts. Most downhill destinations have carved out Nordic routes along the valleys, and there are literally thousands more trails in unmanaged areas of British Columbia.

For cross-country enthusiasts, two of the finest facilities in the province are **Posthill Lake Lodge** (Box 854, Kelowna V1Y 7P5, ☎ 604/860–1655) just east of Kelowna and **Manning Park Resort** (Box 1480, Hope, V0X 1L0, ☎ 604/840–8822) en route to the Okanagan, about 200 kilometers (124 miles) east of Vancouver. Manning Park also has downhill facilities, which are just as popular as the Nordic program. On Vancouver Island, **Mt. Washington** (*see below*) has 36 kilometers (22 miles) of double track–set Nordic trails. **Big White** and **Silver Star Mountain Resort** (*see below*) on the mainland in the Okanagan Valley also have Nordic facilities.

DOWNHILL

With more than half the province higher than 4,200 feet above sea level, new downhill courses are constantly opening. At the moment, more than 40 major resorts have downhill facilities.

In the Comox Valley on Vancouver Island, **Mt. Washington Ski Resort Ltd.** (Box 3069, Courtenay V9N 5N3, ☎ 604/338–1386), with nearly 50 runs and an elevation of 5,200 feet, is the largest ski area on the island, and the third-largest in terms of visitors in the province. It's a modern, well-organized mountain with snowpack averaging 472 inches a year. **Forbidden Plateau** (Box 3268, Courtenay V9N 5N4, ☎ 604/334–4744), near Mt. Washington, has 15 runs and a vertical drop of 1,150 feet.

The Okanagan Valley region, four hours east of Vancouver by car, or one hour by air, offers some of the best ski bargains in the province. **Big White Ski Resort** (Box 2039, Station R, Kelowna V1X 4K5, ☎ 604/765–3101) is the highest ski area in British Columbia, at 7,606 feet, though Whistler (*see* Excursions from Vancouver *in* Chapter 6), the province's best-known resort, has a longer vertical drop. The Big White has almost 60 runs, and, like Whistler, is in the process of rapidly expanding. **Silver Star Mountain Resort** (Box 2, Silver Star Mountain V0E 1G0, ☎ 604/542–0224), with more than 80 runs, offers well-lighted night skiing.

Kootenay Country, a southeastern section of British Columbia that includes the Rockies, Purcells, Selkirks, and Monashees, features two major resorts: **Whitewater** (Box 60, Nelson V1L 5P7, ☎ 604/354–4944), with 28 runs and a lot of powder skiing, and **Red Mountain Resorts** (Box 670, Rossland V0G 1Y0, ☎ 604/362–7700), which spans two mountains and three mountain faces and has 30 marked runs.

The resorts in the High Country reflect British Columbia's most diverse topographical area. With 3,100 feet of vertical drop, **Sun Peaks Resort** (Box 869, Kamloops V2C 5M8, ☎ 604/578–7222) has 63 runs. **Mt. Mackenzie** (Box 1000, Revelstoke V0E 2S0, ☎ 604/837–5268) has 26 runs and offers deep-powder skiing. Revelstoke, 5 kilometers (3 miles) from the base, has a wide selection of lodging.

HELI- AND SNO-CAT SKIING

Heli-skiing operators can often be found at well-established resorts, taking clients into otherwise inaccessible deep-powder regions of the mountains.

In Kootenay Country, try **Kootenay Helicopter Skiing** (Box 717, Nakusp V0G 1R0, ☎ 604/265–3121; 800/663–0100 in Canada and the U.S.). With accommodations at the Tenderfoot Lodge, they run three-, four-, and five-day packages to and from Kelowna and Castlegar and five-day packages from Spokane, Washington.

In the High Country, **Selkirk Tangiers Helicopter Skiing** (Box 1409, Golden V0A 1H0, ☎ 604/344–5016 or 800/663–7080, ☎ 604/344–7012) runs three-, five-, and seven-day all-inclusive packages in the Selkirk and Monashee mountains from their base in Revelstoke. **Cat Powder Skiing** (Box 1479, Revelstoke V0E 2S0, ☎ 604/837–9489) organizes two-, three-, and five-day all-inclusive packages that run into the Selkirks and on the upper slopes of Mt. MacKenzie in Revelstoke.

Whale-Watching

Three resident and several transient pods of orca (killer) whales travel in the waters around Vancouver Island and are the primary focus of nature-watching charter boat tours that depart Victoria from May to October. June and July are actually the best time to see the whales, and harbor seal, sea lion, porpoise, and marine bird sightings are a safe bet anytime. These three-hour Zodiac (an inflatable boat powered by motor) excursions cost around $70 per person ($40–$45 for children). **Five Star Charters** (☎ 604/386–7223) and **Seacoast Expeditions** (☎ 604/383–2254) are the top operators.

DINING AND LODGING

Dining

Throughout British Columbia you'll find a variety of cuisines, from Vancouver Island's seafood places to interior British Columbia's wild game–oriented menus. Prices vary from location to location, but ratings reflect the categories listed on the dining chart.

What to Wear

Restaurants are generally casual in the region; if a restaurant listed below requires jacket or jacket and tie, it is noted in the service information.

Category	Victoria*	Other Areas*
$$$$	over $40	over $35
$$$	$30–$40	$25–$35
$$	$20–$30	$15–$25
$	under $20	under $15

*per person, excluding drinks, service, and 7% GST, in Canadian dollars

Lodging

The lodging possibilities across the region are as diverse as the restaurant menus. Accommodations range from bed-and-breakfasts and rustic cabins to deluxe chain hotels. In the cities, especially, there is an abundance of accommodations, but once you get off the beaten track, guest rooms are often a rare commodity and may require advance booking. The Victoria Visitors Information Centre has a lodging reservations service; call 800/663–3883.

Category	Victoria*	Other Areas*
$$$$	over $180	over $125
$$$	$110–$180	$90–$125
$$	$70–$110	$50–$90
$	under $70	under $50

*All prices are for a standard double room, excluding 10% provincial accommodation tax, service charge, and 7% GST. Prices are in Canadian dollars.

Victoria

Dining

$$$–$$$$ Empress Room. For that special-occasion dinner, reserve a fireside table in the elegant Empress Room. Innovative and beautifully presented Pacific Northwest cuisine vies for attention with the setting when candlelight dances on the tapestried walls beneath an intricately carved mahogany ceiling. Fresh local ingredients go into imaginative seasonal dishes such as house-cured Pacific salmon with wild blackberry-ginger butter, pan-roasted Arctic char with wild-rice polenta and gooseberry chutney, or peppered Vancouver Island venison with black currant sauce, all perfectly complimented by wines from the Empress Hotel's extensive cellar. ✗ *721 Government St.,* ☎ *604/384–8111. Reservations advised. AE, D, DC, MC, V. Closed lunch.*

$$$ Chez Daniel. One of Victoria's old standbys, Chez Daniel offers dishes that are rich, though the nouvelle influence has found its way into some creations. The interior, following a burgundy color scheme, seems to match the traditional caloric cuisine. The wine list is varied, and the menu has a wide selection of basic dishes: rabbit, salmon, duck, steak. The romantic atmosphere here encourages you to linger. ✗ *2524 Estevan Ave.,* ☎ *604/592–7424. Reservations advised. AE, MC, V. Closed lunch and Sun. and Mon.*

$$–$$$ Marina Restaurant. This lovely, round restaurant overlooking the Oak
★   Bay Marina is so popular with the locals that it's always crowded and a bit noisy. While seasonings and presentation often change, best bets on the imaginative menu are warm salmon salad, grilled marlin in citrus sesame vinaigrette, rack of lamb in port glaze, and crab served with drawn butter and Indonesian hot-and-sour sauce. Choose from over 500 wines to complement the meal. If you don't have reservations and the dining room and oyster bar are full, head downstairs to the Café Deli for Mediterranean picnic foods prepared by the chefs upstairs; go early for the best selection. ✗ *1327 Beach Dr.,* ☎ *604/598–8555. Reservations advised. AE, DC, MC, V. Closed Dec. 25.*

$$ Camilles. This restaurant is romantic, intimate, and one of the few West Coast–cuisine restaurants in Victoria. Such house specialties as carrot and smoked Gruyère cheese cake (an appetizer), roast loin of venison with wild-rice risotto, rack of lamb stuffed with mint pesto, and hazelnut crepes are all served in generous portions. Camilles also has an extensive wine cellar. ✗ *45 Bastion Sq.,* ☎ *604/381–3433. Reservations advised. MC, V. Closed lunch and Mon.*

$$ Il Terrazzo. A charming redbrick terrace edged by potted greenery, lit by flickering candles, and warmed by fireplaces and overhead heaters make Il Terrazzo, tucked away off Waddington Alley, the locals' choice for romantic al fresco dining in Victoria. Baked garlic served with warm cambozola cheese and focaccia; scallops dipped in roasted pistachios garnished with arugula, Belgian endive, and mango salsa; grilled lamb chops on angel hair pasta with tomatoes, garlic, mint, and black pepper; and other hearty Northern Italian dishes come piping hot from the restaurant's authentic wood oven. Anything from the daily fresh sheet is worth a try here. ✗ *555 Johnson St. (off Waddington Alley),* ☎ *604/361–0028. Reservations advised. AE, MC, V. Closed lunch Sun.*

$$ Pagliacci's. Another fine Italian bistro in Victoria, Pagliacci's is a must. Dozens of pasta dishes, quiches, veal, and chicken in marsala sauce with fettuccine are standard. The pastas are freshly made in-house. You'll dine surrounded by orange walls covered with photos of Hollywood movie stars. *1011 Broad St.,* ☎ *604/386–1662. MC, V.*

$–$$ Don Mee's. A large neon sign signals guests to Don Mee's, a traditional Chinese restaurant. The long, red staircase leads to an expansive, comfortable restaurant for Szechuan and Cantonese entrées, such as sweet-and-sour chicken, almond duck, and bean curd with broccoli. Dim sum is served daily during lunch hours. ✕ *538 Fisgard St.,* ☎ *604/383–1032. Reservations accepted. AE, DC, MC, V.*

$–$$ **Le Petit Saigon.** This intimate café-style restaurant offers quiet dining with beautifully presented meals and fare that is primarily Vietnamese, with a touch of French. The crab, asparagus, and egg swirl soup is a specialty of the house, and combination meals are cheap and tasty. ✕ *1010 Langley St.,* ☎ *604/386–1412. AE, MC, V. Closed Sat. lunch and Sun.*

$ **Barb's Place.** This funky, rainbow-colored take-out shack on Fisherman's Wharf has been around long enough to become an institution in Victoria, and the authentic fish-and-chips are consistently judged to be the best by the locals. Pick up an order before taking a quick ride on the little harbor ferry across the bay to Songhees Point for a picnic. ✕ *310 Lawrence St.,* ☎ *604/384–6515. No credit cards.*

$ **Cafe Mexico.** Hearty portions of Mexican food, such as *pollo chipotle* (grilled chicken with melted cheddar and spicy sauce, on a bed of rice) are served at this spacious, redbrick dining establishment just off the waterfront. Colorful bullfight ads and cactus plants provide a suitably Mexican atmosphere. ✕ *1425 Store St.,* ☎ *604/386–5454. AE, DC, MC, V.*

$ **Periklis.** Standard Greek cuisine is offered in this warm, taverna-style restaurant, but there are also steaks and ribs on the menu. On weekends you can enjoy Greek and belly dancing, but brace yourself for the hordes of people who come for the entertainment. ✕ *531 Yates St.,* ☎ *604/386–3313. Closed weekend lunch. AE, MC, V.*

$ **Siam.** The Thai chefs at Siam, one block south of the McPherson Playhouse, work wonders with both hot and mild Thai dishes. The *Phad Thai Goong* (fried rice noodles with prawns, tofu, peanuts, eggs, bean sprouts and green onions) and *Panang* (choice of meat in curry and coconut milk) are particularly good options. Mirrored walls give this small, simple restaurant a feeling of space, and there is a well-stocked bar with a variety of beer suited to the spices used here. ✕ *1314 Government St.,* ☎ *604/383–9911. MC, V.*

$ **Six-Mile-House.** While it's a bit of a drive from downtown, this 1855 carriage house is a Victoria landmark. The brass, carved oak moldings, and stained glass set a festive mood for the evening. The menu constantly changes but always includes seafood selections and burgers. Try the cider or one of the many international beers offered. ✕ *494 Island Hwy.,* ☎ *604/478–3121. DC, MC, V.*

Lodging

$$$$ **Bedford Regency.** This European-style hotel in the heart of downtown is reminiscent of San Francisco's small hotels, with personalized service and strict attention to details. Rooms are in earth colors, and many have goose-down comforters, fireplaces, and whirlpool bathtubs. Meeting rooms and small conference facilities are also available, making this a good business traveler's lodging. ▤ *1140 Government St., V8W 1Y2,* ☎ *604/384–6835 or 800/665–6500,* ℻ *604/386–8930. 40 rooms. Restaurant, pub. AE, MC, V.*

$$$$ **Chateau Victoria.** Wonderful views can be had from the upper rooms and rooftop restaurant of this 19-story hotel across from Victoria's new Conference Centre, near the inner harbor and the Royal British Columbia Museum. Rooms are fairly standard in size, and some have balconies or sitting areas and kitchenettes. ▤ *740 Burdett Ave., V8W 1B2,* ☎ *604/382–4221 or 800/663–5891,* ℻ *604/380–1950. 71*

rooms, 107 suites. Restaurant, lounge, indoor pool, meeting rooms, van to ferry, free parking. AE, D, DC, MC, V.

$$$$ **Empress Hotel.** This is Victoria's dowager queen with a face-lift. First opened in 1908, the hotel underwent a major renovation in 1989 that enhanced its Edwardian charm, updated existing guest rooms, and added some 45 new ones (opt for one of the new rooms for more space). Stained glass, carved archways, and hardwood floors are used effectively. The Empress dominates the inner-harbor area and is the city's primary meeting place for politicians, locals, and tourists. Afternoon tea has been a tradition here since 1908, but it's so popular today that reservations are a must. The Bengal Lounge is full of colonial charm from British India, including a stuffed Bengal tiger, overhead fans, and mosquito netting. Award-winning Pacific Northwest cuisine is featured in the elegant Empress Room (*see* Dining, *above*). ⌨ *721 Government St., V8W 1W5, in Canada,* ☎ *604/384–8111 or 800/441–1414,* ℻ *604/381– 4334. 466 rooms, 17 suites. Restaurant, café, 2 lounges, indoor pool, sauna, health club, convention center. AE, D, DC, MC, V.*

$$$–$$$$ ★ **Abigail's.** A Tudor country inn with gardens and crystal chandeliers, Abigail's is not only lovely but also conveniently located four blocks east of downtown. The guest rooms are prettily detailed in contemporary colors. Down comforters, together with Jacuzzis and fireplaces in some, add to the pampering atmosphere. There's a sense of elegant informality about this no-smoking hotel, noticeable especially in the guest library and sitting room. Breakfast, included in the room rate, is served from 8 to 9:30 in the downstairs dining room. ⌨ *906 McClure St., V8V 3E7,* ☎ *604/388–5363,* ℻ *604/361–1905. 16 rooms. Dining room, library. MC, V.*

$$$–$$$$ **Beaconsfield Inn.** Built in 1875 and restored in 1984, the Beaconsfield has retained its Old World charm. Dark mahogany wood appears throughout the house; down comforters and some canopy beds and claw-foot tubs adorn the rooms, reinforcing its Edwardian style. Some of the rooms have fireplaces and whirlpool bathtubs. Added pluses are the guest library and conservatory/sun room. Full breakfast, with homemade croissants or scones, and afternoon tea as well as evening sherry are included in the room rates. This is a no-smoking property. ⌨ *998 Humboldt St., V8V 2Z8,* ☎ *604/384–4044,* ℻ *604/721–2442. 10 rooms, 1 suite. Library. MC, V.*

$$$–$$$$ **Oak Bay Beach Hotel.** This Tudor-style hotel beside the ocean in Oak Bay, on the southwest side of the Saanich Peninsula, is well removed from the bustle of downtown. There's a wonderful atmosphere here, though; the hotel overlooks the Haro Strait and catches the setting sun. The interior decor is as dreamy as the grounds, with antiques and flower prints decorating the rooms. The restaurant, Tudor Room by the Sea, is average, but the bar with its cozy fireplace is truly romantic. ⌨ *1175 Beach Dr., V8S 2N2,* ☎ *and* ℻ *604/598–4556, 800/668–7758 for reservations. 51 rooms. Restaurant, pub, boating. AE, DC, MC, V.*

$$$ **Clarion Hotel Grand Pacific.** This is one of Victoria's newest and finest hotels, with a lot of mahogany woodwork and an elegant ambience. Overlooking the harbor, and adjacent to the legislative buildings, the hotel accommodates business travelers and vacationers looking for comfort, convenience, and great scenery; all rooms have terraces, with views of either the harbor or the Olympic Mountains. The elaborate health club is one of the best in the city. ⌨ *450 Québec St., V8V 1W5,* ☎ *604/386–0450 or 800/424–6423,* ℻ *604/383–7603. 130 rooms, 19 suites. Restaurant, lounge, indoor pool, massage, sauna, aerobics, racquetball, squash, convention center, free parking. AE, D, DC, MC, V.*

$$$ **Holland House Inn.** Two blocks from the inner harbor, legislative buildings, and ferry terminals, this no-smoking hotel has a sense of casual

elegance. Some of the individually designed rooms have original fine art created by the owner, and some have four-poster beds and fireplaces. All rooms have private baths, and all but two have their own balconies. A lavish breakfast is included in room rates. You'll recognize the house by the picket fence around it. ☎ *595 Michigan St., V8V 1S7,* ☎ *604/384–6644,* FAX *604/384–6117. 10 rooms. Lounge. AE, DC, MC, V.*

$$$ **Mulberry Manor.** This Tudor mansion is the last building designed by
★ Victoria architect Simon McClure; the grounds were designed and, until recently, maintained by a gardener at the world-famous Butchart Gardens; and the manor has been restored and decorated to magazine-cover perfection with antiques, sumptuous linens, and tile baths. Charming hosts Susan and Tony Temple provide sumptuous breakfasts with homemade jams and great coffee. ☎ *611 Foul Bay Rd., V8S 1H2,* ☎ *604/370–1918,* FAX *604/370–1968. 3 rooms, 1 suite. MC, V.*

$$$ **Ocean Pointe Resort.** Across the "blue bridge" from downtown Vic-
★ toria, the resort opened in the summer of 1992 on the site of an old shingle mill in an area once claimed by the Songhees natives. Public rooms and half of the guest rooms offer romantic evening views of downtown Victoria and the parliament buildings. Guest rooms are spacious; some come with floor-to-ceiling windows and small balconies. Amenities include several restaurants, extensive fitness facilities, and the best aesthetics spa in town. The housekeeping suites have kitchens. ☎ *45 Songhees Rd., V9A 6T3,* ☎ *604/360–2999 or 800/667–4677,* FAX *604/360–5856. 213 rooms, 37 suites. 2 restaurants, lounge, indoor pool, sauna, spa, 2 tennis courts, exercise room, racquetball, squash. AE, DC, MC, V.*

$$$ **Victoria Regent Hotel.** Originally built as an apartment house, this is now a posh, condo-living hotel that offers views of the harbor or city. The outside is plain, with a glass facade, but the interior is sumptuously decorated with warm earth tones and modern furnishings; each suite has a living room, a dining room, a deck, a kitchen, and one or two bedrooms with bath. It's a good choice for families. ☎ *1234 Wharf St., V8W 3H9,* ☎ *604/386–2211 or 800/663–7472,* FAX *604/386–2622. 15 rooms, 32 suites. Restaurant, coin laundry, free parking. AE, D, DC, MC, V.*

$$–$$$ **Coast Victoria Harbourside.** Built in 1991 on the quieter, more residential
★ section of the harbor front next to Fisherman's Wharf, the hotel enjoys water views while being removed from the bustling traffic and crowds on Government Street. Serene relaxation in modern comfort is a theme here, from the warm mahogany-paneled lobby and soothing shades of blue-gray and pale pink in average-size guest rooms to an extensive health club. Fishing and whale-watching charters and the pudgy little harbor ferries stop at the hotel's marina just outside, and the action of the inner harbor is a leisurely stroll or quick shuttle ride away. ☎ *146 Kingston St., V8V 1V4,* ☎ *604/360–1211 or 800/663–1144,* FAX *604/360–1418. 125 rooms, 7 suites. Restaurant, lounge, health club, meeting rooms, downtown shuttle, free parking. AE, DC, MC, V.*

$–$$ **Admiral Motel.** On Victoria harbor along the tourist strip, this motel is in the center of things, although it is relatively quiet in the evening. If you're looking for basic, clean lodging, the Admiral is just that. The amiable owners take good care of the newly refurbished rooms, and small pets are permitted. ☎ *257 Belleville St., V8V 1X1,* ☎ *and fax 604/388–6267. 29 rooms, 23 with kitchens. Coin laundry, free parking. AE, D, MC, V.*

$ **Cats Meow.** If you're on a tight budget, you may appreciate this small youth hostel just across the bridges in Victoria West. Operated by bubbly Daphne Cuthill and resident meow Rufus, the hostel offers dorm rooms plus two baths, two showers, two kitchens, and a TV room.

Laundry service and breakfast are available at nominal extra cost; Daphne also arranges discounted day trips. It's only a 15-minute walk from downtown. ⌨ *422 Wilson St., V9A 3G5,* ☎ *and* 𝖥𝖠𝖷 *604/380– 1157. 5 dorms with 26 beds. No credit cards.*

Vancouver Island

Campbell River

DINING

$–$$ **Royal Coachman Inn.** Informal, blackboard-menu restaurants like this
★ one dot the landscape of the island. The menu, which changes daily, is surprisingly daring for what is essentially a high-end pub, and the inn draws crowds nightly, especially on Tuesday and Saturday (prime rib nights). Come early for both lunch and dinner to avoid a wait. ✕ *84 Dogwood St.,* ☎ *604/286–0231. No reservations. AE, MC, V.*

DINING AND LODGING

$$$–$$$$ **April Point Lodge and Fishing Resort.** Operated for 50 years by the
★ friendly Peterson family, April Point Lodge has, not surprisingly, developed a tremendous reputation and a whopping amount of repeat business among vacationers. Spread across a point of Quadra Island and stretching into Discovery Passage across from Campbell River, the 1944 cedar lodge is surrounded by refurbished fishermen's cabins and guest houses that have been added over the years. The accommodations are tidy and comfortable; most have kitchen facilities, fireplaces, and sundecks. Kwakiutl and Haida art adorn the comfortable lounge and dining room, where fine regional cuisine is served. Native feasts on the beach on warm summer nights are especially memorable, with spitted salmon roasted over an open fire; fresh steamed scallops, prawns, and clams; and wine from the extensive cellar. ⌨ *1000 April Point Rd., Box 1, V9W 4Z9,* ☎ *604/285–2222,* 𝖥𝖠𝖷 *604/285–2411. 33 units. Restaurant, lounge, pool, exercise room, hiking, dock, fishing, bicycles. AE, D, DC, MC, V. Some units closed Nov.–Mar.*

$$$–$$$$ **Tsa-Kwa-Luten Lodge.** This resort, operated by members of the Kwakiutl tribe, offers authentic Pacific Coast native food and cultural activities. It is located on a high bluff amid 1,100 acres of forest on Quadra Island, a 10-minute ferry ride from Campbell River. Each room in the main lodge has a sea view from a deck or patio; many have a fireplace and loft. There are also four beachfront cabins with fireplaces, whirlpool tubs, kitchen facilities, and private verandas. Guests are invited to take part in traditional dances in the resort's lounge, which resembles a longhouse, and to visit nearby petroglyphs to make rubbings. ⌨ *Lighthouse Rd., Box 460, Quathiaski Cove, V0P 1N0,* ☎ *604/285–2042 or 800/665–7745,* 𝖥𝖠𝖷 *604/285–2532. 26 rooms, 4 cabins. Restaurant, lounge, hot tub, sauna, exercise room, fishing, mountain bikes. AE, DC, MC, V.*

Comox/Courtenay

DINING

$$ **Old House Restaurant.** This bilevel restaurant offers casual dining in
★ a restored 1938 house with large cedar beams and a stone fireplace. People flock here for the West Coast home-style cuisine—pastas, salads, and sandwiches, along with fancier, more innovative dishes (rack of lamb, panfried flounder, California cioppino)—on the fresh-daily sheet. ✕ *1760 Riverside La., Courtenay,* ☎ *604/338–5406. Reservations for parties of 6 or more. AE, DC, MC, V.*

LODGING

$$ **Greystone Manor.** This no-smoking bed-and-breakfast, set in a 78-year-old house with period furnishings, looks out on Comox Harbor, 'where a playful colony of seals is often visible from the house. The antiques, wood stove, and wood paneling add to the hospitable, cozy feel here. Breakfast, which includes fresh fruit, muffins, and fruit pancakes, is enough to keep you filled most of the day. You can go walking in the garden and on trails nearby. ⚏ *4014 Haas Rd., Site 684–C2, R.R. 6, Courtenay V9N 8H9,* ☎ *604/338–1422. 4 rooms share 2 baths. MC, V.*

$$ **Kingfisher.** Ten minutes south of Courtenay, this hotel stands among
★ trees and overlooks the Strait of Georgia. Solid furnishings, clean white-stucco walls, a bright lobby with lots of greenery, and rooms with mountain and ocean views offer a nice change from the majority of plain accommodations lining the main drag. ⚏ *4330 S. Island Hwy. (Site 672, R.R. 6), Courtenay V9N 8H9,* ☎ *604/338–1323 or 800/663–7929 in British Columbia, OR, and WA;* ⚏ *604/338–0058. 30 units. Restaurant, lounge, tennis court, pool. AE, D, DC, MC, V.*

Malahat

DINING AND LODGING

$$$$ **The Aerie.** The million-dollar view of Finlayson Arm and the Gulf Is-
★ lands persuaded Austrians Leo and Maria Schuster to build their small, luxury resort here. In this Mediterranean-style villa, some plush rooms have a patio; others have fireplaces and whirlpool tubs tucked into window nooks to take advantage of the scenery. The dining room is open to the public for stunning dinner views and outstanding cuisine. The maple-smoked salmon, pheasant consommé, medallions of venison in morel sauce, and crème brûlée with fruit sorbet are more than worth the short drive from Victoria. ⚏ *600 Ebedora Ln., V0R 2L0,* ☎ *604/ 743–7115 or 604/743–4055,* ⚏ *604/743–4766. 8 rooms, 14 suites. Restaurant (reservations advised), indoor pool, indoor and outdoor hot tubs, sauna, spa, 2 tennis courts, exercise room, library, helipad. AE, MC, V.*

Nanaimo

DINING

$$ **Mahle House.** This casually elegant place serves innovative Northwest
★ cuisine, such as braised rabbit with Dijon mustard and red wine sauce. Twelve items fill the regular menu, including a succulent carrot and ginger soup and a catch of the day. Care for detail, an intimate setting, and three country-style rooms make this one of the finest dining experiences in the region. ✕ *Cedar and Heemer Rds.,* ☎ *604/722–3621. Reservations advised. MC, V. Closed lunch and Mon. and Tues.*

$–$$ **The Grotto.** A Nanaimo institution that specializes in a variety of
★ seafood, this restaurant is set against a waterfront background. Dining here is relaxed and casual. Try the spare ribs, garlic prawn pasta, or the seafood platter that's big enough for two. ✕ *1511 Stewart Ave.,* ☎ *604/753–3303. AE, MC, V. Closed lunch fall–spring.*

DINING AND LODGING

$$$–$$$$ **La Coast Bastion Inn.** This hotel is conveniently located downtown near the ferry terminal and train and bus stations. Rooms with balconies have views of the old Hudson's Bay fort and the ocean and modern furnishings. Three eating/entertainment establishments are located within the hotel. ⚏ *11 Bastion St., V9R 2Z9,* ☎ *604/753–6601 or 800/663–1144 in the U.S.,* ⚏ *604/753–4155. 179 rooms. Restaurant, lounge, Irish deli/pub, hot tub, sauna, exercise room, meeting rooms. AE, DC, MC, V.*

$–$$$ **Yellow Point Lodge.** Yellow Point is a very popular resort area on a
★ spit of land south of Nanaimo, east of Ladysmith. Rebuilt in 1986 after a fire destroyed the original, the lodge lost almost nothing in ambi-

ence. Nine large lodge rooms and a range of cottages all have private baths and are available year-round. Perched on a rocky knoll overlooking the Stuart Channel are beach cabins, field cabins, and beach barracks for the hardy, which are closed mid-October to mid-April, have no running water, and share a central bathhouse. Beach cabins can be private and include tree-trunk beds and wood-burning stoves; beach barracks are not as solid, and noises carry from unit to unit, but the location along the shore makes them popular. You can stroll and explore on the lodge's 180 acres of land. Three full meals and snacks are included in the rate. ☎ *Yellow Point Rd., R.R. 3, Ladysmith V0R 2E0,* ☎ *604/245–7422. 50 rooms. Restaurant (for guests only), saltwater pool, hot tub, sauna, 2 tennis courts, badminton, jogging, volleyball, boating, mountain bikes. MC, V.*

LODGING

$$$ Best Western Dorchester Hotel. Upbeat Mediterranean tones of champagne, ochre, and teal replace the old drab blue exterior of the Dorchester. Once the Nanaimo Opera House, this elegant hotel in the city center overlooking the harbor has a distinctive character, with gold knockers on each of the doors, winding hallways, and a rooftop patio. The rooms are small but exceptionally comfortable, and most have views of the harbor. ☎ *70 Church St., V9R 5H4,* ☎ *604/754–6835 or 800/528–1234,* FAX *604/754–2638. 64 rooms. Restaurant, lounge, library, meeting rooms. AE, D, DC, MC, V.*

Parksville

LODGING

$$–$$$ Holiday Inn Express. Across the street from the pretty beach in Parksville, this hotel opened in 1994. Kids under 19 stay free with their parents in the motel-modern rooms outfitted with two queen-size beds. King-size rooms have whirlpool tubs. Continental breakfast is also included in the tariff, making this a very affordable choice. ☎ *424 W. Island Hwy., V9P 1K8,* ☎ *604/248–2232 or 800/465–4329,* FAX *604/248–3273. 87 rooms, 3 suites. Indoor pool, hot tub, exercise room. AE, DC, MC, V.*

$–$$ Roadhouse Inn. This small Swiss-style chalet, set on 3 acres, is central to four of the region's golf courses. The rooms, on the second floor, are comfortable, with basic furnishings. ☎ *1223 Smithers Rd., V9P 2C1,* ☎ *604/248–2912. 6 rooms. Restaurant. MC, V.*

Port Hardy

LODGING

$ Glen Lyon Inn. The rooms have a full ocean view of Hardy Bay and, like most area motels, have clean, modern amenities. Eagles often stop here, eyeing the water for fish to prey on. The inn is a short ride from the ferry terminal. ☎ *6435 Hardy Bay Rd., Box 103, V0N 2P0,* ☎ *604/949–7115,* FAX *604/949–7415. 29 rooms. Restaurant, lounge. AE, D, DC, MC, V.*

Sidney

LODGING

$$–$$$ Borthwick Country Manor. Flower boxes and awnings trim the windows
 ★ of this Tudor-style house, built in 1979 on Vancouver Island's Saanich Peninsula in the quiet countryside not far from Victoria. Owners Ann and Brian Reid, originally from England, provide afternoon tea and a hearty English-style breakfast of eggs, sausage, bacon, muffins, fried tomatoes, and home-made jams. Rooms are cheerful, with coordinated floral comforters, shams, and curtains. French doors lead to the back yard, with gardens to admire and a hot tub to enjoy. Smokey, the Reids' watch cat, is friendly, and children are welcome here. ☎ *9750 Ardmore*

Dr., R.R. 2, V8L 3S1, ☎ *604/656–9498. 5 rooms. Breakfast room, hot tub, fishing. MC, V.*

Sooke

DINING AND LODGING

$$$$ **Sooke Harbour House.** This 1931 clapboard farmhouse-turned-inn has
★ three suites, a 10-room addition, and a dining room—all of which exude elegance. One of the finest restaurants in British Columbia, it is well worth the trip to Sooke from Victoria. The seafood is just-caught fresh, and the herbs are grown on the property. Four chefs in the kitchen guarantee an abundance of creative dishes. On a nice summer evening you may want to sit on the terrace, where you can catch a glimpse of the sea mammals that play by the spit of land in front of the restaurant. Equally exquisite are the romantic guest rooms, with natural wood and white finishes adding to each unit's unique theme. Rooms range from the Herb Garden Room—decorated in shades of mint, with French doors opening onto a private patio—to the Longhouse Room, complete with Native American furnishings. All units, with fireplaces and either ocean or mountain views, come with fresh flowers, a decanter of port, and wet bars that include herbal teas and cookies. Breakfast and lunch are included in your room rate, but you must make a reservation for your meals. Likewise, nonguests must make reservations for dinner. ☎ *1528 Whiffen Spit Rd., R.R. 4, V0S 1N0,* ☎ *604/ 642–3421 or 604/642–4944,* FAX *604/642–6988. 13 rooms. Restaurant (closed lunch except for hotel guests). AE, MC, V.*

$$–$$$ **Ocean Wilderness.** This large 1940s log cabin sits on five forested, beachfront acres, 13 kilometers (8 miles) west of Sooke. Auction-buff owner Marion Rolston built a rough cedar addition in 1990 and has furnished her home with a fine collection of Victorian antiques. Romantic canopies and ruffled linens on high beds dominate the spacious guest rooms, which have sitting areas with views of either the Strait of Juan de Fuca or the pretty gardens in the back, as well as private decks or patios. Just outside, a winding path descends to the beach cove where seals make their summer home. The dining room fare is innovative West Coast treatments of fresh local fish and meats. ☎ *109 W. Coast Rd., R.R. 2, V0S 1N0,* ☎ *and* FAX *604/646–2116. 9 rooms. Dining room, hot tub, hiking trails. MC, V.*

Ucluelet/Tofino

DINING

$$ **Whale's Tale.** At this no-frills, dark but warmly decorated down-to-earth place, the cooking and the rustic decor go hand-in-hand. The view isn't much, but the cedar-shingle building, set on pilings, shakes with a good gust of wind. The menu is highlighted by prime rib and a variety of local seafood. ✕ *1861 Peninsula Rd., Ucluelet,* ☎ *604/726–4621. MC, V. Closed lunch and Nov.–Jan.*

$$ **Wickaninnish Restaurant.** Before the Canadian government acquired
★ this wonderful wood building for its interpretive center, it was a unique inn. It is still a restaurant, with an ambience—the beach setting, combined with the building's glass exterior and stone-and-beam interior, accented by a stone fireplace—that cannot be matched anywhere else in the area. Seafood is the primary choice here—especially the West Coast chowder—but if you order the stir-fry, you won't be disappointed. ✕ *Long Beach, 16 km (11 mi) north of Ucluelet,* ☎ *604/726–7706. Reservations advised for 7 or more. AE, MC, V. Closed mid-Oct.–mid-Feb.*

LODGING

$$–$$$ **Canadian Princess Fishing Resort.** If old ships are to your liking, book a berth on this converted survey ship, which has 36 comfortable, but hardly opulent, staterooms. Each offers one to four berths, and all share washrooms; for something a bit more spacious, request the captain's cabin. Roomier than the ship cabins, the resort's deluxe shoreside rooms come complete with more contemporary furnishings. Promising an unusual experience, this spartan resort provides the bare necessities—mostly to the many fishermen who flock here in summer. ☎ *The Boat Basin, Box 939, Ucluelet V0R 3A0, ☎ 604/726–7771 or 800/663–7090, ℻ 604/726–7121. 36 shoreside and 36 ship-board sleeping units. Boating, fishing. AE, DC, MC, V.*

$$–$$$ **Chesterman's Beach Bed and Breakfast.** This is one of several small, ★ romantic bed-and-breakfasts located on the beach, but the front yard— the rolling ocean surf—makes this one unique. You can while away the hours just walking the beach, searching the tidal pools, or—from March to October—watching whales migrate. The self-contained suite in the main house and the separate Lookout Suite are romantic and cozy; both have comfortable beds and a view of the beach. The self-sufficient one-bedroom garden cottage offers no ocean view but accommodates up to four; it's a good option for a family vacation. ☎ *1345 Chesterman's Beach Rd., Tofino V0R 2Z0, ☎ 604/725–3726. 1 room, 2 suites. Beach, surfing, bicycles. V.*

$$–$$$ **Pacific Sands Beach Resort.** Just a mile north of Pacific Rim National Park, this rustic resort has motel suites and individual two-bedroom cottages. The motel rooms are basic with modern furnishings, but fireplaces make them seem cozier. Some of the rooms in the new, three-story addition have hot tubs outside on the deck. Pacific Sands is close to Long Beach golf course and is on the ocean. ☎ *1421 Pacific Rim Hwy., Box 237, Tofino V0R 2Z0, ☎ 604/725–3322 or 800/565–2322, ℻ 604/725–3155. 54 rooms, 10 cottages. Beach. AE, MC, V.*

The Gulf Islands

Mayne

DINING AND LODGING

$$$$ **Fernhill Lodge.** Constructed of wood from the property, this 1983 West Coast cedar contemporary is host to fantastical theme rooms— Moroccan, East Indian, Edwardian, Japanese, Colonial, Jacobean, and French. Two of them have outdoor hot tubs. Outside on the five-acre grounds are a rustic gazebo with a meditation loft, an Elizabethan knot garden, and a medieval "garden of physic." To complete the unique experience, English hosts Mary and Brian Crumblehulme offer historical dinners (Roman, Chaucer, and Cleopatra to name a few) several nights a week; nonguests must make reservations in advance. Breakfasts, which are included in the room rate, are rather less exotic. This is a no-smoking inn, and pets are not allowed. ☎ *Fernhill Rd., R.R. 1 C–4, Mayne Island, V0N 2J0, ☎ 604/539–2544. 7 rooms. Dining room (reservations advised), sauna, bicycles, library. MC, V.*

$$$–$$$$ **Oceanwood Country Inn.** This Tudor-style house on 10 quiet, forested ★ acres overlooking Navy Channel has English country decor throughout. The inviting deluxe guest rooms all have cozy down comforters on comfortable beds, cheerful wall stenciling, and cushioned chairs in brightly lit reading areas. Most overlook grand ocean views. For dinner, the waterfront dining room, which is open to the public, offers fresh regional cuisine emphasizing local ingredients such as grilled salmon, tomato and Dungeness crab soup, and wild mushroom and goat cheese ravioli on the prix-fixe menu. Afternoon tea and breakfast are included in the room rates. There is a guest pay phone, no children or pets are allowed, and smoking is restricted to the library and outdoors. ☎ *630 Dinner Bay Rd., Mayne Island, V0N 2J0,* ☎ *604/539–5074,* FAX *604/539 3002. 9 rooms. Restaurant (reservations required), hot tub, sauna, bicycles, library, meeting room. MC, V.*

Salt Spring

DINING

$$ **House Piccolo.** Blue and white tablecloths and framed pastel prints on whitewashed walls give this cozy restaurant a casual feel. Duckling in Madeira sauce, roasted B.C. venison with juniper berries, and the salmon du jour are good choices from the dinner menu, but save room for *toscano gato* (sponge cake, hazelnuts, chocolate, and Kahlua). ✗ *108 Hereford Ave., Ganges,* ☎ *604/537–1844. Reservations advised. AE, DC, MC, V. Closed lunch.*

$–$$ **Pomodori.** The white and black tile floor, earthenware pots filled with
★ dried flowers, antique farm implements hung from walls, battered wooden tables, bent willow chairs, and international folk music in the background set an eclectic tone for an eatery with an equally unique menu that changes daily. Local favorites such as roasted tomato, red pepper, and Italian feta in balsamic-vinegar and olive-oil dressing with home-baked focaccia for dipping, chicken, prawn, and mussel jambalaya, and fresh vegetable and herb stew appear often. ✗ *Harbour Market Bldg., Fulford–Ganges Rd., Ganges,* ☎ *604/537–2247. No credit cards. Closed Sun. lunch.*

DINING AND LODGING

$$$$ **Hastings House.** One of the finest country inns in North America and
★ a member of the prestigious Relais et Châteaux group, Hastings House knows how to pamper its guests. The centerpiece of this luxurious 30-acre seaside resort is a Tudor-style manor built in 1940. Guests choose from rooms in the manor or the farmhouse; cliff-side or garden cottages; and lovely suites in the reconstructed barn. All are plushly furnished with fine antiques (primarily English) and follow an English country theme, with such extras as eiderdowns, fireplaces, covered porches or decks, and idyllic views of gardens, pastures, or the harbor. Elegant dinners in the manor house are formal: The prix-fixe menu may include grilled eggplant with goat cheese, plum tomato and roasted garlic soup, peppered sea bass on wilted spinach with nasturtium butter, Salt Spring lamb loin with rosemary, and mille-feuille of raspberries with framboise cream. ☎ *160 Upper Ganges Rd., Box 1110, Ganges, V0S 1E0,* ☎ *604/537–2362 or 800/661–9255,* FAX *604/537–5333. 3 rooms, 7 suites, 2 2-bedroom suites. Restaurant (reservations required; jacket and tie), croquet, nature trails, mountain bikes. AE, MC, V. Closed Thanksgiving–mid-March.*

LODGING

$$$$ **Old Farmhouse Bed and Breakfast.** German-born Gerti Fuss operates this delightful bed-and-breakfast with the assistance of her husband, Karl (also from Germany). Their gray-and-white saltbox farmhouse sits in a quiet meadow edged by towering trees. The style of the main house, a registered historic property built in 1895, is echoed in the four-room wing added by Karl in 1989, which has country-comfortable guest rooms furnished with pine bedsteads, down comforters, lace curtains, floral chintz fabrics, and wicker chairs. Breakfast in the dining room begins with Gerti's fresh-daily baked goods, followed by a hot entree such as smoked salmon soufflé. ☎ *1077 Northend Rd., V8K 1L9,* ☎ *604/537–4113,* FAX *604/537–4969. 4 rooms. Boating, ferry pick-up service. MC, V.*

$$$$ **Salty Springs Resort.** Perched on 29 undeveloped acres on the northern shore of Salt Spring, this is the only property to take advantage of the natural mineral springs of the island. The one-, two-, and three-bedroom ponderosa pine cabins have Gothic arch ceilings, fireplaces, kitchenettes, and, best of all, therapeutic whirlpool massage bathtubs tapped into the mineral springs. Outside are flower boxes, gas grills, picnic tables, and unobstructed ocean views. ☎ *1460 North Beach Rd., V8K 1J4,* ☎ *604/537–4111 or 800/665–0039,* ₣ₐₓ *604/537–2939. 12 units. Boating, bicycles, game/music room, coin laundry. MC, V.*

North of Vancouver Island

Prince Rupert

DINING

$$ **Smile's Seafood Café.** If you don't mind walking among the fish-processing plants by the railway, you'll find this place a real change of pace. It has been a mainstay of Prince Rupert since 1935 and has succeeded because it provides small-town friendly service along with its seafood menu. Favorites include the halibut cheeks and the fisherman's platter. ✕ *113 George Hills Way,* ☎ *604/624–3072. MC, V.*

DINING AND LODGING

$$$ **Crest Motor Hotel.** This warm, modern hotel is among the finest in the
★ north. It's a block from the two shopping centers but stands on a bluff overlooking the harbor. The restaurant, pleasantly decorated with brass rails and beam ceilings, has a waterfront view and specializes in seafood; particularly outstanding are the salmon dishes. ☎ *222 1st Ave. W, V8J 3P6,* ☎ *604/624–6771 or 800/663–8150,* ₣ₐₓ *604/627–7666. 103 rooms. Restaurant (reservations required), coffee shop, lounge, hot tub, exercise room. AE, D, DC, MC, V.*

LODGING

$$$ **Best Western Highliner Inn.** This modern high-rise near the waterfront is conveniently situated and relatively well priced. It's in the heart of the downtown shopping district only one block from the airline terminal building. Ask for a room with a private balcony and view of the harbor. ☎ *815 1st Ave. W, V8J 1B3,* ☎ *604/624–9060 or 800/668–3115,* ₣ₐₓ *604/627–7759. 96 rooms. Restaurant, lounge, beauty salon, coin laundry. AE, DC, MC, V.*

Queen Charlotte Islands

DINING AND LODGING

$$ **Tlell River House.** The smell of fresh-cut wood welcomes you into this secluded lodge in the woods overlooking the Tlell River. From the hotel it's only a few hundred feet to the beach (and the shipwreck of the *Pezuta*). The rooms are decorated with wood paneling, floral curtains, and thick down comforters; many have views of the river. The restaurant serves excellent seafood and a variety of deliciously rich cheesecakes. ☎ *Beitush Rd., just south of Tlell River Bridge, Rte. 16, Box 56, Tlell V0T 1Y0,* ☎ *604/557–4211 or 800/667–8906 in Canada,* ₣ₐₓ *604/557–4622. 10 rooms. Restaurant, lounge, fishing, meeting room. AE, MC, V.*

LODGING

$$ **Alaska View Lodge.** On a clear day, you can step onto your porch at this bed-and-breakfast and see the mountains of Alaska in the distance. The lodge is bordered by a long stretch of sandy beach on one side and by woods on the other. For an additional cost, the owner makes a three-course dinner, using classical recipes based on Queen Charlotte fare, such as home-smoked salmon, scallops, and Dungeness crab; plenty of advance notice is necessary for dinners. ☎ *Tow Hill Rd., Box 227, Masset V0T 1M0,* ☎ *604/626–3333 or 800/661–0019 in Canada. 4 rooms. Dining room. MC, V.*

$ **Spruce Point Lodge.** This cedar-sided building, encircled by a balcony, attracts families and couples because of its inexpensive rates and down-home feel. Like most Queen Charlotte accommodations, this one is more rustic than luxurious and features locally made pine furnishings that go with the northern-woods motif. For the money you get a Continental breakfast and an occasional seafood barbecue, with a menu that depends on the daily catch. Kayakers and hikers on a budget should ask about the bunk rooms, usually available at a low nightly rate. ☎ *609 6th Ave., Queen Charlotte V0T 1S0,* ☎ *and fax 604/559–8234. 7 rooms. MC, V.*

Okanagan Valley and Environs, Including Rainbow and High Country

Harrison Hot Springs

DINING

$$–$$$ **Black Forest.** Ask the locals where to dine and they'll send you here, a charming Bavarian dining room on Harrison Village Esplanade, overlooking the lake. It comes as no surprise that the specialties here are German standards, from schnitzels to Black Forest cake, with a few Continental dishes (mainly steaks and seafood) thrown in for good measure. Hearty German beer and an array of wines round out the selection. ✕ *180 Esplanade,* ☎ *604/796–9343. Reservations advised. AE, MC, V. Closed lunch.*

DINING AND LODGING

$$$–$$$$ **Harrison Hot Springs Hotel.** Ever since fur traders and gold miners dis-
★ covered the soothing hot springs in the late 1800s, Harrison has been a favored stopover spot. The St. Alice Hotel, built beside the lake in 1886 to accommodate these weary travelers, was destroyed by fire, and from its ashes rose the Harrison Hot Springs Hotel in the 1920s. The property has continued to grow over the decades, and, for the most part, you can tell from the decor when sections were built. The most reasonably priced rooms, in the original building and the west tower, have an old English look, with Edwardian furnishings and ceiling moldings; those in the east tower (added in 1989) are more modern and plush, with a heftier price tag. All rooms were renovated in 1994 and have new carpet, wallpaper, drapes, and bedspreads in lighter, brighter tones. Amenities include a PGA-rated nine-hole golf course and, of course, hot spring–fed pools. ☎ *100 Esplanade, Harrison Hot Springs V0M 1K0,* ☎ *604/796–2244 or 800/663–2266 in the U.S. and Canada,* FAX *604/796–9374. 290 rooms, 16 cottages. 2 restaurants (reservations advised), lounge, 2 indoor pools, outdoor pool, beauty salon, 2 saunas, 9-hole golf course, 1 indoor and 2 outdoor tennis courts, health club, hiking, bicycles. AE, DC, MC, V.*

Kamloops

DINING AND LODGING

$$$ **Lac le Jeune Resort.** With 160 kilometers (99 miles) of cross-country
★ skiing, a lake stocked with trout, and a restaurant that serves robust helpings, this resort is a good choice if you want to enjoy the outdoors. The rustic, self-sufficient cabins are perfect for families because of their ample size and amenities, and pets are permitted. There are also comfortable, spacious rooms in the main lodge, with no phones or televisions to distract from the beauty of the setting. ☎ *Off Coquihala Hwy., 29 km (18 mi) southwest of Kamloops, Box 3215, Kamloops*

V2C 6B8, ☎ *604/372–2722 or 800/561–5253,* FAX *604/372–8755.*
28 rooms, 4-plex chalet, 6 cabins. Restaurant, lounge, sauna, boating,
cross-country skiing, theater, meeting room. AE, D, DC, MC, V.

Kelowna

DINING

$$–$$$ **Papillon.** This contemporary-looking restaurant has a Continental
menu that offers pasta, seafood, and steak. The Prawns and Scallops
Caribbean is outstanding. The wine list includes a wide selection of
imported and local wines that work nicely with the meals. ✕ *375 Leon*
Ave., ☎ *604/763–3833. Reservations advised. AE, DC, MC, V. Closed*
weekend lunch.

DINING AND LODGING

$$$$ **Lake Okanagan Resort.** This respected Hotels and Resorts property is
★   a popular, self-contained destination on the west side of Okanagan Lake.
The rooms have either kitchens or kitchenettes and range in size from
one-room suites in the main hotel to spacious three-room chalets
spread around the 300 acres. The resort shows some signs of age, particularly in the worn floors; but functional furnishings, wood-burning
fireplaces, perfect views of the lake, and all the resort activities, including
nature and dinner cruises, make this a good choice. Try to book one
of the Lakeside Terrace rooms, renovated in 1993. ⌑ *2751 Westside*
Rd., V1Y 8B2, ☎ *604/769–3511 or 800/663–3273,* FAX *604/769–6665.*
150 rooms. Restaurant, café, poolside lounge, 3 pools, hot tub, sauna,
9-hole golf course, 7 tennis courts, hiking, horseback riding, bicycles.
AE, DC, MC, V.

$$$–$$$$ **Hotel Eldorado.** In 1989, the owners bought the old Eldorado Arms,
built in 1926, and floated it by barge to its present location. Shortly
thereafter, the old property burned down, but a new Eldorado has been
built in its place, with much of the old-style charm intact. Rooms tend
to be small and cozy, with light carpets, floral patterns, and Canadian
heritage furnishings; many have balconies affording superb views of
Okanagan Lake. The Eldorado Dining Room has earned a fine repu-
tation, serving fresh rack of lamb and seafood dishes. Ask for a seat
on the waterfront patio. Full breakfast is included in the room rate.
⌑ *500 Cook Rd., V1W 3G9,* ☎ *604/763–7500,* FAX *604/861–4779.*
20 rooms. Restaurant, lounge, boating. AE, DC, MC, V.

Merritt

DINING AND LODGING

$$ **Corbett Lake Country Inn.** The locals want to keep this one a secret,
★   but not owner Peter McVey, a French-trained chef. His restaurant pre-
sents a different fixed menu every night; favorites include rack of lamb
and chateaubriand. The six single cabins (with extra beds) and two du-
plexes are comfortable and basic (though one duplex renovated in 1993
could now be considered deluxe), and there are rooms in the main lodge.
Fly-fishing for rainbow trout on the private lake is a big attraction here,
and no fishing license is required. Small pets are allowed. ⌑ *Off Rte.*
5A, 11 km (7 mi) south of Merritt, Box 327, V0K 2B0, ☎ *604/378–*
4334. 10 cabins, 3 rooms. Restaurant (reservations required), boat-
ing. V. Closed mid-Jan.–Apr. and mid-Oct.–Dec. 23.

Penticton

DINING

$$–$$$ **Granny Bogner's.** Perhaps the owners got a bit carried away with the
★   homey theme: flowing lace curtains, Oriental rugs, wood chairs, cloth-
covered tables, and waitresses in long skirts. But the food at this mostly
Continental restaurant is excellent and prepared meticulously to order.

The poached halibut and roasted duck have contributed to the widely held belief that this is the best restaurant in the Okanagan. ✗ *302 Eckhardt Ave. W,* ☎ *604/493–2711. Reservations advised. AE, MC, V. Closed lunch; Sun. and Mon.; and Jan.*

LODGING

$$$$ **Coast Lakeside Resort.** On the shore of Okanagan Lake, the inn is both a peaceful retreat and right in the center of the action. The waterfront offers relaxation, and the nearby Penticton Golf and Country Club invites a competitive round of golf. Vancouver businesspeople love this place for its comfort and convention facilities. The rooms are bright and airy, and half of them have lake views; whirlpool bathtubs were added to some in 1994. ⊡ *21 Lakeshore Dr. W, V2A 7M5,* ☎ *604/493–8221 or 800/663–1144,* ℻ *604/493–0607. 204 rooms. 2 restaurants, lounge, indoor pool, beauty salon, hot tub, massage, sauna, 2 tennis courts, health club, shuffleboard, volleyball, windsurfing, boating, waterskiing. AE, DC, MC, V.*

$–$$ **Riordan House.** When John and Donna Ortiz bought and restored the former Tiffin Tea House/Riordan Restaurant for their residence, they didn't expect to give guided tours to the newly spiffed-up 1921 house. But people seemed to like the place, built by a Prohibition rum-runner and furnished now with family antiques, so the Ortizes bowed to the inevitable and opened it as a bed-and-breakfast. One bedroom has a fireplace and one a sitting area; all look out on the surrounding hills. The Continental breakfast stars home-baked croissants, scones, muffins, and a selection of seasonal fruit; box lunches are packed on request (and Granny Bogner's is 60 paces away). Lake Okanagan is only a short walk, and you can drift on a rubber raft down the canal that connects it with Skaha Lake. ⊡ *689 Winnipeg St., V2A 5N1,* ☎ *and* ℻ *604/493–5997. 3 rooms share 3 baths. Airport pickup, beach shuttle. MC, V.*

Silver Star Mountain

DINING

$$ **Craigellachie Dining Room.** The home-cooked meals in the dining room
★ of the Putnam Station Hotel are filling rather than fancy. Soups and sandwiches are on the lunch menu, while old favorites like barbecue ribs, lasagna, pork chops, steaks, and pastas are offered in the evenings. The daily three-course special is generally a good deal. ✗ *Silver Star Mountain Resort,* ☎ *604/542–2459. AE, MC, V.*

DINING AND LODGING

$$$ **Vance Creek Hotel.** Looking more like the set of a spaghetti Western
★ than a modern hotel, the Vance Creek enjoys a prime location in the heart of the gaslight-era-theme village resort atop Silver Star Mountain. Rooms are simple, with coordinated decor, long vanities in the entryway, and boxy bathrooms. Those on the first floor are popular with families because they are equipped with kitchenettes, bunk beds for the kids, and private outside entrances. Willow furniture and fireplaces add a touch more comfort to suites in the annex completed in 1993. ⊡ *Silver Star Mountain Resort, Box 3, Silver Star Mountain V0E 1G0,* ☎ *604/549–5191,* ℻ *604/549–5177. 84 rooms. 2 restaurants, bar, lounge, indoor pool, hot tub, hiking, horseback riding, bicycles, rollerblading, ski storage, meeting room. Closed mid-Apr.–mid-May. AE, D, MC, V.*

$$–$$$ **Silver Lode Inn.** To complete the alpine experience on Silver Star Moun-
★ tain, head to the Silver Lode Restaurant for raclette or fondue. Owners Max Schlaepfer and Trudi Amstutz, originally from Berne, Switzerland, serve hearty helpings of the real thing in the cheerful restaurant of their inn. No-frills rooms offer the basic comforts and

are the most reasonably priced in the village. ⌧ *Silver Star Mountain Resort, Box 5, Silver Star Mountain V0E 1G0,* ☎ *604/549–5105;* FAX *604/549–2163. Restaurant, bar, lounge, indoor pool, hot tub, hiking, horseback riding, bicycles, rollerblading, ski storage, meeting room. AE, MC, V.*

THE ARTS AND NIGHTLIFE

The Arts

GALLERIES

The **Art Gallery of Greater Victoria,** considered one of Canada's finest art museums, is home both to large collections of Chinese and Japanese ceramics and other art and to the only authentic Shinto shrine in North America. The gallery also hosts a permanent Emily Carr exhibit and numerous temporary exhibitions yearly. *1040 Moss St., Victoria,* ☎ *604/384–4101.* ☛ *$4 adults, $2 senior citizens and students, children under 13 free; free Thurs. after 5, though donations are accepted.* ☉ *Mon.–Wed., Fri., and Sat. 10–5; Thurs. 10–9; Sun. 1–5.*

Among the numerous commercial galleries, the **Fran Willis North Park Gallery** (200–1619 Store St., ☎ 604/381–3422) is a good bet. In a gorgeously restored warehouse near the waterfront, it shows contemporary paintings and sculpture by local artists; music is performed from time to time. **Eagle's Moon Gallery** (1010 Government St., ☎ 604/361–4184) showcases the totems, serigraphs, and original paintings of renowned Tsimishian artist Roy Henry Vickers. Original art and fine Canadian crafts are the focus at the **Northern Passage Gallery** (1020 Government St., ☎ 604/381–3380).

MUSIC

The **Victoria Symphony** has a winter schedule and a summer season, playing in the recently refurbished **Royal Theatre** (805 Broughton St., Victoria, ☎ 604/386–6121) and at the **University Centre Auditorium** (Finnerty Rd., Victoria, ☎ 604/721–8480). The **Pacific Opera Victoria** performs three productions a year in the 900-seat **McPherson Playhouse** (3 Centennial Sq., ☎ 604/386–6121), adjoining the Victoria City Hall. The **Victoria International Music Festival** (☎ 604/736–2119) features internationally acclaimed musicians each summer from the first week in July through late August.

The **Victoria Jazz Society** (☎ 604/388–4423) organizes an annual **JazzFest International** in late June, which in the past has featured such jazz, blues, and world-beat artists as Dizzy Gillespie, Frank Morgan, and Ellis Marsalis.

For listings of clubs and restaurants featuring jazz during the year, call **Jazz Hotline** (604/658–5255).

THEATER

Live productions can be seen at the **Belfry Theatre** (1291 Gladstone Ave., ☎ 604/385–6815), the **Phoenix Theatre** (Finnerty Rd., ☎ 604/721–8000) at the University of Victoria, **Langham Court Theatre** (805 Langham Ct., ☎ 604/384–2142), and **McPherson Playhouse** (3 Centennial Sq., ☎ 604/386–6121).

Nightlife

In addition to live music, darts, and brewery tours, **Spinnakers Brew Pub** (308 Catherine St., ☎ 604/386–2739) features plenty of B.C. microbrewery beer, including eight of their own concoctions on tap. **Harpo's** (15 Bastion Sq., ☎ 604/385–5333) has live rock, blues, and jazz, with visits from internationally recognized bands. For dancing, head to **Sweetwater's** (27-560 Johnson St., ☎ 604/383–7844), where a younger crowd moves on two dance floors to taped techno and Top-40.

BRITISH COLUMBIA ESSENTIALS

Arriving and Departing

By Boat
There is year-round passenger service (closed Christmas) between Victoria and Seattle on the *Victoria Clipper* (☎ 604/382–8100 in Victoria or 800/888–2535 in the U.S.).

Washington State Ferries (☎ 604/381–1551 in Victoria, 206/464–6400 in Seattle) cross daily, year-round, between Sidney, just north of Victoria, and Anacortes, Washington. **Black Ball Transport** (☎ 604/386–2202 in Victoria; 206/457–4491 in Port Angeles) operates between Victoria and Port Angeles, Washington.

Direct passenger and vehicle service between Seattle and Victoria is available May 21–September 18 on the *Royal Victorian*, operated by **Victoria Line** (☎ 604/480–5555). Outfitted to carry 192 cars and 1,000 passengers, the ship will make one round-trip daily, departing Victoria at 7:30 AM and returning from Seattle at 1 PM. One-way fares for car and driver are $49. Tickets for additional passengers or foot passengers cost $25 one-way. Reservations are advised if you're traveling with a vehicle.

By Bus
Greyhound (☎ 604/662–3222 in Vancouver, 800/661–8747 in Canada, or 800/231–2222 in the U.S.) connects destinations throughout British Columbia with cities and towns all along the Pacific North Coast.

By Car
Driving time from Seattle to Vancouver is about 3 hours. From other Canadian regions, three main routes lead into British Columbia: through Sparwood, in the south, take Route 3; from Jasper and Banff, in the central region, travel on Route 1 (Trans-Canada) or Route 5; and through Dawson Creek, in the north, follow Routes 2 and 97.

By Plane
British Columbia is served by **Victoria International Airport** and **Vancouver International Airport.** Domestic airports are in most cities. **Air Canada** (☎ 604/688–5515 in Vancouver, 800/776–3000 in the U.S.) and **Canadian Airlines International** (☎ 604/279–6611 in Vancouver, 800/426–7000 in the U.S.) are the two dominant carriers. **Air B.C.** (☎ 604/688–5515 in Vancouver, 604/360–9074 in Victoria, 800/776–3000 in the U.S.) is the major regional line and runs daily flights between Seattle and Victoria. **Kenmore Air** (☎ 206/486–1257 or 800/543–9595 in the U.S. and Canada) offers direct daily flights from Seattle to Victoria, Nanaimo, Campbell River, and Northeast Vancouver Island. **Horizon Air** (☎ 800/547–9308) provides service between Seattle and Victoria airports.

Getting Around

By Bicycle
GULF ISLANDS
Because Mayne Island is so small (only 21 square kilometers), with mild hills and wonderful scenery, it is great territory for a vigorous bike ride.

At 100 kilometers on the circular route, Salt Spring offers more of a challenge. Some bed and breakfasts have bicycles; ask that they be set aside for you when you make your reservations. On Mayne, you can rent bikes at the **Miner's Bay gas station;** on Salt Spring, try **Island Spoke Folk** (☎ 604/537–4664) at the Trading Company Building in Ganges.

By Bus

VICTORIA AND VANCOUVER ISLAND
The **BC Transit System** (☎ 604/382–6161) runs a fairly extensive service throughout Victoria and the surrounding areas, with an all-day pass that costs $4 for adults, $3 for students and senior citizens. Passes are sold at many outlets in downtown Victoria, including Eaton Centre and the Tourist Info Centre.

Pacific Coach Lines (☎ 800/661–1725) operates daily service between Victoria and Vancouver on B.C. Ferries. **Island Coach Lines** (☎ 604/385–4411) serves Vancouver Island. **Maverick Coach Lines** (☎ 604/662–8051) serves Nanaimo from Vancouver on B.C. Ferries (*see below*).

NORTH OF VANCOUVER ISLAND
Greyhound Lines of Canada (☎ 800/231–2222 or 604/662–3222 in Vancouver) serves the area north of Vancouver. Among its hundreds of stops in the province are Prince Rupert, Terrace, and Smithers.

By Car
Major roads in British Columbia, and most secondary roads, are paved and well engineered. Mountain driving is slower but more scenic. There are no roads on the mainland coast once you leave the populated areas of the southwest corner near Vancouver.

VICTORIA
Route 17 connects the Swartz Bay ferry terminal on the Saanich Peninsula with downtown Victoria. The TransCanada Highway, Route 1, runs south from Nanaimo to Victoria. Route 14 connects Sooke to Port Renfrew, on the west coast of Vancouver Island, with Victoria.

GULF ISLANDS
The roads on both islands are narrow and winding. Exercise extreme caution around the many cyclists, especially thick on the roads in summer. Car rentals are available on Salt Spring through **Heritage Rentals** (☎ 604/537–4225, FAX 604/537–4226).

CAR RENTALS
Most major agencies, including **Avis, Budget,** and **Hertz,** serve cities throughout the province (*see* Important Contacts A to Z *in* the Gold Guide).

By Ferry
B.C. Ferries (☎ 604/277–0277 in Vancouver or 604/656-0757 in Victoria for recorded schedule information; 604/669–1211 or 604/629–3215 for reservations; 604/753–6626 in Nanaimo) provides frequent year-round passenger and vehicle service between Vancouver and Vancouver Island, from Tsawwassen (south of Vancouver) to Swartz Bay (30 minutes by car north of Victoria); Tsawwassen to Nanaimo; and Horseshoe Bay (north of Vancouver) to Nanaimo. There are eight round-trips daily between Tsawwassen and Nanaimo and between Horseshoe Bay and Nanaimo, and at least eight round-trips per day between Tsawwassen and Swartz Bay (additional sailings during the summer, on weekends, and during holiday periods). B.C. Ferries also provides service from outside Vancouver and Victoria to the northern and southern Gulf Islands (reserve ahead), the Sunshine Coast, Nanaimo, through the Inside Passage between Port Hardy and Prince Rupert, and

from Prince Rupert to the Queen Charlotte Islands. When you travel with a vehicle in summer, plan to arrive at the terminal well in advance of the scheduled sailing time.

By Plane

VANCOUVER ISLAND

Helijet Airways (☎ 604/273–1414 or 604/382–6222) helicopter service is available from downtown Vancouver to downtown Victoria.

GULF ISLANDS

Harbour Air Ltd. (☎ 604/537–5525 or 800/665–0212 in B.C.) and **Hanna Air Saltspring** (☎ 604/537–9359 or 800/665–2359 in B.C.) provide several regularly scheduled 20- to 30-minute daily floatplane flights from Ganges on Salt Spring Island to Coal Harbor in downtown Vancouver and to Vancouver Airport.

QUEEN CHARLOTTE ISLANDS

Harbour Air (☎ 604/627–1341 in Prince Rupert, 604/637–5355 in Sandspit) runs scheduled floatplanes between Sandspit, Masset, Queen Charlotte City, and Prince Rupert daily except Christmas, Boxing Day (Dec. 26), and New Year's Day. **Air B.C.** (☎ 800/776–3000) provides both airport-to-airport and harbor-to-harbor service from Vancouver to Victoria at least hourly. Both flights take about 35 minutes.

By Train

MAINLAND

BC Rail (☎ 604/984–5246 or 604/631–3500 in Vancouver, 604/564–9080 in Prince George) travels from Vancouver to Prince George, a route of 747 kilometers (463 miles), and offers daily service to Whistler. **Via Rail** (☎ 800/561–8630 in British Columbia) provides service between Prince Rupert and Prince George.

VANCOUVER ISLAND

Esquimalt & Nanaimo Rail Liner (450 Pandora Ave., Victoria V8W 3L5, ☎ 604/383–4324; in British Columbia, 800/561–8630) makes the round-trip from Victoria's Pandora Avenue Station to Courtenay; schedules vary seasonally.

Guided Tours

Orientation

Tally-Ho Horsedrawn Tours (☎ 604/479–1113) offers visitors a get-acquainted session with downtown Victoria that includes Beacon Hill Park. **Victoria's Carriage Tours** (☎ 604/383–2207) is another option for horse-drawn tours. From April through September it's possible to tour downtown Victoria by pedicab; contact **Kabuki Kabs** (☎ 604/385–4243). The best way to see the sights of the inner harbor is by **Harbour Gondola** (☎ 604/361–3511), complete with authentically garbed gondolier to narrate the tour. **Gray Line** (☎ 604/388–5248) offers city tours on double-decker buses that visit the city center, Chinatown, Antique Row, Oak Bay, and Beacon Hill Park; a combination tour stops at Butchart Gardens as well.

Classic Holidays Tour & Travel (102–75 W. Broadway, Vancouver V5Y 1P1, ☎ 604/875–6377) and **Sea to Sky** (1928 Nelson Ave., W. Vancouver V7V 2P4, ☎ 604/922–7339) offer tours throughout the province.

Special Interest

A few Vancouver Island–based companies that conduct whale-watching tours are: **Jamie's Whaling Station** (Box 590, Tofino V0R 2Z0, ☎ 604/725–3919 or 800/667–9913 in Canada), **Tofino Sea-Kayaking Com-**

pany (Box 620, Tofino, VOR 2Z0, ☎ 604/725–4222) on the west coast, **Robson Bight Charter**s (Box 99, Sayward V0P 1R0, ☎ 604/282–3833) near Campbell River, and, near Port Hardy, **Stubbs Island Charters** (Box 7, Telegraph Cove V0N 3J0, ☎ 604/928–3185).

Ecosummer Expeditions (1516 Duranleau St., Vancouver V6H 3S4, ☎ 604/669–7741 or 800/688–8605, FAX 604/669–3244) runs ecological tours of the Queen Charlotte Islands.

The history and culture of the First Nations (native) people of the region are the focus of new summer tours including **Lheit-Lit'en Nation Elders Salmon Camp Tours** (Lheit-Lit'en Native Heritage Society, R.R. 1, Site 27, Comp. 60, Prince George, V2N 2H8, ☎ 604/963–8451, FAX 604/963–8324) on the mainland and **Yuquot History Tours** (Ahaminaquis Tourist Centre, Box 459, Gold River, V0P 1G0, ☎ 604/283–7464, FAX 604/283–2335) on Vancouver Island.

History buffs may prefer looking into Victoria's background on the intriguing guided cemetery tours put together by the **Old Cemeteries Society** (☎ 604/384–0045).

Important Addresses and Numbers

Emergencies
Dial **911** in Vancouver and Victoria; dial **0** elsewhere in the province for **police, ambulance,** or **poison control.** On the Gulf Islands, dial 911 for **police, fire,** or **ambulance service.**

Hospitals
British Columbia has hospitals in virtually every town, including: in Victoria, **Victoria General Hospital** (35 Helmcken Rd., ☎ 604/727–4212); on the Gulf Islands, **Lady Minto Hospital** (☎ 604/537–5545) in Ganges on Salt Spring Island; in Prince George, **Prince George Regional Hospital** (2000 15th Ave., ☎ 604/565–2000 or for emergencies, 604/565–2444); in Chilliwack, **Chilliwack General Hospital** (45600 Menholm Rd., ☎ 604/795–4141); in Kamloops, **Royal Inland Hospital** (311 Columbia St., ☎ 604/374–5111); in Kelowna, **Kelowna General Hospital** (2268 Pandosy St., ☎ 604/862–4000).

Late-Night Pharmacies
In Victoria, **McGill and Orme Pharmacies** (649 Fort St., ☎ 604/384–1195); in Prince George, **Hart Drugs** (3789 W. Austin Rd., ☎ 604/962–9666); in Kamloops, **Kipp-Mallery I.D.A. Pharmacy** (273 Victoria St., ☎ 604/372–2531); in Hope, **Pharmasave Drugs** (235 Wallace St., ☎ 604/869–2486).

Visitor Information
For information concerning the province contact **Discover British Columbia** (Ministry of Tourism, Parliament Buildings, Victoria V8V 1X4, ☎ 604/663-6000 in British Columbia or 800/663–6000 in the U.S.). More than 140 communities in the province have **Travel Infocentres.**

For Victoria, contact **Tourism Victoria** (1175 Douglas St., Suite 710, Victoria V8W 2E1, ☎ 604/382–2160 or 800/663–3883 for reservations, FAX 604/361–9733).

The principal regional tourist offices are: **Tourism Association of Southwestern B.C.** (204–1755 W. Broadway, Vancouver V6J 4S5, ☎ 604/739–9011 or 800/667–3306, FAX 604/739–0153); **Tourism Association of Vancouver Island** (302–45 Bastion Sq., Victoria V8W 1J1, ☎ 604/382–3551, FAX 604/382–3532); **Okanagan–Similkameen Tourist Association**

(104–515 Rte. 97 S, Kelowna V1Z 3J2, ☎ 604/769–5959, FAX 604/861–7493); **High Country Tourist Association** (2–1490 Pearson Pl., Kamloops V2C 6H1, ☎ 604/372–7770 or 800/567–2275, FAX 604/828–4656); **North By Northwest Tourism** (3840 Alfred Ave., Box 1030, Smithers V0J 2N0, ☎ 604/847–5227, FAX 604/847–7585); **Rocky Mountain Visitors Association** (495 Wallinger Ave., Box 10, Kimberley V1A 2Y5, ☎ 604/427–4838, FAX 604/427–3344); **Prince Rupert Convention and Visitors Bureau** (100 McBride St., Box 669 CMG, Prince Rupert V8J 3S1, ☎ 604/624–5637 or 800/667–1994); **Kootenay Country Tourist Association** (610 Railway St., Nelson V1L 1H4, ☎ 604/352–6033, FAX 604/352–1656); **Cariboo Chilcotin Coast Tourist Association** (190 Yorston St., Box 4900, Williams Lake V2G 2V8, ☎ 604/392–2226 or 800/663–5885, FAX 604/392–2838); **Peace River Alaska Highway Tourist Association** (9908 106th Ave., Box 6850, Fort St. John V1J 4J3, ☎ 604/785–2544, FAX 604/785–4424). **Salt Spring Island Chamber of Commerce** (121 Lower Ganges Rd., Box 111, Ganges, V0S 1E0, ☎ 604/537–5252, FAX 604/537–4276) and **Mayne Island Chamber of Commerce** (General Delivery, Mayne Island, V0N 2J0, no ☎) provide information on the Gulf Islands.

8 Southeast Alaska

The Southeast encompasses the Inside Passage—a century ago the traditional route to the Klondike gold fields and today the centerpiece of Alaska cruises. Here are glacier-filled fjords and the justly famous Glacier Bay National Park. Juneau, the state's capital, is also in the Southeast, as are fishing villages such as Petersburg and Ketchikan, which is known for its totem-pole carving. An onion-domed cathedral accents Sitka, the one-time capital of Russian America. Each fall, up to 4,000 eagles gather just outside of Haines.

THE SOUTHEAST STRETCHES BELOW THE STATE like the tail of a kite. It is a world of massive glaciers, fjords, and snowcapped peaks. The largest concentration of coastal glaciers on earth can be viewed at Glacier Bay National Park, one of the region's most prized attractions. Thousands of islands are blanketed with lush stands of spruce, hemlock, and cedar. Bays, coves, lakes of all sizes, and swift, icy rivers provide some of the continent's best fishing grounds—and scenery as majestic and unspoiled as any in North America.

By Mike Miller

Updated by
Dinah Spritzer

Like anywhere else, the Southeast has its drawbacks. For one thing, it rains a lot. If you plan to spend a week or more here, you can count on showers during at least a few of those days. Die-hard southeasterners simply throw on a light slicker and shrug off the rain. Their attitude is philosophical: Without the rain, there would be no forests, no lakes, and no streams running with world-class salmon and trout, no healthy populations of brown and black bear, moose, deer, mountain goats, and wolves.

Another disadvantage—or advantage, depending on your point of view—is an almost total lack of connecting roads between the area's communities. To fill this void, Alaskans created the Marine Highway System of fast, frequent passenger and vehicle ferries. The ships, complete with staterooms, observation decks, cocktail lounges, and heated, glass-enclosed solariums, connect Bellingham, Washington, and Prince Rupert, British Columbia, with the Southeast's Ketchikan, Wrangell, Petersburg, Sitka, Juneau, Haines, and Skagway. Smaller vessels connect remote towns and villages.

The Southeast's natural beauty and abundance of wildlife have made it one of the world's fastest-growing cruise destinations. There are about 20 big cruise ships that ply Southeast waters, known as the Inside Passage, during the height of the summer. Regular air service to the Southeast is available from the lower 48 states and from mainland Alaska. The Southeast is closer to the Lower 48 than the rest of Alaska and is therefore the least costly to reach.

The native peoples you'll meet in the Southeast coastal region are Tlingit, Haida, and Tsimshian Indians. These peoples, like their coastal neighbors in British Columbia, preserve a culture rich in totemic art forms, including deeply carved poles, masks, baskets, and ceremonial objects. Many live among nonnatives in modern towns while continuing their own traditions.

A pioneer spirit dominates the towns of Southeast Alaska, perhaps the last American frontier. Residents, some from other states, some with roots in the Old Country, and some who can trace their ancestors back to the gold-rush days, are an adventurous lot. The rough-and-tumble spirit of the Southeast often combines with a worldly sophistication: Those who fish are also artists, loggers are often business entrepreneurs, and homemakers may be native dance performers. The region has been affected by tourism in many ways—young people from around the country spend summers here working at the hotels, shops, and cafés just to be in such a magnificent setting.

EXPLORING

The Southeast Panhandle stretches some 500 miles from Yakutat at its northernmost to Ketchikan and Metlakatla at the southern end. At its

Southeast Alaska

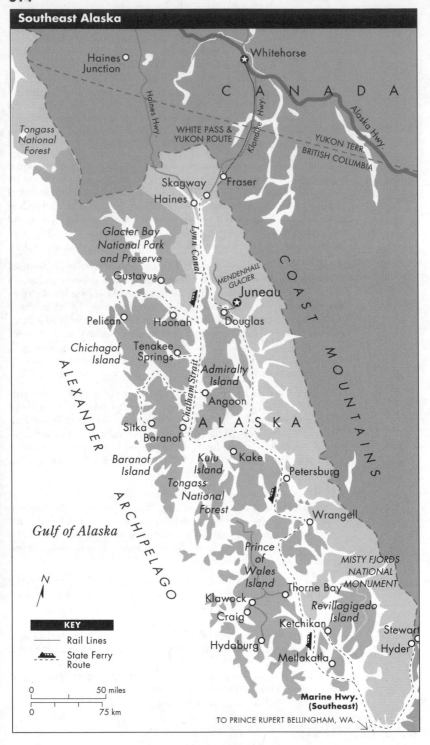

Haines
Junction

Whitehorse

C A N A D A

Tongass
National
Forest

Haines Hwy.

Klondike Hwy.

Alaska Hwy.

WHITE PASS &
YUKON ROUTE

YUKON TERR.
BRITISH COLUMBIA

Skagway
Haines

Fraser

Lynn Canal

Glacier Bay
National Park
and Preserve

MENDENHALL
GLACIER

Juneau

Gustavus

C
O
A
S
T

Pelican

Hoonah

Douglas

Chichagof
Island

Tenakee
Springs

Admiralty
Island

M
O
U
N
T
A
I
N
S

A
L
E
X
A
N
D
E
R

Chatham Strait

Angoon

Sitka

A L A S K A

Baranof

Baranof
Island

Kuiu
Island

Kake

Petersburg

Tongass
National
Forest

A
R
C
H
I
P
E
L
A
G
O

Wrangell

Gulf of Alaska

MISTY FJORDS
NATIONAL
MONUMENT

Prince
of
Wales
Island

Thorne Bay

N

Klawock

Revillagigedo
Island

Craig

Ketchikan

Stewart

KEY

—— Rail Lines

⛴ State Ferry
Route

Hydaburg

Metlakatla

Hyder

0   50 miles

0   75 km

Marine Hwy.
(Southeast)

TO PRINCE RUPERT BELLINGHAM, WA.

widest the region measures only 140 miles, and in the upper Panhandle just south of Yakutat, it's a skinny 30 miles across. Most of the Panhandle consists of a sliver of mainland buffered by offshore islands.

There are more than a thousand islands up and down the Panhandle coast—most of them mountainous with lush covers of timber. Collectively they constitute the Alexander Archipelago. On the mainland to the east of the United States–Canada border lies British Columbia.

You can get to and around the area by ship or by plane, but forget the highway. The roadways that exist in these parts run at most a few dozen miles out from towns and villages, then they dead-end.

Not surprisingly, most of the communities of the region are on islands rather than on the mainland. The principal exceptions are Juneau, Haines, Skagway, and the Indian village of Klukwan. Island outposts include Ketchikan, Wrangell, Petersburg, Sitka, Metlakatla, and a number of other towns, Indian villages, and logging camps. Each town has its own distinct collection of ethnic lore, wildlife, and natural wonders.

If shipboard sightseeing is your pleasure, more than two dozen cruise ships and state ferries await your booking. The usual (though not the only) pattern is for cruising visitors to board ship at Vancouver, British Columbia, or San Francisco, then to set sail on an itinerary that typically includes Ketchikan, Juneau, Skagway, and Sitka. The most popular voyages include a visit to Glacier Bay, where humpback whales and monumental glaciers are the principal attractions. Cruise-ship travel includes a mix of sailing and port visits, which can vary from a few hours to a full day. The state ferries (southern ports of origin: Bellingham, Washington, or Prince Rupert, British Columbia) rarely spend much time in the cities where they call, but you can get off one ship, spend a day or more ashore, then catch another vessel heading north or south to your next destination.

Don't overlook the region's alternative means of travel. Small floatplanes, some carrying five or fewer passengers, and yachts sleeping a half dozen or so ply the routes from the larger population centers to tiny settlements, and to even more remote sites where there are no permanent residents at all (unless you count bears).

The Southeast is a fisherman's paradise. There are saltwater salmon charter boats, salmon fishing lodges (some near the larger communities, others remote and accessible by floatplane), fly-in mountain-lake lodges where the fishing is for trout and char, and—bargain hunters take special note—more than 150 remote but weather-tight cabins operated by the U.S. Forest Service. The USFS rents these units (no electricity or running water) for the absurdly reasonable rate of $25 per night per group (*see* Off the Beaten Track, *below*).

Ketchikan

Numbers in the margin correspond to points of interest on the Ketchikan map.

Alaskans call Ketchikan "the First City," because in the days before air travel it was always the first Alaskan port of call for northbound steamship passengers. For many travelers today—arriving by air, cruise ship, or ferry—the tradition continues.

Ketchikan is also known as the totem-pole port because of its outstanding collection of native totems, which can be viewed at the Totem Heritage Center, Totem Bight State Historical Park, and Saxman Village.

Ketchikan is perched on a large island at the foot of Deer Mountain (3,000 feet). The site at the mouth of Ketchikan Creek was a summer fish camp of the Tlingit Indians until white miners and fishermen came to settle in the town in 1885. Gold discoveries just before the turn of the century brought more immigrants, and valuable timber and commercial fishing resources spurred new industries. By the 1930s the town bragged it was the "Salmon Canning Capital of the World." You will still find some of the Southeast's best salmon fishing here.

Fishing and timber are still the mainstays of Ketchikan's economy, with tourism also playing a major role. If you visit during the summer months, the historic Creek Street may be so packed with cruise passengers that just buying a T-shirt will be an ordeal. Keep in mind that Ketchikan is one of the wettest Southeast cities—the average annual precipitation is more than 150 inches.

There's a lot to be seen on foot in downtown Ketchikan. The best place ❶ to begin is at the **Ketchikan Visitors Bureau** on the dock, where you can pick up a free historic-walking-tour map. Around the corner on ❷ Mill Street is the new **Southeast Alaska Visitor Center,** where the U.S. Forest Service and other federal agencies provide an array of information on the region's history and natural attractions. For $1, you can view a video slide show, "Mystical Alaska," in the center's theater. The show runs every 30 minutes in the summer. ☎ 907/228–6290. ☉ *Summer, daily 8:30–4:30; winter, Tues.–Sat. 8:30–4:30.*

At press time, a development on Mill Street with 1920s-style cannery architecture was scheduled to open in the summer of 1996. Among the development's attractions will be retail shops, eateries, and a luxury hotel with 80 to 90 rooms and an open market with local crafts.

From the visitor center turn onto Main Street and turn right when you hit Mission Street. Walk past the sub–post office in the Trading Post (the main post office is inconveniently located several miles south, near ❸ the ferry terminal) to Bawden Street and **St. John's Church and Seaman's Center.** The 1903 church structure is the oldest remaining house of worship in Ketchikan, its interior formed from red cedar cut in the native-operated sawmill in nearby Saxman. The Seaman's Center, next door to the church, was built in 1904 as a hospital. It later housed the *Alaska Sportsman Magazine* (now *Alaska Magazine*), which began pub❹ lication in Ketchikan in 1936. Catercorner from the church is **Whale Park,** site of the Knox Brother Clock, and the Chief Johnson Totem Pole, raised in 1989 and a replica of the 1901 totem in the same site.

❺ From the Seaman's Center, bear left onto Dock Street to reach the **Tongass Historical Museum and Totem Pole.** Here you can browse among Indian artifacts and pioneer relics of the early mining and fishing era. Among the exhibits are a big and brilliantly polished lens out of Tree Point Lighthouse, the bullet-riddled skull of a notorious and fearsome old brown bear called Old Groaner, Indian ceremonial objects, and a Chilkat blanket. There's even a 14-foot model of a typical Alaskan salmon-fishing seine vessel. *Dock and Bawden Sts.,* ☎ *907/ 225–5600.* ☞ *$2 Mon.–Sat., free Sun.* ☉ *Mon.–Sat. 8–5, Sun. 9–4.*

Continuing north on Bawden, then east on Park Avenue, look up to❻ ward your left to see **Grant Street Trestle,** constructed in 1908. At one time virtually all of Ketchikan's walkways and streets were wooden trestles, but only this one remains. Get out your camera and set it for ❼ fast speed at the **Salmon Falls, Fish Ladder, and Salmon Carving** just off Park Avenue on Married Man's Trail. When the salmon start running in midsummer and later, thousands literally leap the falls (or take

City Park, **11**
Creek Street, **14**
Creek Street
Footbridge, **16**
Deer Mountain
Hatchery, **9**
Dolly's House, **15**
Grant Street
Trestle, **6**
Kyan Totem
Pole, **17**
Monrean
House, **18**
*Return of the
Eagle,* **12**
St. John's
Church, **3**
Salmon Falls, **7**
Scenic
lookout, **19**
Southeast
Alaska Visitor
Center, **2**
Thomas St., **13**
Tongass
Museum, **5**
Totem Heritage
Center, **10**
Visitors
Bureau, **1**
Westmark
Cape Fox
Lodge, **8**
Whale Park, **4**

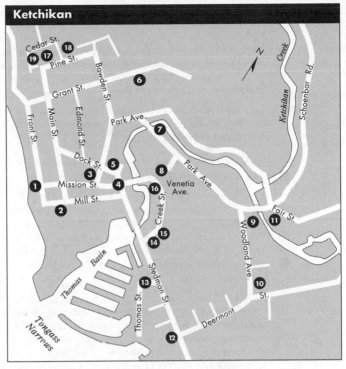

Ketchikan

the easier ladder route) to spawn in Ketchikan Creek's waters farther upstream. Many can also be seen in the creek feeding the falls.

Noting that some of the streets intersecting Park are actually wooden ladders, continue to Venetia Avenue and turn right for a steep climb

8 up to the civic center and **Westmark Cape Fox Lodge** (*see* Lodging, *below*). Besides a stunning view of the harbor and fine dining, the lodge offers funicular rides to and from the popular Creek Street for $1.

9 Go back down Venetia and continue east on Park until you reach **Deer Mountain Hatchery,** where tens of thousands of salmon are annually dispersed into local waters. The hatchery, owned by the Ketchikan Indian Corporation, has exhibits on traditional Native American fish-

10 ing. Just south of the hatchery on Deermont Street is the **Totem Heritage Center and Nature Park** (☛ $2, free on Sun.; ◷ Mon.–Sat. 8–5, Sun. 9–4), where you'll find original totems dating back almost two cen-

11 turies. The Hatchery and Heritage Center lead into **City Park,** at Park and Fair streets. Its small ponds once served as a holding area for the region's first hatchery, open from 1923 to 1928.

Go back to Deermont and head southwest, away from City Park. Turn right onto Stedman Street and you'll pass the colorful wall mural

12 called *Return of the Eagle.* It was created by 21 native artists on the walls of the Robertson Building of the Ketchikan campus, University of Alaska–Southeast.

13 Next comes **Thomas Street** and **Thomas Basin.** The street was constructed in 1913 to be part of the New England Fish Company's cannery here; Thomas Basin is a major, and picture-worthy, harbor. One of four harbors in Ketchikan, it is home port to a wide variety of pleasure and work boats.

⑭ Return to Stedman and head north to **Creek Street,** former site of Ketchikan's infamous red-light district. Today its small, quaint houses, built on stilts over the creek waters, have been restored as trendy
⑮ shops. The street's most famous brothel, **Dolly's House,** has been preserved as a museum, complete with furnishings, beds, and a short history of the life and times of Ketchikan's best-known madam. ☞ *$3.* ⊙ *When cruise ships are in port.*

TIME OUT For a break from the hubbub, duck into the **5-Star Cafe** (5 Creek St.) for the coffee beverage of your choice, or take the funicular up to **Westmark Cape Fox Lodge** (*see above*).

Farther up Creek Street, there's more good salmon-viewing in season
⑯ at the **Creek Street Footbridge.**

If you're into steep street climbing, head left on Mission Street, then
⑰ right up Main Street, past the Ketchikan Fire Department to the **Kyan Totem Pole,** a replica of an 1880s carving that once stood near St. John's
⑱ Church. Adjacent is the **Monrean House,** a 1904 structure that is included in the National Register of Historic Places. Nearby on Cedar
⑲ Street is a **scenic lookout** onto City Float and the waters of Tongass Narrows.

Ketchikan's two most famous totem parks (there are more totems in Ketchikan than anywhere else in the world) are **Totem Bight State Historical Park,** 10 miles north on North Tongass Highway, and the park at **Saxman Indian Village,** 2 miles south on South Tongass Highway. (Don't try walking to Saxman; there are no sidewalks.) The poles at both parks are, for the most part, 50-year-old replicas of even older totems brought in from outlying villages as part of a federal government works–cultural project during the 1930s.

Totem Bight, with its many totems and a hand-hewn Indian tribal house, sits on a particularly scenic spit of land facing the waters of Tongass Narrows.

Saxman Village (named for a missionary who helped Indians settle there before 1900) has added totems to its collection, as well as a large tribal house believed to be the largest in the world. There's also a carver's shed nearby where totems and totemic art objects are created, and a stand-up theater where a multimedia presentation tells the story of Southeast Alaska's Indian peoples.

Out on the highway in either direction, you won't go far before you run out of road. The North Tongass Highway ends about 18 miles from downtown, at Settler's Cove Campground. The South Tongass Highway terminates at a power plant. Side roads soon end at campgrounds and at trailheads, viewpoints, lakes, boat-launching ramps, and private property.

If you're a tough hiker, the 3-mile trail from downtown to the top of **Deer Mountain** will repay your efforts with a spectacular panorama of the city below (facing the water), and the wilderness behind. The trail begins at the corner of Fair and Deermont streets. **Ward Cove Recreation Area,** about 6 miles north of town, offers easier hiking beside lakes and streams and beneath towering spruce and hemlock trees.

Wrangell

Numbers in the margin correspond to points of interest on the Wrangell map.

Next up the line is Wrangell, on an island near the mouth of the fast-flowing Stikine River. A small, unassuming timber and fishing community, the town has had three flags flown over it since the arrival of the Russian traders. Known as Redoubt St. Dionysius when it was part of Russian America, the town was renamed Fort Stikine after the British took it over. The name was changed to Wrangell when Americans bought it.

❶ You can see a lot in Wrangell on foot, and a good place to start your tour is the A-frame **Chamber of Commerce Visitor Information Center** (☎ 907/874–3901) close to the docks at Front Street and Outer Drive.
❷ It's near **City Hall** and its very tall totem pole. The visitor center is open when cruise ships and the ferries are in port and at other times throughout the summer. If you need information and the A-frame is closed, drop by the City Museum where the Wrangell Convention and Visitors Bureau is located (122 2nd St. ☉ Summer, Mon.–Sat. 1–4, and whenever cruise ships or ferries are in port).

❸ Walking up Front Street will bring you to **KikSadi Indian Park,** a pocket park of Alaska greenery and impressive totem poles. This is the spot for a pleasant stroll.

On your way to Wrangell's number-one attraction—Chief Shakes Island—stop at **Chief Shakes's grave site,** uphill from Hansen's Boat Shop
❹ on Case Avenue. Buried here is Shakes V, one of a number of local chiefs to bear that name. He led the local Tlingits during the first half of the 19th century. Two killer-whale totems mark the chief's burial place.

❺ On **Chief Shakes Island,** reached by a footbridge off the harbor dock, you can see some of the finest totem poles in Alaska, as well as a tribal house constructed in the 1930s as a replica of one that was home to many of the various Shakes and their peoples. The interior contains six house totems, two of them more than 100 years old; unfortunately the house is open only when ships are in port or by appointment. ☎ *907/874–2023 or 907/874–3747.* ☛ *$1 donation requested.*

After your visit to the island, wander out to the end of the dock for
❻ ❼ the view and picture taking at the **seaplane float** and **boat harbor.**

❽ The **Wrangell City Museum** (2nd and Bevier Sts., ☎ 907/874–3770; ☛ $2; ☉ Mon. and Wed.–Fri. 10–5, weekends 1–4) contains a historical collection that includes totem fragments, petroglyphs, and other Indian artifacts; a bootlegger's still; a vintage 1800s Linotype and presses.

❾ The **cruise-ship dock** is south and west of the A-frame information cen-
❿ ter; north and west is the **public library** (☎ 907/874–3535), with its small collection of ancient petroglyphs (more about these curious rock carvings later).

Boat harbor, **7**
Chamber of Commerce Visitor Information Center, **1**
Chief Shakes's gravesite, **4**
Chief Shakes Island, **5**
City Hall, **2**
Cruise-ship dock, **9**
KikSadi Indian Park, **3**
"Our Collections", **11**
Petroglyph Beach, **12**
Public library, **10**
Seaplane float, **6**
Wrangell City Museum, **8**

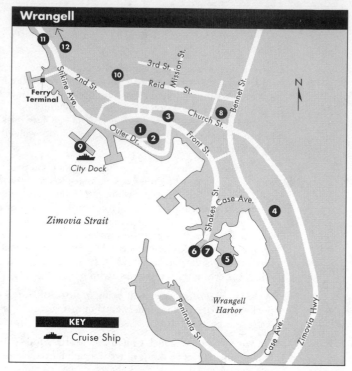

Walking northwest on either 2nd Street or Stikine Avenue, beyond the **state ferry terminal,** you'll discover another museum, called **"Our Collections"** by owner Elva Bigelow. It's in a barnlike building on the water side of Evergreen Avenue (Stikine turns into Evergreen here). To some, the artifacts that comprise the collection constitute less a museum than a garage sale waiting to happen. Still, large numbers of viewers seem quite taken by the literally thousands of unrelated collectibles (clocks, animal traps, waffle irons, tools, etc.) that the Bigelows have gathered in half a century of Alaska living. ☎ *907/874–3646. Call before setting out to visit.* ☞ *Donations accepted.*

A five-minute walk up Evergreen Avenue beyond "Our Collections" brings you (at low tide only) to **Petroglyph Beach,** one of the more curious sights in Southeast Alaska. Here, scattered among other rocks, are three dozen or more large stones bearing designs and pictures chiseled by unknown, ancient artists. No one knows why the rocks were etched the way they are. Perhaps they were boundary markers or messages; possibly they were just primitive doodling. Because the petroglyphs can be damaged by physical contact, the state discourages visitors from creating a "rubbing" off the rocks with rice paper and crayons. Instead, you can purchase a rubber stamp duplicate of selected petroglyphs from the city museum or from a forest service interpreter at the cruise dock for $4.50 to $5.95. Do not, of course, attempt to move any of the petroglyph stones.

There are other stones in Wrangell that you can take with you. These are natural garnets, gathered at Garnet Ledge, facing the Stikine River. The semiprecious gems are sold on the streets for 50¢ to $50, depending on their quality.

Petersburg

Numbers in the margin correspond to points of interest on the Petersburg map.

Getting to Petersburg is an experience, whether you take the "high road" by air or the "low road" by sea. Alaska Airlines claims the shortest jet flight in the world from takeoff at Wrangell to landing at Petersburg. The schedule calls for 20 minutes of flying, but it's usually more like 10. At sea level, only ferries and smaller cruisers can squeak through Wrangell Narrows with the aid of more than 50 buoys and range markers along the 22-mile crossing. At times the channel seems too narrow for ships to pass through, making for a nail-biting—though safe—trip.

The inaccessibility of Petersburg is part of its off-the-beaten-path charm. Unlike at several other Southeast communities, you'll never be overwhelmed by the hordes of cruise passengers here.

At first sight of Petersburg you may think you're in the old country. Neat, white, Scandinavian-style homes and storefronts with steep roofs and bright-colored swirls of leaf and flower designs (called rosemaling) and row upon row of sturdy fishing vessels in the harbor invoke the spirit of Norway. No wonder. This prosperous fishing community was founded by Norwegian Peter Buschmann in 1897.

You may occasionally even hear some Norwegian spoken, especially during the Little Norway Festival held here each year on the weekend closest to May 17. If you're in town during the festival, be sure to partake in one of the fish feeds that highlight the Norwegian Independence Day celebration. You won't find better beer-batter halibut and folk dancing outside of Norway.

Petersburg, like Wrangell, is a destination for travelers who prefer not to be spoon-fed information by a tour guide. On your own, sample the brew at **Kito's Kave** bar on Sing Lee Alley (in the afternoon if you don't like your music in the high-decibel range) and examine the outrageous wall decor there, which varies from Mexican painting on black velvet to mounted Alaska king salmon and two stuffed sailfish from a tropical fishing expedition. Wander, at high tide, to **Hammer Slough** for a vision of houses and buildings on high stilts reflected perfectly in still slough waters. Or simply stroll down Main Street to see shops displaying imported Norwegian wool sweaters or metal Viking helmets, complete with horns.

One of the most pleasant things to do in Petersburg is to roam among the fishing vessels tied up at dockside. This is one of Alaska's busiest, most prosperous fishing communities, and the variety of seacraft is enormous. You'll see small trollers, big halibut vessels, and sleek pleasure craft as well. Wander, too, around the fish-processing structures (though beware of the pungent aroma). Just watching shrimp, salmon, or halibut catches being brought ashore, you can get a real appreciation for this industry and the people who engage in it.

Because of its small size, most of Petersburg can be covered by bicycle. A good route to ride is along the coast on Nordic Drive, past the lovely homes, to the boardwalk and the city dump, where you might spot some bears. Coming back to town, take the interior route and you'll pass the airport and some pretty churches before returning to the waterfront. Tides Inn at 1st and Dolphin streets offers bicycle rentals.

① From the **visitor center** overlooking the city harbor there are great viewing and picture-taking vantage points. For a scenic hike, go north on
② Nordic Drive to get to **Sandy Beach,** where there's frequently good eagle-viewing and access to one of Petersburg's favorite picnic and recreation locales.

Those wanting to do some sightseeing in town should head northeast
③ up the hill from the visitor center to the **Clausen Museum** and the bronze *Fisk* (Norwegian for "fish") sculpture at 2nd and Fram streets. The monument, featuring scores of separately sculpted salmon, halibut, and herring, celebrates the bounty of the sea. It was created in 1967 as part of Petersburg's celebration of the 100th anniversary of the Alaska Purchase from Russia.

The museum—not surprisingly—devotes a lot of its space to fishing and processing. There's an old "iron chink" used in the early days for gutting and cleaning fish, as well as displays that illustrate the workings of several types of fishing boats. A 126½-pound king salmon, the largest ever caught, came out of a fish trap on Prince of Wales Island in 1939 and is on exhibit, as is the world's largest chum salmon—a 36-pounder. There are also displays of native artifacts. *203 Fram St.,* ☎ *907/772–3598.* ☛ *$2.* ☺ *May 13–Sept. 25, Mon.–Sat. 10–4, Sun. 1–4.*

④ ⑤ ⑥ Three pioneer churches— **Catholic, Lutheran,** and **Presbyterian**—are located nearby at Dolphin and 3rd streets, Excel and 5th streets, and on Haugen Street between 2nd and 3rd streets, respectively. Of the three, the 50-year-old Lutheran edifice is the oldest. It is said that boys wheelbarrowed fill from elsewhere in the city for landscaping around the foundation. Their compensation? Ice-cream cones. The enticement was so successful that, after three years of ice-cream rewards, it was necessary to bring in a bulldozer to scrape off the excess dirt.

The large, white, barnlike structure on stilts that stands in Hammer
⑦ Slough off Indian Street is the **Sons of Norway Hall,** the headquarters of an organization devoted to keeping alive the traditions and culture of the old country. North of the hall, from the Nordic Drive bridge, is
⑧ the high-tide **Hammer Slough reflecting pool.**

Other attractions are located south of the city along the Mitkof Highway, where you will pass seafood processing plants and the state ferry terminal (at Mile .8) en route to the **Frank Heintzleman Nursery** at Mile 8.6 (named for a much-loved former territorial governor); the **Fall's Creek fish ladder** at Mile 10.8, where coho and pink salmon migrate upstream in late summer and fall; and the **Crystal Lake State Hatch-**

Catholic church, **4**

Clausen Museum, **3**

Hammer Slough reflecting pool, **8**

Lutheran church, **5**

Presbyterian church, **6**

Sandy Beach, **2**

Sons of Norway Hall, **7**

Visitor center, **1**

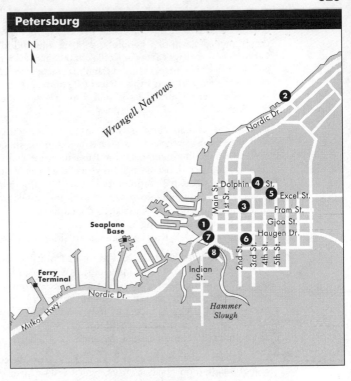

Petersburg

ery/Blind Slough Recreation Area at Mile 17.5, where more than 60,000 pounds of salmon and trout are produced each year.

Petersburg's biggest draw actually lies about 25 miles east of town and is accessible only by water or air. **LeConte Glacier** is the continent's southernmost tidewater glacier and one of its most active, often calving off so many icebergs that the lake at its face is carpeted bank-to-bank with floating bergs. Ferries and cruise ships pass it at a distance. Sightseeing yachts, charter vessels, and flightseeing tours are available (*see* Guided Tours *in* Southeast Essentials, *below,* or contact the visitors bureau).

Sitka

Numbers in the margin correspond to points of interest on the Sitka map.

For centuries before the 18th-century arrival of the Russians, Sitka was the ancestral home of the Tlingit Indian nation. In canoes up to 60 feet long, they successfully fished the Alaskan panhandle. Unfortunately for the Tlingits, Russian Territorial Governor Alexander Baranof coveted the Sitka site for its beauty, mild climate, and economic potential. In the island's massive timbered forests he saw raw materials for shipbuilding; its location offered trading routes as far east as Hawaii and the Orient, and as far south as California.

In 1799 Baranof negotiated with the local chief to build a wooden fort and trading post some 6 miles north of the present town. He called the outpost St. Michael Archangel and moved a large number of his Russian and Aleut fur hunters there from their former base on Kodiak Island.

The Indians soon took exception to the ambitions of their new neighbors. Reluctant to pledge allegiance to the czar and provide free labor, they attacked Baranof's people and burned his buildings in 1802. Baranof, however, was away at Kodiak at the time. He returned in 1804 with a formidable force, including shipboard cannons. He attacked the Indians at their fort near Indian River (site of the present-day 105-acre Sitka National Historical Park) and drove them to the other side of the island.

In 1821 the Tlingits came back to Sitka to trade with the Russians, who were happy to benefit from the tribe's hunting skills. Under Baranof and succeeding managers, the Russian–American Company and the town prospered, becoming known as "the Paris of the Pacific." Besides the fur trade, the community boasted a major shipbuilding and repair facility, sawmills, forges, and a salmon saltery, and even initiated an ice industry. The Russians shipped blocks of ice from nearby Swan Lake to the booming San Francisco market. Baranof eventually shifted the capital of Russian America to Sitka from Kodiak.

The town declined after its 1867 transfer from Russia to the United States but became prosperous again during World War II, when it served as a base for the U.S. effort to drive the Japanese from the Aleutian Islands. Today its important industries are lumber, fishing, and tourism. Sitka's history is best depicted by the totems of the National Historical Park, the artifacts of the Sheldon Jackson Museum, and the Russian architectural landmark, St. Michael's Cathedral.

1 A good place to begin a tour of Sitka is the **Visitors Bureau** in the **Centennial Building** on Harbor Drive, which rests near a big Tlingit Indian war canoe. Inside the building you'll find a museum, an auditorium, an art gallery, and lots of advice on what to see and how to see it. The staff will know if the colorfully costumed New Archangel Russian Dancers are performing, what concerts or recitals are scheduled for the annual Sitka Summer Music Festival, and when logging competitions or the annual salmon derby will be held.

To get a feel for the town, turn left onto Harbor Drive and head for **2** **Castle Hill,** where Alaska was formally handed over to the United States on October 18, 1867, and where the first 49-star U.S. flag was flown on January 3, 1959, signifying Alaska's statehood. In order to reach the hill and get one of Sitka's best views, make the first right off of Harbor Drive just before the John O'Connell Bridge, then go into the Baranof Castle Hill State Historic Site entrance to the left of the Sitka Hotel. A gravel path takes you to the top of the hill, overlooking Crescent Harbor. Several Russian residences were on the hill, including Baranof's castle, which burned down in 1894.

The large four-level, red-roof structure on the northeast side of the hill **3** with the imposing 14-foot statue in front is the **Sitka State Pioneers' Home,** built in 1934 and the first of several state-run retirement homes and medical-care facilities for Alaska's senior citizens. The statue, symbolizing Alaska's frontier sourdough spirit, was modeled by an authentic pioneer, William "Skagway Bill" Fonda. It portrays a determined prospector with pack, pick, rifle, and supplies on his back heading for the gold country.

Go down the Castle Hill steps toward the Pioneer Home and you will be facing **Totem Square,** where there are three anchors discovered in local waters and believed to be 19th-century British in origin. Look for the double-headed eagle of czarist Russia carved into the cedar of the totem pole in the park.

Alaska Raptor
Rehabilitation
Center, **12**

Castle Hill, **2**

Centennial
Building/
Visitors
Bureau, **1**

Russian
Bishop's
House, **7**

Russian
blockhouse, **4**

Russian and
Lutheran
cemeteries, **5**

St. Michael's
Cathedral, **6**

Sheldon
Jackson
College, **8**

Sheldon
Jackson
Museum, **9**

Sitka National
Historical
Park, **10**

Sitka State
Pioneers'
Home, **3**

Tlingit Fort, **11**

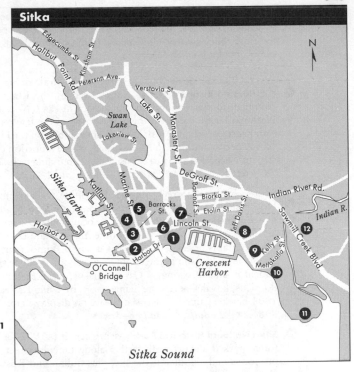

Walk past the Pioneer Home on Lincoln Street and take the first left onto Barracks Street, which turns into Marine Street after a block. On your left is an old **Russian blockhouse,** and on your right are the **Russian and Lutheran cemeteries** where most of Sitka's Russian dignitaries are buried. Make a right from Marine Street and the cemetery entrance will be on your left. The most distinctive grave belongs to Princess Maksutoff, one of the most famous members of the Russian royal family to be buried on Alaskan soil.

Head back down Lincoln Street and turn left to face the house of worship that is one of Southeast Alaska's best-known landmarks. **St. Michael's Cathedral** had its origins in a log-built, frame-covered structure erected between 1844 and 1848. In 1966 the church was totally destroyed in a fire that swept through the downtown business district. As the fire engulfed the building, local townspeople risked their lives and rushed inside to rescue the cathedral's precious icons, religious objects, vestments, and other treasures brought to the church from Russia.

Using original measurements and blueprints, an almost exact replica of onion-domed St. Michael's was built and dedicated in 1976. Today, visitors can see numerous icons, among them the much-prized *Our Lady of Sitka* (also known as the *Sitka Madonna*) and the *Christ Pantocrator* (*Christ the Judge*) on either side of the doors of the interior altar screen. Among other objects to be viewed: ornate Gospel books, chalices, crucifixes, much-used silver-gilt wedding crowns dating back to 1866, and an altar cloth said to have been worked by the first Princess Maksutov (the prince's second wife left Alaska with her husband). This is an active church, so visitors should respect the services and privacy of worshipers. ☎ 907/747–8120. ☛ *$1 donation requested.* ☼ *June–Sept., daily 1:30–5 and when cruise ships are in port.*

TIME OUT You are now in the heart of Sitka. Great views of the harbor, high-quality fashions and collectibles along with a quaint café can be found at the classy **Bayview Trading Company** (407 Lincoln St.), Sitka's version of a mall, not far from St. Michael's.

❼ Several blocks east on Lincoln past the cathedral, facing the harbor, is the **Russian Bishop's House,** constructed by the Russian–American Company for Bishop Innocent Veniaminov in 1842. Now a part of Sitka National Historical Park, the house is one of the few remaining Russian log structures in Alaska. Inside are exhibits on the history of Russian America and the Room Revealed, where a portion of the house's structure is peeled away to expose Russian building techniques. ☎ 907/747–6281. ☛ *Free.* ☉ *Daily 9:30–noon and 1–3.*

❽ South on Lincoln Street, about a 10-minute walk from the Bishop's House, lies the campus of **Sheldon Jackson College,** founded in 1878, **❾** and the **Sheldon Jackson Museum.** The octagonal museum, built in 1895 and now under the jurisdiction of the Alaska State Division of Museums, contains priceless Indian, Aleut, and Eskimo items collected by Dr. Sheldon Jackson in the remote regions of Alaska he traveled as an educator and missionary. Carved masks, Chilkat Indian blankets, dogsleds, kayaks—even the helmet worn by Chief Katlean during the 1804 battle against the Russians—are on display here. ☎ 907/747–8981. ☛ *$2 adults.* ☉ *Daily 8–5.*

❿ **Sitka National Historical Park**'s visitor center (☎ 907/747–6281) and totem park is a short walk farther along Lincoln Street. Audiovisual programs and exhibits at the site, plus Indian and Russian artifacts, give an overview of Southeast Alaska Indian culture, both old and new. Often, Native American artists and craftsmen are on hand to demonstrate and interpret traditional Tlingit crafts such as silversmithing, weaving, and basketry.

⓫ A self-guided trail through the park to the actual site of the **Tlingit Fort** passes by some of the most skillfully carved totems in the state. Some of the 15 poles are quite old, dating back more than eight decades. Others are replicas, copies of those lost to time and a damp climate. ☎ 907/747–6281. ☛ *Free.* ☉ *June–Sept., daily 8–10, visitor center closes at 5; Oct.–May, weekdays 8–5.*

⓬ For die-hard walkers, the 15-minute trek to the **Alaska Raptor Rehabilitation Center** is worth taking; you can see the renowned Buddy, an eagle who thinks he's human. To get there, exit the park onto Sawmill Creek Road, make a left, and walk until you see the entrance across the street. ☎ 907/747–8662. ☛ *$10 adults, $5 children.* ☉ *Daily 7–6.*

About 6 miles from town on Sawmill Creek Road is the newly constructed **Whale Park,** where you can get an excellent view of Sitka's largest annual visitors. Humpback whales frequent Sitka during the fall on their way toward their home in Hawaii. Check with the visitor center to find out about tour operators that offer whale-watching packages.

Juneau

Numbers in the margin correspond to points of interest on the Juneau map.

Juneau, like Haines and Skagway to the north, is located on the North American mainland. Unlike Haines and Skagway, it can't be reached by conventional highway from the rest of the United States and Canada. No matter. There are lots of easy ways to reach Alaska's capital and third largest city. For one, there's the Alaska Marine Highway ferry system, which provides near daily arrivals and departures in the summer. For another, virtually every cruise ship plying Southeast waters calls at Juneau. And two airlines—Alaska and Delta—have several flights daily into Juneau International Airport from other points in Alaska and the other states.

Juneau owes its origins to two colorful sourdoughs, Joe Juneau and Dick Harris, and to a Tlingit chief named Kowee. The chief led the two men to rich reserves of gold in the outwash of the stream that now runs through the middle of town and in quartz rock formations back in the gulches and valleys.

That was 1880, and shortly after the discovery a modest stampede resulted in the formation of first a camp, then a town, then finally the Alaska district government capital in 1906.

For 60 years or so after Juneau's founding, gold was the mainstay of the economy. In its heyday, the AJ (for Alaska Juneau) gold mine was the biggest low-grade ore mine in the world. It was not until World War II, when the government decided it needed Juneau's manpower for the war effort, that the AJ and other mines in the area ceased operations. After the war, mining failed to start up again, and government—first territorial, then state—became the city's principal employer.

These days, government (state, federal, and local) remains Juneau's number-one employer. Tourism, transportation, and trading—even a belated mining revival—provide the other major components of the city's economic picture.

Juneau is full of contrasts—it's a sophisticated and cosmopolitan frontier town. Juneau has one of the best museums in Alaska, is surrounded by beautiful wilderness, and has an accessible glacier (Mendenhall) in its backyard. The town's ambience is best experienced at its celebrated watering hotel, the Red Dog Saloon (*see below*).

❶ Marine Park on the dock where the cruise ships tie up is a little gem of benches, shade trees, and shelter, a great place to enjoy an outdoor meal purchased from Juneau's many street vendors. It also has a visitor kiosk staffed from 9 to 6 daily in the summer months. Planned for summer 1996 is a new aerial tram service that will take visitors from the cruise terminal to the top of Mt. Roberts. After the five-minute ride, passengers will be able to take in a multimedia show on Alaskan wonders and experience mountain-view dining.

❷ The **Log Cabin Visitor Center** (☎ 907/566–2201) up Seward Street at 3rd Street is open weekdays 8:30–5 and weekends 10–5. The cabin is a replica of a 19th-century structure that served first as a Presbyterian church, then as a brewery.

Head east a block from Marine Park to South Franklin Street. Buildings here and on Front Street are among the older and most interesting structures in the city. Many reflect the architecture of the 1920s and '30s, and some are even older. The small (42 rooms) **Alaskan Hotel** at 167 South Franklin Street was called "a pocket edition of any of the best hotels on the Pacific Coast" when it opened in 1913. Owners Mike and Betty Adams have restored the building with period trappings, and it's worth a visit even if you're not looking for lodging. The barroom's massive mirrored, oakwood back bar is accented by Tiffany lights and panels.

Alaska State
Capitol, **4**

Alaska State
Museum, **15**

Centennial
Hall, **16**

Cremation spot
of Chief
Kowee, **12**

Evergreen
Cemetery, **11**

Federal
Building and
Post Office, **13**

Five-story
totem, **6**

Governor's
House, **10**

Juneau-Douglas
City Museum, **9**

Juneau-Harris
Monument, **14**

Log Cabin
Visitor Center, **2**

Marine Park, **1**

Red Dog
Saloon, **3**

St. Nicholas
Russian
Orthodox
Church, **5**

State Office
Building, **8**

Wickersham
House, **7**

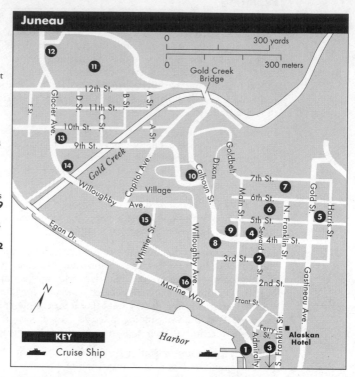

Juneau

Also on South Franklin Street: the **Alaska Steam Laundry Building,** a 1901 structure with a windowed turret that now houses a coffeehouse, a film processor, and other stores. Across the street, the equally venerable **Senate Building mall** contains one of the two Juneau Christmas stores, a children's shop, and a place to buy Russian icons. Close by are numerous other curio and crafts shops, snack shops, and two salmon shops. Alaska's most famous bar, the decades-old and tourist-filled **Red Dog Saloon,** is housed in frontierish quarters at 278 South Franklin Street.

Head uphill on Franklin and turn left onto 4th Street; at the corner of Seward Street is the **Alaska State Capitol,** constructed in 1930, with pillars of southeastern Alaska marble. The building now houses the governor's offices and other state agencies, and the state legislature meets here four months each year. ☎ 907/465–2479. *Tours in summer, daily 8:30–5.*

Uphill one block on Seward and two blocks east on 5th Street stands quaint, onion-domed **St. Nicholas Russian Orthodox Church,** constructed in 1894—the oldest original Russian church in Alaska. *326 5th St.,* ☎ *907/586–1023.* ☛ *Donation requested. Check the visitor center for hrs.*

Directly uphill behind the Capitol Building, between 5th and 6th streets, stands the **five-story totem,** one of Juneau's finer totems, and at the top of the hill on 7th Street stands **Wickersham House,** the former residence of James Wickersham, pioneer judge and delegate to Congress. The home, constructed in 1899, is now a part of Alaska's state park system. Memorabilia from the judge's travels throughout Alaska range from rare native basketry and ivory carvings to historic photos, 47 diaries (maintained even on treks through snow and blizzards), and a Chickering grand piano that came "round the horn" to Alaska while the Russians still ruled here. ☎ *907/586–9001.* ☛ *$2.* ☉ *Mon.–Sat. noon–5.*

8 Back down the hill on 4th Street, you'll pass "the S.O.B."—or **State Office Building.** There on Friday at noon you can have a picnic lunch like the state workers do and listen to organ music played in the four-story atrium on a grand old theater pipe organ, a veteran of the silent-movie era.

9 Head west from the front of the Capitol Building to the **Juneau-Douglas City Museum** (4th and Main Sts., ☎ 907/586–3572), which displays old mining equipment, historic photos, and pioneer artifacts, including a turn-of-the-century store and kitchen. Shortly after passing another totem on Calhoun Street, you'll come to the **Governor's**
10 **House,** a three-level colonial-style home completed in 1912. There are no tours through the house, but the totem pole on the entrance side of the building is surely the only one of its kind to adorn the walls of a U.S. governor's mansion.

If you're still game for walking, continue up Calhoun Street, pass the
11 Gold Creek bridge, and keep going until you come to **Evergreen Cemetery.** A meandering gravel road leads through the graveyard where many Juneau pioneers, including Joe Juneau and Dick Harris, are buried. At the end of the lane you'll come to a monument commemorating the
12 **cremation spot of Chief Kowee.** Turn left here and go south on Glacier
13 Avenue past the **Federal Building and Post Office** at 9th Street, past the
14 **Juneau–Harris Monument** near Gold Creek, then walk on to Whittier
★ **15** Street, where a right turn will take you to the **Alaska State Museum.**

This is one of Alaska's top museums. Whether your tastes run to natural-history exhibits (stuffed brown bears, a replica of a two-story-high eagle nesting tree), native Alaskan exhibits (a 40-foot, walrus-hide umiak [whaling boat] constructed by Eskimos from St. Laurence Island and a re-created interior of a Tlingit tribal house), mining exhibits, or contemporary art, the museum is almost certain to please. *395 Whittier St., ☎ 907/465–2901.* ☛ *$2 adults, children and students free.* ☉ *May 15–Sept. 15, weekdays 9–6, weekends 10–6; Sept. 16–May 14, Tues.–Fri. 10–6.*

16 Finally, on Willoughby Avenue at Egan Drive, there's Juneau's **Centennial Hall**—site of an excellent **information center** operated by the U.S. Forest Service and the U.S. Park Service. Movies, slide shows, and information about recreation in the surrounding Tongass National Forest and in nearby Glacier Bay National Park and Preserve are available here. ☎ *907/586–8751.* ☉ *Summer, daily 8–5; the rest of the year, weekdays 8–5.*

Haines

Numbers in the margin correspond to points of interest on the Haines map.

Missionary S. Hall Young and famed naturalist John Muir picked the site for this town in 1879 as a place to bring Christianity and education to the natives. They could hardly have picked a more beautiful spot. The town sits on a heavily wooded peninsula with magnificent views of Portage Cove and the Coastal Mountain Range. It lies 80 miles north of Juneau via fjordlike Lynn Canal.

Unlike most other cities in Southeast Alaska, Haines can be reached by road (the 152-mile Haines Highway connects at Haines Junction with the Alaska Highway). It's also accessible by the state ferry and by scheduled plane service from Juneau. The Haines ferry terminal is 4½ miles northwest of downtown, and the airport is 3½ miles west.

The town has two distinct personalities. On the northern side of the Haines Highway is the portion of Haines founded by Young and Muir. After its missionary beginnings the town served as the trailhead for the Jack Dalton Trail to the Yukon during the 1897 gold rush to the Klondike. The following year, when gold was discovered in nearby Porcupine (now deserted), the booming community served as a supply center and jumping-off place for those goldfields as well. Today things are quieter; the town's streets are orderly, its homes are well kept, and for the most part it looks a great deal like any other Alaska seacoast community.

South of the highway, the town looks like a military post, which is what it was for nearly half a century. In 1903 the U.S. Army established a post—**Ft. William Henry Seward**—at Portage Cove just south of town. For 17 years (1922–39) the post (renamed Chilkoot Barracks to avoid confusion with the South Central Alaska city of Seward) was the only military base in the territory. That changed with World War II. Following the war the post closed down.

Right after the war a group of veterans purchased the property from the government. They changed its name to Port Chilkoot and created residences, businesses, and an Indian arts center out of the officers' houses and military buildings that surrounded the old fort's parade ground. Eventually Port Chilkoot merged with the city of Haines. Although the two areas are now officially one municipality, the old military post with its still-existing grass parade ground is referred to as Ft. Seward.

The Haines–Ft. Seward community today is recognized for the enormously successful Indian dance and culture center at Ft. Seward, as well as for the superb fishing, camping, and outdoor recreation to be found at Chilkoot Lake, Portage Cove, Mosquito Lake, and Chilkat State Park on the shores of Chilkat Inlet. The last locale, one of the small treasures of the Alaska state park system, features views of the Davidson and Rainbow glaciers across the water.

❶ You can pick up walking-tour maps of both Haines and Ft. Seward at the **visitor center** on 2nd Avenue (☎ 907/766–2234). The easiest place
❷ to start your tour, however, is at the **Sheldon Museum and Cultural Center** near the foot of Main Street. This is another personal Alaskan collection, homegrown by an Alaskan family. Steve Sheldon began assembling Indian artifacts, Russian items, and gold-rush memorabilia, such as Jack Dalton's sawed-off shotgun, in 1924. His daughter, Elisabeth Hakkinen, carries on and is usually on hand to serve Russian tea, to recall the stories behind many of the items on display, and to reminisce about growing up in Haines before World War II. *25 Main St.,* ☎ *907/766–2366. ☛ $2.50. ☉ Summer, daily 1–5; winter, Sun., Mon., and Wed. 1–4 and Tues., Thurs., and Fri. 3–5.*

One of the most rewarding hikes in the area is to the north summit of
❸ **Mt. Ripinsky,** the prominent peak that rises 3,610 feet behind the town. Be warned: It's a strenuous trek and requires a full day. The **trailhead** lies at the top of Young Street, along a pipeline right-of-way. For other hikes, pick up a copy of "Haines Is for Hikers" at the visitor center.

Less than a mile from downtown is Dalton City, an 1890s gold-rush
❹ town re-created from the movie set of *White Fang,* on the **Southeast Alaska State Fairgrounds.** Attractions include carriage rides, gold panning, dogsled demonstrations, native carvers, and keepsakes from the

Chilkat Center for the Arts, **8**

Halsingland Hotel, **6**

Indian tribal house, **7**

Mile 0, **5**

Mt. Ripinsky, **3**

Sheldon Museum and Cultural Center, **2**

Southeast Alaska State Fairgrounds, **4**

Visitor Center, **1**

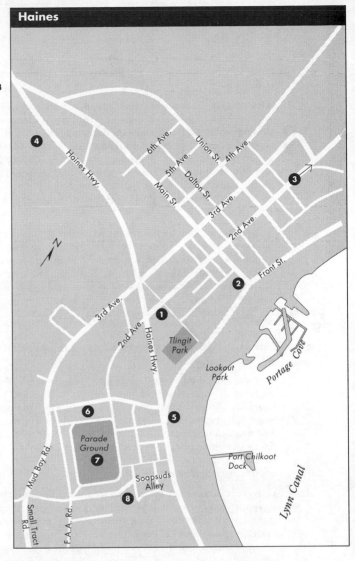

Haines

Dalton City shops. The state fair, held each August, is one of several official regional fall blowouts staged around Alaska, and in its home-grown, homespun way it's a real winner. In addition to the usual collection of barnyard animals (chickens, goats, horses), the fair offers the finest examples of local culinary arts and the chance to see Indian dances, displays of Indian totemic crafts, and some fine art and photography.

As noted, the Haines Highway roughly divides Haines–Ft. Seward. At the base of the highway is **Mile 0,** the starting point of the 152-mile road to the Alaska Highway and the Canadian Yukon. Whether you plan to travel all the way or not, you should spend at least a bit of time on the scenic highway. At about Mile 6 there's a delightful picnic spot near the Chilkat River and an inflowing clear creek; at Mile 9.5 the view of the Takhinsha Mountains across the river is magnificent; and around Mile 19 there is good viewing of the **Alaska Chilkat Bald Eagle Preserve,** where, especially in late fall and early winter, as many as 4,000 of the great birds have been known to assemble. The United States–Canada border lies at Mile 40. If you're traveling on to Canada, stop at Canadian customs and be sure to set your clock ahead one hour.

The Haines Highway is completely paved on the American side of the border and, except for a few remaining stretches, almost entirely paved in Canada.

Back in town, head for Ft. Seward, and wander past the huge, stately, white-columned former commanding officer's home, now a part of the ❻ **Halsingland Hotel** (*see* Dining and Lodging, *below*) on Officer's Row. ❼ Circle the flat but sloping parade ground, with its **Indian tribal house** ❽ and trapper's log cabin. In the evening, visit the **Chilkat Center for the Arts.** This building once was the army post's recreation hall, but now it's the space for Chilkat Indian dancing. Some performances may be at the tribal house next door; check posted notices for performance times.

Between the Chilkat Center for the Arts and the parade ground stands the former fort hospital, now being used as a workshop for the craftsmen of **Alaska Indian Arts,** a nonprofit organization dedicated to the revival of Tlingit Indian art forms. You'll see Indian carvers making totems here, metalsmiths working in silver, and weavers making blankets. ☎ 907/766–2160. ☛ *Free.* ☉ *Weekdays 9–noon and 1–5.*

Skagway

Numbers in the margin correspond to points of interest on the Skagway map.

Skagway lies 13 miles north of Haines by ferry on the Alaska Marine Highway. If you go by road, the distance is 359 miles, as you have to take the Haines Highway up to Haines Junction, Yukon, then take the Alaska Highway 100 miles south to Whitehorse, and then drive a final 100 miles south on the Klondike Highway to Skagway. North country folk call this popular sightseeing route the Golden Horseshoe or Golden Circle tour, because it takes in a lot of gold-rush country in addition to lake, forest, and mountain scenery.

However you get to Skagway, you'll find the town an amazingly preserved artifact from one of North America's biggest, most storied gold rushes. Most of the downtown district forms part of the **Klondike Gold Rush National Historical Park,** a unit of the national park system dedicated to commemorating and interpreting the frenzied stampede that extended to Dawson City in Canada's Yukon. Old false-front stores, saloons, and brothels—built to separate gold-rush prospectors from their grubstakes going north or their gold pokes heading south—have been restored, repainted, and refurnished by the federal government and Skagway's citizens. When you walk down Broadway today, the scene is not appreciably different from what the prospectors saw in the days of 1898, except that the street is now paved to make your exploring easier.

Skagway had only a single cabin, still standing, when the Yukon gold rush began. At first, the argonauts, as they liked to be called, swarmed to Dyea and the Chilkoot Trail, 9 miles west of Skagway. Skagway and its White Pass trail didn't seem as attractive until a dock was built in town. Then it mushroomed overnight into the major gateway to the Klondike, supporting a wild mixture of legitimate businessmen, con artists (among the most cunning was Jefferson "Soapy" Smith), stampeders, and curiosity seekers.

Three months after the first boat landed in July 1897, Skagway numbered perhaps 20,000 persons and had well-laid-out streets, hotels, stores, saloons, gambling houses, and dance halls. By spring of 1898, the superintendent of the Northwest Royal Mounted Police in neighboring Canada would label the town *"little better than a hell on earth."*

A lot of the "hell" ended with a shoot-out one pleasant July evening in 1898. Good guy Frank Reid (the surveyor who laid out Skagway's streets so wide and well) faced down bad guy Soapy Smith on Juneau dock downtown near the present ferry terminal. After a classic exchange of gunfire, Smith lay dead and Reid lay dying. The town built a huge monument at Reid's grave. You can see it in Gold Rush Cemetery and read the inscription on it today: "He gave his life for the honor of Skagway." For Smith, whose tombstone was continually chiseled and stolen by vandals and souvenir seekers, today's grave marker is a simple wooden plank.

When the gold rush played out after a few years, the town of 20,000 dwindled to 700. The White Pass & Yukon Railroad kept the town alive until 1982, when it began to run summers only. By this time, however, tourism revenue was sufficient to compensate for any economic loss suffered as a result of the railroad's more limited schedule.

To begin your visit, head to **City Hall** on 7th Avenue. There, on the first floor of a large granite structure built in 1899 to house McCabe Methodist College, the Skagway Convention and Visitors Bureau will give you maps and lots of suggestions for seeing their town. Your first

❶ stop should be right upstairs in the City Hall building, at the **Trail of '98 Museum.**

Frank Reid's will is preserved under glass here, as are papers disposing of Soapy Smith's estate. Gambling paraphernalia from the old Board of Trade Saloon is on display along with native artifacts, gold scales, a red-and-black sleigh (one-horse variety), a small organ, and a blanket made from the skin of duck necks and fortified by pepper bags sewn behind the skin to afford protection from moths.

After you've browsed in the museum, walk back to Broadway and 6th

❷ Avenue to **Eagles Hall.** Here locals perform a show called "Skagway in the Days of '98." You'll see cancan dancers, learn a little local history, and watch desperado Soapy Smith sent to his reward. ☎ *907/983–2545.* ✆ *$14 adults, $12 senior citizens, $7 children. Posted show hrs depend on ship arrivals and departures. Performances are usually daily at 2 PM and 7:30 PM. There are additional shows at 10:30 AM on Tues., Wed., Thurs.*

❸ Farther south on Broadway you'll come to **Arctic Brotherhood Hall,** the likes of which you'll not see anywhere else in Alaska. The Arctic Brotherhood was a fraternal organization of Alaskan and Yukon pioneers. To decorate the exterior false front of their Skagway lodge building, local members created a mosaic covering out of 20,000 pieces of driftwood and flotsam gathered from local beaches.

❹ **Soapy's Parlor** is on 2nd Avenue just west of Broadway, and the for-
❺ mer **White Pass & Yukon Route rail depot** is on the east side of the main thoroughfare. This building, now the headquarters and information center for the Klondike Gold Rush National Historical Park (☎ 907/983–2921), contains exhibits, photos, and artifacts from the White Pass and Chilkoot trails. This is of special interest if you plan to take a White Pass train ride, drive the nearby Klondike Highway, or hike the Chilkoot Trail.

Arctic
Brotherhood
Hall, **3**

Cruise-ship
dock, **8**

Eagles Hall, **2**

Ferry dock, **7**

Klondike
Highway, **6**

Soapy's
Parlor, **4**

Trail of '98
Museum/
Convention
and Visitors
Bureau, **1**

White Pass &
Yukon Route
rail depot, **5**

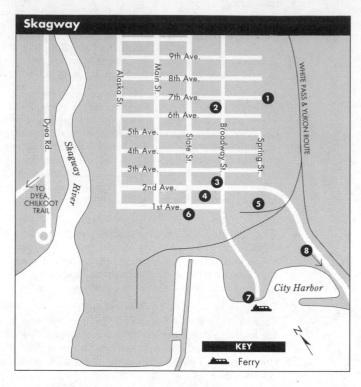

Lots of other stops along Broadway and its side streets merit inspection. For children, the **Sweet Tooth Saloon** with its ice cream and sodas is a special favorite. For adults, the 19th-century **Red Onion Saloon** (with its former brothel upstairs) is an interesting and thirst-quenching stop. The **Golden North Hotel** (*see* Dining and Lodging, *below*) at Broadway and 3rd is Alaska's oldest hotel. Constructed in 1898, it has been lovingly restored to its gold-rush-era milieu. Take a stroll through the lobby even if you're not staying there. Curio shops abound, and among the oldest—probably *the* oldest—in all of Alaska is **Kirmse's** on Broadway. Visit the shop and see the world's largest, heaviest, and most valuable gold-nugget watch chain. On display as well is a companion chain made of the world's tiniest, daintiest little nuggets.

6 At the foot of State Street is the start of the **Klondike Highway.** The Klondike often parallels the older White Pass railway route as it travels northwest to Carcross and Whitehorse in the Canadian Yukon. It merges just south of Whitehorse for a short distance with the Alaska Highway, then heads on its own again to terminate at Dawson City on the shores of the Klondike River. From start to finish, it covers 435 miles.

Along the way the road climbs steeply through forested coastal mountains with jagged, snow-covered peaks. It passes by deep, fish-filled lakes and streams in the Canadian high country, where travelers have a chance of seeing mountain goat, moose, black bear, or grizzly.

If you're driving the Klondike Highway north from Skagway you must stop at **Canadian Customs,** Mile 22. If you're traveling south to Skagway, check in at **U.S. Customs,** Mile 6. And remember that when it's 1 PM in Canada at the border, it's noon in Skagway.

7 Just south of Broadway lies the **ferry dock,** a pleasant half-mile walk
8 from town, and somewhat farther south is the **cruise-ship dock** where
the big ships land. The mountainside cliff behind the cruise-ship dock,
incidentally, is rather incredible, with its scores of advertisements and
ships' names brightly painted on the exposed granite face. Most sin-
gular of all the "murals" at the site is a large skull-like rock formation
that has been painted white, given appropriate cavities, and named
Soapy's Skull.

Two more excursions from Skagway are notable. The first is the
Chilkoot Trail from Dyea to Lake Lindeman, a trek of 33 miles that includes a climb up Chilkoot Pass at the United States–Canada border.
The National Park Service maintains the American side of the pass as
part of the Klondike Gold Rush National Historical Park. The trail is
good; the forest, mountain, and lake country is both scenic and richly
historic, and campsites are strategically located along the way.

The Chilkoot is not, however, an easy walk. There are lots of ups and
downs before you cross the pass and reach the Canadian high country,
and rain is a distinct possibility. To return to Skagway, hikers have three
choices. They can end their trek at Lake Bennett, where a rail motor-
car will transport them to Fraser, with further rail connections to Skagway, or they can walk a cutoff to Log Cabin on the Klondike Highway.
There they can either hitchhike back to town or flag down Gray Line
of Alaska's Alaskon Express motor coach (☎ 907/983–2241 or
800/544–2206; fare $54) heading south to Skagway from Whitehorse.

For the thousands that complete the hike each year, it is the highlight
of a trip to the North country. For details, maps, and references contact the National Park Service information center at 2nd Avenue and
Broadway.

If you're not a hiker, there's an easier way to follow the second excursion,
a prospector's trail to the gold-rush country. You can take the **White
Pass & Yukon Route** (WP & YR) narrow-gauge railroad over the "Trail
of '98."

The historic (started in 1898) gold-rush railroad's diesel locomotives
chug and tow vintage viewing cars up the steep inclines of the route,
hugging the walls of precipitous cliff sides, and providing thousands
of travelers with the view of craggy peaks, plummeting waterfalls, lakes,
and forests. It's a summertime operation only.

Two options are available. Twice daily the WP & YR leaves Skagway
for a three-hour round-trip excursion to the White Pass summit. Sights
along the way include Bridal Veil Falls, Inspiration Point, and Dead
Horse Gulch. The fare is $69. Through service to Whitehorse, Yukon,
is offered daily as well—in the form of a train trip to Fraser where motor-
coach connections are available on to Whitehorse. The one-way fare
to Whitehorse is $95 adults, $42.50 children. For information call
907/983–2217 or 800/343–7373.

Glacier Bay/Gustavus

Visiting Glacier Bay is like discovering the Little Ice Age. It is one of
the few places in the world where you can come within inches (depending
on your mode of transportation) of 16 tidewater glaciers—glaciers that
have their base at the water's edge. They line the 60 miles of narrow
fjords at the northern end of the Inside Passage and rise up to 7,000
feet above the bay. With a noise that sounds like cannons firing, bergs
the size of 10-story office buildings sometimes come crashing from the

"snout" of a glacier. The crash sends tons of water and spray skyward, and it propels mini–tidal waves outward from the point of impact. Johns Hopkins Glacier calves so often and with such volume that the large cruise ships can seldom come within 2 miles of its face.

Nearly 200 years ago, Captain George Vancouver sailed by Glacier Bay and didn't even know it. The bay at that time, 1794, was hidden behind and beneath a vast glacial wall of ice. The glacier was more than 20 miles across its face and, in places, more than 4,000 feet in depth. It extended more than 100 miles to the St. Elias Mountain Range. Over the next 100 years, due to warming weather and other factors not fully understood even now, the face of the glacial ice has melted and retreated with amazing speed, exposing nearly 50 miles of fjords, islands, and inlets.

★   In 1879, about a century after Vancouver's sail-by, one of the earliest white visitors to what is now **Glacier Bay National Park and Preserve** came calling. He was naturalist John Muir, drawn by the flora and fauna that had followed in the wake of glacial withdrawals and fascinated by the vast ice rivers that descended from the mountains to tidewater. Today, the naturalist's namesake glacier, like others in the park, continues to retreat dramatically. Its terminus is now scores of miles farther up bay from the small cabin he built at its face during his time there.

Companies that offer big-ship visits include Holland America Lines, Princess Cruises, Royal Viking Line, and World Explorer Cruises. Other companies, such as Alaska Sightseeing, offer small-ship cruises that allow passengers to get closer to the glaciers. During the several hours that the ships are in the bay, National Park Service naturalists come aboard to explain the great glaciers, to point out features of the forests and islands and mountains, and to help spot black bears, brown bears, mountain goats, whales, porpoises, and the countless species of birds that call the area home.

Smaller, more intimate, and probably more informative (uniformed Park Service naturalists are aboard) is the boat *Spirit of Adventure,* which operates daily from the dock at Bartlett Cove, near Glacier Bay Lodge (☎ 800/622–2042).

At Bartlett Cove, where the glaciers stood and then receded more than two centuries ago, the shore is covered with stands of high-towering spruce and hemlock. This is a climax forest, thick and lush and abounding with the wildlife of Southeast Alaska. As you sail farther into the great bay, the conifers become noticeably smaller, and they are finally replaced by alders and other leafy species, which took root and began growing only a few decades ago. Finally, deep into the bay where the glaciers have withdrawn in very recent years, the shorelines contain only plants and primitive lichens. Given enough time, however, these lands, too, will be covered with the same towering forests that you see at the bay's entrance.

The most adventurous way to see and explore Glacier Bay is up close–really up close, as in paddling your own kayak through the bay's icy waters and inlets. You can book one of **Alaska Discovery's** (234 Gold St., Juneau 99801, ☎ 907/586–1911) four- or seven-day guided expeditions. Unless you really know what you're doing, you're better off signing on with the guided tours. Alaska Discovery provides safe, seaworthy kayaks and tents, gear, and food. Its guides are tough, knowledgeable Alaskans, and they've spent enough time in Glacier Bay's wild country to know what's safe and what's not.

Within Glacier Bay Park and Preserve there's only one overnight facility, **Glacier Bay Lodge.** If it's booked, or too pricey for your budget, don't worry. About a half hour's drive along the 10-mile road that leads out of the park is Gustavus, where additional lodges, inns, and bed-and-breakfasts abound (*see* Dining and Lodging, *below*).

Gustavus calls itself "the way to Glacier Bay," and for airborne visitors the community is indeed the gateway to the park. The long, paved jet airport, built as a refueling strip during World War II, is one of the best and longest in Southeast Alaska, all the more impressive because facilities at the field are so limited. Alaska Airlines, which serves Gustavus daily in the summer, has a large, rustic terminal at the site, and from a free telephone on the front porch of the terminal you can call any of the local hostelries for courtesy pickup. Smaller light-aircraft companies that serve the community out of Juneau also have on-site shelters.

Gustavus boasts no "downtown." In fact, Gustavus is not a town. The 150 or so year-round residents there are most emphatic on this point; they regularly vote down incorporation as a city. Instead, Gustavus is a scattering of homes, farmsteads, arts-and-crafts studios, fishing and guiding charters, and other tiny enterprises peopled by hospitable individualists. It is, in many ways, exemplary of today's version of the frontier spirit in Alaska.

What to See and Do with Children

Canoe rides in the modern equivalent of an Indian war canoe provide fun and exercise for the young and old at a woodsy lake near Ketchikan. Or try a **catamaran trip** to view seabirds near Sitka. *Alaska Travel Adventures,* ☎ *907/789–0052.*

Fishing is one of Alaska's most popular pastimes, and no fishing license is required in Alaska for kids under 16. For the best saltwater shoreline, lake, or stream fishing, call the local Alaska Department of Fish and Game office in the city you're visiting (in Juneau, call 907/465–4112).

Gold panning is fun and sometimes children actually uncover a few flecks of the precious metal in the bottom of their pans. You can buy a pan at almost any Alaska hardware or sporting-goods store. Juneau and Skagway are the best-known gold-panning towns; look for schedules of gold-panning excursions at their visitor information centers.

Indian dancing will dazzle the younger set. Masked performers wearing bearskins and brightly patterned dance blankets act out great hunts, fierce battles, and other stories. Among the best-known dance groups is the Chilkat Indian Dancers of Ft. Seward in Haines. ☎ *907/766–2160.* ☛ *$10. Performance schedules vary depending on when cruises are in port; shows are typically held 4 to 5 nights a wk in summer.*

There are **totem pole parks**—featuring the sometimes fearsome countenances of bears, killer whales, great birds, and legendary hunters—at Ketchikan, Wrangell, Sitka, Juneau, and Haines–Ft. Seward. Other fine examples of the carvers' art can be seen at the Indian villages of Kake, Angoon, and Hoonah (*see* Off the Beaten Track, *below*).

Kayaking in front of Mendenhall Glacier, past Ketchikan's Creek Street, or in Glacier Bay National Park and Preserve is sure to create vivid memories for youngsters as well as active adults (*see* Guided Tours, *below,* and Important Contacts A to Z *in* the Gold Guide).

Summer sports are a passion in Southeast Alaska, and in Petersburg both young and old visitors are welcome to join in recreational softball or volleyball games.

Off the Beaten Track

One of the world's great travel bargains is the network of 150 or so **wilderness cabins** operated by the U.S. Forest Service alongside remote lakes and streams in the **Tongass National Forest** of Southeast Alaska. These cabins are equipped with bunks for six to eight occupants, tables, stoves, and outdoor privies. The cost is only $25 per night per party. Most are fly-in units, accessible by pontoon-equipped aircraft from virtually any community in the Panhandle. You provide your own sleeping bag, food, and cooking utensils. Don't be surprised if the forest service recommends you carry along a 30.06 or larger caliber rifle, in the unlikely event of a bear problem.

If you're a hot-springs or hot-tub enthusiast, **White Sulphur Springs** cabins, out of Sitka, and **Shakes Slough** cabins, accessible from Wrangell or Petersburg, boast these amenities. There's also a hot-springs pool of sorts, big enough for two or three to lounge in, at **Bailey Bay,** just north of Ketchikan's Revilla Island on the mainland. A 10-minute hike from a landing in a nearby lake or a 2-mile trek on an unmaintained but negotiable trail will bring you to the site. Have your pilot fly over to show you your foot route before you land. Shelter here is a three-sided Adirondack lean-to built as a public project during the Depression. *Request details and reservation information from the USFS office in each community or call or write: U.S. Forest Service, 101 Egan Dr., Juneau 99801,* ☎ *907/586–8751.*

Remote, but boasting the ultimate in creature comforts, is the **Waterfall Resort** (Box 6440, Ketchikan 99901, ☎ 907/225–9461 or 800/544–5125, FAX 907/225–8530) on Prince of Wales Island near Ketchikan. At this former commercial salmon cannery you sleep in Cape Cod–style cottages (former cannery workers' cabins, but they never had it so good); eat bountiful meals of salmon, halibut steak, and all the trimmings; and fish from your own private cabin cruiser under the care of your own private fishing guide.

Farther north, **Baranof Wilderness Lodge** (Box 21022, Auke Bay 99824, ☎ 907/586–2660) is one of the Panhandle's newer lodge facilities, located at Warm Springs Bay on Baranof Island. Kayaking, canoeing, hiking, and exploring are all options at this facility, as well as fresh- and saltwater fishing. The most popular activity of all is probably hot-tubbing, in waters supplied by the warm springs.

One of Southeast Alaska's pioneer lodges is **Thayer Lake Lodge** (in summer, Box 211614, Auke Bay 99821, ☎ 907/225–3343; in winter, Box 5416, Ketchikan 99901, ☎ 907/247–8897), on Admiralty Island near Juneau. This is a rustic lodge-and-cabins operation that has been playing host to Juneau folk and Alaskan visitors for decades. Bob and Edith Nelson built this resort after World War II on one of the high-country lakes in the Admiralty Island wilderness. They did it mostly with their own labor, using native timber for their buildings. Lake fishing is unsurpassed for cutthroat and Dolly Varden trout (though they're not overly large). There's also canoeing, hiking, and wildlife photography. Prices are about $150 per day, per person, including three meals daily; children under nine stay for half price.

Tenakee Springs is a tiny little fishing, vacation, and retirement community that clings to (in fact, hangs out over) the shores of Chichagof

Island. The town is accessible from Juneau by air or by the smaller Alaska ferry *LeConte* on an eight-hour run. You won't find any Hilton hotels here, but there is a sportfishing lodge on the beachfront, or the local general store can rent you a cabin. With either type of accommodation comes the privilege of partaking in the town's principal pastime—bathing. Tenakee Springs' bathhouse is the centerpiece of the community's lifestyle. There is no coed time. Use the baths twice in two days and you'll likely meet 75% of the city's population who are of your gender. Use it three times and you'll meet the rest. Between baths you can go crabbing, hiking, berry picking, or fishing for salmon and halibut, while visiting with some of the friendliest townsfolk in the state. *For cabin rentals, write Snyder Mercantile, Box 505, Tenakee Springs 99841, ☎ 907/736–2205.*

Tenakee Hot Springs Lodge, near the water, is a two-story, rustic spruce building with views of the inlet. Sportfishing packages, which include airfare from Juneau and guided fishing off a 42-foot boat, are available. Five-day packages with all meals included start at $2,190 per person. *Box 3, Tenakee Springs 99841, ☎ 907/736–2400.*

In Sitka, Burgess Bauder rents out his hand-built **Rockwell Lighthouse** (Box 277, Sitka 99835, ☎ 907/747–3056) across the sound for $125 per couple or $150 for two couples in winter, and $150 per couple and $200 for two couples in the summer. The lighthouse accommodates eight people, and the price includes the use of a motorboat to get there.

Finally, if you hanker to know how the native Alaskan village peoples of Southeast Alaska live today, you can fly or take the state ferry *LeConte* to **Kake, Angoon,** or **Hoonah.** You won't find much organized touring in any of these communities, but small, clean hotel accommodations are available (advance reservations strongly suggested), and fishing trips can be arranged by asking around. In Kake, contact the Waterfront Lodge (Box 222, Kake 99830, ☎ 907/785–3472); in Angoon, contact Whalers Cove Lodge (Box 101, Angoon 99820, ☎ 907/788–3123); in Hoonah, contact Harbor Lodge (Box 320, Hoonah 99829, ☎ 907/945–3636).

SHOPPING

Art Galleries
Along with the usual array of work by talented but unspectacular artists, Southeast Alaska shops and galleries carry some impressive Alaskan paintings, lithographs, and drawings. Among the best are **Scanlon Gallery,** with locations downtown in Ketchikan (308 Mission St., ☎ 907/225–4730) and in the Plaza Portwest (116 Plaza Portwest, ☎ 907/225–5149), a couple of miles north of downtown. It handles not only major Alaska artists (Byron Birdsall, Rie Munoz, John Fahringer, Nancy Stonington) and local talent but also traditional and contemporary native art, including soapstone, bronze, and ivory earrings. In Juneau, knowledgeable locals frequent the **Rie Munoz Gallery** (233 S. Franklin St., ☎ 907/586–2112) near the cruise-ship dock downtown. Ms. Munoz is one of Alaska's favorite artists, creator of a stylized, simple, and colorful design technique that is much copied but rarely equaled. Other artists' work is also on sale at the Munoz Gallery, including woodblock prints by nationally recognized artist Dale DeArmond. Various books illustrated by Rie Munoz and written by Alaskan children's author Jean Rogers are also available. **David Present's Gallery** on Broadway in Skagway (☎ 907/983–2873) has outstanding and pricey works by Alaskan artists.

Design, art, and clothing convene in Ketchikan's stylish **Soho Coho** shop (5 Creek St., ☎ 907/225–5954). Here you'll find an eclectic collection of art and clothing in modern Alaskan chic. In the same building is the **Ray Troll Gallery** (☎ 907/225–5954). Works by this trendy Alaskan artist are for sale in both establishments.

Books

Book lovers will find fascinating collections of Alaskan lore, native works, and modern literature in the Southeast. In Ketchikan's **Parnassus Bookstore** (28 Creek St., ☎ 907/225–7690), coffee and pastries are served amid the eclectic book selection. A good collection of books about the region can be found in Sitka's **Old Harbor Books** (201 Lincoln St., ☎ 907/747–8808).

Crafts and Gifts

Totem poles, from a few inches to several feet tall, are some of the most popular handicrafts made by the Tlingit and Haida Indians in the Southeast Alaska Panhandle. Other items include wall masks, paddles, dance rattles, baskets, and tapestries with Southeast Alaska Indian designs. You'll find these items at gift shops up and down the coast. If you want to be sure of authenticity, buy items tagged with the state-approved "Authentic Native Handcraft from Alaska" label. Sitka's **Saxman Village** has some of the best prices on superb handcrafted Tlingit merchandise because the artists are local.

On the first floor of the old Senate Building on South Franklin Street in Juneau is the **Russian Shop** (☎ 907/586–2778), a depository of icons, samovars, lacquered boxes, nesting dolls, and other items that reflect Alaska's 18th- and 19th-century Russian heritage. Upstairs is an Irish shop.

For vintage items such as historical photos and old-fashioned newspapers, visit **Dedman's Photo Shop** (☎ 907/983–2353), a Skagway institution. Alaska souvenirs can also be obtained in one of the state's most famous boîtes, the **Red Dog Saloon** in Juneau (*see* Exploring, *above*).

Edibles and Potables

Salmon—smoked, canned, or packaged otherwise—is another popular take-home item. Virtually every community has at least one canning and/or smoking operation that packs and ships local seafood. For some of the best, try **Ketchikan's Salmon Etc.** (322 Mission St., ☎ 907/225–6008). Throughout the region, in food stores and gift shops, you'll also likely run into Silver Lining Seafoods products, a Ketchikan-based company with a consistently high-quality product in attractive packaging.

Another gourmet delicacy is a product southeasterners refer to as Petersburg shrimp. Small (they're seldom larger than half your pinky finger), tender, and succulent, they're much treasured by Alaskans, who often send them "outside" as thank-you gifts. You'll find the little critters fresh in meat departments and canned in gift sections at food stores throughout the Panhandle. You can buy fresh vacuum-packed Petersburg shrimp in Petersburg at **Coastal Cold Storage,** downtown on Main Street, or mail order them (Box 307, Petersburg 99833, ☎ 907/772–4177).

You can't take it with you because of its limited shelf life, but when you're "shopping" the bars and watering holes of Southeast Alaska, ask for Alaskan Beer, an amber beer brewed and bottled in Juneau. Visitors are welcome at the **minibrewery's plant** and can sample the product during the bottling operation on Tuesday and Thursday 11–4. *5429 Shaune Dr., Juneau,* ☎ 907/780–5866.

SPORTS AND THE OUTDOORS

Participant Sports

Bicycling

In spite of sometimes wet weather, bicycling is very popular in Southeast Alaska communities. There are plenty of flat roads to ride and some killer hills, too, if you're game. Cycling beside saltwater bays or within great towering forests can be glorious. Unfortunately, bike rentals in the region seem to cycle in and out of business faster than you can shift gears. Your best bet, if you don't bring your own, is to call bike shops or the parks and recreation departments in the towns you're visiting and ask who is supplying rentals at the moment. Some lodgings in Tenakee, Gustavus, and Petersburg have bikes on hand for the use of their guests.

Canoeing/Kayaking

Paddling has been a pleasant way for visitors to see Southeast Alaska since the first Russians arrived on the scene in 1741 and watched the Indians do it. In Juneau, **Alaska Travel Adventures** (☎ 907/789–0052) has trips in various parts of the region, and **Alaska Discovery** (☎ 907/780–6226) is the company to see for escorted boat excursions in Glacier Bay National Park or Admiralty Island, or for kayaking in the lake in front of Mendenhall Glacier. The **Ketchikan Parks and Recreation Department** (☎ 907/228–6650) and **Southeast Exposure** (☎ 907/225–8829), also in Ketchikan, rent canoes and kayaks. At Sitka, **Baidarka Boats** (☎ 907/747–8996) offers sea-kayak rentals and custom-guided trips.

Kayak rentals for unescorted Glacier Bay exploring and camping can be arranged through **Glacier Bay Sea Kayaks** (Box 26, Gustavus 99826, ☎ 907/697–2257). Twice a day, at 9 AM and 6 PM, its experienced kayakers give orientations on handling the craft plus camping and routing suggestions. The company will also make reservations aboard the regular day boat to drop kayakers off and pick them up in the most scenic country.

Fishing

The prospect of bringing a lunker king salmon or a leaping, diving, fighting rainbow trout to net is the reason many visitors choose an Alaska vacation. Local give-away guidebooks and the State of Alaska's "Vacation Planner" contain the names of scores of reputable charter boats and boat-rental agencies in every community along the Panhandle coast. Your best bet for catching salmon in saltwater is from a boat. Similarly, the very finest angling for freshwater species (rainbows, cutthroat, lake trout) is to be found at fly-in lakes and resorts. Still, there's more than adequate fishing right from saltwater shores or in lakes and streams accessible by roads. To learn where the fish are biting at any given time, call the local office of the Alaska Department of Fish and Game in the community you're visiting, or contact the ADFG's main office (Box 25526, Juneau 99802, ☎ 907/465–4112). For more information on fishing, *see* Important Contacts A to Z *in* the Gold Guide.

Golf

Juneau's par-three nine-hole **Mendenhall Golf course** (2101 Industrial Blvd., ☎ 907/789–7323) is pretty modest. Still, its location on saltwater wetlands beside the waters of Gastineau Channel makes it one of a kind. Club rentals are available.

Hiking and Backpacking

Trekking woods, mountains, and beaches is Southeast Alaska's unofficial regional sport. Many of the trails are old, abandoned mining roads.

Others are natural routes—in some sections, even game trails—meandering over ridges, through forests, and alongside streams and glaciers. A few, like the Chilkoot Trail out of Skagway, rate five stars for historical significance, scenery, and hiker aids en route. There's not a community in Southeast Alaska that doesn't offer some opportunity for hiking or backpacking. The Alaska Division of Parks Southeast regional office in Juneau (400 Willoughby Ave., ☎ 907/465–4563) will send you a list of state-maintained trails and parks in the Panhandle; local visitors bureaus and recreation departments in the communities you're visiting can also help. The Parks and Recreation Department in Juneau (☎ 907/586–2635) sponsors a group hike each Wednesday morning and on Saturdays. For more information on hiking and backpacking, *see* Important Contacts A to Z *in* the Gold Guide.

Running and Jogging

Hotel clerks and visitor information offices will be glad to make route suggestions if you need them. If you plan to run, bring along a light sweatsuit and rain gear as well as shorts and a T-shirt. The weather can be mild one day, chilly and wet the next. If you plan to be in Juneau early in July, call the Parks and Recreation Department (☎ 907/586–5226) and check the date of the annual **Governor's Cup Fun Run.** Hundreds of racers, runners, joggers, race walkers, and mosey-alongers take part in this 3-mile event. Other marathons, half marathons, 5Ks, and similar events take place in various communities throughout the summer. The most grueling race in these parts is the annual September **Klondike Trail of '98 Road Relay** event, spanning 110 miles between Skagway and Whitehorse on the Klondike and Alaska highways. For details contact the Tourism Industry Association of the Yukon (102–302 Steele St., Whitehorse, Yukon, Canada Y1A 2C5, ☎ 403/668–3331).

Scuba Diving

Although the visibility is not very good in most Southeast waters, there's still a lot of scuba and skin-diving activity throughout the region. Quarter-inch wet suits are a must. So is a buddy; stay close together. Local dive shops can steer you to the best places to dive for abalone, scallops, and crabs, and advise you on the delights and dangers of underwater wrecks. Shops that rent tanks and equipment to qualified divers include **Alaska Diving Service** (1601 Tongass Ave., Ketchikan, ☎ 907/225–4667) and **Southeast Diving & Sports** (203 Lincoln Ave., Sitka, ☎ 907/747–8279).

Skiing

CROSS-COUNTRY

Nordic skiing is a favorite winter pastime for outdoor enthusiasts, especially in the northern half of the Panhandle. Although it is promoted mostly by and for the locals, visitors are always welcome. In Petersburg, the favorite locale for Nordic skiing is the end of **Three Lakes Loop.** Old logging roads and trails are popular as well. If you arrive without your skis, call the Chamber of Commerce Visitor Center (☎ 907/772–3646); it will try to line up some loaners for you.

In Juneau, ski rentals are available along with suggestions for touring the trails and ridges around town from **Foggy Mountain Shop** (134 S. Franklin St., ☎ 907/586–6780).

From Haines, **Alaska Nature Tours** (Box 491, Haines 99827, ☎ 907/766–2876) operates a winter Nordic shuttle bus to flat-tracking in the Chilkat Bald Eagle Preserve and across the Canadian border atop Chilkat Pass in British Columbia.

DOWNHILL

Eaglecrest (155 Seward St., Juneau 99801, ☎ 907/586–5284) on Douglas Island, just 30 minutes from downtown Juneau, offers late-November to mid-April skiing and snowboarding on a well-groomed mountain with two double-chairlifts, a beginner's platter-pull, cross-country trails, ski school (including downhill, Nordic, and telemark), ski-rental shop, cafeteria, and trilevel day lodge. Heliskiing is also available. Because this is Southeast Alaska, knowledgeable skiers pack rain slickers along with parkas, hats, gloves, and other gear. On weekends and holidays there are bus pickups at hotels and motels.

Tennis

There are courts in Ketchikan, Wrangell, Petersburg, Juneau, and Skagway. The **Juneau Racquet Club,** about 10 miles north of downtown, adjacent to Mendenhall Mall, will accommodate out-of-towners at its first-class indoor tennis and racquetball courts. Facilities include sauna, Jacuzzi, exercise equipment, snack bar, massage tables, and a sports shop. ☎ 907/789–2181. ☛ *1-day fee for nonmembers: $9.36.*

Spectator Sports

With the possible exception of basketball, Southeast Alaska's spectator sports probably don't offer much excitement for visitors. There are no semipro or professional baseball teams in the Panhandle. The devotion of large numbers of Southeast adults to summer softball, however, borders on addiction.

Basketball

Watching two teams trying to shoot balls through hoops is Southeast Alaska's major spectator sport. Each January in Juneau, the local **Lions Clubs' Golden North** tournament attracts teams from all over the Panhandle and even nearby Canada. And the University of Alaska–Southeast Whales and Lady Whales teams are often in town to offer respectable court action. For schedules, contact University of Alaska–Southeast (11120 Glacier Hwy., Juneau 99801, ☎ 907/465–6457).

DINING AND LODGING

Dining

Reservations are generally not necessary, but you may wish to inquire in advance, particularly in the summer.

Category	Cost*
$$$	over $40
$$	$20–$40
$	under $20

per person for a three-course meal, excluding drinks and service

Lodging

Hotels, motels, lodges, and inns run the gamut in Southeast Alaska from very traditional urban hostelries—the kind you'll find almost anywhere—to charming small-town inns and rustic cabins in the boondocks.

The widest range of options is found in Ketchikan and Juneau. Accommodations in any of the Panhandle communities, however, are usually not hard to come by even in the summer, except when festivals, fishing derbies, fairs, and other special events are under way. To be on the safe side and get your first choice, you should make reservations as early as possible. In addition to the hotels and inns listed here, *see also* Off the Beaten Track, *above,* for more rustic and out-of-the-way accommodations. With the exception of bed-and-breakfasts, most hotels accept the major credit cards. Contact the **Alaska Bed & Breakfast Reservation Service** (369 S. Franklin St., Suite 200, Juneau 99801, ☎ 907/586–2959, FAX 907/463–4453; $–$$) for B&B accommodations in most Southeast communities, as well as Anchorage, Fairbanks, Homer, and Soldotna. Hotels and other lodging are listed under the following categories:

Category	Cost*
$$$$	over $120
$$$	$90–$120
$$	$50–$90
$	under $50

All prices are for a standard double room, excluding 8%–10% tax.

Glacier Bay/Gustavus

DINING

$–$$ **Strawberry Point.** There's nothing fancy here, just good wholesome cooking that the locals seem to like—fresh-baked breads, pastries, and deli sandwiches. Alaskan antiques and knickknacks, such as an eclectic bottle collection, enhance this small, homey establishment. Monday night is pizza night; Saturdays feature seafood. ✕ *On the dock road,* ☎ *907/697–2227. DC, MC, V.*

DINING AND LODGING

$$$$ **Glacier Bay Lodge.** This is the only lodging available within Glacier
★   Bay National Park and Preserve. The lodge is constructed of massive timbers but in spite of its size blends well into the thick rain forest surrounding it on three sides. The fully modern yet rustic rooms (no televisions) are accessible by boardwalk ramps from the main lodge; some have views of Bartlett Cove. From the dock out front, visitors can take day boats, sportfishing trips, whale-watching tours, and overnight cruises up the bay. Reservations for flightseeing can also be made from the lodge. If it swims or crawls in the sea hereabouts, you'll find it on the menu in the rustic dining room of this lodge. A guest favorite is the halibut baked aleyeska, a filet baked in a rich sauce of sour cream, cheddar cheese, mayonnaise, and onions. Steaks and other selections are available as well; everything is made from scratch. The dining room is on the main floor and looks out on the chilly waters of Bartlett Cove. ▦ *At Bartlett Cove (mailing address: Box 108, Gustavus 99826 or 520 Pike Tower, Suite 1610, Seattle, WA 98101),* ☎ *907/697–2226 or 800/451–5952,* FAX *206/623–7809. 55 rooms. Restaurant, lobby lounge, shop. DC, MC, V.*

$$–$$$$ **Glacier Bay Country Inn.** This picturesque but fully modern rambling
★   log structure with marvelous cupolas, dormers, gables, and porches was built from local hand-logged timbers. Innkeepers Al and Annie Unrein have outfitted each room with cozy comforters, warm flannel sheets, and fluffy towels for a homelike, mountain-modern ambience. Some rooms have antiques and open log-beam ceilings; all have views of the Chilkat Mountains's rain forest. The Unreins will arrange sightseeing and flightseeing tours; and they operate charter-boat trips into Glacier Bay and nearby waters aboard their three vessels. Each craft has two staterooms (sleeping four to six) and two bathrooms. Whale-watching, fishing, and kayaking trips are their specialty. Theirs is a gourmet kitchen, with foods fresh from the sea and the inn's own garden (all meals are included in room rate). Among guests' favorites: steamed Dungeness crab, homemade fettuccine, and rhubarb custard pie. Bears and moose might peak in at you from the hay fields beyond. Dinner guests not staying at the inn must make reservations in advance: Tourists flock here for dinner. ▦ *Halfway between the airport and Bartlett Cove (mailing address: Box 5, Gustavus 99826),* ☎ *907/697–2288 or 801/673–*

8480 in winter; FAX *907/697–2289. 9 rooms. Restaurant. Personal checks accepted; no credit cards.*

$$-$$$$ **Gustavus Inn.** Established in 1965 on a pioneer Gustavus homestead,
★ the inn continues a tradition of gracious Alaska rural living. In the original homestead building and in a newer structure, rooms are decorated New England farmhouse–style. Glacier trips, fishing expeditions, bicycle rides around the community, or berry picking in season are offered here. Many guests, however, prefer to do nothing but enjoy the inn's tranquillity and its notable meals, which are included in the room raate. The family-style meals are legendary. Hosts David and Jo Ann Lesh—carrying on a tradition established decades ago by David's parents—heap bountiful servings of seafood and fresh vegetable dishes on the plates of overnight guests and others who reserve in advance. The farmhouse-style dining room is down-home cozy with room for 30; dinnertime is 6:30 sharp. ▦ *On the main road (mailing address: Box 60, Gustavus 99826),* ☎ *907/697–2254,* FAX *907/697–2255; or in winter,* ☎ *913/649–5220,* FAX *913/649–5220. 11 rooms with bath, 2 rooms share a bath. Restaurant, airport shuttle. AE, MC, V accepted, but cash or personal or traveler's checks preferred.*

LODGING

$$ **Puffin Bed & Breakfast.** These attractive cabins are in a wooded homestead and are decorated with Alaskan crafts. There's also a main lodge with a high-end arts-and-crafts shop. Full breakfast is included. The owners also operate Puffin Travel, for fishing, kayaking, and sightseeing charters. ▦ *In central Gustavus (mailing address: Box 3, Gustavus 99826),* ☎ *907/697–2260,* FAX *907/697–2258. 3 cabins with bath, 3 cabins with removed bath. Bicycles, shop. No credit cards.*

Haines
DINING

$$ **Lighthouse Restaurant.** At the foot of Main Street next to the boat harbor, the Lighthouse offers a great view of Lynn Canal, boats, and boaters, along with fine barbecued ribs, steaks, and seafoods. Its Harbor Bar is a popular watering hole for commercial fishermen. It's colorful but can get a little loud at night. ✕ *Front St. on the harbor,* ☎ *907/766–2442. AE, MC, V.*

$ **Bamboo Room.** This unassuming coffee shop is popular for sandwiches, burgers, fried chicken, and seafood, and of course, breakfast. Diners have views of the mountains beyond. ✕ *2nd Ave. near Main St.,* ☎ *907/766–2800. AE, D, DC, MC, V.*

$ **Chilkat Restaurant and Bakery.** Family-style cooking is served in a homelike, no-smoking setting. Lace curtains and plush green carpet add a touch of class. Seafood, steaks, and sandwiches are cooked to order; Friday is all-you-can-eat night. ✕ *5th Ave. near Main St.,* ☎ *907/766–2920. AE, MC, V. Closed Sun., winter hrs vary.*

LODGING

$$-$$$ **Captain's Choice Motel.** This conventional motel in downtown Haines
★ provides amenities such as cable TV and telephones. The motel's decor manages to be contemporary and rustic at the same time. Ask for a room looking out over the waters of Portage Cove. ▦ *2nd and Dalton Sts. (mailing address: Box 392, Haines 99827),* ☎ *907/766–3111, 800/247–7153, or 800/478–2345 in AK. 39 rooms with bath, 5 suites. AE, D, DC, MC, V.*

DINING AND LODGING

$-$$ **Halsingland Hotel.** The officers of old Ft. Seward once lived in the big, white structures that today comprise the Halsingland Hotel, which looks like a Victorian inn. Most of the rooms have private baths; all are carpeted and have wildlife and historic photos on the walls. Many have cast-iron fireplaces (for decoration only) and original claw-foot bathtubs. The hotel is especially popular with European tourists. The Commander's Room Restaurant and Lounge's specialty is seafood; the halibut is a consistent pleaser, as is the extensive wine list and choice of local beers. The restaurant has a full salad bar and full "potato bar" with baked potatoes, boiled red potatoes, rice pilaf, and vegetables with varied toppings (cheese, chili, etc.). Burgers and fish-and-chips are also on the menu. Nearby, at the Indian Tribal House on the parade grounds, the Halsingland also prepares a nightly salmon bake called the Port Chilkoot Potlatch—$20 for all you can eat. ⊡ *On the parade grounds, Ft. Seward (mailing address: Box 1589, Haines 99827),* ☎ *907/766–2000 or 800/542–6363 outside AK,* 🅵🅰🆇 *907/766–2445 or 800/478–5556. 58 rooms. Restaurant, bar. AE, D, DC, MC, V.*

There are several B&Bs in Haines, and one youth hostel. For more information contact the visitor information center (2nd Ave. near Willard St., ☎ 907/766–2234, 🅵🅰🆇 907/766–2404).

Juneau

DINING

$–$$ **The Fiddlehead.** This is probably Juneau's favorite restaurant, a delightful
★ place of light woods, gently patterned wallpaper, stained glass, historic photos, and hanging plants. The food is healthy, generously served, and eclectic. Offerings range from a light dinner of black beans and rice to pasta Greta Garbo (locally smoked salmon tossed with fettuccine in cream sauce) to chicken and eggplant Szechuan (chicken and eggplant sautéed with bean paste and served over rice). Homemade bread from the restaurant's bakery is laudable. ✕ *429 Willoughby Ave.,* ☎ *907/ 586–3150. Reservations recommended. AE, D, MC, V. No smoking.*

$$ **Giorgio at the Pier.** Opened in April 1995, Giorgio combines two ir-
★ resistible elements: fresh Alaskan seafood and authentic Italian preparations. Both Alaskan clam chowder and pasta e fagioli are on the menu at this elegant trattoria with a view of the harbor, as are numerous seafood and salad starters. For an entrée, the baked fresh salmon stuffed with shrimp and halibut and served in a pastry shell is not to be missed. ✕ *544 S. Franklin St.,* ☎ *907/586–4700. AE, MC, V.*

$–$$ **Mike's.** For decades, Mike's, in the former mining community of Douglas across the bridge from Juneau, has been serving up seafood, steaks, and pastas. Its treatment of tiny Petersburg shrimp is particularly noteworthy. Rivaling the food, however, is the view from the picture windows at the rear of the restaurant. Mike's looks over the waters of Gastineau Channel to Juneau and the ruins of the old AJ mine. ✕ *1102 2nd St. in Douglas,* ☎ *907/364–3271. AE, DC, MC, V. Closed Mon. No lunch weekends.*

DINING AND LODGING

$–$$$ **Inn at the Waterfront.** Built in 1898, this inn is home to the Summit,
★ the city's most prestigious dining spot. This small, intimate, candlelit restaurant has 25 entrées on the menu, mostly seafood—including abalone sautéed in butter and almonds; scallops, prawns, halibut, and a tender salmon dish called Salmon Gastineau. For steak lovers, the New York La Bleu is a New York strip steak with blue cheese. The Summit has a luxurious turn-of-the-century brothel decor, and in fact, the inn was a brothel until 1958. Special accents include Italian sconce lamps and lace tablecloths. ⊡ *455 S. Franklin St.,* ☎ *907/586–2050,* 🅵🅰🆇 *907/586–2999. 21 rooms. Restaurant (reservations advised; no lunch). AE, DC, MC, V.*

$–$$ **Silverbow Inn.** This place is popular with locals, so reserve ahead. The
★   decor is "early Juneau," with settings, chairs, and tables (no two are
alike) of the kind you might have found in someone's parlor during
the city's gold-mining era. The main building, for years one of the town's
major bakeries, was built in 1912. The wine list is limited but selec-
tive; dinner entrées change daily, but local fish is a specialty. Favorite
dishes include halibut in berries and port sauce, mixed seafood grill in
lemon-garlic sauce, blackened meats, Alaskan salmon, and rich desserts
such as homemade ice cream. ☎ *120 2nd St.,* ☎ *907/586–4146,* FAX
*907/586–4242. 6 rooms. Restaurant. AE, DC, MC, V. Dining room
hrs vary Oct.–Apr.*

$ **Gold Creek Salmon Bake.** Trees, mountains, and the rushing water of
★   Salmon Creek surround the sheltered, comfortable benches and tables
at this salmon bake—thought to be Alaska's oldest such outdoor offering. Fresh-caught salmon (supplemented sometimes with ribs) is
cooked over an alder fire and served with a simple but succulent sauce
of brown sugar, margarine, and lemon juice. For $22 you can enjoy
the salmon, along with hot baked beans, salad, Jell-O, corn bread, and
your choice of beer, wine, lemonade, tea, or coffee. After dinner you
can pan for gold in the stream (pans are available for no charge and
you can keep any gold you find) or wander up the hill to explore the
remains of AJ gold-mine buildings. *End of Basin Rd.,* ☎ *907/789–0052.
Free bus ride from in front of the Baranof Hotel in downtown Juneau.
No credit cards. Closed mid-Sept.–Apr.*

LODGING

$$$$ **Baranof Hotel.** For half a century the Baranof has been the city's prestige address for business travelers, legislators, lobbyists, and tourists.
That designation has been challenged in recent years by the Westmark
(like the Baranof, a unit of the Westmark chain), but this nine-story
hostelry continues to attract a large proportion of the city's visitors.
The art-deco lobby and most rooms have been extensively refurbished
in recent years in tasteful woods and a lighting style reminiscent of 1939,
when the hotel first opened. The contemporary rooms feature aqua-
blue, pink, or maroon color schemes. Also on site are a travel agency
and an Alaska Airlines ticket office. ☎ *127 N. Franklin St., 99801,* ☎
907/586–2660 or 800/544–0970, FAX *907/586–8315. 194 rooms.
Restaurant, coffee shop, lobby lounge. AE, D, DC, MC, V.*

$$$$ **Westmark Juneau.** A high-rise by Juneau standards, the seven-story
Westmark is across Main Street from Juneau's Centennial Hall and across
Egan Drive from the docks. Rooms are modern in decor; deluxe rooms
have views of the Gastineau Channel. The lobby is distinguished by a
massive carved eagle figure and wood paneling. Extensive wood-mural
carvings adorn the Woodcarver Dining Room. ☎ *51 W. Egan Dr., 99801,*
☎ *907/586–6900 or 800/544–0970,* FAX *907/463–3567. 105 rooms.
Restaurant, lounge. AE, DC, MC, V.*

$$$ **Airport TraveLodge.** The rooms and furnishings here are pretty stan-
dard. The structure, like Fernando's Restaurant inside, is Mexican in
design and decor. The motel is one of only two in the community with
an indoor swimming pool and whirlpool tub—a plus if you want to
unwind after a day of touring. Some rooms have mountain views. ☎
9200 Glacier Hwy., 99801, ☎ *907/789–9700,* FAX *907/789–1969. 86
rooms. Restaurant, indoor pool, hot tub. AE, D, DC, MC, V.*

$$$ **The Prospector.** A short walk west of downtown and next door to the
★   State Museum, this smaller but fully modern hotel is what many busi-
ness travelers and a number of legislators like to call home while they're
in Juneau. Here you'll find very large rooms with contemporary furnishings, bright watercolors of Alaskan nature, and views of the chan-

nel, mountains, or the city. In McGuire's dining room and lounge you can enjoy outstanding prime rib. Steaks and seafood are also popular. ⌧ *375 Whittier St., 99801,* ☎ *907/586–3737 or 800/331–2711,* ℻ *907/586–1204. 60 rooms. Restaurant, lobby lounge. AE, D, MC, V.*

$$–$$$ **Country Lane Inn.** This Best Western property has a charming sitting room–lobby with a couch and reading materials. Baskets of multicolored flowers hang along the entrance walk to rooms, making for a pleasant welcome. Rooms are decorated with mauve and dusty blue fabrics in country style. Furnishings are kept to a minimum, but king- and queen-size beds are available. Some rooms come with whirlpool baths and kitchenettes. ⌧ *9300 Glacier Hwy., 99801,* ☎ *907/789–5005 or 800/528–1234,* ℻ *907/789–2818. 50 rooms. AE, D, DC, MC, V.*

$–$$ **Alaskan Hotel.** This historic 1913 hotel is 15 miles from the ferry ter-
★   minal and 9 miles from the airport (city bus service is available). Rooms, each with a double bed or two twin beds, are on three floors and have turn-of-the-century antiques and iron beds. Four Jacuzzis can be rented by the hour. ⌧ *167 S. Franklin St.,* ☎ *907/586–1000 or 800/327–9347,* ℻ *907/463–3775. 22 rooms with bath, 20 rooms share 5 baths. Bar, 4 hot tubs.*

Ketchikan

DINING

$$ **Salmon Falls Resort.** It's a half-hour drive from town, but the seafood
★   and steaks served up in this huge, octagonal restaurant make the trip more than worthwhile. The restaurant is built of pine logs, and at the center of the dining room, supporting the roof, rises a 40-foot section of 48-inch pipe manufactured to be part of the Alaska pipeline. The dining area overlooks the waters of Clover Passage, where sunsets can be vivid red and remarkable. Seafood caught fresh from adjacent waters is especially good; try the halibut, and prawns stuffed with crabmeat. ⌧ *Mile 17, N. Tongass Hwy.,* ☎ *907/225–2752 or 800/ 247–9059. Reservations recommended. AE, DC, MC, V.*

Other better-than-adequate eating places in the community include the **Clover Pass Resort** (Mile 15, N. Tongass Hwy., ☎ 907/247–2234; $–$$) for excellent seafood and a view of sport fishermen bringing home their catches, and **Kay's Kitchen** (2813 Tongass Ave., ☎ 907/225–5860; $) for homemade soups and generous sandwiches.

DINING AND LODGING

$$–$$$ **Gilmore Hotel.** The Gilmore has a European feel, and because of such features as a 1930s-style lobby, it's on the National Register of Historic Places. Extensive renovations have brought welcome modern touches to the rooms here, but there is no elevator in this three-story building. Annabelle's Keg and Chowder House is really two restaurants. The Keg and Chowder House, with a 1920s-style decor, serves seafood, pasta, steak, and prime rib. Specialties include oysters on the half shell and steamer clams. Annabelle's Parlor is a more formal restaurant frequented by locals for its fine local seafoods in classic preparations. There's also an espresso bar. ⌧ *326 Front St., 99901,* ☎ *907/ 225–9423,* ℻ *907/225–7442. 42 rooms. 2 restaurants, bar. AE, D, MC, V.*

LODGING

$$$$ **Westmark Cape Fox Lodge.** One of Ketchikan's poshest properties offers fantastic views of the town and harbor. Fine dining and a cozy but luxurious setting are also a plus. Rooms are quite spacious with Shaker-style furnishings, the traditional Tlingit tribal colors (red, black, and white), and watercolors of native Alaskan birds. All rooms provide views

of either Tongass Narrows or Deer Mountain. The town's main attractions are within walking distance or guests can take the hotel sky tram directly to Creek Street. ⌕ *800 Venetia Way, 99901,* ☎ *907/225–8001 or 800/544–0970,* ℻ *907/225–8286. 72 rooms. Restaurant, lounge, no-smoking rooms, room service, meeting rooms, free parking. AE, D, MC, V.*

$$$–$$$$ **Cedars Lodge.** Nothing in the plain, square exterior of this hotel building or in its spartan lobby hints at the deluxe accommodations within. Some of the 12 units are split-level with circular stairways; all are carpeted in steel grays or other light colors, with pastel furniture and natural wood trims. Many of the units have full kitchens and whirlpool baths and all guests have access to a hot tub and sauna. Windows are large and give views of the busy water and air traffic in Tongass Narrows. Simple American fare is served at a buffet dinner and breakfast; meals can also be brought to your room from the nearby Roller Bay Cafe, which serves up seafood, steak, and burgers; or from the Galley, which offers pizza and Asian food. ⌕ *1471 Tongass Ave. (mailing address: Box 8331, Ketchikan 99901),* ☎ *907/225–1900,* ℻ *907/225–8604. 12 rooms. AE, D, DC, MC, V.*

$$$ **Ingersoll Hotel.** Old-fashioned patterned wallpaper, wood wainscot-
★   ing, and etched-glass windows on the oak registration desk set an old-fashioned mood for this three-story downtown hotel, built in the 1920s. Room furnishings are standard, with bright Alaskan art on the walls. Some rooms have a view of the cruise-ship dock and the waters of Tongass Narrows. ⌕ *303 Mission St. (mailing address: Box 6440, Ketchikan 99901),* ☎ *907/225–2124,* ℻ *907/225–8530. 58 rooms. Meeting room. AE, D, DC, MC, V.*

$$ **The Landing.** This Best Western property is named for the ferry landing site in the waters of Tongass Narrows across the street. Decor is modern, basic Best Western. Some rooms have microwaves and kitchenettes; suites have all the comforts of home. ⌕ *3434 Tongass Ave.,* ☎ *907/225–5166 or 800/428–8304,* ℻ *907/225–6900. 76 rooms. Café, lobby lounge, exercise room. AE, D, MC, V.*

Petersburg

DINING

$ **Beachcomber Inn.** Seafood, with a distinctly Norwegian flair, is the spe-
★   cialty in this restored cannery building on the shores of Wrangell Narrows. If you're there on a smorgasbord night, you may sample red-snapper fish cakes, salmon loaf, Norwegian (emphatically *not* Swedish) meatballs, creamed potatoes, and sugary desserts such as *sandbakkelse, lefsa,* or *krumkakker.* Petersburg's famed beer-batter halibut is also served here, as are salmon steaks and other traditional seafoods. ✕ *Mile 4, Mitkof Hwy.,* ☎ *907/772–3888. AE, MC, V.*

$ **Helse.** Natural foods, including enormous vegetable-laden sandwiches, are a specialty in this homey cross between a diner and a restaurant. Helse, a favorite lunchtime spot with locals, is filled with plenty of plants and works by local artists. The menu features soups, chowders, home-baked breads, and salads. Espresso makes a nice ending to a meal. Breakfast is not served, excepting raisin bran muffins. ✕ *Sing Lee Alley and Harbor Way,* ☎ *907/772–3444. No credit cards.*

$ **The Homestead.** There's nothing fancy here, just basic American fare: steaks, local prawns and halibut, salad bar, and especially generous breakfasts. Rhubarb pie is the fastest-selling item on the menu. It's a popular place with locals. ✕ *217 Main St.,* ☎ *907/772–3900. DC, MC, V.*

$ **Pellerito's Pizza.** Recommended pizza toppings here include Canadian bacon and pineapple or local shrimp. ✕ *Across from the ferry terminal,* ☎ *907/772–3727. No credit cards.*

$$ **Tides Inn.** This is the largest hotel in town, a block uphill from Pe-
★ tersburg's main thoroughfare. All rooms are modern, with standard
furnishings; some are equipped with kitchens. Rooms in the newer wing
have views of the boat harbor. The coffee is always on in the small, in-
formal lobby, and in the morning you're welcome to complimentary
juices, cereals, and pastries. 🏠 *1st and Dolphin Sts. (mailing address:
Box 1048, Petersburg 99833),* ☎ *907/772–4288,* FAX *907/772–4286.
46 rooms. Car rental. AE, D, DC, MC, V.*

$–$$ **Scandia House.** Exuding a Norwegian, old-country atmosphere, this
hotel on Petersburg's main street has been a local fixture since 1910.
Unfortunately, Scandia House burned down twice in 1994 along with
other nearby buildings, but the owners have worked hard to rebuild
it and re-create its turn-of-the-century charm. The coffee is always on
in a small lobby accented by etched-glass windows on the doors and
large oil paintings depicting local old-timers in colorful Norwegian garb.
Norwegian rosemaling designs ornament the exterior. "American"
units have full toilet facilities; "European" rooms have showers and
toilets down the hall. All the squeaky-clean rooms are a showcase for
traditional Western furnishings. Some rooms have kitchenettes and/or
king-size beds and a view of the harbor. Boat rentals are available on
the premises. 🏠 *110 Nordic Dr. (mailing address: Box 689, Petersburg 99833),* ☎ *907/772–4281 or 800/722–5006,* FAX *907/772–4301.
21 rooms. Car rental. AE, D, DC, MC, V.*

Sitka

DINING

$$–$$$ **Channel Club.** It's a toss-up whether to order steak or seafood here,
★ but whatever you choose will be good. This is Sitka's finest restaurant.
Halibut cheeks are a consistent favorite. If you order steak, don't ask
the chef for his steak seasoning recipe—it's a secret. The decor is nautical, with fishnet floats, whale baleen, and whalebone carvings hanging on the walls. ✗ *Mile 3.5, Halibut Point Rd.,* ☎ *907/747–9916.
AE, DC, MC, V.*

Also recommended: **Marina Restaurant** (205 Harbor Dr., ☎ 907/747–
8840; $) for Mexican or Italian fare and **Van Winkle and Daigler**
(Harbor Dr. and Maksutoff St., ☎ 907/747–3396; $–$$) for steak and
seafood.

DINING AND LODGING

$$–$$$$ **Westmark Shee Atika.** If you stay here for a night or two, you will surely
★ come away with an increased appreciation for Southeast Alaskan In-
dian art and culture. Artwork displayed throughout the hotel illustrate
the history, legends, and exploits of the Tlingit people. Many rooms
overlook Crescent Harbor and the islands in the waters beyond; oth-
ers have mountain and forest views. The Raven Room offers seafood,
pasta, and steaks. Fried halibut nuggets are a top draw. Newly redec-
orated, the restaurant is a pastel-colored room with vaulted ceilings
and watercolors by local artists. Views are of the Sitka Sound and fish-
ing fleets amidst their daily routine. 🏠 *330 Seward St., Sitka 99835,*
☎ *907/747–6241 or 800/544–0970,* FAX *907/747–5486. 100 rooms.
Restaurant, bar. AE, D, DC, MC, V.*

LODGING

A number of B&Bs have sprung up in Sitka in recent years; ask the
visitor center for a referral or write to the **Sitka Convention and Visi-
tors Bureau** (Box 1226, Sitka 99835, ☎ 907/747–5940, FAX 907/747–
3739).

Skagway

DINING

$–$$ **Golden North Restaurant.** To eat in the dining room in the Golden North Hotel is to return to the days of gold-rush con man Soapy Smith, heroic Frank Reid, and the scores of pioneers, stampeders, and dance-hall girls. The decor is *authentically* Days of '98: The hotel was actually built that year and has been tastefully restored to the era. Popular choices include sourdough pancakes for breakfast; soups, salads, and sandwiches for lunch; salmon or other seafood for dinner. ⛩ *3rd Ave. and Broadway,* ☎ *907/983–2294. AE, DC, MC, V.*

$ **Prospector's Sourdough Restaurant.** You'll meet as many Skagway folk here as you will visitors, particularly at breakfast time, when the sourdough hotcakes or snow-crab omelets are on the griddle. At this family-run restaurant of many generations, the sourdough recipes are as old as the town. Salmon steak and halibut are favored in the evening. The decor features colorful works of local artists on the walls. ✕ *4th Ave. and Broadway,* ☎ *907/983–2865. AE, DC, MC, V.*

In the $ category consider the **Northern Lights Pizzeria** (4th St. and Broadway, ☎ 907/983–2225).

DINING AND LODGING

$$–$$$$ **Westmark Inn.** In keeping with the locale, the decor is gold-rush elegant, with rich red carpeting, brass trim, and historical pictures throughout. Gold-rush period furnishings are first class; soothing ivories and soft greens brighten the rooms. When making the required reservation, request a room in the main structure rather than the annex: The rooms are larger and you don't have to leave the building to visit the restaurant or lounge. Formerly called the Klondike Hotel, this is Skagway's largest inn. If it's not packed with tourists (try to avoid the 5:30 PM rush hour), the Chilkoot Dining Room offers some of Skagway's most gracious dining. From Thai sweet noodles to veal pastrami, the diverse menu, full of unusual dishes with nontraditional spice and combinations, is a rare find. If it's on the menu, try the steamed king crab legs with lemongrass sauce. There's also an extensive wine list. Decor here is gold-rush style but grander and more plush than anything the stampeders ever experienced. Highlights include gold-rush photos, lace tablecloths, and floral carpets. ⛩ *3rd St., east of Broadway,* ☎ *907/ 983–2291 or 800/544–0970,* ℻ *907/983–6100, hotel;* ☎ *907/983– 6000, restaurant. 214 rooms. Brasserie, dining room, lobby lounge. AE, D, DC, MC, V. Closed winter.*

LODGING

$$ **Golden North Hotel.** No question about it, this is Alaska's most his-
★   toric hotel. It was built in 1898 in the heyday of the gold rush—golden dome and all—and has been lovingly restored to reflect that period. Pioneer Skagway families have contributed gold-rush furnishings to each of the hotel's rooms, and the stories of those families are posted on the walls of each unit. The third-floor lobby has a view of the Lynn canal. ⛩ *3rd Ave. and Broadway (mailing address: Box 343, Skagway 99840),* ☎ *907/983–2451 or 983–2294,* ℻ *907/983–2755. 32 rooms. Dining room, lobby lounge. AE, DC, MC, V.*

$$ **Skagway Inn Bed & Breakfast.** This downtown Victorian inn lies
★   within the Klondike Gold Rush National Historical Park. Each room is named after a different gold-rush gal. Color schemes vary but rooms share a Victorian motif with antiques and cast-iron beds; some have mountain views. The building was constructed in 1897 and is thus one of Skagway's oldest. The inn attracts hikers and other intrepid travelers. ⛩ *7th Ave. at Broadway (mailing address: Box 500, Skagway*

99840), ☎ 907/983–2289, FAX 907/983–2713. 12 rooms. Restaurant. D, MC, V.

$$ Wind Valley Lodge. A long walk or a short drive from downtown, the Wind Valley Lodge is one of Skagway's newer motels. Rooms are modern with typical motel furniture, and there's a free shuttle to downtown. A restaurant with basic American fare is next door. ⊡ *2nd Ave. and State St. (mailing address: Box 354, Skagway 99840), ☎ 907/983–2236, FAX 907/983–2957. 30 rooms. AE, DC, MC, V.*

Wrangell

DINING

$–$$ Roadhouse Lodge. The walls here are practically a museum of early Alaskan. The food is wholesome, tasty, and ample. Specialties include local prawns (sautéed, deep-fried, or boiled in the shell) and deep-fried Indian fry bread. The lodge is 3½ miles from downtown. ⊡ *Mile 4, Zimovia Hwy., ☎ 907/874–2335. AE, MC, V.*

DINING AND LODGING

$–$$ Stikine Inn. On the dock in the main part of town, this inn offers great views of Wrangell's harbor. Rooms are simply decorated, with plain, modern furnishings. Unless you plan to be among the late-night party crowd, ask the registration clerk to assign you a room away from the bar. There's no charge for children under 12. The Dock Side Restaurant, a coffee shop and dining room, offers good views of the harbor. Seafood and steaks are staples. ⊡ *1 block from ferry terminal; Stikine Ave., Box 990, Wrangell 99929, ☎ 907/874–3388, FAX 907/874–3923. 34 rooms. Restaurant, bar, travel services. AE, DC, MC, V.*

LODGING

$$ Harding's Old Sourdough Lodge. This lodge sits on the docks, in a beautifully converted construction camp. The Harding family welcomes guests in the big open dining-living room with home-baked sourdough breads and local seafood. Guest rooms have rustic paneling and modest country-style furnishings; the exterior is hand-milled cedar. There's a courtesy shuttle. ⊡ *1104 Peninsula St., Box 1062, Wrangell 99929, ☎ 907/874–3613 or 800/874–3613, FAX 907/874–3455. 14 rooms with bath, 5 rooms share 2 baths. Sauna, steam room, boating, meeting room. DC, MC, V.*

THE ARTS AND NIGHTLIFE

The Arts

Theater

Southeast Alaska's only professional theater company, **Perseverance Theater of Juneau** (914 3rd St., ☎ 907/364–2421), presents everything from Broadway plays to Shakespeare to locally written material.

Haines hosts a statewide drama competition called ACTFEST in April of odd-numbered years. The festival is held at the **Chilkat Center for the Arts** at Ft. Seward, with entries from community theaters both large and small. For details write to Mimi Gregg, ACTFEST, Box 75, Haines 99827.

Several communities stage summer musicals or melodramas for the entertainment of visitors. In Haines, there's "The Lust for Dust"; in Juneau, "The Lady Lou Revue"; in Ketchikan, "The Fish Pirate's Daughter"; and in Skagway, the "Days of '98 Show."

For dancing, check out the **Chilkat Indian Dancers,** who demonstrate Tlingit dancing twice weekly in Haines, and the **New Archangel Dancers**

of Sitka, who perform authentic Russian Cossack–type dances whenever cruise ships are in port.

Music Festivals

The annual weeklong **Alaska Folk Festival** (☎ 907/789–0292, Box 21748, Juneau 99802) is staged each April in Juneau, drawing singers, musical storytellers, banjo masters, fiddlers, and even cloggers from all over the state and Yukon Territory.

Early in summer Juneau is the scene of yet another musical gathering, this one called **Juneau Jazz 'n Classics** (Box 22152, Juneau 99802, ☎ 907/364–2801). It celebrates things musical from Bach to Brubeck.

Southeast Alaska's major classical music festival is the annual **Sitka Summer Music Festival** (Box 3333, Sitka 99835, ☎ 907/747–6774), a three-week June celebration of workshops, recitals, and concerts held in the Centennial Building, downtown.

Nightlife

Summer nightlife in Alaska doesn't just mean barhopping: The midnight sun makes possible activities such as late-night fishing, hikes, and strolls alongside the water. In Juneau, state employees pour out of offices after work and head for the water. When in Alaska, do as the Alaskans do, and think of the time after dinner as a bonus afternoon.

Bars and Nightclubs

Socializing at a bar or "saloon" is an old Alaska custom, and the towns and cities of the Southeast Panhandle are no exception. Following are some of the favorite gathering places in these parts:

HAINES/FT. SEWARD

Harbor Bar (Front St. at the Harbor, ☎ 907/766–2444). Commercial fisherfolk gather here nightly at this old (1907) bar and restaurant. Sometimes there is live music.

JUNEAU

Alaskan Hotel Bar (167 S. Franklin St., ☎ 907/586–1000). This spot is popular with locals and distinctly less touristy. If live music isn't playing, an old-fashioned player piano usually is.

Bubble Room (127 N. Franklin St., ☎ 907/586–2660). This comfortable lounge off the lobby in the Baranof Hotel is quiet—and the site (so it is said) of more legislative lobbying and decision making than in the nearby state capitol building. The music from the piano bar is soft.

Galleon Bar (544 S. Franklin St., ☎ 907/586–4700). On the pier adjacent to Giorgio's restaurant, the Galleon has a seafaring motif. Teakwood and potholes adorn the room; booths are designed as ship cabins; and the central bar is a model of a 15th-century galleon, complete with a two-story mast. There's live music nightly and a well-rounded snack menu you can build a meal on.

Red Dog Saloon (278 S. Franklin St., ☎ 907/463–3777). This pub carries on the sawdust-on-the-floor tradition, with mounted bear and other game animal trophies on the walls and lots of historic photos. There's live music and the crowd is lively, particularly when the cruise ships are in port.

KETCHIKAN

Annabelle's (326 Front St., ☎ 907/225–6009). This restaurant-lounge with a jukebox in the Gilmore Hotel blends old and new Alaska in a semiformal atmosphere.

Harbor Bar (Nordic Dr. near Dolphin St., ☎ 907/772–4526). The name suggests the decor here—ship's wheels, ship pictures, and a mounted red snapper.

SITKA
Pilot House (713 Katlean St., ☎ 907/747–7707) is a new dance spot with a waterfront view.

Pioneer Bar (212 Katlean St., ☎ 907/747–3456), across from the harbor, is a hangout for local fishermen. Tourists get a kick out of its authentic Alaskan ambience; the walls are lined with pictures of ships.

Rockies (1615 Sawmill Creek Rd., ☎ 907/747–3285) is a sports bar with pool, air hockey, darts, and plenty of munchies. A DJ plays dance music.

SKAGWAY
Moe's Frontier Bar (Broadway between 4th and 5th Sts., ☎ 907/983–2238). A longtime fixture on the Skagway scene, Moe's is a bar much frequented by the local folk.

Red Onion (Broadway at 2nd St., ☎ 907/983–2222). You'll meet at least as many Skagway people here as you will visitors. There's live music on Thursday nights, ranging from rock and jazz to folk and acoustic. The upstairs was a gold-rush brothel.

WRANGELL
Stikine Bar (107 Front St., ☎ 907/874–3388). This can be a louder-as-the-night-gets-later bar when a rock band is playing on weekends, but it's a friendly place to meet the locals.

SOUTHEAST ESSENTIALS

Getting Around

By Bus
Year-round service between Anchorage and Skagway is available from **Alaska Direct Bus Lines** (Box 501, Anchorage 99510, ☎ 907/277–6652 or 800/770–6652 in Alaska and Canada). **Gray Line of Alaska** (☎ 800/544–2206) offers summertime connections between Whitehorse, Anchorage, Fairbanks, Haines, and Skagway with other stops en route.

Though it's a long ride, you can travel **Greyhound Lines of Canada** (☎ 604/662–3222) from Vancouver or Edmonton to Whitehorse and make connections there with Gray Line buses to Southeast Alaska.

By Car
Only Skagway and Haines, in the northern Panhandle, and tiny little Hyder, just across the border from Stewart, British Columbia, are accessible by conventional highway. To reach Skagway or Haines, take the Alaska Highway to the Canadian Yukon's Whitehorse or Haines Junction, respectively, then drive the Klondike Highway or Haines Highway southwest to the Alaska Panhandle. You can reach Hyder on British Columbia's Cassiar Highway, which can be reached, in turn, from Highway 16 just north of Prince Rupert.

SCENIC DRIVES
The descent (or ascent, depending on which direction you're traveling) from the high, craggy Canadian mountain country to the Southeast Alaska coast makes both the **Klondike Highway** into Skagway or the **Haines Highway** to Haines especially memorable traveling. At the

top of the respective passes, vegetation is sparse and pockets of snow are often present, even in summertime. The scenery is stark, with mountains silhouetted sharply against frequently blue skies. As you near the saltwater coast of the Panhandle, the forest cover becomes tall, thick, and evergreen. Both drives are worth an excursion, even if you don't intend to drive any farther than the Canadian border and return.

Every city, town, and village in Southeast Alaska has one or more waterfront drives that take in bustling dock scenes and tranquil bays and beaches, and they also offer the possibility of seeing wildlife. Inquire at local information centers.

By Cruise Ship
Southeast waters attract cruise ships varying in size from small excursion yachts with the capacity for 100 passengers to huge ocean liners with beds for more than a thousand.

By Ferry
From the south, the **Alaska Marine Highway System** (☎ 800/642–0066) operates stateroom-equipped vehicle and passenger ferries from Bellingham, Washington, and from Prince Rupert, British Columbia. The vessels call at Ketchikan, Wrangell, Petersburg, Juneau, Haines, and Skagway, and they connect with smaller vessels serving bush communities. One of the smaller ferries also operates between Hyder and Ketchikan. In the summer, staterooms on the ferries are always sold out before sailing time; reserve months in advance. For those planning to take cars on the ferry, early reservations are also highly recommended for vehicle space.

BC Ferries (1112 Fort St., Victoria, BC, Canada V8V 4V2, ☎ 604/669–1211) operates similar passenger and vehicle ferries from Vancouver Island, British Columbia, to Prince Rupert, where they connect with the Alaska Marine Highway System.

By Plane
Alaska Airlines (☎ 800/426–0333) operates several flights daily from Seattle and other Pacific Coast and southwestern cities to Ketchikan, Wrangell, Petersburg, Sitka, Glacier Bay, and Juneau. The carrier connects Juneau to the north Alaskan cities of Yakutat, Cordova, Anchorage, Fairbanks, Nome, Kotzebue, and Prudhoe Bay. **Delta Airlines** (☎ 800/221–1212) has at least one flight daily from Seattle to Juneau and from Juneau to Fairbanks.

By Train
At present, Southeast Alaska's only railroad, the **White Pass Yukon Railroad** (☎ 800/343–7373), operates between Skagway and Fraser, British Columbia. The tracks follow the historic path over the White Pass summit—a mountain-climbing, cliff-hanging route of 28 miles each way. Bus connections are available at Fraser to Whitehorse, Yukon.

Guided Tours

The operators listed below offer mainly day trips. For a list of operators offering longer trips, *see* Important Contacts A to Z *in* the Gold Guide. For a more complete listing of yacht charters in Southeast communities, contact visitor information offices in these towns (*see* Important Addresses and Numbers, *below*).

Haines
Alaska Cross-Country Guiding and Rafting (☎ and FAX 907/767–5522) offers fly-in, raft-out trips down the Tsirku River, plus photo trips in the eagle preserve for small groups only.

Alaska Nature Tours (☎ and ℻ 907/766–2876) conducts bird-watching and natural-history tours through the Chilkat Bald Eagle Preserve, home of the largest concentration of bald eagles in the world. Tours include viewing of brown bears, wolves, and other wildlife.

Halsingland Hotel (☎ 907/766–2000 or 800/542–6363) books sightseeing tours for several local operators that visit area attractions.

Juneau

Alaska Rainforest Treks (☎ 907/463–3466, ℻ 907/463–4453) schedules daily escorted hikes on trails around Juneau. Terrain includes mountains, glaciers, forests, and ocean shores. Food and rain gear are provided. The company also takes bookings for other local adventure tour operators.

Alaska Sightseeing/Cruise West (☎ 907/586–6300 or 800/426–7702, ℻ 907/463–3323) and **Gray Line of Alaska** (☎ 907/586–3773 in summer; 800/544–2206 year-round, ℻ 907/463–2516) both offer motorcoach sightseeing tours of Juneau, Mendenhall Glacier, and other points of interest.

Alaska Travel Adventures (☎ 907/789–0052, ℻ 907/789–1749) packages a half-day guided raft trip (bumpy enough to be exciting but well short of a white-knuckle ride) down the Mendenhall River; it includes a mid-trip snack of Alaska smoked salmon, reindeer sausage, cheeses, apple cider, and an alcoholic brew called Mendenhall Madness. Kayaking tours are available as well.

Alaska Up Close (☎ 907/789–9544, ℻ 907/789–3205) arranges half- or full-day nature photography tours. At least a week's notice is recommended.

Beartrack Charters (☎ 907/586–6945) operates four-hour and eight-hour charter fishing excursions.

Juneau Sportfishing (☎ 907/789–7411, ℻ 907/586–9769) also runs charter fishing excursions for salmon and halibut, as well as overnight whale-watching trips on its luxury yachts.

Temsco Helicopters (☎ 907/789–9501, ℻ 907/789–7989) pioneered helicopter sightseeing over Mendenhall Glacier with an actual touchdown and a chance to romp on the glacier. **Era Helicopters** (☎ 907/586–2030, ℻ 907/225–8636) offers a similar trip.

Ketchikan

Alaska Cruises (☎ 907/225–6044, ℻ 907/225–8636) provides cruise or fly-cruise one-day excursions from downtown Ketchikan to Misty Fjords National Monument, a wilderness of steep-walled fjords, mountains, and islands. Boat transport for kayakers is offered to and from Misty Fjords. Harbor cruises of the Ketchikan waterfront are also available.

Alaska Sightseeing/Cruise West (☎ 907/225–2740 or 800/426–7702, ℻ 907/225–1110) offers sightseeing motor-coach tours of downtown Ketchikan, Totem Bight State Historical Park, and Totem Heritage Center. Boat tours of Misty Fjords and the Inside Passage are also available.

Gray Line of Alaska (☎ 907/225–5930 or 800/544–2206, ℻ 907/225–9386) offers all of the above plus a Saxman Native Village tour, flightseeing in Misty Fjords, jet-boat adventures, and canoeing.

Ketchikan Indian Corporation (☎ 907/225–5158 or 800/252–5158, FAX 907/247–0429) conducts Native American heritage tours of town focusing on traditional land and fishery use and native crafts.

Petersburg

Pacific Wing, Inc. (☎ 907/772–9258, FAX 907/772–9282) gets high marks from locals for its flightseeing tours over LeConte Glacier.

Viking Travel (☎ 907/772–3818, FAX 907/772–3940) is a travel agency that books whale-watching, glacier, and kayaking trips with local operators.

Sitka

Alaska Travel Adventures (*see above*) operates a three-hour kayaking tour in protected waters just south of town; no kayaking experience is necessary.

Baidarka Boats (☎ 907/747–8996, FAX 907/747–7510) rents sea kayaks and offers guided custom trips in the island-dotted waters around Sitka.

Prewitt Enterprises (☎ 907/747–8443, FAX 907/747–7510) meets state ferries and provides short city tours while vessels are in port, with stops at Sitka National Historical Park, Sheldon Jackson Museum, and the downtown shopping area. It also offers three-hour tours that visit St. Michael's Cathedral, Old Sitka, Castle Hill, and the old Russian cemetery.

Skagway

Gray Line of Alaska (☎ 907/983–2241 or 800/544–2206, FAX 907/983–2087) provides motor-coach tours through Skagway's historic district, Gold Rush Cemetery (where frontier "bad guy" Soapy Smith lies buried), and from the trailhead of the Chilkoot Trail to the Yukon goldfields. Glacier Bay flightseeing tours are also offered.

Skagway Street Car Co. (☎ and FAX 907/983–2908) lets you revisit the gold-rush days in the original 1937 "White Motor Company" streetcars, complete with costumed conductors who tell the story of the town's tumultuous history while showing you the sights.

Wrangell

Sunrise Aviation (☎ 907/874–2319, FAX 907/874–2546) is a charter-only air carrier that offers trips to the Anan Bear Observatory, Tracy Arm, and the LeConte Glacier and can drop you off at any number of places for a day of secluded fishing and hiking.

TH Charters (☎ 907/874–2085, FAX 907/874–2285) provides a fast-paced jet-boat ride into the Stikine River wilderness country to Shakes Glacier, Shakes Hot Springs, and other historic and natural attractions. Trips to the Anan Bear Observatory are also available.

Important Addresses and Numbers

Emergencies

PHARMACIES

Juneau: Juneau Drug Co., 202 Front Street, downtown, across from McDonald's, ☎ 907/586–1233. **Ron's Apothecary,** 9101 Mendenhall Mall Road, about 10 miles north of downtown in Mendenhall Valley, next to the Super Bear market, ☎ 907/789–0458. For after-hours prescription emergencies, dial 907/789–9522.

Ketchikan: Downtown Pharmacy, 300 Front Street, ☎ 907/225–3144. **Race Pharmacy,** 2300 Tongass Avenue, across from the Plaza Portwest shopping mall, ☎ 907/225–4151. After hours, call Ketchikan General Hospital, ☎ 907/225–5171.

Petersburg: Rexall Drugs, 215 North Nordic Drive, ☎ 907/772–3265. After hours, call Petersburg Medical Center, ☎ 907/772–4291.

Sitka: White's Pharmacy, 705 Halibut Point Road, ☎ 907/747–5755. **Harry Race Pharmacy,** 106 Lincoln Street, ☎ 907/747–8600.

Wrangell: Wrangell Drug, 202 Front Street, ☎ 907/874–3422.

PHYSICIAN AND DENTIST

Haines–Ft. Seward Health Clinic, next to the Visitors Information Center, ☎ 907/766–2521. Pharmacy needs also are cared for. **Skagway Medical Service,** on 11th Avenue between State Street and Broadway, ☎ 907/983–2255. **Wrangell Hospital,** on the airport road, next to the elementary school, ☎ 907/874–3356.

POLICE AND AMBULANCE

In Haines–Ft. Seward, Juneau, Ketchikan, Petersburg, Sitka, and Skagway, dial 911. Gustavus: EMS (☎ 907/697–2222). Wrangell: Police (☎ 907/874–3304); Ambulance and Fire Department (☎ 907/874–2000).

Visitor Information

Southeast Alaska Tourism Council (Box 20710, Juneau 99802, ☎ 907/586–4777 or 800/423–0568).

Glacier Bay National Park and Preserve (Box 140, Gustavus 99826, ☎ 907/697–2230).

Haines/Fort Seward Visitor Information Center (2nd Ave. near Willard St., Box 530, Haines 99827, ☎ 907/766–2234 or 800/458–3579). ☉ June–August, daily 8–8; winter, weekdays 8–5.

Juneau Convention and Visitors Bureau (369 S. Franklin St., Suite 201, Juneau 99801, ☎ 907/586–1737) and **Davis Log Cabin Visitor Center** (134 3rd St., ☎ 907/586–2201). ☉ May–August, daily 8–5; September–April, weekdays 8–5. In the summertime, information is also available at a visitor center on the cruise-ship dock and downtown at a kiosk in Marine Park.

Ketchikan Visitors Bureau (131 Front St., Ketchikan 99901, ☎ 907/225–6166, 800/770–3300). ☉ May 15–September, daily 8–5; October–May 14, weekdays 8–5.

The **Klondike Gold Rush National Historical Park** visitor center (2nd Ave. and Broadway, Box 517, Skagway 99840, ☎ 907/983–2921), which has lots of information on the city as well, is housed in the old White Pass Yukon Route railroad terminal downtown. ☉ Summer, daily 8–8; winter, weekdays 8–5.

Petersburg Visitor Information Center (Box 649, Petersburg 99833, ☎ 907/772–4636) is located at the corner of 1st and Fram streets. ☉ Summer, weekdays 8–5, weekends 10–4; winter, weekdays 10–3.

Sitka Convention and Visitors Bureau (Box 1226, Sitka 99835, ☎ 907/747–5940, located in the new City Hall on Lincoln St., across from Totem Square). ☉ Weekdays 8–5. **Greater Sitka Chamber of Commerce** (Box 638, Sitka 99835, ☎ 907/747–8604, located downtown in the Centennial Building at 330 Harbor Drive, right across from the cruise docks). ☉ Weekdays 9–5. An information booth in the Centennial Building is staffed on weekends and when cruise ships are in town.

Skagway Convention and Visitors Bureau (City Hall, 7th Ave. and Spring St., Box 415, Skagway 99840, ☎ 907/983–2854). ☉ Daily 8–5. From mid-May to mid-September, the bureau moves to Arctic Brotherhood Hall on Broadway between 2nd and 3rd avenues.

Wrangell Chamber of Commerce Visitors Center (Box 49, Wrangell 99929, ☎ 907/874–3901) is in the A-frame on the waterfront next to City Hall. ☉ When cruise ships or ferries are in port, and at other posted times in summer.

9 Portraits of the Pacific North Coast

Pacific Northwest Microbrews: Good for What Ales You

In the Footsteps of the First Settlers

More Portraits

PACIFIC NORTHWEST MICROBREWS: GOOD FOR WHAT ALES YOU

FRESHLY POURED ALE sparkles a rich amber in the light of a sun-dappled May afternoon on the loading-dock beer garden of the Bridgeport Brewpub in Portland, Oregon. To the south rise the office towers of downtown Portland, which supply not a few of Bridgeport's customers. To the north is the graceful span of the Fremont Bridge, from which the tiny brewery takes its name.

The customer tips back his glass and takes a long, thirsty swallow. The ale cascades along his tongue, tweaking taste buds that for years have known only pale, flavorless industrial lagers. A blast of sweet malt explodes at the back of his mouth, counterpointing the citrusy sting of the hops. *This* is flavor, something missing from American beer for far too long.

Sip by sip, beer connoisseurs from all over the world are learning that the Pacific Northwest—particularly Portland and Seattle—has become the best place in the world outside the European continent to imbibe their favorite brew. Microbreweries (companies producing fewer than 20,000 kegs per year) can now be found in Manhattan, Minneapolis, and Maui, from Boulder, Colorado, to the Outer Banks of Cape Hatteras, but it all started in the Pacific Northwest.

There's something inherently noble about a well-crafted pint, something ancient and universal. Anthropologists now theorize that agriculture and brewing may have provided the stimulus for the very foundation of human civilization. Certainly there is nothing new in the idea of a city or region being served by a number of small, distinctive breweries. More than 5,000 years ago, in Egypt, the many breweries of ancient Pelusium were as famous as the city's university. (Even then, books, beer, and scholarly contemplation went hand in hand.) Even the ancient Greeks and Romans, though more partial to wine than grain beverages, drank beer; evidence shows that there were more than 900 public houses in Herculaneum before Mt. Vesuvius sounded its fateful "last call" in AD 79.

Brewing wasn't perfected, however, until it was introduced to northern climes. Teutonic ancestors could imagine no greater paradise than Valhalla, a banquet-hall with 540 doors and an unquenchable supply of ale. For the Tudor English, ale was far more than an amusement—it was a staple of life, "liquid bread," a source of national strength, and brewers who cut corners and overcharged for an inferior product were fined heavily, imprisoned, or both. It may be a coincidence that during the 1970s Britain's Campaign for Real Ale movement—credited with single-handedly restoring fine ale to United Kingdom pubs—paralleled the resurgence in the British economy and national pride. It may also be a coincidence that the return of the microbrewery ale to the Northwest signaled the end of a bitter recession here, and the beginning of a rapid climb into prosperity. Then again, it may not. Who knows how often the Boeing engineer or the Nike designer has, while trading pleasantries with a new acquaintance over a glass of hell-black stout, gotten just the idea he needed for that important project?

The best place to sample the Northwest's hand-crafted ale is a well-run brew pub, which stimulates the human spirit with conviviality, pleasant warmth, intelligent conversation, the scent of malt, and hearty food. Combatting the region's chilly, damp, British-style climate, brew pubs become places of refuge where you can shake the tears of a hostile world from your umbrella, order a pint of cask-conditioned bitter, and savor a complex substance that caresses the senses.

On any given evening, there are at least 40 locally brewed beers and ales available for tasting in pubs in Portland and Seattle, and no fewer than 30 of North America's 150-odd "cottage breweries" are located within 400 miles of Portland, the dynamic center of this brewing storm. There are more brew pubs per capita in

Portland and Seattle than in any other U.S. cities.

And while most East Coast entries in the microbrewing sweepstakes produce German-style lagers—the most familiar brewing style to American palates—the microbrewers of the Pacific Northwest go for wildly adventuresome bitters, stouts, and porters. "We're used to gutsy beers," says Fred Eckhardt, publisher of the Portland-based newsletter "Listen to Your Beer." "When you get grabbed by a new beer in Portland, you know you've been grabbed."

These are beers, it should be noted, that would make a megabrewery marketing consultant blanch. Take Grant's Imperial Stout. So dark that even a blazing summer sun, viewed through a pint glass of the pitch-black stuff, yields not a glimmer, Imperial Stout is heavy with choice whole barley malt, citrusy Cascade hops, and honey; it contains twice the alcohol, four times the calories, and a hundred times the flavor of a Bud Light. At a time when everyone supposedly wants to stay skinny and sober, who in his right mind would brew such a beer?

BACK IN 1982, when Paul Shipman of the Red Hook Brewery in Seattle and Bert Grant of Grant's Ales in Yakima trundled out the first kegs of microbrewery ale tapped in America since Prohibition, they little dreamed that they were ushering in an era of modest revolutionary ferment. Not that these tiny breweries exactly have the Clydesdales quaking in their traces: Anheuser-Busch annually *spills* a thousand times more beer than Bridgeport— one of the most successful microbreweries in America—produces in a year. Still, as America's megabrewers respond to a growing demand for variety by dressing up their beers with labels like "extra gold" and "dry," then actually make their lack of flavor a selling point ("No aftertaste!"), the Northwest's thriving microbrewery industry provides a real alternative for those of us who like beer to taste like *beer*.

"We don't want to take over the beer market," says the most exuberant practitioner of the trade, Oregon brew-pub owner Mike McMenamin. "We just want to have our own identity. It adds a lot of fun, and there's so little fun in the business world today." McMenamin stands in what he calls his "Captain Neon Fermentation Chamber." Tucked away in Portland's West Hills, in the kitchen of a former fast-food restaurant, McMenamin watches the yeast clouds billow across his open fermentation tanks. A weird twisting of neon light—blue, purple, ale-amber—casts a surrealistic pallor over the nascent ale.

"We just love beer—we're experimenting all the time," says the tall, bearded McMenamin. "We want to keep on the cutting edge of what's happening in American brewing. When someone says 'You can't do that,' we know that's a good place to start." Though brewing purists insist that "real beer" should contain only four ingredients—water, malted barley, hops, and yeast—the McMenamins reject such notions out of hand, producing a variety of wildly distinctive brews such as raspberry stout; Java Ale, made with fresh-ground coffee in the mash; and Wisdom Ale, which included a collection of carefully researched ingredients designed, Mike McMenamin says, "to make you smarter." And whether or not the purists approve, the public seems to, for McMenamin's seven tiny breweries—three in Portland, one in suburban Hillsboro, one in Lincoln City at the coast, one in Salem, and one in Eugene—can't keep up with the demand for his products, which are sold only at his network of 21 pubs.

Five years ago, the typical McMenamin pub was an amalgam of fresh local microbrewery beers, cheerfully psychedelic art, wild neon sculptures, classic rock on the jukebox, and sandwiches with names like the Engroovenator and the Captain Neon Burger. At the most recent additions to the McMenamin empire, you can still find the Grateful Dead on the stereo, and fresh microbrewery beer still flows in copious draughts—only now most of it is produced in-house. At outlets such as the brand-new McMenamin's on Broadway and the Thompson Brewery in Salem, a subtle shift in focus is apparent. For one thing, they occupy a brand-new office/retail building and a meticulously restored Victorian house, respectively, rather than the more modest addresses of the earlier pubs. The artwork has also been reined in a bit, at least in the public areas. The

McMenamins employ two house artists, Joe Cotter and Lyle Hehn, who roam from pub to pub late at night adding hand-painted scenes and details as the spirit moves them. Though much of their finest work has now been relegated to back-of-the-house areas (for example, the brewery mural at the Salem location that turns the Capitol Building into a turbo-powered spaceship, with Uncle Sam tipping his hat astride the dome), there is still ample evidence of their work: the grinning imp-face, for example, that's visible only in one of the mirrors at Mc-Menamin's Broadway.

EACH OF PORTLAND'S MICRO-BREWERIES has its own distinctive style, its own array of products, and its own army of followers, ready on the instant to debate the relative merits of Portland Ale versus Widmer Weizen. "The variety does make us work harder," says Art Larrance, one of the founders of Portland Brewing, located in an old creamery just off the railroad tracks. In this ornate pub, the brew kettle shines behind a two-story-high window beneath a skylight, and a music loft provides a view of the after-work crowd bellying up to a brass-railed bar for a pint of Grant's or the popular Portland and Timberline ales. Hot jazz swings out of the music loft every Thursday night for a live radio show sponsored by the brewery.

Inside a historic gray building just across the river from the Portland Brewing Company, Widmer Brewing co-owner and brewmaster Kurt Widmer dons a well-worn pair of Wellington boots and scampers around the wet concrete floor of his brewery preparing to pump the burbling "wort," or raw beer, in his brew-kettle to the stainless-steel fermenting tank a few feet away. The air is thick with steam and the rich fragrance of malt. Widmer tests a bit of the liquid for specific gravity—a measurement of eventual alcohol content—then, satisfied, throws a lever to begin the pumping process.

The redwood-sheathed brew kettle was custom-made to Widmer's specifications at a local metal fabrication company. Until a recent move to ritzier digs, other pieces of his equipment had more check-ered pasts. The whirlpool tank, used to clarify the wort before it is fermented, began its days as a shrimp cooker in a coastal processing plant. Other vats were scavenged from area creameries. And his fermenting tanks? "Those came from the [never-completed] Pebble Springs nuclear power plant," Widmer smiles. "I picked them up for a real good price—and they're built to the highest standards in the land."

Widmer, a former Internal Revenue Service employee and home brewer, is the Portland area's only German-style brewer. While he, like most Northwest brewers, loves the fine local hops, his products tend to emphasize malt flavors and a pleasant yeasty spiciness over the refreshing bitterness of the Northwest's English-style ales. Though one of the most recent micros to come on-line, Widmer has had no difficulty developing a following. After just four years in the marketplace, Widmer is the best-selling microbrew in the state, thanks to an extremely active marketing and distribution team. Production has climbed an average of 30%–40% every year; now that Widmer's dream brewery, located in a historic warehouse just across the Willamette River from his present location, is on-line, the company will soon exceed the legal production for a microbrewery of 20,000 kegs per annum.

"We've already vastly exceeded our projections," Widmer says. "We threw our business plan away a year ago, because it was hopelessly outdated."

Whether it's business or brewing, no Portland micro is more respected than Bridgeport, the oldest. Founded in 1984 by local winemakers Dick and Nancy Ponzi, Bridgeport now combines expertly brewed English-style ales with one of the city's most popular pub operations. As originally conceived by the Ponzis and brewmaster Karl Ockert, the pub was little more than a tasting room, located in the same 1880s-vintage former rope factory as the brewery, with only a single tap, a few tables, and a dart board.

As anyone who has attempted to fight through the crush at the pub's bar on a recent Friday night can tell you, a slightly different attitude prevails at Bridgeport today. Though the atmosphere is still casual, the pub's highly regarded selection of light and dark ales, handmade pizza with a sourdough beer wort crust, and the opportunity to watch the brewers at work through steamy windows behind the bar, pack the place every night of the week.

One of the things that sets Bridgeport apart from other Portland-area breweries is the pub's skill with true cask-conditioned ales, available nowhere else in the city. Made in the traditional English style, these ales are pumped unfiltered directly into the keg at the end of fermentation, to lie undisturbed in a cool cellar for several weeks. There is no added carbon dioxide; cask-conditioned ales contain only the natural carbonation produced during the fermentation process. The result, drawn from one of the antique "beer-engine" hand-pumps at the end of the bar, is a smoother, noticeably less fizzy pint, with all the rich flavors of malt and hops allowed to shine through.

In Seattle, gems such as the Trolleyman Pub keep the Emerald City in the running with other Northwest Coast brew pubs. Tucked away in a corner of Red Hook's state-of-the-art facility in Fremont—just north of downtown Seattle—The Trolleyman poured its inaugural pint in 1988. The popular, low-key pub's five taps dispense brewery-fresh Red Hook ESB, golden Ballard Bitter, coffee-hued Black Hook porter, spicy Wheat Hook, and seasonal brews such as Winter Hook strong ale. There is one cask-conditioned tap, pouring a rotating selection of real ales.

The firelit pub, filled with long trestle tables, comfortable overstuffed furniture, and the sweet, malty aromas of new-brewed ale, is warm and inviting. From the competent kitchen flows a steady stream of hearty pub fare: black bean chili, puff pies crammed with chicken and beef, and a mean lasagna. Of particular interest to those visiting the pub will be the story of the former brewer who invited a young lady for a midnight hot-tub in the mash ton, with results worthy of a segment of the TV show "Cheers." It's a Northwest legend!

So with all these beers to choose from, where do you begin? What should you look for in a microbrewery ale? First and foremost, variety. At any given time in Portland and Seattle, there are 30–40 fresh, locally made brews on tap. They range in color from pale straw to ebony-black, in strength from a standard 3½% alcohol to an ominous 8½%.

And the flavor? Well, you'll just have to taste for yourself. There is the rich sweetness of malt, counterbalanced by good bitter hops. There are the mocha java overtones of roasted barley, used in stouts and porters, and the spiciness of malted wheat. There are sweet ales and tart ales, mild inconsequential ales, and ales so charged with flavor they linger on the palate like a fine Bordeaux.

Above all else, you should look for an ale you can savor, an ale you can taste without wanting to swallow too quickly. The dearest emotion to a brewer's heart is the beer drinker's feeling of regret that the last swig is gone.

By Jeff Kuechle

IN THE FOOTSTEPS OF THE FIRST SETTLERS

THERE'S A SORT OF PRIMEVAL MYSTERY about the majestic landscapes of the Pacific Northwest Coast, something elemental and ancient that can give you a strange sense of being dislocated in time. Drive along the coastal roads of Washington's Olympic Peninsula, for example, and you'll pass magnificent rain forest, pounding surf, and partially submerged chunks of headland stranded at sea. Every bridge you cross takes you over an ancient fishing stream where prehistoric Indians harvested salmon. The oldest trees along the road bear scars where these Indians pulled off bark strips dozens of feet long, which they used for clothing, construction work, and rope making. Stop to look out over the water, and you feel the presence of ancient whale hunters scanning the horizon for spouts among the waves.

It isn't just a question of landscape, either. Elders in the Eskimo (Inuit is the preferred term in Canada) and Indian communities along the coast still pass on stories told to them by their ancestors, stories that can sometimes be traced as far back as 1,000 years, and their tribal art is a living expression of cultures whose origins are lost in the mists of prehistory.

Despite a lack of hard evidence, many archaeologists believe the first people to inhabit the New World arrived by way of the Pacific North Coast. Unlike Columbus and the seafaring Vikings, Polynesians, Chinese, and Japanese, all of whom crossed oceans to arrive at different points in North and South America, it is believed that the first Americans came on foot. If these pioneers had boats at all, they were small ones, not designed for long-distance travel across oceans. They came via Alaska and traveled through Canada into the western United States.

Although these assertions sound feasible, there aren't any known archaeological sites to support them. The oldest documented sites in the New World are believed to be 20,000–13,000 years old; the oldest known sites in the Pacific Northwest are Indian settlements that fall at the younger end of this range, at about 13,000 years old. Why then is the Pacific Northwest Coast believed to be the point of entry for the earliest settlers? Because it's the only place where people could have walked into the New World or used their small boats to travel along the coast without excessive danger.

The last ice age tied up so much water that ocean levels probably dropped by hundreds of feet around the world. On certain winter days today, a person can walk between Alaska and the Soviet Union on ice when the oceans freeze over. But during the Ice Age the oceans were so reduced that the seabed was temporarily exposed as dry land, supporting vegetation and game, with fish in the rivers and sea mammals on the coast. So much ground was exposed, in fact, that the Old World and the New were connected by dry land. And though their languages and blood types differ, evidence strongly suggests that both the Eskimos and Indians have their roots somewhere in Asia. As one Eskimo friend of mine once said, "You know, those Chinese look an awful lot like us. They must be descended from Eskimos."

Why then aren't there any sites to prove this migration theory? All human activity may have been confined to lower ground levels now hidden under the ocean, reason the archaeologists. Or people may have traveled in small numbers, so their remains aren't easily detected. Or we may have already found these sites without recognizing them as such. Even though the two American continents were not inhabited with people at the outset, they did have abundant herds of large game, animals that had no fear of humans. Hunters with such easy prey wouldn't stay in one place for long; as they killed off their local supply of meat, or as the animals learned how to avoid people, the hunters moved on. So it is possible that the settlers arrived in the Pacific Northwest, lived a nomadic life there for a while, and then roamed on to other parts of North America and into South America.

THE FIRST AMERICANS came to a land we wouldn't recognize today. Most of Canada, Alaska, and the northern United States were still under ice. Arctic weather and the forests, animals, and plants that are found in today's far north were prevalent halfway down the lower 48 states. Then the weather changed: The ice sheets melted and the ice receded north. The animal and plant distributions we see today started to become established about 10,000 years ago. Rivers and streams that were previously frozen started to run fast and clear at low temperatures. Conditions for pioneering salmon became so ideal that by 5,000 or so years ago, there were huge runs extending hundreds of miles inland.

For hunters it was a revolutionary time. Herds of large animals started to diminish or disappear, and the big-game hunters were increasingly confronted with more work and less to show for their efforts. Many hunters in the Pacific Northwest Coast, particularly those in Washington, British Columbia, and southeastern Alaska, turned to fishing instead. Their nomadic life following the herds became a more settled one as they switched to fishing. And as they started to settle down, they were able to accumulate more material things.

The first Americans moved north to south, from Alaska to Canada and then to the lower 48 states and finally into Central America and South America. The more recent inhabitants who made their living from salmon fishing, however, headed in the opposite direction, from the lower Pacific Northwest up into Canada and Alaska. The art and culture of these people spread and flourished in the Pacific Northwest and continued to do so in the centuries preceding their contact with European explorers. Archaeological sites of these fishing peoples date back 2,500 years and more.

During this prehistoric fishing era, the most prosperous natives were those of Washington, British Columbia, and southern Alaska. They had the good life, and they flaunted it. Their art was larger than life, while their potlatches (celebratory feasts) gave new meaning to the words conspicuous consumption. The success of the fishing peoples led to imitation. The natives of Kodiak Island were Eskimo, for example, and their ancestors came to the New World to fish and hunt sea mammals along the coast, rather than hunt the big land-bound game as the Indians' ancestors did. Surprising enough, however, the Kodiak people achieved a society in many ways remarkably similar to that of Indian tribes living to the east and south. Their art, archaeology, and legends demonstrate the connections.

One of the best-known archaeological sites of these fishing peoples is Ozette, located on the Makah Reservation in Washington's Olympic Peninsula. The finds of the site can be viewed by the public, and visitors can request permission to visit the site itself. The village of Ozette was partially covered by a mud slide several hundred years ago. This apparent catastrophe ironically turned out to preserve the village, however, for the wet mud provided an anaerobic environment hostile to most decay-causing organisms. As a result, the mud-covered section of Ozette was preserved in its entirety, a kind of New World Pompeii.

Archaeologists usually excavate with masons' trowels because they generally dig up stone and ceramics, objects that a skillfully handled trowel won't harm. But at Ozette in the 1970s, there was a delightful obstacle to overcome. Basketry, cordage, clothing, and all kinds of soft materials had been preserved, but since they were preserved wet, they were particularly soft, and the trowels cut through them like mud. Even experienced excavators couldn't feel the damage they were doing to the objects.

A whole new excavation approach was undertaken, called "wet site" archaeology. Using water hoses to excavate the village, the archaeologists discovered that mud and debris could be washed away, leaving artifacts intact. During the handlers' first clumsy attempts at hosing down the mud, artifacts could be seen tumbling downhill with the water, but after some trial and error, the workers were able to keep even small finds in place.

One of the most exciting aspects of the Ozette excavation was the support archaeologists received from Indians living in the region. The Makah tribe encouraged archaeologists to excavate Ozette and assisted in the fieldwork; tribal members provided logistical support and helped interpret finds. And the tribe even built a museum based on the artifacts on its grounds at Neah Bay.

THE INDIANS ALSO HELPED prepare artifacts for public display, which turned out to be quite a challenge. Generally, archaeological finds of stone and ceramic pieces are preserved simply by being cleaned first in water and then glued together. But Ozette produced all kinds of perishable artifacts, objects that quickly started to deteriorate once they were removed from their muddy entombment. So the Makah Tribe provided laboratory space and helped the archaeologists preserve and stabilize the finds.

These descendants of the ancient Indians went one step further and created a living experiment on the site. The Makah people worked outside to build a plank house, like those in Ozette, and then attempted to use the interior in the same ways their ancestors did. Life in the house was set up based upon the directions of tribal elders, historic accounts, and archaeological interpretations. In the end, the house looked as if one good mud slide would turn it into another ruined Ozette home. After this experimental period, the tribe dismantled the house and rebuilt it inside the Makah museum.

A large dugout canoe was also built for the museum. The art of making canoes had almost died out, but it was revived to capture an important part of life in Ozette. Young and old worked together to build the boat and to pass on these ancient skills.

Other archaeological sites in the area can require a bit more effort to explore. From southern Alaska to Oregon, you can find hundreds of petroglyphs (rock carvings) and pictographs (rock paintings). Only a handful of them can be dated, however, so they can't be attributed to any particular group of people. Some are easily accessible, and seen by the public every day. Others are so hidden you can only find them if you happen to stumble upon them. Still other carvings are positioned at the tidal zone and consequently are under water at high tide. One worthwhile guide to the many accessible rock carvings is Beth and Ray Hill's *Indian Petroglyphs of the Pacific Northwest*.

Prehistoric Indians also carved petroglyphs on land, although mostly facing the ocean, or else overlooking a river or waterway. Pictographs, on the other hand, can be seen throughout the Northwest Coast. Some of these detailed rocks have been jackhammered from their embedded frames and carted away; others have eroded, and still others lie beneath reservoirs. But the vast majority are right where they were created, and with permission from native or nonnative landowners, or government agencies, visitors can examine them. More than 500 sites are known. One protected site open to the public is Petroglyph Park in the town of Nanaimo, on Vancouver Island. Petroglyphs at Wrangell, Alaska, are also open to the public.

The ancient arts of North America's native peoples can provide another avenue of insight into their lives and cultures. The craft of carving giant totem poles out of trees has survived as a living art form, with plenty of demand for new poles. Carvers today often work in public throughout the Pacific Northwest, at museums or on the grounds of institutions that have commissioned their artwork. Young workers aspire to apprentice with master carvers, and gift shops all over the region offer miniature reproductions.

The totem pole is the best-known example of current Northwest Coast tribal art, but masks, tools, and a variety of paintings and prints also continue the artistic tradition of the area. Artwork can be purchased at local galleries, many of which are located on Indian lands and are run by Indians. The choices are broader and the prices lower here than they are in the native art galleries of New York and California. The Dukuah Gallery in Ocluelet, B.C., is run by native Lillian Mac and her husband, Bert Mac, the hereditary chief of the Toquant tribe. Native artists visit and work in the gallery year-round.

Museums offer another glimpse of Inuit and Native American life. The British Columbia Provincial Museum in Victoria, with its unique collection of prehistoric fish bones, is an outstanding research center, with representation from all five species of salmon and almost every other fish that might have been harvested by prehistoric natives. Each fish skeleton has been mounted on wires, with all the bones together in proper anatomical order. While this is a scientific collection, it verges on being a work of art in itself, with skeletal fish elongating and compressing into fantastic shapes.

In Vancouver, at the University of British Columbia's Museum of Anthropology, there's an excellent archaeological collection that's very accessible to the public. Visitors can open any of the Plexiglass-covered drawers to examine even the most delicate artifacts. Other artifacts can be seen at the Thomas Burke Memorial Washington State Museum at the University of Washington in Seattle, and at the Alaska State Museum in Juneau, where they also have a first-rate collection of historic baleen (fibrous plates that hang from the roof of the whale's mouth) baskets. Only native hunters and artisans are legally permitted to own unprocessed baleen.

Any overview of Northwest Coast archaeology inevitably leaves out more than it includes. Paleo-Indian sites, Russian fur-hunting activities, cave sites in Washington's channeled scablands, mastodons and mammoths, and cairns dug up 100 years ago can all be found along the Pacific Northwest Coast. And if you visit the area searching for a glimpse of the past, native people will share their stories, researchers may invite you to observe their work, artisans will explain their ancient crafts, and the museums will let you view even the most fragile artifacts. For here, one thing remains constant: the people's eagerness to document and understand the past.

By Glenn W. Sheehan

MORE PORTRAITS

Fiction & Memoirs

Recommended novels and stories of the Northwest include the imaginative and sometimes surreal creations of novelist Tom Robbins; bittersweet short fiction by Raymond Carver; Ken Kesey's *Sometimes a Great Notion*, about a troubled Oregon logging dynasty; the Jack London classic, *Call of the Wild*; and works by such writers as Annie Dillard, Ursula LeGuin, Aaron Elkin, Frank Herbert, J. A. Jance, W. P. Kinsella, Jack Hodgin, Willo Davis Roberts, William Stafford, Walt Morey, and Norman Maclean. *At the Field's End,* by Nicolas O'Connell, features interviews with 20 leading writers who are all closely connected to the Pacific Northwest and reflect the character of the region. The *Journals of Lewis and Clark* can also make for interesting reading as you follow in the explorers' path.

History & Travel Essays

The late Bill Spiedel, one of Seattle's most colorful characters, wrote about the early history of the city in books replete with lively anecdotes and legends; *Sons of the Profits* and *Doc Maynard* are two of his best. Timothy Egan's *The Good Rain* uses history to explore what the Northwest means. *Washingtonians, A Biographical Portrait of the State,* edited by David Brewster and David M. Buerge, is a series of essays on well-known and influential residents who have left their mark on the state. *Skookum,* by Shannon Applegate, is the history of an Oregon pioneer family. *Whistlepunks and Geoducks—Oral Histories from the Pacific Northwest,* by Ron Strickland, is a collection of stories told by old-timers from all walks of life in Washington State.

Short History of Canada, by Desmond Morton, is a recent historical account of the country. Stephen Brook's *The Maple Leaf Rag* is a collection of idiosyncratic travel essays. *Why We Act Like Canadians: A Personal Exploration of Our National Character,* by Pierre Burton, is one of his many popular nonfiction books focusing on Canada's history and culture. *Local Colour—Writers Discovering Canada,* edited by Carol Marin, is a series of articles about Canadian places by leading travel writers.

Nature & the Outdoors

Gloria Snively's *Exploring the Seashore* offers a guide to shorebirds and intertidal plants and animals in Washington, Oregon, and British Columbia. The *Northwest Sportsman Almanac,* edited by Terry W. Sheely, provides an in-depth guide to fishing and hunting in the Pacific North Coast.

Television & Movies

The Pacific Northwest has provided the setting for a number of television series—*Frasier, Northern Exposure,* and *Twin Peaks,* not to mention the many syndicated series shot (if not set) in Vancouver. For a glimpse of the region on the big screen, check out such recent films as *Sleepless in Seattle, The Hand that Rocks the Cradle, Singles,* and *White Fang.* Idiosyncratic filmmaker and Portland native Gus van Sant has set a number of his movies in the Northwest, including *Drugstore Cowboy* and *My Own Private Idaho.*

A

Abbotsford, B.C., *19*
Aberdeen, WA, *189*
Active Pass Lighthouse, 279
Agness, OR, *65*
Air shows, *19*
Alaska, *4, 313, 315*
  arts, *352–353*
  business hours, *xxix*
  children, attractions for, *337–338*
  emergencies, *357–358*
  festivals, *19, 353*
  guided tours, *355–357*
  hotels, *337, 338–339, 343–352*
  Native culture, *14–15*
  nightlife, *353–354*
  restaurants, *343–352*
  scenic drives, *354–355*
  shopping, *339–340*
  sightseeing, *313–339*
  sports, *341–343*
  tourist information, *358–359*
  transportation, *354–355*
Alaska Chilkat Bald Eagle Preserve, *331–332*
Alaska Indian Arts (workshop), *332*
Alaska Marine Highway System, *281, 355*
Alaskan Hotel, *327*
Alaska Raptor Rehabilitation Center, *326*
Alaska State Capitol, *328*
Alaska State Museum, *329*
Alaska Steam Laundry Building, *328*
Alpine Slide, *96*
American Advertising Museum, *29*
Amusement parks
  British Columbia, *284*
  Portland, *30*
  Vancouver, *232*
Anacortes, WA, *158, 165*
Angoon, AK, *339*
Anne Hathaway's Cottage, *285*
Annie Creek Canyon, *79*
Antiques
  Portland, *32*
  Seattle, *121*
  Tacoma, *179*

Vancouver, *236*
Victoria, *287*
Apartment and villa rentals, *xxi, xxxv*
Aquariums
  Oregon, *61*
  Seattle, *111*
  Tacoma, *178*
  Vancouver, *228–229*
  Washington, *191*
Arctic Brotherhood Hall, *333*
Arlene Schnitzer Concert Hall, *22*
Art Craft (art festival), *279*
Art galleries and museums
  Alaska, *339–340*
  British Columbia, *277*
  Oregon, *78*
  Portland, *24, 32*
  Seattle, *110–111, 116–117, 121*
  Tacoma, *176*
  Vancouver, *221, 231, 232, 236*
  Victoria, *306*
  Washington, *168*
Art Gallery of Greater Victoria, *306*
Artist colonies, *279*
Arts and crafts fairs, *18*
Ashford, WA, *187*
Ashland, OR
  arts, *92*
  bed-and-breakfasts, *85*
  festivals, *18*
  hotels, *86–87*
  nightlife, *92*
  restaurants, *85–86*
  sightseeing, *81–82*
  sports, *84*
  tourist information, *104*
Astoria, OR, *56, 58, 65–66, 67–68*
Astoria Column, *58*
Auctions, *236*
Auto racing, *34, 180*

B

Baby-sitting services, *xxx*
Bailey Bay, *338*
Bainbridge Island Vineyard and Winery, *117*
Ballard Locks, *115*
Ballooning, *149*

Bamfield, B.C., *275*
Bandon, OR, *64–65, 68*
Bandon Historical Museum, *64–65*
Bandon Lighthouse, *64*
Baranov, Alexander, *323–324*
Baseball
  Bellingham, *172*
  Eugene, *85*
  Seattle, *124*
  Tacoma, *180*
  Vancouver, *239*
Basketball
  Alaska, *343*
  Oregon, *85*
  Portland, *34*
  Seattle, *124*
  Vancouver, *239*
Bay Ocean, OR, *60*
B.C. Forest Museum, *275*
B.C. Sports Hall of Fame, *233*
Beaches, *5*
  Alaska, *322*
  British Columbia, *276*
  Oregon, *59, 66, 97*
  Vancouver, *230, 239*
  Washington, *158, 162, 190*
Beacon Hill Park, *271*
Bed-and-breakfasts, *xxi, xxxv*
  Alaska, *345, 350, 351–352*
  Oregon, *67–68, 70, 73, 85, 87, 88, 89–90, 91, 99*
Bellevue, OR, *87*
Bellingham, WA, *167–168*
  arts, *175*
  hotels, *174*
  nightlife, *175*
  restaurants, *173*
  shopping, *171–172*
  sightseeing, *168–169*
  sports, *172*
  tourist information, *217*
Bend, OR, *96–97, 99*
Bennett Pass, *96*
Better Business Bureau, *xv*
Beverly Beach State Park, *66*
Bicycling, *xxiv*
  Alaska, *341*
  British Columbia, *307–308*
  Oregon, *66, 83, 97, 105*
  Portland, *32–33*
  Seattle, *122*
  Vancouver, *237*
  Washington, *158, 163, 172, 179, 201*

Big Time Brewery, *118*
Blackwood Canyon (winery), *213*
Blaine, WA, *174*
Bloedel Reserve, *117*
Blossom Bar, OR, *65*
Blue Heron French Cheese Company, *60*
Boardman State Park, *65*
Board sailing, *122–123*
Boating and sailing, *xxiv, 5*
    Seattle, *122–123*
    Vancouver, *237*
    Washington, *158, 163, 172*
Boeing Field, *118*
Bonair Winery, *211*
Bonneville Dam, *93, 95*
Bonneville Fish Hatchery, *95*
Bookstores
    Alaska, *340*
    Portland, *32*
    Seattle, *121*
    Vancouver, *236*
Bow, WA, *169, 173–174*
Breweries
    Alaska, *340*
    Portland, *48*
    Seattle, *117–118*
    Vancouver, *232*
Bridal Veil Falls, *93*
British Columbia, *4, 266. See also* Vancouver; Victoria; Whistler
    business hours, xxix
    emergencies, 310
    festivals, 18–19
    guided tours, 309–310
    hospitals, 310
    hotels, 291–306
    Native culture, 13–14
    pharmacies, 310
    restaurants, 291–306
    shopping, 286–287
    sightseeing, 267–285
    sports, 287–290
    tourist information, 310–311
    transportation, 307–309
Brockton Point, *228*
Broken Group Islands, *276*
Brookings, OR, *65, 68–69*
Bruce Lee's grave site, *119*
"Bulb Basket of the Nation," *77*
Bullards Beach State Park, *64–65*
Bush House, *76*
Bush's Pasture Park, *76*

Business hours, *xxix. See also under individual cities and areas*
Bus travel
    Alaska, 354
    British Columbia, 307, 308
    Oregon, 103
    within Pacific North Coast region, xv–xvi
    Portland, 49, 50
    Seattle, 147–148
    from U.S., xv, xxix
    Vancouver, 260–261, 262
    Victoria, 308
    Washington, 213, 215
    Whistler, 260
Butchart Gardens, *286*
Butterfly World, *276*
Byrnes Block building, *226*

C

Calona Wines Ltd., *283*
Camcorders, travel with, *xxix*
Cameras, travel with, *xxix*
Campbell Bay, *279*
Campbell River, *14, 277, 296*
Camping, *xxxv*
Camp Six Logging Museum, *178*
Canada Place Pier, *225*
Canadian Craft Museum, *225*
Canadian Imperial Bank of Commerce building, *226*
Canadian Pacific Station, *226*
Candy stores, *121*
Cannon Beach, OR, *18, 59, 66, 69*
Canoeing
    Alaska, 337, 341
    British Columbia, 287–288
    Oregon, 83, 97
    Whistler, 257
Cape Arago State Park, *64*
Cape Blanco Lighthouse, *65*
Cape Blanco State Park, *65*
Cape Disappointment Lighthouse, *198*
Cape Foulweather, *61*
Cape Kiwanda, *60*
Cape Kiwanda State Park, *60*
Cape Lookout, *60*
Cape Meares Lighthouse, *60*
Cape Meares State Park, *60*
Cape Perpetua, *62*
Cape Scott Provincial Park, *278*

Capilano Fish Hatchery, *234–235*
Capitol Mall (Salem), *76*
Car rentals, *xvi, xli*
Car travel
    Alaska, 354–355
    British Columbia, 307, 308
    insurance, xxxii–xxxiii
    Oregon, 103–104
    within Pacific North Coast region, xxxii
    Portland, 49, 50
    Seattle, 147, 148
    speed limits, xxxiii
    from U.S., xxxii
    Vancouver, 261, 262
    Victoria, 308
    Washington, 213, 214, 215, 216
    Whistler, 260
    winter driving, xxxiii
Cascade Locks, OR, *95, 100*
Cash machines, *xxii, xxxvii*
Casinos, *256*
Castle Hill, *324*
Cathedral Grove, *276*
Cathedral Provincial Park, *284*
Caverns, *62–63, 81, 277*
Cedarcreek Estate Winery, *283–284*
Cemeteries
    Alaska, 319, 325, 329
    Seattle, 119
Centennial Building, *324*
Centennial Hall, *329*
Central Washington University, *206*
Champoeg State Park, *75*
Charles H. Scott Gallery, *231*
Charleston, OR, *64, 69–70*
Chateau Ste. Michelle (Grandview), *211*
Chateau Ste. Michelle (Patterson), *213*
Cheese-making, *60*
Chemainus, B.C., *275*
Cheney Discovery Center, *179*
Chief Kowee cremation spot, *329*
Chief Shakes gravesite, *319*
Chief Shakes Island, *319*
Children
    attractions for. See under cities and areas
    traveling with, xvi–xvii, xxix–xxx
Children's Museum (Portland), *30*

Children's Museum of Tacoma, *177*

Chilkat Center for the Arts, *332*

Chilkoot Trail, *335*

Chinatown (Portland), *27*

Chinatown (Vancouver), *227*

Chinatown (Victoria), *272*

Chinese Cultural Center, *227–228*

Chinese Freemasons Building, *227*

Chinese Times Building, *227*

Chinook, WA, *198, 202*

Chinook Wines, *211, 213*

Christ Church Cathedral (Vancouver), *221*

Chuckanut Bay, *168*

Churches
Alaska, 316, 322, 325, 328
British Columbia, 279
Portland, 24
Vancouver, 221
Washington, 201

Clallam County Historical Museum, *191*

Clausen Museum, *322*

Cleawox Lake, *63*

Cle Elum, WA, *205, 207*

Climate, *xlii–xliii*

Clothing for the trip, *xxxix–xl*

Clothing shops
Portland, 32
Seattle, 121
Vancouver, 236–237

Coast Guard Station Cape Disappointment, *200*

Coast Mountain Circle (scenic drive), *257, 285*

Coleman Glacier, *170*

Colleges and universities
Alaska, 326
Oregon, 76, 78, 85
Seattle, 116
Vancouver, 231
Washington, 168, 175, 206

Columbia Gorge Sailpark, *95*

Columbia River Gorge and Oregon Cascades, *93*
hotels, 99–103
restaurants, 99–103
sightseeing, 93–98
sports, 97–98
tourist information, 106–107
transportation, 104

Columbia River Maritime Museum, *56*

Comedy clubs
Portland, 48
Seattle, 145
Vancouver, 256

Comox, B.C., *277, 296–297*

Cooper's Northwest Alehouse, *118*

Coos Bay, OR, *64, 70*

Copalis Beach, *189, 193*

Cornish College of the Arts, *143*

Corvallis, OR, *77, 87*

Coupeville, WA, *156*

Courtenay, B.C., *277, 296–297*

Cowboys Then & Now Museum, *29*

Crafts stores, *121, 340*

Craigdarroch Castle, *272*

Crater Lake National Park, *79*

Cruises, *xvii, xxx*
Alaska, 336, 355, 356

Crystal Gardens, *272*

Crystal Lake State Hatchery/Blind Slough Recreation Area, *322–323*

Currency, U.S. and Canadian, *xxxvii*

Customs, *xvii, xxx–xxxi*

D

The Dalles, OR, *95–96, 100*

Dams, *93, 95*

Dance
Portland, 48–49
Seattle, 142
Vancouver, 254

Dance clubs, *145*

Darlingtona Botanical Wayside, *63*

David Present's Gallery, *339*

Deadman's Island, *228*

Deception Pass State Park, *158*

Deepwood Estate, *76–77*

Deer Mountain, *318*

Deer Mountain Hatchery, *317*

Deighton, Jack, *226*

Della Falls, *277*

Delores Winningstad Theater, *22*

Denman Island, *277*

Department stores
Portland, 31
Vancouver, 236

Depoe Bay, OR, *18, 61*

Devil's Elbow State Park, *62*

Disabilities, hints for travelers with, *xvii–xix, xxxi–xxxii*

Discount clubs, *xxxii*

Discount passes, *xix*

Dr. Sun Yat-sen Classical Chinese Garden, *227–228*

Dog racing, *34*

Dolly's House (brothel), *318*

Douglas County Coastal Visitors Center, *63*

Douglas County Museum, *79*

Duncan, B.C., *14, 273*

Dundee, OR, *75*

Dungeness National Wildlife Refuge, *191–192*

E

Eagles Hall, *333*

East Sooke Park, *273*

Eastsound Village, WA, *161*

Eaton Hill Winery, *211*

Ebey's Landing National Historic Reserve, *156*

Ecola State Park, *59*

Ed Jones Haida Museum, *281–282*

Ellensburg, WA, *15, 206, 207*

Emergencies
Alaska, 357–358
British Columbia, 310
Oregon, 106
Portland, OR, 50
Seattle, WA, 150
Vancouver, BC, 264
Victoria, 310
Washington, 217
Whistler, 260

Emily Carr College of Art and Design, *231*

Empress Hotel, *267*

End of the Trail Interpretive Center, OR, *30*

English Bay, *229*

Eugene, OR
arts, 92
festivals, 18
hotels, 88
restaurants, 78, 87–88
shopping, 82
sightseeing, 78
sports, 83, 84, 85
tourist information, 106
transportation, 103, 104

Evergreen Cemetery, *329*

F

Face Rock Beach, 66
Face Rock Wayside, 64
Fairhaven, WA, 168
Fairhaven Park, 169
Fall's Creek Fish Ladder, 322
Farm tours, 170
Father Pandosy's Mission, 283
Feiro Marine Laboratory, 191
Ferndale, WA, 169–170
Ferry service
Alaska, 355
British Columbia, 280, 281,
  307, 308–309
in Pacific North Coast region,
  xix–xx, xxxiii–xxxiv
Seattle, 148
Vancouver, 261
Washington, 213, 214–215
Festivals and seasonal events,
  18–19
Film
Seattle, 145
Vancouver, 254
Fire stations, 26
Fishing, xxiv, 6
Alaska, 337, 341
British Columbia, 288
Oregon, 66–67, 83, 105
Portland, 33
Seattle, 123
Vancouver, 237
Washington, 158, 163, 172,
  193, 201
Whistler, 257–258
Fish Ladder, 115–116, 316
Flavel House, 58
Flea markets, 236
Float-plane service, xv
Florence, OR, 63, 70–71
Food stores, 340
Football
Oregon, 85
Seattle, 124
Vancouver, 239
Forest Park, 28–29
Forests national
Alaska, 338
Oregon, 96
Washington, 170
Forks, WA, 190, 193–194
Ft. Canby State Park, 198
Ft. Casey State Park, 156
Ft. Clatsop National Memo-
  rial, 58
Fort Columbia State Park,
  198

Ft. Dalles Surgeon's Quarters,
  96
Ft. Nisqually, 178
Forts
Alaska, 326, 330
Oregon, 58
Portland, 29
Tacoma, 178
Washington, 156, 192, 198
Fort Seward, 330, 352, 353,
  358
Ft. Stevens, 58
Fort Vancouver National His-
  toric Site, 29
Fort William Henry Seward,
  330
Ft. Worden, 192
Fountains, 26
Fragrance Garden, 170
Frank Heintzleman Nursery,
  322
Friday Harbor, WA, 161

G

Gabriola Island, 275
Gaches Mansion, 171
Ganges, 279
Gardens
British Columbia, 16–17, 284
Oregon, 63, 76–77
Portland, 27–28
Seattle, 115, 117
Tacoma, 177
Vancouver, 227–228, 233, 234
Victoria, 271, 272
Washington, 16–17, 156, 169,
  170, 171, 177, 189
Garibaldi, OR, 60
Garibaldi Provincial Park, 257
Gay and lesbian travelers,
  hints for, xx–xxi
Geert Maas Sculpture Gar-
  dens, Gallery, and Studio,
  286
Ghost towns, 62
Gift shops
Alaska, 340
Portland, 32
Vancouver, 237
Gig Harbor, WA, 178–179,
  180
Glacier Bay National Park and
  Preserve, 335–337,
  344–345, 358
Glazed Terra Cotta National
  Historic District, 26
Gleneden Beach, OR, 71

Gog-Le-Hi-Te (wetland), 178
Gold Beach, OR, 65, 71–72
Golden and Silver Falls State
  Park, 64
Golden North Hotel, 334
Goldpanning, 337
Gold Rush Trail, 285
Golf, 6
Alaska, 341
British Columbia, 288–289
Leavenworth, 206
Oregon, 33, 67, 83–84
Seattle, 123
Vancouver, 237–238
Victoria, 288
Washington, 172, 179–180,
  201
Whistler, 258
Gordon Southam Observatory,
  235
Government Camp, OR, 96
Governor's House (Juneau),
  329
Governor Tom McCall Water-
  front Park, 25
Grandview, WA, 211
Granger, WA, 211
Grant Street Trestle, AK, 316
Granville Island, 230–232
Granville Island Brewery, 232
Granville Island Information
  Centre, 231
Granville Island Public Mar-
  ket, 230–231
Gray Monk Cellars, 283
Greenbank, WA, 156
Gresham, OR, 18
The Grotto (religious sanctu-
  ary), 29
Grove of the Patriarchs, 183
Gulf Islands
hotels, 300–302
restaurants, 300–301
sightseeing, 278–280
transportation, 308, 309
Gustavus, AK, 335–337,
  344–345, 358

H

Haida Indians, 232, 281–282,
  286
Haines, AK, 329–330
arts, 352
festivals, 19
guided tours, 355–356
hotels, 345–346
nightlife, 353

restaurants, 345–346
sightseeing, 330–332
tourist information, 358
Haines Highway, *354–355*
Hamma Hamma Oyster Company, *192*
Hammer Slough, *321, 322*
Hammond, OR, *58*
Harrison Hot Springs, *284–285, 303*
Hatfield Library, *76*
Hatfield Marine Science Center, *61–62*
Haystack Rock, *59*
Hazelton, B.C., *14, 282*
Health clubs, *238*
Health insurance, *xxxv*
Heceta Head, *62*
Helen Point, *278–279*
Hell's Gate, *284*
Helmecken House, *271*
Hendrix, Jimi, *119*
Henry Art Gallery, *116*
High Desert Museum, *96*
Hiking, *xxiv*
Alaska, 341–342
British Columbia, 289
Leavenworth, 206
Vancouver, 238
Washington, 193, 201
Hinzerling Vineyards, *211*
Historic Kilby Store and Farm, *285*
Hockey
Portland, 34
Vancouver, 239
Washington, 172, 180
Hogue Cellars, *213*
Hoh Rain Forest, *189–190*
Home exchanges, *xxi, xxxv*
Honeyman State Park, *63*
Hood River, OR, *16, 95, 100–101*
Hoodsport, WA, *192*
Hoodsport Winery, *192*
Hoonah, AK, *339*
Hoover-Minthorne House, *75*
Hoquiam, WA, *189*
Horizon's Edge Winery, *211*
Hornby Island, *277*
Horne Lake Caves Provincial Park, *277*
Horseback riding
Leavenworth, 206
Washington, 201
Horse racing, *34*
Horsetail Falls, *93*
Hotel Europe, *226–227*

Hotels, *xxi–xxii, xxxv–xxxvi.*
See also under cities and
areas
Hotel Vancouver, *221*
Hot springs, *191, 284–285*
Houseboat communities, *231*
Houses, historic
Alaska, 318, 326, 328–329
Oregon, 58, 75, 76–77
Portland, 28
Victoria, 271
Washington, 171
Hovander Homestead Park, *170*
Hoyt Arboretum, *28*
Hunting, *xxiv*
Hurricane Ridge, *191*
Hyatt Vineyards Winery, *211*

I

Ilwaco, WA, *198, 203–204*
Ilwaco Heritage Museum, *198*
Indian Beach, *59*
Indians. *See* Native American
headings
Inns, *xxii, xxxvi*
Inside Passage, *280*
Insurance, *xxi*
automobile, xxxii–xxxiii
flight, xxxiv
health, xxxiv
luggage, xxxiv
trip, xxxiv–xxxv
Intermediate Theater, *22*
International District, *114*
International Pinot Noir Celebration, *75*
International Rose Test Garden, *27–28*
Island County Historical Museum, *156*
Itineraries, *13–17*

J

Jacksonville, OR, *81, 82, 89, 92*
Jacksonville Museum, *81*
Japanese garden (Olympia), *189*
Japanese garden (Vancouver), *233*
Japanese Gardens (Portland), *28*
Jazz festivals, *18, 19*
Jeff Morris Memorial Fire Museum, *26*
Jewelry shops

Portland, 32
Seattle, 121
Jimi Hendrix's grave site, *119*
Jogging, *See* Running and jogging
John McLoughlin House National Historic Site, *30*
Juneau, AK, *326–327*
the arts, 352–353
climate, xlii–xliii
emergencies, 357
guided tours, 356
hotels, 346–348
Native culture, 15
nightlife, 353
restaurants, 346–347
shopping, 339–340
sightseeing, 326–329
sports, 341–343
tourist information, 358
Juneau Douglas City Museum, *329*
Juneau-Harris monument, *329*
Justice Center (Portland), *25*

K

Kakali, *232*
Kake, AK, *339*
Kalaloch, WA, *189*
Kalamalka Lake Provincial Park, *283*
Kamloops, B.C., *283, 303–304*
Kamloops Wildlife Park, *283*
Kayaking
Alaska, 337, 341
British Columbia, 287–288
Seattle, 123
Vancouver, 238
Washington, 163
Whistler, B.C., 257
Kelowna, B.C., *283, 304*
Ketchikan, AK, *315–316*
emergencies, 357–358
guided tours, 356–357
hotels, 348–349
Native culture, 14
nightlife, 353
restaurants, 348
sightseeing, 315–318
tourist information, 316, 358
Kettle Valley Steam Railroad, *284*
Keystone, WA, *156*
Kids Only Market, *232*
KikSadi Indian Park, *319*
Kingdome, *114*

Kiona Vineyards, 213
Kirmse's (shop), 334
Kite festivals, 18
Kitimat, B.C., 282
Kitsilano Beach, 239
Klondike Gold Rush National Historical Park (Alaska), 332–333
Klondike Gold Rush National Historical Park (Seattle), 114
Klondike Highway, 334, 354–355
'Ksan Village, 282
Kyan Totem Pole, 318

L

La Conner, WA, 171, 174–175
La Conner Flats (commercial garden), 171
Ladybug Theater, 30
Lady Rose (cruise ship), 275
Lake Bonneville, 95
Lake Crescent, 191
Lake Cushman, 192
Lakes District, B.C., 282
Lake Terrell Wildlife Preserve, 170
Lake Whatcom Steam Train, 171
Langley, WA, 156
Language, *xxxv*
La Push, WA, 190
Latourell Falls, 93
Leadbetter State Park, 201
Leather and luggage stores, 121
Leavenworth, WA,
hotels, 208–209
restaurants, 207–208
sightseeing, 205
sports, 206
tourist information, 218
LeConte Glacier, 323
Lee, Bruce, 119
Legislative Building (Olympia), 188–189
Legislative Parliament Buildings (Victoria), 271
Lewis & Clark Interpretive Center, 200
Libraries
Alaska, 319
Oregon, 76
Washington, 189
Lighthouses
Alaska, 339
British Columbia, 279

Oregon, 59, 60, 62, 63, 64, 65
Washington, 198, 200
Lime Kiln Point State Park, 162
Lincoln City, OR, 61, 72
Linfield College, 75
Lions Gate Bridge, 229
Lithia Park, 82
Lodge facilities, 338–339
Lodging, *xxi–xxii, xxxv–xxxvi. See also* hotels *under cities and areas*
Loeb State Park, 65
Loganberry Farm, 156
Log Cabin Visitor Center, 327
Long Beach, B.C., 276
Long Beach, WA, 18, 200, 201, 202, 203
Long Beach Peninsula region, 197–198
festival, 18
hotels, 203–204
restaurants, 202–203
shopping, 201
sightseeing, 198–201
sports, 201–202
tourist information, 218
transportation, 215
Longmire, 187
Longmire Museum, 183
Lopez Island, 161, 162, 163, 164, 165
Lost Lagoon, 228
Lost Lake, 95
Luggage
airline rules, xl
insurance for, xxxv
Lumberman's Arch, 228
Lummi Island, 169
Lynden, WA, 170
Lynn Canyon Suspension Bridge, 234

M

Mail, *xxxvi*
Malahat, BC, 297
Malkin Bowl, 228
Manzanita, OR, 72
Maplewood Farms, 234
Marine Building, 225
Marine Park, 327
Marion County Museum of History, 76
Maritime Heritage Center (Bellingham), 168
Maritime Museum (Vancouver), 232–233

Maritime Museum of British Columbia, 272
Maude I. Kerns Art Center, 78
Mayne Island, 278–279, 300–301
McKenzie Bridge, OR, 89
McLoughlin Historic District, OR, 30
McMinnville, OR, 16, 75, 82, 83, 89–90
Medford, OR, 79, 81, 90
Medical care. *See* emergencies *under cities and areas*
Meerkerk Rhododendron Gardens, 156
Merritt, B.C., 304
Metropolitan Center for Public Art (Portland), 24
Mile 0, 331
Mill Ends Park, 25
Miners Bay, 279
Mission Mill Village, 76
Moclips, WA, 189, 194
Money, *xxii, xxxvi–xxxviii*
Monrean House, 318
Moran State Park, 161
Motels/motor inns, *xxii, xxxvi*
Motor lifeboats, 200
Mountain climbing, 4
Washington, 172, 183, 186
Mt. Baker-Snoqualmie National Forest, 170, 175
Mt. Baker Theater, 175
Mt. Constitution, 161
Mt. Golden Hinde, 277
Mt. Hood, 18, 96, 101–102
Mt. Hood National Forest, 96
Mt. Maxwell Provincial Park, 280
Mount Parke, 279
Mt. Rainier National Park, 182
hotels, 185–187
restaurants, 185–186
sightseeing, 182–183
sports, 183, 186
tourist information, 217
transportation, 215
Mt. Ripinsky, 330
Mt. Shuksan, 170
Muir, John, 329, 336
Multnomah Falls, 93
Museum of Anthropology (Vancouver), 233
Museum of Flight (Seattle), 118–119
Museum of History and Industry (Seattle), 117

Museum of Natural History (Eugene), 78
Museum of Northern British Columbia, 280–281
Museums. *See also* Art galleries and museums
Alaska, 316, 319, 322, 326, 329, 330, 333
British Columbia, 273, 275, 280–281, 282, 285
Native culture displays, 13–15
Oregon, 56, 60, 64–65, 76, 78, 81, 82, 96, 97
Portland, 24, 25, 26, 29, 30
Seattle, 110–111, 114, 115, 116, 117, 118–119
Tacoma, 176
Vancouver, 225, 232, 233
Victoria, 271, 272
Washington, 156, 161, 168, 171, 175, 183, 189, 191, 192, 198
Music, classical
festivals, 18, 19
Oregon, 92
Portland, 48
Seattle, 142–143
Vancouver, 254–255
Victoria, 306
Music, popular
Alaska, 353–354
festivals, 18, 19
Portland, 47
Seattle, 146–147
Vancouver, 256
Victoria, 306–307

N

Nahcotta, WA, 200, 202–203
Naikoon Provincial Park, 281
Nanaimo, B.C., 14, 275, 297–298
Nanaimo District Museum, 275
National Exhibition Centre and Museum, 282
National Motor Life Boat School, 200
Native American dancing, 332, 337
Native American sites
Alaska, 318, 319, 326, 332, 339
British Columbia, 273, 281–282
Vancouver, 228

Native Heritage Centre, 273
Naval bases, 158
Neahkahnie Mountain, 59
Newberg, OR, 75, 82, 83
Newcastle Island, 275
New Market Theater Building, 27
Newport, OR, 61, 66, 72–73
Nike Town (factory outlet), 22
Nine O'Clock Gun, 228
Nitobe Garden, 233
Nooksack Falls, 170
North Bend, OR, 64
North Head Lighthouse, 200
Northwest Trek Wildlife Park, 179
Norwegian Independence Day celebration, 321

O

Oak Harbor, WA, 156, 158
Oakland, OR, 90
Oakridge, OR, 78
Oaks Amusement Park, 30
Oakwood Cellars, 213
Ocean Park, WA, 200
Odlin County Park, 161
Odyssey Contemporary Maritime Museum, 114
Officers' Row Historic District, 30
Okanagan Game Farm, 284
Okanagan Valley region
hotels, 303–306
restaurants, 303–306
shopping, 286
sightseeing, 282–285
sports, 288
O'Keefe Historic Ranch, 283
Old Church (Portland), 24
Old School House Gallery and Art Centre, 277
Olympia, WA, 188, 194
Olympic Peninsula region, 188
arts, 197
hotels, 193–196
nightlife, 197
restaurants, 193–197
shopping, 193
sightseeing, 188–192
sports, 193
tourist information, 218
transportation, 215
Omnidome Film Experience, 111
Oneonta Gorge, 93

Opera
Portland, 48
Seattle, 142–143
Vancouver, 255
Orcas Island, 161, 162, 163, 164, 165–166
Oregon, 4, 53, 56. *See also* Columbia River Gorge and Oregon Cascades; Oregon Coast; Portland; Willamette Valley and the Wine Country
business hours, xxix
emergencies, 106
festivals, 18
guided tours, 104–105
hotels, 105
restaurants, 105
sports, 105
tourist information, 106–107
transportation, 103–104
Oregon Caves National Monument, 81
Oregon City, 30
Oregon Coast, 56
hotels, 67–74
restaurants, 63, 67–74
shopping, 65–66
sightseeing, 56–65
sports, 66–67
tourist information, 106
transportation in, 103
Oregon Coast Aquarium, 61
Oregon Dunes National Recreation Area, 63, 66
Oregon Historical Center, 24
Oregon Maritime Center and Museum, 26
Oregon Museum of Science and Industry, 29
Oregon Shakespeare Festival, 18, 81, 92
Oregon Trail, 30
Oregon Wine Center, 104
Oswald West State Park, 59
Otter Crest Loop, 61
"Our Collections" (museum), 320
Outdoor equipment stores, 122
Oyama, B.C., 282
Oysterville, WA, 200–201
Ozette Lake, 190

P

Pacific Beach, WA, 189
Pacific Center Mall, 235
Pacific City, OR, 60–61

Pacific Crest Trail, 96
Pacific Northwest Brewing Co., 118
Pacific Northwest Museum of Natural History, 82
Pacific Rim National Park, 276
Pacific Spirit Park, 233–234
Pacific Undersea Garden, 271
Package deals, xxvi, xxxviii–xxxix
Pantages Theater, 176–177
Paradise, WA, 183, 187–188
Parks, national
  Alaska, 326, 332–333
  British Columbia, 276
  Oregon, 79
  Washington, 162, 182–188
Parks, state and provincial
  British Columbia, 257, 275, 276, 277, 278, 280, 281, 283, 284
  Oregon, 59, 60, 62, 63, 64, 65, 75, 77
  Washington, 156, 158, 161, 162, 198, 201
Parksville, B.C., 276, 298
Parliament Buildings (Victoria), 271
Passports, xxii, xl–xli
Peachland, B.C., 282
Penticton, B.C., 284, 304–305
Perfume shops, 32
Peter Britt Festival, 18, 81, 92
Petersburg, AK, 321–322
  emergencies, 358
  festivals, 19
  guided tours, 357
  hotels, 350
  nightlife, 354
  restaurants, 349
  sightseeing, 321–323
  tourist information, 358
Petroglyph Beach, 320–321
Petroglyph Provincial Park, 275
Photographers, tips for, xxii, xxix
Pike Place Market, 111
Pioneer Museum, 60
Pioneer Park (Ferndale), 169–170
Pioneer Park (Seattle), 114
Pittock Mansion, 28
Planetariums and observatories, 235
Plane travel
  airports and airlines, xiv–xv
  Alaska, 355

British Columbia, 307, 309
  with children, xvi, xxx
  discount flights, xv, xxviii–xxix
  float-plane service, xv
  luggage, xl
  Oregon, 103
  in Pacific North Coast region, xiv–xv
  Portland, 49
  Seattle, 147
  from U.K., xiv
  Vancouver, 261
  Washington, 213–214, 215
Plumbers Pass Lockup, 279
Point Defiance Park, 178
Point Defiance Zoo and Aquarium, 178
Point Grey Beaches, 239
Police Museum, 25
Pontin del Rosa (winery), 211
Port Alberni, B.C., 275
Port Angeles, WA, 191, 194–195
Port Hardy, B.C., 14, 278, 298
Portland, OR, 4, 21–22
  arts, 47–49
  Chapman Square, 24
  children, attractions for, 30
  Chinatown, 27
  climate, xlii–xliii
  emergencies, 50
  festivals, 18
  Forest Park, 28–29
  Glazed Terra Cotta National Historic District, 26
  guided tours, 50
  hotels, 40–47
  Japanese-American Historical Plaza, 27
  Lownsdale Square, 24
  nightlife, 47–49
  Officers' Row Historic District, 30
  pharmacies, 51
  Pioneer Courthouse Square, 22
  radio stations, 50
  restaurants, 26, 34–40
  Salmon Street Plaza, 25
  shopping, 22, 27, 31–32
  sightseeing, 22–30
  Skidmore Old Town National Historic District, 26
  South Park Blocks, 24
  sports, 32–34
  Terry Shrunk Park, 24
  tourist information, 51

transportation, 49–50
  Washington Park, 27
  wineries, 16
  Yamhill National Historic District, 25
Portland Art Museum, 24
Portland Audubon Society, 28–29
Portland Building, 24
Portland Center for the Performing Arts, 22
Portlandia (statue), 24
Portland Saturday Market, 27
Port McNeill, B.C., 14
Port of Tacoma, 178
Port Orford, OR, 65
Portteus Vineyards, 211
Port Townsend, WA, 18, 192, 193, 195–196, 197
Poulsbo, WA, 18
Powell River, B.C., 277
Prince George, B.C., 282
Prince Rupert, B.C., 14, 280–281, 286, 302
Prospect Point, 229
Puget Sound region. See San Juan Islands; Whidbey Island
Puyallup, WA, 18

Q

Quail Run Vintners, 211
Qualicum Beach, 276–277
Queen Charlotte Islands, 281–282, 286, 302–303, 309
Queen Charlotte Islands Museum, 281
Queen Elizabeth Park, 234
Queets, WA, 189
Quinault, WA, 196

R

Rafting
  British Columbia, 289
  Leavenworth, 206
  Oregon, 83, 97
Rail passes, xix, xxiii
Railroads
  Alaska, 335, 355
  Washington, 171, 205
Rainbow Country, 284
Ranches, 283
Rathtrevor Provincial Park, 276
Record shops, 32
Red Dog Saloon, 328

Red Onion Saloon, *334*
Reid, Bill, *232*
Reid, Frank, *333*
Resorts, *xxxvi*
Restaurants, *5–6. See also
    under cities and areas*
Return of the Eagle (mural),
    317
Rialto Beach, *190*
Richmond Nature Park, *234*
Rie Munoz Gallery, *339*
River Trail, *205*
Roche Harbor, WA, *162*
Rock and Roll Heaven, *235*
Rock climbing, *172, 183, 186,
    206*
Rockwell Lighthouse, *339*
Rodeo, *206*
Roderick Haig-Brown Conser-
    vation Area, *283*
Rollerskating, *123*
Rooster Rock State Park, *97*
Roozengaarde (commercial
    garden), *171*
Roseburg, OR, *79*
Rose festival, *18*
Rose Garden at Fairhaven
    Park, *169*
Roslyn, WA, *205, 209*
Royal Bank building, *226*
Royal British Columbia Mu-
    seum, *271*
Royal London Wax Museum,
    267
Ruckle Provincial Park, *280*
Running and jogging
Alaska, 342
Seattle, 123
Vancouver, 238
Russian and Lutheran ceme-
    teries, *325*
Russian Bishop's House,
    326
Russian blockhouse and ceme-
    tery, *325*

S

Sailboarding, *6, 122–123*
Sailing. *See* Boating and sailing
Ste. Michelle Winery, *118*
St. John's Church and Sea-
    man's Center, *316*
St. Mary Magdalene Church,
    279
St. Michael's Cathedral, *325*
St. Nicholas Russian Ortho-
    dox Church, *328*

Salem, OR
festivals, 18
hotels, 91
nightlife, 92
restaurants, 90–91
shopping, 82
sightseeing, 75–77
sports, 83–84
tourist information, 106
wineries, 16
Salishan, OR, *61*
Salmon Falls, Fish Ladder, and
    Salmon Carving, *316*
Salmon Harbor, *63*
Salmon Street Fountain, *25*
Salt Spring, *279–280,
    301–302*
Sam Kee Building, *227*
Sandcastle Contest, *18, 59*
Sandy Beach, *322*
San Juan Island National His-
    toric Park, *162*
San Juan Islands, *160*
beaches, 162
guided tours, 216
hotels, 164–167
restaurants, 164
shopping, 162
sightseeing, 161–162
sports, 162–163
tourist information, 217
transportation, 214–215
Sappho, WA, *190*
Saturday markets, *279*
Saxman Indian Village, *318*
Scanlon Gallery, *339*
Schreiner's Iris Gardens, *77*
Science World (museum), *233*
Scuba diving, *xxiv*
Alaska, 342
Sea Gulch (ghost town), *62*
Sea Lion Caves, *62–63*
Seal Rock (chain-saw carving),
    62
Sea Resources Hatchery Com-
    plex, *198*
Seaside, OR, *58–59*
Seattle, WA, *4, 109–110*
arts, 141–144
Bainbridge Island, 167
*children, attractions for,
    119–120*
climate, xlii–xliii
downtown, 110–115
emergencies, 150
festivals, 18
gardens, 17
guided tours, 148–150

hospitals, 150
hotels, 133–141
International District, 114
monorail, 148
nightlife, 144–147
pharmacies, 150
Pioneer Square, 114
radio stations, 150
restaurants, 115, 124–133
shopping, 120–122
sightseeing, 110–120
sports, 122–124
*tourist information, 110,
    150–151*
transportation, 147–148
wine tour, 15
Seattle Aquarium, *111*
Seattle Art Museum, *110–111*
Seattle Center, *110, 139–140*
Seattle Children's Museum,
    119
Seattle Children's Theatre,
    119–120
Seaview, WA, *200, 203, 204*
Second Beach, *230*
Senate Building mall (Juneau),
    328
Senior citizens, hints for, *xxiii,
    xli*
Sequim, WA, *191–192, 196*
Sequim-Dungeness Museum,
    192
Seymour Botanical Conserva-
    tory, *177*
Shakespeare Festival Exhibit
    Center, *81–82*
Shakes Slough, *338*
Shaw Island, *161*
Sheldon Jackson College, *326*
Sheldon Jackson Museum, *326*
Sheldon Museum and Cultural
    Center, *330*
Shelton, WA, *192*
Shopping, *6–7. See also under
    cities and areas*
Shore Acres State Park, *64*
Sidney, B.C., *298–299*
Silver Falls State Park, *77*
Silver Star Mountain, *305–306*
Sinclair Centre, *226, 235*
Sitka, AK, *323–324*
arts, 353
emergencies, 358
festivals, 19
guided tours, 357
hotels, 350
native culture, 15
nightlife, 354

restaurants, 350
sightseeing, 324–326
tourist information, 358
Sitka National Historical Park, 326
Sitka State Pioneers' Home, 324
Siwash Rock, 229
Skagit County Historical Museum, 171
Skagway, AK, 332–333
emergencies, 358
guided tours, 357
hotels, 351–352
nightlife, 354
restaurants, 351
sightseeing, 332–335
tourist information, 359
Skating, 123
Skidmore Fountain, 26
Skidmore Fountain Building, 27
Skidmore Old Town National Historic District, 26
Skiing, xxiv–xxv, 7
Alaska, 342–343
British Columbia, 289–291
Leavenworth, 206
Oregon, 84–85, 98
Portland, 33
Seattle, 123–124
Vancouver, 238
Washington, 172, 186, 193
Whistler, 258
Smith, Jefferson "Soapy," 332–333
Snoqualmie
arts and nightlife in, 210
hotels, 210
restaurants, 209–210
sightseeing, 204–205
Snoqualmie Falls, 204–205
Snoqualmie Falls Forest Theater, 210
Snoqualmie Valley Railway, 205
Snowmobiling, 186
Snowshoeing, 186
Soapy's Parlor, 333
Sol Duc Hot Springs, 191
Soleduck Hatchery, 190–191
Sons of Norway Hall, 322
Sooke, B.C., 273, 299
Sooke Regional Museum and Travel Infocentre, 273
Southeast Alaska. See Alaska
Southeast Alaska State Fairgrounds, 19, 330–331

South Slough National Estuarine Reserve, 64
Space Needle, 110
Spencer Spit State Park, 161
Splashdown Park, 234
Sports, xxiv–xxv. See also specific sports; under cities and areas
halls of fame, 25
Spouting Horn, 61
Sri Lankan Gem Museum, 225
Stadium High School, 177
Staircase Rapids, 192
Stanley Park, 228–230
State Capitol (Salem), 76
State Capitol Museum (Olympia), 189
State Library (Olympia), 189
State Office Building (Juneau), 329
State of Oregon Sports Hall of Fame, 25
Staton Hills Winery, 211
Steamboat, OR, 91
Steam trains, 171, 234, 284
Stewart Winery, 211
Strathcona Provincial Park, 277
Student and youth travel, xxv, xli–xlii
Summerland, B.C., 282
Sunset Bay State Park, 64
Sun Yat-sen, Dr., 227–228
Swan Lake Christmas Hill Nature Sanctuary, 286
Sweet Tooth Saloon, 334
Swimming, 7

T

Tacoma, WA, 175–176
hotels, 181–182
restaurants, 176, 180–181
shopping, 179
sightseeing, 176–179
sports, 179–180
tourist information, 217
transportation, 215
Tacoma Art Museum, 176
Taholah, WA, 189
Taxes, xxxvii–xxxviii
Taxis
Portland, 49, 50
Seattle, 147, 148
Vancouver, 261, 262
Telephones, xlii
Tenakee Springs, AK, 338–339
Tenino, WA, 197

Tennant Lake Natural History Interpretive Center, 170
Tennis
Alaska, 343
Portland, 33
Seattle, 124
Vancouver, 238
Terrace, B.C., 282
Theater
Alaska, 352–353
British Columbia, 306
Oregon, 18, 92
Portland, 48–49
Seattle, 119–120, 143–144
Vancouver, 232, 255
Victoria, 306
Washington, 175, 210
Theater on the Square (Tacoma), 177
Thomas Basin, 317
Thomas Burke Memorial Washington State Museum, 116
Thomas Creek Bridge, 65
Thomas Kay Woolen Mill Museum, 76
Three Capes Loop, 60
Thunderbird Park, 271
Tillamook, OR, 60
Tillamook Bay, 60
Tillamook County Creamery, 60
Tillamook Head, 59
Tillamook Rock Light Station, 59
Timberline Lodge, 96, 98
Tipping, xlii
Tlingit Fort, 327
Tlingit Indians, 323–324, 327, 332
Tofino, B.C., 276, 299–300
Tongass Historical Museum, 316
Tongass National Forest, 338
Toronto-Dominion Bank building, 226
Totem Bight State Historical Park, 318
Totem Heritage Center and Nature Path, 317
Totem poles
Alaska, 316, 317, 318, 319, 324, 328, 337
British Columbia, 267, 271
Vancouver, 228
Totem Square, 324
Tour groups, xxv–xxvi

Tourist information, *xxvii. See also under cities and areas*
Tour operators, *xxv–xxvii*
Toy shops
Portland, 32
Seattle, 122
Trail of '98 Museum, *333*
Trail of Shadows, *183*
Trains, miniature, *234*
Train travel. *See also* Railroads
Alaska, 355
British Columbia, 309
Oregon, 103, 104
in Pacific North Coast region, xxiii
Portland, 49, 50
rail passes, xix, xxiii
Seattle, 148
from U.S., xxii
Vancouver, 261–262
Washington, 214
Whistler, 260
Trans-Canada Waterslides, *284*
Travel agencies, *xxvii*
Traveler's checks, *xxxviii*
Trillium Lake, *96*
Trolleyman brew pub, *118*
Trolleys, *148, 263*
Troutdale, OR, *93, 102*
Tucker Cellars, *211*
Tulip festival, *18*

U

Ucluelet, B.C., *275–276, 299–300*
Umpqua Lighthouse Park, *63*
Umpqua River Lighthouse, *63*
Union Station, *176*
United Kingdom
customs, xvii, xxxi
insurance, xxi, xxxiv
passports and visas, xxii, xl–xli
plane travel from, xiv
tourist information, xxvii
University of Oregon, *18, 78, 85*
University of Oregon Museum of Art, *78*
University of Washington, *116*
Uwajimaya (Japanese store), *114–115*

V

Vancouver, B.C., *4, 220*
air tours, 262
arts, 254–255

beaches, 230
Blood Alley, 226
boat tours, 262–263
business hours, 264
Cathedral Place, 221
children, attractions for, 234
Chinatown, 227, 235
climate, xlii–xliii
consulates, 264
downtown, 220–221, 225–228
East Indian district, 235
emergencies, 264
excursions, 256–260
festivals, 18, 19
Gaoler's Mews, 226
Gastown, 226
Granville Island, 230–232
guided tours, 262–263
hotels, 221, 226–227, 249–254
Japantown, 235
Little Italy, 235
medical assistance, 264
Native culture, 13–14
nightlife, 255–256
parks and gardens, 16, 233–234
radio stations, 264
restaurants, 221, 229, 232, 239–249
Robson Square, 221
Robson Street, 221
SeaBus, 262
shopping, 235–237
sightseeing, 220–235
sports, 237–239
Stanley Park, 228–230
subway, 262
taxis, 261, 262
tourist information, 264
transportation in, 262
transportation to, 260–262
travel agencies, 264
West End, 230
Vancouver Aquarium, *228–229*
Vancouver Art Gallery, *221*
Vancouver Children's Festival, *19*
Vancouver Club, *225*
Vancouver Island. *See also* British Columbia; Victoria
hotels, 296–300
restaurants, 296–299
shopping, 286
sightseeing, 273–278
sports, 289

transportation, 308, 309
Vancouver Museum, *233*
Vancouver Rowing Club, *228*
Van Dusen Botanical Garden, *234*
Vernon, B.C., *283*
Victoria, B.C. *See also* Vancouver Island
arts, 306
Bastion Square, 272
children, attractions for, 285–286
Chinatown, 272
emergencies, 310
festivals, 19
gardens, 16–17
guided tours, 309–310
hospitals, 310
hotels, 293–296
Market Square, 272
native culture, 14
nightlife, 306–307
restaurants, 292–293
shopping, 286–287
sightseeing, 267, 270–272
sports, 288
tourist information, 310
transportation, 307, 308
Viking festivals, *18*
Village Bay, *279*
Visas, *xxii, xl–xli*
Volunteer Fireman's Museum, *171*

W

W. W. Seymour Botanical Conservatory, *177*
Wahkeena Falls, *93*
Wah Mee Club, *114*
Waldo Lake, *79*
Waldport, OR, *73*
Ward Cove Recreation Area, *318*
Warm Springs, OR, *102*
Wasco County Courthouse, *96*
Washington, *4, 153. See also* Seattle
business hours, xxix
emergencies, 217
festivals, 18
guided tours, 216–217
hotels, 217
restaurants, 217
tourist information, 217–218
transportation, 213–216
Washington Hills (winery), *211*

Washington Park (Portland), 27

Washington Park Arboretum (Seattle), 117

Washington Park Zoo, 28

Washington State Historical Society, 176

Waterfalls
British Columbia, 277
Oregon, 64, 77, 93
Washington, 170, 204–205

Wax museums, 267

Weather information, xxvii

Wedderburn, OR, 65

Welches, OR, 102–103

Welcome Totem, 267

Westbank, B.C., 282

West Coast Trail, 276

West End Beaches, 239

Western Washington University, 168, 175

Westlake Center, 110, 120

Whale Museum, 161

Whale Park (Ketchikan), 316

Whale Park (Sitka), 326

Whale-watching tours
British Columbia, 275–276, 277, 291
Washington, 172, 202, 216

Whatcom and Skagit Counties, WA, 167–168
arts, 175
hotels, 174–175
nightlife, 175
restaurants, 172–174
shopping, 171–172
sightseeing, 168–171
sports, 172
tourist information, 217

Whatcom Museum of History and Art, 168, 175

Whidbey Island, 153, 156
hotels, 159–160
restaurants, 159
shopping, 158
sightseeing, 156, 158

sports, 158
transportation, 214

Whidbey Island Naval Air Station, 158

Whistler, B.C.
emergencies, 260
hotels, 259–260
restaurants, 258–259
scenic drives, 257
sightseeing, 256–257
sports, 257–258
tourist information, 260
transportation, 260

White Pass and Yukon Route, 333, 335

White Sulphur Springs, 338

Wickersham House, 328–329

Wildlife preserves
Alaska, 331–332
British Columbia, 283
Oregon, 64
Victoria, 286
Washington, 170, 191–192

Wildlife viewing, 7

Willamette Science and Technology Center, 78

Willamette University, 76

Willamette Valley and the Wine Country, 74–75
arts, 92
hotels, 85–92
nightlife, 92
restaurants, 85–91
shopping, 82–83
sightseeing, 75–82
sports, 83–85
tourist information, 106
transportation in, 104

Winchester Bay, 63

Windsurfing, 239

Wineries, 15–16
British Columbia, 283–284
Oregon, 16, 104–105
Seattle, 118
Washington, 15, 192, 210–211, 213, 216–217

Wine shops, 122

Wing Luke Museum, 115

Winslow, 117

Wiring money, xxii, xxxviii

Wolfhaven, WA, 189

Woodland Park Zoo, 116

World Forestry Center, 28

Wrangell, AK, 319
emergencies, 358
guided tours, 357
hotels, 352
Native culture, 14–15
nightlife, 354
restaurants, 352
sightseeing, 319–321
tourist information, 319, 359

Wrangell City Museum, 319

Wright Park, 177

Y

Yachats, OR, 62, 74

Yakima, WA, 15

Yakima River Winery, 211

Yakima Valley wine country, 15, 210–211, 213
guided tours, 216–217
tourist information, 218
transportation, 216

Yamhill, OR, 91–92

Yamhill National Historic District, 25

Yaquina Head, 61

YMCAs/YWCAs, 139

Young, S. Hall, 329

Youth hostels, xxv, 139

Z

Zillah, WA, 211

Zillah Oakes Winery, 211

Zoos
Portland, 28
Seattle, 116
Tacoma, 178

NOTES

NOTES

NOTES

NOTES

NOTES

Fodor's Travel Publications

Available at bookstores everywhere, or call 1–800–533–6478, 24 hours a day.

Gold Guides

U.S.

Alaska

Arizona

Boston

California

Cape Cod, Martha's
Vineyard, Nantucket

The Carolinas & the
Georgia Coast

Chicago

Colorado

Florida

Hawaii

Las Vegas, Reno,
Tahoe

Los Angeles

Maine, Vermont,
New Hampshire

Maui

Miami & the Keys

New England

New Orleans

New York City

Pacific North Coast

Philadelphia & the
Pennsylvania Dutch
Country

The Rockies

San Diego

San Francisco

Santa Fe, Taos,
Albuquerque

Seattle & Vancouver

The South

U.S. & British Virgin
Islands

USA

Virginia & Maryland

Waikiki

Washington, D.C.

Foreign

Australia &
New Zealand

Austria

The Bahamas

Bermuda

Budapest

Canada

Cancún, Cozumel,
Yucatán Peninsula

Caribbean

China

Costa Rica, Belize,
Guatemala

Cuba

The Czech Republic
& Slovakia

Eastern Europe

Egypt

Europe

Florence, Tuscany
& Umbria

France

Germany

Great Britain

Greece

Hong Kong

India

Ireland

Israel

Italy

Japan

Kenya & Tanzania

Korea

London

Madrid & Barcelona

Mexico

Montréal &
Québec City

Moscow, St.
Petersburg, Kiev

The Netherlands,
Belgium &
Luxembourg

New Zealand

Norway

Nova Scotia, New
Brunswick, Prince
Edward Island

Paris

Portugal

Provence &
the Riviera

Scandinavia

Scotland

Singapore

South America

South Pacific

Southeast Asia

Spain

Sweden

Switzerland

Thailand

Tokyo

Toronto

Turkey

Vienna &
the Danube

Fodor's Special-Interest Guides

Branson

Caribbean Ports
of Call

The Complete Guide
to America's
National Parks

Condé Nast Traveler
Caribbean Resort and
Cruise Ship Finder

Cruises and Ports
of Call

Fodor's London
Companion

France by Train

Halliday's New
England Food
Explorer

Healthy Escapes

Italy by Train

Kodak Guide to
Shooting Great
Travel Pictures

Shadow Traffic's
New York Shortcuts
and Traffic Tips

Sunday in New York

Sunday in
San Francisco

Walt Disney World,
Universal Studios
and Orlando

Walt Disney World
for Adults

Where Should We
Take the Kids?
California

Where Should We
Take the Kids?
Northeast

Special Series

Affordables

Caribbean

Europe

Florida

France

Germany

Great Britain

Italy

London

Paris

Fodor's Bed & Breakfasts and Country Inns

America's Best B&Bs

California's Best B&Bs

Canada's Great Country Inns

Cottages, B&Bs and Country Inns of England and Wales

The Mid-Atlantic's Best B&Bs

New England's Best B&Bs

The Pacific Northwest's Best B&Bs

The South's Best B&Bs

The Southwest's Best B&Bs

The Upper Great Lakes' Best B&Bs

The Berkeley Guides

California

Central America

Eastern Europe

Europe

France

Germany & Austria

Great Britain & Ireland

Italy

London

Mexico

Pacific Northwest & Alaska

Paris

San Francisco

Compass American Guides

Arizona

Chicago

Colorado

Hawaii

Hollywood

Las Vegas

Maine

Manhattan

Montana

New Mexico

New Orleans

Oregon

San Francisco

Santa Fe

South Carolina

South Dakota

Southwest

Texas

Utah

Virginia

Washington

Wine Country

Wisconsin

Wyoming

Fodor's Español

California

Caribe Occidental

Caribe Oriental

Gran Bretaña

Londres

Mexico

Nueva York

Paris

Fodor's Exploring Guides

Australia

Boston & New England

Britain

California

Caribbean

China

Egypt

Florence & Tuscany

Florida

France

Germany

Ireland

Israel

Italy

Japan

London

Mexico

Moscow & St. Petersburg

New York City

Paris

Prague

Provence

Rome

San Francisco

Scotland

Singapore & Malaysia

Spain

Thailand

Turkey

Venice

Fodor's Flashmaps

Boston

New York

San Francisco

Washington, D.C.

Fodor's Pocket Guides

Acapulco

Atlanta

Barbados

Jamaica

London

New York City

Paris

Prague

Puerto Rico

Rome

San Francisco

Washington, D.C.

Rivages Guides

Bed and Breakfasts of Character and Charm in France

Hotels and Country Inns of Character and Charm in France

Hotels and Country Inns of Character and Charm in Italy

Short Escapes

Country Getaways in Britain

Country Getaways in France

Country Getaways Near New York City

Fodor's Sports

Golf Digest's Best Places to Play

Skiing USA

USA Today The Complete Four Sport Stadium Guide

Fodor's Vacation Planners

Great American Learning Vacations

Great American Sports & Adventure Vacations

Great American Vacations

National Parks and Seashores of the East

National Parks of the West